$$\text{Debt/Equity Ratio} = \frac{\text{Total Liabilities}}{\text{Stockholders' Equity}}$$

$$\text{Debt to Tangible Net Worth Ratio} = \frac{\text{Total Liabilities}}{\text{Stockholders' Equity} - \text{Intangible Assets}}$$

$$\text{Operating Cash Flow/Total Debt} = \frac{\text{Operating Cash Flow}}{\text{Total Debt}}$$

PROFITABILITY

$$\text{Net Profit Margin} = \frac{\text{Net Income Before Minority Share of Earnings, Equity Income and Nonrecurring Items}}{\text{Net Sales}}$$

$$\text{Total Asset Turnover} = \frac{\text{Net Sales}}{\text{Average Total Assets}}$$

$$\text{Return on Assets} = \frac{\text{Net Income Before Minority Share of Earnings and Nonrecurring Items}}{\text{Average Total Assets}}$$

$$\text{Operating Income Margin} = \frac{\text{Operating Income}}{\text{Net Sales}}$$

$$\text{Operating Asset Turnover} = \frac{\text{Net Sales}}{\text{Average Operating Assets}}$$

$$\text{Return on Operating Assets} = \frac{\text{Operating Income}}{\text{Average Operating Assets}}$$

$$\text{DuPont Return on Operating Assets} = \text{Operating Income Margin} \times \text{Operating Asset Turnover}$$

$$\text{Sales to Fixed Assets} = \frac{\text{Net Sales}}{\text{Average Net Fixed Assets (Exclude Construction in Progress)}}$$

$$\text{Return on Investment} = \frac{\text{Net Income Before Minority Share of Earnings and Nonrecurring Items} + [(\text{Interest Expense}) \times (1 - \text{Tax Rate})]}{\text{Average (Long-Term Liabilities} + \text{Equity)}}$$

$$\text{Return on Total Equity} = \frac{\text{Net Income Before Nonrecurring Items} - \text{Dividends on Redeemable Preferred Stock}}{\text{Average Total Equity}}$$

$$\text{Return on Common Equity} = \frac{\text{Net Income Before Nonrecurring Items} - \text{Preferred Dividends}}{\text{Average Common Equity}}$$

$$\text{Gross Profit Margin} = \frac{\text{Gross Profit}}{\text{Net Sales}}$$

Financial Reporting & Analysis

Using Financial Accounting Information

11th Edition

Charles H. Gibson

The University of Toledo, Emeritus

SOUTH-WESTERN
CENGAGE Learning™

Australia • Brazil • Japan • Korea • Mexico • Singapore • Spain • United Kingdom • United States

SOUTH-WESTERN
CENGAGE Learning

Financial Reporting & Analysis,
Eleventh Edition
Charles H. Gibson

VP/Editorial Director: Jack W. Calhoun

Editor-in-Chief: Rob Dewey

Acquisitions Editor: Matt Filimonov

Developmental Editor: Peggy Hussey

Editorial Assistant: Heather McAuliffe

Marketing Communications Manager:
Libby Shipp

Marketing Manager: Kristen Hurd

Marketing Coordinator: Gretchen Wildauer

Content Project Managers: Emily Nesheim,
Jacquelyn Featherly

Production Technology Analyst: Adam Grafa

Sr. Manufacturing Coordinator: Doug Wilke

Production Service: LEAP Publishing Services,
Inc.

Compositor: International Typesetting and
Composition

Art Director: Linda Helcher

Internal Designer: Mike Stratton

Cover Designer: Beckmeyer Design

Cover Image: Daryl Benson/The Image Bank/
Getty Images

For product information and technology assistance, contact us at
Cengage Learning Academic Resource Center, 1-800-423-0563

For permission to use material from this text or product,
submit all requests online at **www.cengage.com/permissions**
Further permissions questions can be emailed to
permissionrequest@cengage.com

Library of Congress Control Number: 2008922184
PKG ISBN-13: 978-0-324-65742-5
PKG ISBN-10: 0-324-65742-0
Text only ISBN 13: 978-0-324-66083-8
Text only ISBN 10: 0-324-66083-9

South-Western Cengage Learning
5191 Natorp Boulevard
Mason, OH 45040
USA

Cengage Learning products are represented in Canada by Nelson Education, Ltd.

For your course and learning solutions, visit **academic.cengage.com**

Purchase any of our products at your local college store or at our preferred
online store **www.ichapters.com**

Material from the Certified Management Accountant Examination, Copyright
© 1973, 1975, 1976, 1977, 1978, 1979, 1980, 1984, 1988, by the Institute of
Certified Management Accountants, is reprinted and/or adapted with
permission.

Material copyrighted by the Financial Accounting Standards Board, 401
Merritt 7, P.O. Box 5116, Norwalk, Connecticut 06856-5116, U.S.A., is reprinted
with permission. Copies of the complete documents are available from the
FASB.

Printed in the United States of America
2 3 4 5 6 7 12 11 10 09 08

Charles Gibson is a certified public accountant who practiced with a Big Four accounting firm for four years and has had more than 30 years of teaching experience. His teaching experience encompasses a variety of accounting courses, including financial, managerial, tax, cost, and financial analysis.

Professor Gibson has taught seminars on financial analysis to financial executives, bank commercial loan officers, lawyers, and others. He has also taught financial reporting seminars for CPAs and review courses for both CPAs and CMAs. He has authored several problems used on the CMA exam.

Charles Gibson has written more than 60 articles in such journals as the *Journal of Accountancy, Accounting Horizons, Journal of Commercial Bank Lending, CPA Journal, Ohio CPA, Management Accounting, Risk Management, Taxation for Accountants, Advanced Management Journal, Taxation for Lawyers, California Management Review*, and *Journal of Small Business Management*. He is a co-author of the Financial Executives Research Foundation Study entitled, "Discounting in Financial Accounting and Reporting."

Dr. Gibson co-authored *Cases in Financial Reporting* (PWS-KENT Publishing Company). He has also co-authored two continuing education courses consisting of books and cassette tapes, published by the American Institute of Certified Public Accountants. These courses are entitled "Funds Flow Evaluation" and "Profitability and the Quality of Earnings."

Professor Gibson is a member of the American Accounting Association, American Institute of Certified Public Accountants, Ohio Society of Certified Public Accountants, and Financial Executives Institute. In the past, he has been particularly active in the American Accounting Association and the Ohio Society of Certified Public Accountants.

Dr. Gibson received the 1989 Outstanding Ohio Accounting Educator Award jointly presented by The Ohio Society of Certified Public Accountants and the Ohio Regional American Accounting Association. In 1993, he received the College of Business Research Award at The University of Toledo. In 1996, Dr. Gibson was honored as an "Accomplished Graduate" of the College of Business at Bowling Green State University. In 1999, he was honored by The Gamma Epsilon Chapter of Beta Alpha Psi of The University of Toledo.

Dedication

This book is dedicated to my wife Patricia and daughters Ann Elizabeth and Laura.

Special Dedication

To professors and students who have provided comments on this edition and prior editions. Their comments have contributed to the quality of this book.

Brief Contents

Contents

Chapter 5   Basics of Analysis   177

Chapter 6   Liquidity of Short-Term Assets; Related Debt-Paying Ability   201

Preface

This book teaches financial accounting from both the user's perspective and preparer's perspective. It includes the language and the preparation of financial statements. Reliance is placed on actual annual reports, 10-Ks, and proxy statements. Sufficient background material is included, enabling it for use with students who do not have prior courses in accounting or finance.

Tell me, I'll forget.
Show me, I may remember.
Involve me, I'll understand.

This proverb describes the approach of this book—involving students in actual financial statements and their analysis and interpretation. Its premise is that students are better prepared to understand and analyze real financial reports when learning is not based on oversimplified financial statements.

From this basic premise come the many changes to this edition. Those changes, supported by our technology tools, focus on the goal of this text, which is to involve students in actively learning how to read, understand, and analyze the financial statements of actual companies. These changes are discussed below.

Significant Items

The following notable items are available in this edition to increase its relevance to students and its flexibility for instructors:

- FASB Accounting Standards Codification™ has been introduced
- Coverage of ethics has been expanded
- International accounting has been updated to reflect the substantial changes that have taken place
- Internet exercises have been updated and new exercises added
- Questions have been updated and new questions added
- Problems have been updated and new problems added
- Where appropriate, cases have been updated and new cases added
- Exhibits and cases are extensively based on real companies to which students would relate

- **Access to Thomson One—Business School Edition**™ This high-tech feature is available with every new book. This access to a version of the professional research tool allows students to become familiar with the software that is used in practice. Chapter cases on the text web site, for every chapter with the exception of Chapter 13, walk users step-by-step through those databases as they learn how to access financial information covered in the text. Thomson One—Business School Edition provides information on 500 companies, combining a full range of fundamental financials, earnings estimates, market data, and source documents with powerful functionality.

    Market index information is available for a variety of indices. The database gives you the ability to compare firms against their peers in a portfolio context. There are detailed historical and current financial statements from several different sources. Also available as summary information is financial ratio analysis. Historical stock price information and analysis, along with earnings estimates, is presented. Both fundamental and technical financial analysis is provided. Recent news reports are available. Filings the company has made with the SEC, such as 10-K and 10-Q are also available.

    The Thomson One—Business School Edition provides information on market indices such as the Dow Jones Industrial Average and the Standard and Poor's 500.

    It also provides a powerful and customizable report writing function that enables you to develop custom financial reports for the firm.

- **FinSAS Financial Statement Analysis Spreadsheets** (by Donald V. Saftner, University of Toledo) allow students to perform analysis on any set of financial statements using the ratios covered in the text. Users enter income statement, balance sheet, and other data for two to five years. The result is a 2- to 5-year ratio comparison by liquidity, long-term debt-paying ability, profitability, and investor analysis. The result also includes common-size analysis of the income statement (horizontal and vertical) and common-size analysis of the balance sheet (horizontal and vertical). Downloadable in Excel® from the product web site, *FinSAS* can save users hours of number crunching, allowing them to concentrate on analysis and interpretation.

- **Flexible** (by Donald V. Saftner, University of Toledo) is designed to accompany and complement FinSAS. *Flexible* allows for common-size analysis (horizontal and vertical) of any financial schedule as well as statements. *Flexible* can be used to analyze financial statements (common-size) in a different format (user-defined) from the format of *FinSAS*. Downloadable in Excel® from the product web site, like FinSAS, *Flexible* can save users hours of number crunching, allowing them to concentrate on analysis and interpretation.

Actual Companies

The text explains financial reporting differences among industries, including manufacturing, retailing, service firms, and regulated and nonregulated industries. This text also covers personal financial reports and financial reporting for governments and other not-for-profit institutions.

Statements of actual companies are used in illustrations, cases, and "To The Net" exercises. The actual financial statements highlight current financial reporting problems, including guidelines for consolidated statements, stock-based compensation, postretirement benefits, and the harmonization of international accounting standards.

Extensive Use of One Firm

An important feature of this text is that one firm, Nike, Inc., is used extensively as an illustration. By using Nike's 2007 financial report and industry data, readers become familiar with a typical competitive market and a meaningful example for reviewing financial statement analysis as a whole. (See Chapters 6 through 10 and Summary Analysis—Nike Inc.)

Flexible Organization

This text is used in a variety of courses with a variety of approaches to financial statement reporting and analysis. It provides the flexibility necessary to meet the needs of accounting and finance courses varying in content and length. Sufficient text, questions, "To the Net" exercises, problem materials, and cases are presented to allow the instructor latitude in the depth of coverage. Access to Thomson One—Business School Edition™ is also included with every new book. Accounting principles are the basis for all discussion so that students may understand the methods used as well as the implications for analysis. Following is an outline of our chapter coverage.

Chapter 1 develops the basic principles of accounting on which financial reports are based. A review of the evolution of GAAP and the traditional assumptions of the accounting model helps the reader understand the statements and thus analyze them better.

Chapter 2 describes the forms of business entities and introduces financial reports. This chapter also reviews the sequence of accounting procedures completed during each accounting period. It includes other financial reporting topics that contribute to the understanding of financial reporting, such as the auditor's report, management's discussion, management's responsibility for financial statements, and summary annual report. The efficient market hypothesis, ethics, harmonization of international accounting standards, consolidated statements, and accounting for business combinations are also covered.

Chapter 3 presents an in-depth review of the balance sheet, statement of stockholders' equity, and problems in balance sheet presentation. This chapter gives special emphasis to inventories and tangible assets.

Chapter 4 presents an in-depth review of the income statement, including special income statement items. Other topics included are earnings per share, retained earnings, dividends and stock splits, legality of distributions to stockholders, and comprehensive income.

Chapter 5 is an introduction to analysis and comparative statistics. Techniques include ratio analysis, common-size analysis, year-to-year change analysis, financial statement variations by type of industry, review of descriptive information, comparisons including Standard Industrial Classification (SIC) Manual and North American Industry Classification System (NAICS), relative size of firm, and many library sources of industry data.

Chapter 6 covers short-term liquidity. This chapter includes suggested procedures for analyzing short-term assets and the short-term debt-paying ability of an entity. This chapter discusses in detail four very important assets: cash, marketable securities, accounts receivable, and inventory. It is the first to extensively use Nike as an illustration.

Chapter 7 covers long-term debt-paying ability. This includes the income statement consideration and the balance sheet consideration. Topics include long-term leasing, pension plans, joint ventures, contingencies, financial instruments with off-balance-sheet risk, financial instruments with concentrations of credit risk, and disclosures about fair value of financial instruments.

Chapter 8 covers the analysis of profitability, which is of vital concern to stockholders, creditors, and management. Besides profitability ratios, this chapter covers trends in profitability, segment reporting, gains and losses from prior-period adjustments, comprehensive income, pro forma financial information, and interim reports.

Chapter 9, although not intended as a comprehensive guide to investment analysis, introduces analyses useful to the investor. Besides ratios, this chapter covers leverage and its effect on earnings, earnings per share, stock-based compensations, and stock appreciation rights.

Chapter 10 reviews the statement of cash flows, including ratios that relate to this statement. This chapter also covers procedures for developing the statement of cash flows.

A summary analysis of Nike is presented after Chapter 10, along with the Nike 2007 financial statements. The summary analysis includes Nike background information.

Chapter 11 covers an expanded utility of financial ratios. This includes the perception of financial ratios, the degree of conservatism and quality of earnings, forecasting financial failure, analytical review procedures, management's use of analysis, use of LIFO reserves, graphing financial information, and management of earnings. New to the tenth edition, valuation is included in this chapter.

Chapter 12 covers problems in analyzing six specialized industries: banks, electric utilities, oil and gas, transportation, insurance, and real estate. The chapter notes the differences in statements and suggests changes or additions to their analysis.

Chapter 13 covers personal financial statements and financial reporting for governments and other not-for-profit institutions.

A very extensive **Glossary** defines terms explained in the text and terms frequently found in annual reports and the financial literature. The text also includes a **Bibliography** of references that can be used in exploring further the topics in the text.

Product Web Site: academic.cengage.com/accounting/gibson

Students and instructors have immediate access to financial statement analysis and classroom tools needed for the course at academic.cengage.com/accounting/gibson. This web site contains the following supplementary materials available to both instructors and students:

- *FinSAS*—financial statement analysis spreadsheets (both blank and sample Nike versions) designed to perform analysis using ratios covered in the text
- *Flexible*—allows for common-size analysis (horizontal and vertical) of any financial schedule as well as statements
- Thomson One—Business School Edition™—provides online cases tied to the book's chapter content for users of new books, utilizing its powerful suite of research tools for 500 companies

Other supplementary materials that are password protected for adopting instructors:

- Solutions Manual—prepared by the author and includes a suggested solution for each "To the Net" exercise, question, problem, and case
- PowerPoint® Slides—available to enrich classroom teaching of concepts and practice
- Test Bank—prepared by the author and includes problems, multiple-choice, true/false, and other objective material for each chapter. The Test Bank is available in Microsoft® Word
- Thomson One—Business School Edition™—suggested solutions to the online cases

Acknowledgments

I am grateful to many people for their help and encouragement during the writing of this book. I want to extend my appreciation to the numerous firms and organizations that granted permission to reproduce their material. Special thanks go to the American Institute of Certified Public Accountants, the Institute of Certified Management Accountants, and the Financial Accounting Standards Board. Permission has been received from the Institute of Management Accountants to use questions and/or unofficial answers from past CMA examinations.

I am grateful to the following individuals for their useful and perceptive comments during the making of the eleventh edition: Joyce S. Allen (Xavier University), Segundo I. Fernandez (New York University), Umit Gurun (University of Texas at Dallas), Deborah Leitsch (Goldey-Beacom College), Frederic Lerner (New York University), Anastasios Moysidis (Florida International University), John J. Surdick (Xavier University), James A. Taibleson (New York University), and Oktay Urcan (University of Texas at Dallas).

I am very grateful to Donald Saftner (University of Toledo) for his careful, timely, and effective revision of the *FinSAS* spreadsheet tool and *Flexible* for this edition.

Thanks to Dianne Feldman for accuracy verification of the solutions manual and test bank. Thanks also to the following at South-Western Cengage Learning for their hard work on this edition: Matt Filimonov (Acquisitions Editor), Jessica Kempf and Peggy Hussey (Developmental Editors), Kristen Hurd (Marketing Manager), Emily Nesheim and Jacquelyn Featherly (Content Project Managers), Adam Grafa (Production Technology Analyst), and Stacy Shirley (Art Director).

Charles H. Gibson

Actual Companies and Organizations

Real-world business examples are used extensively in the text, illustrations, and cases.

3M Company
Abbott Laboratories
Advances Micro Devices
AK Steel
Alexander & Baldwin, Inc.
Algoma Steel Inc.
Amazon.com, Inc.
American Greetings Corporation
American Institute of Certified
    Public Accountants (AICPA)
Ann Taylor Stores Corporation
Apple Computer
Arden Group, Inc.
Balden
Baldor Electric Company
Bank of America
Baytex Entity Trust
Bemis Company
Best Buy, Inc.
Blair Corporation
Borders Group, Inc.
Briggs & Stratton
CA, Inc.
Cabot Oil & Gas Corporation
Carl and Lawrence Zicklin Center
    for Business Ethics Research
Casey's General Stores
Celtics Basketball Holdings, L.P.
Circuit City
City of Toledo, Ohio
Columbia Bancorp
Conoco Phillips
Cooper Tire
Crown Holdings, Inc.
Daimler Chrysler
Daktronics, Inc.
Dana Corporation
Dell, Inc.
Diodes Incorporated
Diversified Technology
Dow Chemical Co.
Dow Jones Company
Dynatronics Corporation
Earthlink, Inc.
Eastman Kodak Company
El Paso Corporation
Emerging Issues Task Force (EITF)
Enbridge, Inc.
Enron
Financial Accounting Standards
    Board (FASB)
Flowers Foods, Inc.
Foot Locker, Inc.

Ford Motor Company
Frisch's Restaurants
Gannett Co., Inc.
Gateway, Inc.
General Electric Company
General Motors
Genesee & Wyoming, Inc.
Gentex Corporation
Goodyear Tire & Rubber
Google, Inc.
Government Accounting Standards
    Board (GASB)
Harley Davidson
Harrah's Entertainment
Hershey Company
Hess Corporation
Hewlett-Packard
Hormel Foods
ICT Group, Inc.
Ides Corporation
Independent Bank Corporation
Indymac Bancorp
Intel Corporation
International Accounting
    Standards Board (IASB)
Isle of Capri Casinos, Inc.
JLG
Johnson & Johnson
KB Home
Kellogg Company
Kelly Services
Kohl's Corporation
Kroger Company
Lands' End
Lennox Corporation
Lucas County, Ohio
Maine & Maritime Corporation
Maintowac Company
McDonald's Corporation
McKinsey & Company, Inc.
Medical University of Ohio
Met-Pro
Milacron, Inc.
Molson Coors Brewing Company
Motorola
MSC Software
Myers Industries
National City
Newmont Mining
Nike, Inc.
Nordson Corporation
Northrop Grumman
Occidental Petroleum Corporation

Ohio Society of Certified Public
    Accountants (OSCPA)
Omnova Solutions
Owens Corning
Panera Bread
Perry Ellis International
PFG
PG&E Corporation
Private Securities Litigation Reform
    Act
Public Company Accounting
    Oversight Board (PCAOB)
Quantum Corporation
Reliance Steel & Aluminum
Royal Ahold
Safeway, Inc.
Seachange International
Securities and Exchange
    Commission (SEC)
Shaw Communications
Sherwin-Williams Company
Skechers U.S.A.
Southwest Airlines Company
Sovereign Bancorp
Starbucks Corporation
Steel Dynamics, Inc.
Sun Hydraulics® Corporation
T. Rowe Price Group
Taser International, Inc.
Tech Data Corporation
The Boeing Company
The Chubb Corporation
Toledo Mud Hens Baseball
    Club, Inc.
Transact Technologies
Treadway Commission
Tribune Company
TRM Corporation
Trump Hotels & Casino
    Resorts, Inc.
United Airlines
United States Steel Corporation
United Stationers
Vulcan Materials Company
Walt Disney
Weyerhaeuser Company
Winnebago Industries
Wisconsin Energy
WorldCom
World Wrestling Entertainment
Yahoo, Inc.
Yums Brands, Inc.
Zebra Designs

Chapter 1

Introduction to Financial Reporting

Users of financial statements include a company's managers, stockholders, bondholders, security analysts, suppliers, lending institutions, employees, labor unions, regulatory authorities, and the general public. These are internal and external stakeholder groups. They use the financial reports to make decisions. For example, potential investors use the financial reports as an aid in deciding whether to buy the stock. Suppliers use the financial reports to decide whether to sell merchandise to a company on credit. Labor unions use the financial reports to help determine their demands when they negotiate for employees. Management could use the financial reports to determine the company's profitability.

Demand for financial reports exists because users believe that the reports help them in decision making. In addition to the financial reports, users often consult competing information sources, such as new wage contracts and economy-oriented releases.

This book concentrates on using financial accounting information properly. A basic understanding of generally accepted accounting principles and traditional assumptions of the accounting model are introduced. This aids the user in recognizing the limits of financial reports.

The ideas that underlie financial reports have developed over several hundred years. This development continues today to meet the needs of a changing society. A review of the evolution of generally accepted accounting principles and the traditional assumptions of the accounting model should help the reader understand the financial reports and thus analyze them better.

Development of Generally Accepted Accounting Principles (GAAP) in the United States

Generally accepted accounting principles (GAAP) are accounting principles that have substantial authoritative support: The accountant must be familiar with acceptable reference sources in order to decide whether any particular accounting principle has substantial authoritative support.

The formal process of developing accounting principles that exist today in the United States began with the Securities Acts of 1933 and 1934. Prior to these securities acts, the New York Stock Exchange (NYSE), which was established in 1792, was the primary mechanism for establishing specific requirements for the disclosure of financial information. These requirements could be described as minimal and only applied to corporations whose shares were listed on the NYSE. The prevailing view of management was that financial information was for management's use.

The stock market crash of 1929 provoked widespread concern about external financial disclosure. Some alleged that the stock market crash was substantially influenced by the lack of adequate financial reporting requirements to investors and creditors. The Securities Act of 1933 was designed to protect investors from abuses in financial reporting that developed in the United States. This act was intended to regulate the initial offering and sale of securities in interstate commerce.

In general, the Securities Exchange Act of 1934 was intended to regulate securities trading on the national exchanges, and it was under this authority that the **Securities and Exchange Commission (SEC)** was created. In effect, the SEC has the authority to determine GAAP and to regulate the accounting profession. The SEC has elected to leave much of the determination of GAAP and the regulation of the accounting profession to the private sector. At times, the SEC will issue its own standards.

Currently, the SEC issues Regulation S-X, which describes the primary formal financial disclosure requirements for companies. The SEC also issues Financial Reporting Releases (FRRs) that pertain to financial reporting requirements. Regulation S-X and FRRs are part of GAAP and are used to give the SEC's official position on matters relating to financial statements. The formal process that exists today is a blend of the private and public sectors.

A number of parties in the private sector have played a role in the development of GAAP. The American Institute of Certified Public Accountants (AICPA) and the Financial Accounting Standards Board (FASB) have had the most influence.

AMERICAN INSTITUTE OF CERTIFIED PUBLIC ACCOUNTANTS (AICPA)

The **AICPA** is a professional accounting organization whose members are certified public accountants (CPAs). During the 1930s, the AICPA had a special committee working with the New York Stock Exchange on matters of common interest. An outgrowth of this special committee was the establishment in 1939 of two standing committees, the **Committee on Accounting Procedures** and the **Committee on Accounting Terminology**. These committees were active from 1939 to 1959 and issued 51 Accounting Research Bulletins (ARBs). These committees took a problem-by-problem approach, because they tended to review an issue only when there was a problem related to that issue. This method became known as the **brushfire approach.** They were only partially successful in developing a well-structured body of accounting principles. ARBs are part of GAAP unless they have been superseded.

In 1959, the AICPA replaced the two committees with the **Accounting Principles Board (APB)** and the **Accounting Research Division**. The Accounting Research Division provided research to aid the APB in making decisions regarding accounting principles. Basic postulates would be developed that would aid in the development of accounting principles, and the entire process was intended to be based on research prior to an APB decision. However, the APB and the Accounting Research Division were not successful in formulating broad principles.

The combination of the APB and the Accounting Research Division lasted from 1959 to 1973. During this time, the Accounting Research Division issued 14 Accounting Research Studies. The APB issued 31 Opinions (APBOs) and four Statements (APBSs). The Opinions represented official positions of the Board, whereas the Statements represented the views of the Board but not the official opinions. APBOs are part of GAAP unless they have been superseded.

Various sources, including the public, generated pressure to find another way of developing GAAP. In 1972, a special study group of the AICPA recommended another approach—the establishment of the **Financial Accounting Standards Board (FASB)**. The AICPA adopted these recommendations in 1973.

FINANCIAL ACCOUNTING STANDARDS BOARD (FASB)

The structure of the FASB is as follows: A panel of electors is selected from nine organizations. They are the AICPA, the Financial Executives Institute, the Institute of Management Accountants, the Financial Analysts Federation, the American Accounting Association, the Security Industry Association, and three not-for-profit organizations. The electors appoint the board of trustees that governs the **Financial Accounting Foundation (FAF)**. There are 16 trustees.

The FAF appoints the **Financial Accounting Standards Advisory Council (FASAC)** and the FASB.

There are approximately 30 members of the FASAC. This relatively large number is to obtain representation from a wide group of interested parties. The FASAC is responsible for advising the FASB. There are seven members of the FASB. Exhibit 1-1 illustrates the structure of the FASB.

Exhibit   1-1   STRUCTURE OF THE FASB

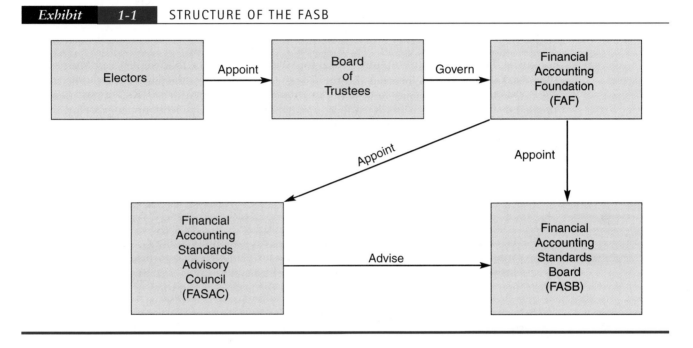

The FASB issues four types of pronouncements:

1. **Statements of Financial Accounting Standards (SFASs).** These Statements establish GAAP for specific accounting issues. SFASs are part of GAAP unless they have been superseded.

2. **Interpretations.** These pronouncements provide clarifications to previously issued standards, including SFASs, APB Opinions, and Accounting Research Bulletins. The interpretations have the same authority and require the same majority votes for passage as standards (a super-majority of five or more of the seven members). Interpretations are part of GAAP unless they have been superseded.

3. **Technical bulletins.** These bulletins provide timely guidance on financial accounting and reporting problems. They may be used when the effect will not cause a major change in accounting practice for a number of companies and when they do not conflict with any broad fundamental accounting principle. Technical bulletins are part of GAAP unless they have been superseded.

4. **Statements of Financial Accounting Concepts (SFACs).** These Statements provide a theoretical foundation upon which to base GAAP. They are the output of the FASB's Conceptual Framework project, but they are not part of GAAP.

OPERATING PROCEDURE FOR STATEMENTS OF FINANCIAL ACCOUNTING STANDARDS (SFASs)

The process of considering a SFAS begins when the Board elects to add a topic to its technical agenda. The Board receives suggestions and advice on topics from many sources, including the FASAC, the SEC, the AICPA, and industry organizations.

For its technical agenda, the Board considers only "broken" items. In other words, the Board must be convinced that a major issue needs to be addressed in a new area or an old issue needs to be reexamined.

The Board must rely on staff members for the day-to-day work on projects. A project is assigned a staff project manager, and informal discussions frequently take place among Board members, the staff project manager, and staff. In this way, Board members gain an understanding of the accounting issues and the economic relationships that underlie those issues.

On projects with a broad impact, a **Discussion Memorandum (DM)** or an **Invitation to Comment** is issued. A Discussion Memorandum presents all known facts and points of view on a topic. An Invitation to Comment sets forth the Board's tentative conclusions on some issues related to the topic or represents the views of others.

The Discussion Memorandum or Invitation to Comment is distributed as a basis for public comment. There is usually a 60-day period for written comments, followed by a public hearing. A transcript of the public hearing and the written comments become part of the public record. Then the Board begins deliberations on an **Exposure Draft (ED)** of a proposed Statement of Financial Accounting Standards. When completed, the Exposure Draft is issued for public comment. The Board may call for written comments only, or it may announce another public hearing. After considering the written comments and the public hearing comments, the Board resumes deliberations in one or more public Board meetings. The final Statement must receive affirmative votes from five of the seven members of the Board. The Rules of Procedure require dissenting Board members to set forth their reasons in the Statement. Developing a Statement on a major project generally takes at least two years, sometimes much longer. Some people believe that the time should be shortened to permit faster decision making.

The FASB standard-setting process includes aspects of accounting theory and political aspects. Many organizations, companies, and individuals have input into the process. Some input is directed toward achieving a standard less than desirable in terms of a strict accounting perspective. Often, the end result is a standard that is not the best representation of economic reality.

FASB CONCEPTUAL FRAMEWORK

The Conceptual Framework for Accounting and Reporting was on the agenda of the FASB from its inception in 1973. The Framework is intended to set forth a system of interrelated objectives and underlying concepts that will serve as the basis for evaluating existing standards of financial accounting and reporting.

Under this project, the FASB has established a series of pronouncements, **Statements of Financial Accounting Concepts (SFACs)**, intended to provide the Board with a common foundation and the basic reasons for considering the merits of various alternative accounting principles. SFACs do *not* establish GAAP; rather, the FASB eventually intends to evaluate current principles in terms of the concepts established.

To date, the Framework project has issued seven Concept Statements:

1. *Statement of Financial Accounting Concepts No. 1*, "Objectives of Financial Reporting by Business Enterprises."
2. *Statement of Financial Accounting Concepts No. 2*, "Qualitative Characteristics of Accounting Information."
3. *Statement of Financial Accounting Concepts No. 3*, "Elements of Financial Statements of Business Enterprises."
4. *Statement of Financial Accounting Concepts No. 4*, "Objectives of Financial Reporting by Nonbusiness Organizations."
5. *Statement of Financial Accounting Concepts No. 5*, "Recognition and Measurement in Financial Statements of Business Enterprises."
6. *Statement of Financial Accounting Concepts No. 6*, "Elements of Financial Statements" (a replacement of No. 3).
7. *Statement of Financial Accounting Concepts No. 7*, "Using Cash Flow Information and Present Value in Accounting Measurements."

Concepts Statement No. 1, issued in 1978, deals with identifying the objectives of financial reporting for business entities and establishes the focus for subsequent concept projects for business entities. Concepts Statement No. 1 pertains to general-purpose external financial reporting and is not restricted to financial statements. The following is a summary of the highlights of Concepts Statement No. 1.[1]

1. Financial reporting is intended to provide information useful in making business and economic decisions.
2. The information should be comprehensible to those having a reasonable understanding of business and economic activities. These individuals should be willing to study the information with reasonable diligence.
3. Financial reporting should be helpful to users in assessing the amounts, timing, and uncertainty of future cash flows.
4. The primary focus is information about earnings and its components.
5. Information should be provided about the economic resources of an enterprise and the claims against those resources.

Issued in May 1980, "Qualitative Characteristics of Accounting Information" (SFAC No. 2) examines the characteristics that make accounting information useful for investment, credit, and similar decisions. Those characteristics of information that make it a desirable commodity can be viewed as a hierarchy of qualities, with *understandability* and *usefulness for decision making* of most importance (see Exhibit 1-2).

Relevance and reliability, the two primary qualities, make accounting information useful for decision making. To be relevant, the information needs to have *predictive* and feedback value and must be *timely*. To be reliable, the information must be *verifiable*, subject to representational faithfulness, and *neutral*. Comparability, which includes consistency, interacts with relevance and reliability to contribute to the usefulness of information.

The hierarchy includes *two constraints*. To be useful and worth providing, the information should have *benefits that exceed its cost*. In addition, all of the qualities of information shown are *subject to a materiality threshold*.

SFAC No. 6, "Elements of Financial Statements," which replaced SFAC No. 3 in 1985, defines 10 interrelated elements directly related to measuring performance and financial status of an enterprise. The 10 elements are defined as follows:[2]

1. **Assets.** Assets are probable future economic benefits obtained or controlled by a particular entity as a result of past transactions or events.
2. **Liabilities.** Liabilities are probable future sacrifices of economic benefits arising from present obligations of a particular entity to transfer assets or provide services to other entities in the future as a result of past transactions or events.
3. **Equity.** Equity is the residual interest in the assets of an entity that remains after deducting its liabilities:

$$Equity = Assets - Liabilities$$

4. **Investments by owners.** Investments by owners are increases in equity of a particular business enterprise resulting from transfers to the enterprise from other entities of something of value to obtain or increase ownership interests (or equity) in it. Assets, most commonly received as investments by owners, may also include services or satisfaction or conversion of liabilities of the enterprise.
5. **Distribution to owners.** Distribution to owners is a decrease in equity of a particular business enterprise resulting from transferring assets, rendering services, or incurring liabilities by the enterprise to owners. Distributions to owners decrease ownership interest (or equity) in an enterprise.
6. **Comprehensive income.** Comprehensive income is the change in equity (net assets) of a business enterprise during a period from transactions and other events and circumstances from nonowner sources. It includes all changes in equity during a period except those resulting from investments by owners and distributions to owners.

Exhibit   1-2   A HIERARCHY OF ACCOUNTING QUALITIES

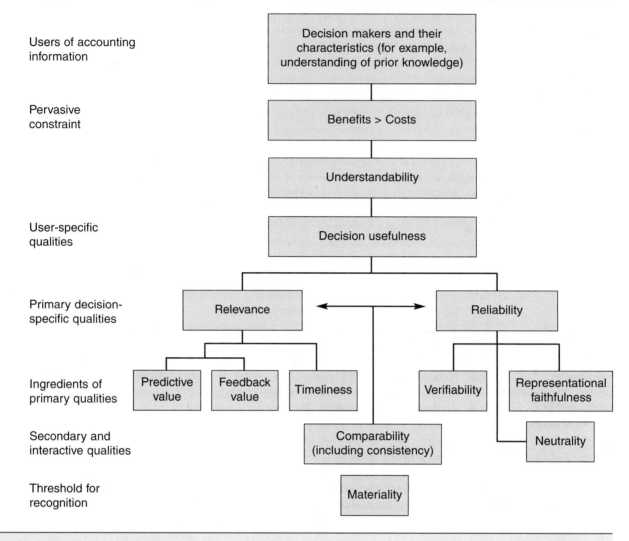

Source: "Qualitative Characteristics of Accounting Information." Adapted from Figure 1 in FASB *Statement of Financial Accounting Concepts No. 2* (Stamford, Conn.: Financial Accounting Standards Board, 1980).

7. **Revenues.** Revenues are inflows or other enhancements of assets of an entity or settlements of its liabilities (or a combination of both) from delivering or producing goods, rendering services, or other activities that constitute the entity's ongoing major or central operations.

8. **Expenses.** Expenses are outflows or other consumption or using up of assets or incurrences of liabilities (or a combination of both) from delivering or producing goods, rendering services, or carrying out other activities that constitute the entity's ongoing major or central operations.

9. **Gains.** Gains are increases in equity (net assets) from peripheral or incidental transactions of an entity and from all other transactions and other events and circumstances affecting the entity during a period except those that result from revenues or investments by owners.

10. **Losses.** Losses are decreases in equity (net assets) from peripheral or incidental transactions of an entity and from all other transactions and other events and circumstances affecting the entity during a period except those that result from expenses or distributions to owners.

"Objectives of Financial Reporting by Nonbusiness Organizations" (SFAC No. 4) was completed in 1980. Organizations that fall within the focus of this statement include churches, foundations, and human-service organizations. Performance indicators for nonbusiness organizations include formal budgets and donor restrictions. These types of indicators are not ordinarily related to competition in markets.

Issued in 1984, "Recognition and Measurement in Financial Statements of Business Enterprises" (SFAC No. 5) indicates that an item, to be recognized, should meet four criteria, subject to the cost-benefit constraint and materiality threshold:[3]

1. **Definition.** The item fits one of the definitions of the elements.
2. **Measurability.** The item has a relevant attribute measurable with sufficient reliability.
3. **Relevance.** The information related to the item is relevant.
4. **Reliability.** The information related to the item is reliable.

This concept statement identifies *five* different *measurement attributes* currently used in practice and recommends the composition of a full set of financial statements for a period.

The following are five different measurement attributes currently used in practice:[4]

1. Historical cost (historical proceeds)
2. Current cost
3. Current market value
4. Net realizable (settlement) value
5. Present (or discounted) value of future cash flows

This concept statement probably accomplished little, relating to measurement attributes, because a firm, consistent position on recognition and measurement could not be agreed upon. It states: "Rather than attempt to select a single attribute and force changes in practice so that all classes of assets and liabilities use that attribute, this concept statement suggests that use of different attributes will continue."[5]

SFAC No. 5 recommended that a full set of financial statements for a period should show the following:[6]

1. Financial position at the end of the period
2. Earnings (net income)
3. Comprehensive income (total nonowner change in equity)
4. Cash flows during the period
5. Investments by and distributions to owners during the period

At the time of issuance of SFAC No. 5, financial position at the end of the period and earnings (net income) were financial statements being presented. Comprehensive income, cash flows during the period, and investments by and distributions to owners during the period are financial statements (disclosures) that have been subsequently developed. All of these financial statements (disclosures) will be extensively covered in this book.

SFAC No. 7, issued in February 2000, provides general principles for using present values for accounting measurements. It describes techniques for estimating cash flows and interest rates and applying present value in measuring liabilities.

The FASB Conceptual Framework for Accounting and Reporting project represents the most extensive effort undertaken to provide a conceptual framework for financial accounting. Potentially, the project can have a significant influence on financial accounting.

Additional Input—American Institute of Certified Public Accountants (AICPA)

As indicated earlier, the AICPA played the primary role in the private sector in establishing GAAP prior to 1973. However, the AICPA continues to play a part, primarily through its Accounting Standards Division. The Accounting Standards Executive Committee (AcSEC) serves as the official voice of the AICPA in matters relating to financial accounting and reporting standards.

The Accounting Standards Division published numerous documents considered as sources of GAAP. These include Industry Audit Guides, Industry Accounting Guides, and Statements of Position (SOPs).

Industry Audit Guides and Industry Accounting Guides are designed to assist auditors in examining and reporting on financial statements of companies in specialized industries, such as insurance. SOPs were issued to influence the development of accounting standards. Some SOPs were revisions or clarifications to recommendations on accounting standards contained in Industry Audit Guides and Industry Accounting Guides.

Industry Audit Guides, Industry Accounting Guides, and SOPs were considered a lower level of authority than FASB Statements of Financial Accounting Standards, FASB Interpretations, APB Opinions, and Accounting Research Bulletins. However, since the Industry Audit Guides, Industry Accounting Guides, and SOPs deal with material not covered in the primary sources, they, in effect, became the guide to standards for the areas they cover. They are part of GAAP unless they have been superseded.

Emerging Issues Task Force (EITF)

The FASB established the Emerging Issues Task Force (EITF) in July 1984 to help identify emerging issues affecting reporting and problems in implementing authoritative pronouncements. The Task Force has 15 members—senior technical partners of major national CPA firms and representatives of major associations of preparers of financial statements. The FASB's Director of Research and Technical Activities serves as Task Force chairperson. The SEC's Chief Accountant and the chairperson of the AICPA's Accounting Standards Executive Committee participate in Task Force meetings as observers.

The SEC's Chief Accountant has stated that any accounting that conflicts with the position of a consensus of the Task Force would be challenged. Agreement of the Task Force is recognized as a consensus if no more than two members disagree with a position.

Task Force meetings are held about once every six weeks. Issues come to the Task Force from a variety of sources, including the EITF members, the SEC, and other federal agencies. The FASB also brings issues to the EITF in response to issues submitted by auditors and preparers of financial statements.

The EITF statements have become a very important source of GAAP. The Task Force has the capability to review a number of issues within a relatively short period of time, in contrast to the lengthy deliberations that go into an SFAS.

EITF statements are considered to be less authoritative than the sources previously discussed in this chapter. However, since the EITF addresses issues not covered by the other sources, its statements become important guidelines to standards for the areas they cover.

A New Reality

In November 2001, Enron, one of the largest companies in the United States, recognized in a federal filing that it had overstated earnings by nearly $600 million since 1997. Within a month, Enron declared bankruptcy. The Enron bankruptcy probably received more publicity than any prior bankruptcy in U.S. history. This was influenced by the size of Enron, the role of the auditors, the financial loss of investors, and the losses sustained by Enron employees. Many Enron employees lost their jobs and their pensions. There were approximately two dozen guilty pleas or convictions in the Enron case including Ken Lay, former Enron chairman. Ken Lay died before he was sentenced; therefore, Judge Sim Lake erased his convictions.

In June 2002, WorldCom announced that it had inflated profits by $3.8 billion over the previous five quarters. This represented the largest financial fraud in corporate history. Soon after the WorldCom fraud announcement, WorldCom declared bankruptcy. (In November 2002, a special bankruptcy court examiner indicated that the restatement would likely exceed $7.2 billion.) On July 13, 2005, Bernard J. Ebbers, founder and former chief executive of WorldCom, was sentenced to 25 years in prison for orchestrating the biggest corporate accounting fraud in U.S. history.

The WorldCom fraud compelled Congress and President George W. Bush to take action. Congress acted swiftly, with the support of President Bush, to pass legislation now known as the Sarbanes-Oxley Act of 2002.

The Sarbanes-Oxley Act has many provisions. While it is not practical to review the Act in detail, it is clear that it has far-reaching consequences for financial reporting and the CPA profession. Because of the importance of the Sarbanes-Oxley Act to financial reporting, some additional comments are in order.

Sarbanes-Oxley Section 404 requires companies to document adequate internal controls and procedures for financial reporting. They must be able to assess the effectiveness of the internal controls and financial reporting.

Companies have found it difficult to comply with Section 404 for many reasons. Internal auditing departments have been reduced or eliminated at many companies. Some companies do not have the personnel to confront complex accounting issues. This lack of adequate competent personnel to confront complex accounting issues in itself represents an internal control weakness.

Sarbanes-Oxley makes it an administrative responsibility to have adequate internal controls and procedures in place. Management must acknowledge their responsibility and assert the effectiveness of internal controls and procedures in writing.

The SEC requires companies to file an annual report on their internal control systems. The report should contain the following:[7]

1. A statement of management's responsibilities for establishing and maintaining an adequate system.
2. Identification of the framework used to evaluate the internal controls.
3. A statement as to whether or not the internal control system is effective as of year-end.
4. The disclosure of any material weaknesses in the system.
5. A statement that the company's auditors have issued an audit report on management's assessment.

The financial statements auditor must report on management's assertion as to the effectiveness of the internal controls and procedures as of the company's year-end. Sarbanes-Oxley has changed the relationship between the company and the external auditor. Prior to Sarbanes-Oxley, some companies relied on the external auditor to determine the accounting for complex accounting issues. This was a form of conflict of interest, as the auditor surrendered independence in assessing the company's controls, procedures, and reporting.

Not only have some companies found that they did not have adequately trained personnel to confront complex accounting issues, but external auditors have also been pressed to provide trained accounting personnel. This has led some auditing firms to reduce the number and type of companies that they will audit.

The spring of 2005 represented the first reporting season under Sarbanes-Oxley. Hundreds of companies acknowledged that they had "material weaknesses" in their controls and processes. In some cases, this led to financial statements being restated.

Implementing Sarbanes-Oxley has resulted in several benefits. Companies have improved their internal controls, procedures, and financial reporting. Many companies have also improved their fraud prevention. Systems put in place to review budgets will enable companies to be more proactive in preventing potential problems. Users of financial statements benefit from an improved financial product that they review and analyze to make investment decisions.

Unfortunately, implementing Sarbanes-Oxley has been quite costly. Some firms question the cost/benefit of compliance with Sarbanes-Oxley. In time, we will know how much of the cost was represented by start-up cost and how much was annual recurring costs. The substantial cost of implementing Sarbanes-Oxley will likely result in future changes to this law.

Publicly held companies are required to report under Sarbanes-Oxley, whereas private companies are not. Many state-level legislators have proposed extending certain provisions of Sarbanes-Oxley to private companies. Such proposals are controversial because of the cost. Some private companies support these proposals.

Most of the publicity relating to Sarbanes-Oxley has been related to Section 404, but the Act includes many other sections. This book will revisit Sarbanes-Oxley when covering other areas, such as ethics, in Chapter 2.

Sarbanes-Oxley created a five-person oversight board, the Public Company Accounting Oversight Board (PCAOB). The PCAOB consists of five members appointed by the SEC. Two must be CPAs, but the others cannot be CPAs.

Among the many responsibilities of the PCAOB is to adopt auditing standards. This will materially decrease or eliminate the role of the AICPA in setting auditing standards.

The PCAOB sets an annual accounting support fee for the standard-setting body (FASB). The PCAOB also establishes an annual accounting support fee for the PCAOB. These fees are assessed against each issuer.

The chief executive officer (CEO), and the chief financial officer (CFO), of each issuer must prepare a statement to accompany the audit report to certify disclosures fairly present, in all material respects, the operations and financial condition of the issuer.

In addition to appointing the five members of the PCAOB, the SEC is responsible for the oversight and enforcement authority over the Board. In effect, the PCAOB is an arm of the SEC.

As described in this chapter, the setting of accounting standards has been divided among the SEC, FASB, EITF, and AcSEC. By law, the setting of accounting standards is the responsibility of the SEC. The SEC elected to have most of the accounting standards developed in the private sector with the oversight of the SEC. This substantially meant that the SEC allowed the FASB to determine accounting standards. The FASB allowed some of the standards to be determined by the EITF, and the AcSEC of the AICPA.

The FASB has announced that it was streamlining the accounting rule-making process by taking back powers it had vested to AcSEC (an arm of the AICPA). The AcSEC will be allowed to continue with industry-specific accounting and audit guides (A&A guides). The AICPA is to stop issuing general-purpose accounting Statements of Position (SOPs).

The FASB also streamlined the accounting rule-making process by taking back powers it had vested to EITF (an arm of the FASB). Two FASB members will be involved in the agenda-setting process of the EITF. Statements of the EITF will go to the FASB before release.

FASB Accounting Standards Codification™ (Codification)

As indicated in this chapter, there have been many sources of authoritative U.S. GAAP. This has resulted in thousands of pages addressing U.S. GAAP and some confusion as to the level of authoritative GAAP.

To provide a single source of authoritative U.S. GAAP, the FASB commenced a project to provide a Codification of U.S. GAAP. The result will be one source and one level of authoritative GAAP. The Codification does not change GAAP.

This project reached a verification stage in late 2007. During a one-year verification period the Codification is available to solicit feedback and confirm that the Codification is accurate. The Codification will likely become the single authoritative source of U.S. GAAP in 2009.

The Codification reorganizes the accounting pronouncements into approximately 90 accounting topics. A separate section of the Codification will include SEC guidance. The SEC guidance will use the same 90 accounting topics. The Codification addresses U.S. GAAP for nongovernmental entities.

Traditional Assumptions of the Accounting Model

The FASB's Conceptual Framework was influenced by several underlying assumptions. Some of these assumptions were addressed in the Conceptual Framework, and others are implicit in the Framework. These assumptions, along with the Conceptual Framework, are considered when a GAAP is established. Accountants, when confronted with a situation lacking an explicit standard, should resolve the situation by considering the Conceptual Framework and the traditional assumptions of the accounting model.

In all cases, the reports are to be a "fair representation." Even when there is an explicit GAAP, following the GAAP is not appropriate unless the end result is a "fair representation." Following GAAP is not an appropriate legal defense unless the statements represent a "fair representation."

BUSINESS ENTITY

The concept of separate **entity** means that the business or entity for which the financial statements are prepared is separate and distinct from the owners of the entity. In other words, the entity is viewed as an economic unit that stands on its own.

For example, an individual may own a grocery store, a farm, and numerous personal assets. To determine the economic success of the grocery store, we would view it separately from the other resources owned by the individual. The grocery store would be treated as a separate entity.

A corporation such as Ford Motor Company has many owners (stockholders). The entity concept enables us to account for the Ford Motor Company entity separately from the transactions of the owners of Ford Motor Company.

GOING CONCERN OR CONTINUITY

The **going-concern assumption,** that the entity in question will remain in business for an indefinite period of time, provides perspective on the future of the entity. The going-concern assumption deliberately disregards the possibility that the entity will go bankrupt or be liquidated. If a particular entity is in fact threatened with bankruptcy or liquidation, then the going-concern assumption should be dropped. In such a case, the reader of the financial statements is interested in the liquidation values, not the values that can be used when making the assumption that the business will continue indefinitely. If the going-concern assumption has not been used for a particular set of financial statements, because of the threat of liquidation or bankruptcy, the financial statements must clearly disclose that the statements were prepared with the view that the entity will be liquidated or that it is a failing concern. In this case, conventional financial report analysis would not apply.

Many of our present financial statement figures would be misleading if it were not for the going-concern assumption. For instance, under the going-concern assumption, the value of prepaid insurance is computed by spreading the cost of the insurance over the period of the policy. If the entity were liquidated, then only the cancellation value of the policy would be meaningful. Inventories are basically carried at their accumulated cost. If the entity were liquidated, then the amount realized from the sale of the inventory, in a manner other than through the usual channels, usually would be substantially less than the cost. Therefore, to carry the inventory at cost would fail to recognize the loss that is represented by the difference between the liquidation value and the cost.

The going-concern assumption also influences liabilities. If the entity were liquidating, some liabilities would have to be stated at amounts in excess of those stated on the conventional statement. Also, the amounts provided for warranties and guarantees would not be realistic if the entity were liquidating.

The going-concern assumption also influences the classification of assets and liabilities. Without the going-concern assumption, all assets and liabilities would be current, with the expectation that the assets would be liquidated and the liabilities paid in the near future.

The audit opinion for a particular firm may indicate that the auditors have reservations as to the going-concern status of the firm. This puts the reader on guard that the statements are misleading if the firm does not continue as a going concern. For example, the annual report of Trump Hotels & Casino Resorts, Inc. indicated a concern over the company's ability to continue as a going concern.

The Trump Hotels & Casino Resorts, Inc. annual report included these comments in Note 1 and the auditor's report.

Trump Hotels & Casino Resorts, Inc.
Notes to Consolidated Financial Statements (in Part)
December 31, 2004

Accounting Impact of Chapter 11 Filing (Part of Note 1)

The accompanying consolidated financial statements have been prepared in accordance with AICPA Statement of Position No. (SOP) 90-7, "Financial Reporting by Entities in Reorganization under the Bankruptcy Code" ("SOP 90-7") and on a going concern basis, which contemplates continuity of operations, realization of assets and liquidation of liabilities in the ordinary course of business. The ability of the Company, both during and after the chapter 11 cases, to continue as a going concern is dependent upon, among other things, (i) the ability of the Company to successfully achieve required cost savings to complete its restructuring; (ii) the ability of the Company to maintain adequate cash on hand; (iii) the ability of the Company to generate cash from operations; (iv) the ability of the Company to confirm a plan of reorganization under the Bankruptcy Code and obtain emergency financing; (v) the ability of the Company to maintain its customer base; and (vi) the Company's ability to achieve profitability. There can be no assurance that the Company will be able to successfully achieve these objectives in order to continue as a going concern. The accompanying consolidated financial statements do not include any adjustments that might result should the Company be unable to continue as a going concern.

Report of Independent Registered Public Accounting Firm (in Part)
Board of Directors
Trump Hotels & Casino Resorts, Inc.

We have audited the accompanying consolidated balance sheets of Trump Hotels & Casino Resorts, Inc. as of December 31, 2003 and 2004, and the related consolidated statements of operations, stockholders' equity/deficit, and cash flows for each of the three years in the period ended December 31, 2004. Our audits also included the financial statement schedules as listed in the index at item 15(a). These financial statements and schedule are the responsibility of the Company's management. Our responsibility is to express an opinion on these financial statements and schedule based on our audits.

The accompanying consolidated financial statements have been prepared assuming that the Company will continue as a going concern. As more fully described in Note 1, the Company has experienced increased competition, incurred significant recurring losses from operations, has an accumulated deficit and has filed a voluntary petition seeking to reorganize under chapter 11 of the federal bankruptcy laws. Such circumstances raise substantial doubt about its ability to continue as a going concern. Although the Company is currently operating as a debtor-in-possession under the jurisdiction of the Bankruptcy Court, the continuation of the business as a going concern is contingent upon, among other things: (1) the ability of the Company to maintain compliance with all terms of its current debt structure; (2) the ability of the Company to generate cash from operations and to maintain adequate cash on hand; (3) the resolution of the uncertainty as to the amount of claims that will be allowed; (4) the ability of the Company to confirm a plan of reorganization under the Bankruptcy Code and obtain the required debt and equity financing to emerge from bankruptcy protection; and (5) the Company's ability to achieve profitability. Management's plans in regard to these matters are also described in Note 1. The accompanying consolidated financial statements do not include any adjustments to reflect the possible future effects on the recoverability and classification of assets or the amounts and classification of liabilities that may result from the outcome of this uncertainty.

Ernst & Young, LLP
Philadelphia, Pennsylvania
March 30, 2005

TIME PERIOD

The only accurate way to account for the success or failure of an entity is to accumulate all transactions from the opening of business until the business eventually liquidates. Many years ago, this time period for reporting was acceptable, because it would be feasible to account for and divide up what remained at the completion of the venture. Today, the typical business has a relatively long duration, so it is not feasible to wait until the business liquidates before accounting for its success or failure.

This presents a problem: Accounting for the success or failure of the business in midstream involves inaccuracies. Many transactions and commitments are incomplete at any particular time between the opening and the closing of business. An attempt is made to eliminate the inaccuracies when statements are prepared for a period of time short of an entity's life span, but the inaccuracies cannot be eliminated completely. For example, the entity typically carries accounts receivable at the amount expected to be collected. Only when the receivables are collected can the entity account for them accurately. Until receivables are collected, there exists the possibility that collection cannot be made. The entity will have outstanding obligations at any time, and these obligations cannot be accurately accounted for until they are met. An example would be a warranty on products sold. An entity may also have a considerable investment in the production of inventories. Usually, until the inventory is sold in the normal course of business, the entity cannot accurately account for the investment in inventory.

With the time period assumption, we accept some inaccuracies of accounting for the entity short of its complete life span. We assume that the entity can be accounted for with reasonable accuracy for a particular period of time. In other words, the decision is made to accept some inaccuracy, because of incomplete information about the future, in exchange for more timely reporting.

Some businesses select an accounting period, known as a **natural business year,** that ends when operations are at a low ebb in order to facilitate a better measurement of income and financial position. In many instances, the natural business year of a company ends on December 31. Other businesses use the **calendar year** and thus end the accounting period on December 31. Thus, for many companies that use December 31, we cannot tell if December 31 was selected because it represents a natural business year or if it was selected to represent a calendar year. Some select a 12-month accounting period, known as a **fiscal year,** which closes at the end of a month other than December. The accounting period may be shorter than a year, such as a month. The shorter the period of time, the more inaccuracies we typically expect in the reporting.

At times, this text will refer to *Accounting Trends & Techniques.* This is a book compiled annually by the American Institute of Certified Public Accountants, Inc. *Accounting Trends & Techniques* is "a compilation of data obtained by a survey of 600 annual reports to stockholders undertaken for the purpose of analyzing the accounting information disclosed in such reports. The annual reports surveyed were those of selected industrial, merchandising, technology, and service companies for fiscal periods ending between February 25, 2005, and February 3, 2006."[8]

Exhibit 1-3 summarizes month of fiscal year-end from a financial statement compilation in *Accounting Trends & Techniques.* In Exhibit 1-3 for 2005, 171 survey companies were on a 52- to 53-week fiscal year.[9] Jack in the Box Inc. was one of those companies. Jack in the Box disclosed in its notes to consolidated financial statements: "Our fiscal year is 52 or 53 weeks ending the Sunday closest to September 30. Fiscal years 2005 and 2003 includes 52 weeks, and fiscal year 2004 includes 53 weeks."[10]

Exhibit 1-3 MONTH OF FISCAL YEAR-END*				
	2005	2004	2003	2002
January	30	30	30	31
February	8	8	9	9
March	17	17	16	16
April	8	9	8	7
May	18	18	18	21
June	41	41	49	49
July	13	11	8	8
August	12	11	14	14
September	49	44	42	42
October	17	19	17	16
November	12	12	13	13
Subtotal	225	220	224	226
December	375	380	376	374
Total companies	**600**	**600**	**600**	**600**

*If a fiscal year ended on the first week of a month, the fiscal year was considered to have ended in the preceding month.

Source: *Accounting Trends & Techniques,* copyright © 2006 by American Institute of Certified Public Accountants, Inc., p. ATT-SEC 1.31. Reprinted with permission.

Monetary Unit

Accountants need some standard of measure to bring financial transactions together in a meaningful way. Without some standard of measure, accountants would be forced to report in such terms as 5 cars, 1 factory, and 100 acres. This type of reporting would not be very meaningful.

There are a number of standards of measure, such as a yard, a gallon, and money. Of the possible standards of measure, accountants have concluded that money is the best for the purpose of measuring financial transactions.

Different countries call their monetary units by different names. For example, Japan uses the yen. Different countries also attach different values to their money—1 dollar is not equal to 1 yen. Thus, financial transactions may be measured in terms of money in each country, but the statements from various countries cannot be compared directly or added together until they are converted to a common monetary unit, such as the U.S. dollar.

In various countries, the stability of the monetary unit has been a problem. The loss in value of money is called inflation. In some countries, inflation has been more than 300% per year. In countries where inflation has been significant, financial statements are adjusted by an inflation factor that restores the significance of money as a measuring unit. However, a completely acceptable restoration of money as a measuring unit cannot be made in such cases because of the problems involved in determining an accurate index. To indicate one such problem, consider the price of a car in 1997 and in 2007. The price of the car in 2007 would be higher, but the explanation would not be simply that the general price level has increased. Part of the reason for the price increase would be that the type and quality of the equipment have changed between 1997 and 2007. Thus, an index that relates the 2007 price to the 1997 price is a mixture of inflation, technological advancement, and quality changes.

The rate of inflation in the United States prior to the 1970s was relatively low. Therefore, it was thought that an adjustment of money as a measuring unit was not appropriate, because the added expense and inaccuracies of adjusting for inflation were greater than the benefits. During the 1970s, however, the United States experienced double-digit inflation. This made it increasingly desirable to implement some formal recognition of inflation.

In September 1979, the FASB issued *Statement of Financial Accounting Standards No. 33,* "Financial Reporting and Changing Prices," which required that certain large, publicly held companies disclose certain supplementary information concerning the impact of changing prices in their annual reports for fiscal years ending on or after December 25, 1979. This disclosure later became optional in 1986. Currently, no U.S. company provides this supplementary information.

Historical Cost

SFAC No. 5 identified five different measurement attributes currently used in practice: historical cost, current cost, current market value, net realizable value, and present value. Often, historical cost is used in practice because it is objective and determinable. A deviation from historical cost is accepted when it becomes apparent that the historical cost cannot be recovered. This deviation is justified by the conservatism concept. A deviation from historical cost is also found in practice where specific standards call for another measurement attribute such as current market value, net realizable value, or present value.

Conservatism

The accountant is often faced with a choice of different measurements of a situation, with each measurement having reasonable support. According to the concept of conservatism, the accountant must select the measurement with the least favorable effect on net income and financial position in the current period.

To apply the concept of conservatism to any given situation, there must be alternative measurements, each of which must have reasonable support. The accountant cannot use the conservatism concept to justify arbitrarily low figures. For example, writing inventory down to an arbitrarily low figure in order to recognize any possible loss from selling the inventory constitutes inaccurate accounting and cannot be justified under the concept of conservatism. An acceptable use of conservatism would be to value inventory at the lower of historical cost or market value.

The conservatism concept is used in many other situations, such as writing down or writing off obsolete inventory prior to sale, recognizing a loss on a long-term construction contract when it can be reasonably anticipated, and taking a conservative approach in determining the application of overhead to inventory. Conservatism requires that the estimate of warranty expense reflects the least favorable effect on net income and the financial position of the current period.

REALIZATION

Accountants face a problem of when to recognize revenue. All parts of an entity contribute to revenue, including the janitor, the receiving department, and the production employees. The problem becomes how to determine objectively the contribution of each of the segments toward revenue. Since this is not practical, accountants must determine *when* it is practical to recognize revenue.

In practice, revenue recognition has been the subject of much debate. This has resulted in fairly wide interpretations. The issue of revenue recognition has represented the basis of many SEC enforcement actions. In general, the point of recognition of revenue should be the point in time when revenue can be reasonably and objectively determined. It is essential that there be some uniformity regarding when revenue is recognized, so as to make financial statements meaningful and comparable.

Point of Sale

Revenue is usually recognized at the point of sale. At this time, the earning process is virtually complete, and the exchange value can be determined.

There are times when the use of the point-of-sale approach does not give a fair result. An example would be the sale of land on credit to a buyer who does not have a reasonable ability to pay. If revenue were recognized at the point of sale, there would be a reasonable chance that sales had been overstated because of the material risk of default. There are many other acceptable methods of recognizing revenue that should be considered, such as the following:

1. End of production
2. Receipt of cash
3. During production
4. Cost recovery

End of Production

The recognition of revenue at the completion of the production process is acceptable when the price of the item is known and there is a ready market. The mining of gold or silver is an example, and the harvesting of some farm products would also fit these criteria. If corn is harvested in the fall and held over the winter in order to obtain a higher price in the spring, the realization of revenue from the growing of corn should be recognized in the fall, at the point of harvest. The gain or loss from the holding of the corn represents a separate consideration from the growing of the corn.

Receipt of Cash

The receipt of cash is another basis for revenue recognition. This method should be used when collection is not capable of reasonable estimation at the time of sale. The land sales business, where the purchaser makes only a nominal down payment, is one type of business where the collection of the full amount is especially doubtful. Experience has shown that many purchasers default on the contract.

During Production

Some long-term construction projects recognize revenue as the construction progresses. This exception tends to give a fairer picture of the results for a given period of time. For example, in the building of a utility plant, which may take several years, recognizing revenue as work progresses gives a fairer picture of the results than does having the entire revenue recognized in the period when the plant is completed.

Cost Recovery

The cost recovery approach is acceptable for highly speculative transactions. For example, an entity may invest in a venture search for gold, the outcome of which is completely unpredictable. In this case, the first revenue can be handled as a return of the investment. If more is received than has been invested, the excess would be considered revenue.

In addition to the methods of recognizing revenue described in this chapter, there are many other methods that are usually industry-specific. Being aware of the method(s) used by a specific firm can be important to your understanding of the financial reports.

MATCHING

The revenue realization concept involves when to recognize revenue. Accountants need a related concept that addresses when to recognize the costs associated with the recognized revenue: the **matching concept**. The basic intent is to determine the revenue first and then match the appropriate costs against this revenue.

Some costs, such as the cost of inventory, can be easily matched with revenue. When we sell the inventory and recognize the revenue, the cost of the inventory can be matched against the revenue. Other costs have no direct connection with revenue, so some systematic policy must be adopted in order to allocate these costs reasonably against revenues. Examples are research and development costs and public relations costs. Both research and development costs and public relations costs are charged off in the period incurred. This is inconsistent with the matching concept because the cost would benefit beyond the current period, but it is in accordance with the concept of conservatism.

CONSISTENCY

The **consistency concept** requires the entity to give the same treatment to comparable transactions from period to period. This adds to the usefulness of the reports, since the reports from one period are comparable to the reports from another period. It also facilitates the detection of trends.

Many accounting methods could be used for any single item, such as inventory. If inventory were determined in one period on one basis and in the next period on a different basis, the resulting inventory and profits would not be comparable from period to period.

Entities sometimes need to change particular accounting methods in order to adapt to changing environments. If the entity can justify the use of an alternative accounting method, the change can be made. The entity must be ready to defend the change—a responsibility that should not be taken lightly in view of the liability for misleading financial statements. Sometimes the change will be based on a new accounting pronouncement. When an entity makes a change in accounting methods, the justification for the change must be disclosed, along with an explanation of the effect on the statements.

FULL DISCLOSURE

The accounting reports must disclose all facts that may influence the judgment of an informed reader. If the entity uses an accounting method that represents a departure from the official position of the FASB, disclosure of the departure must be made, along with the justification for it.

Several methods of disclosure exist, such as parenthetical explanations, supporting schedules, cross-references, and notes. Often, the additional disclosures must be made by a note in order to explain the situation properly. For example, details of a pension plan, long-term leases, and provisions of a bond issue are often disclosed in notes.

The financial statements are expected to summarize significant financial information. If all the financial information is presented in detail, it could be misleading. Excessive disclosure could violate the concept of **full disclosure**. Therefore, a reasonable summarization of financial information is required.

Because of the complexity of many businesses and the increased expectations of the public, full disclosure has become one of the most difficult concepts for the accountant to apply. Lawsuits frequently charge accountants with failure to make proper disclosure. Since disclosure is often a judgment decision, it is not surprising that others (especially those who have suffered losses) would disagree with the adequacy of the disclosure.

MATERIALITY

The accountant must consider many concepts and principles when determining how to handle a particular item. The proper use of the various concepts and principles may be costly and time-consuming. The **materiality concept** involves the relative size and importance of an item to a firm. A material item to one entity may not be material to another. For example, an item that costs $100 might be expensed by General Motors, but the same item might be carried as an asset by a small entity.

It is essential that material items be properly handled on the financial statements. Immaterial items are not subject to the concepts and principles that bind the accountant. They may be handled in the most economical and expedient manner possible. However, the accountant faces a judgment situation when determining materiality. It is better to err in favor of an item being material than the other way around.

A basic question when determining whether an item is material is: "Would this item influence an informed reader of the financial statements?" In answering this question, the accountant should consider the statements as a whole.

The Sarbanes-Oxley Act has materiality implications. "The Sarbanes-Oxley Act of 2002 has put demands on management to detect and prevent material control weaknesses in a timely manner. To help management fulfill this responsibility, CPAs are creating monthly key control processes to asses and report on risk. When management finds a key control that does not meet the required minimum quality standard, it must classify the result as a key control exception."[11]

INDUSTRY PRACTICES

Some **industry practices** lead to accounting reports that do not conform to the general theory that underlies accounting. Some of these practices are the result of government regulation. For example, some differences can be found in highly regulated industries, such as insurance, railroad, and utilities.

In the utility industry, an allowance for funds used during the construction period of a new plant is treated as part of the cost of the plant. The offsetting amount is reflected as other income. This amount is based on the utility's hypothetical cost of funds, including funds from debt and stock. This type of accounting is found only in the utility industry.

In some industries, it is very difficult to determine the cost of the inventory. Examples include the meat-packing industry, the flower industry, and farming. In these areas, it may be necessary to determine the inventory value by working backward from the anticipated selling price and subtracting the estimated cost to complete and dispose of the inventory. The inventory would thus be valued at a net realizable value, which would depart from the cost concept and the usual interpretation of the revenue realization concept. If inventory is valued at net realizable value, then the profit has already been recognized and is part of the inventory amount.

The accounting profession is making an effort to reduce or eliminate specific industry practices. However, industry practices that depart from typical accounting procedures will probably never be eliminated completely. Some industries have legitimate peculiarities that call for accounting procedures other than the customary ones.

TRANSACTION APPROACH

The accountant records only events that affect the financial position of the entity and, at the same time, can be reasonably determined in monetary terms. For example, if the entity purchases merchandise on account (on credit), the financial position of the entity changes. This change can be determined in monetary terms as the inventory asset is obtained and the liability, accounts payable, is incurred.

Many important events that influence the prospects for the entity are not recorded and, therefore, are not reflected in the financial statements because they fall outside the transaction approach. The death of a top executive could have a material influence on future prospects, especially for a small company. One of the company's major suppliers could go bankrupt at a time when the entity does not have an alternative source. The entity may have experienced a long strike by its employees or have a history of labor problems. A major competitor may go out of business. All these events may be significant to the entity. They are not recorded because they are not transactions. When projecting the future prospects of an entity, it is necessary to go beyond current financial reports.

Some of the items not recorded will be disclosed. This is done under the full disclosure assumption.

CASH BASIS

The cash basis recognizes revenue when cash is received and recognizes expenses when cash is paid. The cash basis usually does *not* provide reasonable information about the earning capability of the entity in the short run. Therefore, the cash basis is usually *not* acceptable.

ACCRUAL BASIS

The accrual basis of accounting recognizes revenue when realized (realization concept) and expenses when incurred (matching concept). If the difference between the accrual basis and the cash basis is not material, the entity may use the cash basis as an alternative to the accrual basis for income determination. Usually, the difference between the accrual basis and the cash basis is material.

A modified cash basis is sometimes used by professional practices and service organizations. The modified cash basis adjusts for such items as buildings and equipment.

The accrual basis requires numerous adjustments at the end of the accounting period. For example, if insurance has been paid for in advance, the accountant must determine the amounts that belong in prepaid insurance and insurance expense. If employees have not been paid all of their wages, the unpaid wages must be determined and recorded as an expense and as a liability. If revenue has been collected in advance, such as rent received in advance, this revenue relates to future periods and must, therefore, be deferred to those periods. At the end of the accounting period, the unearned rent would be considered a liability.

The use of the accrual basis complicates the accounting process, but the end result is more representative of an entity's financial condition than the cash basis. Without the accrual basis, accountants would not usually be able to make the time period assumption—that the entity can be accounted for with reasonable accuracy for a particular period of time.

The following illustration indicates why the accrual basis is generally regarded as a better measure of a firm's performance than the cash basis.

Assumptions:

1. Sold merchandise (inventory) for $25,000 on credit this year. The merchandise cost $12,500 when purchased in the prior year.
2. Purchased merchandise this year in the amount of $30,000 on credit.
3. Paid suppliers of merchandise $18,000 this year.
4. Collected $15,000 from sales.

	Accrual Basis		Cash Basis
Sales	$ 25,000	Receipts	$ 15,000
Cost of sales (expenses)	(12,500)	Expenditures	(18,000)
Income	$ 12,500	Loss	$ (3,000)

The accrual basis indicates a profitable business, whereas the cash basis indicates a loss. The cash basis does not reasonably indicate when the revenue was earned or when to recognize the cost that relates to the earned revenue. The cash basis does indicate when the receipts and payments (disbursements) occurred. The points in time when cash is received and paid do not usually constitute a good gauge of profitability. However, knowing the points in time is important; the flow of cash will be presented in a separate financial statement (statement of cash flows).

In practice, the accrual basis is modified. Immaterial items are frequently handled on a cash basis, and some specific standards have allowed the cash basis.

Using the Internet

The **Internet** is a global collection of computer networks linked together and available for your use. Information passes easily among these networks because all connected networks use a common communication protocol. The Internet includes local, regional, national, and international backbone networks.

There are many reasons for using the Internet. Some of these reasons include (1) retrieving information, (2) finding information, (3) sending and receiving electronic mail, (4) conducting research, and (5) accessing information databases.

COMPANIES' INTERNET WEB SITES

The majority of publicly held companies in the United States have established a Web site on the Internet. The contents of these Web sites vary. A few companies only provide advertisements and product information. In these cases, a phone number may be given to order more information. Other companies provide limited financial information, such as total revenues, net income, and earnings per share. These companies may also provide advertisements and a phone number for more information. Many companies provide comprehensive financial information and possibly advertisements. The comprehensive financial information may include the annual report and quarterly reports. It may also include the current stock price and the history of the stock price.

HELPFUL WEB SITES

A number of Web sites can be very useful when performing analysis. Many of these Web sites have highlighted text or graphics that can be clicked to go to another related site. Several excellent Web sites follow:

1. **SEC Edgar Database:** http://www.sec.gov. The Securities and Exchange Commission provides a Web site that includes its Edgar Database. This site allows users to download publicly available electronic filings submitted to the SEC from 1994 to the present. By citing the company name, you can select from a menu of recent filings. This will include the 10-K report and the 10-Q.
2. **Rutgers Accounting Web (RAW):** http://accounting.rutgers.edu. This site provides links to many other accounting sites. RAW provides rapid access to many accounting sites without separately targeting each site. These include Edgar, the International Accounting Network, and many other accounting resources. Accounting organizations include the American Accounting Association, American Institute of Certified Public Accountants, and Institute of Management Accountants.
3. **Report Gallery:** http://www.reportgallery.com. This site lists Web sites and annual reports of publicly traded companies.
4. **Financial Accounting Standards Board (FASB):** http://www.fasb.org. Many useful items can be found here including publications, technical projects, and international activities.

5. **U.S. General Services Administration:** http://www.info.gov. This site serves as an entry point to find state, federal, and foreign government information.

6. **U.S. Government Accountability Office (GAO):** http://www.gao.gov/. This is an independent, nonpartisan agency that works for Congress. The GAO issues more than 1,000 reports each year.

7. **Virtual Finance Library:** http://fisher.osu.edu/fin/overview.htm. Contains substantial financial information.

8. **Financial Markets/Stock Exchanges**
   a. **American Stock Exchange:** http://www.amex.com
   b. **Chicago Mercantile Exchange:** http://www.cme.com
   c. **NASDAQ Stock Market:** http://www.nasdaq.com
   d. **New York Stock Exchange:** http://www.nyse.com
   e. **Chicago Board of Trade:** http://www.cbot.com
   The contents of the financial markets/stock exchange sites vary and are expanding.

9. **Newspapers**
   a. *The Wall Street Journal:* http://www.wsj.com (subscription-only site)
   b. *The New York Times:* http://www.nytimes.com
   c. *Financial Times:* http://news.ft.com
   d. *Investor's Business Daily:* http://www.investors.com
   These sites contain substantial financial information including information on the economy, specific companies, and industries.

10. **American Institute of Certified Public Accountants (AICPA):** http://www.aicpa.org. The AICPA is the national organization for U.S. certified public accountants. This site contains substantial information relating to the accounting profession.

11. **International Accounting Standards Board (IASB):** http://www.iasb.org. The IASB sets global financial accounting and reporting standards. This site helps accountants keep abreast of financial accounting and reporting standards worldwide.

12. **Public Company Accounting Oversight Board (PCAOB):** http://www.pcaobus.org. The PCAOB is the private-sector corporation created by the Sarbanes-Oxley Act of 2002. This board is responsible for overseeing the audits of public companies and has broad authority over public accounting firms and auditors. Its actions are subject to the approval of the Securities and Exchange Commission.

13. **Global Accounting Digital Archive Network (GADAN):** http://raw.rutgers.edu/digitallibrary. Combines sources of available digital information and archives related to accounting in various parts of the world.

14. **Financial Portals**
   a. **The Street.com:** http://www.thestreet.com
   b. **Smart Money's Map of the Market:** http://www.smartmoney.com
   c. **Yahoo! Finance:** http://finance.yahoo.com
   d. **Morningstar.com:** http://www.morningstar.com
   e. **MSN Money:** http://moneycentral.msn.com
   f. **MarketWatch.com:** http://www.marketwatch.com
   g. **Reuters:** http://www.investor.reuters.com
   h. **Briefing.com:** http://www.briefing.com
   i. **Zacks Investment Research:** http://www.zacks.com
   j. **BigCharts:** http://www.bigcharts.com
   k. **Dow Jones Indexes:** http://www.djindexes.com
   l. **Russell Investments:** http://www.russell.com
   m. **Standard & Poor's:** http://www.standardandpoors.com
   n. **Wilshire Associates:** http://www.wilshire.com
   o. **Bloomberg.com:** http://www.bloomberg.com
   These financial portals provide information on stock quotes, individual companies, industries, and much more.

Summary

This chapter has reviewed the development of U.S. generally accepted accounting principles and the traditional assumptions of the accounting model. You need a broad understanding of GAAP and the traditional assumptions to reasonably understand financial reports. The financial reports can be no better than the accounting principles and the assumptions of the accounting model that are the basis for preparation.

This chapter also introduced helpful Web sites that can be very useful when performing analysis.

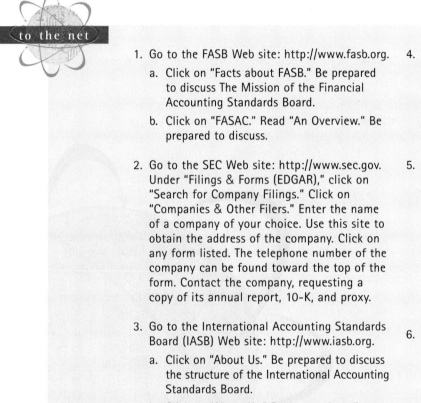

to the net

1. Go to the FASB Web site: http://www.fasb.org.
   a. Click on "Facts about FASB." Be prepared to discuss The Mission of the Financial Accounting Standards Board.
   b. Click on "FASAC." Read "An Overview." Be prepared to discuss.

2. Go to the SEC Web site: http://www.sec.gov. Under "Filings & Forms (EDGAR)," click on "Search for Company Filings." Click on "Companies & Other Filers." Enter the name of a company of your choice. Use this site to obtain the address of the company. Click on any form listed. The telephone number of the company can be found toward the top of the form. Contact the company, requesting a copy of its annual report, 10-K, and proxy.

3. Go to the International Accounting Standards Board (IASB) Web site: http://www.iasb.org.
   a. Click on "About Us." Be prepared to discuss the structure of the International Accounting Standards Board.
   b. Click on "About Us." Be prepared to discuss the history of the International Accounting Standards Board.

4. Go to the Public Company Accounting Oversight Board (PCAOB) Web site: http://www.pcaobus.org.
   a. What is the mission of the Public Company Accounting Oversight Board?
   b. Click on "Rules." Comment on the PCAOB's rule-making process.

5. Go to the American Institute of Certified Public Accountants (AICPA) Web site: http://www.aicpa.org.
   a. Click on "About the AICPA." Click on "AICPA Mission." Be prepared to discuss the mission of the AICPA.
   b. Click on "About the AICPA." Click on "Understanding the Organization." Click on "History." Be prepared to discuss the history of the AICPA.

6. Go to the Yahoo! Finance Web site: http://finance.yahoo.com.
   a. Enter the name of a company in the "Get Quotes" box. Click on "Get Quotes." Comment on what you found.
   b. Click on "Finance Search." Search—"Yahoo! Finance" for—type in "Airbus"—click on "Search." Comment on what you found.

Questions

Q 1-1.   Discuss the role of each of the following in the formulation of accounting principles:
   a. American Institute of Certified Public Accountants
   b. Financial Accounting Standards Board
   c. Securities and Exchange Commission

Q 1-2.   How does the concept of consistency aid in the analysis of financial statements? What type of accounting disclosure is required if this concept is not applied?

Q 1-3.   The president of your firm, Lesky and Lesky, has little background in accounting. Today, he walked into your office and said, "A year ago we bought a piece of land for $100,000. This year, inflation has driven prices up by

6%, and an appraiser just told us we could easily resell the land for $115,000. Yet our balance sheet still shows it at $100,000. It should be valued at $115,000. That's what it's worth. Or, at a minimum, at $106,000." Respond to this statement with specific reference to accounting principles applicable in this situation.

Q 1-4.   Identify the accounting principle(s) applicable to each of the following situations:

a.   Tim Roberts owns a bar and a rental apartment and operates a consulting service. He has separate financial statements for each.

b.   An advance collection for magazine subscriptions is reported as a liability titled Unearned Subscriptions.

c.   Purchases for office or store equipment for less than $25 are entered in Miscellaneous Expense.

d.   A company uses the lower of cost or market for valuation of its inventory.

e.   Partially completed television sets are carried at the sum of the cost incurred to date.

f.   Land purchased 15 years ago for $40,500 is now worth $346,000. It is still carried on the books at $40,500.

g.   Zero Corporation is being sued for $1,000,000 for breach of contract. Its lawyers believe that the damages will be minimal. Zero reports the possible loss in a note.

Q 1-5.   A corporation like General Motors has many owners (stockholders). Which concept enables the accountant to account for transactions of General Motors, separate and distinct from the personal transactions of the owners of General Motors?

Q 1-6.   Zebra Company has incurred substantial financial losses in recent years. Because of its financial condition, the ability of the company to keep operating is in question. Management prepares a set of financial statements that conform to generally accepted accounting principles. Comment on the use of GAAP under these conditions.

Q 1-7.   Because of assumptions and estimates that go into the preparation of financial statements, the statements are inaccurate and are, therefore, not a very meaningful tool to determine the profits or losses of an entity or the financial position of an entity. Comment.

Q 1-8.   The only accurate way to account for the success or failure of an entity is to accumulate all transactions from the opening of business until the business eventually liquidates. Comment on whether this is true. Discuss the necessity of having completely accurate statements.

Q 1-9.   Describe the following terms, which indicate the period of time included in the financial statements:

a.   Natural business year

b.   Calendar year

c.   Fiscal year

Q 1-10.   Which standard of measure is the best for measuring financial transactions?

Q 1-11.   Countries have had problems with the stability of their money. Briefly describe the problem caused for financial statements when money does not hold a stable value.

Q 1-12.   In some countries where inflation has been material, an effort has been made to retain the significance of money as a measuring unit by adjusting the financial statements by an inflation factor. Can an accurate adjustment for inflation be made to the statements? Can a reasonable adjustment to the statements be made? Discuss.

Q 1-13.   An arbitrary write-off of inventory can be justified under the conservatism concept. Is this statement true or false? Discuss.

Q 1-14.   Inventory that has a market value below the historical cost should be written down in order to recognize a loss. Comment.

Q 1-15.   There are other acceptable methods of recognizing revenue when the point of sale is not acceptable. List and discuss the other methods reviewed in this chapter, and indicate when they can be used.

Q 1-16.   The matching concept involves the determination of when to recognize the costs associated with the revenue that is being recognized. For some costs, such as administrative costs, the matching concept is difficult to apply. Comment on when it is difficult to apply the matching concept. What do accountants often do under these circumstances?

Q 1-17. The consistency concept requires the entity to give the same treatment to comparable transactions from period to period. Under what circumstances can an entity change its accounting methods, provided it makes full disclosure?

Q 1-18. Discuss why the concept of full disclosure is difficult to apply.

Q 1-19. No estimates or subjectivity is allowed in the preparation of financial statements. Discuss.

Q 1-20. It is proper to handle immaterial items in the most economical, expedient manner possible. In other words, generally accepted accounting principles do not apply. Comment, including a concept that justifies your answer.

Q 1-21. The same generally accepted accounting principles apply to all companies. Comment.

Q 1-22. Many important events that influence the prospect for the entity are not recorded in the financial records. Comment and give an example.

Q 1-23. Some industry practices lead to accounting reports that do not conform to the general theory that underlies accounting. Comment.

Q 1-24. An entity may choose between the use of the accrual basis of accounting and the cash basis. Comment.

Q 1-25. Generally accepted accounting principles have substantial authoritative support. Indicate the problem with determining substantial authoritative support.

Q 1-26. Would an accountant record the personal assets and liabilities of the owners in the accounts of the business? Explain.

Q 1-27. At which point is revenue from sales on account (credit sales) commonly recognized?

Q 1-28. Elliott Company constructed a building at a cost of $50,000. A local contractor had submitted a bid to construct it for $60,000.
   a. At what amount should the building be recorded?
   b. Should revenue be recorded for the savings between the cost of $50,000 and the bid of $60,000?

Q 1-29. Dexter Company charges to expense all equipment that costs $25 or less. What concept supports this policy?

Q 1-30. Which U.S. government body has the legal power to determine generally accepted accounting principles?

Q 1-31. What is the basic problem with the monetary assumption when there has been significant inflation?

Q 1-32. Explain the matching principle. How is the matching principle related to the realization concept?

Q 1-33. Briefly explain the term generally accepted accounting principles.

Q 1-34. Briefly describe the operating procedure for Statements of Financial Accounting Standards.

Q 1-35. What is the FASB Conceptual Framework for Accounting and Reporting intended to provide?

Q 1-36. Briefly describe the following:
   a. Committee on Accounting Procedures
   b. Committee on Accounting Terminology
   c. Accounting Principles Board
   d. Financial Accounting Standards Board

Q 1-37. The objectives of general-purpose external financial reporting are primarily to serve the needs of management. Comment.

Q 1-38. Financial accounting is designed to measure directly the value of a business enterprise. Comment.

Q 1-39.   According to SFAC No. 2, relevance and reliability are the two primary qualities that make accounting information useful for decision making. Comment on what is meant by relevance and reliability.

Q 1-40.   SFAC No. 5 indicates that, to be recognized, an item should meet four criteria, subject to the cost-benefit constraint and materiality threshold. List these criteria.

Q 1-41.   There are five different measurement attributes currently used in practice. List these measurement attributes.

Q 1-42.   Briefly explain the difference between an accrual basis income statement and a cash basis income statement.

Q 1-43.   The cash basis does not reasonably indicate when the revenue was earned and when the cost should be recognized. Comment.

Q 1-44.   It is not important to know when cash is received and when payment is made. Comment.

Q 1-45.   Comment on what Section 404 of the Sarbanes-Oxley Act requires of companies.

Q 1-46.   Under the Sarbanes-Oxley Act, what must the financial statement auditor do in relation to the company's internal control?

Q 1-47.   Comment on perceived benefits from Section 404 of the Sarbanes-Oxley Act.

Q 1-48.   Comment on the responsibility of private companies under the Sarbanes-Oxley Act.

Q 1-49.   If its accounting period ends December 31, would a company be using a natural business year or a fiscal year?

Q 1-50.   Describe the book *Accounting Trends & Techniques*.

Q 1-51.   Comment on the materiality implications of the Sarbanes-Oxley Act.

Q 1-52.   Briefly describe the Public Company Accounting Oversight Board (PCAOB).

Q 1-53.   Why did the FASB commence the Accounting Standards Codification™ project?

Problems

P 1-1.   FASB Statement of Concepts No. 2 indicates several qualitative characteristics of useful accounting information. Following is a list of some of these qualities, as well as a list of statements and phrases describing the qualities.

a. Benefits > costs
b. Decision usefulness
c. Relevance
d. Reliability
e. Predictive value, feedback value, timeliness

f. Verifiability, neutrality, representational faithfulness
g. Comparability
h. Materiality
i. Relevance, reliability

_____ 1. Without usefulness, there would be no benefits from information to set against its cost.
_____ 2. Pervasive constraint imposed upon financial accounting information.
_____ 3. Constraint that guides the threshold for recognition.
_____ 4. A quality requiring that the information be timely and that it also have predictive value, or feedback value, or both.
_____ 5. A quality requiring that the information have representational faithfulness and that it be verifiable and neutral.
_____ 6. These are the two primary qualities that make accounting information useful for decision making.
_____ 7. These are the ingredients needed to ensure that the information is relevant.
_____ 8. These are the ingredients needed to ensure that the information is reliable.
_____ 9. Includes consistency and interacts with relevance and reliability to contribute to the usefulness of information.

Required   Place the appropriate letter identifying each quality on the line in front of the statement or phrase describing the quality.

P 1-2.   Certain underlying considerations have had an important impact on the development of generally accepted accounting principles. Following is a list of these underlying considerations, as well as a list of statements describing them.

a. Going concern or continuity
b. Monetary unit
c. Conservatism
d. Matching
e. Full disclosure
f. Materiality
g. Transaction approach
h. Accrual basis

i. Industry practices
j. Verifiability
k. Consistency
l. Realization
m. Historical cost
n. Time period
o. Business entity

_____ 1. The business for which the financial statements are prepared is separate and distinct from the owners.
_____ 2. The assumption is made that the entity will remain in business for an indefinite period of time.
_____ 3. Accountants need some standard of measure to bring financial transactions together in a meaningful way.
_____ 4. Revenue should be recognized when the earning process is virtually complete and the exchange value can be objectively determined.
_____ 5. This concept deals with when to recognize the costs that are associated with the recognized revenue.
_____ 6. Accounting reports must disclose all facts that may influence the judgment of an informed reader.
_____ 7. This concept involves the relative size and importance of an item to a firm.
_____ 8. The accountant is required to adhere as closely as possible to verifiable data.
_____ 9. Some companies use accounting reports that do not conform to the general theory that underlies accounting.
_____ 10. The accountant records only events that affect the financial position of the entity and, at the same time, can be reasonably determined in monetary terms.
_____ 11. Revenue must be recognized when it is realized (realization concept), and expenses are recognized when incurred (matching concept).
_____ 12. The entity must give the same treatment to comparable transactions from period to period.
_____ 13. The measurement with the least favorable effect on net income and financial position in the current period must be selected.
_____ 14. Of the various values that could be used, this value has been selected because it is objective and determinable.
_____ 15. With this assumption, inaccuracies of accounting for the entity short of its complete life span are accepted.

Required   Place the appropriate letter identifying each quality on the line in front of the statement describing the quality.

P 1-3.

Required   Answer the following multiple-choice questions:
a. Which of the following is a characteristic of information provided by external financial reports?
   1. The information is exact and not subject to change.
   2. The information is frequently the result of reasonable estimates.
   3. The information pertains to the economy as a whole.
   4. The information is provided at the least possible cost.
   5. None of the above.
b. Which of the following is *not* an objective of financial reporting?
   1. Financial reporting should provide information that is useful to present and potential investors and creditors and other users in making rational investment, credit, and similar decisions.
   2. Financial reporting should provide information to help present and potential investors and creditors and other users in assessing the amounts, timing, and uncertainty of prospective cash receipts from dividends or interest and the proceeds from the sale, redemption, or maturity of securities or loans.

      3. Financial reporting should provide information about the economic resources of an enterprise, the claims against those resources, and the effects of transactions, events, and circumstances that change the resources and claims against those resources.

      4. Financial accounting is designed to measure directly the value of a business enterprise.

      5. None of the above.

c. According to FASB Statement of Concepts No. 2, which of the following is an ingredient of the quality of relevance?

      1. Verifiability

      2. Representational faithfulness

      3. Neutrality

      4. Timeliness

      5. None of the above

d. The primary current source of generally accepted accounting principles for nongovernment operations is the

      1. New York Stock Exchange

      2. Financial Accounting Standards Board

      3. Securities and Exchange Commission

      4. American Institute of Certified Public Accountants

      5. None of the above

e. What is the underlying concept that supports the immediate recognition of a loss?

      1. Matching

      2. Consistency

      3. Judgment

      4. Conservatism

      5. Going concern

f. Which statement is *not* true?

      1. The Securities and Exchange Commission is a source of some generally accepted accounting principles.

      2. The American Institute of Certified Public Accountants is a source of some generally accepted accounting principles.

      3. The Internal Revenue Service is a source of some generally accepted accounting principles.

      4. The Financial Accounting Standards Board is a source of some generally accepted accounting principles.

      5. Numbers 1, 2, and 4 are sources of generally accepted accounting principles.

g. Which pronouncements are *not* issued by the Financial Accounting Standards Board?

      1. Statements of Financial Accounting Standards

      2. Statements of Financial Accounting Concepts

      3. Technical bulletins

      4. Interpretations

      5. Opinions

P 1-4.

Required   Answer the following multiple-choice questions:

a. Which of the following does the Financial Accounting Standards Board *not* issue?

      1. Statements of Position (SOPs)

      2. Statements of Financial Accounting Standards (SFASs)

      3. Interpretations

      4. Technical bulletins

      5. Statements of Financial Accounting Concepts (SFACs)

b. According to SFAC No. 6, assets can be defined by which of the following?

      1. Probable future sacrifices of economic benefits arising from present obligations of a particular entity to transfer assets or provide services to other entities in the future as a result of past transactions or events.

      2. Probable future economic benefits obtained or controlled by a particular entity as a result of past transactions or events.

      3. Residual interest on the assets of an entity that remains after deducting its liabilities.

4. Increases in equity of a particular business enterprise resulting from transfers to the enterprise from other entities of something of value to obtain or increase ownership interests (or equity) in it.

5. Decrease in equity of a particular business enterprise resulting from transferring assets, rendering services, or incurring liabilities by the enterprise.

c. According to SFAC No. 6, expenses can be defined by which of the following?

1. Inflows or other enhancements of assets of an entity or settlements of its liabilities (or a combination of both) from delivering or producing goods, rendering services, or other activities that constitute the entity's ongoing major or central operations.

2. Outflows or other consumption or using up of assets or incurrences of liabilities (or a combination of both) from delivering or producing goods, rendering services, or carrying out other activities that constitute the entity's ongoing major or central operations.

3. Increases in equity (net assets) from peripheral or incidental transactions of an entity and from all other transactions and other events and circumstances affecting the entity during a period, except those that result from revenues or investments.

4. Decreases in equity (net assets) from peripheral or incidental transactions of an entity and from all other transactions and other events and circumstances affecting the entity during a period, except those that result from expenses or distributions to owners.

5. Probable future economic benefits obtained or controlled by a particular entity as a result of past transactions or events.

d. SFAC No. 5 indicates that an item, to be recognized, should meet four criteria, subject to the cost-benefit constraint and the materiality threshold. Which of the following is *not* one of the four criteria?

1. The item fits one of the definitions of the elements.
2. The item has a relevant attribute measurable with sufficient reliability.
3. The information related to the item is relevant.
4. The information related to the item is reliable.
5. The item has comparability, including consistency.

e. SFAC No. 5 identifies five different measurement attributes currently used in practice. Which of the following is *not* one of the measurement attributes currently used in practice?

1. Historical cost
2. Future cost
3. Current market value
4. Net realizable value
5. Present, or discounted, value of future cash flows

f. Which of the following indicates how revenue is usually recognized?

1. Point of sale
2. End of production
3. Receipt of cash
4. During production
5. Cost recovery

g. *Statement of Financial Accounting Concepts No. 1,* "Objectives of Financial Reporting by Business Enterprises," includes all of the following objectives, except one. Which objective does it *not* include?

1. Financial accounting is designed to measure directly the value of a business enterprise.

2. Investors, creditors, and others may use reported earnings and information about the elements of financial statements in various ways to assess the prospects for cash flows.

3. The primary focus of financial reporting is information about earnings and its components.

4. Financial reporting should provide information that is useful to present and potential investors and creditors and other users in making rational investment, credit, and similar decisions.

5. The objectives are those of general-purpose external financial reporting by business enterprises.

P 1-5. The following data relate to Jones Company for the year ended December 31, 2007:

Sales on credit	$80,000
Cost of inventory sold on credit	65,000
Collections from customers	60,000
Purchase of inventory on credit	50,000
Payment for purchases	55,000
Cash collections for common stock	30,000
Dividends paid	10,000
Payment to salesclerk	10,000

Required   a. Determine income on an accrual basis.

              b. Determine income on a cash basis.

P 1-6.   Matching Acronyms

Required   Listed below are phrases with the appropriate acronym. Match the letter that goes with each definition.

              a. Generally accepted accounting principles (GAAP)
              b. Securities and Exchange Commission (SEC)
              c. Financial Reporting Releases (FRRs)
              d. American Institute of Certified Public Accountants (AICPA)
              e. Certified public accountants (CPAs)
              f. Accounting Principles Board (APB)
              g. Accounting Principles Board Opinions (APBOs)
              h. Accounting Principles Board Statements (APBSs)
              i. Financial Accounting Standards Board (FASB)
              j. Financial Accounting Foundation (FAF)
              k. Financial Accounting Standards Advisory Council (FASAC)
              l. Statements of Financial Standards (SFASs)
              m. Statements of Financial Accounting Concepts (SFACs)
              n. Discussion Memorandum (DM)
              o. Exposure Draft (ED)
              p. Accounting Standards Executive Committee (AcSEC)
              q. Statements of Position (SOP)
              r. Emerging Issues Task Force (EITF)
              s. The Public Company Accounting Oversight Board (PCAOB)

              _____ 1. Accounting principles that have substantial authoritative support.
              _____ 2. A task force of representatives from the accounting profession created by the FASB to deal with emerging issues of financial reporting.
              _____ 3. A proposed Statement of Financial Accounting Standards.
              _____ 4. Issued by the Accounting Standards Division of the AICPA to influence the development of accounting standards.
              _____ 5. Created by the Securities Exchange Act of 1934.
              _____ 6. A professional accounting organization whose members are certified public accountants.
              _____ 7. Issued official opinions on accounting standards between 1959–1973.
              _____ 8. Represent views of the Accounting Principles Board but not the official opinions.
              _____ 9. This board issues four types of pronouncements: (1) Statements of Financial Accounting Standards, (2) Interpretations, (3) Technical bulletins, and (4) Statements of Financial Accounting Concepts.
              _____ 10. Governs the Financial Accounting Standards Board.
              _____ 11. These statements are issued by the Financial Accounting Standards Board and establish GAAP for specific accounting issues.
              _____ 12. These statements are issued by the Financial Accounting Standards Board and provide a theoretical foundation upon which to base GAAP. They are not part of GAAP.
              _____ 13. Serves as the official voice of the AICPA in matters relating to financial accounting and reporting standards.
              _____ 14. Presents all known facts and points of view on a topic. Issued by the FASB.
              _____ 15. Responsible for advising the FASB.
              _____ 16. Represented official positions of the APB.
              _____ 17. An accountant who has received a certificate stating that he/she has met the requirements of state law.
              _____ 18. Issued by the SEC and give the SEC's official position on matters relating to financial statements.
              _____ 19. Adopts auditing standards.

Case 1-1

STANDARDS OVERLOAD?*

Even though accounting records go back hundreds of years, there was little effort to develop accounting standards until the 1900s. The first major effort to develop accounting standards in the United States came in 1939 when the American Institute of Certified Public Accountants formed the Committee on Accounting Procedures.

As the number of standards increased, an issue called "standards overload" emerged. Essentially, the charge of "standards overload" is that there are too many accounting standards and that the standards are too complicated. Many individuals charging that standards overload is a problem maintain that more professional judgment should be allowed in financial accounting. Some individuals take a position that selected standards should not apply to nonpublic companies. Others take a position that "little" companies should be exempt from selected standards. There has been some selective exclusion from standards in the past. Examples of selective exclusion are the following:

1. *Statement of Financial Accounting Standards No. 21,* "Suspension of the Reporting of Earnings per Share and Segment Information by Nonpublic Enterprises."
   "Although the presentation of earnings per share and segment information is not required in the financial statements of nonpublic enterprises, any such information that is presented in the financial statements of nonpublic enterprises shall be consistent with the requirements of APB Opinion No. 15 and FASB Statement No. 14."
2. *Statement of Financial Accounting Standards No. 33,* "Financial Reporting and Changing Prices."
   This statement required supplemental reporting on the effects of price changes. Only large public companies were required to present this information on a supplementary basis.

Required   a. Financial statements should aid the user of the statements in making decisions. In your opinion, would the user of the statements be aided if there were a distinction between financial reporting standards for public vs. nonpublic companies? Between little and big companies?
   b. In your opinion, would CPAs favor a distinction between financial reporting standards for public vs. nonpublic companies? Discuss.
   c. In your opinion, would small business owner-managers favor a distinction between financial reporting standards for small and large companies? Discuss.
   d. In your opinion, would CPAs in a small CPA firm view standards overload as a bigger problem than CPAs in a large CPA firm? Discuss.
   e. Comment on standards overload, considering *Statement of Financial Accounting Concepts No. 1,* "Objectives of Financial Reporting by Business Enterprises." Particularly consider the following objective:
   Financial reporting should provide information useful to present and potential investors and creditors and other users in making rational investment, credit, and similar decisions. The information should be comprehensible to those having a reasonable understanding of business and economic activities and willing to study the information with reasonable diligence.

*The standards referenced in this case should not be considered current standards. The financial reporting issues referenced in this case are discussed in later chapters, using current requirements.

Case 1-2

STANDARD SETTING: "A POLITICAL ASPECT"

This case consists of a letter from Dennis R. Beresford, chairperson of the Financial Accounting Standards Board, to Senator Joseph I. Lieberman. The specific issue was proposed legislation relating to the accounting for employee stock options.

Permission to reprint the following letter was obtained from the Financial Accounting Standards Board.

(continued)

Case	STANDARD SETTING: "A POLITICAL ASPECT" (Continued)
1-2	

August 3, 1993

Senator Joseph I. Lieberman
United States Senate
Hart Senate Office Building
Room 316
Washington, DC 20510

Dear Senator Lieberman:

Members of the Financial Accounting Standards Board (the FASB or the Board) and its staff routinely consult with members of Congress, their staffs, and other government officials on matters involving financial accounting. For example, FASB members and staff met with Senator Levin both before and after the introduction of his proposed legislation, Senate Bill 259, which also addresses accounting for employee stock options.

The attachment to this letter discusses the accounting issues (we have not addressed the tax issues) raised in your proposed legislation, Senate Bill 1175, and issues raised in remarks introduced in the *Congressional Record*. My comments in this letter address an issue that is more important than any particular legislation or any particular accounting issue: why we have a defined process for setting financial reporting standards and why it is harmful to the public interest to distort accounting reports in an attempt to attain other worthwhile goals.

Financial Reporting

Markets are enormously efficient information processors—when they have the information and that information faithfully portrays economic events. Financial statements are one of the basic tools for communicating that information. The U.S. capital market system is well-developed and efficient because of users' confidence that the financial information they receive is reliable. Common accounting standards for the preparation of financial reports contribute to their credibility. The mission of the FASB, an organization designed to be independent of all other business and professional organizations, is to establish and improve financial accounting and reporting standards in the United States.

Investors, creditors, regulators, and other users of financial reports make business and economic decisions based on information in financial statements. Credibility is critical whether the user is an individual contemplating a stock investment, a bank making lending decisions, or a regulatory agency reviewing solvency. Users count on financial reports that are evenhanded, neutral, and unbiased.

An efficiently functioning economy requires credible financial information as a basis for decisions about allocation of resources. If financial statements are to be useful, they must report economic activity without coloring the message to influence behavior in a particular direction. They must not intentionally favor one party over another. Financial statements must provide a neutral scorecard of the effects of transactions.

Economic Consequences of Accounting Standards

The Board often hears that we should take a broader view, that we must consider the economic consequences of a new accounting standard. The FASB should not act, critics maintain, if a new accounting standard would have undesirable economic consequences. We have been told that the effects of accounting standards could cause lasting damage to American companies and their employees. Some have suggested, for example, that recording the liability for retiree health care or the costs for stock-based compensation will place U.S. companies at a competitive disadvantage. These critics suggest that because of accounting standards, companies may reduce benefits or move operations overseas to areas where workers do not demand the same benefits. These assertions are usually combined with statements about desirable goals, like providing retiree health care or creating employee incentives.

(continued)

There is a common element in those assertions. The goals are desirable, but the means require that the Board abandon neutrality and establish reporting standards that conceal the financial impact of certain transactions from those who use financial statements. Costs of transactions exist whether or not the FASB mandates their recognition in financial statements. For example, not requiring the recognition of the cost of stock options or ignoring the liabilities for retiree health benefits does not alter the economics of the transactions. It only withholds information from investors, creditors, policy makers, and others who need to make informed decisions and, eventually, impairs the credibility of financial reports.

One need only look to the collapse of the thrift industry to demonstrate the consequences of abandoning neutrality. During the 1970s and 1980s, regulatory accounting principles (RAP) were altered to obscure problems in troubled institutions. Preserving the industry was considered a "greater good." Many observers believe that the effect was to delay action and hide the true dimensions of the problem. The public interest is best served by neutral accounting standards that inform policy rather than promote it. Stated simply, truth in accounting is always good policy.

Neutrality does not mean that accounting should not influence human behavior. We expect that changes in financial reporting will have economic consequences, just as economic consequences are inherent in existing financial reporting practices. Changes in behavior naturally flow from more complete and representationally faithful financial statements. The fundamental question, however, is whether those who measure and report on economic events should somehow screen the information before reporting it to achieve some objective. In FASB Concepts Statement No. 2, "Qualitative Characteristics of Accounting Information" (paragraph 102), the Board observed:

> *Indeed, most people are repelled by the notion that some "big brother," whether government or private, would tamper with scales or speedometers surreptitiously to induce people to lose weight or obey speed limits or would slant the scoring of athletic events or examinations to enhance or decrease someone's chances of winning or graduating. There is no more reason to abandon neutrality in accounting measurement.*

The Board continues to hold that view. The Board does not set out to achieve particular economic results through accounting pronouncements. We could not if we tried. Beyond that, it is seldom clear which result we should seek because our constituents often have opposing viewpoints. Governments, and the policy goals they adopt, frequently change.

Standard Setting in the Private Sector

While the SEC and congressional committees maintain active oversight of the FASB to ensure that the public interest is served, throughout its history the SEC has relied on the Board and its predecessors in the private sector to establish and improve financial accounting and reporting standards. In fulfilling the Board's mission of improving financial reporting, accounting standards are established through a system of due process and open deliberation. On all of our major projects, this involves open Board meetings, proposals published for comment, "field testing" of proposals, public hearings, and redeliberation of the issues in light of comments.

Our due process has allowed us to deal with complex and highly controversial accounting issues, ranging from pensions and retiree health care to abandonment of nuclear power plants. This open, orderly process for standard setting precludes placing any particular special interest above the interests of the many who rely on financial information. The Board believes that the public interest is best served by developing neutral accounting standards that result in accounting for similar transactions similarly and different transactions differently. The resulting financial statements provide as complete and faithful a picture of an entity as possible.

Corporations, accounting firms, users of financial statements, and most other interested parties have long supported the process of establishing accounting standards in the private

(continued)

Case 1-2   STANDARD SETTING: "A POLITICAL ASPECT" (Continued)

sector without intervention by Congress or other branches of government. Despite numerous individual issues on which the FASB and many of its constituents have disagreed, that support has continued. The resulting system of accounting standards and financial reporting, while not perfect, is the best in the world.

Conclusion

We understand that there are a number of people who believe that their particular short-term interests are more important than an effectively functioning financial reporting system. We sincerely hope, however, that you and others in the Congress will review the reasons that have led generations of lawmakers and regulators to conclude that neutral financial reporting is critical to the functioning of our economic system and that the best way to achieve that end is to allow the existing private sector process to proceed. We respectfully submit that the public interest will be best served by that course. As former SEC Chairman Richard Breeden said in testimony to the Senate Banking Committee in 1990:

> *The purpose of accounting standards is to assure that financial information is presented in a way that enables decision-makers to make informed judgments. To the extent that accounting standards are subverted to achieve objectives unrelated to a fair and accurate presentation, they fail in their purpose.*

The attachment to this letter discusses your proposed legislation. It also describes some aspects of our project on stock compensation and the steps in our due process procedures that remain before the project will be completed. In your remarks in the Congressional Record, you said that you will address future issues, including an examination of the current treatment of employee stock options, over the next weeks and months. We would be pleased to meet with you or your staff to discuss these topics and the details of our project. I will phone your appointments person in the next two weeks to see if it is convenient for you to meet with me.

Sincerely,

Dennis R. Beresford

Dennis R. Beresford

Enclosure
cc: The Honorable Connie Mack
       The Honorable Dianne Feinstein
       The Honorable Barbara Boxer
       The Honorable Carl S. Levin
       The Honorable Christopher J. Dodd
       The Honorable Arthur J. Levitt

Required
   a. "Financial statements must provide a neutral scorecard of the effects of transactions." Comment.
   b. "Costs of transactions exist whether or not the FASB mandates their recognition in financial statements." Comment.
   c. In the United States, standard setting is in the private sector. Comment.
   d. Few, if any, accounting standards are without some economic impact. Comment.

Case 1-3   STANDARD SETTING: "BY THE WAY OF THE UNITED STATES CONGRESS"

In the summer of 1993, the Senate and the House introduced identical bills to amend the Internal Revenue Code of 1986. Section 4 of these bills addressed stock option compensation and financial reporting.

(continued)

SEC. 4 Stock Option Compensation.

Section 14 of the Securities Exchange Act of 1934 (15 U.S.C. 78n) is amended by adding at the end the following new subsection:

"(h) STOCK OPTION COMPENSATION—The Commission shall not require or permit an issuer to recognize any expense or other charge in financial statements furnished to its security holders resulting from, or attributable to, either the grant, vesting, or exercise of any option or other right to acquire any equity security of such issuer (even if the right to exercise such option or right is subject to any conditions, contingencies or other criteria including, without limitation, the continued performance of services, achievement of performance objectives, or the occurrence of any event) which is granted to its directors, officers, employees, or other persons in connection with the performance of services, where the exercise price of such option or right is not less than the fair market value of the underlying security at the time such option or right is granted."

Required
   a. The United States Congress is well qualified to debate and set generally accepted accounting principles. Comment.
   b. Speculate on why these bills were directed to amend the Securities Exchange Act of 1934.

Case 1-4

FLYING HIGH*

Note 1

Summary of Significant Accounting Policies (in Part)

Contract accounting—Contract accounting is used for development and production activities predominately by the Aircraft and Weapons Systems (A&WS), Network Systems, Support Systems, and Launch and Orbital Systems (L&OS) segments within Integrated Defense Systems (IDS). These activities include the following products and systems: military aircraft, helicopters, missiles, space systems, missile defense systems, satellites, rocket engines, and information and battle management systems. The majority of business conducted in these segments is performed under contracts with the U.S. Government and foreign governments that extend over a number of years. Contract accounting involves a judgmental process of estimating the total sales and costs for each contract, which results in the development of estimated cost of sales percentages. For each sale contract, the amount reported as cost of sales is determined by applying the estimated cost of sales percentage to the amount of revenue recognized.

Sales related to contracts with fixed prices are recognized as deliveries are made, except for certain fixed-price contracts that require substantial performance over an extended period before deliveries begin, for which sales are recorded based on the attainment of performance milestones. Sales related to contracts in which we are reimbursed for costs incurred plus an agreed upon profit are recorded as costs are incurred. The majority of these contracts are with the U.S. Government. The Federal Acquisition regulations provide guidance on the types of cost that will be reimbursed in establishing contract price. Contracts may contain provisions to earn incentive and award fees if targets are achieved. Incentive and award fees that can be reasonably estimated are recorded over the performance period of the contract. Incentive and award fees that cannot be reasonably estimated are recorded when awarded.

*"The Boeing Company, together with its subsidiaries . . . is one of the world's major aerospace firms." 10-K

(continued)

Program accounting—We use program accounting to account for sales and cost of sales related to all our commercial airplane programs by the Commercial Airplanes segment. Program accounting is a method of accounting applicable to products manufactured for delivery under production-type contracts where profitability is realized over multiple contracts and years. Under program accounting, inventoriable production costs, program tooling costs and warranty costs are accumulated and charged as cost of sales by program instead of by individual units or contracts. A program consists of the estimated number of units (accounting quantity) of a product to be produced in a continuing, long-term production effort for delivery under existing and anticipated contracts. To establish the relationship of sales to cost of sales, program accounting requires estimates of (a) the number of units to be produced and sold in a program, (b) the period over which the units can reasonably be expected to be produced, and (c) the units' expected sales prices, production costs, program tooling, and warranty costs for the total program.

We recognize sales for commercial airplane deliveries as each unit is completed and accepted by the customer. Sales recognized represent the price negotiated with the customer, adjusted by an escalation formula. The amount reported as cost of sales is determined by applying the estimated cost of sales percentage for the total remaining program to the amount of sales recognized for airplanes delivered and accepted by the customer.

Service revenue—Service revenue is recognized when the service is performed. This method is predominately used by our Support Systems, L&OS and Commercial Airplanes segments. Service activities include the following: Delta launches, ongoing maintenance of International Space Station, Space Shuttle and explosive detection systems, support agreements associated with military aircraft and helicopter contracts and technical and flight operation services for commercial aircraft. BCC lease and financing revenue is also included in "Service revenue" on the Consolidated Statements of Operations. See the "Lease and financing arrangements" section below for a discussion of BCC's revenue recognition policies.

Notes receivable—At commencement of a note receivable issued for the purchase of aircraft or equipment, we record the note and any unamortized discounts. Interest income and amortization of any discounts are recorded ratably over the related term of the note.

Required

a. **Contract Accounting (in Part)**

"Contracts may contain provisions to earn incentive and award fees if targets are achieved. Incentive and award fees that can be reasonably estimated are recorded over the performance period of the contract. Incentive and award fees that cannot be reasonably estimated are recorded when awarded."

Comment on the difficulty in determining which incentive and award fees can be reasonably estimated.

b. **Program Accounting (in Part)**

"We recognize sales for commercial airplane deliveries as each unit is completed and accepted by the customer. Sales recognized represent the price negotiated with the customer, adjusted by an escalation formula."

Comment on the difficulty in determining the sales amount.

"The amount reported as cost of sales is determined by applying the estimated cost of sales percentage for the total remaining program to the amount of sales recognized for airplanes delivered and accepted by the customer."

Does it appear more difficult to determine the sales or cost of sales? Comment.

c. **Service Revenue (in Part)**

"Service revenue is recognized when the service is performed."

Is it difficult to determine service revenue? Comment.

d. **Notes Receivable**

"At commencement of a note receivable issued for the purchase of aircraft or equipment, we record the note and any unamortized discounts. Interest income and amortization of any discounts are recorded ratably over the related term of the note."

Is it difficult to determine revenue from notes receivable? Comment.

HAWAII CENTERED

Alexander & Baldwin, Inc.*

Notes to Consolidated Financial Statements (in Part)
1. Summary of Significant Accounting Policies (in Part)

Real Estate Sales Revenue Recognition: Sales are recorded when the risks and benefits of ownership have passed to the buyers (generally on closing dates), adequate down payments have been received, and collection of remaining balances is reasonably assured.

Real Estate Leasing Revenue Recognition: Rental revenue is recognized on a straight-line basis over the terms of the related leases, including periods for which no rent is due (typically referred to as "rent holidays"). Differences between revenue recognized and amounts due under respective lease agreements are recorded as increases or decreases, as applicable, to deferred rent receivable. Also included in rental revenue are certain tenant reimbursements and percentage rents determined in accordance with the terms of the leases. Income arising from tenant rents that are contingent upon the sales of the tenant exceeding a defined threshold are recognized in accordance with Staff Accounting Bulletin 101, which states that this income is to be recognized only after the contingency has been removed (i.e., sales thresholds have been achieved).

Sugar and Coffee Revenue Recognition: Revenue from bulk raw sugar sales is recorded when delivered to the cooperative of Hawaiian producers, based on the estimated net return to producers in accordance with contractual agreements. Revenue from coffee is recorded when the title to the product and risk of loss passes to third parties (generally this occurs when the product is shipped or delivered to customers) and when collection is reasonably assured.

Required
a. Real Estate Sales Revenue Recognition—Conservative? Reasonable?
b. Real Estate Leasing Revenue Recognition—Why is income arising from tenant rents that are contingent upon the sales of the tenant exceeding a defined threshold handled differently than the "normal" real estate leasing?
c. Sugar and Coffee Revenue Recognition
1. Bulk raw sugar sales (why recorded based on the estimated net return to producers)?
2. Revenue from coffee (revenue recognition reasonable)?

*"Alexander & Baldwin, Inc. ('A&B') is a diversified corporation with most of its operations centered in Hawaii. It was founded in 1870 and incorporated in 1900. Ocean transportation operations, related shoreside operations in Hawaii, and intermodal, truck brokerage and logistics services are conducted by a wholly-owned subsidiary, Matson Navigation Company, Inc. ('Matson') and two Matson subsidiaries. Property development and food products operations are conducted by A&B and certain other subsidiaries of A&B." 10-K

GOING CONCERN?

TRM Corporation

Annual report to the United States Securities and Exchange Commission
For the fiscal year ended December 31, 2006

Part I (in Part)

ITEM 1. BUSINESS (in Part)

General

Where you can find more information. We file annual, quarterly and other reports, proxy statements and other information with the Securities and Exchange Commission ("SEC"). We also make available free of charge through our website at www.trm.com, our annual report on Form 10-K, quarterly

(continued)

reports on Form 10-Q, current reports on Form 8-K, and amendments to those reports filed or furnished pursuant to Section 13(a) or 15(d) of the Exchange Act as soon as reasonably practicable after they are filed electronically with the SEC.

Overview. We are an owner and operator of off-premises networks of automated teller machines, or ATMs. We expanded into the ATM business in 1999, leveraging the experience and infrastructure we had established in developing our photocopier operations, which began in 1981. During 2006 we operated ATM networks in the United States, United Kingdom, Canada and Germany, and operated photocopier networks in the United States, United Kingdom and Canada. From 2001 to 2005, we expanded our ATM operations through both internal growth and through acquisitions including, in November 2004, the acquisition of a network of over 15,000 ATMs from eFunds Corporation. However, as a result of financial difficulties that we encountered beginning in 2005, in 2006 we determined to sell assets in order to reduce debt and to focus our business on our U.S. ATM operations. As a result, we sold our United Kingdom photocopy business in June 2006, our United Kingdom, Canadian and German ATM businesses in January 2007, and our United States photocopy business in January 2007. Currently, we operate ATMs in the United States and photocopiers in Canada. During 2006 our United States ATM networks had an average of 12,378 transacting ATMs and our Canadian photocopy network had an average of 2,751 photocopiers.

We locate our ATMs and photocopiers in high traffic retail environments through national merchants such as The Pantry, Cumberland Farms, and Wal-Mart, and through regional and locally-owned supermarkets, convenience and other stores. In addition to providing our merchant customers with supplemental revenues from shared transaction fees, we believe that the presence of ATMs and photocopiers in a merchant's store helps to promote higher foot traffic, increased impulse purchases and longer shopping times since they often make the retail site a destination for cash and photocopies. We attempt to maximize the usefulness of our ATMs to our customers by participating in as many electronic funds transfer networks, or EFTNs, as practical, including NYCE, Visa, Mastercard, Cirrus, Plus, American Express, Discover/Novus, and STAR.

Net sales from our ATM operations accounted for 93% of our net sales from continuing operations in both 2005 and 2006.

Net sales from our photocopier operations accounted for 7% of our net sales from continuing operations in both 2005 and 2006.

ITEM 8. FINANCIAL STATEMENTS AND SUPPLEMENT DATA (in Part)

Report of Independent Registered Public Accounting Firm (in Part)

To the Board of Directors and Shareholders of TRM Corporation:

We have completed integrated audits of TRM Corporation's 2006 and 2005 consolidated financial statements and of its internal control over financial reporting as of December 31, 2006 and an audit of its 2004 consolidated financial statements in accordance with the standards of the Public Company Accounting Oversight Board (United States). Our opinions, based upon our audits, are presented below.

Consolidated financial statements and financial statement schedule

In our opinion, the consolidated financial statements listed in the index appearing under item 15(a)(1) present fairly, in all material respects, the financial position of TRM Corporation and its subsidiaries at December 31, 2006 and 2005, and the results of their operations and their cash flows for each of the three years in the period ended December 31, 2006 in conformity with accounting principles generally accepted in the United States of America. In addition, in our opinion, the financial statement schedule listed in the index appearing under item 15(a)(2) presents fairly, in all material respects, the information set forth therein when read in conjunction with the related consolidated financial statements. These financial statements and financial statement schedule are the responsibility of the Company's management. Our responsibility is to express an opinion on these financial statements and financial statement schedule based on our audits. We conducted our audits of these statements in accordance with the standards of the Public Company Accounting Oversight Board (United States). Those standards require that we plan and perform the audit to obtain reasonable assurance about whether the evidence supporting the amounts and disclosures in the financial statements assessing the accounting principles used and significant estimates made by management, and evaluating the overall financial statement presentation. We believe that our audits provide a reasonable basis for our opinion.

(continued)

The accompanying financial statements have been prepared assuming that the Company will continue as a going concern. As discussed in Note 1 to the consolidated financial statements, the Company incurred a net loss for 2006 resulting in its inability to meet certain financial covenants of its financing agreement with GSO Origination Funding Partners LP and other lenders, and based on its projections the Company does not expect to meet the required financial covenants during 2007, which may render the debt callable by the lenders and trigger the cross-default provisions in TRM Funding Trust's Loan and Servicing Agreement. This raises substantial doubt about the Company's ability to continue as a going concern. Management's plans in regard to these matters are also described in Note 1. The financial statements do not include any adjustments that might result from the outcome of this uncertainty.

Notes to Consolidated Financial Statements (in Part)

1.   Description of Business and Summary of Significant Accounting Policies (in Part)
Description of Business and Basis of Presentation

TRM Corporation ("we" or "TRM") delivers convenience services to consumers in retail environments. We currently deliver self-service cash delivery and account balance inquiry through ATM machines and photocopy services.

As of December 2006 we offered our services in retail locations in the United States, the United Kingdom, Germany and Canada. We provide the equipment, maintenance, supplies and point of sale materials required for each of our installations, while the retailer oversees the daily operation of the equipment, provides the necessary floor space and shares in the revenue generated by our offerings.

In June 2006 we sold our United Kingdom photocopy business. In January 2007 we sold our ATM businesses in the United Kingdom, Germany and Canada and our United States photocopy business. The results of the businesses we have sold are reflected as discontinued operations in our consolidated statement of operations. Our remaining businesses operate ATMs in the United States and photocopiers in Canada. During 2006 our United States ATM networks had an average of 12,378 transacting ATMs and our Canadian photocopy network had an average of 2,751 photocopiers.

During the fourth quarter of 2004, we decided to discontinue efforts in the software development segment of our business. In December 2004, the last employee of this segment was terminated and we negotiated the termination of its office lease and accrued a related termination payment. Therefore, results of the software development segment have been reflected as discontinued operations in 2004.

We incurred a net loss of $120.1 million in the year ended December 31, 2006. As a result of our financial performance for the three months ended September 20, 2006, we failed to meet certain financial covenants of our financing agreements with GSO Origination Funding Partners LP and other lenders. On November 20, 2006, we entered into amendments that restructured our loans and waived the failure to meet the loan covenants. Under the restructured loan agreements principal payments of $69.9 million were due in the first quarter of 2007. During January 2007 we sold our Canadian, United Kingdom and German ATM businesses and our United States photocopy business and used $98.5 million from the proceeds of those sales to make principal and interest payments under these loans, leaving a remaining balance of principal plus accrued interest of $2.0 million. We are uncertain whether our remaining operations can generate sufficient cash to comply with the covenants of our restructured loan agreements and to pay our obligations on an ongoing basis. Because there are cross-default provisions in TRM Inventory Funding Trust's Loan and Servicing Agreement, if we fail to comply with the covenants of our restructured loan agreements and are declared to be in default by GSO Origination Funding Partners LP and other lenders, we may be declared in default of the provisions of the Loan and Servicing Agreement as well, and the lender may be able to demand payment. These factors, among others, may indicate that we may be unable to continue as a going concern for a reasonable period of time. Our financial statements do not include any adjustments relating to the recoverability and classification of recorded asset amounts or the amounts and classification of liabilities that may be necessary should we be unable to continue as a going concern. Our continuation as a going concern is contingent upon our ability to generate sufficient cash to pay our obligations on an ongoing basis.

In connection with the sales of our ATM businesses in the United Kingdom, Germany and Canada, and our photocopy business in the United States in January 2007, we have made various representations and warranties and/or provided indemnities including those relating to taxation matters. Further, the sales prices may be subject to adjustment based on working capital

(continued)

Case GOING CONCERN? (Continued)
1-6

amounts, the value of accounts receivable as of the closing of the sale or other factors which have not yet been agreed upon. The purchasers may make claims against us relating to the representations or warranties or provisions for adjustment of the sales prices, and those claims could be substantial. Because we used substantially all of the net proceeds from the business sales to reduce our debt, we might not have sufficient cash to pay such claims without additional financing.

In November 2006 we announced the implementation of a corporate restructuring plan involving an initial reduction of then-existing controllable selling, general and administrative expenses of approximately 15%. Subsequent to that announcement, we have sold operations that accounted for approximately 58% of our net sales in 2006. In connection with our restructuring plan and the sales of a substantial part of our operations, we have reduced our number of employees from 364 as of December 31, 2006 to 91 as of March 31, 2007, and we anticipate additional staff reductions during the second quarter of 2007.

We expect to be able to refinance the outstanding balances under our financing agreement and have begun initial efforts to do so. However, we can provide no assurance that we will be able to do so. If we are unable to refinance our debt or to get our lenders to agree to any further forbearance from calling our loans, we might be forced to seek protection of the courts through reorganization, bankruptcy or insolvency proceedings.

Required
    a. What is the going-concern assumption?
    b. Has TRM Corporation prepared financial statements using the going-concern assumption? Comment.
    c. What is the significance of the disclosure that this company may not be able to continue as a going concern?

Case ECONOMICS AND ACCOUNTING: THE UNCONGENIAL TWINS*
1-7

"Economics and accountancy are two disciplines which draw their raw material from much the same mines. From these raw materials, however, they seem to fashion remarkably different products. They both study the operations of firms; they both are concerned with such concepts as income, expenditure, profits, capital, value, and prices. In spite of an apparently common subject-matter, however, they often seem to inhabit totally different worlds, between which there is remarkably little communication."

"It is not surprising that the economist regards much accounting procedure as in the nature of ritual. To call these procedures ritualistic is in no way to deny or decry their validity. Ritual is always the proper response when a man has to give an answer to a question, the answer to which he cannot really know. Ritual under these circumstances has two functions. It is comforting (and in the face of the great uncertainties of the future, comfort is not to be despised), and it is also an answer sufficient for action. It is the sufficient answer rather than the right answer which the accountant really seeks. Under these circumstances, however, it is important that we should know what the accountant's answer means, which means that we should know what procedure he has employed. The wise businessman will not believe his accountant although he takes what his accountant tells him as important evidence. The quality of that evidence, however, depends in considerable degree on the simplicity of the procedures and the awareness which we have of them. What the accountant tells us may not be true, but, if we know what he has done, we have a fair idea of what it means. For this reason, I am somewhat suspicious of many current efforts to reform accounting in the direction of making it more 'accurate'."

"If accounts are bound to be untruths anyhow, as I have argued, there is much to be said for the simple untruth as against a complicated untruth, for if the untruth is simple, it seems to me that we have a fair chance of knowing what kind of an untruth it is. A known untruth

*Source: Quotes from the article "Economics and Accounting: The Uncongenial Twins," in *Accounting Theory*, edited by W. T. Baxter and Sidney Davidson (Homewood, IL., R. D. Irwin, 1962), pp. 44–55.

(continued)

Case	**ECONOMICS AND ACCOUNTING: THE UNCONGENIAL TWINS (Continued)**
1-7	

is much better than a lie, and provided that the accounting rituals are well known and understood, accounting may be untrue but it is not lies; it does not deceive because we know that it does not tell the truth, and we are able to make our own adjustment in each individual case, using the results of the accountant as evidence rather than as definitive information."

Required   a. Assume that accounting procedures are in the form of ritual. Does this imply that the accountant's product does not serve a useful function? Discuss.

              b. Does it appear that Kenneth Boulding would support complicated procedures and a complicated end product for the accountant? Discuss.

              c. Accounting reports must be accurate in order to serve a useful function. Discuss.

Case	**I OFTEN PAINT FAKES***
1-8	

An art dealer bought a canvas signed "Picasso" and traveled all the way to Cannes to discover whether it was genuine. Picasso was working in his studio. He cast a single look at the canvas and said, "It's a fake."

A few months later, the dealer bought another canvas signed "Picasso." Again he traveled to Cannes, and again Picasso, after a single glance, grunted: "It's a fake."

"But cher maitre," expostulated the dealer, "it so happens that I saw you with my own eyes working on this very picture several years ago."

Picasso shrugged: "I often paint fakes."

Required   a. Assume that the accounting report was prepared using generally accepted accounting principles. Does this imply that the report is exactly accurate? Discuss.

              b. In your opinion, do accountants paint fakes? Discuss.

*This case consists of a quote from *The Act of Creation*, Arthur Koestler (New York: Macmillan, 1964), p. 82.

Case	**OVERSIGHT**
1-9	**Selected sections of the Sarbanes-Oxley Act follow:**

Public Law 107-204—July 30, 2002
Section 1. Short title. This Act may be cited as the "Sarbanes-Oxley Act of 2002"

TITLE I—Public Company Accounting Oversight Board

Sec.101. Establishment; Administrative Provisions
(a) Establishment of Board—There is established the Public Company Accounting Oversight Board, to oversee the audit of public companies that are subject to the securities laws, and related matters, in order to protect the interests of investors and further the public interest in the preparation of informative, accurate, and independent audit reports for companies the securities of which are sold to, and held by and for, public investors. The Board shall be a body corporate, operate as a nonprofit corporation, and have succession until dissolved by an Act of Congress.
(b) Duties of the Board—The Board shall, subject to action by the Commission under section 107, and once a determination is made by the Commission under subsection (d) of this section—
    (1) register public accounting firms that prepare audit reports for issuers, in accordance with section 102;
    (2) establish or adopt, or both, by rule, auditing, quality control, ethics, independence, and other standards relating to the preparation of audit reports for issuers, in accordance with section 103;

(continued)

(3) conduct inspections of registered public accounting firms, in accordance with section 104 and the rules of the Board;

(4) conduct investigations and disciplinary proceedings concerning, and impose appropriate sanctions where justified upon, registered public accounting firms and associated persons of such firms, in accordance with section 105;

(5) perform such other duties or functions as the Board (or the Commission, by rule or order) determines are necessary or appropriate to promote high professional standards among, and improve the quality of audit services offered by, registered public accounting firms and associated persons thereof, or otherwise to carry out this Act, in order to protect investors, or to further the public interest;

(6) enforce compliance with this Act, the rules of the Board, professional standards, and the securities laws relating to the preparation and issuance of audit reports and the obligations and liabilities of accountants with respect thereto, by registered public accounting firms and associated persons thereof; and

(7) set the budget and manage the operations of the Board and the staff of the Board.

Sec.102. Registration with the Board

(a) Mandatory Registration—Beginning 180 days after the date of the determination of the Commission under section 101(d), it shall be unlawful for any person that is not a registered public accounting firm to prepare or issue, or to participate in the preparation or issuance of, any audit report with respect to any issuer.

Sec.103. Auditing, Quality Control, and Independence Standards and Rules

(a) Auditing, quality control, and ethics standards

(1) In General—The Board shall, by rule, establish, including, to the extent it determines appropriate, through adoption of standards proposed by 1 or more professional groups of accountants designated pursuant to paragraph (3)(A) or advisory groups convened pursuant to paragraph (4), and amend or otherwise modify or alter, such auditing and related attestation standards, such quality control standards, and such ethics standards to be used by registered public accounting firms in the preparation and issuance of audit reports, as required by this Act or the rules of the Commission, or as may be necessary or appropriate in the public interest or for the protection of investors.

Sec.104. Inspections of Registered Public Accounting Firms

(a) In General—The Board shall conduct a continuing program of inspections to assess the degree of compliance of each registered public accounting firm and associated persons of that firm with this Act, the rules of the Board, the rules of the Commission, or professional standards, in connection with its performance of audits, issuance of audit reports, and related matters involving issuers.

Sec.105. Investigations and Disciplinary Proceedings

(a) In General—The Board shall establish, by rule, subject to the requirements of this section, fair procedures for the investigation and disciplining of registered public accounting firms and associated persons of such firms.

(3) Noncooperation with Investigations

(A) In General—If a registered public accounting firm or any associated person thereof refuses to testify, produce documents, or otherwise cooperate with the Board in connection with an investigation under this section, the Board may—

(i) suspend or bar such person from being associated with a registered public accounting firm, or require the registered public accounting firm to end such association;

(ii) suspend or revoke the registration of the public accounting firm; and

(iii) invoke such other lesser sanctions as the Board considers appropriate, and as specified by rule of the Board.

(continued)

OVERSIGHT (Continued)

Sec. 106. Foreign Public Accounting Firms

(a) Applicability to Certain Foreign Firms

    (1) In General—Any foreign public accounting firm that prepares or furnishes an audit report with respect to any issuer, shall be subject to this Act and the rules of the Board and the Commission issued under this Act, in the same manner and to the same extent as a public accounting firm that is organized and operates under the laws of the United States or any State, except that registration pursuant to section 102 shall not by itself provide a basis for subjecting such a foreign public accounting firm to the jurisdiction of the Federal or State courts, other than with respect to controversies between such firms and the Board.

Sec. 107. Commission Oversight of the Board

(a) General Oversight Responsibility—The Commission shall have oversight and enforcement authority over the Board, as provided in this Act.

Sec. 108. Accounting Standards

(a) Amendment to Securities Act of 1933—Section 19 of the Securities Act of 1933 (15 U.S.C. 77s) is amended

(b) Recognition of Accounting Standards

    (1) In General—In carrying out its authority under subsection (a) and under section 13(b) of the Securities Exchange Act of 1934, the Commission may recognize, as "generally accepted" for purposes of the securities laws, any accounting principles established by a standard setting body—

        (A) that—

            (i) is organized as a private entity;

            (ii) has, for administrative and operational purposes, a board of trustees (or equivalent body) serving in the public interest, the majority of whom are not, concurrent with their service on such board, and have not been during the 2-year period preceding such service, associated persons of any registered public accounting firm;

            (iii) is funded as provided in section 109 of the Sarbanes-Oxley Act of 2002;

            (iv) has adopted procedures to ensure prompt consideration, by majority vote of its members, of changes to accounting principles necessary to reflect emerging accounting issues and changing business practices; and

            (v) considers, in adopting accounting principles, the need to keep standards current in order to reflect changes in the business environment, the extent to which international convergence on high quality accounting standards is necessary or appropriate in the public interest and for the protection of investors; and

        (B) that the Commission determines has the capacity to assist the Commission in fulfilling the requirements of subsection (a) and section 13(b) of the Securities Exchange Act of 1934, because, at a minimum, the standard setting body is capable of improving the accuracy and effectiveness of financial reporting and the protection of investors under the securities laws.

Sec. 109. Funding

(a) In General—The Board, and the standard setting body designated pursuant to section 19(b) of the Securities Act of 1933, as amended by section 108, shall be funded as provided in this section.

(d) Annual Accounting Support Fee for the Board

    (1) Establishment of Fee—The Board shall establish, with the approval of the Commission, a reasonable annual accounting support fee (or a formula for the computation thereof), as may be necessary or appropriate to establish and maintain the Board. Such fee may also cover costs incurred in the Board's first fiscal year (which may be a short fiscal year), or may be levied separately with respect to such short fiscal year.

(continued)

(2) Assessments—The rules of the Board under paragraph (1) shall provide for the equitable allocation, assessment, and collection by the Board (or an agent appointed by the Board) of the fee established under paragraph (1), among issuers, in accordance with subsection (g), allowing for differentiation among classes of issuers, as appropriate.

(e) Annual Accounting Support Fee for Standard Setting Body—The annual accounting support fee for the standard setting body referred to in subsection (a)—

(1) shall be allocated in accordance with subsection (g), and assessed and collected against each issuer, on behalf of the standard setting body, by 1 or more appropriate designated collection agents, as may be necessary or appropriate to pay for the budget and provide for the expenses of that standard setting body, and to provide for an independent, stable source of funding for such body, subject to review by the Commission; and

(2) may differentiate among different classes of issuers.

TITLE II—Auditor Independence

Sec. 201. Services Outside the Scope of Practice of Auditors

(a) Prohibited Activities—Section 10A of the Securities Exchange Act of 1934 (15 U.S.C. 78j–1) is amended by adding at the end the following:

(g) Prohibited Activities—Except as provided in subsection (h), it shall be unlawful for a registered public accounting firm (and any associated person of that firm, to the extent determined appropriate by the Commission) that performs for any issuer any audit required by this title or the rules of the Commission under this title or, beginning 180 days after the date of commencement of the operations of the Public Company Accounting Oversight Board established under section 101 of the Sarbanes-Oxley Act of 2002 (in this section referred to as the "Board"), the rules of the Board, to provide to that issuer, contemporaneously with the audit, any non-audit service, including—

(1) bookkeeping or other services related to the accounting records or financial statements of the audit client;

(2) financial information systems design and implementation;

(3) appraisal or valuation services, fairness opinions, or contribution-in-kind reports;

(4) actuarial services;

(5) internal audit outsourcing services;

(6) management functions or human resources;

(7) broker or dealer, investment adviser, or investment banking services;

(8) legal services and expert services unrelated to the audit; and

(9) any other service that the Board determines, by regulation, is impermissible.

(h) Preapproval Required for Non-Audit Services—A registered public accounting firm may engage in any non-audit service, including tax services, that is not described in any of paragraphs (1) through (9) of subsection (g) for an audit client, only if the activity is approved in advance by the audit committee of the issuer, in accordance with subsection (i).

TITLE IV—Enhanced Financial Disclosures

Sec. 404. Management Assessment of Internal Controls

(a) RULES REQUIRED—The Commission shall prescribe rules requiring each annual report required by section 13(a) or 15(d) of the Securities Exchange Act of 1934 [15 U.S.C. 78m or 78o(d)] to contain an internal control report, which shall—

(1) state the responsibility of management for establishing and maintaining an adequate internal control structure and procedures for financial reporting; and

(2) contain an assessment, as of the end of the most recent fiscal year of the issuer, of the effectiveness of the internal control structure and procedures of the issuer for financial reporting.

(continued)

Case 1-9	OVERSIGHT (Continued)

(b) INTERNAL CONTROL EVALUATION AND REPORTING—With respect to the internal control assessment required by subsection (a), each registered public accounting firm that prepares or issues the audit report for the issuer shall attest to, and report on, the assessment made by the management of the issuer. An attestation made under this subsection shall be made in accordance with standards for attestation engagements issued or adopted by the Board. Any such attestation shall not be the subject of a separate engagement.

Required

a. The Sarbanes-Oxley Act refers to "the Commission" in several sections. To what Commission is the Sarbanes-Oxley Act referring?
b. Describe the responsibility of the Commission in relation to the "Board."
c. Describe the Board.
d. Describe the duties of the Board.
e. Who must register with the Board?
f. Describe the Board's responsibility as to the inspection of those registered with the Board.
g. Describe the responsibilities of the Board in relation to auditing standards.
h. Contrast the applicability of the Sarbanes-Oxley Act to domestic public accounting firms versus foreign public accounting firms.
i. Describe the recognition of accounting standards by the Commission as provided.
j. Comment on the funding for the:
   1. Board.
   2. Financial Accounting Standards Board.
k. Describe prohibited activities of the independent auditor. Can the independent auditor perform tax services for an audit client?
l. Describe management's responsibility in relation to internal controls.
m. Speculate on why Title IV, Section 404, "Management Assessment of Internal Controls," has received substantial criticism.

Case 1-10	REGULATION OF SMALLER PUBLIC COMPANIES

The U.S. Securities and Exchange Commission (SEC) chartered the Advisory Committee on Smaller Public Companies on March 23, 2005. The charter provided an objective of assessing the regulatory system for smaller companies under the securities laws of the United States, and makes recommendations for changes.

The SEC Advisory Committee gave its final recommendations to the SEC in April 2006. These recommendations included several primary recommendations including: establish a scaled or proportional securities regulation for smaller public companies based on a stratification of smaller public companies into two groups; micro cap companies and small cap companies.*

The report indicates that a scales or proportional securities regulation for smaller public companies assures the full benefits and protection of federal securities regulation for investors in large companies that make up 94% of the total public U.S. equity capital markets. . . .†

The committee acknowledges the relative risk to investors and the capital markets as it's currently used by professional investors when using proportional securities regulations.

Required   It is perceived that the risk is greater when investing in smaller public companies with proportional securities regulations than in larger companies. Speculate on why the committee considers this risk worth taking.

*Final Report of the Advisory Committee on Smaller Public Companies to the U.S. Securities and Exchange Commission (April 23, 2006), p. 4.
†Ibid., p. 16.

Thomson One *Business School Edition*

Please complete the Web case that covers material discussed in this chapter at academic.cengage.com/accounting/Gibson. You'll be using Thomson One Business School Edition, a powerful tool, that combines a full range of fundamental financial information, earnings estimates, market data, and source documents for 500 publicly traded companies.

Endnotes

1. *Statement of Financial Accounting Concepts No. 1*, "Objectives of Financial Reporting by Business Enterprises" (Stamford, Conn.: Financial Accounting Standards Board, 1978).
2. *Statement of Financial Accounting Concepts No. 6*, "Elements of Financial Statements" (Stamford, Conn.: Financial Accounting Standards Board, 1985).
3. *Statement of Financial Accounting Concepts No. 5*, "Recognition and Measurement in Financial Statements of Business Enterprises" (Stamford, Conn.: Financial Accounting Standards Board, 1984), par. 63.
4. *Statement of Financial Accounting Concepts No. 5*, par. 67.
5. *Statement of Financial Accounting Concepts No. 5*, par. 70.
6. *Statement of Financial Accounting Concepts No. 5*, par. 13.
7. Release No. 33-8238, February 24, 2004, Securities and Exchange Commission, Final Rule: "Management's Reports on Internal Control Over Financial Reporting and Certification of Disclosure in Exchange Act Periodic Reports," http://www.sec.gov.
8. *Accounting Trends & Techniques* (New York: American Institute of Certified Public Accountants, Inc., 2006), preface.
9. Ibid., p. 39.
10. Ibid., p. 40.
11. James Brady Vorhies, "The New Importance of Materiality," *Journal of Accounting* (May 2005), pp. 53–59.

Chapter 2

Introduction to Financial Statements and Other Financial Reporting Topics

This chapter introduces financial statements. Subsequent chapters present a detailed review of the principal financial statements. Chapter 3 covers the balance sheet, Chapter 4 covers the income statement, and Chapter 10 covers the statement of cash flows.

This chapter also reviews the forms of business entities and the sequence of accounting procedures (called the accounting cycle). Other financial reporting topics included in this chapter that contribute to the understanding of financial reporting are: Treadway Commission, auditor's opinion, auditor's report on the firm's internal controls, Report of Management on Internal Control over Financial Reporting, management's responsibility for financial statements, the SEC's integrated disclosure system, proxy, the summary annual report, the efficient market hypothesis, ethics, harmonization of international accounting standards, consolidated statements, and accounting for business combinations.

Forms of Business Entities

A business entity may be a sole proprietorship, a partnership, or a corporation. A sole proprietorship, a business owned by one person, is not a legal entity separate from its owner, but the accountant treats the business as a separate accounting entity. The profit or loss of the proprietorship goes on the income tax return of the owner. The owner is responsible for the debts of the sole proprietorship.

In the United States, a sole proprietorship may qualify to be treated as a limited liability company (LLC). As an LLC, the owner may limit the liability of the sole proprietor, but may increase the tax exposure of the proprietorship.

A partnership is a business owned by two or more individuals. Each owner, called a partner, is personally responsible for the debts of the partnership. The accountant treats the partners and the business as separate accounting entities. The profit or loss of the partnership goes on the individual income tax return of the partners. Like a proprietorship, a partnership may qualify to be treated as an LLC. As an LLC, the owners may limit the liability of the partners, but may increase the tax exposure of the partnership.

In the United States, a business corporation is a legal entity incorporated in a particular state. Ownership is evidenced by shares of stock. A corporation is considered to be separate and distinct from the stockholders. The stockholders risk only their investment; they are not responsible for the debts of the corporation.

Since a corporation is a legal entity, the profits or losses are treated as a separate entity on an income tax return. The owners are not taxed until profits are distributed to the owners (dividends). In the United States, some corporations qualify to be treated as a subchapter S corporation. These corporations do not pay a corporate income tax. The profits or losses go directly on the income tax returns of the owners.

In the United States, most businesses operate as proprietorships, but corporations perform the bulk of business activity. Since the bulk of business activity is carried on in corporations and because much of financial accounting is concerned with reporting to the public, this book focuses on the corporate form of business.

Accounting for corporations, sole proprietorships, and partnerships is the same, except for the owners' equity section of the balance sheet. The owners' equity section for a sole proprietorship consists of the owners' capital account, while the owners' equity section for a partnership has a capital account for each partner. The more complicated owners' equity section for a corporation will be described in detail in this book.

The Financial Statements

The principal financial statements of a corporation are the balance sheet, income statement, and statement of cash flows. Notes accompany these financial statements. To evaluate the financial condition, the profitability, and cash flows of an entity, the user needs to understand the statements and related notes.

Exhibit 2-1 illustrates the interrelationship of the balance sheet, income statement, and statement of cash flows. The most basic statement is the balance sheet. The other statements explain the changes between two balance sheet dates.

BALANCE SHEET (STATEMENT OF FINANCIAL POSITION)

A balance sheet shows the financial condition of an accounting entity as of a particular date. The balance sheet consists of three major sections: assets, the resources of the firm; liabilities, the debts of the firm; and stockholders' equity, the owners' interest in the firm.

At any point in time, the total assets amount must equal the total amount of the contributions of the creditors and owners. This is expressed in the accounting equation:

Assets = Liabilities + Stockholders' Equity

In simplistic form, the stockholders' equity of a corporation appears as follows:

Stockholders' Equity	
Common stock	$200,000
Retained earnings	50,000
	$250,000

This indicates that stockholders contributed (invested) $200,000, and prior earnings less prior dividends have been retained in the entity in the net amount of $50,000 (retained earnings).

STATEMENT OF STOCKHOLDERS' EQUITY (RECONCILIATION OF STOCKHOLDERS' EQUITY ACCOUNTS)

Firms are required to present reconciliations of the beginning and ending balances of their stockholders' equity accounts. This is accomplished by presenting a "statement of stockholders' equity." Retained earnings is one of the accounts in stockholders' equity.

Retained earnings links the balance sheet to the income statement. Retained earnings is increased by net income and decreased by net losses and dividends paid to stockholders. There are some other possible increases or decreases to retained earnings besides income (losses) and dividends. For the purposes of this chapter, retained earnings will be described as prior earnings less prior dividends.

| Exhibit | 2-1 | ABC COMPANY |

The Interrelationship of Financial Statements

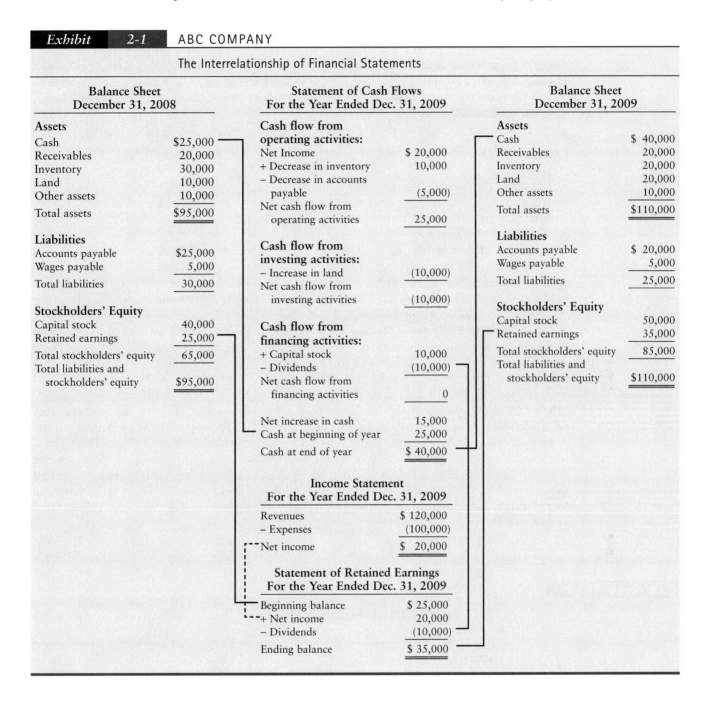

Balance Sheet **December 31, 2008**		**Statement of Cash Flows** **For the Year Ended Dec. 31, 2009**		**Balance Sheet** **December 31, 2009**	
Assets		**Cash flow from** **operating activities:**		**Assets**	
Cash	$25,000	Net Income	$ 20,000	Cash	$ 40,000
Receivables	20,000	+ Decrease in inventory	10,000	Receivables	20,000
Inventory	30,000	– Decrease in accounts		Inventory	20,000
Land	10,000	payable	(5,000)	Land	20,000
Other assets	10,000	Net cash flow from		Other assets	10,000
Total assets	$95,000	operating activities	25,000	Total assets	$110,000
Liabilities		**Cash flow from**		**Liabilities**	
Accounts payable	$25,000	**investing activities:**		Accounts payable	$ 20,000
Wages payable	5,000	– Increase in land	(10,000)	Wages payable	5,000
Total liabilities	30,000	Net cash flow from		Total liabilities	25,000
		investing activities	(10,000)		
Stockholders' Equity				**Stockholders' Equity**	
Capital stock	40,000	**Cash flow from**		Capital stock	50,000
Retained earnings	25,000	**financing activities:**		Retained earnings	35,000
Total stockholders' equity	65,000	+ Capital stock	10,000	Total stockholders' equity	85,000
Total liabilities and		– Dividends	(10,000)	Total liabilities and	
stockholders' equity	$95,000	Net cash flow from		stockholders' equity	$110,000
		financing activities	0		
		Net increase in cash	15,000		
		Cash at beginning of year	25,000		
		Cash at end of year	$ 40,000		

Income Statement
For the Year Ended Dec. 31, 2009

Revenues	$ 120,000
– Expenses	(100,000)
Net income	$ 20,000

Statement of Retained Earnings
For the Year Ended Dec. 31, 2009

Beginning balance	$ 25,000
+ Net income	20,000
– Dividends	(10,000)
Ending balance	$ 35,000

Firms usually present the reconciliation of retained earnings within a "statement of stockholders' equity." Some firms present the reconciliation of retained earnings at the bottom of the income statement (combined income statement and retained earnings). In this case, the other stockholders' equity accounts may be reconciled in a statement that excludes retained earnings. An additional review of the statement of stockholders' equity is in Chapter 3.

INCOME STATEMENT (STATEMENT OF EARNINGS)

The income statement summarizes revenues and expenses and gains and losses, ending with net income. It summarizes the results of operations for a particular period of time. Net income is included in retained earnings in the stockholders' equity section of the balance sheet. (This is necessary for the balance sheet to balance.)

STATEMENT OF CASH FLOWS (STATEMENT OF INFLOWS AND OUTFLOWS OF CASH)

The **statement of cash flows** details the inflows and outflows of cash during a specified period of time—the same period that is used for the income statement. The statement of cash flows consists of three sections: cash flows from operating activities, cash flows from investing activities, and cash flows from financing activities.

NOTES

The notes to the financial statements are used to present additional information about items included in the financial statements and to present additional financial information. Notes are an integral part of financial statements. A detailed review of notes is essential to understanding the financial statements.

Certain information must be presented in notes. Accounting policies are to be disclosed as the first note or be disclosed in a separate summary of significant accounting policies (preceding the first note). Accounting policies include such items as the method of inventory valuation and depreciation policies. Other information specifically requiring note disclosure is the existence of contingent liabilities and some subsequent events.

Contingent liabilities are dependent upon the occurrence or nonoccurrence of one or more future events to confirm the liability. The settlement of litigation or the ruling of a tax court would be examples of the confirmation of a contingent liability. Signing as guarantor on a loan creates another type of contingent liability.

An estimated loss from a contingent liability should be charged to income and be established as a liability only if the loss is considered probable and the amount is reasonably determinable. A contingent liability that is recorded is also frequently described in a note. A loss contingency that is reasonably possible, but not probable, must be disclosed even if the loss is not reasonably estimable. (This loss contingency is not charged to income or established as a liability.) A loss contingency that is less than reasonably possible does not need to be disclosed, but disclosure may be desirable if there is an unusually large potential loss. Exhibit 2-2 illustrates a contingent liability note for Intel Corporation whose fiscal year ended December 30, 2006.

Exhibit 2-2	INTEL CORPORATION*

For the Fiscal Year Ended December 30, 2006
Contingences (in Part)

Tax Matters
In connection with the regular examination of Intel's tax returns for the years 1999 through 2005, the IRS formally assessed, in 2005 and 2006, certain adjustments to the amounts reflected by Intel on those returns as a tax benefit for its export sales. The company does not agree with these adjustments and has appealed the assessments. If the IRS prevails in its position, Intel's federal income tax due for 1999 through 2005 would increase by approximately $2.2 billion, plus interest. In addition, the IRS will likely make a similar claim for 2006, and if the IRS prevails, income tax due for 2006 would increase by approximately $200 million, plus interest.

Although the final resolution of the adjustments is uncertain, based on currently available information, management believes that the ultimate outcome will not have a material adverse effect on the company's financial position, cash flows, or overall trends in results of operations. There is the possibility of a material adverse impact on the results of operations for the period in which the matter is ultimately resolved, if it is resolved unfavorably, or in the period in which an unfavorable outcome becomes probable and reasonably estimable.

*"We are the world's largest semiconductor chip maker, based on revenue." 10-K

Subsequent events occur after the balance sheet date, but before the statements are issued. Two varieties of subsequent events occur. The first type consists of events related to conditions that existed at the balance sheet date, affect the estimates in the statements, and require adjustment of the statements before issuance. For example, if additional information is obtained indicating that a major customer's account receivable is not collectible, an adjustment would be made. The second type consists of events that provide evidence about conditions that did not exist at the balance sheet date and do not require adjustment of the statements. If failure to disclose these events would be misleading, disclosure should take the form of notes or supplementary schedules. Examples of the second type of such events include the sale of securities, the settlement of litigation, or casualty loss. Other examples of subsequent events might be debt incurred, reduced, or refinanced; business combinations pending or effected; discontinued operations; employee benefit plans; and capital stock issued or purchased. Exhibit 2-3 describes a subsequent event for Kellogg Company, whose year-end was December 30, 2006.

Exhibit	**2-3**	KELLOGG COMPANY*

For the Fiscal Year Ended December 30, 2006

Subsequent Events

As discussed in preceding subnote (d), on January 31, 2007, a subsidiary of the Company announced an early redemption, effective February 28, 2007, of Euro 550 million of Guaranteed Floating Rate Notes otherwise due May 2007. To partially refinance this redemption, the Company and two of its subsidiaries (the "Issuers") established a program under which the Issuers may issue euro-commercial paper notes up to a maximum aggregate amount outstanding at any time of $750 million or its equivalent in alternative currencies. The notes may have maturities ranging up to 364 days and will be senior unsecured obligations of the applicable issuer. Notes issued by subsidiary Issuers will be guaranteed by the Company. The notes may be issued at a discount or may bear fixed or floating rate interest or a coupon calculated by reference to an index or formula.

In connection with these financing activities, the Company increased its short-term lines of credit from $2.2 billion at December 30, 2006 to approximately $2.6 billion, via a $400 million unsecured 364-Day Credit Agreement effective January 31, 2007. The 364-Day Agreement contains customary covenants, warranties, and restrictions similar to those described herein for the Five-Year Credit Agreement. The facility is available for general corporate purposes, including commercial paper back-up, although the Company does not currently anticipate any usage under the facility.

*"Kellogg Company, founded in 1906 and incorporated in Delaware in 1922, and its subsidiaries are engaged in the manufacture and marketing of ready-to-eat cereal and convenience foods." 10-K

The Accounting Cycle

The sequence of accounting procedures completed during each accounting period is called the accounting cycle. A broad summary of the steps of the accounting cycle includes:

1. Recording transactions
2. Recording adjusting entries
3. Preparing the financial statements

RECORDING TRANSACTIONS

A **transaction** is an event that causes a change in a company's assets, liabilities, or stockholders' equity, thus changing the company's financial position. Transactions may be external or internal to the company. External transactions involve outside parties, while internal transactions are confined within the company. For example, sales is an external transaction, while the use of equipment is internal.

Transactions must be recorded in a journal (book of original entry). All transactions could be recorded in the general journal. However, companies use a number of special journals to record most transactions. The special journals are designed to improve record-keeping efficiency that could not be obtained by using only the general journal. The general journal is then used only to record transactions for which the company does not have a special journal. A transaction recorded in a journal is referred to as a journal entry.

All transactions are recorded in a journal (journal entry) and are later posted from the journals to a general ledger (group of accounts for a company). After posting, the general ledger accounts contain the same information as the journals, but the information has been summarized by account.

Accounts store the monetary information from the recording of transactions. Examples of accounts include Cash, Land, and Buildings. An accounting system can be computerized or manual. A manual system using T-accounts is usually used for textbook explanations because a T-account is a logical format.

T-accounts have a left (debit) side and a right (credit) side. An example T-account follows:

Cash	
Debit	Credit

A double-entry system has been devised to handle the recording of transactions. In a double-entry system, each transaction is recorded with the total dollar amount of the debits equal to the total dollar amount of the credits. The scheme of the double-entry system revolves around the accounting equation:

$$\text{Assets} = \text{Liabilities} + \text{Stockholders' Equity}$$

With the double-entry system, *debit* merely means the left side of an account, while *credit* means the right side. Each transaction recorded must have an equal number of dollars on the left side as it does on the right side. Several accounts could be involved in a single transaction, but the debits and credits must still be equal.

The debit and credit approach is a technique that has gained acceptance over a long period of time. This book will not make you competent in the use of the double-entry (debit and credit) technique. It will enhance your understanding of the end result of the accounting process and enable you to use the financial accounting information in a meaningful way.

Asset, liability, and stockholders' equity accounts are referred to as **permanent accounts** because the balances in these accounts carry forward to the next accounting period. Balances in revenue, expense, gain, loss, and dividend accounts, described as **temporary accounts,** are closed to retained earnings and not carried into the next period.

Exhibit 2-4 illustrates the double-entry system. Notice that the permanent accounts are represented by the accounting equation: assets = liabilities + stockholders' equity. The temporary accounts are represented by revenue, expense, and dividends. (Gains and losses would be treated like revenue and expense, respectively.) The balance sheet will not balance until the temporary accounts are closed to retained earnings.

RECORDING ADJUSTING ENTRIES

Earlier, a distinction was made between the accrual basis of accounting and the cash basis. It was indicated that the accrual basis requires that revenue be recognized when realized (realization concept) and expenses recognized when incurred (matching concept). The point of cash receipt for revenue and cash disbursement for expenses is not important under the accrual basis when determining income. Usually, a company must use the accrual basis to achieve a reasonable result for the balance sheet and the income statement.

The accrual basis needs numerous adjustments to account balances at the end of the accounting period. For example, $1,000 paid for insurance on October 1 for a one-year period (October 1–September 30) could have been recorded as a debit to Insurance Expense ($1,000) and a credit to Cash ($1,000). If this company prepares financial statements on December 31, it would be necessary to adjust Insurance Expense because not all of the insurance expense should be recognized in the three-month period October 1–December 31. The adjustment would debit Prepaid Insurance, an asset account, for $750 and credit

Exhibit	2-4	DOUBLE-ENTRY SYSTEM

(Illustrating Relationship Between Permanent and Temporary Accounts)

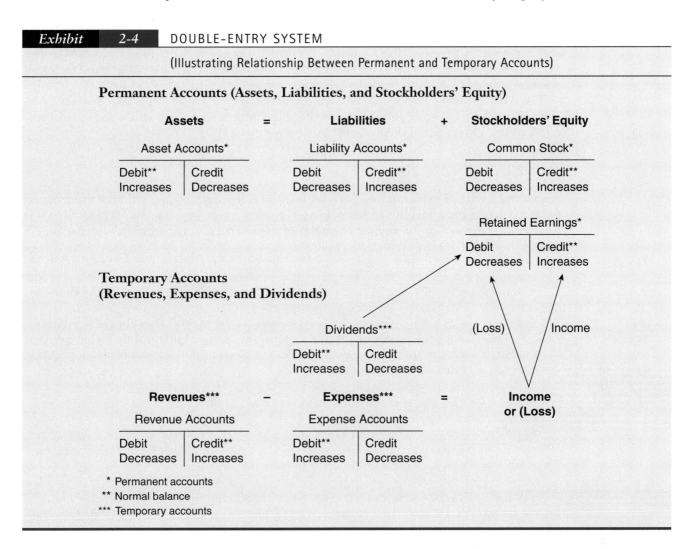

Permanent Accounts (Assets, Liabilities, and Stockholders' Equity)

* Permanent accounts
** Normal balance
*** Temporary accounts

Insurance Expense for $750. Thus, insurance expense would be presented on the income statement for this period as $250, and an asset, prepaid insurance, would be presented on the balance sheet as $750.

Adjusting entries are recorded in the general journal and then posted to the general ledger. Once the accounts are adjusted to the accrual basis, the financial statements can be prepared.

PREPARING THE FINANCIAL STATEMENTS

The accountant uses the accounts after the adjustments have been made to prepare the financial statements. These statements represent the output of the accounting system. Two of the principal financial statements, the income statement and the balance sheet, can be prepared directly from the adjusted accounts. Preparation of the statement of cash flows requires further analysis of the accounts.

TREADWAY COMMISSION

Treadway Commission is the popular name for the National Commission on Fraudulent Reporting named after its first chairman, former SEC Commissioner James C. Treadway. The Commission has issued a number of recommendations for the prevention of fraud in financial reports, ethics, and effective internal controls. The Treadway Commission is a voluntary private-sector organization formed in 1985.[1]

The Committee of Sponsoring Organizations of the Treadway Commission (COSO) has released reports detailing internal control systems. These reports represent the standard for evaluating the effectiveness of internal control systems.

Section 404 of the Sarbanes-Oxley Act emphasizes the importance of internal control and makes management responsible for internal controls. The independent public accounting firm is required to give an opinion as to management's assessment of internal control and the effectiveness of internal control over financial reporting as of the balance sheet date.

The Management's Report on Internal Control over Financial Reporting and the independent public accounting firm report to the shareholders, and the board of directors often refers to the criteria established on internal control by COSO.

Auditor's Opinion

An auditor (certified public accountant) conducts an independent examination of the accounting information presented by the business and issues a report thereon. An auditor's report is the formal statement of the auditor's opinion of the financial statements after conducting an audit. Audit opinions are classified as follows:

1. **Unqualified opinion.** This opinion states that the financial statements present fairly, in all material respects, the financial position, results of operations, and cash flows of the entity, in conformity with generally accepted accounting principles.
2. **Qualified opinion.** A qualified opinion states that, except for the effects of the matter(s) to which the qualification relates, the financial statements present fairly, in all material respects, the financial position, results of operations, and cash flows of the entity, in conformity with generally accepted accounting principles.
3. **Adverse opinion.** This opinion states that the financial statements do *not* present fairly the financial position, results of operations, and cash flows of the entity, in conformity with generally accepted accounting principles.
4. **Disclaimer of opinion.** A disclaimer of opinion states that the auditor does not express an opinion on the financial statements. A disclaimer of opinion is rendered when the auditor has not performed an audit sufficient in scope to form an opinion.

Since the passage of Sarbanes-Oxley, the form of the audit opinion can vary substantially. Private companies are not under Sarbanes-Oxley, but an increasing number of private companies are complying with parts of the law. Some of the reasons for private companies to follow the law are the following:

1. Owners hope to sell the company or take it public.
2. Directors who sit on public-company boards see the law's benefits.
3. Executives believe strong internal controls will improve efficiency.
4. Customers require strong internal controls.
5. Lenders are more likely to approve loans.[2]

The typical unqualified (or clean) opinion for private companies has three paragraphs. The first paragraph indicates that the financial statements have been audited and are the responsibility of the company's management. This paragraph states that the auditors have the responsibility to either express an opinion on these statements based on the audit or to disclaim an opinion.

The second paragraph indicates that the audit has been conducted in accordance with generally accepted auditing standards. This will typically be expressed in terms of standards of the Public Company Accounting Oversight Board (United States). These standards require the auditor to plan and perform the audit to obtain reasonable assurance about whether the financial statements are free of material misstatement. This paragraph also confirms that the audit provided a reasonable basis for an opinion.

The third paragraph gives an opinion on the statements—that they are in conformity with GAAP. In certain circumstances, an unqualified opinion on the financial statements may require that the auditor add an explanatory paragraph after the opinion paragraph. In this paragraph, the auditor may express agreement with a departure from a designated principle, describe a material uncertainty, describe a change in accounting principle, or express doubt as to the ability of the entity to continue as a going concern. An explanatory paragraph may also be added to emphasize a particular matter.

The audit opinion of a public company is similar to an opinion for a private company except that the public company comments will be added as to the effectiveness of internal control over financial reporting. An opinion is expressed as to management's assessment of, and the effective operation of, internal control over financial reporting.

When examining financial statements, review the independent auditor's report. It can be important to your analysis. From the point of view of analysis, financial statements accompanied by an unqualified opinion without an explanatory paragraph or explanatory language carry the highest degree of reliability. This type of report indicates that the financial statements do not contain a material departure from GAAP and that the audit was not limited as to scope.

When an unqualified opinion contains an explanatory paragraph or explanatory language, try to decide how seriously to regard the departure from a straight unqualified opinion. For example, an explanatory paragraph because of a change in accounting principle would not usually be regarded as serious, although it would be important to your analysis. An explanatory paragraph because of a material uncertainty would often be regarded as a serious matter.

You are likely to regard a qualified opinion or an adverse opinion as casting serious doubts on the reliability of the financial statements. In each case, you must read the auditor's report carefully to form your opinion.

A disclaimer of opinion indicates that you should not look to the auditor's report as an indication of the reliability of the statements. When rendering this type of report, the auditor has not performed an audit sufficient in scope to form an opinion, or the auditor is not independent.

In some cases, outside accountants are associated with financial statements when they have performed less than an audit. The accountant's report then indicates that the financial statements have been reviewed or compiled.

A review consists principally of inquiries made to company personnel and analytical procedures applied to financial data. It has substantially less scope than an examination in accordance with generally accepted auditing standards, the objective of which is the expression of an opinion regarding the financial statements taken as a whole. Accordingly, the accountant does not express an opinion. The accountant's report will indicate that the accountants are not aware of any material modifications that should be made to the financial statements in order for them to be in conformity with GAAP; or the report will indicate departures from GAAP. A departure from GAAP may result from using one or more accounting principles without reasonable justification, the omission of necessary note disclosures, or the omission of the statement of cash flows.

In general, the reliance that can be placed on financial statements accompanied by an accountant's review report is substantially less than those accompanied by an audit report. Remember that the accountant's report does not express an opinion on reviewed financial statements.

When the outside accountant presents only financial information as provided by management, he or she is said to have compiled the financial statements. The compilation report states that the accountant has not audited or reviewed the financial statements. Therefore, the accountant does not express an opinion or any other form of assurance about them. If an accountant performs a compilation and becomes aware of deficiencies in the statements, then the accountant's report characterizes the deficiencies as follows:

- Omission of substantially all disclosures
- Omission of statement of cash flows
- Accounting principles not generally accepted

Sometimes financial statements are presented without an accompanying accountant's report. This means that the statements have not been audited, reviewed, or compiled. Such statements are solely the representation of management.

AUDITOR'S REPORT ON THE FIRM'S INTERNAL CONTROLS

For public companies reporting under Sarbanes-Oxley, a report on the firm's internal controls is required in addition to the audit report. The internal control report is usually much longer than the audit report. For some firms, the audit opinion and the report on the firm's internal controls have been combined. This results in one audit report that can be very long.

Exhibit 2-5 presents the audit report for T. Rowe Price Group, Inc. It is an unqualified opinion. T. Rowe Price Group, Inc., is a public company reporting under Sarbanes-Oxley. Exhibit 2-6 presents the auditor's report on T. Rowe Price Group, Inc.'s internal controls.

Exhibit	2-5	T. ROWE PRICE GROUP, INC.*

Audit Opinion
Unqualified Opinion—2006 Annual Report

Report of Independent Registered Public Accounting Firm

The Board of Directors and Stockholders
T. Rowe Price Group, Inc.

We have audited the accompanying consolidated balance sheets of T. Rowe Price Group, Inc. and subsidiaries ("the Company") as of December 31, 2006 and 2005, and the related consolidated statements of income, stockholders' equity, and cash flows for each of the years in the three-year period ended December 31, 2006. These consolidated financial statements are the responsibility of the Company's management. Our responsibility is to express an opinion on these consolidated financial statements based on our audits.

We conducted our audits in accordance with the standards of the Public Company Accounting Oversight Board (United States). Those standards require that we plan and perform the audit to obtain reasonable assurance about whether the financial statements are free of material misstatement. An audit includes examining, on a test basis, evidence supporting the amounts and disclosures in the financial statements. An audit also includes assessing the accounting principles used and significant estimates made by management, as well as evaluating the overall financial statement presentation. We believe that our audits provide a reasonable basis for our opinion.

In our opinion, the consolidated financial statements referred to above present fairly, in all material respects, the financial position of T. Rowe Price Group, Inc. and subsidiaries as of December 31, 2006 and 2005, and the results of their operations and their cash flows for each of the years in the three-year period ended December 31, 2006, in conformity with U.S. generally accepted accounting principles.

As discussed in the summary of significant accounting policies accompanying the consolidated financial statements, effective January 1, 2006, the Company changed its method of accounting for stock-based compensation with the adoption of Statement of Financial Accounting Standards No. 123R, *Share-Based Payment.*

We also have audited, in accordance with the standards of the Public Company Accounting Oversight Board (United States), the effectiveness of the Company's internal control over financial reporting as of December 31, 2006, based on criteria established in *Internal Control—Integrated Framework* issued by the Committee of Sponsoring Organizations of the Treadway Commission (COSO), and our report dated February 7, 2007, expressed an unqualified opinion on management's assessment of, and the effective operation of, internal control over financial reporting.

/s/ KPMG LLP

Baltimore, Maryland
February 7, 2007

*"T. Rowe Price Group is a financial services holding company that derives its consolidated revenues and net income primarily from investment advisory services that its subsidiaries provide to individual and institutional investors in the sponsored T. Rowe Price mutual funds and other investment portfolios." 10-K

| Exhibit | 2-6 | T. ROWE PRICE GROUP, INC.* |

Auditor's Report on the Firm's Internal Controls–2006 Annual Report

---

Report of Independent Registered Public Accounting Firm

The Board of Directors and Stockholders
T. Rowe Price Group, Inc.

We have audited management's assessment, included in the accompanying Report on Internal Control Over Financial Reporting, that T. Rowe Price Group, Inc. and subsidiaries ("the Company") maintained effective internal control over financial reporting as of December 31, 2006, based on criteria established in *Internal Control—Integrated Framework* issued by the Committee of Sponsoring Organizations of the Treadway Commission (COSO). The Company's management is responsible for maintaining effective internal control over financial reporting and for its assessment of the effectiveness of internal control over financial reporting. Our responsibility is to express an opinion on management's assessment and an opinion on the effectiveness of the Company's internal control over financial reporting based on our audit.

We conducted our audit in accordance with the standards of the Public Company Accounting Oversight Board (United States). Those standards require that we plan and perform the audit to obtain reasonable assurance about whether effective internal control over financial reporting was maintained in all material respects. Our audit included obtaining an understanding of internal control over financial reporting, evaluating management's assessment, testing and evaluating the design and operating effectiveness of internal control, and performing such other procedures as we considered necessary in the circumstances. We believe that our audit provides a reasonable basis for our opinion.

A company's internal control over financial reporting is a process designed to provide reasonable assurance regarding the reliability of financial reporting and the preparation of financial statements for external purposes in accordance with generally accepted accounting principles. A company's internal control over financial reporting includes those policies and procedures that (1) pertain to the maintenance of records that, in reasonable detail, accurately and fairly reflect the transactions and dispositions of the assets of the company; (2) provide reasonable assurance that transactions are recorded as necessary to permit preparation of financial statements in accordance with generally accepted accounting principles, and that receipts and expenditures of the company are being made only in accordance with authorizations of management and directors of the company; and (3) provide reasonable assurance regarding prevention or timely detection of unauthorized acquisition, use, or disposition of the company's assets that could have a material effect on the financial statements.

Because of its inherent limitations, internal control over financial reporting may not prevent or detect misstatements. Also, projections of any evaluation of effectiveness to future periods are subject to the risk that controls may become inadequate because of changes in conditions, or that the degree of compliance with the policies or procedures may deteriorate.

In our opinion, management's assessment that the Company maintained effective internal control over financial reporting as of December 31, 2006, is fairly stated, in all material respects, based on criteria established in *Internal Control—Integrated Framework* issued by the Committee of Sponsoring Organizations of the Treadway Commission (COSO). Also, in our opinion, the Company maintained, in all material respects, effective internal control over financial reporting as of December 31, 2006, based on criteria established in *Internal Control—Integrated Framework* issued by the Committee of Sponsoring Organizations of the Treadway Commission (COSO).

---

*"T. Rowe Price Group is a financial services holding company that derives its consolidated revenues and net income primarily from investment advisory services that its subsidiaries provide to individual and institutional investors in the sponsored T. Rowe Price mutual funds and other investment portfolios." 10-K

(continued)

Exhibit   2-6   T. ROWE PRICE GROUP, INC. (Continued)

> We also have audited, in accordance with the standards of the Public Company Accounting Oversight Board (United States), the consolidated balance sheets of T. Rowe Price Group, Inc. and subsidiaries as of December 31, 2006 and 2005, and the related consolidated statements of income, stockholders' equity, and cash flows for each of the years in the three-year period ended December 31, 2006, and our report dated February 7, 2007, expressed an unqualified opinion on those consolidated financial statements.
>
> /s/ KPMG LLP
>
> Baltimore, Maryland
> February 7, 2007

REPORT OF MANAGEMENT ON INTERNAL CONTROL OVER FINANCIAL REPORTING

Under Sarbanes-Oxley, management of public companies must present a Report of Management on Internal Control over Financial Reporting. Exhibit 2-7 presents the internal control report of management for T. Rowe Price Group, Inc., that was presented with its 2006 annual report.

Management's Responsibility for Financial Statements

The responsibility for the preparation and for the integrity of financial statements rests with management. The auditor is responsible for conducting an independent examination of the statements and expressing an opinion on the financial statements based on the audit. To make financial statement users aware of management's responsibility, some companies have presented management statements to shareholders as part of the annual report. Exhibit 2-8 shows an example of a report of management's responsibility for financial statements as presented by Kellogg Company in its 2006 annual report.

The SEC's Integrated Disclosure System

In general, in the United States, the SEC has the authority to prescribe external financial reporting requirements for companies with securities sold to the general public. Under this jurisdiction, the SEC requires that certain financial statement information be included in the annual report to shareholders. This annual report, along with certain supplementary information, must then be included, or incorporated by reference, in the annual filing to the SEC, known as the 10-K report or Form 10-K. The Form 10-K is due 60 days, 75 days, or 90 days following the end of the company's fiscal year, depending on the market value of the common stock (see Exhibit 2-9). The annual report and the Form 10-K include audited financial statements.

The SEC promotes an integrated disclosure system between the annual report and the Form 10-K. The goals are to improve the quality of disclosure, lighten the disclosure load, standardize information requirements, and achieve uniformity of annual reports and Form 10-K filings.

In addition to the company's primary financial statements, the Form 10-K must include the following:

1. Information on the market for holders of common stock and related securities, including high and low sales price, frequency and amount of dividends, and number of shares.

2. Five-year summary of selected financial data, including net sales or operating revenues, income from continuing operations, total assets, long-term obligations, redeemable preferred stock, and cash dividends per share. (Some companies elect to present data for more than five years and/or expand the disclosure.) Trend analysis is emphasized.

Exhibit	2-7	T. ROWE PRICE GROUP, INC.*

Report of Management on Internal Control over Financial Reporting—2006 Annual Report

Report of Management on Internal Control over Financial Reporting

To the Stockholders of T. Rowe Price Group, Inc.

We, together with other members of management of T. Rowe Price Group, are responsible for establishing and maintaining adequate internal control over the company's financial reporting. Internal control over financial reporting is the process designed under our supervision, and effected by the company's board of directors, management and other personnel, to provide reasonable assurance regarding the reliability of financial reporting and the preparation of the company's financial statements for external purposes in accordance with accounting principles generally accepted in the United States of America.

There are inherent limitations in the effectiveness of internal control over financial reporting, including the possibility that misstatements may not be prevented or detected. Accordingly, even effective internal controls over financial reporting can provide only reasonable assurance with respect to financial statement preparation. Furthermore, the effectiveness of internal controls can change with circumstances.

Management has evaluated the effectiveness of internal control over financial reporting as of December 31, 2006, in relation to criteria described in *Internal Control—Integrated Framework* issued by the Committee of Sponsoring Organizations of the Treadway Commission (COSO). Based on management's assessment, we believe that the company's internal control over financial reporting was effective as of December 31, 2006.

KPMG LLP, an independent registered public accounting firm, has audited our financial statements that are included in this annual report and expressed an unqualified opinion thereon. KPMG LLP has also expressed an unqualified opinion on management's assessment of, and the effective operation of, our internal control over financial reporting as of December 31, 2006.

February 7, 2007

/s/ James A. C. Kennedy
Chief Executive Officer and President

/s/ Kenneth V. Moreland
Vice President and Chief Financial Officer

*"T. Rowe Price Group is a financial services holding company that derives its consolidated revenues and net income primarily from investment advisory services that its subsidiaries provide to individual and institutional investors in the sponsored T. Rowe Price mutual funds and other investment portfolios." 10-K

3. Management's discussion and analysis (MDA) of financial condition and results of operations. Specifically required is discussion of liquidity, capital resources, and results of operations.

4. Two years of audited balance sheets and three years of audited income statements and statements of cash flow.

5. Disclosure of the domestic and foreign components of pretax income, unless foreign components are considered to be immaterial.

SEC requirements force management to focus on the financial statements as a whole, rather than on just the income statement and operations. Where trend information is relevant, discussion should center on the five-year summary. Emphasis should be on favorable or unfavorable trends and on identification of significant events or uncertainties. This discussion should provide the analyst with a reasonable summary of the position of the firm.

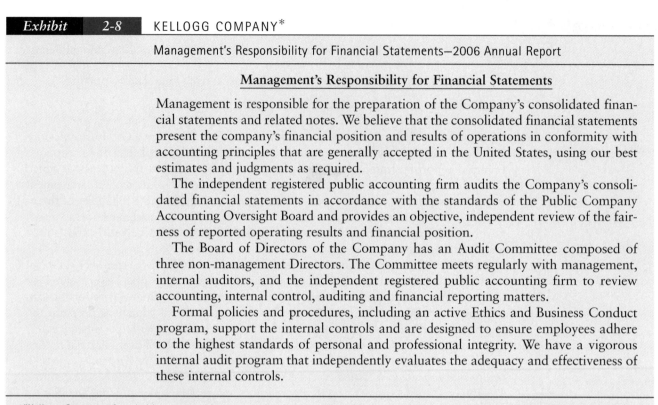

| Exhibit | 2-8 | KELLOGG COMPANY* |

Management's Responsibility for Financial Statements—2006 Annual Report

Management's Responsibility for Financial Statements

Management is responsible for the preparation of the Company's consolidated financial statements and related notes. We believe that the consolidated financial statements present the company's financial position and results of operations in conformity with accounting principles that are generally accepted in the United States, using our best estimates and judgments as required.

The independent registered public accounting firm audits the Company's consolidated financial statements in accordance with the standards of the Public Company Accounting Oversight Board and provides an objective, independent review of the fairness of reported operating results and financial position.

The Board of Directors of the Company has an Audit Committee composed of three non-management Directors. The Committee meets regularly with management, internal auditors, and the independent registered public accounting firm to review accounting, internal control, auditing and financial reporting matters.

Formal policies and procedures, including an active Ethics and Business Conduct program, support the internal controls and are designed to ensure employees adhere to the highest standards of personal and professional integrity. We have a vigorous internal audit program that independently evaluates the adequacy and effectiveness of these internal controls.

*"Kellogg Company, founded in 1906 and incorporated in Delaware in 1922, and its subsidiaries are engaged in the manufacture and marketing of ready-to-eat cereal and convenience foods." 10-K

| Exhibit | 2-9 | FORM 10-K AND 10-Q DEADLINE |

Category of Filer	Form 10-K Deadline	Form 10-Q Deadline
Large accelerated filer ($700 million or more market value*)	60 days	40 days
Accelerated filer ($75 million or more and less than $700 million market value*)	75 days	40 days
Non-accelerated filer (less than $75 million market value*)	90 days	45 days

*Market value is the worldwide market value of outstanding voting and non-voting common equity held by non-affiliates.

Source: Adapted from Securities and Exchange Commission Release No. 33-8644, Revisions to Accelerated Filer Definition and Accelerated Deadlines for Filing Periodic Reports, December 21, 2005.

Exhibit 2-10 presents a summary of the major parts of the Form 10-K. In practice, some of the required information in the Form 10-K is incorporated by reference. Incorporated by reference means that the information is presented outside the Form 10-K, and a reference in the Form 10-K indicates where the information can be found.

A review of a company's Form 10-K can reveal information that is not available in the annual report. For example, Item 2 of the Form 10-K reveals a detailed listing of properties and indicates if the property is leased or owned.

The SEC requires that a quarterly report (Form 10-Q), containing financial statements and a management discussion and analysis, be submitted within either 40 or 45 days following the end of the quarter, depending on the market value of the common stock (see Exhibit 2-9). (The Form 10-Q is not required for the fourth quarter of the fiscal year.) Most companies also issue a quarterly report to stockholders. The Form 10-Q and quarterly reports are unaudited.

Exhibit	2-10	GENERAL SUMMARY OF FORM 10-K

Part I

Item 1. Business.

Item 1A. Risk Factors.

Item 1B. Unresolved Staff Comments.

Item 2. Properties.

Item 3. Legal Proceedings.

Item 4. Submission of Matters to a Vote of Security Holders.

Part II

Item 5. Market for Registrant's Common Equity, Related Stockholder Matters, and Issuer Purchases of Equity Securities.

Item 6. Selected Financial Data.

Item 7. Management's Discussion and Analysis of Financial Condition and Results of Operations.

Item 7A. Qualitative and Quantitative Disclosures About Market Risk.

Item 8. Financial Statements and Supplementary Data.

Item 9. Changes in and Disagreements with Accountants on Accounting and Financial Disclosure.

Item 9A. Controls and Procedures.

Item 9B. Other Information.

Part III

Item 10. Directors, Executive Officers, and Corporate Governance.

Item 11. Executive Compensation.

Item 12. Security Ownership of Certain Beneficial Owners and Management and Related Stockholders' Matters.

Item 13. Certain Relationships and Related Transactions, and Director Independence.

Item 14. Principal Accountant Fees and Services.

Part IV

Item 15. Exhibits and Financial Statement Schedules.

Signatures

Exhibit Index

In addition to the Form 10-K and Form 10-Q, a Form 8-K must be submitted to the SEC to report special events. Some events required to be reported are changes in principal stockholders, changes in auditors, acquisitions and divestitures, bankruptcy, and resignation of directors. The Form 8-K is due 15 days following the event.

The Forms 10-K, 10-Q, and 8-K filings are available to the public. Many companies are reluctant to send these reports to nonstockholders. In public companies, these reports can be found at http://www.sec.gov.

Proxy

The **proxy**, the solicitation sent to stockholders for the election of directors and for the approval of other corporation actions, represents the shareholder authorization regarding the casting of that shareholder's vote. The proxy contains notice of the annual meeting, beneficial ownership (name, address, and share ownership data of shareholders holding more than 5% of outstanding shares), board of directors, standing committees, compensation of directors, compensation of executive officers, employee benefit plans, certain transactions with officers and directors, relationship with independent accountants, and other business.

The proxy rules provided under the 1934 Securities Exchange Act are applicable to all securities registered under Section 12 of the Act. The SEC gains its influence over the annual report through provisions of the Act that cover proxy statements.

The SEC's proxy rules of particular interest to investors involve executive compensation disclosure, performance graph, and retirement plans for executive officers. These rules are designed to improve shareholders' understanding of the compensation paid to senior executives and directors, the criteria used in reaching compensation decisions, and the relationship between compensation and corporate performance.

Among other matters, the executive compensation rules call for four highly formatted disclosure tables and the disclosure of the compensation committee's basis for compensation decisions.

The four tables disclosing executive compensation are:

- A summary executive compensation table covering compensation for the company's chief executive officer and its four other most highly compensated executives for the last three years.
- Two tables detailing options and stock appreciation rights.
- A long-term incentive plan award table.

The performance graph is a line graph comparing the cumulative total shareholder return with performance indicators of the overall stock market and either the published industry index or the registrant-determined peer comparison. This performance graph must be presented for a five-year period.

The pension plan table for executive officers discloses the estimated annual benefits payable upon retirement for any defined benefit or actuarial plan under which benefits are determined primarily by final compensation (or average final compensation) and years of service. Immediately following the table, additional disclosure is required. This disclosure includes items such as the relationship of the covered compensation to the compensation reported in the summary compensation table and the estimated credited years of service for each of the named executive officers.

For public companies, the proxy can be found at http://www.sec.gov.

Summary Annual Report

A reporting option available to public companies is to issue a summary annual report. A summary annual report, a condensed report, omits much of the financial information typically included in an annual report. A typical full annual report has more financial pages than nonfinancial pages. A summary annual report generally has more nonfinancial pages.[3] When a company issues a summary annual report, the proxy materials it sends to shareholders must include a set of fully audited statements and other required financial disclosures.

A summary annual report is *not* adequate for reasonable analysis. For companies that issue a summary annual report, request a copy of their proxy and the Form 10-K. Even for companies that issue a full annual report, it is also good to obtain a copy of the proxy materials and the Form 10-K. Some companies issue a joint annual report and Form 10-K, while other companies issue a joint annual report and proxy. A few companies issue a joint annual report, Form 10-K, and proxy. These joint reports are usually labeled as the annual report.

The Efficient Market Hypothesis

The efficient market hypothesis (EMH) relates to the ability of capital markets to generate prices for securities that reflect worth. The EMH implies that publicly available information is fully reflected in share prices. The market will not be efficient if the market does not have access to relevant information or if fraudulent information is provided.

There seems to be little doubt that the FASB and the SEC assess the impact of their actions on security prices. The SEC has been particularly sensitive to insider trading because abnormal returns could be achieved by the use of insider information.

If the market is efficient, investors may be harmed when firms do not follow a full disclosure policy. In an efficient market, the method of disclosure is not as important as whether the item is disclosed. It should not matter whether an item is disclosed in the body of the financial statements or in the notes. It is the disclosure rather than how to disclose that is the substantive issue.

Usually, there is a cost to disclose. An attempt should be made to determine the value of additional disclosure in relation to the additional cost. Disclosure should be made when the perceived benefits exceed the additional cost to provide the disclosure.

It is generally recognized that the market is more efficient when dealing with large firms trading on large organized stock markets than it is for small firms that are not trading on large organized stock markets.

Although the research evidence regarding the EMH is conflicting, this hypothesis has taken on an important role in financial reporting in the United States.

Ethics

"Ethics and morals are synonymous. While *ethics* is derived from Greek, *morals* is derived from Latin. They are interchangeable terms referring to ideals of character and conduct. These ideals, in the form of codes of conduct, furnish criteria for distinguishing between right and wrong."[4] Ethics has been a subject of investigation for hundreds of years. Individuals in financial positions must be able to recognize ethical issues and resolve them in an appropriate manner.

Ethics affect all individuals—from the financial clerk to the high-level financial executive. Individuals make daily decisions based on their individual values. Some companies and professional organizations have formulated a code of ethics as a statement of aspirations and a standard of integrity beyond that required by law (which can be viewed as the minimum standard of ethics).

Ten essential values can be considered central to relations between people.[5]

1. Caring
2. Honesty
3. Accountability
4. Promise keeping
5. Pursuit of excellence
6. Loyalty
7. Fairness
8. Integrity
9. Respect for others
10. Responsible citizenship

Ethics can be a particular problem with financial reports. Accepted accounting principles leave ample room for arriving at different results in the short run. Highly subjective estimates can substantially influence earnings. What provision should be made for warranty costs? What should be the loan loss reserve? What should be the allowance for doubtful accounts?

The American Accounting Association initiated a project in 1988 on professionalism and ethics. One of the goals of this project was to provide students with a framework for evaluating their courses of action when encountering ethical dilemmas. The American Accounting Association developed a decision model for focusing on ethical issues.[6]

1. Determine the facts—what, who, where, when, how.
2. Define the ethical issues (includes identifying the identifiable parties affected by the decision made or action taken).

3. Identify major principles, rules, and values.
4. Specify the alternatives.
5. Compare norms, principles, and values with alternatives to see if a clear decision can be reached.
6. Assess the consequences.
7. Make your decision.

Example 1: Questionable Ethics in Savings and Loans

In connection with the savings and loan (S&L) scandal, it was revealed that several auditors of thrift institutions borrowed substantial amounts from the S&L that their firm was auditing. It was charged that some of the loans involved special consideration.[7] In one case, dozens of partners of a major accounting firm borrowed money for commercial real estate loans, and some of the partners defaulted on their loans when the real estate market collapsed.[8] It was not clear whether these particular loans violated professional ethics standards. The AICPA subsequently changed its ethics standards to ban all such loans.

In another case, an accounting firm paid $1.5 million to settle charges by the California State Board of Accountancy that the accounting firm was grossly negligent in its audit of Lincoln Savings & Loan. The accounting board charged that the firm had agreed to the improper recognition of approximately $62 million in profits.[9]

Example 2: Questionable Ethics in the Motion Picture Industry

Hollywood's accounting practices have often been labeled "mysterious."[10] A case in point is Art Buchwald's lawsuit against Paramount Pictures for breach of contract regarding the film *Coming to America*. Paramount took an option on Buchwald's story "King for a Day" in 1983 and promised Buchwald 1.5% of the net profits of the film. Buchwald's attorney, Pierce O'Donnell, accused Paramount Studios of "fatal subtraction" in determining the amount of profit. Although the film grossed $350 million worldwide, Paramount claimed an $18 million net loss. As a result of the studio's accounting practices, Buchwald was to get 1.5% of nothing.[11] Buchwald was eventually awarded $150,000 in a 1992 court decision.[12]

Many Hollywood celebrities, in addition to Art Buchwald, have sued over Hollywood-style accounting. These include Winston Groom over the movie rights to *Forrest Gump*, Jane Fonda over a larger share of profits relating to *On Golden Pond*, and James Garner over his share of profits from *The Rockford Files* (a television program). Some of the best creative work in Hollywood is in accounting.

SEC REQUIREMENTS—CODE OF ETHICS

In January 2003, the SEC voted to require disclosure in a company's annual report whether it has a code of ethics that applies to the company's principal executive officer, principal financial officer, principal accounting officer or controller, or persons performing similar functions. The rules will define a code of ethics as written standards that are reasonably necessary to deter wrongdoing and to promote:

1. Honest and ethical conduct, including the ethical handling of actual or apparent conflicts of interest between personal and professional relationships;
2. Full, fair, accurate, timely, and understandable disclosure in reports and documents that a company files with, or submits to, the Commission and in other public communications made by the company;
3. Compliance with applicable governmental laws, rules, and regulations;
4. The prompt internal reporting of code violations to an appropriate person or persons identified in the code; and
5. Accountability for adherence to the code.[13]

The SEC requires that a copy of the company's code of ethics be made available by filing an exhibit with its annual report (10-K), or by providing it on the company's Web site.

The SEC requirements were an outcome of the Sarbanes-Oxley Act. Exhibit 2-11 presents NIKE's code of ethics.

Exhibit **2-11**	THE NIKE CODE OF ETHICS*

Defining the NIKE Playing Field and the Rules of the Game

Do the Right Thing

A Message from Phil

At NIKE, we are on the offense, always. We play hard, we play to win, but we play by the rules of the game.

This Code of Ethics is vitally important. It contains the rules of the game for NIKE, the rules we live by and what we stand for. Please read it, and if you've read it before, read it again.

Then take some time to think about what it says and make a commitment to play by it. Defining the NIKE playing field ensures no matter how dynamic and challenging NIKE may be, our actions and decisions fit with our shared values.

Thank you for your commitment.

Philip H. Knight

Note: Philip H. Knight is the Chairman of the Board of Directors of NIKE.

The NIKE Code of Ethics is backed by a twenty-one page "Defining the NIKE Playing Field and the Rules of the Game."

The NIKE Code of Ethics can be found at http://www.nikebiz.com. Click on "Investors," click on "Corporate Governance," click on "Code of Ethics," and click on "Code of Business Conduct & Ethics."

*Our principal business activity is the design, development and worldwide marketing of high-quality footwear, apparel, equipment, and accessory products." 10-K

Harmonization of International Accounting Standards

The impetus for changes in accounting practice has come from the needs of the business community and governments. With the expansion of international business and global capital markets, the business community and governments have shown an increased interest in the harmonization of international accounting standards.

Suggested problems caused by the lack of harmonization of international accounting standards include the following:

1. A need for employment of key personnel in multinational companies to bridge the "gap" in accounting requirements between countries.
2. Difficulties in reconciling local standards for access to other capital markets.
3. Difficulties in accessing capital markets for companies from less-developed countries.[14]
4. Negative effect on the international trade of accounting practice and services.[15]

Domestic accounting standards have developed to meet the needs of domestic environments. A few of the factors that influence accounting standards locally are as follows:

1. A litigious environment in the United States that has led to a demand for more detailed standards in many cases.
2. High rates of inflation in some countries that have resulted in periodic revaluation of fixed assets and other price-level adjustments or disclosures.
3. More emphasis on financial reporting/income tax conformity in certain countries (for example, Japan and Germany) that no doubt greatly influences domestic financial reporting.
4. Reliance on open markets as the principal means of intermediating capital flows that has increased the demand for information to be included in financial reports in the United States and some other developed countries.[16]

The following have been observed to have an impact on a country's financial accounting operation:

1. Who the investors and creditors—the information users—are (individuals, banks, the government).
2. How many investors and creditors there are.
3. How close the relationship is between businesses and the investor/creditor group.
4. How developed the stock exchanges and bond markets are.
5. The extent of use of international financial markets.[17]

With this backdrop of fragmentation, it has been difficult in the short run, if not impossible, to bring all national standards into agreement with a meaningful body of international standards. But many see benefits to harmonization of international accounting standards and feel that accounting must move in that direction. In the short run, ways exist to cope with incomparable standards. One possible interim solution involves dual standards. International companies would prepare two sets of financial statements. One would be prepared under domestic GAAP, while the other would be prepared under international GAAP. This would likely put pressure on domestic GAAP to move toward international GAAP.

In the United States, a conflict exists between the SEC and the securities exchanges, such as the New York Stock Exchange (NYSE). In general, the SEC has required foreign registrants to conform to U.S. GAAP, either directly or by reconciliation. This approach achieved a degree of comparability in the U.S. capital market, but it did not achieve comparability for investors who want to invest in several national capital markets. This approach poses a problem for U.S. securities exchanges, because the U.S. standards are perceived to be the most stringent. This puts exchanges such as the NYSE at a competitive disadvantage with foreign exchanges that have lower standards. The development of international standards would alleviate this problem.

The United Nations (UN) has shown a substantial interest in the harmonization of international accounting standards. The UN appointed a group to study harmonization of international accounting standards in 1973. This has evolved into an ad hoc working group. Members of the working group represent governments and not the private sector. The working group does not issue standards but rather facilitates their development. The UN's concern is with how multinational corporations affect the developing countries.[18]

Many other organizations, in addition to the IASB and the UN, have played a role in the harmonization of international accounting standards. Some of these organizations include the Financial Accounting Standards Board (FASB), the European Economic Community (EEC), the Organization for Economic Cooperation and Development (OECD), and the International Federation of Accountants (IFAC).

In 1973, nine countries, including the United States, formed the International Accounting Standards Committee (IASC). The IASC included approximately 100 member nations and well over 100 professional accounting bodies. The IASC was the only private-sector body involved in setting international accounting standards. International Accounting Standards (IAS) were issued by the IASC from 1973 to 2000.

The IASC's objectives included the following:

1. Developing international accounting standards and disclosure to meet the needs of international capital markets and the international business community.
2. Developing accounting standards to meet the needs of developing and newly industrialized countries.
3. Working toward increased comparability between national and international accounting standards.[19]

The International Accounting Standards Board (IASB) was established in January 2001 to replace the IASC. The IASB arose from a review of the structure of the IASC. The new structure has characteristics similar to that of the FASB. The IASB basically continues the objectives of the IASC.

The IASB does not have authority to enforce its standards, but these standards have been adopted in whole or in part by approximately 100 countries. Some see the lack of enforcement authority as a positive factor because it enables the passing of standards that would have not had the necessary votes if they could be enforced. This allows standards to be more ideal than they would otherwise be if they were enforceable. The IASB issues International Financial Reporting Standards (IFRSs). The term IFRSs now refers to the entire body of international standards.

The IASB follows a due-process procedure similar to that of the FASB. This includes Exposure Drafts and a comment period. All proposed standards and guidelines are exposed for comment for about six months.

The Financial Accounting Standards Board and the International Accounting Standards Board met jointly in Norwalk, Connecticut, on September 18, 2002. They acknowledge their commitment to the development of high-quality, compatible accounting standards that could be used for both domestic and cross-border financial reporting. (This is known as the Norwalk Agreement.)

Since the Norwalk Agreement, the FASB and IASB have made significant progress. In joint meetings in April and October 2005, the FASB and the IASB reaffirmed their commitment to the convergence of U.S. GAAP and International Financial Reporting Standards. In a joint meeting February 27, 2006, they agreed on a road map for convergence between U.S. GAAP and IFRS during 2006–2008. Some topics identified for short-term convergence include the following:[20]

To Be Examined by the FASB	To Be Examined by the IASB
1. Fair value option	1. Borrowing costs
2. Impairment	2. Impairment
3. Income tax	3. Income tax
4. Investment properties	4. Government grants
5. Research and development	5. Joint ventures
6. Subsequent events	6. Segment reporting

The FASB and IASB also agreed on major joint topics. Those topics are as follows:[21]

1. Business combinations
2. Consolidations
3. Fair value measurement guidance
4. Liabilities and equity distinctions
5. Performance reporting
6. Postretirement benefits
7. Revenue recognition
8. Derecognition
9. Financial instruments
10. Intangible assets
11. Leases

The major joint topic performance reporting—financial statement presentation—was updated July 2007. This project includes the presentation and display on the face of the financial statements that constitute a complete set of financial statements. This project would drastically alter and change the presentation and display on the face of the financial statements as now presented by U.S. GAAP and IFRSs.

Completion of these major projects will take several years. They will substantially alter IFRSs and likely eliminate U.S. GAAP.

In 2007, the Securities and Exchange Commission announced that it would accept financial statements from foreign private issuers without reconciliation to U.S. GAAP if they are prepared using IFRSs as issued by the International Accounting Standards Board. It is also considering allowing U.S. companies to use U.S. GAAP or IFRSs. Also in 2007, President Bush signed an agreement between the United States and the European Union that sets the stage to allow many public companies to drop U.S. GAAP in favor of more flexible international rules. Some of these international accounting issues will be covered in subsequent chapters.

Consolidated Statements

Financial statements of legally separate entities may be issued to show financial position, income, and cash flow as they would appear if the companies were a single entity (consolidated). Such statements reflect an economic, rather than a legal, concept of the entity. For consolidated statements, all transactions between the entities being consolidated—intercompany transactions—must be eliminated.

When a subsidiary is less than 100% owned and its statements are consolidated, minority shareholders must be recognized in the consolidated financial statements by showing the minority interest in net assets on the balance sheet and the minority share of earnings on the income statement. Minority-related accounts are discussed in detail in Chapter 3.

Consolidated statements are financial statements that a parent company produces when its financial statements and those of a subsidiary are added together. This portrays the resulting financial statements as a single company. The parent company concept emphasizes the interests of the controlling shareholders (the parent's shareholders). A subsidiary is a company controlled by another company. An unconsolidated subsidiary is accounted for as an investment on the parent's balance sheet.

There are two reporting approaches to presenting consolidated statements. In one approach, the subsidiary's accounts are shown separately from the parent's. This format is logical when the parent has a subsidiary in a different line of business. Ford Motor Company consolidates presenting the automotive and financial services category separately.

Most companies consolidate the parents and subsidiary accounts summed. The Dow Chemical Company consolidates summing the accounts.

The parent company can have legal control with ownership of a majority of the subsidiary's outstanding voting shares. The parent company can have effective control when a majority of the subsidiary board of directors can be elected by means other than by having legal control.

A company could have ownership of the majority voting shares and not have control. Such a situation would be a subsidiary that has filed for bankruptcy protection. In the bankruptcy situation, the judge in the bankruptcy court has assumed control.

Control can be gained by means other than obtaining majority stock ownership. The FASB recognizes a risks, rewards, decision-making ability and the primary beneficiary. Thus, consolidation would be required when a firm bears the majority (over 50%) of the risks and/or rewards of ownership. Examples of consolidating because of risks, rewards, and decision-making ability would be a contractual situation to accept substantial production or a loan situation which grants substantial control.

The consolidation of financial statements has been a practice in the United States for years; however, this has not been the case for many other nations. Some countries do not consolidate. Other countries use consolidation with different rules. Countries such as Canada, France, Germany, Italy, Japan, and the United Kingdom do consolidate, but each has different consolidation standards.

The IASC passed a standard that requires that all controlled subsidiaries be consolidated. Although IASC standards cannot be enforced, this standard will likely increase the acceptance of consolidation.

Accounting for Business Combinations

The combination of business entities by merger or acquisition is very frequent. There are many possible reasons for this external business expansion, including achieving economies of scale and savings of time in entering a new market. The combination must be accounted for using the purchase method.

The purchase method views the business combination as the acquisition of one entity by another. The firm doing the acquiring records the identifiable assets and liabilities at fair value at the date of acquisition. The difference between the fair value of the identifiable assets and liabilities and the amount paid is recorded as goodwill (an asset).

With a purchase, the acquiring firm picks up the income of the acquired firm from the date of acquisition. Retained earnings of the acquired firm do not continue.

Summary

This chapter includes an introduction to the basic financial statements. Later chapters will cover these statements in detail.

An understanding of the sequence of accounting procedures completed during each accounting period, called the accounting cycle, will help in understanding the end result—financial statements.

This chapter describes the forms of business entities, which are sole proprietorship, partnership, and corporation.

Management is responsible for financial statements. These statements are examined by auditors who express an opinion regarding the statements' conformity to GAAP in the auditor's report. The auditor's report often points out key factors that can affect financial statement analysis. The SEC has begun a program to integrate the Form 10-K requirements with those of the annual report.

A reporting option available to public companies, a summary annual report (a condensed annual report), omits much of the financial information included in a typical annual report.

The EMH relates to the ability of capital markets to generate prices for securities that reflect worth. The market will not be efficient if the market does not have access to relevant information or if fraudulent information is provided.

Individuals in financial positions must be able to recognize ethical issues and resolve them appropriately.

With the expansion of international business and global capital markets, the business community and governments have shown an increased interest in the harmonization of international accounting standards.

Financial statements of legally separate entities may be issued to show financial position, income, and cash flow as they would appear if the companies were a single entity (consolidated).

The combination of business entities by merger or acquisition is very frequent. An understanding of how a business combination can impact the basic statements is important to the analyst.

to the net

1. Go to the Carol and Lawrence Zicklin Center for Business Ethics Research Web site: http://www.zicklincenter.org. Copy the mission statement. Click on "Links." Click on "Publications & Journals." Choose a journal from the list provided. Go to a library and review an article in the journal selected. Summarize the information provided by the article.

2. Go to the Carol and Lawrence Zicklin Center for Business Ethics Research Web site: http://www.zicklincenter.org. Click on "Links." Under "Codes of Conduct, Online Resources," select a company. Summarize that company's code of conduct.

3. Go to the Carol and Lawrence Zicklin Center for Business Ethics Research Web site: http://www.zicklincenter.org. Click on "Links." Under "Corporate Scandals," select a company. Write a summary of the corporate scandal.

4. The following Web sites provide for an in-depth review of the emergence of IFRSs:

a. Go to the International Accounting Standards Board (IASB) Web site: http://www.iasb.org. Click on "About Us." Comment on the IASB structure.

b. Go to the FASB Web site: http://www.fasb.org. Click on "International." Click on "Convergence with the IASB." Write a summary of the convergence with the IASB.

c. Go to the Web site http://www.iasplus.com/country/useias.htm. Comment on the adoption status of IFRSs by country. (IFRSs not permitted, IFRSs permitted, IFRSs required for some, IFRSs required for all, use of IFRSs by unlisted companies.)

d. Go to the Web site http://www.iasplus.com/standard/standard.htm. Select a recent IFRS and comment on the contents of the summary.

e. Go to the Web site http://www.iasplus.com/fs/fs.htm. What do the IFRS Model Financial Statements illustrate?

5. Go to the COSO Web site: http://www.coso.org. What is COSO? List the five major professional associations that sponsored COSO.

6. Consolidated Statement Presentation

Go to the SEC Web site: http://www.sec.gov. Under "Filings & Forms (EDGAR)," click on "Search for Company Filings." Click on "Companies & Other Filers."

a. Under Company Name, enter "Ford Motor Co" (or under Ticker Symbol, enter "F"). Select the 2006 10-K. Review the Sector Statement of Income found a little over half-way through the document. Describe in some detail the consolidation presentation. (Refer to comments in this chapter.)

b. Type in "Dow Chemical Co" (or under Ticker Symbol, enter "DOW"). Select the 2006 10-K. Review the consolidated statements of income. Describe in some detail the reconsolidation presentation. (Refer to comments in this chapter.)

7. Proxy

Go to the SEC Web site: http://www.sec.gov. Under "Filings & Forms (EDGAR)," click on "Search for Company Filings." Click on "Companies & Other Filers." Under Company Name, enter "Gorman-Rupp Company" (or under Ticker Symbol, enter "GRC"). Select the 2006 proxy. Go to Executive Compensation within the proxy. Describe the executive compensation.

8. Audit Report and Auditor's Report on the Firm's Internal Controls

Go to the SEC Web site: http://www.sec.gov. Under "Filings & Forms (EDGAR)," click on "Search for Company Filings." Click on "Companies & Other Filers." Under Company Name, enter "Bemis Company" (or under Ticker Symbol, enter "BMS"). Select the 2006 10-K. Go to Report of Independent Registered Public Accounting Firm. Compare this report with Exhibit 2-5 (Audit Opinion) and Exhibit 2-6 (Auditor's Report on the Firm's Internal Controls). What is the basic difference in presentation?

Questions

Q 2-1. Name the type of opinion indicated by each of the following situations:
a. There is a material uncertainty.
b. There was a change in accounting principle.
c. There is no material scope limitation or material departure from GAAP.
d. The financial statements do not present fairly the financial position, results of operations, or cash flows of the entity in conformity with GAAP.
e. Except for the effects of the matter(s) to which the qualification relates, the financial statements present fairly, in all material respects, the financial position, results of operations, and cash flows of the entity, in conformity with GAAP.

Q 2-2. What are the roles of management and the auditor in the preparation and integrity of the financial statements?

Q 2-3. What is the purpose of the SEC's integrated disclosure system for financial reporting?

Q 2-4. Why do some unqualified opinions have explanatory paragraphs?

Q 2-5. Describe an auditor's review of financial statements.

Q 2-6. Will the accountant express an opinion on reviewed financial statements? Describe the accountant's report for reviewed financial statements.

Q 2-7. What type of opinion is expressed on a compilation?

Q 2-8. Are all financial statements presented with some kind of an accountant's report? Explain.

Q 2-9. What are the three principal financial statements of a corporation? Briefly describe the purpose of each statement.

Q 2-10.   Why are notes to statements necessary?

Q 2-11.   What are contingent liabilities? Are lawsuits against the firm contingent liabilities?

Q 2-12.   Which of the following events, occurring subsequent to the balance sheet date, would require a note?
a. Major fire in one of the firm's plants
b. Increase in competitor's advertising
c. Purchase of another company
d. Introduction of new management techniques
e. Death of the corporate treasurer

Q 2-13.   Describe a proxy statement.

Q 2-14.   Briefly describe a summary annual report.

Q 2-15.   If a company issues a summary annual report, where can the more extensive financial information be found?

Q 2-16.   Comment on the typical number of financial pages in a summary annual report as compared to a full annual report.

Q 2-17.   What are the major sections of a statement of cash flows?

Q 2-18.   Which two principal financial statements explain the difference between two balance sheet dates? Describe how these financial statements explain the difference between two balance sheet dates.

Q 2-19.   What are the three major categories on a balance sheet?

Q 2-20.   Can cash dividends be paid from retained earnings? Comment.

Q 2-21.   Why review notes to financial statements?

Q 2-22.   Where do we find a description of a firm's accounting policies?

Q 2-23.   Describe the relationship between the terms *ethics* and *morals*.

Q 2-24.   What is the relationship between ethics and law?

Q 2-25.   Identify the basic accounting equation.

Q 2-26.   What is the relationship between the accounting equation and the double-entry system of recording transactions?

Q 2-27.   Define the following:
a. Permanent accounts
b. Temporary accounts

Q 2-28.   A typical accrual recognition for salaries is as follows:

Salaries Expense $1,000 (increase)
Salaries Payable   1,000 (increase)

Explain how the matching concept applies in this situation.

Q 2-29.   Why are adjusting entries necessary?

Q 2-30.   Why aren't all transactions recorded in the general journal?

Q 2-31.   The NYSE has trouble competing with many foreign exchanges in the listing of foreign stocks. Discuss.

Q 2-32.   Identify the usual forms of a business entity and describe the ownership characteristic of each.

Q 2-33.   Why would the use of insider information be of concern if the market is efficient?

Q 2-34.   Considering the EMH, it is best if financial disclosure is made in the body of the financial statements. Comment.

Q 2-35.   Considering the EMH, how could abnormal returns be achieved?

Q 2-36.   Describe the purchase method of accounting for a business combination.

Q 2-37.   Consolidated statements may be issued to show financial position as it would appear if two or more companies were one entity. What is the objective of these statements?

Q 2-38.   What is the basic guideline for consolidation?

Q 2-39.   Where must a company's code of ethics be made available?

Q 2-40.   Describe the Treadway Commission.

Q 2-41.   Why is the COSO report on internal control systems important under requirements of the Sarbanes-Oxley Act?

Q 2-42.   Under Sarbanes-Oxley, the auditing firm will include which two reports with the audited statements? (*Note:* These two reports can be combined into one report.)

Q 2-43.   Under Sarbanes-Oxley, management must include what report with the audited statements?

Q 2-44.   Private companies are not under Sarbanes-Oxley. Why do some private companies follow the law?

Q 2-45.   Indicate the two approaches to presenting consolidated statements.

Q 2-46.   Describe how a company could be required to consolidate another company in which it has no or minor voting stock.

Q 2-47.   Consolidation rules are similar between countries. Comment.

Q 2-48.   Describe the filing deadline for Form 10-K.

Q 2-49.   Describe the Norwalk Agreement.

Q 2-50.   Comment on the impact on U.S. GAAP if the short-term convergence and the major topics are completed.

Problems

P 2-1.   Mike Szabo Company engaged in the following transactions during the month of December:

December   2   Made credit sales of $4,000 (accepted accounts receivable).
            6   Made cash sales of $2,500.
           10   Paid office salaries of $500.
           14   Sold land that originally cost $2,200 for $3,000 cash.
           17   Paid $6,000 for equipment.
           21   Billed clients $900 for services (accepted accounts receivable).
           24   Collected $1,200 on an account receivable.
           28   Paid an account payable of $700.

Required   Record the transactions, using T-accounts.

P 2-2. Darlene Cook Company engaged in the following transactions during the month of July:

July   1 Acquired land for $10,000. The company paid cash.

   8 Billed customers for $3,000. This represents an increase in revenue. The customer has been billed and will pay at a later date. An asset, accounts receivable, has been created.

  12 Incurred a repair expense for repairs of $600. Darlene Cook Company agreed to pay in 60 days. This transaction involves an increase in accounts payable and repair expense.

  15 Received a check for $500 from a customer who was previously billed. This is a reduction in accounts receivable.

  20 Paid $300 for supplies. This was previously established as a liability, account payable.

  24 Paid wages in the amount of $400. This was for work performed during July.

Required Record the transactions, using T-accounts.

P 2-3. Gaffney Company had these adjusting entry situations at the end of December.

1. On July 1, Gaffney Company paid $1,200 for a one-year insurance policy. The policy was for the period July 1 through June 30. The transaction was recorded as prepaid insurance and a reduction in cash.

2. On September 10, Gaffney Company purchased $500 of supplies for cash. The purchase was recorded as supplies. On December 31, it was determined that various supplies had been consumed in operations and that supplies costing $200 remained on hand.

3. Gaffney Company received $1,000 on December 1 for services to be performed in the following year. This was recorded on December 1 as an increase in cash and as revenue. As of December 31, this needs to be recognized as Unearned Revenue, a liability account.

4. As of December 31, interest charges of $200 have been incurred because of borrowed funds. Payment will not be made until February. A liability for the interest needs to be recognized as does the interest expense.

5. As of December 31, a $500 liability for salaries needs to be recognized.

6. As of December 31, Gaffney Company had provided services in the amount of $400 for Jones Company. An asset, Accounts Receivable, needs to be recognized along with the revenue.

Required Record the adjusting entries at December 31, using T-accounts.

P 2-4. DeCort Company had these adjusting entry situations at the end of December:

1. On May 1, DeCort Company paid $960 for a two-year insurance policy. The policy was for the period May 1 through April 30 (2 years). This is the first year of the policy. The transaction was recorded as insurance expense.

2. On December 1, DeCort Company purchased $400 of supplies for cash. The purchase was recorded as an asset, supplies. On December 31, it was determined that various supplies had been consumed in operations and that supplies costing $300 remained on hand.

3. DeCort Company holds a note receivable for $4,000. This note is interest-bearing. The interest will be received when the note matures. The note is a one-year note receivable made on June 30, bearing 5% simple interest.

4. DeCort Company owes salaries in the amount of $800 at the end of December.

5. As of December 31, DeCort Company had received $600 for services to be performed. These services had not been performed as of December 31. A liability, Unearned Revenue, needs to be recognized, and revenue needs to be reduced.

6. On December 20, DeCort Company received a $400 bill for advertising in December. The liability account, Accounts Payable, needs to be recognized along with the related expense.

Required Record the adjusting entries at December 31, using T-accounts.

P 2-5.

Required Answer the following multiple-choice questions:

a. The balance sheet equation can be defined as which of the following?

   1. Assets + Stockholders' Equity = Liabilities
   2. Assets + Liabilities = Stockholders' Equity
   3. Assets = Liabilities − Stockholders' Equity
   4. Assets − Liabilities = Stockholders' Equity
   5. None of the above

b. If assets are $40,000 and stockholders' equity is $10,000, how much are liabilities?
   1. $30,000
   2. $50,000
   3. $20,000
   4. $60,000
   5. $10,000

c. If assets are $100,000 and liabilities are $40,000, how much is stockholders' equity?
   1. $40,000
   2. $50,000
   3. $60,000
   4. $30,000
   5. $140,000

d. Which is a permanent account?
   1. Revenue
   2. Advertising Expense
   3. Accounts Receivable
   4. Dividends
   5. Insurance Expense

e. Which is a temporary account?
   1. Cash
   2. Accounts Receivable
   3. Insurance Expense
   4. Accounts Payable
   5. Notes Payable

f. In terms of debits and credits, which accounts have the same normal balances?
   1. Dividends, retained earnings, liabilities
   2. Capital stock, liabilities, expenses
   3. Revenues, capital stock, expenses
   4. Expenses, assets, dividends
   5. Dividends, assets, liabilities

P 2-6.

Required   Answer the following multiple-choice questions:

a. Audit opinions cannot be classified as which of the following?
   1. All-purpose
   2. Disclaimer of opinion
   3. Adverse opinion
   4. Qualified opinion
   5. Unqualified opinion

b. From the point of view of analysis, which classification of an audit opinion indicates that the financial statements carry the highest degree of reliability?
   1. Unqualified opinion
   2. All-purpose
   3. Disclaimer of opinion
   4. Qualified opinion
   5. Adverse opinion

c. Which one of the following statements is false?
   1. The reliance that can be placed on financial statements that have been reviewed is substantially less than for those that have been audited.
   2. An accountant's report described as a compilation presents only financial information as provided by management.
   3. A disclaimer of opinion indicates that you should not look to the auditor's report as an indication of the reliability of the statements.
   4. A review has substantially less scope than an examination in accordance with generally accepted auditing standards.
   5. The typical unqualified opinion has one paragraph.

    d. If an accountant performs a compilation and becomes aware of deficiencies in the statements, the accountant's report characterizes the deficiencies by all but one of the following:
1. Omission of substantially all disclosures
2. Omission of statement of cash flows
3. Accounting principles not generally accepted
4. All of the above
5. None of the above

    e. In addition to the company's principal financial statements, the Form 10-K and shareholder annual reports must include all but one of the following:
1. Information on the market for holders of common stock and related securities, including high and low sales price, frequency and amount of dividends, and number of shares
2. Five-year summary of selected financial data
3. Management's discussion and analysis of financial condition and results of operations
4. Two years of audited balance sheets, three years of audited statements of income, and two years of statements of cash flows
5. Disclosure of the domestic and foreign components of pretax income

    f. Which of these is *not* a suggested problem caused by lack of harmonization of international accounting standards?
1. Positive effect on the international trade of accounting practice and services
2. A need for employment of key personnel in multinational companies to bridge the "gap" in accounting requirements between countries
3. Difficulties in reconciling local standards for access to other capital markets
4. Difficulties in accessing capital markets for companies from less-developed countries
5. Negative effect on the international trade of accounting practice and services

    g. Which of these organizations has *not* played a role in the harmonization of international accounting standards?
1. United Nations
2. Internal Revenue Service
3. International Accounting Standards Board
4. Financial Accounting Standards Board
5. European Economic Community

    h. The Form 10-K is submitted to the:
1. American Institute of Certified Public Accountants
2. Securities and Exchange Commission
3. Internal Revenue Service
4. American Accounting Association
5. Emerging Issues Task Force

P 2-7.

Required   Answer the following multiple-choice questions:

    a. Which party has the primary responsibility for the financial statements?
1. Bookkeeper
2. Auditor
3. Management
4. Cost accountant
5. None of the above

    b. Which of the following is a type of audit opinion that a firm would usually prefer?
1. Unqualified opinion
2. Qualified opinion
3. Adverse opinion
4. Clear opinion
5. None of the above

    c. Which of the following statements is true?
1. You are likely to regard an adverse opinion as an immaterial issue as to the reliability of the financial statements.
2. A disclaimer of opinion indicates that you should look to the auditor's report as an indication of the reliability of the statements.

3. A review consists principally of inquiries made to company personal and analytical procedures applied to financial data.
4. When the outside accountant presents only financial information as provided by management, he or she is said to have reviewed the financial statements.
5. None of the above

d. This item need *not* be provided with a complete set of financial statements:
1. A 20-year summary of operations
2. Note disclosure of such items as accounting policies
3. Balance sheet
4. Income statement
5. Statement of cash flows

e. Which of the following statements is true?
1. Financial statements of legally separate entities may be issued to show financial position, income, and cash flow as they would appear if the companies were a single entity (consolidated).
2. Consolidated statements reflect a legal, rather than an economic, concept of the entity.
3. The financial statements of the parent and the subsidiary are consolidated for all majority-owned subsidiaries.
4. Consolidated statements are rare in the United States.
5. The acceptance of consolidation has been decreasing.

f. Domestic accounting standards developed to meet the needs of domestic environments. Which of these factors did *not* influence accounting standards locally?
1. A litigious environment in the United States that led to a demand for more detailed standards in many cases
2. High rates of inflation in some countries that resulted in periodic revaluation of fixed assets and other price-level adjustments or disclosures
3. Income tax conformity in certain countries that no doubt greatly influenced domestic financial reporting
4. Reliance on open markets as the principal means of intermediating capital flows that increased the demand for information to be included in financial reports in the United States
5. The need to have standards different from the U.S. standards

P 2-8.   The following are selected accounts of Laura Gibson Company on December 31:

	Permanent (P) or Temporary (T)	Normal Balance (Dr.) or (Cr.)
Cash	_____	_____
Accounts Receivable	_____	_____
Equipment	_____	_____
Accounts Payable	_____	_____
Common Stock	_____	_____
Sales	_____	_____
Purchases	_____	_____
Rent Expense	_____	_____
Utility Expense	_____	_____
Selling Expense	_____	_____

Required   In the space provided:
1. Indicate if the account is a permanent (P) or temporary (T) account.
2. Indicate the normal balance in terms of debit (Dr.) or credit (Cr.).

P 2-9.   An auditor's report is the formal presentation of all the effort that goes into an audit. Below is a list of the classifications of audit opinions that can be found in an auditor's report as well as a list of phrases describing the opinions.

Classifications of Audit Opinions
a. Unqualified opinion
b. Qualified opinion
c. Adverse opinion
d. Disclaimer of opinion

Phrases

_____ 1. This opinion states that the financial statements do not present fairly the financial position, results of operations, or cash flows of the entity, in conformity with generally accepted accounting principles.

_____ 2. This type of report is rendered when the auditor has not performed an audit sufficient in scope to form an opinion.

_____ 3. This opinion states that, except for the effects of the matters to which the qualification relates, the financial statements present fairly, in all material respects, the financial position, results of operations, and cash flows of the entity, in conformity with generally accepted accounting principles.

_____ 4. This opinion states that the financial statements present fairly, in all material respects, the financial position, results of operations, and cash flows of the entity, in conformity with generally accepted accounting principles.

Required   Place the appropriate letter identifying each type of opinion on the line in front of the statement or phrase describing the type of opinion.

P 2-10.   A company prepares financial statements in order to summarize financial information. Below is a list of financial statements and a list of descriptions.

Financial Statements

a. Balance sheet

b. Income statement

c. Statement of cash flows

d. Statement of stockholders' equity

Descriptions

_____ 1. Details the sources and uses of cash during a specified period of time.

_____ 2. Summary of revenues and expenses and gains and losses for a specific period of time.

_____ 3. Shows the financial condition of an accounting entity as of a specific date.

_____ 4. Presents reconciliation of the beginning and ending balances of the stockholders' equity accounts.

Required   Match each financial statement with its description.

Case
2-1

THE CEO RETIRES*

Dan Murphy awoke at 5:45 A.M., just like he did every workday morning. No matter that he went to sleep only four hours ago. The Orange Bowl game had gone late into the evening, and the New Year's Day party was so good, no one wanted to leave. At least Dan could awake easily this morning. Some of his guests had lost a little control celebrating the first day of the new year, and Dan was not a person who ever lost control.

The drive to the office was easier than most days. Perhaps there were a great many parties last night. All the better as it gave Dan time to think. The dawn of a new year; his last year. Dan would turn 65 next December, and the company had a mandatory retirement policy. A good idea he thought; to get new blood in the organization. At least that's what he thought on the climb up. From just another college graduate within the corporate staff, all the way to the chief executive officer's suite. It certainly is a magnificent view from the top.

To be CEO of his own company. Well, not really, as it was the stockholders' company, but he had been CEO for the past eight years. Now he, too, must turn the reins over. "Must," now that's the operative word. He knew it was the best thing for the company. Turnover kept middle management aggressive, but he also knew that he wouldn't leave if he had a choice. So Dan resolved to make his last year the company's best year ever.

Prepared by Professor William H. Coyle, Babson College.

*Source: "Ethics in the Accounting Curriculum: Cases & Readings," American Accounting Association.

(continued)

It was that thought that kept his attention, yet the focus of consideration and related motivations supporting such a strategy changed as he continued to strategize. At first, Dan thought that it would be a fine way to give something back to a company that had given him so much. His 43 years with the company had given him challenges which filled his life with meaning and satisfaction, provided him with a good living, and made him a man respected and listened to in the business community. But the thought that the company was also forcing him to give all that up made his thoughts turn more inward.

Of course, the company had done many things for him, but what of all the sacrifices he had made? His whole heart and soul were tied to the company. In fact, one could hardly think of Dan Murphy without thinking of the company, in much the same way as prominent corporate leaders and their firms are intrinsically linked. But the company would still be here this time next year, and what of him? Yes, he would leave the company strong, because by leaving it strong, it would strengthen his reputation as a great leader. His legacy would carry and sustain him over the years. But would it? One must also live in a manner consistent with such esteem.

Being the CEO of a major company also has its creature comforts. Dan was accustomed to a certain style of living. How much will that suffer after the salary, bonuses, and stock options are no more?

Arriving at the office by 7:30 A.M., he left a note for his secretary that he was not to be disturbed until 9 A.M. He pulled out the compensation file and examined the incentive clauses in his own contract. The contract was created by the compensation committee of the Board of Directors. All of the committee members were outsiders; that is, not a part of the company's management. This lends the appearance of independence, but most were CEOs of their own companies, and Dan knew that, by and large, CEOs take care of their own. His suspicions were confirmed. If the company's financial results were the best ever this year, then so, too, would be his own personal compensation.

Yet what if there were uncontrollable problems? The general economy appeared fairly stable. However, another oil shock, some more bank failures, or a list of other disasters could turn things into a downward spiral quickly. Economies are easily influenced and consumer and corporate psychology can play a large part in determining outcomes. But even in apparently uncontrollable circumstances, Dan knew he could protect himself and the financial fortunes of his company during the short term, which after all, was the only thing that mattered.

Upon further review of his compensation contract, Dan saw that a large portion of his bonus and stock options was a function of operating income levels, earnings per share, and return on assets. So the trick was to maximize those items. If he did, the company would appear vibrant and poised for future growth at the time of his forced retirement, he reminded himself. Furthermore, his total compensation in the last year of his employment would reach record proportions. Additionally, since his pension is based on the average of his last three years' compensation, Dan will continue to reap the benefits of this year's results for hopefully a long time to come. And who says CEOs don't think long term?

Two remaining issues needed to be addressed. Those were (1) how to ensure a record-breaking year and (2) how to overcome any objections raised in attaining those results. Actually, the former was a relatively simple goal to achieve. Since accounting allows so many alternatives in the way financial events are measured, Dan could just select a package of alternatives, which would maximize the company's earnings and return on assets. Some alternatives may result in changing an accounting method, but since the new auditing standards were issued, his company could still receive an unqualified opinion from his auditors, with only a passing reference to any accounting changes in the auditor's opinion and its effects disclosed in the footnotes. As long as the alternative was allowed by generally accepted accounting principles, and the justification for the change was reasonable, the auditors should not object. If there were objections, Dan could always threaten to change auditors. But still the best avenue to pursue would be a change in accounting estimates, since those changes did not even need to be explicitly disclosed.

So Dan began to mull over what changes in estimates or methods he could employ in order to maximize his firm's financial appearance. In the area of accounting estimates, Dan could

(continued)

Case	THE CEO RETIRES (Continued)
2-1	

lower the rate of estimated default on his accounts receivable, thus lowering bad debt expense. The estimated useful lives of his plant and equipment could be extended, thus lowering depreciation expense. In arguing that quality improvements have been implemented in the manufacturing process, the warranty expense on the products sold could also be lowered. In examining pension expense, he noted that the assumed rate of return on pension assets was at a modest 6.5%, so if that rate could be increased, the corresponding pension expense could be reduced.

Other possibilities occurred to Murphy. Perhaps items normally expensed, such as repairs, could be capitalized. Those repairs that could not be capitalized could simply be deferred. The company could also defer short-term expenses for the training of staff. Since research and development costs must now be fully expensed as incurred, a reduction in those expenditures would increase net income. Return on assets would be increased by not acquiring any new fixed assets. Production levels for inventory could be increased, thus spreading fixed costs over a greater number of units and reducing the total average cost per unit. Therefore, gross profit per unit will increase. Inventory levels would be a little bloated, but that should be easily handled by Dan's successor.

The prior examples are subtle changes that could be made. As a last resort, a change in accounting methods could be employed. This would require explicit footnote disclosure and a comment in the auditor's report, but if it came to that, it would still be tolerable. Examples of such changes would be to switch from accelerated to straight-line depreciation or to change from LIFO to FIFO.

How to make changes to the financial results of the company appeared easier than he first thought. Now back to the other potential problem of "getting away with it." At first thought, Dan considered the degree of resistance by the other members of top management. Mike Harrington, Dan's chief financial officer, would have to review any accounting changes that he suggested. Since Dan had brought Mike up the organization with him, Dan didn't foresee any strong resistance from Mike. As for the others, Dan believed he had two things going for him. One was their ambition. Dan knew that they all coveted his job, and a clear successor to Dan had yet to be chosen. Dan would only make a recommendation to the promotion committee of the Board of Directors, but everyone knew his recommendation carried a great deal of weight. Therefore, resistance to any accounting changes by any individual would surely end his or her hope to succeed him as CEO. Secondly, although not as lucrative as Dan's, their bonus package is tied to the exact same accounting numbers. So any actions taken by Dan to increase his compensation will also increase theirs.

Dan was actually beginning to enjoy this situation, even considering it one of his final challenges. Dan realized that any changes he implemented would have the tendency to reverse themselves over time. That would undoubtedly hurt the company's performance down the road, but all of his potential successors were in their mid-to-late 50s, so there would be plenty of time for them to turn things around in the years ahead. Besides, any near-term reversals would merely enhance his reputation as an excellent corporate leader, as problems would arise after his departure.

At that moment, his secretary called to inform him that Mike Harrington wanted to see him. Mike was just the man Dan wanted to see.

What are the ethical issues?

What should Mike do?

Required
a. Determine the facts—what, who, where, when, and how.
b. Define the ethical issues.
c. Identify major principles, rules, and values.
d. Specify the alternatives.
e. Compare norms, principles, and values with alternatives to see if a clear decision can be reached.
f. Assess the consequences.
g. Make your decision.

Case 2-2	THE DANGEROUS MORALITY OF MANAGING EARNINGS*
	The Majority of Managers Surveyed Say It's Not Wrong to Manage Earnings

Occasionally, the morals and ethics executives use to manage their businesses are examined and discussed. Unfortunately, the morals that guide the timing of nonoperating events and choices of accounting policies largely have been ignored.

The ethical framework used by managers in reporting short-term earnings probably has received less attention than its operating counterpart because accountants prepare financial disclosures consistent with laws and generally accepted accounting principles (GAAP). Those disclosures are reviewed by objective auditors.

Managers determine the short-term reported earnings of their companies by:

- Managing, providing leadership, and directing the use of resources in operations.
- Selecting the timing of some nonoperating events, such as the sale of excess assets or the placement of gains or losses into a particular reporting period.
- Choosing the accounting methods that are used to measure short-term earnings.

Casual observers of the financial reporting process may assume that time, laws, regulation, and professional standards have restricted accounting practices to those that are moral, ethical, fair, and precise. But most managers and their accountants know otherwise—that managing short-term earnings can be part of a manager's job.

To understand the morals of short-term earnings management, we surveyed general managers and finance, control, and audit managers. The results are frightening.

We found striking disagreements among managers in all groups. Furthermore, the liberal definitions revealed in many responses of what is moral or ethical should raise profound questions about the quality of financial information that is used for decision-making purposes by parties both inside and outside a company. It seems many managers are convinced that if a practice is not explicitly prohibited or is only a slight deviation from rules, it is an ethical practice regardless of who might be affected either by the practice or the information that flows from it. This means that anyone who uses information on short-term earnings is vulnerable to misinterpretation, manipulation, or deliberate deception.

The Morals of Managing Earnings

To find a "revealed" consensus concerning the morality of engaging in earnings-management activities, we prepared a questionnaire describing 13 earnings-management situations we had observed either directly or indirectly. The actions described in the incidents were all legal (although some were in violation of GAAP), but each could be construed as involving short-term earnings management.

A total of 649 managers completed our questionnaire. Table 2-1 classifies respondents by job function. Table 2-2 summarizes the views on the acceptability of various earnings-management practices.

A major finding of the survey was a striking lack of agreement. None of the respondent groups viewed any of the 13 practices unanimously as an ethical or unethical practice. The

Table 2-1	SURVEY RESPONDENTS

Total Sample	
General Managers	119
Finance, Control, & Audit Managers	262
Others or Position Not Known	268
	649

*Source: Reprinted from *Management Accounting*, August 1990. Copyright by National Association of Accountants, Montvale, NJ.

(continued)

THE DANGEROUS MORALITY OF MANAGING EARNINGS (Continued)

dispersion of judgments about many of the incidents was great. For example, here is one hypothetical earnings-management practice described in the questionnaire:

> *In September, a general manager realized that his division would need a strong perform-ance in the last quarter of the year in order to reach its budget targets. He decided to implement a sales program offering liberal payment terms to pull some sales that would normally occur next year into the current year. Customers accepting delivery in the fourth quarter would not have to pay the invoice for 120 days.*

Table   2-2   MANAGING SHORT-TERM EARNINGS

Proportion of Managers Who Judge the Practice*

	Ethical	Questionable, or a Minor Infraction	Unethical, or a Serious Infraction
1. Managing short-term earnings by changing or manipulating operating decisions or procedures:			
When the result is to reduce earnings	79%	19%	2%
When the result is to increase earnings	57%	31%	12%
2. Managing short-term earnings by changing or manipulating accounting methods:			
When the change to earnings is small	5%	45%	50%
When the change to earnings is large	3%	21%	76%
3. Managing short-term earnings by deferring discretionary expenditures into the next accounting period:			
To meet an interim quarterly budget target	47%	41%	12%
To meet an annual budget target	41%	35%	24%
4. Increasing short-term earnings to meet a budget target:			
By selling excess assets and realizing a profit	80%	16%	4%
By ordering overtime work at year-end to ship as much as possible	74%	21%	5%
By offering customers special credit terms to accept delivery without obligation to pay until the following year	43%	44%	15%

*Percentages are calculated from *Harvard Business Review* readers' sample.

The survey respondents' judgments of the acceptability of this practice were distributed as follows:

Ethical	279
Questionable	288
Unethical	82
Total	649

Perhaps you are not surprised by these data. The ethical basis of an early shipment/liberal payment program may not be something you have considered, but, with the prevalence of such diverse views, how can any user of a short-term earnings report know the quality of the information?

Although the judgments about all earnings-management practices varied considerably, there are some other generalizations that can be made from the findings summarized in Table 2-2.

- On average, the respondents viewed management of short-term earnings by *accounting* methods as significantly less acceptable than accomplishing the same ends by changing or manipulating *operating decisions or procedures.*
- The direction of the effect on earnings matters. *Increasing* earnings is judged less acceptable than *reducing* earnings.

(continued)

- Materiality matters. Short-term earnings management is judged less acceptable if the earnings effect is *large* rather than *small*.
- The time period of the effect may affect ethical judgments. Managing short-term earnings at the end of an interim *quarterly* reporting period is viewed as somewhat more acceptable than engaging in the same activity at the end of an *annual* reporting period.
- The method of managing earnings has an effect. Increasing profits by offering *extended credit terms* is seen as less acceptable than accomplishing the same end by *selling excess assets or using overtime* to increase shipments.

Managers Interviewed

Were the survey results simply hypothetical, or did managers recognize they can manage earnings and choose to do so? To find the answers, we talked to a large number of the respondents. What they told us was rarely reassuring.

On accounting manipulations, a profit center controller reported:

> *"Accounting is grey. Very little is absolute . . . You can save your company by doing things with sales and expenses, and, if it's legal, then you are justified in doing it."*

A divisional general manager spoke to us about squeezing reserves to generate additional reported profit:

> *"If we get a call asking for additional profit, and that's not inconceivable, I would look at our reserves. Our reserves tend to be realistic, but we may have a product claim that could range from $50,000 to $500,000. Who knows what the right amount for something like that is? We would review our reserves, and if we felt some were on the high side, we would not be uncomfortable reducing them."*

We also heard about operating manipulations. One corporate group controller noted:

> *"[To boost sales] we have paid overtime and shipped on Saturday, the last day of the fiscal quarter. If we totally left responsibility for the shipping function to the divisions, it could even slip over to 12:30 A.M. Sunday. There are people who would do that and not know it's wrong."*

Managers often recognize that such actions "move" earnings from one period to another. For example, a division controller told us:

> *"Last year we called our customers and asked if they would take early delivery. We generated an extra $300,000 in sales at the last minute. We were scratching for everything. We made our plans, but we cleaned out our backlog and started in the hole this year. We missed our first quarter sales plan. We will catch up by the end of the second quarter."*

And a group vice president said:

> *"I recently was involved in a situation where the manager wanted to delay the production costs for the advertising that would appear in the fall [so that he could meet his quarterly budget]."*

Thus, in practice, it appears that a large majority of managers use at least some methods to manage short-term earnings. Although legal, these methods do not seem to be consistent with a strict ethical framework. While the managers' actions have the desired effect on reported earnings, the managers know there are no real positive economic benefits, and the actions might actually be quite costly in the long run. These actions are at best questionable because they involve deceptions that are not disclosed. Most managers who manage earnings, however, do not believe they are doing anything wrong.

We see two major problems. The most important is the generally high tolerance for operating manipulations. The other is the dispersion in managers' views about which practices are moral and ethical.

(continued)

The Dangerous Allure

The essence of a moral or ethical approach to management is achieving a balance between individual interests and obligations to those who have a stake in what happens in the corporation (or what happens to a division or group within the corporation). These stakeholders include not only people who work in the firm, but customers, suppliers, creditors, shareholders, and investors as well.

Managers who take unproductive actions to boost short-term earnings may be acting totally within the laws and rules. Also they may be acting in the best interest of the corporation. But, if they fail to consider the adverse effects of their actions on other stakeholders, we may conclude that they are acting unethically.

The managers we interviewed explained that they rated accounting manipulations harshly because in such cases the "truth" has somehow been denied or misstated. The recipients of the earnings reports do not know what earnings would have been if no manipulation had taken place. Even if the accounting methods used are consistent with GAAP, they reason, the actions are not ethical because the interests of major stakeholder groups—including the recipients of the earnings reports—have been ignored.

The managers judge the operating manipulations more favorably because the earnings numbers are indicative of what actually took place. The operating manipulations have changed reality, and "truth" is fairly reported.

We see flaws in that reasoning. One is that the truth has not necessarily been disclosed completely. When sales and profits are borrowed from the future, for example, it is a rare company that discloses the borrowed nature of some of the profits reported.

A second flaw in the reasoning about the acceptability of operating manipulations is that it ignores a few or all of the effects of some types of operating manipulations on the full range of stakeholders. Many managers consider operating manipulations as a kind of "victimless crime."

But victims do exist. Consider, for example, the relatively common operating manipulation of early shipments. As one manager told us:

> *"Would I ship extra product if I was faced with a sales shortfall? You have to be careful there; you're playing with fire. I would let whatever happened fall to the bottom line. I've been in companies that did whatever they could to make the sales number, such as shipping lower quality product. That's way too short term. You have to draw the line there. You must maintain the level of quality and customer service. You'll end up paying for bad shipments eventually. You'll have returns, repairs, adjustments, ill will that will cause you to lose the account . . . [In addition] it's tough to go to your employees one day and say ship everything you can and then turn around the next day and say that the quality standards must be maintained."*

Another reported:

> *"We've had to go to [one of our biggest customers] and say we need an order. That kills us in the negotiations. Our last sale was at a price just over our cost of materials."*

These comments point out that customers—and sometimes even the corporation—may be victims.

Without a full analysis of the costs of operating manipulations, the dangers of such manipulations to the corporation are easily underestimated. Mistakes will be made because the quality of information is misjudged. The short term will be emphasized at the expense of the long term. If managers consistently manage short-term earnings, the messages sent to other employees create a corporate culture that lacks mutual trust, integrity, and loyalty.

A Lack of Moral Agreement

We also are troubled by the managers' inability to agree on the types of earnings-management activities that are acceptable. This lack of agreement exists even within corporations.

(continued)

Case	THE DANGEROUS MORALITY OF MANAGING EARNINGS (Continued)
2-2	

What this suggests is that many managers are doing their analyses in different ways. The danger is obfuscation of the reality behind the financial reports. Because managers are using different standards, individuals who try to use the information reported may be unable to assess accurately the quality of that information.

If differences in opinions exist, it is likely that financial reporting practices will sink to their lowest and most manipulative level. As a result, managers with strict definitions of what is moral and ethical will find it difficult to compete with managers who are not playing by the same rules. Ethical managers either will loosen their moral standards or fail to be promoted into positions of greater power.

Actions for Concerned Managers

We believe most corporations would benefit if they established clearer accounting and operating standards for all employees to follow. The standard-setting process should involve managers in discussions of the practices related to short-term earnings measurements.

Until these standards are in place, different managers will use widely varying criteria in assessing the acceptability of various earnings-management practices. These variations will have an adverse effect on the quality of the firm's financial information. Companies can use a questionnaire similar to the one in our study to encourage discussion and to communicate corporate standards and the reason for them.

Standards also enable internal and external auditors and management to judge whether the desired quality of earnings is being maintained. In most companies, auditors can depend on good standards to identify and judge the acceptability of the operating manipulations.

Ultimately, the line management chain-of-command, not auditors or financial staff, bears the primary responsibility for controlling operating manipulations. Often managers must rely on their prior experience and good judgment to distinguish between a decision that will have positive long-term benefits and one that has a positive short-term effect but a deleterious long-term effect.

Finally, it is important to manage the corporate culture. A culture that promotes openness and cooperative problem solving among managers is likely to result in less short-term earnings management than one that is more competitive and where annual, and even quarterly, performance shortfalls are punished. A corporate culture that is more concerned with managing for excellence rather than for reporting short-term profits will be less likely to support the widespread use of immoral earnings-management practices.

Required
a. Time, laws, regulation, and professional standards have restricted accounting practices to those that are moral, ethical, fair, and precise. Comment.
b. Most managers surveyed had a conservative, strict interpretation of what is moral or ethical in financial reporting. Comment.
c. The managers surveyed exhibited a surprising agreement as to what constitutes an ethical or unethical practice. Comment.
d. List the five generalizations from the findings in this study relating to managing earnings.
e. Comment on management's ability to manage earnings in the long run by influencing financial accounting.

Case	FIRM COMMITMENT?
2-3	

In the early 1980s, airlines introduced frequent-flier awards to develop passenger loyalty to a single airline. Free tickets and possibly other awards were made available to passengers when they accumulated a certain number of miles or flights on a particular air carrier. These programs were potentially good for the passenger and the airline as long as the awards were not too generous and the airlines could minimize revenue displacement from a paying passenger.

These programs were introduced by American Airlines in 1981. Originally, there were no restrictions. Anyone with the necessary miles could take any flight that had an available seat.

(continued)

Case	FIRM COMMITMENT? (Continued)
2-3	

In the late 1980s, most airlines changed their no-restriction programs to programs with restrictions and blackout days. The airlines also added partners in frequent-flier programs, such as car rental companies and hotels. These partners handed out frequent-flier miles compensating the airlines in some manner for the miles distributed. Airlines also added triple-mileage deals.

A consequence of these expanding frequent-flier programs was a surge in the number of passengers flying free and a surge in unused miles. To get a handle on the cost and the unused miles, airlines increased the frequent-flier miles needed for a flight and placed time limits on the award miles.

The increased frequent-flier miles needed for a flight and the time limits prompted lawsuits. Many of these lawsuits were filed in state courts. One of the suits filed in the District Court in Chicago in 1989 made its way to the U.S. Supreme Court. In 1995, the Supreme Court ruled that federal airline deregulation law would not bar the breach-of-contract claim in the state court. In June of 1995, a District Court in Dallas ruled in favor of the airline in a case involving an increase in miles needed to earn a trip. Airlines interpret this decision as upholding their right to make changes to their frequent-flier programs.

Required   a. In your opinion, are the outstanding (unused) miles a liability to the airline? (Substantiate your answer.)

              b. Comment on the potential problems involved in estimating the dollar amount of any potential liability.

              c. 1. What is a contingent liability?

                   2. In your opinion, are unused miles a contingent liability to the air carrier?

                   3. Recommend the recognition (if any) for unused miles.

Case	RULES OR FEEL?
2-4	

The FASB and the IASB have made progress towards convergence. The IFRS standards are considered to be more principles based than the U.S. rules-based GAAP. As of 2007, the IFRSs filled approximately 2,000 pages of accounting regulations.[*] When an IFRS or interpretation does not exist, then judgment must be used when applying an accounting policy.

As of 2007, U.S. GAAP comprised over 2,000 separate pronouncements.[†] Many of the U.S. pronouncements were dozens of pages, issued by numerous bodies.[‡]

Required   a. "The IFRS standards are considered to be more principles based than the U.S. rules-based GAAP." Comment on the implications of this statement, including the legal implications.

              b. U.S. GAAP has been considered by many to be the best GAAP in the world. Should the United States give up its GAAP?

[*]Lawrence M. Gill, "IFRS: Coming to America," *Journal of Accountancy* (June 2007), p. 71.
[†]Ibid.
[‡]Ibid.

Case	MATERIALITY: IN PRACTICE
2-5	

Professional standards require auditors to make a preliminary judgment about materiality levels during the planning of an audit. Statement of Auditing Standards (SAS) No. 47 states that "the auditor plans the audit to obtain reasonable assurance of detecting misstatements that he/she believes could be large enough, individually or in the aggregate, to be quantitatively material to the financial statements."[*]

[*]This case is based on SAS No. 47 as updated and presented in AV312 of the *Codification of Statements on Auditing Standards* (American Institute of Certified Public Accountants, January 1989).

(continued)

| Case 2-5 | MATERIALITY: IN PRACTICE (Continued) |

SAS No. 47 indicates that materiality judgments involve both quantitative and qualitative considerations. This statement recognizes that it ordinarily is not practical to design procedures to detect misstatements that could be qualitatively material.

A number of rule-of-thumb materiality calculations have emerged, such as percentages of income, total assets, revenues, and equity. These rule-of-thumb calculations result in differing amounts for audit planning purposes. In fact, sizeable differences can result, depending on the rule of thumb and the industry.

Required

a. It would seem prudent for auditors to give careful consideration to planning materiality decisions. Comment.

b. It is difficult to design procedures to detect misstatements that could be qualitatively material. Comment.

c. It is difficult to design procedures to detect misstatements that could be quantitatively material. Comment.

d. In your opinion, would the application of materiality be a frequent issue in court cases involving financial statements? Comment.

e. Comment on materiality implications of the Sarbanes-Oxly Act as it relates to control weaknesses.

| Case 2-6 | MANAGEMENT'S RESPONSIBILITY |

3M* included these reports with its 2006 annual report:

Management's Responsibility for Financial Reporting

Management is responsible for the integrity and objectivity of the financial information included in this report. The financial statements have been prepared in accordance with accounting principles generally accepted in the Unites States of America. Where necessary, the financial statements reflect estimates based on management's judgment.

Management has established and maintains a system of internal accounting and other controls for the Company and its subsidiaries. This system and its established accounting procedures and related controls are designed to provide reasonable assurance that assets are safeguarded, that the books and records properly reflect all transactions, that policies and procedures are implemented by qualified personnel, and that published financial statements are properly prepared and fairly presented. The Company's system of internal control is supported by widely communicated written policies, including business conduct policies, which are designed to require all employees to maintain high ethical standards in the conduct of Company affairs. Internal auditors continually review the accounting and control system.

3M Company

Management's Report on Internal Control over Financial Reporting

Management is responsible for establishing and maintaining an adequate system of internal control over financial reporting. Management conducted an assessment of the Company's internal control over financial reporting based on the framework established by the Committee of Sponsoring Organizations of the Treadway Commission in *Internal Control—Integrated Framework*. Based on the assessment, management concluded that, as of December 31, 2006, the Company's internal control over financial reporting is effective.

---

*"3M is a diversified technology company with a global presence in the following businesses: industrial and transportation; health care; display and graphics; consumer and office; safety, security and protection services; and electro and communications." 10-K

(continued)

Case 2-6	MANAGEMENT'S RESPONSIBILITY (Continued)

Management's assessment of the effectiveness of the Company's internal control over financial reporting as of December 31, 2006 has been audited by PricewaterhouseCoopers LLP, an independent registered public accounting firm, as stated in their report which is included herein.

3M Company

Required
a. Who has the responsibility for the financial statements?
b. What is the role of the accountant (auditor) as to the financial statements?
c. Accountants (auditors) are often included as defendants in lawsuits that relate to the financial statements. Speculate as to why this is the case.
d. Why did 3M include the report "Management's Report on Internal Control over Financial Reporting"?

Case 2-7	SAFE HARBOR

In 1995, Congress passed the Private Securities Litigation Reform Act (the Act). The principal provisions of the Act are intended to curb abusive litigation and improve the quality of information available to investors through the creation of a safe harbor for forward-looking statements.

Forward-looking statements were defined to include statements relating to projections of revenues and other financial items, plans and objectives, future economic performance, assumptions, reports issued by outside reviewers, or other projections or estimates specified by rule of the SEC. The safe harbor applies to both oral and written statements.

Management frequently uses signals as "we estimate," "we project," and the like, where forward-looking statements are not otherwise identified as such. The forward-looking statements must be accompanied by meaningful cautionary statements. The cautionary statement may be contained in a separate risk section elsewhere in the disclosure document.

Southwest Airlines Co.* included this statement with its 2006 Form 10-K.

Forward-Looking Statements

Some statements in this Form 10-K (or otherwise made by the Company or on the Company's behalf from time to time in other reports, filings with the Securities and Exchange Commission, news releases, conferences, World Wide Web postings or otherwise) which are not historical facts, may be "forward-looking statements" within the meaning of Section 27A of the Securities Act of 1933, as amended, Section 21E of the Securities Exchange Act of 1934, and the Private Securities Litigation Reform Act of 1995. Forward-looking statements are based on, and include statements about, Southwest's estimates, expectations, beliefs, intentions or strategies for the future, and the assumptions underlying these forward-looking statements. Specific forward-looking statements can be identified by the fact that they do not relate strictly to historical or current facts and include, without limitation, words such as "anticipates," "believes," "estimates," "expects," "intends," "forecasts," "may," "will," "should," and similar expressions. Forward-looking statements are not guarantees of future performance and involve risks and uncertainties that are difficult to predict. Therefore, actual results may differ materially from what is expressed in or indicated by Southwest's forward-looking statements or from historical experience or the Company's present expectations. Factors that could cause these differences include, but are not limited to, those set forth under item 1A–Risk Factors.

*"Southwest Airlines Co. is a major passenger airline that provides scheduled air transportation in the United States." 10-K

(continued)

Case	SAFE HARBOR (Continued)
2-7	

Caution should be taken not to place undue reliance on the Company's forward-looking statements, which represent the Company's views only as of the date this report is filed. The Company undertakes no obligation to update publicly or revise any forward-looking statement.

Required

a. Demand for financial reports exists because users believe that the reports help them in decision making. In your opinion, will forward-looking statements as provided by the Private Securities Litigation Reform Act aid users of financial reports in decision making?

b. To some extent, investors' rights are limited by the curb of abusive litigation. In your opinion, is there a net benefit to investors from a safe harbor for forward-looking statements?

Case	ENFORCEMENT
2-8	

This case includes a news release issued by the Public Company Accounting Oversight Board. This news release comments on the first disciplines of an accounting firm and auditors under the Sarbanes-Oxley Act of 2002.

Board Revokes Firm's Registration, Disciplines Three Accountants for Failure to Cooperate

Washington, DC, May 24, 2005—The Public Company Accounting Oversight Board today revoked the registration of a public accounting firm and barred the firm's managing partner from association with a registered accounting firm after finding that they concealed information from the Board and submitted false information in connection with a PCAOB inspection.

The Board also censured two former partners in the firm, finding that they participated in the misconduct but noting that they promptly alerted the PCAOB and cooperated in the Board's investigation.

"Registered accounting firms and their associated persons have a duty to cooperate in PCAOB inspections," said Claudius Modesti, director of the PCAOB's Division of Enforcement and Investigations. "The findings in this case demonstrate that the Board will not tolerate conduct aimed at thwarting the Board's inspections."

The accounting firm, Goldstein and Morris CPAs, P.C., based in New York City, was notified in September 2004 that the firm would be inspected by the PCAOB in November 2004.

The PCAOB's Division of Registration and Inspections directed a request for information and documents to the firm's managing partner, Edward B. Morris. The Board found that, in responding to the request, Mr. Morris and two partners, Alan J. Goldberger and William A. Postelnik, were aware that the firm had prepared the financial statements of two of its public company audit clients, contrary to auditor independence requirements of federal law. The Board found that Messrs. Morris, Goldberger, and Postelnik took steps to conceal that fact from the Board by omitting certain requested information from the firm's written response to the inspection request.

The Board also found that the partners, after learning of the imminent inspection, formulated and carried out a plan to create and back-date certain documents and place them in the firm's audit files. The Board found that Messrs. Morris, Goldberger, and Postelnik took these steps to conceal from the Board the firm's failure to comply with certain auditing standards.

Messrs. Goldberger and Postelnik notified the PCAOB of the omitted and falsified information. Both resigned from the firm.

The accounting firm and Mr. Morris consented to a Board order making the findings and imposing sanctions, without admitting or denying the findings. The order bars Mr. Morris from association with a registered accounting firm and revokes the firm's registration. Firms that are not registered with the PCAOB are prohibited from auditing the financial statements of public companies.

(continued)

Case	ENFORCEMENT (Continued)
2-8	

Messrs. Goldberger and Postelnik each consented to a Board order making the findings and imposing the censures without admitting or denying the findings. The Board limited the sanctions of the two men to censures because they "promptly and voluntarily brought the matter to the Board's attention, disclosed their own misconduct and the misconduct of others, and made affirmative efforts to provide the Board with relevant information."

The Board's orders are available under Enforcement at www.pcaobus.org.

Suspected misconduct by auditors can be reported to the PCAOB Center for Enforcement Tips, Complaints and Other Information by e-mail or by phone to 800-741-3158.

Media Inquiries: Public Affairs, 202-207-9227

Required

a. Does it appear that Mr. Morris and the accounting firm can continue to function in public accounting? Comment.

b. It appears that Mr. Morris, Goldberger, and Postelnik can continue to function as certified public accountants. Speculate on what may happen to their ability to function as certified public accountants. (*Hint:* Certification is granted by individual states.)

Case	WATCH–DOLLARS–AUDITING STANDARDS–GAAP
2-9	

Information reported in some Canadian companies' 2006 annual reports follows:

1. Enbridge Inc.
2. Baytex Energy Trust
3. Algoma Steel Inc.

1. Enbridge Inc.

Corporate Head Office
3000, 425—1st Street S.W.
Calgary, Alberta, Canada T2P3L8

Exchange Listing

Enbridge common shares trade on the Toronto Stock Exchange in Canada and on the New York Stock Exchange in the United States under the symbol "ENB."

Management's Report (in Part)

"The consolidated financial statements have been prepared in accordance with Canadian generally accepted accounting principles . . . PricewaterhouseCoopers LLP, independent auditors appointed by the shareholders of the Company, conducts an examination of the consolidated financial statements in accordance with Canadian generally accepted auditing standards."

Auditor's Report (in Part)

"In accordance with Canadian generally accepted auditing standards and the standards of The Public Company Accounting Oversight Board (United States) . . . in accordance with Canadian generally accepted accounting principles."

Enbridge Inc.

Consolidated Statements of Earnings (in Part)
(Millions of Canadian dollars, except per share amounts)

(continued)

Notes to the Consolidated Financial Statements (in Part)

"Enbridge, Inc. . . . is one of North America's largest energy transportation and distribution companies."

1. Summary of Significant Accounting Policies (in Part)

"The consolidated financial statements of the Company are prepared in accordance with Canadian generally accepted accounting principles (Canadian GAAP). These accounting principles are different in some respects from United States generally accepted accounting principles (U.S. GAAP) and the significant differences that impact the company's financial statements are described in Note 26. Amounts are stated in Canadian dollars unless otherwise noted."

2. Baytex Energy Trust

Corporate Head Office
Suite 2200, Bow Valley Square II
205—5th Avenue S.W.
Calgary, Alberta, Canada T2P2U7

Exchange Listing

Toronto Stock Exchange
New York Stock Exchange

Management's Report (in Part)

"Management, in accordance with Canadian generally accepted accounting principles"

Auditor's Report (in Part)

"We conducted our audits in accordance with Canadian generally accepted auditing standards . . . conducted in accordance with Canadian generally accepted auditing standards and the standards of the Public Company Oversight Board (United States) on the consolidated financial statements for the same period, prepared in accordance with Canadian generally accepted accounting principles but which included Note 17, Differences Between Canadian and United States Generally Accepted Accounting Principles."

Baytex Energy Trust
Consolidated Statements of Operations and Deficit (in Part)
Years Ended December 31 (thousands, except per unit data)

Note to the Consolidated Financial Statements (in Part)
Years ended December 31, 2006 and 2005
(All tabular amounts in thousands of Canadian dollars, except per unit amounts)
1. Basis of Presentation (in Part)

"Baytex Energy Trust (the 'Trust') was established on September 2, 2003 under a plan of arrangement involving the trust and Baytex Energy Ltd. (the 'Company')."

"The consolidated financial statements include the accounts of the trust and its subsidiaries and have been prepared by management in accordance with Canadian generally accepted accounting principles ('GAAP') as described in note 2."

(continued)

WATCH—DOLLARS—AUDITING STANDARDS—GAAP (Continued)

17. Differences Between Canadian and United States Generally Accepted Accounting Principles (in Part)

"The consolidated financial statements have been prepared in accordance with accounting principles generally accepted in Canada ('Canadian GAAP'). The significant differences between Canadian and United States GAAP, as applicable to these consolidated financial statements and notes, are described in the trust's Form 40-F, which is filed with the United States Securities and Exchange Commission."

3. Algoma Steel Inc.

Corporate Head Office
Sault Ste. Marie
Ontario, Canada P6A7B4

Share Listings

Algoma Steel Inc. trades on the Toronto Stock Exchange under the symbol AGA.

Management's Responsibility for Financial Reporting (in Part)

"The consolidated financial statements of Algoma Steel Inc. ('Algoma') have been prepared in accordance with Canadian generally accepted accounting principles."

Auditor's Report to the Shareholders (in Part)

"We conducted our audits in accordance with Canadian generally accepted auditing standards . . . in accordance with Canadian generally accepted accounting principles."

Algoma Steel Inc.

Consolidated Statements of Income and Retained Earnings (in Part)

Expressed in millions of Canadian dollars, except per share amounts

Notes to Consolidated Financial Statements (in Part)

1. Nature of Operations

    "Algoma Steel Inc. is an integrated steel producer with operations located entirely in Canada. The Company produces sheet and plate products that are sold primarily in Canada and the United States."

2. Summary of Significant Accounting Policies (in Part)

    "The consolidated financial statements have been prepared by the Company with Canadian generally accepted accounting principles."

Required
a. Indicate if Canadian or U.S. dollars are used for these companies' financial statements.
    1. Enbridge Inc.
    2. Baytex Energy Trust
    3. Algoma Steel Inc.
b. Indicate if Canadian or U.S. GAAP was used for these companies.
    1. Enbridge Inc.
    2. Baytex Energy Trust
    3. Algoma Steel Inc.

(continued)

Case
2-9

WATCH—DOLLARS—AUDITING STANDARDS—GAAP (Continued)

    c. Indicate if Canadian or U.S. generally accepted auditing standards were used for these companies.

       1. Enbridge Inc.

       2. Baytex Energy Trust

       3. Algoma Steel Inc.

    d. Can the operating results be determined in U.S. GAAP? Comment on each.

       1. Enbridge Inc.

       2. Baytex Energy Trust

       3. Algoma Steel Inc.

    e. Consider the stock exchanges where the respective shares are listed. Does the stock exchange used contribute to the complexity? Comment.

Case
2-10

MULTIPLE COUNTRY ENFORCEMENT*

SEC Charges Royal Ahold and Three Former Top Executives with Fraud; Former Audit Committee Member Charged with Causing Violations of the Securities Laws for Immediate Release

2004-144

Washington, D.C., Oct. 13, 2004—The Securities and Exchange Commission today announced the filing of enforcement actions alleging fraud and other violations against Royal Ahold (Koninklijke Ahold N.V.) (Ahold) and three former top executives: Cees van der Hoeven, former CEO and chairman of executive board; A. Michiel Meurs, former CFO and executive board member; and Jan Andreae, former executive vice president and executive board member. The Commission also charged Roland Fahlin, former member of Ahold's supervisory board and audit committee, with causing violations of the reporting, books and records, and internal controls provisions of the securities laws.

The SEC's complaints, filed in the United States District Court for the District of Columbia, allege that, as a result of the fraudulent inflation of promotional allowances at U.S. Foodservice, Ahold's wholly-owned subsidiary, the improper consolidation of joint ventures through fraudulent side letters, and other accounting errors and irregularities, Ahold's original SEC filings for at least fiscal years 2000 through 2002 were materially false and misleading. For fiscal years 2000 through 2002, Ahold overstated net sales by approximately EUR 33 billion ($30 billion). For fiscal years 2000 and 2001 and the first three quarters of 2002, Ahold overstated operating income by approximately EUR 3.6 billion ($3.3 billion) and net income by approximately EUR 900 million ($829 million).

The Commission has not sought penalties in the enforcement actions against the individuals because the Dutch Public Prosecutor's Office, which is conducting a parallel criminal investigation in The Netherlands, has requested that the Commission not seek penalties against the individuals because of potential double jeopardy issues under Dutch law. Because of the importance of this case in The Netherlands and the need for continued cooperation between the SEC and regulatory authorities in other countries, the Commission has agreed to the Dutch prosecutor's request.

Required   a. Why can the SEC charge a company in The Netherlands with U.S. security violations?

    b. Why is The Netherlands conducting a parallel criminal investigation?

    c. Speculate on how many countries may be running a parallel criminal investigation relating to securities sold.

*Dr. Thomas Klein, Emeritus, the University of Toledo, assisted with this case.

Case 2-11	NOTIFY THE SEC

Summary

"This matter involves Hewlett-Packard's failure to disclose the circumstances surrounding a board member's resignation amidst the company's controversial investigation into boardroom leaks. On May 18, 2006, HP's Board of Directors learned the findings of the company's leak investigation and voted to request the resignation of a director believed to have violated HP's policies by providing confidential information to the press. Silicon Valley venture capitalist and fellow director Thomas Perkins (not the source of the leak) voiced his strong objections to the handling of the matter, announced his resignation, and walked out of the Board meeting. Contrary to the reporting requirements of the federal securities laws, HP failed to disclose to investors the circumstances of Mr. Perkins' disagreement with the company."*

Required
    a. What form reviewed in this chapter would be used to disclose the resignation of a board member?
    b. Comment on why it would be in the public interest to know the circumstances surrounding the resignation of this board member.

*SEC Administrative Proceeding, File No. 3-12643, May 23, 2007.

Web Case	**Thomson One** *Business School Edition*

Please complete the Web case that covers material discussed in this chapter at academic.cengage.com/accounting/Gibson. You'll be using Thomson One Business School Edition, a powerful tool, that combines a full range of fundamental financial information, earnings estimates, market data, and source documents for 500 publicly traded companies.

Endnotes

1. http://www.coso.org.
2. Jaclyne Badal and Phred Dvorak, "Sarbanes-Oxley Gains Adherents," *The Wall Street Journal* (August 14, 2006), p. B3.
3. Charles H. Gibson and Nicholas Schroeder, "How 21 Companies Handled Their Summary Annual Reports," *Financial Executive* (November/December 1989), pp. 45–46.
4. Mary E. Guy, *Ethical Decision Making in Everyday Work Situations* (New York: Quarum Books, 1990), p. 5.
5. Ibid., p. 14.
6. William W. May, ed., *Ethics in the Accounting Curriculum: Cases & Readings* (Sarasota, FL: American Accounting Association, 1990), pp. 1–2.
7. "Regulators Investigate Peat on Its Auditing of S&L," *The New York Times* (May 23, 1991), p. D-1.
8. "S.E.C. Inquiry Is Reported on Loans to Accountants," *The New York Times* (February 7, 1991), p. D-1.
9. "Ernst & Young Settles Negligence Charge," *Business Insurance* (May 6, 1991), p. 2.
10. Ronald Grover, "Curtains for Tinseltown Accounting?" *Business Week* (January 14, 1991), p. 35.
11. Shahram Victory, "Pierce O'Donnell Pans 'Fatal Subtraction,'" *American Lawyer* (March 1991), p. 43.
12. "Buchwald Wins Just $150,000 in Film Lawsuit," *The Wall Street Journal* (March 17, 1992), p. B-1.
13. SEC Adopts Rules on Provisions of Sarbanes-Oxley Act, SEC Web site, http://www.sec.gov/. The SEC News Digest Archive, January 16, 2003.
14. Dennis E. Peavey and Stuart K. Webster, "Is GAAP the Gap to International Markets?" *Management Accounting* (August 1990), pp. 31–32.

15. John Hagarty, "Why We Can't Let GATT Die," *Journal of Accountancy* (April 1991), p. 74.

16. Dennis Beresford, "Internationalization of Accounting Standards," *Accounting Horizons* (March 1990), p. 10.

17. Gerhard G. Mueller, Helen Gernan, and Gary Meek, *Accounting: An International Perspective*, 2d ed. (Homewood, IL: Richard D. Irwin, Inc., 1991), pp. 11–12.

18. Ibid., pp. 45–46.

19. Peavey and Webster, "Is GAAP the GAP to International Markets?" p. 34.

20. http://www.fasb.org, Financial Accounting Standards Board, *International Overview of FASB's Memorandum of Understanding, A Roadmap for Convergence Between IFRSs and U.S. GAAP— 2006–2008, Memorandum of Understanding Between the FASB and IASB* (February 27, 2006), p. 2.

21. Ibid., p. 3.

Chapter 3

Balance Sheet

The principal financial statements are the balance sheet, income statement, and statement of cash flows. This chapter will review the balance sheet in detail. Other titles used for the balance sheet are statement of financial position and statement of financial condition. The title *balance sheet* is the predominant title used.[1]

Another statement, called the statement of stockholders' equity, reconciles the changes in stockholders' equity, a section of the balance sheet. This statement will also be reviewed in this chapter. Many alternative titles are used for the statement of stockholders' equity. The title most frequently used is the statement of shareholders' equity.[2]

Basic Elements of the Balance Sheet

A **balance sheet** shows the financial condition of an accounting entity as of a particular date. The balance sheet consists of assets, the resources of the firm; liabilities, the debts of the firm; and stockholders' equity, the owners' interest in the firm.

The assets are derived from two sources, creditors and owners. At any point in time, the assets must equal the contribution of the creditors and owners. The accounting equation expresses this relationship:

$$\text{Assets} = \text{Liabilities} + \text{Stockholders' Equity}$$

On the balance sheet, the assets equal the liabilities plus the stockholders' equity. This may be presented side by side (account form) or with the assets at the top and the liabilities and stockholders' equity at the bottom (report form). Exhibit 3-1 presents a typical report form format, and Exhibit 3-2 presents a typical account form format.

Balance sheet formats differ across nations. For example, nations influenced by British financial reporting report the least liquid assets first and cash last. Nations influenced by the United States report a balance sheet emphasizing liquidity, as illustrated in this chapter.

ASSETS

Assets are probable future economic benefits obtained or controlled by an entity as a result of past transactions or events.[3] Assets may be *physical*, such as land, buildings, inventory of supplies, material, or finished products. Assets may also be *intangible*, such as patents and trademarks.

| Exhibit | 3-1 | MILACRON INC. AND SUBSIDIARIES* |

Consolidated Balance Sheets, Report Form

MILACRON INC. AND SUBSIDIARIES
CONSOLIDATED BALANCE SHEET
December 31, 2006 and 2005

	2006	2005
	(In millions, except par value)	
ASSETS		
Current Assets		
Cash and cash equivalents	$ 38.5	$ 45.7
Notes and accounts receivable, less allowances of $7.3 in 2006 and $9.0 in 2005	114.5	117.7
Inventories		
Raw materials	7.6	8.2
Work-in-process and finished parts	88.4	83.6
Finished products	74.7	69.3
Total inventories	170.7	161.1
Other current assets	41.9	44.3
Total current assets	365.6	368.8
Property, plant and equipment—net	114.3	114.2
Goodwill	87.3	83.7
Other noncurrent assets	83.3	104.9
Total assets	$ 650.5	$ 671.6
LIABILITIES AND SHAREHOLDERS' DEFICIT		
Current Liabilities		
Short-term borrowings	$ 25.5	$ 4.1
Long-term debt and capital lease obligations due within one year	2.2	2.6
Trade accounts payable	77.8	76.4
Advanced billings and deposits	24.4	22.6
Accrued and other current liabilities	82.6	76.3
Total current liabilities	212.5	182.0
Long-term accrued liabilities	226.5	261.4
Long-term debt	232.8	233.3
Total liabilities	671.8	676.7
Commitments and contingencies	—	—
Shareholders' deficit		
4% Cumulative Preferred Shares	6.0	6.0
6% Series B Convertible Preferred Stock, $.01 par value (outstanding: .5 in both 2006 and 2005)	116.1	112.9
Common shares, $.01 par value (outstanding: 52.3 in 2006 and 50.1 in 2005)	0.5	0.5
Capital in excess of par value	351.1	348.0
Contingent warrants	0.5	0.5
Accumulated deficit	(381.9)	(332.8)
Accumulated other comprehensive loss	(113.6)	(140.2)
Total shareholders' deficit	(21.3)	(5.1)
Total liabilities and shareholders' deficit	$ 650.5	$ 671.6

*"Milacron is a major solutions provider to the plastics-processing industries and a leading supplier of premium fluids to the networking industries." 10-K

Assets are normally divided into two major categories: current and noncurrent (long-term). **Current assets** are assets (1) in the form of cash, (2) that will normally be realized in cash, or (3) that conserve the use of cash during the operating cycle of a firm or for one year, whichever is longer. The *operating cycle* covers the time between the acquisition of inventory and the realization of cash from selling the inventory. **Noncurrent** or **long-term assets** take longer than a year or an operating cycle to be converted to cash or to conserve cash. Some industries, such as banking (financial institutions), insurance, and real estate, do not divide assets (or liabilities) into current and noncurrent. Chapter 12 reviews specialized industries.

Exhibit 3-2   CABOT CORPORATION*

Consolidated Balance Sheets, Account Form

CABOT CORPORATION
CONSOLIDATED BALANCE SHEETS

Assets	September 30, 2006	September 30, 2005
	(In millions, except share and per share amounts)	
Current Assets:		
Cash and cash equivalents	$ 189	$ 181
Short-term marketable securities investments	1	30
Accounts and notes receivable, net of reserve for doubtful accounts of $6 and $4	534	430
Inventories	420	493
Prepaid expenses and other current assets	75	80
Deferred income taxes	36	27
Assets held for sale	—	5
Total current assets	1,255	1,246
Investments:		
Equity affiliates	59	63
Long-term marketable securities and cost investments	3	6
Total investments	62	69
Property, plant and equipment	2,531	2,264
Accumulated depreciation and amortization	(1,567)	(1,430)
Net property, plant and equipment	964	834
Goodwill	31	25
Intangible assets, net of accumulated amortization of $10 and $9	5	6
Assets held for rent	40	37
Deferred income taxes	100	108
Other assets	77	49
Total assets	$2,534	$2,374

Liabilities and Stockholders' Equity	September 30, 2006	September 30, 2005
	(In millions, except share and per share amounts)	
Current Liabilities:		
Notes payable to banks	$ 58	$ 34
Accounts payable and accrued liabilities	384	321
Income taxes payable	27	30
Deferred income taxes	2	1
Current portion of long-term debt	34	47
Total current liabilities	505	433
Long-term debt	459	463
Deferred income taxes	20	15
Other liabilities	286	307
Commitments and contingencies (Note S)		
Minority interest	68	57
Stockholders' Equity:		
Preferred stock:		
Authorized: 2,000,000 shares of $1 par value		
Series B ESOP Convertible Preferred Stock 7.75% Cumulative:		
Authorized: 2,000,000 shares		
Issued and outstanding: 38,734 and 43,907 shares		
(aggregate redemption value of $39 and $44)	56	61
Less cost of 17,161 shares of preferred treasury stock	(38)	(38)
Common stock:		
Authorized: 200,000,000 shares of $1 par value		
Issued: 63,432,651 and 62,819,715 shares	64	63
Less cost of 146,389 and 152,121 shares of common treasury stock	(5)	(5)
Additional paid-in capital	7	32
Retained earnings	1,160	1,127
Unearned compensation	—	(41)
Deferred employee benefits	(38)	(42)
Notes receivable for restricted stock	(20)	(19)
Accumulated other comprehensive income (loss)	10	(39)
Total stockholders' equity	1,196	1,099
Total liabilities and stockholders' equity	$2,534	$2,374

*"Cabot is a global specialty chemicals and performance materials company headquartered in Boston, Massachusetts." 10-K

When a significant subsidiary is consolidated from an industry that does not use the concept of current and noncurrent, then the consolidated statements will not use the concept of current and noncurrent. These companies often present supplementary statements, handling the subsidiary as an investment (nonconsolidated).

For example, General Electric does not use the concept of current and noncurrent. General Electric Company's consolidated financial statements represent the combination of manufacturing and nonfinancial services businesses of General Electric Company (GE) and the accounts of General Electric Capital Services, Inc. (GECS).

Current Assets

Current assets are listed on the balance sheet in order of liquidity (the ability to be converted to cash). Current assets typically include cash, marketable securities, short-term receivables, inventories, and prepaids. In some cases, assets other than these may be classified as current. If so, management is indicating that it expects the asset to be converted into cash during the operating cycle or within a year, whichever is longer. An example is land held for immediate disposal. Exhibit 3-3 includes the items that the 2006 edition of *Accounting Trends & Techniques* reported as being disclosed as other current assets. The definition of current assets excludes restricted cash, investments for purposes of control, long-term receivables, the cash surrender value of life insurance, land and other natural resources, depreciable assets, and long-term prepayments.

| Exhibit | 3-3 | OTHER CURRENT ASSET ITEMS |

Nature of Asset	Number of Companies			
	2005	2004	2003	2002
Deferred income taxes	424	422	387	399
Property held for sale	95	93	67	62
Derivatives	49	41	34	23
Advances or deposits	22	10	10	15
Unbilled costs	18	15	13	10
Other—identified	33	32	50	49

Source: *Accounting Trends & Techniques,* copyright © 2006 by American Institute of Certified Public Accountants, Inc., p. ATT-SEC 1.31. Reprinted with permission.

Cash

Cash, the most liquid asset, includes negotiable checks and unrestricted balances in checking accounts, as well as cash on hand. Savings accounts are classified as cash even though the bank may not release the money for a specific period of time. Exhibit 3-4 illustrates the presentation of cash.

Marketable Securities

Marketable securities (also labeled short-term investments) are characterized by their marketability at a readily determinable market price. A firm holds marketable securities to earn a return on near-cash resources. Management must intend to convert these assets to cash during the current period for them to be classified as marketable securities.

The carrying basis of debt and equity marketable securities is fair value. Refer to Exhibit 3-4 for a presentation of marketable securities.

Accounts Receivable

Accounts receivable are monies due on accounts that arise from sales or services rendered to customers. Accounts receivable are shown net of allowances to reflect their realizable value.

Exhibit	3-4	SEACHANGE INTERNATIONAL, INC.*

Consolidated Balance Sheet (in Part)
Illustration of cash, marketable securities, and accounts receivable

SEACHANGE INTERNATIONAL, INC.
CONSOLIDATED BALANCE SHEET
(In thousands, except share and per share data)

ASSETS	January 31, 2007	January 31, 2006
Current Assets:		
Cash and cash equivalents	$31,179	$21,594
Restricted cash	—	500
Marketable securities	11,231	14,596
Accounts receivable, net of allowance for doubtful accounts of $466 at January 31, 2007 and $405 at January 31, 2006	28,854	30,109
Unbilled receivables	5,562	4,363
Inventories, net	19,350	19,299
Income taxes receivable	409	2,781
Prepaid expenses and other current assets	2,990	4,594
Total current assets	$99,575	$97,836

*"Seachange International, Inc. . . . a Delaware corporation founded on July 9, 1993, is a leading developer, manufacturer and marketer of digital video systems and services." 10-K

This amount is expected to be collected. The most typical allowances are for bad debts (uncollectible accounts). Other allowances may account for expected sales discounts, which are given for prompt payment or for sales returns. These types of allowances recognize expenses in the period of sale, at which time the allowance is established. In future periods, when the losses occur, they are charged to the allowance. All of the allowances are presented in one allowance account. Exhibit 3-4 presents the accounts receivable of Seachange International, Inc. (less allowances). At January 31, 2007, the firm expects to realize $28,854,000. The gross receivables can be reconciled as follows:

Receivables, net	$28,854,000
Plus: Allowances	466,000
Receivables, gross	$29,320,000

Other receivables may also be included in current assets. These receivables may result from tax refund claims, investees/affiliates, contracts, finance, retained interest in sold receivables, insurance claims, installment notes or accounts, asset disposals, and employees.[4]

Inventories

Inventories are the balance of goods on hand. In a manufacturing firm, they include raw materials, work in process, and finished goods. Inventories will be carried at cost, expressed in terms of lower-of-cost-or-market. (Cost methods and lower-of-cost-or-market are covered in Chapter 7.) Refer to Exhibit 3-5 for a presentation of inventory.

Raw Materials   These are goods purchased for direct use in manufacturing a product, and they become part of the product. For example, in the manufacture of shirts, the fabric and buttons would be raw materials.

Work in Process   Work in process represents goods started but not ready for sale. Work in process includes the cost of materials, labor costs for workers directly involved in the manufacture, and factory overhead. Factory overhead includes such cost items as rent, indirect wages, and maintenance.

Exhibit	3-5	STEEL DYNAMICS, INC.*

Consolidated Balance Sheets (in Part)
Illustration of Inventory

STEEL DYNAMICS, INC.
CONSOLIDATED BALANCE SHEETS
(In thousands, except share data)

	December 31,	
ASSETS	2006	2005
Current assets:		
Cash and equivalents	$ 29,373	$ 65,518
Accounts receivable, net of related allowances of $6,863 and $5,727 as of December 31, 2006 and 2005, respectively	355,011	214,670
Accounts receivable—related parties	53,365	38,830
Inventories	569,317	386,892
Deferred income taxes	13,964	6,516
Other current assets	15,167	13,307
Total current assets	$1,036,197	$725,733

NOTES TO CONSOLIDATED FINANCIAL STATEMENTS (in Part)

Note 1.   Description of the Business and Summary of Significant Accounting Policies (in Part)

Inventories. Inventories are stated at lower of cost or market. Cost is determined principally on a first-in, first-out, basis. Inventory consisted of the following at December 31 (in thousands):

	2006	2005
Raw materials	$243,770	$184,518
Supplies	130,373	97,627
Work in progress	54,555	38,221
Finished goods	140,619	66,526
	$569,317	$386,892

*"We are one of the largest steel producers in the United States based on an estimated annual steelmaking capability of approximately 5.2 million tons, with actual 2006 shipments from steel operations totaling 4.8 million tons." 10-K

Finished Goods   Finished goods are inventory ready for sale. These inventory costs also include the cost of materials, labor costs for workers directly involved in the manufacture, and a portion of factory overhead.

Since retailing and wholesaling firms do not engage in the manufacture of a product but only in the sale, their only inventory item is merchandise. These firms do not have raw materials, work in process inventory, or finished goods.

Supplies   In addition to goods on hand, the firm may have supplies. Supplies could include register tapes, pencils, or sewing machine needles for the shirt factory. Details relating to inventory are usually disclosed in a note.

Prepaids

A **prepaid** is an expenditure made in advance of the use of the service or goods. It represents future benefits that have resulted from past transactions. For example, if insurance is paid in advance for three years, at the end of the first year, two years' worth of the outlay will be prepaid. The entity retains the right to be covered by insurance for two more years.

Typical prepaids include advertising, taxes, insurance, promotion costs, and early payments on long-term contracts. Prepaids are often not disclosed separately. In Exhibit 3-1, the prepaid account is not disclosed separately. In Exhibit 3-2, prepaids are part of prepaid expenses and other current assets.

Long-Term Assets

Long-term assets are usually divided into four categories: tangible assets, investments, intangible assets, and other.

Tangible Assets

These are the physical facilities used in the operations of the business. The tangible assets of land, buildings, machinery, and construction in progress will now be reviewed. Accumulated depreciation related to buildings and machinery will also be reviewed.

Land   Land is shown at acquisition cost and is not depreciated because land does not get used up. Land containing resources that will be used up, however, such as mineral deposits and timberlands, is subject to depletion. Depletion expense attempts to measure the wearing away of these resources. It is similar to depreciation except that depreciation deals with a tangible fixed asset and depletion deals with a natural resource.

Buildings   Structures are presented at cost plus the cost of permanent improvements. Buildings are depreciated (expensed) over their estimated useful life.

Machinery   Machinery is listed at historical cost, including delivery and installation, plus any material improvements that extend its life or increase the quantity or quality of service. Machinery is depreciated over its estimated useful life.

Construction in Progress   Construction in progress represents cost incurred for projects under construction. These costs will be transferred to the proper tangible asset account upon completion of construction. The firm cannot use these assets while they are under construction. Some analysis is directed at how efficiently the company is using operating assets. This analysis can be distorted by construction in progress, since construction in progress is classified as part of tangible assets. To avoid this distortion, classify construction in progress under long-term assets, other.

Accumulated Depreciation   Depreciation is the process of allocating the cost of buildings and machinery over the periods benefited. The depreciation expense taken each period is accumulated in a separate account (Accumulated Depreciation). Accumulated depreciation is subtracted from the cost of plant and equipment. The net amount is the **book value** of the asset. It does not represent the current market value of the asset.

There are a number of depreciation methods that a firm can use. Often, a firm depreciates an asset under one method for financial statements and another for income tax returns. A firm often wants to depreciate slowly for the financial statements because this results in the highest immediate income and highest asset balance. The same firm would want to depreciate faster for income tax returns because this results in the lowest immediate income and thus lower income taxes. Over the life of an asset, the total depreciation will be the same regardless of the depreciation method selected.

Three factors are usually considered when computing depreciation: (1) the asset cost, (2) length of the life of the asset, and (3) its salvage value when retired from service. The length of the asset's life and the salvage value must be estimated at the time that the asset is placed in service. These estimates may be later changed if warranted.

Exhibit 3-6 indicates the depreciation methods used for financial reporting purposes by the firms surveyed for the 2006 edition of *Accounting Trends & Techniques*. The most popular method was straight-line. Many firms use more than one depreciation method.

The following assumptions will be made to illustrate some depreciation methods:

1. Cost of asset—$10,000
2. Estimated life of asset—5 years
3. Estimated salvage (or residual) value—$2,000
4. Estimated total hours of use—16,000

Exhibit	3-6	DEPRECIATION METHODS

	Number of Companies			
	2005	2004	2003	2002
Straight-line	592	586	580	579
Declining-balance	14	16	22	22
Sum-of-the-years'-digits	4	6	5	5
Accelerated method—not specified	30	32	41	44
Unit-of-production	24	22	30	32
Other	10	8	4	7

Source: *Accounting Trends & Techniques,* copyright © 2006 by American Institute of Certified Public Accountants, Inc., p. ATT-SEC 1.31. Reprinted with permission.

Straight-Line Method   The **straight-line method** recognizes depreciation in equal amounts over the estimated life of the asset. Compute depreciation using the straight-line method as follows:

$$\frac{\text{Cost} - \text{Salvage Value}}{\text{Estimated Life}} = \text{Annual Depreciation}$$

For the asset used for illustration, the annual depreciation would be computed as follows:

$$\frac{\$10,000 - \$2,000}{5 \text{ years}} = \$1,600$$

The $1,600 depreciation amount would be recognized each year of the five-year life of the asset. Do not depreciate the salvage value.

Declining-Balance Method   The **declining-balance method**, an accelerated method, applies a multiple times the straight-line rate to the declining book value (cost minus accumulated depreciation) to achieve a declining depreciation charge over the estimated life of the asset. This book will use double the straight-line rate, which is the maximum rate that can be used. Compute depreciation using the declining-balance method as follows:

$$\frac{1}{\text{Estimated Life of Asset}} \times 2 \times \text{Book Amount at Beginning of the Year} = \text{Annual Depreciation}$$

For the asset used for illustration, the first year's depreciation would be computed as follows:

$$\frac{1}{5} \times 2 \times (\$10,000 - 0) = \$4,000$$

The declining-balance method results in the following depreciation amounts for each of the five years of the asset's life:

Year	Cost	Accumulated Depreciation at Beginning of Year	Book Amount at Beginning of Year	Depreciation for Year	Book Amount at End of Year
1	$10,000	—	$10,000	$4,000	$6,000
2	10,000	$4,000	6,000	2,400	3,600
3	10,000	6,400	3,600	1,440	2,160
4	10,000	7,840	2,160	160	2,000
5	10,000	8,000	2,000	—	2,000

Estimated salvage value is not considered in the formula, but the asset should not be depreciated below the estimated salvage value. For the sample asset, the formula produced a depreciation amount of $864 in the fourth year. Only $160 depreciation can be used in the fourth year because the $160 amount brings the book amount of the asset down to the salvage value. Once the book amount is equal to the salvage value, no additional depreciation may be taken.

Sum-of-the-Years'-Digits Method   The **sum-of-the-years'-digits method** is an accelerated depreciation method. Thus, the depreciation expense declines steadily over the estimated life of the asset. This method takes a fraction each year times the cost less salvage value. The numerator of the fraction changes each year. It is the remaining number of years of the asset's life. The denominator of the fraction remains constant; it is the sum of the digits representing the years of the asset's life. Compute depreciation using the sum-of-the-years'-digits method as follows:

$$\frac{\text{Remaining Number of Years of Life}}{\text{Sum of the Digits Representing the Years of Life}} \times (\text{Cost} - \text{Salvage}) = \text{Annual Depreciation}$$

For the asset used for illustration, the first year's depreciation would be computed as follows:

$$\frac{5}{(5 + 4 + 3 + 2 + 1) \text{ or } 15} \times (\$10,000 - \$2,000) = \$2,666.67$$

The sum-of-the-years'-digits method results in the following depreciation amounts for each year of the five years of the asset's life:

Year	Cost Less Salvage Value	Fraction	Depreciation for Year	Accumulated Depreciation at End of Year	Book Amount at End of Year
1	$8,000	5/15	$2,666.67	$2,666.67	$7,333.33
2	8,000	4/15	2,133.33	4,800.00	5,200.00
3	8,000	3/15	1,600.00	6,400.00	3,600.00
4	8,000	2/15	1,066.67	7,466.67	2,533.33
5	8,000	1/15	533.33	8,000.00	2,000.00

Unit-of-Production Method   The **unit-of-production method** relates depreciation to the output capacity of the asset, estimated for the life of the asset. The capacity is stated in terms most appropriate for the asset, such as units of production, hours of use, or miles. Hours of use will be used for the asset in our example. For the life of the asset, it is estimated that there will be 16,000 hours of use. The estimated output capacity is divided into the cost of the asset less the salvage value to determine the depreciation per unit of output. For the example asset, the depreciation per hour of use would be $0.50 [(cost of asset, $10,000 − salvage, $2,000) divided by 16,000 hours].

The depreciation for each year is then determined by multiplying the depreciation per unit of output by the output for that year. Assuming that the output was 2,000 hours during the first year, the depreciation for that year would be $1,000 ($0.50 × 2,000). Further depreciation cannot be taken when the accumulated depreciation equals the cost of the asset less the salvage value. For the example asset, this will be when accumulated depreciation equals $8,000.

In Exhibit 3-7, Lennox International, Inc., presents these assets as property, plant, and equipment at cost. Added detail information is disclosed in the notes.

Leases

Leases are classified as *operating* leases or *capital* leases. If the lease is in substance an ownership arrangement, it is a capital lease; otherwise, the lease is an operating lease. Assets leased under a capital lease are classified as long-term assets. They are shown net of amortization (depreciation) and listed with plant, property, and equipment. (The discounted value of the obligation, a liability, will be part current and part long term.) Chapter 7 covers the topic of leases in more length.

Exhibit	3-7	LENNOX INTERNATIONAL, INC., AND SUBSIDIARIES*

Consolidated Balance Sheets (in Part)
Properties and Depreciation

CONSOLIDATED BALANCE SHEETS
As of December 31, 2006 and 2005
(In millions, except share and per share data)

	As of December 31,	
	2006	2005
ASSETS		
Current assets:		
Cash and equivalents	$ 144.3	$ 213.5
Accounts and notes receivable, net	502.6	508.4
Inventories	305.5	242.4
Deferred income taxes	22.2	20.3
Other assets	43.8	62.6
Total current assets	1,018.4	1,047.2
Property, plant and equipment, net	288.2	255.7
Goodwill	239.8	223.9
Deferred income taxes	104.3	71.9
Other assets	69.1	138.9
Total assets	$1,719.8	$1,737.6

Notes to Consolidated Financial Statements (in Part)

2. Summary of Significant Accounting Policies (in Part)

Property, Plant and Equipment (in Part)

Property, plant and equipment are stated at cost, net of accumulated depreciation. Expenditures for renewals and betterments are capitalized and expenditures for maintenance and repairs are charged to expense as incurred. Depreciation is computed using the straight-line method over the following estimated useful lives:

Buildings and improvements	10 to 39 years
Machinery and equipment	3 to 10 years

5. Property, Plant and Equipment

	As of December 31,	
	2006	2005
Land	$ 32.7	$ 30.3
Buildings and improvements	181.6	177.1
Machinery and equipment	526.6	487.8
Construction in progress and equipment not yet in service	36.1	25.1
Total	777.0	720.3
Less—accumulated depreciation	(488.8)	(464.6)
Property, plant and equipment, net	$ 288.2	$ 255.7

*"Through our subsidiaries, we are a leading global provider of climate control solutions." 10-K

Investments

Long-term investments, usually stocks and bonds of other companies, are often held to maintain a business relationship or to exercise control. Long-term investments are different from marketable securities, where the intent is to hold for short-term profits and to achieve liquidity. (Financial reports often refer to marketable securities as investments.)

Debt securities under investments are to be classified as held-to-maturity securities or available-for-sale securities. *Held-to-maturity securities* are securities that the firm has the intent and ability to hold to maturity. Debt securities classified as held-to-maturity securities are carried at amortized cost. Debt securities classified as available-for-sale securities are carried at fair value.

Equity securities under investments are to be carried at fair value. An exception for fair value is used for common stock where there is significant influence. For these common stock investments, the investment is carried under the equity method. Under the equity method, the cost is adjusted for the proportionate share of the rise (fall) in retained profits of the subsidiary (investee). For example, a parent company owns 40% of a subsidiary company, purchased at a cost of $400,000. When the subsidiary company earns $100,000, the parent company increases the investment account by 40% of $100,000, or $40,000. When the subsidiary company declares dividends of $20,000, the parent company decreases the investment account by 40% of $20,000, or $8,000. This decrease occurs because the investment account changes in direct proportion to the retained earnings of the subsidiary.

Investments can also include tangible assets not currently used in operations, such as an idle plant, as well as monies set aside in special funds, such as pensions. The investments of Gentex Corporation are illustrated in Exhibit 3-8.

Intangibles

Intangibles are nonphysical assets, such as patents and copyrights. Intangibles are recorded at historical cost and amortized over their useful lives or their legal lives, whichever is shorter. Purchased goodwill resulting from an acquisition represents an exception to amortization. Research and development costs must be expensed as incurred. Thus, research and development costs in the United States represent an immediate expense, not an intangible. This requirement is not common in many other countries. The following are examples of intangibles that are recorded in the United States.

Exhibit **3-8**	GENTEX CORPORATION*

Consolidated Balance Sheets (in Part)
As of December 31, 2006 and 2005
Investments

GENTEX CORPORATION AND SUBSIDIARIES
CONSOLIDATED BALANCE SHEETS
AS OF DECEMBER 31, 2006 AND 2005

Assets	2006	2005
Current Assets:		
Cash and cash equivalents	$245,499,783	$439,681,693
Short-term investments	82,727,927	67,331,928
Accounts receivable	58,337,396	60,924,437
Inventories	48,805,398	39,836,822
Prepaid expenses and other	11,507,590	11,212,647
Total current assets	446,878,094	618,987,527
Plant and Equipment:		
Land, buildings and improvements	95,998,488	57,544,173
Machinery and equipment	231,526,281	196,878,770
Construction-in-process	12,393,019	40,858,633
	339,917,788	295,281,576
Less—accumulated depreciation and amortization	(155,783,415)	(131,251,235)
Other Assets:		
Long-term investments	146,215,929	132,524,966
Patents and other assets, net	7,800,004	7,102,968
	154,015,933	139,627,934
	$785,028,400	$922,645,802

*"Gentex Corporation . . . designs, develops, manufactures and markets proprietary products employing electro-optic technology: automatic-dimming rearview automotive mirrors and fire protected products." 10-K

(continued)

Exhibit   3-8   GENTEX CORPORATION (Continued)

Notes to Consolidated Financial Statements (in Part)

(1) Summary of Significant Accounting and Reporting Policies (in Part)

Investments

At December 31, 2006, investment securities are available for sale and are stated at fair value based on quoted market prices. Adjustments to the fair value of investments are recorded as increases or decreases, net of income taxes, within accumulated other comprehensive income (loss) in shareholders' investment.

The amortized cost, unrealized gains and losses, and market value of investment securities are shown as of December 31, 2006 and 2005:

2006	Cost	Gains	Unrealized Losses	Market Value
Government Agency	$ 8,992,336	$ —	$ (3,796)	$ 8,988,540
Certificates of Deposit	71,200,000	—	—	71,200,000
Corporate Bonds	297,579	—	(4,926)	292,653
Other Fixed Income	2,539,387	—	—	2,539,387
Equity	110,150,262	36,173,199	(400,185)	145,923,276
	$193,179,564	$36,173,199	$ (408,907)	$228,943,856

2005	Cost	Gains	Losses	Market Value
U.S. Government	$ 5,000,000	$ —	$ —	$ 5,000,000
Government Agency	18,024,332	—	(33,462)	17,990,870
Certificates of Deposit	26,200,000	—	—	26,200,000
Corporate Bonds	17,288,250	—	(93,899)	17,194,351
Other Fixed Income	1,215,708	—	—	1,215,708
Equity	103,212,665	30,802,826	(1,759,526)	132,255,965
	$170,940,955	$30,802,826	$(1,886,887)	$199,856,894

Unrealized losses on investments as of December 31, 2006, are as follows:

	Aggregate Unrealized Losses	Aggregate Fair Value
Less than one year	$351,434	$ 7,451,508
Greater than one year	57,473	10,210,915

Management has reviewed the unrealized losses in the Company's fixed-income and equity securities as of December 31, 2006, and has determined that they are temporary in nature; accordingly, no losses have been recognized in income as of December 31, 2006.

Fixed income securities as of December 31, 2006, have contractual maturities as follows:

Due within one year	$82,731,723
Due between one and five years	297,579
Due over five years	—
	$83,029,302

Fair Value of Financial Instruments

The Company's financial instruments consist of cash and cash equivalents, investments, accounts receivable and accounts payable. The Company's estimate of the fair values of these financial instruments approximates their carrying amounts at December 31, 2006 and 2005.

Goodwill   Goodwill arises from the acquisition of a business for a sum greater than the physical asset value, usually because the business has unusual earning power. It may result from good customer relations, a well-respected owner, and so on. Purchased goodwill is not amortized but is subject to annual impairment reviews.[5]

The global treatment of goodwill varies significantly. In some countries, goodwill is not recorded because it is charged to stockholders' equity. In this case, there is no influence to reported income. In some countries, goodwill is expensed in the year acquired. In many countries, goodwill is recorded and amortized.

Patents   Patents, exclusive legal rights granted to an inventor for a period of 20 years, are valued at their acquisition cost. The cost of a patent should be amortized over its legal life or its useful life, whichever is shorter.

Trademarks   Trademarks are distinctive names or symbols. Rights are granted indefinitely as long as the owner uses it in connection with the product or service and files the paperwork. Since a trademark has an indefinite life, it should not be amortized. Trademarks should be tested for impairment at least annually.

Franchises   Franchises are the legal right to operate under a particular corporate name, providing trade-name products or services. The cost of a franchise with a limited life should be amortized over the life of the franchise.

Copyrights   Copyrights are rights that authors, painters, musicians, sculptors, and other artists have in their creations and expressions. A copyright is granted for the life of the creator, plus 70 years. The costs of the copyright should be amortized over the period of expected benefit.

Exhibit 3-9 displays the 3M Company presentation of intangibles. It consists of goodwill and other intangibles.

Exhibit	3-9	3M COMPANY*

Balance Sheet
Intangibles

Consolidated Balance Sheet
3M Company and Subsidiaries
At December 31

(Dollars in millions, except per share amount)	2006	2005
ASSETS		
Current assets:		
Cash and cash equivalents	$ 1,447	$ 1,072
Marketable securities—current	471	—
Accounts receivable—net of allowance of $71 and $73	3,102	2,838
Inventories		
Finished goods	1,235	1,050
Work in progress	795	706
Raw materials and supplies	571	406
Total inventories	2,601	2,162
Other current assets	1,325	1,043
Total current assets	8,946	7,115
Marketable securities—noncurrent	166	—
Investments	314	272
Property, plant and equipment	17,017	16,127
Less: Accumulated depreciation	(11,110)	(10,534)
Property, plant and equipment—net	5,907	5,593
Goodwill	4,082	3,530
Intangible assets—net	708	486
Prepaid pension and postretirement benefits	395	2,905
Other assets	776	640
Total assets	$21,294	$20,541

*"3M is a diversified technology company with a global presence in the following businesses: industrial and transportation; health care; display and graphics; consumer and office; safety, security and protection services; and electro and communications." 10-K

(continued)

| Exhibit | 3-9 | 3M COMPANY (Continued) |

Notes to Consolidated Financial Statements (in Part)

Note 1. Significant Accounting Policies (in Part)

Goodwill

Goodwill: Goodwill is the excess of cost of an acquired entity over the amounts assigned to assets acquired and liabilities assumed in a business combination. Goodwill is not amortized. Goodwill is tested for impairment annually, and will be tested for impairment between annual tests if an event occurs or circumstances change that would indicate the carrying amount may be impaired. Impairment testing for goodwill is done at a reporting unit level. Reporting units are one level below the business segment level, but can be combined when reporting units within the same segment have similar economic characteristics. The majority of goodwill relates to and is assigned directly to specific reporting units. An impairment loss generally would be recognized when the carrying amount of the reporting unit's net assets exceeds the estimated fair value of the reporting unit. The estimated fair value of a reporting unit is determined using earnings for the reporting unit multiplied by a price/earnings ratio for comparable industry groups, or by using a discounted cash flow analysis. The Company completed its annual goodwill impairment test in the fourth quarter of 2006 and determined that no goodwill was impaired.

Intangible asset: Intangible assets include patents, tradenames and other intangible assets acquired from an independent party. Intangible assets with an indefinite life, namely certain tradenames, are not amortized. Intangible assets with a definite life are amortized on a straight-line basis, with estimated useful lives ranging from one to 20 years. Indefinite-lived intangible assets are tested for impairment annually, and will be tested for impairment between annual tests if an event occurs or circumstances change that would indicate that the carrying amount may be impaired. Intangible assets with a definite life are tested for impairment whenever events or circumstances indicate that the carrying amount of an asset (asset group) may not be recoverable. An impairment loss is recognized when the carrying amount of an asset exceeds the estimated undiscounted cash flows used in determining the fair value of the asset. The amount of the impairment loss to be recorded is calculated by the excess of the asset's carrying value over its fair value. Fair value is generally determined using a discounted cash flow analysis. Costs related to internally developed intangible assets, such as patents, are expensed as incurred, primarily in "Research, development and related expenses."

Note 3. Goodwill and Intangible Assets

Purchased goodwill from acquisitions totaled $536 million in 2006, $41 million of which is deductible for tax purposes. Purchased goodwill in 2005 totaled $1.002 billion, primarily related to CUNO, none of which is deductible for tax purposes. The sale of 3M's global branded pharmaceuticals business (Health Care) resulted in the write-off of $54 million in goodwill, which is reflected in the translation and other column below. Changes in foreign currency exchange rates impacted both 2006 and 2005 goodwill balances. The goodwill balance by business segment follows:

Millions	Dec. 31, 2004 Balance	2005 Acqui-sition Activity	2005 Trans-lation and Other	Dec. 31, 2005 Balance	2006 Acqui-sition Activity	2006 Trans-lation and Other	Dec. 31, 2006 Balance
Industrial and Transportation	$ 375	$ 992	$ (27)	$1,340	$ 51	$ (7)	$1,384
Health Care	634	—	(75)	559	191	(37)	713
Display and Graphics	885	—	(14)	871	12	3	886
Consumer and Office	68	—	(5)	63	11	8	82
Safety, Security and Protection Services	193	—	(21)	172	239	26	437
Electro and Communications	566	10	(51)	525	32	23	580
Total Company	$2,721	$1,002	$(193)	$3,530	$536	$16	$4,082

Exhibit 3-9 3M COMPANY (Continued)

Acquired Intangible Assets

The carrying amount and accumulated amortization of acquired intangible assets as of December 31 follow:

Millions	2006	2005
Patents	$ 419	$378
Other amortizable intangible assets (primarily		
tradenames and customer-related intangibles)	641	369
Non-amortizable intangible assets (tradenames)	68	60
Total gross carrying amount	$1,128	$807
Accumulated amortization—patents	(266)	(205)
Accumulated amortization—other	(154)	(116)
Total accumulated amortization	(420)	(321)
Total intangible assets—net	$ 708	$486

Amortization expense for acquired intangible assets for the years ended December 31 follows:

Millions	2006	2005	2004
Amortization expense	$ 89	$ 48	$ 43

Expected amortization expense for acquired intangible assets recorded as of December 31, 2006, follows:

(Millions)	2007	2008	2009	2010	2011	After 2044
Amortization expense	$69	$67	$66	$57	$50	$331

The preceding expected amortization expense is an estimate. Actual amounts of amortization expense may differ from estimated amounts due to additional intangible asset acquisitions, changes in foreign currency exchange rates, impairment of intangible assets, accelerated amortization of intangible assets and other events.

Other Assets

Firms will occasionally have assets that do not fit into one of the previously discussed classifications. These assets, termed "other," might include noncurrent receivables and noncurrent prepaids. Exhibit 3-10 summarizes types of other assets from a financial statement compilation in *Accounting Trends & Techniques*.

LIABILITIES

Liabilities are probable future sacrifices of economic benefits arising from present obligations of a particular entity to transfer assets or provide services to other entities in the future as a result of past transactions or events.[6] Liabilities are usually classified as either current or long-term liabilities.

Current Liabilities

Current liabilities are obligations whose liquidation is reasonably expected to require the use of existing current assets or the creation of other current liabilities within a year or an operating cycle, whichever is longer. They include the following items. Exhibit 3-11 shows the current liabilities of Starbucks Corporation.

| Exhibit | 3-10 | OTHER NONCURRENT ASSETS |

	\multicolumn{4}{c}{**Number of Companies**}
	2005	**2004**	**2003**	**2002**
Deferred income taxes	243	237	212	195
Prepaid pension costs	193	151	147	146
Software	118	132	124	128
Debt issue costs	89	69	57	64
Segregated cash or securities	73	75	61	69
Derivatives	68	88	54	61
Property held for sale	47	52	49	43
Cash surrender value of life insurance	35	40	31	33
Contracts	12	16	8	13
Assets leased to others	11	12	11	16
Estimated insurance recoveries	11	7	8	9
Assets of nonhomogeneous operations	8	7	3	6
Other identified noncurrent assets	62	66	53	59

Source: *Accounting Trends & Techniques,* copyright © 2006 by American Institute of Certified Public Accountants, Inc., p. ATT-SEC 1.31. Reprinted with permission.

| Exhibit | 3-11 | STARBUCKS CORPORATION* |

Current Liabilities

(In thousands)	October 1, 2006	October 2, 2005
Current Liabilities		
Accounts payable	$ 340,937	$ 220,975
Accrued compensation and related costs	288,963	232,354
Accrued occupancy costs	54,868	44,496
Accrued taxes	94,010	78,293
Short-term borrowings	700,000	277,000
Other accrued expenses	224,154	198,082
Deferred revenue	231,926	175,048
Current portion of long-term debt	762	748
Total current liabilities	$1,935,620	$1,226,996

*"Starbucks purchases and roasts high-quality whole bean coffees and sells them, along with fresh, rich-brewed coffees, Italian style espresso beverages, cold blended beverages, a variety of complementary food items, coffee-related accessories and equipment, a selection of premium teas and a line of compact discs, primarily through company-operated retail stores." 10-K

Payables

These include short-term obligations created by the acquisition of goods and services, such as accounts payable (for materials or goods bought for use or resale), wages payable, and taxes payable. Payables may also be in the form of a written promissory note, notes payable.

Unearned Income

Payments collected in advance of the performance of service are termed unearned. They include rent income and subscription income. Rather than cash, a future service or good is due the customer.

Other Current Liabilities

There are many other current obligations requiring payment during the year. Exhibit 3-12 displays other current liabilities reported by *Accounting Trends & Techniques* in 2006.

Exhibit	3-12	OTHER CURRENT LIABILITIES

	Number of Companies			
	2005	**2004**	**2003**	**2002**
Deferred revenue	162	144	127	116
Costs related to discontinued operations/restructuring	161	163	151	157
Interest	137	141	130	122
Taxes other than federal income taxes	127	121	117	112
Warranties	126	122	126	104
Insurance	125	96	89	76
Deferred taxes	82	72	69	61
Customer advances, deposits	68	63	64	60
Advertising	66	63	60	51
Derivatives	64	61	52	45
Rebates	59	45	40	21
Dividends	58	62	56	52
Environmental costs	56	53	48	50
Litigation	46	47	30	37
Billings on uncompleted contracts	28	30	19	18
Royalties	25	22	20	19
Due to affiliated companies	18	14	22	20
Asset retirement obligations	11	11	6	—
Other—described	139	167	153	164

Source: *Accounting Trends & Techniques,* copyright © 2006 by American Institute of Certified Public Accountants, Inc., p. ATT-SEC 1.31. Reprinted with permission.

Long-Term Liabilities

Long-term liabilities are those due in a period exceeding one year or one operating cycle, whichever is longer. Long-term liabilities are generally of two types: financing arrangements of assets and operational obligations.

Liabilities Relating to Financing Agreements

The long-term liabilities that are financing arrangements of assets usually require systematic payment of principal and interest. They include notes payable, bonds payable, and credit agreements.

Notes Payable   Promissory notes due in periods greater than one year or one operating cycle, whichever is longer, are classified as long term. If secured by a claim against real property, they are called mortgage notes.

Bonds Payable   A **bond** is a debt security normally issued with $1,000 par per bond and requiring semiannual interest payments based on the coupon rate. Bonds payable is similar to notes payable. Bonds payable are usually for a longer duration than notes payable.

Bonds are not necessarily sold at par. They are sold at a premium if the stated rate of interest exceeds the market rate and at a discount if the stated rate of interest is less than the market rate. If sold for more than par, a premium on bonds payable arises and increases bonds payable to obtain the current carrying value. Similarly, if sold at less than par, a discount on bonds payable arises and decreases bonds payable on the balance sheet. Each of these accounts, discount or premium, will be gradually written off (amortized) to interest expense over the life of the bond. At the maturity date, the carrying value of bonds payable will be equal to the par value. Amortization of bond discount increases interest expense; amortization of bond premium reduces it. Exhibit 3-13 illustrates bonds sold at par, premium, or discount.

Bonds that are convertible into common stock at the option of the bondholder (creditor) are exchanged for a specified number of common shares, and the bondholder becomes a common stockholder. Often, convertible bonds are issued when the common stock price is low, in management's opinion, and the firm eventually wants to increase its common equity. By issuing a convertible bond, the firm may get more for the specified number of common shares than could be obtained by issuing the common shares. The conversion feature allows the firm to issue the bond

| Exhibit | 3-13 | BONDS AT PAR, PREMIUM, OR DISCOUNT |

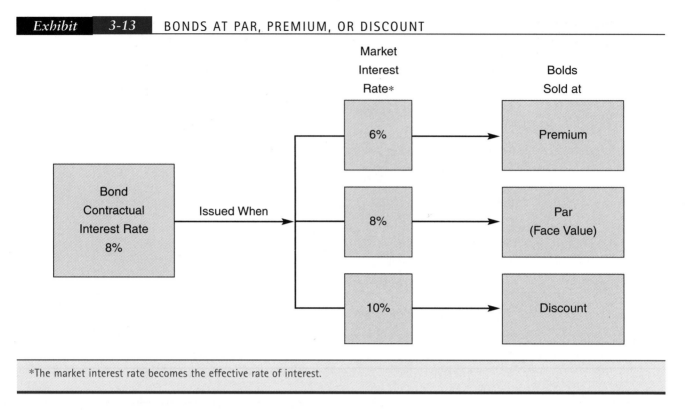

*The market interest rate becomes the effective rate of interest.

at a more favorable interest rate than would be the case with a bond lacking the conversion feature. Also, the tax deductible interest paid on the convertible bond reduces the firm's cost for these funds. If common stock had been issued, the dividend on the common stock would not be tax deductible. Thus, a firm may find that issuing a convertible bond can be an attractive means of raising common equity funds in the long run. However, if the firm's stock price stays depressed after issuing a convertible bond, then the firm will have the convertible bond liability until the bond comes due. Convertible bonds of Quantum Corporation are displayed in Exhibit 3-14.

| Exhibit | 3-14 | QUANTUM CORPORATION* |

Convertible Bonds

| | (In thousands) | |
Liabilities	March 31, 2007	March 31, 2006
Current liabilities:		
Accounts payable	$ 98,757	$ 67,306
Accrued warranty	30,669	32,422
Accrued compensation	32,814	24,903
Income taxes payable	15,490	8,627
Deferred revenue, current	57,617	22,107
Current portion of long-term debt	25,000	—
Accrued restructuring charges	13,289	13,019
Other accrued liabilities	55,814	46,825
Total current liabilities	329,450	215,209
Long-term liabilities:		
Deferred income taxes	16,751	6,995
Long-term debt	337,500	—
Convertible subordinated debt	160,000	160,000
Deferred revenue, long-term	27,634	—
Other long-term liabilities	53	69
Total long-term liabilities	541,938	167,064

*"Quantum Corporation . . . is a leading global storage company specializing in backup, recovery and archive." 10-K

Credit Agreements   Many firms arrange loan commitments from banks or insurance companies for future loans. Often, the firm does not intend to obtain these loans but has arranged the credit agreement just in case a need exists for additional funds. Such credit agreements do not represent a liability unless the firm actually requests the funds. From the point of view of analysis, the existence of a substantial credit agreement is a positive condition in that it could relieve pressure on the firm if there is a problem in meeting existing liabilities.

In return for giving a credit agreement, the bank or insurance company obtains a fee. This commitment fee is usually a percentage of the unused portion of the commitment. Also, banks often require the firm to keep a specified sum in its bank account, referred to as a compensating balance. Exhibit 3-15 shows credit agreements.

Liabilities Relating to Operational Obligations

Long-term liabilities relating to operational obligations include obligations arising from the operation of a business, mostly of a service nature, such as pension obligations, postretirement benefit obligations other than pension plans, deferred taxes, and service warranties. Chapter 7 covers at length pensions and postretirement benefit obligations other than pension plans.

Deferred Taxes   Deferred taxes are caused by using different accounting methods for tax and reporting purposes. For example, a firm may use accelerated depreciation for tax purposes and straight-line depreciation for reporting purposes. This causes tax expense for reporting purposes to be higher than taxes payable according to the tax return. The difference is deferred tax. Any situation where revenue or expense is recognized in the financial statements in a different time period than for the tax return will create a deferred tax situation (asset or liability). For example, in the later years of the life of a fixed asset, straight-line depreciation will give higher depreciation and, therefore, lower net income than an accelerated method. Then tax expense for reporting purposes will be lower than taxes payable, and the deferred tax will be reduced (paid). Since firms often buy more and higher-priced assets, however, the increase in deferred taxes may exceed the decrease. In this case, a partial or a total reversal will not occur. The taxes may be deferred for a very long time, perhaps permanently. Chapter 7 covers deferred taxes in more detail.

Warranty Obligations   Warranty obligations are estimated obligations arising out of product warranties. Product warranties require the seller to correct any deficiencies in quantity, quality, or performance of the product or service for a specific period of time after the sale. Warranty obligations are estimated in order to recognize the obligation at the balance sheet date and to charge the expense to the period of the sale.

Exhibit 3-16 shows warranty obligations of Ford Motor Company.

Minority Interest

Minority interest reflects the ownership of minority shareholders in the equity of consolidated subsidiaries less than wholly owned. Minority interest does not represent a liability or stockholders' equity in the firm being analyzed. Consider the following simple example. Parent P owns 90% of the common stock of Subsidiary S.

	Parent P Balance Sheet December 31, 2008	Subsidiary S Balance Sheet December 31, 2008
	(In millions)	
Current assets	$100	$10
Investment in Subsidiary S	18	—
Other long-term assets	382	40
	$500	$50
Current liabilities	$100	$10
Long-term liabilities	200	20
Stockholders' equity	200	20
	$500	$50

Exhibit   **3-15**   UNITED STATIONERS*

Credit Agreements

For the Fiscal Year Ended December 31, 2006

Notes to consolidated financial statements (in Part)

10. Long-Term Debt (in Part)

Credit Agreement and Other Debt (in Part)

On November 10, 2006, the Registrant and its wholly owned subsidiary, United Stationers Supply Co. ("USSC"), entered into Amendment No. 1 to the Amended and Restated Five-Year Revolving Credit Agreement (the "Amendment" or the "Revolving Credit Facility") with certain financial institutions listed and JPMorgan Chase Bank, National Association [successor by merger to Bank One, NA (Illinois)], as Agent. The Amendment modifies an existing Amended and Restated Five-Year Revolving Credit Agreement (the "2005 Agreement") originally entered into on October 12, 2005. As of December 31, 2006 and 2005, the Company had $110.5 million and $14.2 million, respectively, outstanding under the Revolving Credit Facility. The facility matures in October 2010.

USSC exercised its right under the 2005 Agreement to seek additional commitments to increase the aggregate committed principal amount under a revolving credit facility. The Amendment increased the aggregate committed principal amount from $275 million to $325 million, a $50 million increase. The Amendment also increased the permitted amount of additional commitments USSC may seek under the revolving credit facility to a total amount of up to $425 million, a $50 million increase from the $375 million limit under the 2005 Agreement. In addition, the Amendment increased the permitted size of USSC's third-party receivables securitization program to $350 million, a $75 million increase from the $275 million limit under the 2005 Agreement. All other provisions of the 2005 Agreement, as disclosed in previous filings with the Securities and Exchange Commission, remain unchanged.

The Amended Agreement provides for the issuance of letters of credit in an aggregate amount of up to a sublimit of $90 million. It also provides a sublimit for swingline loans in an aggregate outstanding principal amount not to exceed $25 million at any one time. These amounts, as sublimits, do not increase the maximum aggregate principal amount, and any undrawn issued letters of credit and all outstanding swingline loans under the facility reduce the remaining availability under the Revolving Credit Facility provided for in the Amended Agreement. As of December 31, 2006 and 2005, the Company had outstanding letters of credit of $17.3 million and $16.0 million, respectively.

Obligations of USSC under the Amended Agreement are guaranteed by USI and certain of USSC's domestic subsidiaries. USSC's obligations under the Amended Agreement and the guarantors' obligations under the guaranty are secured by liens on substantially all Company assets, including accounts receivable, chattel paper, commercial tort claims, documents, equipment, fixtures, instruments, inventory, investment property, pledged deposits and all other tangible and intangible personal property (including proceeds) and certain real property, but excluding accounts receivable (and related credit support) subject to any accounts receivable securitization program permitted under the Amended Agreement. Also securing these obligations are first priority pledges of all of the capital stock of USSC and the domestic subsidiaries of USSC.

*"United Stationers Inc. is North America's largest broad line wholesale distributor of business products, with consolidated net sales of approximately $4.5 billion." 10-K

In consolidation, the assets and liabilities of the subsidiary are added to those of the parent, with the elimination of the investment in Subsidiary S. Parent P owns 90% of the subsidiary's net assets of $20 ($50 − $30), and the minority shareholders own 10%.

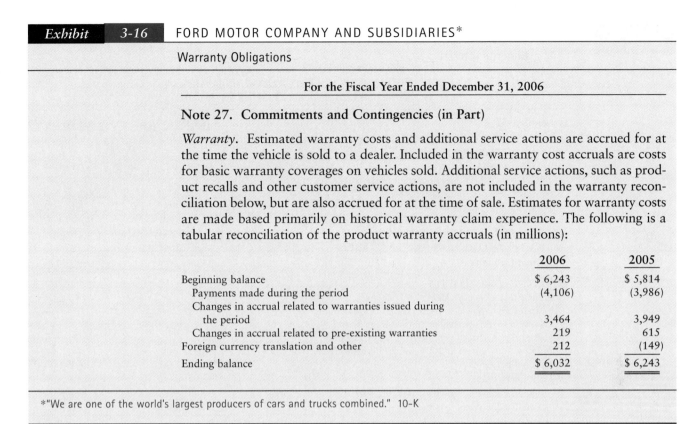

Exhibit	3-16	FORD MOTOR COMPANY AND SUBSIDIARIES*

Warranty Obligations

For the Fiscal Year Ended December 31, 2006

Note 27. Commitments and Contingencies (in Part)

Warranty. Estimated warranty costs and additional service actions are accrued for at the time the vehicle is sold to a dealer. Included in the warranty cost accruals are costs for basic warranty coverages on vehicles sold. Additional service actions, such as product recalls and other customer service actions, are not included in the warranty reconciliation below, but are also accrued for at the time of sale. Estimates for warranty costs are made based primarily on historical warranty claim experience. The following is a tabular reconciliation of the product warranty accruals (in millions):

	2006	2005
Beginning balance	$ 6,243	$ 5,814
Payments made during the period	(4,106)	(3,986)
Changes in accrual related to warranties issued during the period	3,464	3,949
Changes in accrual related to pre-existing warranties	219	615
Foreign currency translation and other	212	(149)
Ending balance	$ 6,032	$ 6,243

*"We are one of the world's largest producers of cars and trucks combined." 10-K

This will be shown on the consolidated balance sheet as follows:

PARENT P AND SUBSIDIARY
Consolidated Balance Sheet
December 31, 2008

	(In millions)
Current assets	$110
Long-term assets	422
	$532
Current liabilities	$110
Long-term liabilities	220
Minority interest	2
Stockholders' equity	200
	$532

Because of the nature of minority interest, it has usually been presented after liabilities and before stockholders' equity.

Minority interest is seldom material. In a firm where minority interest is material, the analysis can be performed twice—once with minority interest as a liability to be conservative, and then as a stockholders' equity item. Refer to Exhibit 3-17 for an illustration of minority interest.

Other Noncurrent Liabilities

Many other noncurrent liabilities may be disclosed. It would not be practical to discuss all of the possibilities. An example would be deferred profit on sales.

Redeemable Preferred Stock

Redeemable preferred stock is subject to mandatory redemption requirements or has a redemption feature outside the control of the issuer. If this feature is coupled with such characteristics as no vote or fixed return, often preferred stock and bond characteristics, then this type of preferred stock is more like debt than equity. For this reason, the SEC directs that the three categories of stock—redeemable preferred stock, nonredeemable preferred stock, and

Exhibit	3-17	DIODES INCORPORATED AND SUBSIDIARIES*

Minority Interest

DIODES INCORPORATED AND SUBSIDIARIES*
CONSOLIDATED BALANCE SHEETS (in Part)

December 31,	2005	2006
LIABILITIES AND STOCKHOLDERS' EQUITY (in Part)		
CURRENT LIABILITIES (in Part)		
Total Current Liabilities	$ 54,081,000	$ 83,492,000
LONG-TERM DEBT, net of current portion 2.25%		
convertible senior notes due 2026		230,000,000
Others	4,865,000	7,115,000
CAPITAL LEASE OBLIGATIONS, net of current portion	1,618,000	1,477,000
OTHER LONG-TERM LIABILITIES	—	1,101,000
MINORITY INTEREST IN JOINT VENTURE	3,477,000	4,787,000
Total Liabilities	64,041,000	327,972,000
STOCKHOLDERS' EQUITY		
Preferred stock—par value $1.00 per share, 1,000,000		
shares authorized; no shares issued or outstanding	—	—
Common stock—par value $0.66 2/3 per share;		
70,000,000 shares authorized, 25,258,119 and		
25,961,267 issued at 2005 and 2006, respectively	16,839,000	17,308,000
Additional paid-in capital	94,664,000	113,449,000
Retained earnings	114,659,000	162,802,000
Accumulated other comprehensive gain (loss)	(688,000)	608,000
Total stockholders' equity	225,474,000	294,167,000
Total liabilities and stockholders' equity	$289,515,000	$622,139,000

*"We are a global supplier of low pin-count standard semiconductor products."   10-K

common stock—not be totaled in the balance sheet. Further, the stockholders' equity section should not include redeemable preferred stock. Redeemable preferred stock is illustrated in Exhibit 3-18. Because redeemable preferred stock is more like debt than equity, consider it as part of total liabilities for purposes of financial statement analysis.

STOCKHOLDERS' EQUITY

Stockholders' equity is the residual ownership interest in the assets of an entity that remains after deducting its liabilities.[7] Usually divided into two basic categories, paid-in capital and retained earnings, other accounts may appear in stockholders' equity that are usually presented separately from paid-in capital and retained earnings. Other accounts include accumulated other comprehensive income, equity-oriented deferred compensation, and employee stock ownership plans (ESOPs).

Paid-In Capital

The first type of paid-in capital account is capital stock. Two basic types of capital stock are preferred and common.

Both preferred stock and common stock may be issued as par-value stock. (Some states call this *stated value stock*.) The articles of incorporation establish the par value, a designated dollar amount per share. Many states stipulate that the par value of issued stock times the number of shares outstanding constitutes the legal capital. Many states also designate that, if original-issue stock is sold below par value, the buyer is contingently liable for the difference between the par value and the lower amount paid. This does not usually pose a problem because the par value has no direct relationship to market value, the selling price of the stock. To avoid selling a stock below par, the par value is usually set very low in relation to the intended selling price. For example, the intended selling price may be $25.00, and the par value may be $1.00.

Exhibit   3-18   NIKE, INC.*

Redeemable Preferred Stock

NIKE, INC.
Consolidated Balance Sheet

	May 31,	
	2007	2006
	(In millions)	
Total current liabilities	2,584.0	2,612.4
Long-term debt (Note 7)	409.9	410.7
Deferred income taxes and other liabilities (Note 8)	668.7	561.0
Commitments and contingencies (Notes 14 and 16)	—	—
Redeemable Preferred Stock (Note 9)	0.3	0.3
Shareholders' equity:		
Common stock at stated value (Note 10):		
Class A convertible—117.6 and 127.8 shares outstanding	0.1	0.1
Class B—384.1 and 384.2 shares outstanding	2.7	2.7
Capital in excess of stated value	1,960.0	1,447.3
Accumulated other comprehensive income (Note 13)	177.4	121.7
Retained earnings	4,885.2	4,713.4
Total shareholders' equity	7,025.4	6,285.2
Total liabilities and shareholders' equity	$10,688.3	$9,869.6

Notes to Consolidated Financial Statements (in Part)

Note 9—Redeemable Preferred Stock

Sojitz America is the sole owner of the company's authorized Redeemable Preferred Stock, $1 par value, which is redeemable at the option of Sojitz America or the Company at par value aggregating $0.3 million. A cumulative dividend of $0.10 per share is payable annually on May 31 and no dividends may be declared or paid on the common stock of the Company unless dividends on the Redeemable Preferred Stock have been declared and paid in full. There have been no changes in the Redeemable Preferred Stock in the three years ended May 31, 2007, 2006, and 2005. As the holder of the Redeemable Preferred Stock, Sojitz America does not have general voting rights but does have the right to vote as a separate class on the sale of all or substantially all of the assets of the Company and its subsidiaries, on merger, con-solidation, liquidation or dissolution of the Company or on the sale or assignment of the NIKE trademark for athletic footwear sold in the United States.

*"Our principal business activity is the design, development and worldwide marketing of high quality footwear, apparel, equipment, and accessory products." 10-K

Some states allow the issuance of no-par stock (either common or preferred). Some of these states require that the entire proceeds received from the sale of the no-par stock be designated as legal capital.

Additional paid-in capital arises from the excess of amounts paid for stock over the par or stated value of the common and preferred stock. Also included here are amounts over cost from the sale of treasury stock (discussed later in this chapter), capital arising from the dona-tion of assets to the firm, and transfer from retained earnings through stock dividends when the market price of the stock exceeds par.

Common Stock

Common stock shares in all the stockholders' rights and represents ownership that has voting and liquidation rights. Common stockholders elect the board of directors and vote on major corporate decisions. In the event of liquidation, the liquidation rights of common stockholders give them claims to company assets after all creditors' and preferred stockholders' rights have been fulfilled.

Preferred Stock

Preferred stock seldom has voting rights. When preferred stock has voting rights, it is usually because of missed dividends. For example, the preferred stockholders may possibly receive voting rights if their dividends have been missed two consecutive times. Some other preferred stock characteristics include the following:

- Preference as to dividends
- Accumulation of dividends
- Participation in excess of stated dividend rate
- Convertibility into common stock
- Callability by the corporation
- Redemption at future maturity date (see the previous discussion of redeemable preferred stock)
- Preference in liquidation

Preference as to Dividends

When preferred stock has a preference as to dividends, the current year's preferred dividend must be paid before a dividend can be paid to common stockholders. For par-value (or stated value) stock, the dividend rate is usually stated as a percentage of par. For example, if the dividend rate were 6% and the par were $100 per share, then the dividend per share would be $6. For no-par stock, if the dividend rate is stated as $5, then each share should receive $5 if a dividend is paid. A preference as to dividends does not guarantee that a preferred dividend will be paid in a given year. The Board of Directors must declare a dividend before a dividend is paid. The lack of a fixed commitment to pay dividends and the lack of a due date on the principal are the primary reasons that many firms elect to issue preferred stock instead of bonds. Preferred stock usually represents an expensive source of funds, compared to bonds. The preferred stock dividends are not tax deductible, while interest on bonds is deductible.

Accumulation of Dividends

If the Board of Directors does not declare dividends in a particular year, a holder of noncumulative preferred stock will never be paid that dividend. To make the preferred stock more attractive to investors, a corporation typically issues cumulative preferred stock. If a corporation fails to declare the usual dividend on the cumulative preferred stock, the amount of passed dividends becomes **dividends in arrears**. Common stockholders cannot be paid any dividends until the preferred dividends in arrears and the current preferred dividends are paid.

To illustrate dividends in arrears, assume a corporation has outstanding 10,000 shares of 8%, $100 par cumulative preferred stock. If dividends are not declared in 2006 and 2007, but are declared in 2008, the preferred stockholders would be entitled to dividends in arrears of $160,000 and current dividends in 2008 of $80,000 before any dividends could be paid to common stockholders.

Participation in Excess of Stated Dividend Rate

When preferred stock is participating, preferred stockholders may receive an extra dividend beyond the stated dividend rate. The terms of the participation depend on the terms included with the stock certificate. For example, the terms may state that any dividend to common stockholders over $10 per share will also be given to preferred stockholders.

To illustrate participating preferred stock, assume that a corporation has 8%, $100 par preferred stock. The terms of the participation are that any dividend paid on common shares over $10 per share will also be paid to preferred stockholders. For the current year, a dividend of $12 per share is declared on the common stock. Therefore, a dividend of $10 must be paid per share of preferred stock for the current year: $(8\% \times \$100) + \$2.00 = \$10.00$.

Convertibility into Common Stock

Convertible preferred stock contains a provision that allows the preferred stockholders, at their option, to convert the share of preferred stock at a specific exchange ratio into another security of the corporation. The other security is almost always common stock. The conversion feature is very attractive to investors. For example, the terms may be that each share of preferred stock can be converted to four shares of common stock.

Convertible preferred stock is similar to a convertible bond, except that there are no fixed payout commitments with the convertible preferred stock. The preferred dividend need not be declared, and the preferred stock does not have a due date. The major reason for issuing convertible preferred stock is similar to that for issuing convertible bonds: If the current common stock price is low, in the opinion of management, and the firm eventually wants to increase its common equity, then the firm can raise more money for a given number of common shares by first issuing convertible preferred stock.

A firm usually prefers to issue convertible bonds rather than convertible preferred stock if its capital structure can carry more debt without taking on too much risk. The interest on the convertible bond is tax deductible, while the dividend on the preferred stock is not.

Callability by the Corporation

Callable preferred stock may be retired (recalled) by the corporation at its option. The call price is part of the original stock contract. When the preferred stock is also cumulative, the call terms normally require payment of dividends in arrears before the call is executed.

The call provision favors the company because the company decides when to call. Investors do not like call provisions. Therefore, to make a security that has a call provision marketable, the call provision can normally not be exercised for a given number of years. For example, callable preferred stock issued in 2007 may have a provision that the call option cannot be exercised prior to 2017.

Preference in Liquidation

Should the corporation liquidate, the preferred stockholders normally have priority over common stockholders for settlement of claims. However, the claims of preferred stockholders are secondary to the claims of creditors, including bondholders.

Preference in liquidation for preferred stock over common stock is not usually considered to be an important provision. This is because often, in liquidation, funds are not sufficient to pay claims of preferred stock. Even creditors may receive only a few cents on the dollar in satisfaction of their claims.

Disclosures

Preferred stock may carry various combinations of provisions. The provisions of each preferred stock issue should be disclosed either parenthetically in the stockholders' equity section of the balance sheet or in a note. A company may have various preferred stock issues, each with different provisions. Preferred stock is illustrated in Exhibit 3-19.

Donated Capital

Donated capital may be included in the paid-in capital. Capital is donated to the company by stockholders, creditors, or other parties (such as a city). For example, a city may offer land to a company as an inducement to locate a factory there to increase the level of employment. The firm records the donated land at the appraised amount and records an equal amount as donated capital in stockholders' equity.

Another example would be a company that needs to increase its available cash. A plan is devised, calling for existing common stockholders to donate a percentage of their stock to the company. When the stock is sold, the proceeds are added to the cash account, and the donated capital in stockholders' equity is increased. Exhibit 3-20 illustrates the presentation of donated capital by Lands' End.

Retained Earnings

Retained earnings are the undistributed earnings of the corporation—that is, the net income for all past periods minus the dividends (both cash and stock) that have been declared. Retained earnings, cash dividends, and stock dividends are reviewed in more detail in Chapter 4. Exhibit 3-20 illustrates the presentation of retained earnings.

Exhibit	3-19	UNITED STATES STEEL CORPORATION*

Consolidated Balance Sheet (in Part)
Preferred Stock

(Dollars in millions)	December 31,	
	2006	**2005**
Stockholders' Equity		
Series B Mandatory Convertible Preferred shares (no par value, zero and 5,000,000 shares issued, 40,000,000 shares authorized, liquidation preference $50 per share) (*Note 17*)	—	216
Common stock issued—123,785,911 shares and 114,585,727 shares (par value $1 per share, authorized 400,000,000 shares) (*Note 17*)	124	115
Treasury stock, at cost (5,240,810 and 5,799,650 shares)	(317)	(253)
Additional paid-in capital	2,942	3,061
Retained earnings	2,902	1,605
Accumulated other comprehensive loss	(1,286)	(1,418)
Deferred compensation	—	(2)
Total stockholders' equity	4,365	3,324

*"U.S. Steel is an integrated steel producer with major production operations in the United States (U.S.) and Central Europe." 10-K

Exhibit	3-20	LANDS' END, INC. AND SUBSIDIARIES—2002 ANNUAL REPORT

Donated Capital

Consolidated Balance Sheets (in Part)

(In thousands)	February 1, 2002	January 26, 2001
Shareholders' investment		
Common stock, 40,221 shares issued	$ 402	$ 402
Donated capital	8,400	8,400
Additional paid-in capital	39,568	31,908
Deferred compensation	(56)	(121)
Accumulated other comprehensive income	3,343	5,974
Retained earnings	556,003	489,087
Treasury stock, 10,236 and 10,945 shares at cost, respectively	(206,942)	(221,462)
Total shareholders' investment	$ 400,718	$ 314,188

QUASI-REORGANIZATION

A quasi-reorganization is an accounting procedure equivalent to an accounting fresh start. A company with a deficit balance in retained earnings "starts over" with a zero balance rather than a deficit. A quasi-reorganization involves the reclassification of a deficit in retained earnings. It removes the deficit and an equal amount from paid-in capital. A quasi-reorganization may also include a restatement of the carrying values of assets and liabilities to reflect current values.

When a quasi-reorganization is performed, the retained earnings should be dated as of the readjustment date and disclosed in the financial statements for a period of five to ten years. Exhibit 3-21 illustrates a quasi-reorganization of Owens Corning.

ACCUMULATED OTHER COMPREHENSIVE INCOME

Conceptually, accumulated other comprehensive income represents retained earnings from other comprehensive income. In addition to the aggregate amount, companies are required to

| *Exhibit* | *3-21* | OWENS CORNING* |

Quasi-Reorganization
For the Fiscal Year Ended December 31, 2006

Owens Corning and Subsidiaries
Notes to Consolidated Financial Statements (in Part)

3. FRESH-START ACCOUNTING (in Part)

On the Effective Date, the Company adopted fresh-start accounting in accordance with SoP 90-7. This resulted in a new reporting entity on November 1, 2006, which has a new basis of accounting, a new capital structure and no retained earnings or accumulated losses. The Company was required to implement fresh-start accounting as the holders of existing voting shares immediately before confirmation received less than 50% of the voting shares of the Successor Company. The fresh-start accounting principles pursuant to SoP 90-7 provide, among other things, for the Company to determine the value to be assigned to the equity of the reorganized Company as of a date selected for financial reporting purposes.

The reorganization value represents the amount of resources available for the satisfaction of post-petition liabilities and allowed claims, as negotiated between the Company and its creditors. The Company's total enterprise value at the time of emergence was $5.8 billion, with a total value for common equity of $3.7 billion, including the estimated fair value of the Series A Warrants and Service B Warrants issued on the Effective Date.

In accordance with fresh-start accounting, the reorganization value of the Company was allocated based on the fair market values of the assets and liabilities in accordance with SFAS 141. The fair values represented the Company's best estimates at the Effective Date based on internal and external appraisals and valuations. Liabilities existing at the Effective Date, other than deferred taxes, were stated at present values of amounts to be paid determined at appropriate current interest rates. Any portion not attributed to specific tangible or identified intangible assets was recorded as goodwill. While the Company believes that the enterprise value approximates fair value, differences between the methodology used in testing for goodwill impairment, as discussed in Note 10, and the negotiated value could adversely impact the Company's results of operations.

Pursuant to SoP 90-7, the results of operations of the ten months ended October 31, 2006 include a pre-emergence gain on the cancellation of debt of $5.9 billion resulting from the discharge of liabilities subject to compromise and other liabilities under the Plan; and a pre-emergence gain of $2.2 billion, net of tax, resulting from the aggregate remaining changes to the net carrying value of the Company's pre-emergence assets and liabilities to reflect the fair values under fresh-start accounting.

**Application of fresh-start accounting at October 31, 2006.

*"Owens Corning, a global company incorporated in Delaware, is headquartered in Toledo, Ohio, and is a leading producer of residential and commercial building materials and glass fiber reinforcements and other similar materials for composite systems." 10-K

disclose the separate categories that make up accumulated other comprehensive income. The disclosure of the separate components can be made on the face of the balance sheet, in the statement of stockholders' equity, or in the notes. Chapter 4 covers comprehensive income. Exhibit 3-20 illustrates the presentation of accumulated other comprehensive income.

EQUITY-ORIENTED DEFERRED COMPENSATION

Equity-oriented deferred compensation arrangements encompass a wide variety of plans. The deferred compensation element of an equity-based deferred compensation arrangement is the amount of compensation cost deferred and amortized (expensed) to future periods as the services are provided.

If stock is issued in a plan before some or all of the services are performed, the unearned compensation should be shown as a reduction to stockholders' equity. This unearned compensation amount should be accounted for as an expense of future period(s) as services are performed. Thus, the unearned compensation amount is removed from stockholders' equity (amortized) and is recognized as an expense in future periods.

When a plan involves the potential issuance of only stock, then the unearned compensation is shown as a reduction in stockholders' equity, and the offsetting amount is also in the stockholders' equity section. If the plan involves cash or a subsequent election of either cash or stock, the unearned compensation appears as a reduction in stockholders' equity, and the offsetting amount appears as a liability.

Exhibit 3-22 illustrates an equity-oriented deferred compensation plan for Isle of Capri Casinos, Inc. It is apparently a stock-only plan. The deferred compensation will be amortized to expense over subsequent periods.

Exhibit 3-22	ISLE OF CAPRI CASINOS, INC.*

Equity-Oriented Deferred Revenue Compensation

(In thousands)	April 24, 2005	April 25, 2004
Stockholders' equity:		
Preferred stock, $.01 par value; 2,000 shares authorized; none issued	—	—
Common stock, $.01 par value; 45,000 shares authorized; shares issued and outstanding: 33,528 at April 24, 2005 and 33,055 at April 25, 2004	$ 335	$ 330
Class B common stock, $.01 par value; 3,000 shares authorized; none issued	—	—
Additional paid-in capital	148,177	143,385
Unearned compensation	(1,488)	(1,413)
Retained earnings	146,133	128,095
Accumulated other comprehensive income	2,858	521
	296,015	270,918
Treasury stock, 3,607 shares at April 24, 2005 and 3,338 shares at April 25, 2004	(34,619)	(29,512)
Total stockholders' equity	$261,396	$241,406

Notes to Consolidated Financial Statements (in Part)

II. Common Stock (in Part)

Stock-Based Compensation—Deferred Bonus Plan

In the fiscal 2001, the Company's stockholders approved the Deferred Bonus Plan. The Plan provides for the issuance of non-vested stock to eligible officers and employees who agree to receive a deferred bonus in the form of non-vested stock. The vesting of the stock is dependent upon continued service to the Company for a period of five years. At April 24, 2005, the non-vested stock issued in connection with the Plan totaled 203,687 shares, of which 36,400 shares were issued during fiscal year ended April 24, 2005 at $23.80, the weighted-average fair value of the non-vested stock at the grant date. For the fiscal year ended April 24, 2005, the Company recorded an unearned compensation contra account in consolidated stockholders' equity equal to the fair value of the non-vested award and recorded compensation expense for the portion of unearned compensation that had been earned through April 24, 2005. Compensation expense related to stock-based compensation under the Deferred Bonus Plan totaled $606,000 in fiscal 2005, $605,000 in fiscal 2004, and $617,000 in fiscal 2003.

*"We are a leading developer, owner and operator of branded games facilities and related lodging and entertainment facilities in growing markets in the United States and internationally." 10-K

Employee Stock Ownership Plans (ESOPs)

An **employee stock ownership plan (ESOP)** is a qualified stock-bonus, or combination stock-bonus and money-purchase pension plan, designed to invest primarily in the employer's securities. A qualified plan must satisfy certain requirements of the Internal Revenue Code. An ESOP must be a permanent trusteed plan for the exclusive benefit of the employees.

The trust that is part of the plan is exempt from tax on its income, and the employer/sponsor gets a current deduction for contributions to the plan. The plan participants become eligible for favorable taxation of distributions from the plan.

An ESOP may borrow the funds necessary to purchase the employer stock. These funds may be borrowed from the company, its stockholders, or a third party such as a bank. The company can guarantee the loan to the ESOP. Financial leverage—the ability of the ESOP to borrow in order to buy employer securities—is an important aspect.

The Internal Revenue Code favors borrowing for an ESOP. Commercial lending institutions, insurance companies, and mutual funds are permitted an exclusion from income for 50% of the interest received on loans used to finance an ESOP's acquisition of company stock. Thus, these institutions are willing to charge a reduced rate of interest for the loan.

From a company's perspective, there are advantages and disadvantages to an ESOP. One advantage is that an ESOP serves as a source of funds for expansion at a reasonable rate. Other possible advantages follow:

1. A means to buy the stock from a major shareholder or possibly an unwanted shareholder.
2. Help financing a leveraged buyout.
3. Reduction of potential of an unfriendly takeover.
4. Help in creating a market for the company's stock.

Some firms do not find an ESOP attractive, because it can result in a significant amount of voting stock in the hands of their employees. Existing stockholders may not find an ESOP desirable because it will probably dilute their proportional ownership.

The employer contribution to an ESOP reduces cash, and an unearned compensation item decreases stockholders' equity. The unearned compensation is amortized on the income statement in subsequent periods. When an ESOP borrows funds and the firm (in either an informal or formal guarantee) commits to future contributions to the ESOP to meet the debt-service requirements, then the firm records this commitment as a liability and as a deferred compensation deduction within stockholders' equity. As the debt is liquidated, the liability and deferred compensation are reduced.

Exhibit 3-23 shows the reporting of the ESOP of The Hershey Company.

Treasury Stock

A firm creates **treasury stock** when it repurchases its own stock and does not retire it. Since treasury stock lowers the stock outstanding, it is subtracted from stockholders' equity. Treasury stock is, in essence, a reduction in paid-in capital.

A firm may record treasury stock in two ways. One method records the treasury stock at par or stated value, referred to as the par value method of recording treasury stock. This method removes the paid-in capital in excess of par (or stated value) from the original issue. The treasury stock appears as a reduction of paid-in capital.

The other method, referred to as the *cost method*, records treasury stock at the cost of the stock (presented as a reduction of stockholders' equity). Most firms record treasury stock at cost.

Exhibit 3-24 illustrates the presentation of treasury stock for Dow Jones & Company. Note that a firm cannot record gains or losses from dealing in its own stock. Any apparent gains or losses related to treasury stock must impact stockholders' equity, such as a reduction in retained earnings.

Stockholders' Equity in Unincorporated Firms

These firms do not have stockholders. Stockholders' equity in an unincorporated firm is termed capital. The amount invested by the owner plus the retained earnings may be shown

Exhibit 3-23	THE HERSHEY COMPANY*

Employee Stock Ownership (ESOP)

(In thousands of dollars)	December 31,	
	2006	**2005**
Stockholders' Equity:		
Preferred Stock, shares issued: none in 2006 and 2005	—	—
Common Stock, shares issued: 299,085,666 in 2006 and 299,083,266 in 2005	299,085	299,083
Class B Common Stock, shares issued: 60,816,078 in 2006 and 60,818,478 in 2005	60,816	60,818
Additional paid-in capital	298,243	252,374
Unearned ESOP compensation	—	(3,193)
Retained earnings	3,965,415	3,641,483
Treasury—Common Stock shares, at cost: 129,638,183 in 2006 and 119,377,690 in 2005	(3,801,947)	(3,224,863)
Accumulated other comprehensive loss	(138,189)	(9,322)
Total stockholders' equity	683,423	1,016,380

Notes to Consolidated Financial Statements (in Part)

13. EMPLOYEE STOCK OWNERSHIP TRUST

Our Company's employee stock ownership trust ("ESOP") serves as the primary vehicle for employer contributions to The Hershey Company 401(k) Plan (formerly known as The Hershey Company Employee Savings Stock Investment and Ownership Plan) for participating domestic salaried and hourly employees. In December 1991, we funded the ESOP by providing a 15-year, 7.75% loan of $47.9 million. The ESOP used the proceeds of the loan to purchase our Common Stock. During 2006 and 2005, the ESOP received a combination of dividends on unallocated shares of our Common Stock and contributions from us. This equals the amount required to meet principal and interest payments under the loan. Simultaneously, the ESOP allocated to participants 318,351 shares of our Common Stock each year. As of December 31, 2006, all shares had been allocated. We consider all ESOP shares as outstanding for income per share computations.

The following table summarizes our ESOP expense and dividends:

For the year ended December 31,	2006	2005	2004
In millions of dollars			
Compensation (income) expense related to ESOP	$(.3)	$.4	$(.1)
Dividends paid on unallocated ESOP shares	.3	.5	.7

- We recognized net compensation expense equal to the shares allocated multiplied by the original cost of $10.03 per share less dividends received by the ESOP on unallocated shares.
- We reflect dividends paid on all ESOP shares as a reduction to retained earnings.

*"We are the largest North American manufacturer of quality chocolate and confectionery products and a leading snack food company." 10-K

as one sum. A sole proprietorship form of business has only one owner (one capital account). A partnership form of business has more than one owner (capital account for each owner). Chapter 2 reviewed these forms of business.

Statement of Stockholders' Equity

Firms are required to present reconciliations of the beginning and ending balances of their stockholder accounts. This is accomplished by presenting a "statement of stockholders' equity."

Exhibit	3-24	DOW JONES & COMPANY*

Treasury Stock

Consolidated Balance Sheets (in Part)
(Dollars in thousands, except per share amounts)

Stockholders' Equity	As of December 31,	
	2006	2005
Common stock, par value $1 per share; authorized 135,000,000 shares; issued 82,095,954 in 2006 and 81,737,520 in 2005	$ 82,096	$ 81,738
Class B common stock, convertible, par value $1 per share; authorized 25,000,000 shares; issued 20,085,067 in 2006 and 20,443,501 in 2005	20,085	20,443
	102,181	102,181
Additional paid-in capital	141,628	137,290
Retained earnings	1,120,165	817,168
Accumulated other comprehensive income, net of taxes:		
Unrealized gain on investments	563	2,636
Unrealized gain (loss) on hedging	175	(198)
Foreign currency translation adjustment	3,682	3,430
Defined benefit plan adjustments	(20,141)	(28,861)
	1,348,253	1,033,646
Less, treasury stock, at cost; 18,534,499 shares in 2006 and 19,074,641 shares in 2005	849,280	871,381
Total stockholders' equity	498,973	162,265
Total liabilities and stockholders' equity	$1,955,562	$1,781,972

*"We are a provider of global business and financial news, information and insight through multiple channels of media." 10-K

This statement will include all of the stockholders' equity accounts. It is important when performing analysis to be aware of changes in these accounts. For example, common stock will indicate changes in common stock, retained earnings will indicate changes in retained earnings, and treasury stock will indicate changes in treasury stock. This statement is illustrated in Chapter 4.

For many firms, changes to the account Accumulated Other Comprehensive Income (Loss) will be important to observe. This account is related to comprehensive income, which is covered in Chapter 4.

Problems in Balance Sheet Presentation

Numerous problems inherent in balance sheet presentation may cause difficulty in analysis. First, many assets are valued at cost, so one cannot determine the market value or replacement cost of many assets and should not assume that their balance sheet amount approximates current valuation.

Second, varying methods are used for asset valuation. For example, inventories may be valued differently from firm to firm and, within a firm, from product to product. Similar problems exist with long-term asset valuation and the related depreciation alternatives.

A different type of problem exists in that not all items of value to the firm are included as assets. For example, such characteristics as good employees, outstanding management, and a well-chosen location do not appear on the balance sheet. In the same vein, liabilities related to contingencies also may not appear on the balance sheet. Chapters 6 and 7 present many of the problems of the balance sheet.

These problems do not make statement analysis impossible. They merely require that qualitative judgment be applied to quantitative data in order to assess the impact of these problem areas.

Summary

The balance sheet shows the financial condition of an accounting entity as of a particular date. It is the most basic financial statement, and it is read by various users as part of their decision-making process.

to the net

1. Go to the SEC Web site (http://www.sec.gov). Under "Filings & Forms (EDGAR)," click on "Search for Company Filings." Click on "Companies & Other Filers." Under Company Name, enter "Cooper Tire" (or under Ticker Symbol, enter "CTB"). Select the 10-K filed March 1, 2007.

   a. What is the total stockholders' equity at December 31, 2006?

   b. What is the cost of treasury shares at December 31, 2006?

   c. Why is treasury stock subtracted from stockholders' equity?

2. Go to the SEC Web site (http://www.sec.gov). Under "Filings & Forms (EDGAR)," click on "Search for Company Filings." Click on "Companies & Other Filers." Under Company Name, enter "Yahoo" (or under Ticker Symbol, enter "YHOO"). Select the 10-K filed February 23, 2007.

   a. What is the total current assets at December 31, 2006?

   b. What is the net intangibles at December 31, 2006?

   c. Why are intangibles amortized?

3. Go to the SEC Web site (http://www.sec.gov). Under "Filings & Forms (EDGAR)," click on "Search for Company Filings." Click on "Companies & Other Filers." Under Company Name, enter "Boeing Co" (or under Ticker Symbol, enter "BA"). Select the 10-K filed February 16, 2007.

   a. What is the total for inventories at December 31, 2006?

   b. Go to Note 1, Summary of Significant Accounting Policies. Go to Inventories. Describe the inventory policy, consistent with industry practice, that is unique for this industry. How does this practice impact liquidity appearance?

4. Go to the SEC Web site (http://www.sec.gov). Under "Filings & Forms (EDGAR)," click on "Search for Company Filings." Click on "Companies & Other Filers." Under Company Name, enter "Gateway Inc" (or under Ticker Symbol, enter "GTW"). Select the 10-K filed February 26, 2007.

   a. What is the balance in accrued warranty at December 31, 2006?

   b. Comment on the subjectivity in determining this balance.

5. Go to the SEC Web site (http://www.sec.gov). Under "Filings & Forms (EDGAR)," click on "Search for Company Filings." Click on "Companies & Other Filers." Under Company Name, enter "McDonalds" (or under Ticker Symbol, enter "MCD"). Select the 10-K filed February 26, 2007.

   a. What is the total assets at December 31, 2006?

   b. What is the total for investments in and advances to affiliates at December 31, 2006?

   c. In your opinion, are the companies receiving the "investments in and advances to affiliates" consolidated with McDonald's Corporation? Comment.

   d. Considering the balance in "investments in and advances to affiliates" in relation to "total assets," does this relationship of dollars likely represent the importance of affiliates to McDonald's Corporation? Comment.

6. Go to the SEC Web site (http://www.sec.gov). Under "Filings & Forms (EDGAR)," click on "Search for Company Filings." Click on "Companies & Other Filers." Under Company Name, enter "Hershey Food" (or under Ticker Symbol, enter "HSY"). Select the 10-K filed February 23, 2007.

   a. Note 13. Employee Stock Ownership Trust. Briefly describe the purpose of this plan.

   b. Note 14. Capital Stock and Net Income per Share. Comment on the voting control of Milton Hershey School Trust.

Questions

Q 3-1.   Name and describe the three major categories of balance sheet accounts.

Q 3-2.   Are the following balance sheet items (A) assets, (L) liabilities, or (E) stockholders' equity?
      a. Cash dividends payable
      b. Mortgage notes payable
      c. Investments in stock
      d. Cash
      e. Land
      f. Inventory
      g. Unearned rent
      h. Marketable securities
      i. Patents
      j. Capital stock
      k. Retained earnings
      l. Donated capital
      m. Accounts receivable
      n. Taxes payable
      o. Accounts payable
      p. Organizational costs
      q. Prepaid expenses
      r. Goodwill
      s. Tools
      t. Buildings

Q 3-3.   Classify the following as (CA) current asset, (IV) investments, (IA) intangible asset, or (TA) tangible asset:
      a. Land
      b. Cash
      c. Copyrights
      d. Marketable securities
      e. Goodwill
      f. Inventories
      g. Tools
      h. Prepaids
      i. Buildings
      j. Accounts receivable
      k. Long-term investment in stock
      l. Machinery

Q 3-4.   Usually, current assets are listed in a specific order, starting with cash. What is the objective of this order of listing?

Q 3-5.   Differentiate between marketable securities and long-term investments. What is the purpose of owning each?

Q 3-6.   Differentiate between accounts receivable and accounts payable.

Q 3-7.   What types of inventory will a retailing firm have? A manufacturing firm?

Q 3-8.   What is depreciation? Which tangible assets are depreciated, and which are not? Why?

Q 3-9.   For reporting purposes, management prefers higher profits; for tax purposes, lower taxable income is desired. To meet these goals, firms often use different methods of depreciation for tax and reporting purposes. Which depreciation method is best for reporting and which for tax purposes? Why?

Q 3-10.   A rental agency collects rent in advance. Why is the rent collected treated as a liability?

Q 3-11.   A bond carries a stated rate of interest of 6% and par of $1,000. It matures in 20 years. It is sold at 83 (83% of $1,000, or $830).
      a. Under normal conditions, why would the bond sell at less than par?
      b. How would the discount be disclosed on the statements?

Q 3-12.   To be conservative, how should minority interest on the balance sheet be handled for primary analysis?

Q 3-13.   Many assets are presented at historical cost. Why does this accounting principle cause difficulties in financial statement analysis?

Q 3-14.   Explain how the issuance of a convertible bond can be a very attractive means of raising common equity funds.

Q 3-15.   Classify each of the following as a (CA) current asset, (NA) noncurrent asset, (CL) current liability, (NL) noncurrent liability, or (E) equity account. Choose the best or most frequently used classification.

a. Supplies   k. Wages payable
b. Notes receivable   l. Mortgage bonds payable
c. Unearned subscription revenue   m. Unearned interest
d. Accounts payable   n. Marketable securities
e. Retained earnings   o. Paid-in capital from sale of treasury stock
f. Accounts receivable   p. Land
g. Preferred stock   q. Inventories
h. Plant   r. Taxes accrued
i. Prepaid rent   s. Cash
j. Capital

Q 3-16.   Explain these preferred stock characteristics:
a. Accumulation of dividends
b. Participation in excess of stated dividend rate
c. Convertibility into common stock
d. Callability by the corporation
e. Preference in liquidation

Q 3-17.   Describe the account Unrealized Exchange Gains or Losses.

Q 3-18.   What is treasury stock? Why is it deducted from stockholders' equity?

Q 3-19.   A firm, with no opening inventory, buys 10 units at $6 each during the period. In which accounts might the $60 appear on the financial statements?

Q 3-20.   How is an unconsolidated subsidiary presented on a balance sheet?

Q 3-21.   When would minority interest be presented on a balance sheet?

Q 3-22.   DeLand Company owns 100% of Little Florida, Inc. Will DeLand Company show a minority interest on its balance sheet? Would the answer change if it owned only 60%? Will there ever be a case in which the subsidiary, Little Florida, is not consolidated?

Q 3-23.   Describe the item Unrealized Decline in Market Value of Noncurrent Equity Investments.

Q 3-24.   What is redeemable preferred stock? Why should it be included with debt for purposes of financial statement analysis?

Q 3-25.   Describe donated capital.

Q 3-26.   Assume that a city donated land to a company. What accounts would be affected by this donation, and what would be the value?

Q 3-27.   Describe quasi-reorganization.

Q 3-28.   Assume that an equity-oriented deferred compensation plan involves cash or a subsequent election of either cash or stock. Describe the presentation of this plan on the balance sheet.

Q 3-29.   Describe employee stock ownership plans (ESOPs).

Q 3-30.   Why are commercial lending institutions, insurance companies, and mutual funds willing to grant loans to an employee stock ownership plan at favorable rates?

Q 3-31.   What are some possible disadvantages of an employee stock ownership plan?

Q 3-32.   How does a company recognize, in an informal or a formal way, that it has guaranteed commitments to future contributions to an ESOP to meet debt-service requirements?

Q 3-33.   Describe depreciation, amortization, and depletion. How do they differ?

Q 3-34.   What are the three factors usually considered when computing depreciation?

Q 3-35.   An accelerated system of depreciation is often used for income tax purposes but not for financial reporting. Why?

Q 3-36.   Which depreciation method will result in the most depreciation over the life of an asset?

Q-3-37.   Should depreciation be recognized on a building in a year in which the cost of replacing the building rises? Explain.

Q 3-38.   Describe the account Accumulated Other Comprehensive Income.

Problems

P 3-1.   The following information was obtained from the accounts of Airlines International dated December 31, 2008. It is presented in alphabetical order.

Accounts payable	$ 77,916
Accounts receivable	67,551
Accrued expenses	23,952
Accumulated depreciation	220,541
Allowance for doubtful accounts	248
Capital in excess of par	72,913
Cash	28,837
Common stock (par $0.50, authorized 20,000 shares, issued 14,304 shares)	7,152
Current installments of long-term debt	36,875
Deferred income tax liability (long term)	42,070
Inventory	16,643
Investments and special funds	11,901
Long-term debt, less current portion	393,808
Marketable securities	10,042
Other assets	727
Prepaid expenses	3,963
Property, plant, and equipment at cost	809,980
Retained earnings	67,361
Unearned transportation revenue (airline tickets expiring within one year)	6,808

Required   Prepare a classified balance sheet in report form.

P 3-2.   The following information was obtained from the accounts of Lukes, Inc., as of December 31, 2008. It is presented in scrambled order.

Common stock, no par value, 10,000 shares authorized, 5,724 shares issued	$ 3,180
Retained earnings	129,950
Deferred income tax liability (long term)	24,000
Long-term debt	99,870
Accounts payable	35,000
Buildings	75,000
Machinery and equipment	300,000
Land	11,000
Accumulated depreciation	200,000
Cash	3,000
Receivables, less allowance of $3,000	58,000
Accrued income taxes	3,000
Inventory	54,000
Other accrued expenses	8,000
Current portion of long-term debt	7,000
Prepaid expenses	2,000
Other assets (long term)	7,000

Required   Prepare a classified balance sheet in report form. For assets, use the classifications of current assets, plant and equipment, and other assets. For liabilities, use the classifications of current liabilities and long-term liabilities.

P 3-3.   The following information was obtained from the accounts of Alleg, Inc., as of December 31, 2008. It is presented in scrambled order.

Common stock, authorized 21,000 shares at $1 par value, issued 10,000 shares	$ 10,000
Additional paid-in capital	38,000
Cash	13,000
Marketable securities	17,000
Accounts receivable	26,000
Accounts payable	15,000
Current maturities of long-term debt	11,000
Mortgages payable	80,000
Bonds payable	70,000
Inventory	30,000
Land and buildings	57,000
Machinery and equipment	125,000
Goodwill	8,000
Patents	10,000
Other assets	50,000
Deferred income taxes (long-term liability)	18,000
Retained earnings	33,000
Accumulated depreciation	61,000

Required   Prepare a classified balance sheet in report form. For assets, use the classifications of current assets, plant and equipment, intangibles, and other assets. For liabilities, use the classifications of current liabilities and long-term liabilities.

P 3-4.   The following is the balance sheet of Ingram Industries:

INGRAM INDUSTRIES
Balance Sheet
June 30, 2008

Assets

Current assets:		
Cash (including $13,000 in sinking fund for bonds payable)	$ 70,000	
Marketable securities	23,400	
Investment in subsidiary company	23,000	
Accounts receivable	21,000	
Inventories (lower-of-cost-or-market)	117,000	$254,400
Plant assets:		
Land and buildings	$160,000	
Less: Accumulated depreciation	100,000	60,000
Investments:		
Treasury stock		4,000
Deferred charges:		
Discount on bonds payable	$ 6,000	
Prepaid expenses	2,000	8,000
		$326,400

Liabilities and Stockholders' Equity

Liabilities:		
Notes payable to bank	$ 60,000	
Accounts payable	18,000	
Bonds payable	61,000	
Total liabilities		$139,000
Stockholders' equity:		
Preferred and common (each $10 par, 5,000 shares preferred and 6,000 shares common)	$110,000	
Capital in excess of par	61,000	
Retained earnings	16,400	
		187,400
Total liabilities and stockholders' equity		$326,400

Required   Indicate your criticisms of the balance sheet and briefly explain the proper treatment of any item criticized.

P 3-5.   The following is the balance sheet of Rubber Industries:

RUBBER INDUSTRIES
Balance Sheet
For the Year Ended December 31, 2008

Assets

Current assets:	
Cash	$ 50,000
Marketable equity securities	19,000
Accounts receivable, net	60,000
Inventory	30,000
Treasury stock	20,000
Total current assets	$179,000
Plant assets:	
Land and buildings, net	160,000
Investments:	
Short-term U.S. notes	20,000
Other assets:	
Supplies	4,000
Total assets	$363,000

Liabilities and Stockholders' Equity

Liabilities:	
Bonds payable	$123,000
Accounts payable	40,000
Wages payable	10,000
Total liabilities	$173,000
Stockholders' equity:	
Common stock ($20 par, 20,000 shares authorized,	
6,000 shares outstanding)	120,000
Retained earnings	50,000
Redeemable preferred stock	20,000
Total liabilities and stockholders' equity	$363,000

Required   Indicate your criticisms of the balance sheet and briefly explain the proper treatment of any item criticized.

P 3-6.   The following is the balance sheet of McDonald Company:

McDONALD COMPANY
December 31, 2008

Assets

Current assets:			
Cash (including $10,000 restricted for payment of note)		$ 40,000	
Marketable equity securities		20,000	
Accounts receivable, less allowance			
for doubtful accounts of $12,000		70,000	
Inventory		60,000	
Total current assets			$190,000
Plant assets:			
Land		$ 40,000	
Buildings, net		100,000	
Equipment	$80,000		
Less: Accumulated depreciation	20,000	60,000	
Patent		20,000	
Organizational costs		15,000	
			235,000
Other assets:			
Prepaid insurance			5,000
Total assets			$430,000

(continued)

Liabilities and Stockholders' Equity

Current liabilities:		
Accounts payable	$ 60,000	
Wages payable	10,000	
Notes payable, due July 1, 2012	20,000	
Bonds payable, due December 2016	100,000	
Total current liabilities		$190,000
Dividends payable		4,000
Deferred tax liability, long term		30,000
Stockholders' equity:		
Common stock ($10 par, 10,000		
shares authorized, 5,000 shares outstanding)	$ 50,000	
Retained earnings	156,000	
Total stockholders' equity		206,000
Total liabilities and stockholders' equity		$430,000

Required Indicate your criticisms of the balance sheet and briefly explain the proper treatment of any item criticized.

P 3-7. You have just started as a staff auditor for a small CPA firm. During the course of the audit, you discover the following items related to a single client firm:

a. During the year, the firm declared and paid $10,000 in dividends.

b. Your client has been named defendant in a legal suit involving a material amount. You have received from the client's counsel a statement indicating little likelihood of loss.

c. Because of cost control actions and general employee dissatisfaction, it is likely that the client will suffer a costly strike in the near future.

d. Twenty days after closing, the client suffered a major fire in one of its plants.

e. The cash account includes a substantial amount set aside for payment of pension obligations.

f. Marketable securities include a large quantity of shares of stock purchased for control purposes.

g. Land is listed on the balance sheet at its market value of $1,000,000. It cost $670,000 to purchase 12 years ago.

h. During the year, the government of Uganda expropriated a plant located in that country. There was substantial loss.

Required How would each of these items be reflected in the year-end balance sheet, including notes?

P 3-8. Corvallis Corporation owns 80% of the stock of Little Harrisburg, Inc. At December 31, 2008, Little Harrisburg had the following summarized balance sheet:

LITTLE HARRISBURG, INC.
Balance Sheet
December 31, 2008

Current assets	$100,000	Current liabilities	$ 50,000
Property, plant, and		Long-term debt	150,000
equipment (net)	400,000	Capital stock	50,000
		Retained earnings	250,000
	$500,000		$500,000

The earnings of Little Harrisburg, Inc., for 2008 were $50,000 after tax.

Required a. What would be the amount of minority interest on the balance sheet of Corvallis Corporation? How should minority interest be classified for financial statement analysis purposes?

b. What would be the minority share of earnings on the income statement of Corvallis Corporation?

P 3-9. Aggarwal Company has had 10,000 shares of 10%, $100 par-value preferred stock and 80,000 shares of $5 stated-value common stock outstanding for the last three years. During that period, dividends paid totaled $0, $200,000, and $220,000 for each year, respectively.

Required Compute the amount of dividends that must have been paid to preferred stockholders and common stockholders in each of the three years, given the following four independent assumptions:

a. Preferred stock is nonparticipating and cumulative.

b. Preferred stock participates up to 12% of its par value and is cumulative.

c. Preferred stock is fully participating and cumulative.

d. Preferred stock is nonparticipating and noncumulative.

P 3-10.   Rosewell Company has had 5,000 shares of 9%, $100 par-value preferred stock and 10,000 shares of $10 par-value common stock outstanding for the last two years. During the most recent year, dividends paid totaled $65,000; in the prior year, dividends paid totaled $40,000.

Required   Compute the amount of dividends that must have been paid to preferred stockholders and common stock-holders in each year, given the following independent assumptions:
a. Preferred stock is fully participating and cumulative.
b. Preferred stock is nonparticipating and noncumulative.
c. Preferred stock participates up to 10% of its par value and is cumulative.
d. Preferred stock is nonparticipating and cumulative.

P 3-11.   An item of equipment acquired on January 1 at a cost of $100,000 has an estimated life of 10 years.

Required   Assuming that the equipment will have a salvage value of $10,000, determine the depreciation for each of the first three years by the:
a. Straight-line method
b. Declining-balance method
c. Sum-of-the-years'-digits method

P 3-12.   An item of equipment acquired on January 1 at a cost of $60,000 has an estimated use of 25,000 hours. During the first three years, the equipment was used 5,000 hours, 6,000 hours, and 4,000 hours, respectively. The estimated salvage value of the equipment is $10,000.

Required   Determine the depreciation for each of the three years, using the unit-of-production method.

P 3-13.   An item of equipment acquired on January 1 at a cost of $50,000 has an estimated life of five years and an estimated salvage of $10,000.

Required   a. From a management perspective, from among the straight-line method, declining-balance method, and sum-of-the-years'-digits method of depreciation, which method should be chosen for the financial statements if income is to be at a maximum the first year? Which method should be chosen for the income tax returns, assuming that the tax rate stays the same each year? Explain and show computations.
b. Is it permissible to use different depreciation methods in financial statements than those used in tax returns?

P 3-14.

Required   Answer the following multiple-choice questions:
a. Which of the following accounts would *not* appear on a conventional balance sheet?
    1. Accounts Receivable
    2. Accounts Payable
    3. Patents
    4. Gain from Sale of Land
    5. Common Stock
b. Current assets typically include all but which of the following assets?
    1. Cash restricted for the retirement of bonds
    2. Unrestricted cash
    3. Marketable securities
    4. Receivables
    5. Inventories
c. The Current Liabilities section of the balance sheet should include
    1. Land.
    2. Cash Surrender Value of Life Insurance.
    3. Accounts Payable.
    4. Bonds Payable.
    5. Preferred Stock.

d. Inventories are the balance of goods on hand. In a manufacturing firm, they include all but which of the following?
   1. Raw materials
   2. Work in process
   3. Finished goods
   4. Supplies
   5. Construction in process

e. Which of the following accounts would *not* usually be classified as a current liability?
   1. Accounts Payable
   2. Wages Payable
   3. Unearned Rent Income
   4. Bonds Payable
   5. Taxes Payable

f. For the issuing firm, redeemable preferred stock should be classified where for analysis purposes?
   1. Marketable security
   2. Long-term investment
   3. Intangible
   4. Liabilities
   5. Shareholders' equity

g. Which of the following accounts would *not* be classified as an intangible?
   1. Goodwill
   2. Patent
   3. Accounts Receivable
   4. Trademarks
   5. Franchises

h. Which of the following is *not* true relating to intangibles?
   1. Research and development usually represents a significant intangible on the financial statements.
   2. Goodwill arises from the acquisition of a business for a sum greater than the physical asset value.
   3. Purchased goodwill is not amortized but is subject to annual impairment reviews.
   4. The global treatment of goodwill varies significantly.
   5. Intangibles are usually amortized over their useful lives or legal lives, whichever is shorter.

i. Growth Company had total assets of $100,000 and total liabilities of $60,000. What is the balance of the stockholders' equity?
   1. $0
   2. $40,000
   3. $60,000
   4. $100,000
   5. None of the above

j. The Current Assets section of the balance sheet should include
   1. Inventory.
   2. Taxes Payable.
   3. Land.
   4. Patents.
   5. Bonds Payable.

k. Which of the following is *not* a typical current liability?
   1. Accounts payable
   2. Wages payable
   3. Interest payable
   4. Pension liabilities
   5. Taxes payable

l. Which of the following is a current liability?
   1. Unearned rent income
   2. Prepaid interest
   3. Land
   4. Common stock
   5. None of the above

m. Treasury stock is best classified as a
   1. Current liability.
   2. Current asset.
   3. Reduction of stockholders' equity.
   4. Contra asset.
   5. Contra liability.

IT'S A TRIP

The August 26, 2006, and August 27, 2005, consolidated balance sheets of Winnebago Industries, Inc.* follow:

Winnebago Industries, Inc.
Consolidated Balance Sheets

(In thousands, except per share data)	August 26, 2006	August 27, 2005
Assets		
Current assets:		
Cash and cash equivalents	$ 24,934	$ 19,484
Short-term investments	129,950	93,100
Receivables, less allowance for doubtful accounts ($164 and $270, respectively)	20,859	40,910
Inventories	77,081	120,655
Prepaid expenses and other assets	5,269	4,333
Deferred income taxes	9,067	9,610
Total current assets	267,160	288,092
Property and equipment, at cost:		
Land	946	1,000
Buildings	59,378	60,282
Machinery and equipment	99,839	100,601
Transportation equipment	9,561	9,487
Total property and equipment, at cost	169,724	171,370
Accumulated depreciation	(112,817)	(107,517)
Total property and equipment, net	56,907	63,853
Investment in life insurance	20,814	22,066
Deferred income taxes	25,002	24,997
Other assets	14,832	13,952
Total assets	$ 384,715	$ 412,960
Liabilities and Stockholders' Equity		
Current liabilities:		
Accounts payable	$ 27,923	$ 34,660
Income taxes payable	7,876	4,458
Accrued expenses:		
Accrued compensation	12,498	16,380
Product warranties	9,523	12,183
Self-insurance	7,842	6,728
Promotional	5,253	5,495
Accrued dividends	3,109	2,963
Other	6,098	7,756
Total current liabilities	80,122	90,623
Postretirement health care and deferred compensation benefits, net of current portion	86,271	86,450
Contingent liabilities and commitments		
Stockholders' equity:		
Capital stock common, par value $0.50; authorized 60,000 shares, issued 51,776 shares	25,888	25,888
Additional paid-in capital	22,268	16,811
Retained earnings	480,446	447,518
Treasury stock, at cost (20,633 and 18,787 shares, respectively)	(310,280)	(254,330)
Total stockholders' equity	218,322	235,887
Total liabilities and stockholders' equity	$ 384,715	$ 412,960

*"Winnebago Industries, Inc., headquartered in Forest City, Iowa, is a leading United States manufacturer of motor homes which are self-contained recreation vehicles used primarily in leisure travel and outdoor recreation activities." 10-K

(continued)

IT'S A TRIP (Continued)

Winnebago Industries, Inc.

Notes to Consolidated Financial Statements (in Part)

Note 1: Nature of Business and Significant Accounting Policies (in Part)

We are a leading U.S. manufacturer of motor homes, self-contained RVs used primarily in leisure travel and outdoor recreation activities. The RV market is highly competitive, both as to price and quality of the product. We believe our principal competitive advantages are our brand name recognition, the quality of our products and our warranty and service capability. We also believe that our prices are competitive with the competitions' units of comparable size and quality.

Principles of Consolidation

The consolidated financial statements include the parent company and subsidiary companies. All material intercompany balances and transactions with subsidiaries have been eliminated.

Fiscal Period

We follow a 52/53-week fiscal year period. The financial statements presented are all 52-week periods.

Allowance for Doubtful Accounts

The allowance for doubtful accounts is based on historical loss experience and any specific customer collection issues identified. Additional amounts are provided through charges to income as we believe necessary after evaluation of receivables and current economic conditions. Amounts which are considered to be uncollectible are written off and recoveries of amounts previously written off are credited to the allowance upon recovery.

Inventories

Inventories are valued at the lower of cost or market, with cost being determined by using the last-in, first-out (LIFO) method and market defined as net realizable value.

Property and Equipment

Depreciation of property and equipment is computed using the straight-line method on the cost of the assets, less allowance for salvage value where appropriate, at rates based upon their estimated service lives as follows:

Asset Class	Asset Life
Buildings	10–30 yrs.
Machinery and equipment	3–10 yrs.
Transportation equipment	3–6 yrs.

We review our long-lived depreciable assets for impairment annually or whenever events or changes in circumstances indicate that the carrying value of an asset may not be recoverable from future cash flows. As of August 26, 2006, and August 27, 2005, we have determined there were no impairments.

Note 3: Inventories

Inventories consist of the following:

(In thousands)	August 26, 2006	August 27, 2005
Finished goods	$ 33,420	$ 67,998
Work-in-process	35,166	45,657
Raw materials	40,080	38,461
	108,666	152,116
LIFO reserve	(31,585)	(31,461)
	$ 77,081	$120,655

The above value of inventories, before reduction for the LIFO reserve, approximates replacement cost at the respective dates.

(continued)

Case 3-1	IT'S A TRIP (Continued)

During Fiscal 2006, inventory quantities were reduced. This reduction resulted in a liquidation of LIFO inventory values, the effect of which decreased cost of goods sold by $4.0 million and increased net income by $2.6 million or $0.08 per share.

Required

a. 1. The statement is entitled "Consolidated Balance Sheets." What does it mean to have a consolidated balance sheet?

    2. For subsidiaries (affiliates), where control is present, does Winnebago have 100% ownership? Explain.

    3. For subsidiaries (affiliates) where control is not present, have these investments been consolidated?

b. 1. What are the gross receivables at August 26, 2006?

    2. What is the estimated amount that will be collected on receivables outstanding at August 26, 2006?

c. 1. What is the total amount of inventory at August 26, 2006?

    2. What is the approximate replacement cost of inventory at August 26, 2006?

    3. What is the trend in inventory balance? Comment.

d. 1. What is the net property and equipment at August 26, 2006?

    2. What is the gross property and equipment at August 26, 2006?

    3. What depreciation method is used for financial reporting purposes?

    4. Does it appear that property and equipment is relatively old at August 26, 2006?

    5. What is the accumulated depreciation on the land at August 26, 2006?

e. 1. What is the balance of product warranties at August 26, 2006?

    2. Why is a product warranties account provided under accrued expenses?

f. 1. Describe the treasury stock account.

    2. What method is used to record treasury stock?

    3. Why is treasury stock presented as a reduction in stockholders' equity?

g. 1. What is the fiscal year?

    2. How many weeks are included for the fiscal years ended August 26, 2006, and August 27, 2005?

Case 3-2	UP, UP, AND AWAY

The December 31, 2006 and 2005 consolidated balance sheets of The Goodyear Tire & Rubber Company* included the following assets and notes:

THE GOODYEAR TIRE & RUBBER COMPANY AND SUBSIDIARIES
CONSOLIDATED BALANCE SHEETS

(Dollars in millions)	December 31,	
	2006	2005
Assets		
Current Assets:		
Cash and cash equivalents (Note 1)	$ 3,899	$ 2,162
Restricted cash (Note 1)	214	241
Accounts and notes receivable (Note 5)	2,973	3,158
Inventories (Note 6)	2,789	2,810
Prepaid expenses and other current assets	304	245
Total Current Assets	10,179	8,616

*"We are one of the world's leading manufacturers of tires and rubber products, engaging in operations in most regions of the world." 10-K

(continued)

UP, UP, AND AWAY (Continued)

(Dollars in millions)	December 31,	
	2006	**2005**
Goodwill (Note 7)	685	637
Intangible Assets (Note 7)	166	159
Deferred Income Tax (Note 14)	155	102
Other Assets and Deferred Pension Costs (Notes 8 and 13)	467	860
Properties and Plants (Note 9)	5,377	5,231
Total Assets	**$ 17,029**	**$ 15,605**
Liabilities		
Current Liabilities:		
Accounts payable—trade	$ 2,037	$ 1,939
Compensation and benefits (Notes 12 and 13)	905	1,773
Other current liabilities	839	671
Unites States and foreign taxes	225	393
Notes payable and overdrafts (Note 11)	255	217
Long term debt and capital leases due within 1 year (Note 11)	405	448
Total Current Liabilities	4,666	5,441
Long Term Debt and Capital Leases (Note 11)	6,563	4,742
Compensation and Benefits (Notes 12 and 13)	4,965	3,828
Deferred and Other Noncurrent Income Taxes (Note 14)	333	304
Other Long Term Liabilities	383	426
Minority Equity in Subsidiaries	877	791
Total Liabilities	17,787	15,532
Commitments and Contingent Liabilities (Note 18)		
Shareholders' (Deficit) Equity		
Preferred Stock, no par value:		
Authorized 50,000,000 shares, unissued	—	—
Common Stock, no par value:		
Authorized, 450,000,000 shares (300,000,000 in 2005)		
Outstanding shares, 178,218,970 (176,509,751 in 2005)		
(Note 21)	178	177
Capital Surplus	1,427	1,398
Retained Earnings	968	1,298
Accumulated Other Comprehensive Loss (Note 17)	(3,331)	(2,800)
Total Shareholders' (Deficit) Equity	(758)	73
Total Liabilities and Shareholders' (Deficit) Equity	**$ 17,029**	**$ 15,605**

THE GOODYEAR TIRE & RUBBER COMPANY AND SUBSIDIARIES
NOTES TO CONSOLIDATED FINANCIAL STATEMENTS (in Part)

Note 1. Accounting Policies (in Part)

A summary of the significant accounting policies used in the preparation of the accompanying consolidated financial statements follows:

Principles of Consolidation

The consolidated financial statements include the accounts of all majority-owned subsidiaries in which no substantive participating rights are held by minority shareholders. All intercompany transactions have been eliminated. Our investments in companies in which we do not own a majority and we have the ability to exercise significant influence over operating and financial policies are accounted for using the equity method. Accordingly, our share of the earnings of these companies is included in the Consolidated Statement of Operations. Investments in other companies are carried at cost.

The consolidated financial statements also include the accounts of entities consolidated pursuant to the provisions of Interpretation No. 46 of the Financial Accounting Standards Board,

(continued)

UP, UP, AND AWAY (Continued)

"Consolidation of Variable Interest Entities ("VIEs")—an Interpretation of ARB No. 51," as amended by FASB Interpretation No. 46R (collectively, "FIN 46"). FIN 46 requires consolidation of VIEs in which a company holds a controlling financial interest through means other than the majority ownership of voting equity. Entities consolidated under FIN 46 include South Pacific Tyres ("SPT") and Tire and Wheel Assembly ("T&WA"). Effective in January 2006, we purchased the remaining 50% interest in SPT and no longer consolidate SPT under FIN 46.

Refer to Note 8.

Warranty

Warranties are provided on the sale of certain of our products and services and an accrual for estimated future claims is recorded at the time revenue is recognized. Tire replacement under most of the warranties we offer is on a prorated basis. Warranty reserves are based on past claims experience, sales history and other considerations. Refer to Note 18.

Inventories

Inventories are stated at the lower of cost or market. Cost is determined using the first-in, first-out or the average cost method. Costs include direct material, direct labor and applicable manufacturing and engineering overhead. We recognize abnormal manufacturing costs as period costs and allocate fixed manufacturing overheads based on normal production capacity. We determine a provision for excess and obsolete inventory based on management's review of inventories on hand compared to estimated future usage and sales. Refer to Note 6.

Goodwill and Other Intangible Assets (in Part)

Goodwill is recorded when the cost of acquired businesses exceeds the fair value of the identifiable net assets acquired. Goodwill and intangible assets with indefinite useful lives are not amortized, but are tested for impairment annually or when events or circumstances indicate that impairment may have occurred, as provided in Statement of Financial Accounting Standards No. 142, "Goodwill and Other Intangible Assets." We perform the goodwill and intangible assets with indefinite useful lives impairment tests annually as of July 31.

Properties and Plants

Properties and plants are stated at cost. Depreciation is computed using the straight-line method. Additions and improvements that substantially extend the useful life of properties and plants, and interest costs incurred during the construction period of major projects, are capitalized. Repair and maintenance costs are expensed as incurred. Properties and plants are depreciated to their estimated residual values over their estimated useful lives, and reviewed for impairment in accordance with Statement of Financial Accounting Standards No. 144, "Accounting for the Impairment or Disposal of Long-Lived Assets." Refer to Notes 9 and 15.

Note 5. Accounts and Notes Receivable (in Part)

(In millions)	2006	2005
Accounts and notes receivable	$3,076	$3,288
Allowance for doubtful accounts	(103)	(130)
	$2,973	$3,158

(continued)

Accounts and Notes Receivable included non-trade receivables totaling $301 million and $300 million at December 31, 2006 and 2005 respectively. These amounts primarily related to value-added taxes and tax receivables.

Note 6. Inventories

(In millions)	2006	2005
Raw materials	$ 722	$ 587
Work in process	156	137
Finished products	1,911	2,086
	$2,789	$2,810

Note 9. Properties and Plants

	2006			2005		
(In millions)	Owned	Capital Leases	Total	Owned	Capital Leases	Total
Properties and plants, at cost:						
Land and improvements	$ 442	$ 5	$ 447	$ 415	$ 9	$ 424
Buildings and improvements	1,902	84	1,986	1,856	91	1,947
Machinery and equipment	10,408	108	10,516	9,885	110	9,995
Construction in progress	442	—	442	445	—	445
	13,194	197	13,391	12,601	210	12,811
Accumulated depreciation	(8,064)	(99)	(8,163)	(7,635)	(94)	(7,729)
	5,130	98	5,228	4,966	116	5,082
Spare parts	149	—	149	149	—	149
	$ 5,279	$ 98	$ 5,377	$ 5,115	$ 116	$ 5,231

The range of useful lives of property used in arriving at the annual amount of depreciation provided are as follows: buildings and improvements, 8 to 45 years; machinery and equipment, 3 to 30 years.

Required

a. The statement is entitled "Consolidated Balance Sheets." What does it mean to have a consolidated balance sheet?

b. 1. What is the gross amount for accounts and notes receivable at December 31, 2006?

   2. What is the net amount for accounts and notes receivable at December 31, 2006?

   3. What is the December 31, 2006, balance for allowance for doubtful accounts?

c. 1. What is the gross amount of properties and plants at December 31, 2006?

   2. What is the net amount of properties and plants at December 31, 2006?

   3. Describe the account Accumulated Depreciation.

   4. What would be the accumulated depreciation at December 31, 2006?

   5. Does it appear that properties and plants is relatively old at December 31, 2006?

d. 1. What is the amount of total assets at December 31, 2006?

   2. What is the amount of current assets at December 31, 2006?

   3. What is the depreciation method?

e. 1. What is the inventory cost method?

   2. What is the dominant inventory category at December 31, 2006?

f. Warranty. When is the warranty liability recorded?

Case 3-3

LINE OF HEALTH

The December 31, 2006 liabilities and shareholders' investment of the consolidated balance sheet for Abbot Laboratories and Subsidiaries* follow:

Abbott Laboratories and Subsidiaries
Consolidated Balance Sheet
(dollars in thousands)

	December 31, 2006	2005	2004
Liabilities and Shareholders' Investment			
Current Liabilities:			
Short-term borrowings	$ 5,305,985	$ 212, 447	$ 1,836,649
Trade accounts payable	1,175,590	1,032,516	1,054,464
Salaries, wages and commissions	807,283	625,254	637,333
Other accrued liabilities	3,850,723	2,722,685	2,491,956
Dividends payable	453,994	423,335	405,730
Income taxes payable	262,344	488,926	156,417
Current portion of long-term debt	95,276	1,849,563	156,034
Liabilities of operations held for sale	—	60,788	87,061
Total Current Liabilities	11,951,195	7,415,514	6,825,644
Long-Term Debt	7,009,664	4,571,504	4,787,934
Post-Employment Obligations and Other Long-Term Liabilities	3,163,127	2,154,775	2,606,410
Liabilities of Operations Held for Sale	—	1,062	1,644
Deferred Income Taxes	—	583,077	220,079
Commitments and Contingencies			
Shareholders' Investment:			
Preferred shares, one dollar par value Authorized—1,000,000 shares, none issued	—	—	—
Common shares, without par value Authorized—2,400,000,000 shares Issued at stated capital amount— Shares: 2006: 1,550,590,438; 2005: 1,553,769,958; 2004: 1,575,147,418	4,290,929	3,477,460	3,189,465
Common shares held in treasury, at cost— Shares: 2006: 13,347,272; 2005: 14,534,979; 2004: 15,123,800	(195,237)	(212,255)	(220,854)
Earnings employed in the business	9,568,728	10,404,568	10,033,440
Accumulated other comprehensive income (loss)	389,766	745,498	1,323,732
Total Shareholders' Investment	14,054,186	14,415,271	14,325,783
	$36,178,172	$29,141,203	$28,767,494

Required a. 1. The statement is entitled "Consolidated Balance Sheet." What does it mean to have a consolidated balance sheet?

   2. Does it appear that the subsidiary is wholly owned?

 b. 1. Describe the trend in current liabilities.

   2. What current liability increased the most for the year ended December 31, 2006?

 c. 1. How many commons shares had been issued as of December 31, 2006?

   2. How many shares were held in the treasury at December 31, 2006?

   3. How many shares were outstanding at December 31, 2006?

   4. What is the treasury stock method?

 d. Abbott Laboratories discloses the account Earnings Employed in the Business. What is this account usually called?

*"Abbott's principal business is the discovery, development, manufacture, and sale of a broad and diversified line of health care products." 10-K

Case 3-4

BUY NOW

The Best Buy* liabilities and shareholders' equity for the fiscal year ended March 31, 2007, follow:

Liabilities and Shareholders' Equity

(In millions, except per share amounts)	March 3, 2007	February 25, 2006
Current Liabilities		
Accounts payable	$ 3,934	$ 3,234
Unredeemed gift card liabilities	496	469
Accrued compensation and related expenses	332	354
Accrued liabilities	990	878
Accrued income taxes	489	703
Short-term debt	41	—
Current portion of long-term debt	19	418
Total current liabilities	6,301	6,056
Long-Term Liabilities	443	373
Long-Term Debt	590	178
Minority Interests	35	—
Shareholders' Equity		
Preferred stock, $1.00 par value: Authorized—		
400,000 shares; Issued and outstanding—none	—	—
Common stock, $.10 par value: Authorized—		
1 billion shares; Issued and outstanding—		
480,655,000 and 485,098,000 shares, respectively	48	49
Additional paid-in capital	430	643
Retained earnings	5,507	4,304
Accumulated other comprehensive income	216	261
Total shareholders' equity	6,201	5,257
Total Liabilities and Shareholders' Equity	$13,570	$11,864

Required

a. Describe the following accounts:
   1. Shareholders' Equity
   2. Common Stock, $.10 par value
   3. Additional Paid-In Capital
   4. Minority Interests (balance sheet account)

b. Determine the number of shares of:
   1. Common stock authorized at March 3, 2007.
   2. Common stock issued and outstanding at March 3, 2007.

c. 1. What is the dollar amount of shareholders' equity at March 3, 2007?
   2. Would the dollar amount of shareholders' equity at March 3, 2007, equal the market value of shareholders' equity at March 3, 2007? Comment.

d. Compute the common stock amount of $48 (in millions) at March 3, 2007.

e. What is the total long-term debt at March 3, 2007?

f. Describe the account Unredeemed Gift Card Liabilities. Why is this a current liability?

*"Best Buy Co., Inc. . . . is a specialty retailer of consumer electronics, home-office products, entertainment software, appliance and related services." 10-K

Case 3-5

OUR PRINCIPAL ASSET IS OUR PEOPLE

Dana Corporation included the following in its 2001 financial report:

Foundation Business: Focused Excellence

Dana's foundation businesses are: axles, drive shafts, structures, brake and chassis products, fluid systems, filtration products, and bearing and sealing products.

These products hold strong market positions—number one or two in the markets they serve. They provide value-added manufacturing, are technically advanced, and each has features that are unique and patented.

(continued)

| Case 3-5 | OUR PRINCIPAL ASSET IS OUR PEOPLE (Continued) |

Management Statement (in Part)

We believe people are Dana's most important asset. The proper selection, training and development of our people as a means of ensuring that effective internal controls are fair, uniform reporting are maintained as standard practice throughout the Company.

Required   a. Dana states that "We believe people are Dana's most important asset." Currently, generally accepted accounting principles do not recognize people as an asset. Speculate on why people are not considered to be an asset.
   b. Speculate on what concept of an asset Dana is considering when it states "We believe people are Dana's most important asset."

| Case 3-6 | BRANDS ARE DEAD? |

The September 1, 1993, issue of *Financial World* estimated that the brand value of Intel was $178 billion. *Financial World* arrived at this estimate using a valuation method developed by London-based Interbrand Group.

Required   a. Define an asset.
   b. In your opinion, do brands represent a valuable asset? Comment.
   c. Under generally accepted accounting principles, should an internally generated brand value be recognized as an asset? Comment.
   d. If the brand was purchased, should it be recognized as an asset? Comment.

| Case 3-7 | ADVERTISING—ASSET? |

Big Car Company did substantial advertising in late December. The company's year-end date was December 31. The president of the firm was concerned that this advertising campaign would reduce profits.

Required   a. Define an asset.
   b. Would the advertising represent an asset? Comment.

| Case 3-8 | IFRS MODEL BALANCE SHEET* |
| | Presented below is an outline of a balance sheet that conforms to IFRSs at December 31, 2006. |

Consolidated Balance Sheet
at December 31, 2006

	31/12/06
Assets:	
Non-current assets	
Current assets	
Total assets	

Consolidated Balance Sheet
at December 31, 2006—continued

	31/12/06
Equity and liabilities:	
Capital and reserves	
Non-current liabilities	
Current liabilities:	
Total equity and liabilities	

*Adapted from IFRS Model Financial Statements, 2006 (http://www.iasplus.com/fs/fs.htm).

Required   a. Construct the balance sheet similar to a balance sheet presented under U.S. GAAP.
   b. Does the IFRS balance sheet emphasize liquidity?

CANADIAN GAAP VS. U.S. GAAP

Shaw Communications Inc.* included Note 21, "United States Accounting Principles," in its 2004 annual report.

21. United States Accounting Principles (in Part)
August 31, 2004, and 2003
(All amounts in thousands of Canadian dollars except per share amounts)

Balance sheet items using U.S. GAAP

	2004		2003	
	Canadian GAAP	U.S. GAAP	Canadian GAAP	U.S. GAAP
Investments and other assets (7)	$ 43,965	$ 72,998	$ 49,415	$ 74,758
Deferred charges (2) (10) (12) (13)	267,439	147,353	293,065	161,122
Broadcast licenses (1) (5) (6)	4,685,582	4,660,348	4,627,728	4,602,494
Other long-term liability (13)	16,993	51,345	9,409	40,397
Deferred credits (10) (12)	898,980	674,718	850,991	696,884
Derivatives instruments liability (9)	—	250,160	—	168,757
Future income taxes	982,281	943,531	939,281	896,263
Long-term debt (8)	2,344,025	3,037,603	2,645,548	3,363,685
Shareholders' equity	2,492,018	1,660,593	2,498,665	1,646,074

The cumulative effect of these adjustments on consolidated shareholders' equity is as follows:

	2004	2003
Shareholders' equity using Canadian GAAP	$2,492,018	$2,498,665
Amortization of intangible assets (1)	(124,179)	(123,542)
Deferred changes (2)	(35,817)	(44,973)
Equity in loss of investees (4)	(35,710)	(36,202)
Gain on sale of subsidiary (5)	15,309	13,822
Gain on sale of cable systems (6)	47,745	47,501
Equity instruments (3)(8)	(688,520)	(709,540)
Accumulated other comprehensive income	(9,809)	825
Cumulative translation adjustment	(444)	(482)
Shareholders' equity using U.S. GAAP	1,660,593	1,646,074

Required
    a. In your opinion, is there a material difference between shareholders' equity at the end of 2004 using Canadian GAAP vs. U.S. GAAP? Comment.
    b. The disclosure indicates "all amounts in thousands of Canadian dollars." In your opinion, does this present a challenge to U.S. investors?

*"Shaw Communications . . . is a diversified Canadian communications company whose core business is providing broadband cable television, internet and satellite, to direct-to-home ("DTH") services to over three million customers (from 2004 annual report). Annual report obtained from The Wall Street Journal annual report service."

Thomson One *Business School Edition*

Endnotes

1. *Accounting Trends & Techniques* (New York, NY: American Institute of Certified Public Accountants, 2006), p. 149.
2. Ibid., p. 307.
3. *Statement of Financial Accounting Concepts No. 6*, "Elements of Financial Statements" (Stamford, Conn.: Financial Accounting Standards Board, 1985), par. 25.
4. *Accounting Trends & Techniques* (New York, NY: American Institute of Certified Public Accountants, 2006), p. 141.
5. *Statement of Financial Accounting Standards No. 142*, "Goodwill and Other Intangible Assets," issued June 1, 2001, represents the current standard relating to goodwill. Prior to this standard, goodwill was amortized over a period of 40 years or less. SFAS No. 142 was required to be applied starting with fiscal years beginning after December 15, 2001.
6. *Statement of Financial Accounting Concepts No. 6*, par. 35.
7. *Statement of Financial Accounting Concepts No. 6*, par. 212.

Chapter 4

Income Statement

The income statement is often considered to be the most important financial statement. Frequently used titles for this statement include statement of operations, statement of income, and statement of earnings. Both the statement of operations and statement of income are very popular titles.[1]

Basic Elements of the Income Statement

An income statement summarizes revenues and expenses and gains and losses, and ends with the net income for a specific period. A multiple-step income statement usually presents separately the gross profit, operating income, income before income taxes, and net income.

A simplified multiple-step income statement might look as follows:

	Net Sales (Revenues)	$XXX
−	*Cost of Goods Sold (cost of sales)*	XXX
	Gross Profit	XXX
−	*Operating Expenses (selling and administrative)*	XXX
	Operating Income	XXX
+(−)	*Other Income or Expense*	XXX
	Income Before Income Taxes	XXX
−	*Income Taxes*	XXX
	Net Income	$XXX
	Earnings per Share	$XXX

Some firms use a single-step income statement, which totals revenues and gains (sales, other income, etc.) and then deducts total expenses and losses (cost of goods sold, operating expenses, other expenses, etc.). A simplified single-step income statement might look as follows:

Revenue:	
Net Sales	$XXX
Other Income	XXX
Total Revenue	XXX

Expenses:	
Cost of Goods Sold (cost of sales)	XXX
Operating Expenses (selling and administrative)	XXX
Other Expense	XXX
Income Tax Expense	XXX
Total Expenses	XXX
Net Income	$XXX
Earnings per Share	$XXX

A single-step income statement lists all revenues and gains (usually in order of amount), then lists all expenses and losses (usually in order of amount). Total expense and loss items deducted from total revenue and gain items determine the net income. Most firms that present a single-step income statement modify it in some way, such as presenting federal income tax expense as a separate item.

Exhibits 4-1 and 4-2 illustrate the different types of income statements. In Exhibit 4-1, Blair Corporation uses a single-step income statement, while in Exhibit 4-2, Sun Hydraulics® Corporation uses a multiple-step format.

Exhibit **4-1** BLAIR CORPORATION*

Single-Step Income Statement

Blair Corporation and Subsidiaries
Consolidated Statements of Income

	Years Ended December 31,		
	2006	**2005**	**2004**
Net sales	$426,425,708	$456,625,397	$496,120,207
Other revenue	6,849,913	36,072,657	44,714,912
	433,275,621	492,698,054	540,835,119
Cost and expenses:			
Cost of goods sold	190,831,333	204,121,644	234,972,079
Advertising	126,119,487	119,321,916	128,324,650
General and administrative	116,901,838	135,588,219	131,408,753
Provision for doubtful accounts	687,399	11,669,552	22,664,048
Gain on sale of receivables	—	(27,747,513)	—
Interest (income) expense, net	(1,292,447)	568,466	(122,757)
Other expense, net	477,801	46,833	221,699
	433,725,411	443,569,117	517,468,472
(Loss) income before income taxes	(449,790)	49,128,937	23,366,647
Income tax (benefit) provision	(666,000)	17,583,000	8,498,000
Net income	$ 216,210	$ 31,545,937	$ 14,868,647
Basic earnings per share based on weighted average shares outstanding	$ 0.06	$ 4.79	$ 1.83
Diluted earnings per share based on weighted average shares outstanding and assumed conversions	$ 0.06	$ 4.71	$ 1.80

*"The Company's business consists of the sale of fashion apparel for men and women, plus a wide range of home products." 10-K

For firms that have cost of goods sold, cost of goods manufactured, or cost of services, a multiple-step income statement should be used for analysis. The multiple-step provides intermediate profit figures useful in analysis. You may need to construct the multiple-step format from the single-step.

Exhibit 4-3 (page 148) contains a comprehensive multiple-step income statement illustration. This illustration resembles the vast majority of income statements as presented in the United States. Be familiar with this illustration. It serves as a guide to much of our analysis.

Exhibit	4-2	SUN HYDRAULICS® CORPORATION*

Multiple-Step Income Statement

Sun Hydraulics Corporation
Consolidated Statements of Operations
(In thousands, except per share data)

	For the Year Ended		
	December 30, 2006	December 31, 2005	December 25, 2004
Net sales	$142,282	$116,757	$94,503
Cost of sales	98,350	79,839	65,968
Gross profit	43,932	36,918	28,535
Selling, engineering and administrative expenses	18,881	17,738	16,241
Operating income	25,051	19,180	12,294
Interest expense	312	441	527
Foreign currency transaction (gain) loss	187	(362)	0
Miscellaneous (income) expense	(351)	(36)	35
Income before income taxes	24,903	19,137	11,732
Income tax provision	8,680	6,329	3,902
Net income	$ 16,223	$ 12,808	$ 7,830
Basic net income per common share	$ 1.49	$ 1.18	$ 0.76
Weighted average basic shares outstanding	10,878	10,827	10,269
Diluted net income per common share	$ 1.48	$ 1.17	$ 0.76
Weighted average diluted shares outstanding	10,939	10,918	10,346
Dividends declared per share	$ 0.400	$ 0.300	$ 0.143

*"The Company is a leading designer and manufacturer of high-performance screw-in hydraulic cartridge valves and manifolds, which control force, speed, and motion as integral components in fluid power systems." 10-K

NET SALES (REVENUES)

Sales (revenues) represent revenue from goods or services sold to customers. The firm earns revenue from the sale of its principal products. Sales are usually shown net of any discounts, returns, and allowances.

COST OF GOODS SOLD (COST OF SALES)

This category shows the cost of goods sold to produce revenue. For a retailing firm, the cost of goods sold equals beginning inventory plus purchases minus ending inventory. In a manufacturing firm, the cost of goods manufactured replaces purchases since the goods are produced rather than purchased. A service firm will not have cost of goods sold or cost of sales, but it will often have cost of services.

OTHER OPERATING REVENUE

Depending on the operations of the business, there may be other operating revenue, such as lease revenue and royalties.

OPERATING EXPENSES

Operating expenses consist of two types: selling and administrative. **Selling expenses**, resulting from the company's effort to create sales, include advertising, sales commissions, sales supplies used, and so on. **Administrative expenses** relate to the general administration of the company's operation. They include office salaries, insurance, telephone, bad debt expense, and other costs difficult to allocate.

| Exhibit | 4-3 | ILLUSTRATION OF SPECIAL ITEMS |

G AND F COMPANY
Income Statement (Multiple-Step Format)
For the Year Ended December 31, 2007

Net sales		$ XXX
Cost of products sold (cost of sales)		(XXX)
Gross profit		XXX
Other operating revenue		XXX
Operating expenses:		
Selling expenses	$ XXX	
General expenses	XXX	(XXX)
Operating income		XXX
Other income (includes interest income)		XXX
Other expenses (includes interest expense)		(XXX)
[A] Unusual or infrequent item disclosed separately [loss]		(XXX)
[B] Equity in earnings of nonconsolidated subsidiaries [loss]		XXX
Income before taxes		XXX
Income taxes related to operations		(XXX)
Net income from operations		XXX
[C] Discontinued operations:		
Income [loss] from operations of discontinued segment		
(less applicable income taxes of $XXX)	$(XXX)	
Income [loss] on disposal of division X (less applicable		
income taxes of $XXX)	(XXX)	(XXX)
[D] Extraordinary gain [loss] (less applicable income taxes of $XXX)		(XXX)
[E] Cumulative effect of change in accounting principle [loss]		
(less applicable income taxes of $XXX)		XXX
Net income before minority interest		$ XXX
[F] Minority share of earnings (income) loss		(XXX)
Net income		$ XXX
Earnings per share		$ XXX

OTHER INCOME OR EXPENSE

In this category are secondary activities of the firm, not directly related to the operations. For example, if a manufacturing firm has a warehouse rented, this lease income would be other income. Dividend and interest income and gains and losses from the sale of assets are also included here. Interest expense is categorized as other expense.

Special Income Statement Items

To comprehend and analyze profits, you need to understand income statement items that require special disclosure. Exhibit 4-3 contains items that require special disclosure. These items are lettered to identify them for discussion. Note that some of these items are presented before tax and some are presented net of tax.

(A) UNUSUAL OR INFREQUENT ITEM DISCLOSED SEPARATELY

Certain income statement items are either unusual or occur infrequently. They might include such items as a gain on sale of securities, write-downs of receivables, or write-downs of inventory. These items are shown with normal, recurring revenues and expenses, and gains and losses. If material, they will be disclosed separately, before tax. Unusual or infrequent items are typically left in primary analysis because they relate to operations.

In supplementary analysis, unusual or infrequent items should be removed net after tax. Usually, an estimate of the tax effect will be necessary. A reasonable estimate of the tax effect can be made by using the effective income tax rate, usually disclosed in a note, or by dividing income taxes by income before taxes.

Refer to Exhibit 4-4, which illustrates an unusual or infrequent item disclosed separately for Taser International, Inc. The unusual or infrequent item was a shareholder litigation expense.

The unusual or infrequent item in 2006 would be removed as follows:

Shareholder litigation settlement expense	$17,650,000
Less estimated tax effect (17.98% × $17,650,000)	3,173,470
Net expense of litigation settlement	$14,476,530

Taser International reported a net loss of $4,087,679 in 2006. Removing the unusual or infrequent item results in a gain of $10,388,851.

Exhibit	**4-4**	TASER INTERNATIONAL, INC.*

Unusual or Infrequent Item

TASER INTERNATIONAL, INC.
STATEMENTS OF OPERATIONS

	For the Years Ended December 31,		
	2006	2005	2004
		(As restated)	
Net sales	$16,717,851	$47,694,181	$67,639,879
Cost of products sold:			
Direct manufacturing expense	18,296,039	12,843,816	16,898,559
Indirect manufacturing expense (1)	6,242,751	5,252,470	5,556,937
Total cost of products sold	24,538,790	18,096,286	22,455,496
Gross margin	43,179,061	29,597,895	45,184,383
Sales, general and administrative expenses (1)	29,680,764	26,483,485	13,880,322
Research and development expenses (1)	2,704,521	1,574,048	823,593
Shareholder litigation settlement expense	17,650,000	—	—
Income (loss) from operations	(6,856,224)	1,540,362	30,480,468
Interest income	1,880,407	1,229,044	439,450
Interest expense	(7,281)	(4,208)	(1,485)
Other income (expense), net	(481)	(59,772)	2,309
Income (loss) before provision for income taxes	(4,983,579)	2,705,426	30,920,742
Provision (benefit) for income taxes	(895,900)	1,648,910	12,039,000
Net income (loss)	$ (4,087,679)	$ 1,056,516	$18,881,742
Income (loss) per common and common equivalent shares			
Basic	$ (0.07)	$ 0.02	$ 0.33
Diluted	$ (0.07)	$ 0.02	$ 0.30
Weighted average number of common and common equivalent shares outstanding			
Basic	61,984,240	61,303,939	57,232,329
Diluted	61,984,240	63,556,246	62,319,590
(1) Stock-based compensation was allocated as follows:			
Indirect manufacturing expense	$ 131,086	$ —	$ —
Sales, general and administrative	808,341	—	—
Research and development expenses	199,418	—	—
	$ 1,138,845	$ —	$ —

*"Taser International, Inc. . . . is a global leader in the development and manufacture of advanced electronic control devices designed for use in law enforcement." 10-K

(B) EQUITY IN EARNINGS OF NONCONSOLIDATED SUBSIDIARIES

When a firm accounts for its investments in stocks using the equity method (the investment is not consolidated), the investor reports equity earnings (losses). **Equity earnings** (losses) are the investor's proportionate share of the investee's earnings (losses). If the investor owns 20% of the stock of the investee, for example, and the investee reports income of $100,000, then the investor reports $20,000 on its income statement. In this book, the term "equity earnings" will be used unless equity losses are specifically intended.

To the extent that equity earnings are not accompanied by cash dividends, the investor reports earnings greater than the cash flow from the investment. If an investor company reports material equity earnings, its net income could be much greater than its ability to pay dividends or cover maturing liabilities.

For purposes of analysis, the equity in the net income of nonconsolidated subsidiaries raises practical problems. For example, the equity earnings represent earnings of other companies, not earnings from the operations of the business. Thus, equity earnings can distort the reported results of a business's operations. For each ratio influenced by equity earnings, this book suggests a recommended approach described when the ratio is introduced.

Refer to Exhibit 4-5, which illustrates equity in earnings of nonconsolidated subsidiaries for Hormel Foods. Leaving these accounts in the statements presents a problem for profitability analysis because most of the profitability measures relate income figures to other figures (usually balance sheet figures). Because these earnings are from nonconsolidated subsidiaries, an inconsistency can result between the numerator and the denominator when computing a ratio. (Chapter 5 presents a detailed discussion of ratios.)

Exhibit	4-5	HORMEL FOODS*

Equity Income

Consolidated Statements of Operations			
	Fiscal Year Ended		
	October 29,	October 30,	October 30,
(In thousands, except per share amounts)	2006	2005	2004
Net sales	$5,745,481	$5,413,997	$4,779,875
Cost of products sold	4,362,291	4,129,549	3,655,837
Gross Profit	1,383,190	1,284,448	1,124,038
Expenses:			
Selling and delivery	754,143	691,792	621,694
Administrative and general	182,891	172,242	146,488
Gain on sale of business	0	0	(18,063)
Total Expenses and Gain on Sale of Business	937,034	864,034	750,119
Equity in earnings of affiliates	4,553	5,525	6,458
Operating Income	450,709	425,939	380,377
Other income and expense:			
Interest and investment income	5,470	8,531	14,363
Interest expense	(25,636)	(27,744)	(27,142)
Earnings Before Income Taxes	430,543	406,726	367,598
Provision for income taxes	144,404	152,123	134,048
Net Earnings	$ 286,139	$ 254,603	$ 233,550
Net Earnings Per Share:			
Basic	$ 2.08	$ 1.84	$ 1.69
Diluted	$ 2.05	$ 1.82	$ 1.67
Weighted Average Shares Outstanding:			
Basic	137,845	138,040	138,596
Diluted	139,561	139,577	140,179

*"The Company started as a processor of meat and food products and continues in this line of business." 10-K

Some ratios are distorted more than others by equity earnings. For example, the ratio that relates income to sales can be distorted because of equity earnings. The numerator of the ratio includes the earnings of the operating company and the equity earnings of nonconsolidated subsidiaries. The denominator (sales) includes only the sales of the operating company. The sales of the unconsolidated subsidiaries will not appear on the investor's income statement because the subsidiary was not consolidated. This causes the ratio to be distorted.

Equity in earnings of nonconsolidated subsidiaries (equity earnings) will be presented before tax. Any tax will be related to the dividend received, and it will typically be immaterial. When removing equity earnings for analysis, do not attempt a tax computation.

INCOME TAXES RELATED TO OPERATIONS

Federal, state, and local income taxes, based on reported accounting profit, are shown here. Income tax expense includes taxes paid and taxes deferred. Income taxes reported here will not include taxes on items presented net of tax.

(C) DISCONTINUED OPERATIONS

A common type of unusual item is the disposal of a business or product line. If the disposal meets the criteria of a discontinued operation, then a separate income statement category for the gain or loss from disposal of a segment of the business must be provided. In addition, the results of operations of the segment that has been or will be disposed of are reported in conjunction with the gain or loss on disposal. These effects appear as a separate category after continuing operations.

Discontinued operations pose a problem for profitability analysis. Ideally, income from continuing operations would be the better figure to use to project future income. Several practical problems associated with the removal of a gain or loss from the discontinued operations occur in the primary profitability analysis. These problems revolve around two points: (1) an inadequate disclosure of data related to the discontinued operations, in order to remove the balance sheet amounts associated with the discontinued operations; and (2) the lack of past profit and loss data associated with the discontinued operations.

Exhibit 4-6 illustrates the presentation of discontinued operations in net income. The best analysis would remove the income statement items that relate to the discontinued operations.

The income statement items that relate to a discontinued operation are always presented net of applicable income taxes. Therefore, the items as presented on the income statement can be removed for primary analysis without further adjustment for income taxes. Supplementary analysis considers discontinued operations in order to avoid disregarding these items.

Ideally, the balance sheet accounts that relate to the discontinued operations should be removed for primary analysis. Consider these items on a supplemental basis because they will not contribute to future operating revenue. However, inadequate disclosure often makes it impossible to remove these items from your analysis.

The balance sheet items related to discontinued operations are frequently disposed of when the business or product line has been disposed of prior to the year-end balance sheet date. In this case, the balance sheet accounts related to discontinued operations do not present a problem for the current year.

(D) EXTRAORDINARY ITEMS

Extraordinary items are material events and transactions distinguished by their unusual nature and by the infrequency of their occurrence. Examples include a major casualty (such as a fire), prohibition under a newly enacted law, or an expropriation. These items, net of their tax effects, must be shown separately. Some pronouncements have specified items that must be considered extraordinary; an example is a material tax loss carryover. The effect of an extraordinary item on earnings per share must also be shown separately. Exhibit 4-7 presents an extraordinary gain.

In analysis of income for purposes of determining a trend, extraordinary items should be eliminated since the extraordinary item is not expected to recur. In supplementary analysis, these extraordinary items should be considered, as this approach avoids disregarding these items.

Extraordinary items are always presented net of applicable income taxes. Therefore, the items as presented on the income statement are removed without further adjustment for income taxes.

Exhibit	4-6	CROWN HOLDINGS, INC.*

Discontinued Operations

CONSOLIDATED STATEMENTS OF OPERATIONS
(In millions, except per share amounts)

For the years ended December 31	2006	2005	2004
Net sales	$6,982	$6,675	$6,285
Cost of products sold, excluding depreciation and amortization	5,863	5,535	5,244
Depreciation and amortization	227	237	247
Gross profit	892	903	794
Selling and administrative expense	316	339	307
Provision for asbestos	10	10	35
Provision for restructuring	15	13	6
Provision for asset impairments and loss/gain on sale of assets	(64)	(18)	31
Loss from early extinguishments of debt		383	39
Interest expense	286	361	361
Interest income	(12)	(9)	(8)
Translation and exchange adjustments	6	94	(98)
Income/(loss) from continuing operations before income taxes, minority interests and equity earnings	335	(270)	121
Provision/(benefit) for income taxes	(62)	11	67
Minority interests	(55)	(51)	(41)
Equity earnings		12	14
Income/(loss) from continuing operations	342	(320)	27
Discontinued operations			
Income/(loss) before income taxes	(34)	(21)	40
Provision/(benefit) for income taxes	(1)	21	16
Income/(loss) from discontinued operations	(33)	(42)	24
Net income/(loss)	$ 309	$ (362)	$ 51
Per common share data:			
Earnings/(loss)			
Basic—Continuing operations	$ 2.07	$ (1.93)	$ 0.16
—Discontinued operations	(0.20)	(0.25)	(0.15)
	$ 1.87	$ (2.18)	$ 0.31
Diluted—Continuing operations	$ 2.01	$ (1.93)	$ 0.16
—Discontinued operations	(0.19)	(0.25)	0.14
	$ 1.82	$ (2.18)	$ 0.30

*"The Company is a worldwide leader in the design, manufacture and sale of packaging products for consumer goods." 10-K

(E) CUMULATIVE EFFECT OF CHANGE IN ACCOUNTING PRINCIPLE

There are two possible methods to disclose a change in accounting principle. These are the retrospective application and the prospective application.

With the retrospective application, the accounts of each prior period are adjusted to reflect the effects of applying the new accounting principle. The new accounting principle is used in the current financial statements.

With the prospective application, the accounts of each prior period are *not* adjusted to reflect the effects of applying the new accounting principle. The new accounting principle is used in the current financial statements, and the income effect of using the new principle in prior financial statements is disclosed on the current income statement as a cumulative effect of change in accounting principle, net of tax. This presents a comparability problem between accounting periods.

A change from one generally accepted principle to another can be the result of a voluntary change in accounting principle, or a mandatory change because the FASB has adopted a new principle.

| Exhibit | 4-7 | BRIGGS & STRATTON CORPORATION* |

Extraordinary Item

BRIGGS & STRATTON CORPORATION
Consolidated Statements of Earnings

FOR THE FISCAL YEARS ENDED JULY 2, 2006, JULY 3, 2005 AND JUNE 27, 2004

(In thousands, except per share data)	2006	2005	2004
NET SALES	$2,542,171	$2,654,875	$1,947,364
Cost of Goods Sold	2,050,487	2,149,984	1,507,492
Gross Profit	491,684	504,891	439,872
ENGINEERING, SELLING, GENERAL AND ADMINISTRATIVE EXPENSES	315,718	314,123	205,663
Income from Operations	175,966	190,768	234,209
INTEREST EXPENSE	(42,091)	(36,883)	(37,665)
OTHER INCOME, Net	18,491	20,430	8,460
Income Before Provision for Income Taxes	152,366	174,315	205,004
PROVISION FOR INCOME TAXES	50,020	57,548	68,890
Income Before Extraordinary Item	102,346	116,767	136,114
EXTRAORDINARY GAIN—NEGATIVE GOODWILL	—	19,800	—
NET INCOME	$ 102,346	$ 136,567	$ 136,114
EARNINGS PER SHARE DATA*			
Weighted Average Shares Outstanding	51,479	51,472	45,286
Income Before Extraordinary Item	$ 1.99	$ 2.27	$ 3.01
Extraordinary Gain	—	.38	—
Basic Earnings Per Share	$ 1.99	$ 2.65	$ 3.01
Diluted Average Shares Outstanding	51,594	51,954	50,680
Income Before Extraordinary Item	$ 1.98	$ 2.25	$ 2.77
Extraordinary Gain	—	.38	—
Diluted Earnings Per Share	$ 1.98	$ 2.63	$ 2.77

*Share data adjusted for effect of 2-for-1 stock split effective October 29, 2004.

*"Briggs & Stratton is the world's largest producer of air-cooled gasoline engines for outdoor power equipment." 10-K

An FASB standard issued in May 2005 requires retrospective application to prior periods' financial statements of a voluntary change in accounting principle unless it is impracticable. This standard does not rule out the possibility that a new accounting pronouncement could include specific directions on how to report a change in principle.

Prior to the 2005 standard, voluntary changes in accounting principle were presented using the prospective method in the United States. This was inconsistent with the reporting under the International Accounting Standards Board (IASB). Reporting of a voluntary change in accounting principle was identified as an area in which financial reporting in the United States could be improved by eliminating the differences between the United States and the IASB. The new standard for reporting a voluntary change in accounting principle was effective for changes in fiscal years beginning after December 15, 2005.

A review of 2006 annual reports revealed that a cumulative effect of change in accounting principle was present in the 2006, 2005, and 2004 columns of the statement of income. Exhibit 4-8 illustrates a cumulative effect of change in accounting principle.

Because of the new standard, it is reasonable to expect the number of companies reporting a cumulative effect of change in accounting principle to be substantially reduced. When it is present, it will still be important to know how to treat this item when doing analysis.

(F) MINORITY SHARE OF EARNINGS

If a firm consolidates subsidiaries not wholly owned, the total revenues and expenses of the subsidiaries are included with those of the parent. However, to determine the income that would accrue to the parent, it is necessary to deduct the portion of income that would belong

| *Exhibit* | 4-8 | ZEBRA DESIGNS* |

Cumulative Effect of Change in Accounting Principle

ZEBRA TECHNOLOGIES CORPORATION
Consolidated Statements of Earnings (in Part)
(In thousands, except per share data)

	Year Ended December 31,		
	2006	2005 (restated see Note 2)	2004 (restated see Note 2)
Net sales	$759,524	$702,271	$663,054
Cost of sales	401,104	348,851	320,951
Gross profit	358,420	353,420	342,103
Operating expenses:			
Selling and marketing	96,788	91,630	79,111
Research and development	48,959	47,359	38,609
General and administrative	62,656	64,050	53,083
Amortization of intangible assets	3,653	2,341	2,569
Litigation settlement	53,392	—	—
Insurance receivable reserve	12,543	—	—
Acquired in-process technology	—	—	22
Exit costs	—	2,012	2,100
Total operating expenses	277,991	207,392	175,494
Operating income	80,429	146,028	166,609
Other income (expense):			
Investment income	23,182	13,417	10,628
Interest expense	(252)	(79)	(44)
Foreign exchange gain (loss)	(635)	1,286	485
Other, net	(1,082)	(370)	(1,594)
Total other income	21,213	14,254	9,475
Income before income taxes and cumulative effect of accounting change	101,642	160,282	176,084
Income taxes	32,015	54,098	60,943
Income before cumulative effect of accounting change	69,627	106,184	115,141
Cumulative effect of accounting change, net of income taxes of $694 (See Note 2)	1,319	—	—
Net income	$ 70,946	$106,184	$115,141

Notes to Consolidated Financial Statements (in Part)

Note 2 Summary of Significant Accounting Policies (in Part)

SFAS No. 123(R) requires entities to estimate the number of forfeitures expected to occur and record expense based upon the number of awards expected to vest. Prior to the adoption of SFAS No. 123(R), Zebra accounted for forfeitures as they occurred as permitted under previous accounting standards. The requirement to estimate forfeitures is classified as an accounting change under APB Opinion No. 20, Accounting Changes, which requires a one-time adjustment in the period of adoption. The one-time adjustment (cumulative effect of accounting change) related to the change in estimating forfeitures increased income by $1,319,000, net of applicable taxes, for the year ended December 31, 2006.

*"Zebra Technologies Corporation and its wholly-owned subsidiaries (Zebra) design, manufacture, sell and support a broad range of direct thermal and thermal transfer label printers, radio frequency identification printer/encoders, dye sublimation card printers, digital photo printers and related accessories and support software." 10-K

to the minority owners. This is labeled "minority share of earnings" or "minority interest." Note that this item sometimes appears before and sometimes after the tax provision on the income statement. When presented before the tax provision, it is usually presented gross of tax. When presented after the tax provision, it is presented net of tax. In this book, assume net-of-tax treatment. Exhibit 4-9 illustrates minority share of earnings.

Some ratios can be materially distorted because of a minority share of earnings. For each ratio influenced by a minority share of earnings, this book suggests a recommended approach.

Earnings per Share

In general, **earnings per share** is earnings divided by the number of shares of outstanding common stock. Chapter 9 presents earnings per share in detail and explains its computation. Meanwhile, use the formula of net income divided by outstanding shares of common stock.

Retained Earnings

Retained Earnings, an account on the balance sheet, represents the undistributed earnings of the corporation. A reconciliation of retained earnings summarizes the changes in retained earnings. It shows the retained earnings at the beginning of the year, the net income for the year as an addition, the dividends as a subtraction, and concludes with end-of-year retained earnings. It also includes, if appropriate, prior period adjustments (net of tax) and some adjustments for changes in accounting principles (net of tax). These restate beginning retained earnings. Other possible changes to retained earnings are beyond the scope of this book.

Sometimes a portion of retained earnings may be unavailable for dividends because it has been appropriated (restricted). Appropriated retained earnings remain part of retained earnings. The appropriation of retained earnings may or may not have significance.

Appropriations that result from legal requirements (usually state law) and appropriations that result from contractual agreements are potentially significant. They may leave unappropriated retained earnings inadequate to pay dividends. (*Note:* A corporation will not be able to pay a cash dividend even with an adequate unrestricted balance in retained earnings unless it has adequate cash or ability to raise cash and has complied with the state law where it is incorporated.)

Most appropriations result from management decisions. These are usually not significant because management can choose to remove the appropriation.

Caution should be exercised not to confuse retained earnings or appropriated retained earnings with cash or any other asset. There is no cash or any other asset in retained earnings. The reason for an appropriation will be disclosed either in the reconciliation of retained earnings or in a note. From this disclosure, try to arrive at an opinion as to the significance, if any.

The reconciliation of retained earnings usually appears as part of a statement of stockholders' equity. Sometimes it is combined with the income statement. Exhibit 4-10 gives an example of a reconciliation of retained earnings being presented with a stockholders' equity statement.

Dividends and Stock Splits

Dividends return profits to the owners of a corporation. A cash dividend declared by the Board of Directors reduces retained earnings by the amount of the dividends declared and creates the current liability, dividends payable. The date of payment occurs after the date of declaration. The dividend payment eliminates the liability, dividends payable, and reduces cash. Note that the date of the declaration of dividends, not the date of the dividend payment, affects retained earnings and creates the liability.

The Board of Directors may elect to declare and issue another type of dividend, termed a *stock dividend*. The firm issues a percentage of outstanding stock as new shares to existing shareholders. If the Board declares a 10% stock dividend, for example, an owner holding 1,000 shares would receive an additional 100 shares of new stock. The accounting for a stock dividend, assuming a relatively small distribution (less than 25% of the existing stock), requires removing the fair market value of the stock at the date of declaration from retained earnings and transferring it to paid-in capital. With a material stock dividend, the amount removed from retained earnings and transferred to paid-in capital is determined by

| Exhibit | 4-9 | NEWMONT MINING CORPORATION* |

Minority Interest

STATEMENTS OF CONSOLIDATED INCOME

	Years Ended December 31,		
	2006	2005	2004
	(In millions, except per share data)		
Revenues			
Sales—gold, net	$4,316	$3,680	$3,540
Sales—copper, net	671	672	786
	4,987	4,352	4,326
Cost and expenses			
Costs applicable to sales (exclusive of depreciation, depletion and amortization shown separately below)			
Gold	2,207	1,990	1,878
Copper	308	303	305
Depreciation, depletion and amortization	636	635	652
Exploration	170	147	107
Advanced projects, research and development	94	73	80
General and administrative	149	134	116
Write-down of goodwill (Note 18)	—	41	52
Write-down of long-lived assets (Note 4)	3	43	39
Other expense, net (Note 5)	149	112	34
	3,716	3,478	3,263
Other income (expense)			
Other income, net (Note 6)	451	269	102
Interest expense, net of capitalized interest of $57, $39, and $13, respectively	(97)	(97)	(97)
	354	172	5
Income from continuing operations before income tax, minority interest and equity income of affiliates	1,625	1,046	1,068
Income tax expense (Note 7)	(424)	(310)	(324)
Minority interest in income of consolidated subsidiaries	(363)	(380)	(335)
Equity income of affiliates (Note 8)	2	4	2
Income from continuing operations	840	360	411
(Loss) income from discontinued operations (Note 9)	(49)	(38)	79
Cumulative effect of a change in accounting principle, net of tax of $25 in 2004 (Note 3)	—	—	(47)
Net income	$ 791	$ 322	$ 443
Income from continuing operations per common share, basic	$ 1.87	$ 0.81	$ 0.93
(Loss) income from discontinued operations per common share, basic	(0.11)	(0.09)	0.18
Cumulative effect of a change in accounting principle per common share, basic	—	—	(0.11)
Net income per common share, basic (Note 10)	$ 1.76	$ 0.72	$ 1.00
Income from continuing operations per common share, diluted	$ 1.86	$ 0.80	$ 0.92
(Loss) income from discontinued operations per common share, diluted	(0.11)	(0.08)	0.18
Cumulative effect of a change in accounting principle per common share, diluted	—	—	(0.11)
Net income per common share, diluted (Note 10)	$ 1.75	$ 0.72	$ 0.99
Basic weighted-average common shares outstanding	450	446	443
Diluted weighted-average common shares outstanding	452	449	447
Cash dividends declared per common share	$ 0.40	$ 0.40	$ 0.30

*"Newmont Mining Corporation is primarily a gold producer with significant assets or operations in the United States, Australia, Peru, Indonesia, Ghana, Canada, Bolivia, New Zealand, and Mexico." 10-K

| Exhibit | 4-10 | RELIANCE STEEL & ALUMINUM CO.* |

Consolidated Statements of Shareholders' Equity

RELIANCE STEEL & ALUMINUM CO.
CONSOLIDATED STATEMENTS OF SHAREHOLDERS' EQUITY
(In thousands, except share and per share amounts)

	Common Stock Shares	Common Stock Amount	Retained Earnings	Accumulated Other Comprehensive Income (Loss)	Total
Balance at January 1, 2004	64,451,744	$303,587	$ 344,962	$ (930)	$ 647,619
Net income for the year	—	—	169,728	—	169,728
Other comprehensive income (loss):					
Foreign currency translation gain	—	—	—	1,476	1,476
Unrealized loss on investments	—	—	—	(166)	(166)
Minimum pension liability	—	—	—	72	72
Comprehensive income					171,110
Stock options exercised	873,600	10,130	1,905	—	12,035
Stock issued under incentive bonus plan	14,590	236	—	—	236
Cash dividends—$.13 per share	—	—	(8,448)	—	(8,448)
Balance at December 31, 2004	65,339,934	313,953	508,147	452	822,552
Net income for the year	—	—	205,437	—	205,437
Other comprehensive income (loss):					
Foreign currency translation gain	—	—	—	1	1
Unrealized gain on investments	—	—	—	40	40
Minimum pension liability	—	—	—	(168)	(168)
Comprehensive income					205,310
Stock options exercised	866,900	10,811	3,476	—	14,287
Stock issued under incentive bonus plan	11,164	246	—	—	246
Cash dividends—$.19 per share	—	—	(12,530)	—	(12,530)
Balance at December 31, 2005	66,217,998	$325,010	$ 704,530	$ 325	$1,029,865
Net income for the year	—	—	354,507	—	354,507
Other comprehensive income (loss):					
Foreign currency translation gain	—	—	—	1,221	1,221
Unrealized gain on investments	—	—	—	116	116
Minimum pension liability	—	—	—	423	423
Comprehensive income					356,267
Adjustment to initially apply SFAS No. 158, net of tax	—	—	—	(3,716)	(3,716)
Stock options exercised	438,290	7,115	3,446	—	10,561
Stock based compensation	—	6,060	—	—	6,060
Stock and stock options issued in connection with business acquisition	8,962,268	360,453	—	—	360,453
Stock issued to a retirement savings plan	78,288	2,830	—	—	2,830
Stock issued under incentive bonus plan	5,202	222	—	—	222
Cash dividends—$22 per share	—	—	(16,144)	—	(16,144)
Balance at December 31, 2006	75,702,046	$701,690	$1,046,339	$(1,631)	$1,746,398

*"We are one of the largest metals service center companies in the United States." 10-K

multiplying the par value of the stock by the number of additional shares. Note that the overall effect of a stock dividend leaves total stockholders' equity and each owner's share of stockholders' equity unchanged. However, the total number of outstanding shares increases.

A stock dividend should reduce the market value of individual shares by the percentage of the stock dividend. Total market value considering all outstanding shares should not change in theory. In practice, the market value change may not be the same percentage as the stock dividend.

A more drastic device to change the market value of individual shares is by declaring a stock split. A 2-for-1 split should reduce the market value per share to one-half the amount prior to the split. The market value per share in practice may not change exactly in proportion to the split. The market value will result from the supply and demand for the stock.

Lowering the market value is sometimes desirable for stocks selling at high prices (as perceived by management). Stocks with high prices are less readily traded. A stock dividend or stock split can influence the demand for the stock.

A stock split merely increases the number of shares of stock. It does not usually change retained earnings or paid-in capital. For example, if a firm had 1,000 shares of common stock, a 2-for-1 stock split would result in 2,000 shares.

For a stock split, the par or stated value of the stock is changed in proportion to the stock split, and no change is made to retained earnings, additional paid-in capital, or capital stock. For example, a firm with $10 par common stock that declares a 2-for-1 stock split would reduce the par value to $5.

Since the number of shares changes under both a stock dividend and stock split, any ratio based on the number of shares must be restated for a meaningful comparison. For example, if a firm had earnings per share of $4 in 2007, a 2-for-1 stock split in 2008 would require restatement of the earnings per share to $2 in 2007 because of the increase in the shares. Restatement will be made for all prior financial statements presented with the current financial statements, including a 5- or 10-year summary.

Legality of Distributions to Stockholders

The legality of distributions to stockholders is governed by applicable state law. Currently, the 50 states may be classified into one of three groups for purposes of distributions to stockholders. These groups are the following:[2]

1. Distributions to stockholders are acceptable as long as the firm has the ability to pay debts as they come due in the normal course of business.
2. Distributions to stockholders are acceptable as long as the firm is solvent and the distributions do not exceed the fair value of net assets.
3. Distributions consist of solvency and balance sheet tests of liquidity and risk.

Thus, the appropriateness of a distribution to stockholders is a legal interpretation. Accountants have not accepted the role of disclosing the firm's capacity to make distributions to stockholders. Accountants have accepted the role of disclosing appropriations (restrictions) of retained earnings. Appropriations can temporarily limit the firm's ability to make distributions. These appropriations are typically directed toward limiting or prohibiting the payment of cash dividends.

During the 1980s and 1990s, there were many distributions to stockholders that exceeded the net book value of the firm's assets. These were often accompanied by debt-financed restructurings. Often, the result was a deficit balance in retained earnings and sometimes a deficit balance in total stockholders' equity.

During 1988, Holiday Corporation (owner of Holiday Inns of America) distributed a $65 per share dividend to prevent a hostile takeover. The result was a substantial deficit to retained earnings and approximately a $770 million deficit to total stockholders' equity.[3]

A similar situation took place at Owens Corning during the 1980s as it made a substantial distribution to stockholders by way of a debt-financed restructuring. Owens Corning also had substantial expenses related to asbestos-related illnesses. At the end of 1995, Owens Corning had a deficit in retained earnings of $781,000,000, and a deficit in total stockholders' equity of $212,000,000.

An Owens Corning news release of June 20, 1996, stated (in Part):

The Board of Directors has approved an annual dividend policy of 25 cents per share and declared a quarterly dividend of 6-1/4 cents per share payable on October 15, 1996 to shareholders of record as of September 30, 1996.

In reference to the dividend, we were able to initiate this action because debt has been reduced to target levels and cash flow from operations will be in excess of internal funding requirements.

We are delighted to be able to reward our shareholders with a dividend. Reinstating the dividend has been a priority of mine since joining the company and I am pleased that we now are in a position to set the date.

Comprehensive Income

Chapter 1 described the Concept Statements that serve as the basis for evaluating existing standards of financial accounting and reports. Concept Statement Nos. 5 and 6 included the concept of comprehensive income. Comprehensive income was described in SFAC No. 6 as the change in equity of a business enterprise during a period from transactions and other events and circumstances from nonowner sources.

Subsequently, SFAS No. 130 was issued that required the reporting of comprehensive income, but using a narrower definition than in SFAC No. 6. Under SFAS No. 130, comprehensive income is net income plus the period's change in accumulated other comprehensive income. Accumulated other comprehensive income is a category within stockholders' equity, described in Chapter 3.

Categories within accumulated other comprehensive income are:

1. *Foreign currency translation adjustments.* The expansion of international business and extensive currency realignment have created special accounting problems. The biggest difficulty has been related to translating foreign financial statements into the financial statements of a U.S. enterprise.

   U.S. financial reporting calls for postponing the recognition of unrealized exchange gains and losses until the foreign operation is substantially liquidated. This postponement is accomplished by creating a separate category within stockholders' equity to carry unrealized exchange gains and losses. This method eliminates the wide fluctuations in earnings from translation adjustments for most firms. For subsidiaries operating in highly inflationary economies, translation adjustments are charged to net earnings. Also, actual foreign currency exchange gains (losses) are included in net earnings.

2. *Unrealized holding gains and losses on available-for-sale marketable securities.* Debt and equity securities classified as available-for-sale securities are carried at fair value. Unrealized holding gains and losses are included in a separate category within stockholders' equity until realized. Thus, the unrealized holding gains and losses are not included in net earnings. Note that this accounting only applies to securities available for sale. Trading securities are reported at their fair values on the balance sheet date, and unrealized holding gains and losses are included in income of the current period. Debt securities held to maturity are reported at their amortized cost on the balance sheet date.

3. *Changes to stockholders' equity resulting from additional minimum pension liability adjustments.* Accounting standards require a reduction in stockholders' equity for a minimum pension liability under a defined benefit plan. Accounting for a defined benefit plan is reviewed in Chapter 7.

4. *Unrealized gains and losses from derivative instruments.* Derivative instruments are financial instruments or other contracts where rights or obligations meet the definitions of assets or liabilities. The gain or loss for some derivative instruments is reported in current earnings. For other derivative instruments, the gain or loss is reported as a component of other comprehensive income. The gain or loss for these instruments is recognized in subsequent periods in income as the hedged forecasted transactions affect earnings.

   Required disclosures are the following:

   • Comprehensive income
   • Each category of other comprehensive income
   • Reclassification adjustments for categories of other comprehensive income
   • Tax effects for each category of other comprehensive income
   • Balances for each category of accumulated other comprehensive income

The accounting standard provides considerable flexibility in reporting comprehensive income. One format uses a single income statement to report net income and comprehensive income. The second format reports comprehensive income in a separate statement of financial activity. The third format reports comprehensive income within the statement of changes in stockholders' equity. Exhibit 4-11 illustrates the three format options provided for in the accounting standard. Exhibit 4-10 presents the accumulated other comprehensive income (loss) of Reliance Steel & Aluminum Co. Reliance presents this within its consolidated statements of shareholders' equity.

The first two options are not popular because comprehensive income would be closely tied to the income statement. Comprehensive income will typically be more volatile than net

Exhibit	4-11	REPORTING COMPREHENSIVE INCOME

Format A Single Income Statement
to Report Net Income and Comprehensive Income

XYZ Corporation
Statement of Income and Comprehensive Income
For the Year Ended December 31, 2008

(Dollars in thousands, except per share)

Sales	$230,000
Cost of goods sold	140,000
Gross profit	90,000
Operating expenses	40,000
Operating income	50,000
Other income	4,000
Income before income taxes	54,000
Income taxes	20,000
Net income	34,000

Other comprehensive income

Available-for-sale securities adjustment, net of $2,500 income tax	5,500
Minimum pension liability adjustment, net of $1,000 income tax	3,500
Foreign currency translation adjustment, net of $1,500 income tax benefit	(5,000)
Other comprehensive income	4,000
Comprehensive income	$ 38,000

Earnings per share

(Earnings per share continue to be calculated based on net income.)	$2.80

Format B Separate Comprehensive
Income Statement

XYZ Corporation
Statement of Comprehensive Income
For the Year Ended December 31, 2008

(Dollars in thousands)

Net income		$34,000
Other comprehensive income		
Available-for-sale securities adjustment, net of $2,500 income tax	$5,500	
Minimum pension liability adjustment, net of $1,000 income tax	3,500	
Foreign currency translation adjustments, net of $1,500 income tax benefit	(5,000)	
Total other comprehensive income		4,000
Comprehensive income		$38,000

Format C Comprehensive Income Presented with
Statement of Changes in Stockholders' Equity

XYZ Corporation
Statement of Stockholders' Equity for the Year Ended December 31, 2008

(Dollars in thousands)	Total	Retained Earnings	Accumulated Other Comprehensive Income	Common Stock Amount	Shares
Beginning balance	$180,000	$60,000	$10,000	$110,000	55,000
Net income	34,000	34,000			
Other comprehensive income:					
Available-for-sale securities adjustment, net of $2,500 income tax	5,500		5,500		
Minimum pension liability adjustment, net of $1,000 income tax	3,500		3,500		
Foreign currency translation adjustment, net of $1,500 income tax benefit	(5,000)		(5,000)		
Comprehensive income	38,000				
Ending balance	$218,000	$94,000	$14,000	$110,000	55,000

income. This is because the items within accumulated other comprehensive income have the potential to be volatile. A good case could be made that comprehensive income is a better indication of long-run profitability than is net income. Some firms have elected to disclose comprehensive income as a note to the financial statements. The coverage of comprehensive income in analysis is in Chapter 12.

Summary

The income statement summarizes the profit for a specific period of time. To understand and analyze profitability, the reader must be familiar with the components of income, as well as income statement items that require special disclosure. This chapter presented special income statement items, such as unusual or infrequent items disclosed separately, equity in earnings of nonconsolidated subsidiaries, discontinued operations, extraordinary items, and minority shares of earnings. This chapter also covered the reconciliation of retained earnings, dividends and stock splits, and comprehensive income.

to the net

1. Go to the SEC Web site (http://www.sec.gov). Under "Filings & Forms (EDGAR)," click on "Search for Company Filings." Click on "Companies & Other Filers." Under Company Name, enter "KB Home" (or under Ticker Symbol, enter "KBH"). Select the 10-K filed February 13, 2007.

   a. What is the amount of minority interests for 2007?

   b. What is the amount of equity earnings for 2007? Describe equity earnings.

2. Go to the SEC Web site (http://www.sec.gov). Under "Filings & Forms (EDGAR)," click on "Search for Company Filings." Click on "Companies & Other Filers." Under Company Name, enter "Amazoncom Inc" (or under Ticker Symbol, enter "AMZN"). Select the 10-K filed February 16, 2007.

   a. What were the net sales for 2006, 2005, and 2004?

   b. What were the gross profits for 2006, 2005, and 2004?

   c. What were the income from operations for 2006, 2005, and 2004?

   d. What were the interest expenses for 2006, 2005, and 2004?

   e. Comment considering the data in (a), (b), (c), and (d).

3. Go to the SEC Web site (http://www.sec.gov). Under "Filings & Forms (EDGAR)," click on "Search for Company Filings." Click on "Companies & Other Filers." Under Company Name, enter "Alexander & Baldwin, Inc." (or under Ticker Symbol, enter "ALEX"). Select the 10-K filed February 26, 2007.

   a. Describe the account Equity in Income of Real Estate Affiliates.

   b. For 2006, would you describe Income from Discontinued Operations Net of Income Taxes to be material?

   c. For 2005, identify an unusual or infrequent item.

   d. What is the major operating revenue?

   e. What are the major operating costs and expenses?

4. Go to the SEC Web site (http://www.sec.gov). Under "Filings & Forms (EDGAR)," click on "Search for Company Filings." Click on "Companies & Other Filers." Under Company Name, enter "Kroger Co" (or under Ticker Symbol, enter "KR"). Select the 10-K filed April 4, 2007.

   a. Why is the goodwill account on the balance sheet?

   b. Why is the goodwill impairment charge on the consolidated statements of earnings for 2004? (Review Note 2—Goodwill.)

   c. Why is the goodwill impairment charge described as a noncash impairment?

5. Go to the SEC Web site (http://www.sec.gov). Under "Filings & Forms (EDGAR)," click on "Search for Company Filings." Click on "Companies & Other Filers."

   This exercise will view the presentation format of three firms as to how they present comprehensive income.

   Firm #1—Occidental Petroleum Corporation

   Under Company Name, enter "Occidental Petroleum" (or under Ticker Symbol, enter "OXY"). Select the 10-K filed February 27, 2007.

   a. Indicate the format presentation selected by Occidental Petroleum Corporation.

   Firm #2—El Paso Corporation

   Under Company Name, enter "El Paso Corporation" (or under Ticker Symbol, enter "El"). Select the 10-K filed February 28, 2007.

b. Indicate the format presentation selected by El Paso Corporation.

Firm #3—Arden Group, Inc.

Under Company Name, enter "Arden Group Inc." (or under Ticker Symbol, enter "ARDNA"). Select the 10-K filed April 16, 2007.

c. Indicate the format presentation selected by Arden Group Inc.

In your opinion, which of the three alternative format presentations is the best for the user of the statement?

6. Go to http://www.iasplus.com/fs/fs.htm. Click on "IFRS Model Financial Statements." Use the most recent year presented.

a. Review the consolidated income statement, expenses analyzed by function. Comment on similarities and differences to the U.S. GAAP income statement.

b. Review the consolidated income statement, expenses analyzed by nature. Comment on similarities and difference to the U.S. GAAP income statement.

Questions

Q 4-1. What are extraordinary items? How are they shown on the income statement? Why are they shown in that manner?

Q 4-2. Which of the following would be classified as extraordinary?
a. Selling expense
b. Interest expense
c. Gain on the sale of marketable securities
d. Loss from flood
e. Income tax expense
f. Loss from prohibition of red dye
g. Loss from the write-down of inventory

Q 4-3. Give three examples of unusual or infrequent items that are disclosed separately. Why are they shown separately? Are they presented before or after tax? Why or why not?

Q 4-4. Why is the equity in earnings of nonconsolidated subsidiaries sometimes a problem in profitability analysis? Discuss with respect to income versus cash flow.

Q 4-5. A health food distributor selling wholesale dairy products and vitamins decides to discontinue the division that sells vitamins. How should this discontinuance be classified on the income statement?

Q 4-6. Why are unusual or infrequent items disclosed before tax?

Q 4-7. In the future, we should expect few presentations of a "cumulative effect of change in accounting principle." Comment.

Q 4-8. How does the declaration of a cash dividend affect the financial statements? How does the payment of a cash dividend affect the financial statements?

Q 4-9. What is the difference in the impact on financial statements of a stock dividend versus a stock split?

Q 4-10. Why is minority share of earnings deducted before arriving at net income?

Q 4-11. Explain the relationship between the income statement and the reconciliation of retained earnings.

Q 4-12. List the three types of appropriated retained earnings accounts. Which of these types is most likely not a detriment to the payment of a dividend? Explain.

Q 4-13. A balance sheet represents a specific date, such as "December 31," while an income statement covers a period of time, such as "For the Year Ended December 31, 2008." Why does this difference exist?

Q 4-14.   Describe the following items:
a. Minority share of earnings
b. Equity in earnings of nonconsolidated subsidiaries

Q 4-15.   An income statement is a summary of revenues and expenses and gains and losses, ending with net income for a specific period of time. Indicate the two traditional formats for presenting the income statement. Which of these formats is preferable for analysis? Why?

Q 4-16.   Melcher Company reported earnings per share in 2008 and 2007 of $2.00 and $1.60, respectively. In 2009, there was a 2-for-1 stock split, and the earnings per share for 2009 were reported to be $1.40. Give a three-year presentation of earnings per share (2007–2009).

Q 4-17.   Comment on your ability to determine a firm's capacity to make distributions to stockholders, using published financial statements.

Q 4-18.   Management does not usually like to tie comprehensive income closely with the income statement. Comment.

Problems

P 4-1.   The following information for Decher Automotives covers the year ended 2008:

Administrative expense	$ 62,000
Dividend income	10,000
Income taxes	100,000
Interest expense	20,000
Merchandise inventory, 1/1	650,000
Merchandise inventory, 12/31	440,000
Flood loss (net of tax)	30,000
Purchases	460,000
Sales	1,000,000
Selling expenses	43,000

Required
a. Prepare a multiple-step income statement.
b. Assuming that 100,000 shares of common stock are outstanding, calculate the earnings per share before extraordinary items and the net earnings per share.
c. Prepare a single-step income statement.

P 4-2.   The following information for Lesky Corporation covers the year ended December 31, 2008:

LESKY CORPORATION
Income Statement
For the Year Ended December 31, 2008

Revenue:		
Revenues from sales		$362,000
Rental income		1,000
Interest		2,400
Total revenue		365,400
Expenses:		
Cost of products sold	$242,000	
Selling expenses	47,000	
Administrative and general expenses	11,400	
Interest expense	2,200	
Federal and state income taxes	20,300	
Total expenses		322,900
Net income		$ 42,500

Required   Change this statement to a multiple-step format, as illustrated in this chapter.

P 4-3.   The accounts of Consolidated Can contain the following amounts at December 31, 2008:

Cost of products sold	$410,000
Dividends	3,000
Extraordinary gain (net of tax)	1,000
Income taxes	9,300
Interest expense	8,700
Other income	1,600
Retained earnings, 1/1	270,000
Sales	480,000
Selling and administrative expense	42,000

Required   Prepare a multiple-step income statement combined with a reconciliation of retained earnings for the year ended December 31, 2008.

P 4-4.   The following items are from Taperline Corporation on December 31, 2008. Assume a flat 40% corporate tax rate on all items, including the casualty loss.

Sales	$670,000
Rental income	3,600
Gain on the sale of fixed assets	3,000
General and administrative expenses	110,000
Selling expenses	97,000
Interest expense	1,900
Depreciation for the period	10,000
Extraordinary item (casualty loss—pretax)	30,000
Cost of sales	300,000
Common stock (30,000 shares outstanding)	150,000

Required   a. Prepare a single-step income statement for the year ended December 31, 2008. Include earnings per share for earnings before extraordinary items and net income.

b. Prepare a multiple-step income statement. Include earnings per share for earnings before extraordinary items and net income.

P 4-5.   The income statement of Rawl Company for the year ended December 31, 2008, shows the following:

Net sales	$360,000
Cost of sales	190,000
Gross profit	170,000
Selling, general, and administrative expense	80,000
Income before unusual write-offs	90,000
Provision for unusual write-offs	50,000
Earnings from operations before income taxes	40,000
Income taxes	20,000
Net earnings from operations before extraordinary charge	20,000
Extraordinary charge, net of tax of $10,000	(50,000)
Net earnings (loss)	$ (30,000)

Required   Compute the net earnings remaining after removing unusual write-offs and the extraordinary charge. Remove these items net of tax. Estimate the tax rate for unusual write-offs based on the taxes on operating income.

P 4-6.   At the end of 2008, vandals destroyed your financial records. Fortunately, the controller had kept certain statistical data related to the income statement, as follows:

a. Cost of goods sold was $2,000,000.

b. Administrative expenses were 20% of the cost of sales but only 10% of sales.

c. Selling expenses were 150% of administrative expenses.

d. Bonds payable were $1,000,000, with an average interest rate of 11%.

e. The tax rate was 48%.

f. 50,000 shares of common stock were outstanding for the entire year.

Required   From the information given, reconstruct a multiple-step income statement for the year. Include earnings per share.

P 4-7.   The following information applies to Bowling Green Metals Corporation for the year ended December 31, 2008:

Total revenues from regular operations	$832,000
Total expenses from regular operations	776,000
Extraordinary gain, net of applicable income taxes	30,000
Dividends paid	20,000
Number of shares of common stock outstanding during the year	10,000

Required   Compute earnings per share before extraordinary items and net earnings. Show how this might be presented in the financial statements.

P 4-8.   You were recently hired as the assistant treasurer for Victor, Inc. Yesterday, the treasurer was injured in a bicycle accident and is now hospitalized, unconscious. Your boss, Mr. Fernandes, just informed you that the financial statements are due today. Searching through the treasurer's desk, you find the following notes:

a. Income from continuing operations, based on computations done so far, is $400,000. No taxes are accounted for yet. The tax rate is 30%.

b. Dividends declared and paid were $20,000. During the year, 100,000 shares of stock were outstanding.

c. The corporation experienced an uninsured $20,000 pretax loss from a freak hailstorm. Such a storm is considered to be unusual and infrequent.

d. The company decided to change its inventory pricing method from average cost to the FIFO method. The effect of this change is to increase prior years' income by $30,000 pretax. The FIFO method has been used for 2008. (*Hint:* This adjustment should be placed just prior to net income.)

e. In 2008, the company settled a lawsuit against it for $10,000 pretax. The settlement was not previously accrued and is due for payment in February 2009.

f. In 2008, the firm sold a portion of its long-term securities at a gain of $30,000 pretax.

g. The corporation disposed of its consumer products division in August 2008, at a loss of $90,000 pretax. The loss from operations through August was $60,000 pretax.

Required   Prepare an income statement for 2008, in good form, starting with income from continuing operations. Compute earnings per share for income from continuing operations, discontinued operations, extraordinary loss, cumulative effect of a change in accounting principle, and net income.

P 4-9.   List the statement on which each of the following items may appear. Choose from (A) income statement, (B) balance sheet, or (C) neither.

a. Net income
b. Cost of goods sold
c. Gross profit
d. Retained earnings
e. Paid-in capital in excess of par
f. Sales
g. Supplies expense
h. Investment in G. Company
i. Dividends
j. Inventory
k. Common stock

l. Interest payable
m. Loss from flood
n. Land
o. Taxes payable
p. Interest income
q. Gain on sale of property
r. Dividend income
s. Depreciation expense
t. Accounts receivable
u. Accumulated depreciation
v. Sales commissions

P 4-10.   List where each of the following items may appear. Choose from (A) income statement, (B) balance sheet, or (C) reconciliation of retained earnings.

a. Dividends paid
b. Notes payable
c. Minority share of earnings
d. Accrued payrolls
e. Loss on disposal of equipment
f. Minority interest in consolidated subsidiary
g. Adjustments of prior periods
h. Redeemable preferred stock
i. Treasury stock
j. Extraordinary loss

k. Unrealized exchange gains and losses
l. Equity in net income of affiliates
m. Goodwill
n. Unrealized decline in market value of equity investment
o. Cumulative effect of change in accounting principle
p. Common stock
q. Cost of goods sold
r. Supplies
s. Land

P 4-11.   The income statement of Tawls Company for the year ended December 31, 2008, shows the following:

Revenue from sales		$ 980,000
Cost of products sold		510,000
Gross profit		470,000
Operating expenses:		
Selling expenses	$110,000	
General expenses	140,000	250,000
Operating income		220,000
Equity on earnings of nonconsolidated subsidiary		60,000
Operating income before income taxes		280,000
Taxes related to operations		100,000
Net income from operations		180,000
Extraordinary loss from flood		
(less applicable taxes of $50,000)		(120,000)
Minority share of earnings		(40,000)
Net income		$ 20,000

Required   a. Compute the net earnings remaining after removing nonrecurring items.
b. Determine the earnings from the nonconsolidated subsidiary.
c. For the subsidiary that was not consolidated, what amount of income would have been included if this subsidiary had been consolidated?
d. What earnings relate to minority shareholders of a subsidiary that was consolidated?
e. Determine the total tax amount.

P 4-12.   The income statement of Jones Company for the year ended December 31, 2008, follows.

Revenue from sales		$790,000
Cost of products sold		410,000
Gross profit		380,000
Operating expenses:		
Selling expenses	$ 40,000	
General expenses	80,000	120,000
Operating income		260,000
Equity in earnings of nonconsolidated		
subsidiaries (loss)		(20,000)
Operating income before income taxes		240,000
Taxes related to operations		(94,000)
Net income from operations		146,000
Discontinued operations:		
Loss from operations of discontinued segment		
(less applicable income tax credit of $30,000)	$ (70,000)	
Loss on disposal of segment (less applicable		
income tax credit of $50,000)	(100,000)	(170,000)
Income before cumulative effect of change		
in accounting principle		(24,000)
Cumulative effect of change in accounting principle		
(less applicable income taxes of $25,000)		50,000
Net income		$ 26,000

Required   a. Compute the net earnings remaining after removing nonrecurring items.
b. Determine the earnings (loss) from the nonconsolidated subsidiary.
c. Determine the total tax amount.

P 4-13.   Uranium Mining Company, founded in 1980 to mine and market uranium, purchased a mine in 1981 for $900 million. It estimated that the uranium had a market value of $150 per ounce. By 2008, the market value had increased to $300 per ounce. Records for 2008 indicate the following:

Production	200,000 ounces
Sales	230,000 ounces
Deliveries	190,000 ounces

Cash collection	210,000 ounces
Costs of production including depletion*	$50,000,000
Selling expense	$2,000,000
Administrative expenses	$1,250,000
Tax rate	50%

*Production cost per ounce has remained constant over the last few years, and the company has maintained the same production level.

Required   a. Compute the income for 2008, using each of the following bases:
   1. Receipt of cash
   2. Point of sale
   3. End of production
   4. Based on delivery
   b. Comment on when each of the methods should be used. Which method should be used by Uranium Mining Company?

P 4-14.   Each of the following statements represents a decision made by the accountant of Growth Industries:
   a. A tornado destroyed $200,000 in uninsured inventory. This loss is included in the cost of goods sold.
   b. Land was purchased 10 years ago for $50,000. The accountant adjusts the land account to $100,000, which is the estimated current value.
   c. The cost of machinery and equipment is charged to a fixed asset account. The machinery and equipment will be expensed over the period of use.
   d. The value of equipment increased this year, so no depreciation of equipment was recorded this year.
   e. During the year, inventory that cost $5,000 was stolen by employees. This loss has been included in the cost of goods sold for the financial statements. The total amount of the cost of goods sold was $1,000,000.
   f. The president of the company, who owns the business, used company funds to buy a car for personal use. The car was recorded on the company's books.

Required   State whether you agree or disagree with each decision.

P 4-15.   The following information for Gaffney Corporation covers the year ended December 31, 2008:

GAFFNEY CORPORATION
Income Statement
For the Year Ended December 31, 2008

Revenue:		
Revenues from sales		$450,000
Other		5,000
Total revenue		455,000
Expenses:		
Cost of products sold	$280,000	
Selling expenses	50,000	
Administrative and general expenses	20,000	
Federal and state income taxes	30,000	
Total expenses		380,000
Net income		75,000
Other comprehensive income		
Available-for-sale securities adjustment, net of $5,000 income tax	$ 7,000	
Foreign currency translation adjustment, net of $3,000 income tax	8,000	
Other comprehensive income		15,000
Comprehensive income		$ 90,000

Required   a. Will net income or comprehensive income tend to be more volatile? Comment.

b. Which income figure will be used to compute earnings per share?

c. What is the total tax expense reported?

d. Will the items within other comprehensive income always net out as an addition to net income? Comment.

P 4-16.

Required   Answer the following multiple-choice questions:

a. Which of the following items would be classified as operating revenue or expense on an income statement of a manufacturing firm?

1. Interest expense

2. Advertising expense

3. Equity income

4. Dividend income

5. Cumulative effect of change in accounting principle

b. Which of the following is a recurring item?

1. Error of a prior period

2. Equity in earnings of nonconsolidated subsidiaries

3. Extraordinary loss

4. Cumulative effect of change in accounting principle

5. Discontinued operations

c. The following relate to the income statement of Growth Company for the year ended 2008. What is the beginning inventory?

Purchases	$180,000
Purchase returns	5,000
Sales	240,000
Cost of goods sold	210,000
Ending inventory	30,000

1. $6,000

2. $65,000

3. $50,000

4. $55,000

5. $70,000

d. Which of the following items are considered to be nonrecurring items?

1. Equity earnings

2. Unusual or infrequent item disclosed separately

3. Discontinued operations

4. Extraordinary item

5. Cumulative effect of change in accounting principle

e. If the investor company owns 30% of the stock of the investee company and the investee company reports profits of $150,000, then the investor company reports equity income of

1. $25,000.

2. $35,000.

3. $45,000.

4. $50,000.

5. $55,000.

f. Which of the following would be classified as an extraordinary item on the income statement?

1. Loss from tornado

2. Loss on disposal of a segment of business

3. Write-down of inventory

4. Correction of an error of the current period

5. Loss from strike

g. Which of the following is true when a cash dividend is declared and paid?
   1. The firm is left with a liability to pay the dividend.
   2. Retained earnings is reduced by the amount of the dividend.
   3. Retained earnings is increased by the amount of the dividend.
   4. Retained earnings is not influenced by the dividend.
   5. Stockholders' equity is increased.

h. Which of the following is true when a 10% stock dividend is declared and distributed?
   1. Retained earnings is increased.
   2. Stockholders' equity is increased.
   3. Stockholders' equity is decreased.
   4. Authorized shares are increased.
   5. The overall effect is to leave stockholders' equity in total and each owner's share of stockholders' equity is unchanged; however, the total number of shares increases.

P 4-17.

Required   Answer the following multiple-choice questions:

a. The following relate to Owens data in 2008. What is the ending inventory?

Purchases	$580,000
Beginning inventory	80,000
Purchase returns	8,000
Sales	900,000
Cost of goods sold	520,000

   1. $150,000
   2. $132,000
   3. $152,000
   4. $170,000
   5. $142,000

b. Changes in account balances of Gross Flowers during 2008 were as follows:

	Increase
Assets	$400,000
Liabilities	150,000
Capital stock	120,000
Additional paid-in capital	110,000

   Assuming there were no charges to retained earnings other than dividends of $20,000, the net income (loss) for 2008 was
   1. $(20,000).
   2. $(40,000).
   3. $20,000.
   4. $40,000.
   5. $60,000.

c. Which of the following would be classified as an extraordinary item on the income statement?
   1. Loss on disposal of a segment of business
   2. Cumulative effect of a change in accounting principle
   3. A sale of fixed assets
   4. An error correction that relates to a prior year
   5. A loss from a flood in a location that would not be expected to flood

d. Minority share of earnings comes from which of the following situations?
   1. A company has been consolidated with our income statement, and our company owns less than 100% of the other company.

2. A company has been consolidated with our income statement, and our company owns 100% of the other company.

3. Our company owns less than 100% of another company, and the statements are not consolidated.

4. Our company owns 100% of another company, and the statements are not consolidated.

5. None of the above

e. Which of the following will *not* be disclosed in retained earnings?

1. Declaration of a stock dividend

2. Adjustment for an error of the current period

3. Adjustment for an error of a prior period

4. Net income

5. Net loss

f. Bell Company has 2,000,000 shares of common stock with par of $10. Additional paid-in capital totals $15,000,000, and retained earnings is $15,000,000. The directors declare a 5% stock dividend when the market value is $10. The reduction of retained earnings as a result of the declaration will be

1. $0.

2. $1,000,000.

3. $800,000.

4. $600,000.

5. None of the above.

g. The stockholders' equity of Gaffney Company at November 30, 2008, is presented below.

Common stock, par value $5, authorized 200,000 shares, 100,000 shares issued and outstanding	$500,000
Paid-in capital in excess of par	100,000
Retained earnings	300,000
	$900,000

On December 1, 2008, the board of directors of Gaffney Company declared a 5% stock dividend, to be distributed on December 20. The market price of the common stock was $10 on December 1 and $12 on December 20. What is the amount of the change to retained earnings as a result of the declaration and distribution of this stock dividend?

1. $0

2. $40,000

3. $50,000

4. $60,000

5. None of the above

h. Schroeder Company had 200,000 shares of common stock outstanding with a $2 par value and retained earnings of $90,000. In 2006, earnings per share were $0.50. In 2007, the company split the stock 2 for 1. Which of the following would result from the stock split?

1. Retained earnings will decrease as a result of the stock split.

2. A total of 400,000 shares of common stock will be outstanding.

3. The par value would become $4 par.

4. Retained earnings will increase as a result of the stock split.

5. None of the above

i. Which of the following is *not* a category within accumulated other comprehensive income?

1. Foreign currency translation adjustments

2. Unrealized holding gains and losses on available-for-sale marketable securities

3. Changes to stockholders' equity resulting from additional minimum pension liability

4. Unrealized gains and losses from derivative instruments

5. Extraordinary item

Case	HOME BUILDING BLUES
4-1	

LENNAR CORPORATION AND SUBSIDIARIES*
CONSOLIDATED STATEMENTS OF EARNINGS (in Part)
Years Ended November 30, 2006, 2005, and 2004

	2006	2005	2004
	(Dollars in thousands, except per share amounts)		
Revenues:			
Homebuilding	$15,623,040	$13,304,599	$10,000,632
Financial services	643,622	562,372	500,336
Total revenues	16,266,662	13,866,971	10,500,968
Costs and expenses:			
Homebuilding (1)	14,677,565	11,215,244	8,629,767
Financial services	493,819	457,604	389,605
Corporate general and administrative	193,307	187,257	141,722
Total costs and expenses	15,364,691	11,860,105	9,161,094
Equity in earnings (loss) from unconsolidated entities (2)	(12,536)	133,814	90,739
Management fees and other income, net	66,629	98,952	97,680
Minority interest expense, net	13,415	45,030	10,796
Loss on redemption of 9.95% senior notes	—	34,908	—
Earnings from continuing operations before provision for income taxes	942,649	2,159,694	1,517,497
Provision for income taxes	348,780	815,284	572,855
Net earnings from continuing operations	593,869	1,344,410	944,642
Discontinued operations:			
Earnings from discontinued operations before provision for income taxes	—	17,261	1,570
Provision for income taxes	—	6,516	593
Net earnings from discontinued operations	—	10,745	977
Net earnings	$ 593,869	$ 1,355,155	$ 945,619

(1) Homebuilding costs and expenses include $501.8 million, $20.5 million, and $16.8 million, respectively, of inventory valuation adjustments for the years ended November 30, 2006, 2005, and 2004.

(2) Equity in earnings (loss) from unconsolidated entities includes $126.4 million of valuation adjustments to the Company's investments in unconsolidated entities for the year ended November 30, 2006. There were no material valuation adjustments for the years ended November 30, 2005 and 2004.

Required   a. Would you consider the presentation to be a multiple-step income statement or a single-step income statement? Comment.

b. Does it appear that there is a 100% ownership in all consolidated subsidiaries?

c. If a subsidiary were not consolidated but rather accounted for using the equity method, would this change net income? Explain.

d. Describe equity earnings. Why were these entities not consolidated?

e. What type of "special item" would be Loss on Redemption of 9.95% Senior Notes?

f. Which would likely be considered more important when looking to the future—net earnings from continuing operations or net earnings?

g. Consider homebuilding revenue and homebuilding costs. Comment on the trend in profitability between 2005 and 2006.

*"We are one of the nation's largest homebuilders and a provider of financial services." 10-K

ENTERTAINMENT PROVIDER

HARRAH'S ENTERTAINMENT, INC.*
CONSOLIDATED STATEMENTS OF INCOME (in Part)

	Years Ended December 31,		
	2006	2005	2004
	(In millions except per share amounts)		
Revenues			
Casino	$ 7,868.6	$ 5,966.5	$3,922.9
Food and beverage	1,577.7	1,086.7	650.9
Rooms	1,240.7	786.2	382.2
Management fees	89.1	75.6	60.6
Other	611.0	424.7	215.9
Less: Casino promotional allowances	(1,713.2)	(1,329.7)	(835.7)
Net revenues	9,673.9	7,010.0	4,396.8
Operating expenses			
Direct			
Casino	3,902.6	2,984.6	1,972.5
Food and beverage	697.6	482.3	275.1
Rooms	256.6	151.5	66.7
Property general, administrative and other	2,206.8	1,464.4	898.1
Depreciation and amortization	667.9	485.7	313.1
Write-downs, reserves and recoveries (Note 10)	83.3	194.7	9.6
Project opening costs	20.9	16.4	9.4
Corporate expense	177.5	97.7	66.8
Merger and integration costs	37.0	55.0	2.3
(Income)/losses on interests in nonconsolidated affiliates (Note 16)	(3.6)	(1.2)	0.9
Amortization of intangible assets (Note 5)	70.7	49.9	9.5
Total operating expenses	8,117.3	5,981.0	3,624.0
Income from operations	1,556.6	1,029.0	772.8
Interest expense, net of interest capitalized (Note 12)	(670.5)	(479.6)	(269.3)
Losses on early extinguishments of debt (Note 8)	(62.0)	(3.3)	—
Other income, including interest income	10.7	8.0	9.5
Income from continuing operations before income taxes and minority interests	834.8	554.1	513.0
Provision for income taxes (Note 11)	(295.6)	(225.9)	(185.1)
Minority interests	(15.3)	(11.9)	(8.6)
Income from continuing operations	523.9	316.3	319.3
Discontinued operations (Note 4)			
Income from discontinued operations (including gains on disposals of $10.9, $119.6 and $0.0)	16.4	16.6	72.4
Provisions for income taxes	(4.5)	(96.5)	(24.0)
Income/(loss) from discontinued operations	11.9	(79.9)	48.4
Net income	$ 535.8	$ 236.4	$ 367.7

Required
   a. Would you consider the presentation to be a multiple-step income statement or a single-step income statement?

   b. Does it appear there is a 100% ownership in all consolidated subsidiaries? Comment.

   c. If a subsidiary were not consolidated but rather accounted for using the equity method, would this change net income? Explain.

   d. Describe (Income)/Losses on Interests in Nonconsolidated Affiliates. What is this account normally called?

   e. What type of "special item" is Losses on Early Extinguishments of Debt?

   f. Which would likely be considered more important when looking to the future— income from continuing operations or net income?

*"Harrah's Entertainment, Inc. . . . is one of the largest casino entertainment providers in the world." 10-K

Case	APPAREL EXTRAORDINARY
4-3	

PERRY ELLIS INTERNATIONAL, INC. AND SUBSIDIARIES*
CONSOLIDATED STATEMENTS OF INCOME (in Part)
FOR THE YEARS ENDED JANUARY 31,
(Amounts in thousands, except per share data)

	2007	2006	2005
Revenues			
Net sales	$807,616	$827,504	$633,774
Royalty income	22,226	21,910	22,807
Total revenues	829,842	849,414	656,581
Cost of sales	554,046	586,900	448,531
Gross profit	275,796	262,514	208,050
Operating expenses			
Selling, general and administrative expenses	204,883	195,236	153,282
Depreciation and amortization	11,608	9,557	6,557
Total operating expense	216,491	204,793	159,839
Operating income	59,305	57,721	48,211
Costs on early extinguishment of debt	2,963	—	—
Interest expense	21,114	21,930	14,575
Income before minority interest and income tax provision	35,228	35,791	33,636
Minority interest	508	470	467
Income tax provision	12,311	12,639	12,207
Net income	$ 22,409	$ 22,682	$ 20,962

Required   a. What type of "special item" would be Costs on Early Extinguishment of Debt?

b. Does it appear that there is a 100% ownership in all consolidated subsidiaries? Comment.

c. What type of year-end is being used?

*"We are one of the leading apparel companies in the United States." 10-K

Case	THE BIG ORDER
4-4	

On October 15, 1990, United Airlines (UAL Corporation) placed the largest wide-body aircraft order in commercial aviation history—60 Boeing 747-400s and 68 Boeing 777s—with an estimated value of $22 billion. With this order, United became the launch customer for the B777. This order was equally split between firm orders and options.

Required   a. Comment on when United Airlines should record the purchase of these planes.

b. Comment on when Boeing should record the revenue from selling these planes.

c. Speculate on how firm the commitment was on the part of United Airlines to accept delivery of these planes.

d. 1. Speculate on the disclosure for this order in the 1990 financial statements and notes of United Airlines.

2. Speculate on the disclosure for this order in the 1990 annual report of United Airlines. (Exclude the financial statements and notes.)

e. 1. Speculate on the disclosure for this order in the 1990 financial statements and notes of Boeing.

2. Speculate on the disclosure for this order in the 1990 annual report of Boeing. (Exclude the financial statements and notes.)

CELTICS

Boston Celtics Limited Partnership II and Subsidiaries presented these consolidated
statements of income for 1998, 1997, and 1996.

BOSTON CELTICS LIMITED PARTNERSHIP II AND SUBSIDIARIES
CONSOLIDATED STATEMENTS OF INCOME

	For the Year Ended		
	June 30, 1998	June 30, 1997	June 30, 1996
Revenues:			
Basketball regular season	$39,107,960	$31,813,019	$35,249,625
Ticket sales	28,002,469	23,269,159	22,071,992
Television and radio broadcast rights fees	8,569,485	7,915,626	7,458,651
Other, principally promotional advertising	75,679,914	62,997,804	64,780,268
Costs and expenses:			
Basketball regular season			
Team	40,401,643	40,941,156	27,891,264
Game	2,820,107	2,386,042	2,606,218
General and administrative	13,464,566	13,913,893	15,053,333
Selling and promotional	4,819,478	4,680,168	2,973,488
Depreciation	208,162	189,324	140,894
Amortization of NBA franchise and other intangible assets	165,035	164,702	164,703
	61,878,991	62,275,285	48,829,900
	13,800,923	722,519	15,950,368
Interest expense	(6,017,737)	(5,872,805)	(6,387,598)
Interest income	6,402,366	6,609,541	8,175,184
Net realized gains (losses) on disposition of marketable securities and other short-term investments	(18,235)	361,051	(101,138)
Income from continuing operations before income taxes	14,167,317	1,820,306	17,636,816
Provision for income taxes	1,900,000	1,400,000	1,850,000
Income from continuing operations	12,267,317	420,306	15,786,816
Discontinued operations:			
Income from discontinued operations (less applicable income taxes of $30,000)			82,806
Gain from disposal of discontinued operations (less applicable income taxes of $17,770,000)			38,330,907
NET INCOME	12,267,317	420,306	54,200,529
Net income applicable to interests of General Partners	306,216	62,246	1,291,014
Net income applicable to interests of Limited Partners	$11,961,101	$ 358,060	$52,909,515
Per unit:			
Income from continuing operations—basic	$2.45	$0.07	$2.68
Income from continuing operations—diluted	$2.17	$0.06	$2.59
Net income—basic	$2.45	$0.07	$9.18
Net income—diluted	$2.17	$0.06	$8.89
Distributions declared	$2.00	$1.00	$1.50

Required

a. Comment on Amortization of NBA Franchise and Other Intangible Assets.

b. Would the discontinued operations be included in projecting the future? Comment.

c. The costs and expenses include team costs and expenses. Speculate on the major reason for the increase in this expense between 1996 and 1997.

d. What were the major reasons for the increase in income from continuing operations between 1997 and 1998?

e. Speculate on why distributions declared were higher in 1998 than 1996. (Notice that net income was substantially higher in 1996.)

Case
4-6

POLYMER PRODUCTS

MYERS INDUSTRIES, INC. AND SUBSIDIARIES*
Statements of Consolidated Income (in Part)
For the Years Ended December 31, 2006, 2005, and 2004

	2006	2005	2004
Net sales	$779,984,388	$736,880,105	$635,912,379
Cost of sales	572,438,757	555,687,606	464,565,836
Gross profit	207,545,631	181,192,499	171,346,543
Selling	79,340,520	71,796,860	66,631,978
General and administrative	67,282,548	62,400,646	60,071,564
Gain on sale of plants	0	(740,386)	(1,524,598)
	146,623,068	133,457,120	125,178,944
Operating income	60,922,563	47,735,379	46,167,599
Interest			
Income	(146,343)	(340,173)	(434,854)
Expense	15,994,763	15,803,452	13,490,294
	15,848,426	15,463,279	13,055,440
Income from continuing operations before income taxes	45,074,143	32,272,100	33,112,159
Income taxes	16,363,613	12,907,205	12,925,464
Income from continuing operations	28,710,531	19,364,895	20,186,695
Income (loss) from discontinued operations, net of tax	(97,734,686)	7,190,611	5,523,065
Net income (loss)	$ (69,024,155)	$ 26,555,506	$ 25,709,760

Required
a. Comment on Income from Continuing Operations versus Net Income (Loss). Which of these would best reflect the future?
b. What type of "special item" would be Gain on Sale of Plants?
c. Comment on the trend in gross profit.

*"The Company conducts its business activities in four distinct business segments, including three in manufacturing and one in distribution. . . . In our manufacturing segments, we design, manufacture, and market a variety of plastic and rubber products." 10-K

Case
4-7

MULTIPLE INCOME

Shaw Communications, Inc.,* included this information in its annual report.

NOTES TO CONSOLIDATED FINANCIAL STATEMENTS (in Part)

August 31, 2004, 2003, and 2002

[all amounts in thousands of Canadian dollars except per share amounts]

21. UNITED STATES ACCOUNTING PRINCIPLES (in Part)

The consolidated financial statements of the Company are prepared in Canadian dollars in accordance with accounting principles generally accepted in Canada ("Canadian GAAP"). The following adjustments and disclosures would be required in order to present these consolidated financial statements in accordance with accounting principles generally accepted in the United States ("US GAAP").

*"Shaw Communications . . . is a diversified Canadian Communications company whose core business is providing broadband cable television, internet and satellite direct-to-home ("DTH") services to over three million customers." Annual report 2004.

(continued)

(a) Reconciliation to accounting principles generally accepted in the United States

	2004	2003	2002
Net income (loss) using Canadian GAAP	$ 90,909	$ (46,864)	$(284,629)
Add (deduct) adjustments for:			
Deferred charges (2)	14,424	(9,849)	35,594
Foreign exchange gains (3)	22,899	54,527	1,370
Equity in losses of investees (4)	—	2,001	(19,901)
Entitlement payments on equity instruments (8)	(62,302)	(64,827)	(70,551)
Adjustment to write-down of GT Group			
Telecom Inc. (11)	—	—	28,374
Income tax effect of adjustments	15,724	18,005	13,631
Effect of future income tax rate reductions			
on differences	(534)	—	—
Net income (loss) using U.S. GAAP	81,120	(47,007)	(296,112)
Unrealized foreign exchange gain (loss) on			
translation of self-sustaining foreign operations	(38)	(1,031)	1,513
Unrealized gains on available-for-sale securities, net of tax (7)			
Unrealized holding gains arising during the year	5,456	1,361	59,406
Less: Reclassification adjustments for gains			
included in net income	(1,055)	(95,879)	(180,425)
	4,363	(95,549)	(119,506)
Adjustment to fair value of derivatives (9)	(67,408)	(224,341)	53,293
Foreign exchange gains on hedged long-term debt (10)	57,704	136,975	—
Minimum liability for pension plan (13)	(3,864)	(1,928)	—
Effect of future income tax rate reductions on differences	(63)	—	—
	(9,268)	(184,843)	(66,213)
Comprehensive income (loss) using U.S. GAAP	$ 71,852	$(231,850)	$(362,325)
Earnings (loss) per share—basic and diluted			
Net income (loss) per share using U.S. GAAP	$0.35	$(0.20)	$(1.28)
Comprehensive income (loss) per share using U.S. GAAP	$0.31	$(1.00)	$(1.56)

Required

a. Observe net income (loss) using Canadian GAAP, net income (loss) using U.S. GAAP, and comprehensive income (loss) using U.S. GAAP. Comment on the materiality of the difference between these numbers.

b. Harmonization of international accounting standards has been a goal for many years. Considering the substantial commerce and flow of capital between Canada and the United States, would it be desirable to have similar accounting standards? Comment.

c. Do you think that harmonization of international accounting will be achieved in the near future? In the long run? Comment.

Thomson One *Business School Edition*

Please complete the Web case that covers material discussed in this chapter at academic.cengage.com/accounting/Gibson. You'll be using Thomson One Business School Edition, a powerful tool, that combines a full range of fundamental financial information, earnings estimates, market data, and source documents for 500 publicly traded companies.

Endnotes

1. *Accounting Trends & Techniques* (New York, NY: American Institute of Certified Public Accountants, 2006), p. 295.
2. Michael L. Roberts, William D. Samson, and Michael T. Dugan, "The Stockholders' Equity Section: Form Without Substance," *Accounting Horizon* (December 1990), pp. 35–46.
3. Ibid., p. 36.

Chapter 5

Basics of Analysis

The analysis of financial data employs various techniques to emphasize the comparative and relative importance of the data presented and to evaluate the position of the firm. These techniques include ratio analysis, common-size analysis, study of differences in components of financial statements among industries, review of descriptive material, and comparisons of results with other types of data. The information derived from these types of analysis should be blended to determine the overall financial position. No one type of analysis supports overall findings or serves all types of users. This chapter provides an introduction to different analyses and uses of financial information.

Financial statement analysis is a judgmental process. One of the primary objectives is identification of major changes (turning points) in trends, amounts, and relationships and investigation of the reasons underlying those changes. Often, a turning point may signal an early warning of a significant shift in the future success or failure of the business. The judgment process can be improved by experience and by the use of analytical tools.

Ratio Analysis

Financial ratios are usually expressed as a percent or as times per period. The following ratios will be discussed fully in future chapters.

1. Liquidity ratios measure a firm's ability to meet its current obligations. They may include ratios that measure the efficiency of the use of current assets and current liabilities (Chapter 6).
2. Borrowing capacity (leverage) ratios measure the degree of protection of suppliers of long-term funds (Chapter 7).
3. Profitability ratios measure the earning ability of a firm. Discussion will include measures of the use of assets in general (Chapter 8).
4. Investors are interested in a special group of ratios, in addition to liquidity, debt, and profitability ratios (Chapter 9).
5. Cash flow ratios can indicate liquidity, borrowing capacity, or profitability (Chapter 10).

A ratio can be computed from any pair of numbers. Given the large quantity of variables included in financial statements, a very long list of meaningful ratios can be derived. A standard list of ratios or standard computation of them does not exist. Each author and source on financial analysis uses a different list and often a different computation of the same ratio. This book presents frequently utilized and discussed ratios.

Ratios are interpretable in comparison with (1) prior ratios, (2) ratios of competitors, (3) industry ratios, and (4) predetermined standards. The trend of a ratio and the variability of a ratio are important considerations.

Comparison of income statement and balance sheet numbers, in the form of ratios, can create difficulties due to the timing of the financial statements. Specifically, the income statement covers the entire fiscal period; whereas, the balance sheet applies to a single point in time, the end of the period. Ideally, then, to compare an income statement figure such as sales to a balance sheet figure such as receivables, we need to know the average receivables for the year that the sales figure covers. However, these data are not available to the external analyst. In some cases, the analyst uses an average of the beginning and ending balance sheet figures. This approach smooths out changes from beginning to end, but it does not eliminate problems due to seasonal and cyclical changes. It also does not reflect changes that occur unevenly throughout the year.

Be aware that computing averages from two similar balance sheet dates can be misleading. It is possible that a representative average cannot be computed from externally published statements.

A ratio will usually represent a fairly accurate trend, even when the ratio is distorted. If the ratio is distorted, then it does not represent a good absolute number.

Applying the U.S. techniques of ratio analysis to statements prepared in other countries can be misleading. The ratio analysis must be understood in terms of the accounting principles used and the business practices and culture of the country.

Common-Size Analysis (Vertical and Horizontal)

Common-size analysis expresses comparisons in percentages. For example, if cash is $40,000 and total assets is $1,000,000, then cash represents 4% of total assets. The use of percentages is usually preferable to the use of absolute amounts. An illustration will make this clear. If Firm A earns $10,000 and Firm B earns $1,000, which is more profitable? Firm A is probably your response. However, the total owners' equity of A is $1,000,000, and B's is $10,000. The return on owners' equity is as follows:

	Firm A	Firm B
$\dfrac{\text{Earnings}}{\text{Owners' Equity}}$	$\dfrac{\$10,000}{\$1,000,000} = 1\%$	$\dfrac{\$1,000}{\$10,000} = 10\%$

The use of common-size analysis makes comparisons of firms of different sizes much more meaningful. Care must be exercised in the use of common-size analysis with small absolute amounts because a small change in amount can result in a very substantial percentage change. For example, if profits last year amounted to $100 and increased this year to $500, this would be an increase of only $400 in profits, but it would represent a substantial percentage increase.

Vertical analysis compares each amount with a base amount selected from the same year. For example, if advertising expenses were $1,000 in 2007 and sales were $100,000, the advertising would have been 1% of sales.

Horizontal analysis compares each amount with a base amount for a selected base year. For example, if sales were $400,000 in 2006 and $600,000 in 2007, then sales increased to 150% of the 2006 level in 2007, an increase of 50%.

Exhibit 5-1 illustrates common-size analysis (vertical and horizontal).

Year-to-Year Change Analysis

Comparing financial statements over two time periods using absolute amounts and percentages can be meaningful. This approach aids in keeping absolute and percentage changes in perspective. For example, a substantial percentage change may not be relevant because of an immaterial absolute change. When performing year-to-year change analysis, follow these rules:

1. When an item has value in the base year and none in the next period, the decrease is 100%.
2. A meaningful percent change cannot be computed when one number is positive and the other number is negative.
3. No percent change is computable when there is no figure for the base year.

These rules are illustrated in Exhibit 5-2.

| Exhibit | 5-1 | MELCHER COMPANY |

Income Statement

Illustration of Common-Size Analysis (Vertical and Horizontal)

	For the Years Ended December 31,		
(Absolute dollars)	**2007**	**2006**	**2005**
Revenue from sales	$100,000	$95,000	$91,000
Cost of products sold	65,000	60,800	56,420
Gross profit	35,000	34,200	34,580
Operating expenses			
Selling expenses	14,000	11,400	10,000
General expenses	16,000	15,200	13,650
Total operating expenses	30,000	26,600	23,650
Operating income before income taxes	5,000	7,600	10,930
Taxes related to operations	1,500	2,280	3,279
Net income	$ 3,500	$ 5,320	$ 7,651
Vertical Common Size			
Revenue from sales	100.0%	100.0%	100.0%
Cost of goods sold	65.0	64.0	62.0
Gross profit	35.0	36.0	38.0
Operating expenses			
Selling expenses	14.0	12.0	11.0
General expenses	16.0	16.0	15.0
Total operating expenses	30.0	28.0	26.0
Operating income before income taxes	5.0	8.0	12.0
Taxes related to operations	1.5	2.4	3.6
Net income	3.5%	5.6%	8.4%
Horizontal Common Size			
Revenue from sales	109.9%	104.4%	100.0%
Cost of goods sold	115.2	107.8	100.0
Gross profit	101.2	98.9	100.0
Operating expenses			
Selling expenses	140.0	114.0	100.0
General expenses	117.2	111.4	100.0
Total operating expenses	126.8	112.5	100.0
Operating income before income taxes	45.7	69.5	100.0
Taxes related to operations	45.7	69.5	100.0
Net income	45.7	69.5	100.0

| Exhibit | 5-2 | YEAR-TO-YEAR CHANGE ANALYSIS |

(Illustrating Rules)

Item	Year 1	Year 2	Change Analysis Amount	Percent
Advertising expense	$20,000	$ —	$(20,000)	(100%)
Operating income	6,000	(3,000)	(9,000)	—
Net income	(7,000)	8,000	15,000	—
Other	—	4,000	4,000	—

Financial Statement Variation by Type of Industry

The components of financial statements, especially the balance sheet and the income statement, will vary by type of industry. Exhibits 5-3, 5-4, and 5-5 (pages 180–185) illustrate, respectively, a merchandising firm (Best Buy Co., Inc.), a service firm (Kelly Services, Inc. and Subsidiaries), and a manufacturing firm (Cooper Tire & Rubber Company).

Merchandising (retail-wholesale) firms sell products purchased from other firms. A principal asset is inventory, which consists of merchandise inventories. For some merchandising firms, a large amount of sales may be for cash. In such cases, the receivables balance will be relatively low. Other merchandising firms have a large amount of sales charged but also accept credit

Exhibit	5-3	BEST BUY CO., INC.*

Merchandising Firm

Best Buy Co., Inc.
Consolidated Balance Sheets
($ in millions, except per share amounts)

	March 3, 2007	February 25, 2006
Assets		
Current Assets		
Cash and cash equivalents	$ 1,205	$ 748
Short-term investments	2,588	3,041
Receivables	548	449
Merchandise inventories	4,028	3,338
Other current assets	712	409
Total current assets	9,081	7,985
Property and Equipment		
Land and buildings	705	580
Leasehold improvements	1,540	1,325
Fixtures and equipment	2,627	2,898
Property under capital lease	32	33
	4,904	4,836
Less accumulated depreciation	1,966	2,124
Net property and equipment	2,938	2,712
Goodwill	919	557
Tradenames	81	44
Long-Term Investments	318	218
Other Assets	233	348
Total Assets	$ 13,570	$ 11,864
Liabilities and Shareholders' Equity		
Current Liabilities		
Accounts payable	$ 3,934	$ 3,234
Unredeemed gift card liabilities	496	469
Accrued compensation and related expenses	332	354
Accrued liabilities	990	878
Accrued income taxes	489	703
Short-term debt	41	—
Current portion of long-term debt	19	418
Total current liabilities	6,301	6,056
Long-Term Liabilities	443	373
Long-Term Debt	590	178
Minority Interests	35	—
Shareholders' Equity		
Preferred stock, $1.00 par value: Authorized—400,000 shares; Issued and outstanding—none	—	—
Common stock, $.10 par value; Authorized—1 billion shares; Issued and outstanding—480,655,000 and 485,098,000 shares, respectively	48	49
Additional paid-in capital	430	643
Retained earnings	5,507	4,304
Accumulated other comprehensive income	216	261
Total shareholders' equity	6,201	5,257
Total Liabilities and Shareholders' Equity	$13,570	$11,864

*"Best Buy Co., Inc. . . . is a specialty retailer of consumer electronics, home-office products, entertainment software, appliances and related services." 10-K

| Exhibit | 5-3 | BEST BUY CO., INC. (Continued) |

Best Buy Co., Inc.
Consolidated Statements of Earnings
($ in millions, except per share amounts)

Fiscal Years Ended	March 3, 2007	February 25, 2006	February 26, 2005
Revenue	$35,934	$30,848	$27,433
Cost of goods sold	27,165	23,122	20,938
Gross profit	8,769	7,726	6,495
Selling, general and administrative expenses	6,770	6,082	5,053
Operating income	1,999	1,644	1,442
Net interest income	111	77	1
Gain on investments	20	—	—
Earnings from continuing operations before income tax expense	2,130	1,721	1,443
Income tax expense	752	581	509
Minority interest in earnings	1	—	—
Earnings from continuing operations	1,377	1,140	934
Gain on disposal of discontinued operations (Note 2), net of tax	—	—	50
Net earnings	$ 1,377	$ 1,140	$ 984
Basic earnings per share:			
Continuing operations	$ 2.86	$ 2.33	$ 1.91
Gain on disposal of discontinued operations	—	—	0.10
Basic earnings per share	$ 2.86	$ 2.33	$ 2.01
Diluted earnings per share:			
Continuing operations	$ 2.79	$ 2.27	$ 1.86
Gain on disposal of discontinued operations	—	—	0.10
Diluted earnings per share	$ 2.79	$ 2.27	$ 1.96
Basic weighted-average common shares outstanding (in millions)	482.1	490.3	488.9
Diluted weighted-average common shares outstanding (in millions)	496.2	504.8	505.0

cards such as VISA, so they also have a relatively low balance in receivables. Other firms extend credit and carry the accounts receivable and thus have a relatively large receivables balance. Because of the competitive nature of the industry, profit ratios on the income statement are often quite low, with the cost of sales and operating expenses constituting a large portion of expenses. Refer to Exhibit 5-3, Best Buy Co., Inc.

A service firm generates its revenue from the service provided. Because service cannot typically be stored, inventory is low or nonexistent. In people-intensive services, such as advertising, investment in property and equipment is also low compared with that of manufacturing firms. Refer to Exhibit 5-4, Kelly Services, Inc. and Subsidiaries.

A manufacturing firm will usually have large inventories composed of raw materials, work in process, and finished goods, as well as a material investment in property, plant, and equipment. Notes and accounts receivable may also be material, depending on the terms of sale. The cost of sales often represents the major expense. Refer to Exhibit 5-5, Cooper Tire & Rubber Company.

Review of Descriptive Information

The descriptive information found in an annual report, in trade periodicals, and in industry reviews helps us understand the financial position of a firm. Descriptive material might discuss the role of research and development in producing future sales, present data on capital expansion and the goals related thereto, discuss aspects of employee relations such as minority hiring or union negotiations, or help explain the dividend policy of the firm. In its annual report, a company must present a section called Management Discussion and Analysis (MD&A). This section provides an overview of the previous year and an overview of future goals and new projects. Although the MD&A is unaudited, the information it contains can be very useful.

Exhibit	5-4	KELLY SERVICES, INC. AND SUBSIDIARIES*

Service Firm

BALANCE SHEETS
Kelly Services, Inc. and Subsidiaries

	2006	2005
	(In thousands of dollars)	
ASSETS		
Current Assets		
Cash and equivalents	$ 118,428	$ 63,699
Trade accounts receivable, less allowances of $16,818 and		
$16,648, respectively	838,246	803,812
Prepaid expenses and other current assets	45,316	47,588
Deferred taxes	29,543	33,805
Total current assets	1,031,533	948,904
Property and Equipment		
Land and buildings	61,410	58,461
Equipment, furniture and leasehold improvements	311,244	297,980
Accumulated depreciation	(202,366)	(190,684)
Net property and equipment	170,288	165,757
Noncurrent Deferred Taxes	35,437	22,088
Goodwill, net	96,504	88,217
Other Assets	135,662	87,891
Total Assets	$1,469,424	$1,312,857
LIABILITIES AND STOCKHOLDERS' EQUITY		
Current Liabilities		
Short-term borrowings	$ 68,928	$ 56,644
Accounts payable	132,819	110,411
Accrued payroll and related taxes	274,284	263,112
Accrued insurance	24,191	34,097
Income and other taxes	68,055	56,651
Total current liabilities	568,277	520,915
Noncurrent Liabilities		
Accrued insurance	57,277	54,517
Accrued retirement benefits	71,990	57,443
Other long-term liabilities	13,323	7,939
Total noncurrent liabilities	142,590	119,899
Stockholders' Equity		
Capital stock, $1.00 par value		
Class A common stock, shares issued 36,632,768 at 2006		
and 36,620,146 at 2005	36,633	36,620
Class B common stock, shares issued 3,483,098 at 2006		
and 3,495,720 at 2005	3,483	3,496
Treasury stock, at cost		
Class A common stock, 3,698,781 shares at 2006 and		
4,269,753 at 2005	(78,241)	(90,319)
Class B common stock, 22,575 shares at 2006 and 2005	(600)	(600)
Paid-in capital	32,048	27,015
Earnings invested in the business	735,104	688,033
Accumulated other comprehensive income	30,130	7,798
Total stockholders' equity	758,557	672,043
Total Liabilities and Stockholders' Equity	$1,469,424	$1,312,857

*"We have evolved from a United States-based company concentrating primarily on traditional office services into a global staffing leader with a breadth of specialty businesses. We now assign professional and technical employees in the fields of finance and accounting, education, engineering, information technology, legal, science, health and home care." 10-K

| Exhibit | 5-4 | KELLY SERVICES, INC. AND SUBSIDIARIES (Continued) |

STATEMENTS OF EARNINGS
For the three fiscal years ended December 31, 2006
Kelly Services, Inc. and Subsidiaries

	2006	2005	2004(1)
	(In thousands of dollars except per share items)		
Revenue from services	$5,605,752	$5,251,712	$4,932,650
Cost of services	4,680,538	4,402,618	4,143,411
Gross profit	925,214	849,094	789,239
Selling, general and administrative expenses	846,198	797,813	758,128
Earnings from operations	79,016	51,281	31,111
Other income (expense), net	1,471	(187)	(861)
Earnings from continuing operations before taxes	80,487	51,094	30,250
Income taxes	23,112	14,813	10,780
Earnings from continuing operations	57,375	36,281	19,470
Earnings from discontinued operations, net of tax	6,116	2,982	1,741
Net earnings	$ 63,491	$ 39,263	$ 21,211
Basic earnings per share			
Earnings from continuing operations	$ 1.59	$ 1.02	$ .55
Earnings from discontinued operations	.17	.08	.05
Net earnings	$ 1.76	$ 1.10	$ .60
Diluted earnings per share			
Earnings from continuing operations	$ 1.58	$ 1.01	$ .55
Earnings from discontinued operations	.17	.08	.05
Net earnings	$ 1.75	$ 1.09	$ .60
Dividends per share	$ .45	$ .40	$ .40
Average shares outstanding (thousands):			
Basic	35,999	35,667	35,115
Diluted	36,314	35,949	35,461
(1) Fiscal year included 53 weeks			

Comparisons

Absolute figures or ratios appear meaningless unless compared to other figures or ratios. If a person were asked if $10 is a lot of money, the frame of reference would determine the answer. To a small child, still in awe of a quarter, $10 is a lot. To a millionaire, a $10 bill is nothing. Similarly, having 60% of total assets composed of buildings and equipment would be normal for some firms but disastrous for others. One must have a guide to determine the meaning of the ratios and other measures. Several types of comparisons offer insight.

TREND ANALYSIS

Trend analysis studies the financial history of a firm for comparison. By looking at the trend of a particular ratio, one sees whether that ratio is falling, rising, or remaining relatively constant. This helps detect problems or observe good management.

STANDARD INDUSTRIAL CLASSIFICATION (SIC) MANUAL

The Standard Industrial Classification is a statistical classification of business by industry. The National Technical Information Service publishes the classification manual. The manual is the responsibility of the Office of Management and Budget, which is under the executive office of the president.

Exhibit   5-5   COOPER TIRE & RUBBER COMPANY*

Manufacturing Firm

CONSOLIDATED BALANCE SHEETS
December 31
(Dollar amounts in thousands, except par value amounts)

	2005	2006
ASSETS		
Current Assets:		
Cash and cash equivalents	$ 280,712	$ 221,655
Accounts receivable, less allowances of $5,765 in 2005 and		
$8,880 in 2006	338,793	414,096
Inventories at lower of cost or market:		
Finished goods	221,968	240,100
Work in progress	21,820	28,458
Raw materials and supplies	62,258	83,129
	306,046	351,687
Other current assets	20,120	21,686
Deferred income taxes	23,130	—
Total current assets	968,801	1,009,124
Property, plant and equipment:		
Land and land improvements	39,152	41,553
Buildings	266,364	298,706
Machinery and equipment	1,396,248	1,636,091
Molds, cores and rings	225,555	268,158
	1,927,319	2,244,508
Less accumulated depreciation and amortization	1,141,094	1,252,692
Net property, plant and equipment	786,225	991,816
Goodwill	48,172	24,439
Intangibles, net of accumulated amortization of $18,028 in 2005		
and $22,446 in 2006	31,108	37,399
Restricted cash	12,382	7,550
Other assets	305,498	164,951
	$2,152,186	$2,235,279
LIABILITIES AND STOCKHOLDERS' EQUITY		
Current Liabilities:		
Notes payable	$ 79	$ 112,803
Payable to non-controlling owner of subsidiary	—	51,527
Accounts payable	157,785	238,181
Accrued liabilities	99,659	117,005
Income taxes	15,390	4,698
Liabilities related to the sale of automotive operations	4,684	3,038
Total current liabilities	277,597	527,252
Long-term debt	491,618	513,213
Postretirement benefits other than pensions	181,997	258,579
Other long-term liabilities	220,896	217,743
Long-term liabilities related to the sale of automotive		
operations	14,407	8,913
Deferred income taxes	21,941	—
Minority interests in consolidated subsidiaries	4,954	69,688
Stockholders' equity:		
Preferred stock, $1 par value; 5,000,000 shares authorized; none		
issued	—	—
Common stock, $1 par value; 300,000,000 shares authorized;		
86,322,514 shares issued in 2005 and 2006	86,323	86,323
Capital in excess of par value	37,667	38,144
Retained earnings	1,361,269	1,256,971
Cumulative other comprehensive loss	(86,323)	(282,552)
	1,398,936	1,098,886

*"Cooper Tire & Rubber Company . . . is a leading manufacturer of replacement tires. It is the fourth largest tire manufacturer in North America and, according to a recognized trade source, is the ninth largest tire company in the world based on jobs." 10-K

Exhibit   5-5   COOPER TIRE & RUBBER COMPANY (Continued)

	2005	2006
Less: common shares in treasury at cost (25,001,503 in 2005 and 24,943,265 in 2006)	$ (460,160)	$ (458,995)
Total stockholders' equity	938,776	639,891
	$2,152,186	$2,235,279

CONSOLIDATED STATEMENTS OF OPERATIONS
Years ended December 31
(Dollar amounts in thousands except per share amounts)

	2004	2005	2006
Net sales	$2,081,609	$2,155,185	$2,676,242
Cost of products sold	1,848,616	1,967,835	2,478,679
Gross profit	232,993	187,350	197,563
Selling, general and administrative	171,689	161,192	192,737
Adjustments to class action warranty	(11,273)	(277)	—
Restructuring	9,353	—	14,575
Operating profit	63,224	26,435	(9,749)
Interest expense	27,569	54,511	47,166
Debt extinguishment costs	—	4,228	(77)
Interest income	(2,068)	(18,541)	(10,067)
Dividend from unconsolidated subsidiary	—	—	(4,286)
Impairment of goodwill and indefinite-lived intangible asset	—	—	51,546
Other—net	2,717	588	(2,077)
Income/(loss) from continuing operations before income taxes	35,006	(14,351)	(91,954)
Provision (benefit) for income taxes	7,560	704	(9,727)
Income/(loss) from continuing operations before minority interests	27,446	(15,055)	(82,227)
Minority interests	—	22	(3,663)
Income/(loss) from continuing operations	27,446	(15,033)	(85,890)
Income from discontinued operations, net of income taxes	61,478	—	7,379
Gain on sale of discontinued operations including income tax benefit	112,448	5,677	—
Net income/(loss)	$ 201,372	$ (9,356)	$ (78,511)
Basic earnings (loss) per share:			
Income/(loss) from continuing operations	$ 0.37	$ (0.24	$ (1.40)
Income from discontinued operations	0.83	—	0.12
Gain on sale of discontinued operations	1.52	0.09	—
Net income/(loss)	$ 2.71**	$ (0.15)	$ (1.28)
Diluted earnings (loss) per share:			
Income/(loss) from continuing operations	$ 0.37	$ (0.24)	$ (1.40)
Income from discontinued operations	0.82	—	0.12
Gain on sale of discontinued operations	1.50	0.09	—
Net income/(loss)	$ 2.68**	$ (0.15)	$ (1.28)

**Amounts do not add due to rounding.

Use of the SIC promotes comparability of various facets of the U.S. economy and defines industries in accordance with the composition and structure of the economy. An organization's SIC consists of a two-digit major group number, a three-digit industry group number, and a four-digit industry number. These numbers describe the business's identifiable level of industrial detail.

Determining a company's SIC is a good starting point in researching a company, an industry, or a product. Many library sources use the SIC number as a method of classification.

NORTH AMERICAN INDUSTRY CLASSIFICATION SYSTEM (NAICS)

The North American Industry Classification System (NAICS) was created jointly by the United States, Canada, and Mexico. It is to replace the existing classification of each country: the Standard Industrial Classification of Canada (1980), the Mexican Classification of Activities and Products (1994), and the Standard Industrial Classification of the United States (1987).

For the NAICS, economic units with similar production processes are classified in the same industry, and the lines drawn between industries demarcate differences in production processes. This supply-based economic concept was adopted because an industry classification system is a framework for collecting information on both inputs and outputs. This will aid in the collection of statistics on such things as productivity, unit labor costs, and capital intensity.

NAICS provides enhanced industry comparability among the three NAFTA trading partners. It also increases compatibility with the two-digit level of the International Standard Industrial Classification (ISIC Rev. 3) of the United Nations.

NAICS divides the economy into 20 sectors. Industries within these sectors are grouped according to the production criterion. Four sectors are largely goods-producing and 16 are entirely services-producing industries.

In most sectors, NAICS provides for compatibility at the industry (five-digit) level. For some sectors, the compatibility level is less at four-digit, three-digit, or two-digit levels. Each country can add additional detailed industries, provided the additional detail aggregates to the NAICS level.

The United States adopted the NAICS in 1997 for statistical agencies. Most of the U.S. government agencies now use the NAICS in place of the Standard Industrial Classification. A major exception is the Securities and Exchange Commission (SEC). Companies reporting to the SEC include their SIC. For private companies that publish industry data, some now only use the NAICS, some use the SIC, and some include both the NAICS and the SIC.

INDUSTRY AVERAGES AND COMPARISON WITH COMPETITORS

The analysis of an entity's financial statements is more meaningful if the results are compared with industry averages and with results of competitors. Several financial services provide composite data on various industries.

The analyst faces a problem when the industries reported do not clearly include the company being examined because the company is diversified into many industrial areas. Since many companies do not clearly fit into any one industry, it is often necessary to use an industry that best fits the firm. The financial services have a similar problem in selecting an industry in which to place a company. Thus, a financial service uses its best judgment as to which industry the firm best fits.

This section briefly describes some financial services. For a more extensive explanation, consult the service's literature. Each service explains how it computes its ratios and the data it provides.

The Department of Commerce Financial Report is a publication of the federal government for manufacturing, mining, and trade corporations. Published by the Economic Surveys Division of the Bureau of the Census, it includes income statement data and balance sheet data in total industry dollars. It also includes an industry-wide common-size vertical income statement (Income Statement in Ratio Format) and an industry-wide common-size vertical balance sheet (Selected Balance Sheet Ratios). This source also includes selected operating and balance sheet ratios. This government publication uses NAICS for classification.

This report, updated quarterly, probably offers the most current source. It typically becomes available within six or seven months after the end of the quarter. It is a unique source of industry data in total dollars and would enable a company to compare its dollars (such as sales) with the industry dollars (sales). This service is free and is now on the Internet at http://www.census.gov/csd/qfr.

Annual Statement Studies is published by the Risk Management Association, the association of lending and credit risk professionals. Submitted by institutional members of the Risk

Management Association, the data cover several hundred different industries in manufacturing, wholesaling, retailing, service, agriculture, and construction.

Annual Statement Studies groups the data by industry, using the SIC number, and the NAICS number. It provides common-size balance sheets, income statements, and 16 selected ratios.

The data are sorted by assets and sales and are particularly useful because the financial position and operations of small firms are often quite different from those of larger firms. The presentation also includes a five-year comparison of historical data that presents all firms under a particular NAICS or SIC code.

In each category, the ratios are computed for the median and the upper and lower quartiles. For example:

Number of firms (9)

Ratio—Return on total assets

Results for the nine firms (in order, from highest to lowest):

    12%, 11%, 10.5%, 10%, 9.8%, 9.7%, 9.6%, 7.0%, 6.5%

The middle result is the median: 9.8%

The result halfway between the top result and the median is the upper quartile: 10.5%

The result halfway between the bottom result and the median is the lower quartile: 9.6%

For ratios in which a low value is desirable, the results are presented from low values to high: For example, 2% (upper quartile), 5% (median), and 8% (lower quartile). For ratios in which a high value is desirable, the results are presented from high values to low; for example, 10.5% (upper quartile), 9.8% (median), and 9.6% (lower quartile).

Because of the combination of common-size statements, selected ratios, and comparative historical data, *Annual Statement Studies* is one of the most extensively used sources of industry data. Commercial loan officers in banks frequently use this source.

Standard & Poor's Industry Surveys contains information of particular interest to investors. This includes a write-up by industry, statistics for companies in an industry, and specific company by industry.

Almanac of Business and Industrial Financial Ratios, published by CCH Incorporated, is a compilation of corporate tax return data. It includes nearly 200 industries and presents 50 statistics for 11 size categories of firms. Some of the industries include manufacturing, construction, transportation, retail trade, banking, and wholesale trade.

Beginning with the 2002 edition, each *Almanac* industry is cross-referenced to a NAICS number. The IRS's condensed NAICS represents the classification system used in the *Almanac*.

Industry Norms and Key Business Ratios, desktop edition published by Dun & Bradstreet, includes over 800 different lines of business as defined by the SIC code numbers. It includes one-year data consisting of a condensed balance sheet and income statement in dollars and common size. It also includes working capital and ratios.

There are 14 ratios presented for the upper quartile, median, and lower quartile. The 14 ratios are as follows:

Solvency
    Quick Ratio (Times)
    Current Ratio (Times)
    Current Liabilities to Net Worth (%)
    Current Liabilities to Inventory (%)
    Total Liabilities to Net Worth (%)
    Fixed Assets to Net Worth (%)

Efficiency
    Collection Period (days)
    Sales to Inventory (times)
    Assets to Sales (%)
    Sales to Net Working Capital (times)
    Accounts Payable to Sales (%)

Profitability
>   Return on Sales (%)
>   Return on Assets (%)
>   Return on Net Working Capital (%)

Dun & Bradstreet advises that the industry norms and key business ratios are to be used as yardsticks and not as absolutes. *Industry Norms and Key Business Ratios* is also published in an expanded set in the following five segments:

1. Agriculture/Mining/Construction/Transportation/Communication/Utilities
2. Manufacturing
3. Wholesaling
4. Retailing
5. Finance/Real Estate/Services

All five segments are available in three different formats, for a total of 15 books. The three formats follow:

1. Industry Norms and Key Business Ratios, three-year edition
2. Industry Norms and Key Business Ratios, one-year edition
3. Key Business Ratios, one-year edition

Value Line Investment Survey is in two editions; the Standard Edition and the Small & Mid-Cap Edition. The Standard Edition places companies in 1 of 97 industries. The Small & Mid-Cap Edition places companies in 1 of 84 industries. There are approximately 1,700 stocks in the Standard Edition and approximately 1,800 stocks in the Small & Mid-Cap Edition. The *Value Line Investment Survey* is very popular with investors.

The full-page Ratings & Reports are similar for the Standard Edition and the Small & Mid-Cap Edition. Each stock is rated for timeliness, safety, and technical. The Standard Edition includes an analyst's comments, while the Small & Mid-Cap Edition does not include an analyst's comments.

The data included in *Value Line* for a company are largely for a relatively long period of time (11 to 17 years). The data provided vary somewhat by industry. Some of the data provided for many companies are as follows:

1. Revenues per share
2. Cash flow per share
3. Earnings per share
4. Dividends declared per share
5. Capital spending per share
6. Book value per share
7. Common shares outstanding
8. Average annual P/E ratio
9. Relative P/E ratio
10. Average annual dividend yield
11. Revenues
12. Operating margin
13. Depreciation
14. Net profit
15. Income tax rate
16. Net profit margin
17. Working capital
18. Long-term debt
19. Shareholders' equity

20. Return on total capitalization
21. Return on shareholders' equity
22. Retained to common equity
23. All dividends to net profit

As indicated previously, comparison has become more difficult in recent years as more firms become conglomerates and diversify into many product lines. To counteract this problem, the SEC has implemented line-of-business reporting requirements for companies that must submit their reports to the SEC. These reports are made available to the public. SFAS No. 14 also addresses line-of-business reporting requirements. Such reporting requirements ease the analysis problem created by conglomerates but cannot eliminate it because the entity must decide how to allocate administrative and joint costs.

If industry figures are unavailable or if comparison with a competitor is desired, another firm's statements may be analyzed. Remember, however, that the other firm is not necessarily good or bad, nor does it represent a norm or standard for its industry. It also can be said that industry figures do not necessarily represent good or bad, nor do they represent a standard for its industry.

Alternative accounting methods are acceptable in many situations. Since identical companies may use different valuation or expense methods, read statements and notes carefully to determine if the statements are reasonably comparable.

Ideally, the use of all types of comparison would be best. Using trend analysis, industry averages, and comparisons with a major competitor will give support to findings and will provide a concrete basis for analysis.

In analyzing ratios, the analyst will sometimes encounter negative profit figures. **Analysis of ratios that have negative numerators or denominators is meaningless, and the negative sign of the ratio should simply be noted.**

CAUTION IN USING INDUSTRY AVERAGES

Financial analysis requires judgment decisions on the part of the analyst. Users of financial statements must be careful not to place under confidence in ratios or comparisons.

Remember that ratios are simply fractions with a numerator (top) and a denominator (bottom). There are as many for financial analysis as there are pairs of figures. There is no set group, nor is a particular ratio always computed using the same figures. Even the industry ratio formulas vary from source to source. Adequate detailed disclosure of how the industry ratios are computed is often lacking. Major problems can result from analyzing a firm according to the recommendations of a book and then making comparisons to industry ratios that may have been computed differently.

The use of different accounting methods causes a problem. For example, identical firms may use different valuation or revenue recognition methods. Read statements and notes carefully to determine the degree of comparability between statements. Trend analysis for each firm, however, will usually be meaningful. Industry averages group firms together that use different accounting principles.

Different year-ends can also produce different results. Consider the difference in the inventory of two toy stores if one ends November 30 and the other ends December 31. The ratios of firms with differing year-ends are all grouped together in industry averages.

Firms with differing financial policies might be included in the same industry average. Possibly capital-intensive firms are grouped with labor-intensive companies. Firms with large amounts of debt may be included in the same average as firms that prefer to avoid the risk of debt.

Some industry averages come from small samples that may not be representative of the industry. An extreme statement, such as one containing a large loss, can also distort industry data.

Ratios may have alternative forms of computation. In comparing one year to the next, one firm to another, or a company to its industry, meaningful analysis requires that the ratios be computed using the same formula. For example, *Annual Statement Studies* computes income ratios before tax; Dun & Bradstreet profit figures are after tax. The analyst should compute the enterprise ratios on the same basis as is used for industry comparisons, but this is often not possible.

Finally, ratios are not absolute norms. They are general guidelines to be combined with other methods in formulating an evaluation of the financial condition of a firm. Despite the problems with using ratios, they can be very informative if reasonably used.

Relative Size of Firm

Comparisons of firms of different sizes may be more difficult than comparisons of firms of equal size. For example, larger firms often have access to wider and more sophisticated capital markets, can buy in large quantities, and service wider markets. Ratios and common-size analysis help to eliminate some of the problems related to the use of absolute numbers.

Be aware of the different sizes of firms under comparison. These differences can be seen by looking at relative sales, assets, or profit sizes. Investment services such as *Value Line* often make available another meaningful figure—percent of market.

Other Library Sources

The typical business library has many sources of information relating to a particular company, industry, and product. Some of these sources are described here to aid you in your search for information about a company, its industry, and its products.

WARD'S BUSINESS DIRECTORY

Ward's Business Directory covers domestic private and public companies. Up to 20 items of information are provided for each company listed. The data may include names, addresses, telephone numbers, e-mails and URLs, sales, employee figures, and up to five names and titles of executive officers.

The directory is published in eight volumes. Volumes 1, 2, and 3 contain profiles of private and public companies arranged alphabetically. Volume 4 provides profiles of all the companies listed in Volumes 1, 2, and 3 organized by state and lists each company in ascending ZIP Code order. Volume 5 organizes the companies by the 4-digit SIC code that most closely resembles their principal industry and ranks them according to revenue. Volumes 6 and 7 organize the companies by state, then by the 4-digit SIC code. Volume 8 organizes the companies by the 5- or 6-digit NAICS code and ranks them according to revenue. A number of the volumes include special features that are too extensive to describe here.

Ward's Business Directory is good for obtaining the SIC and NAICS codes for a company. It also includes a conversion guide from SIC to NAICS codes, and from NAICS to SIC codes. The directory is a very good source for information on private companies.

STANDARD & POOR'S STOCK REPORTS

Standard & Poor's Reports covers companies on the New York Stock Exchange, American Stock Exchange, NASDAQ stock market, and regional exchanges. Arranged alphabetically by stock exchange, it contains a brief narrative analysis of companies regularly traded. It provides key financial data relating to the income statement, balance sheet, and per-share data. Other comments cover management, company's business, product lines, and other important factors.

STANDARD & POOR'S REGISTER OF CORPORATIONS, DIRECTORS, AND EXECUTIVES

This annual source is arranged in two volumes. Volume 1 contains an alphabetical list of approximately 75,000 corporations, including such data as ZIP Codes, telephone numbers, and functions of officers, directors, and other principals. The NAICS code is included at the end of each listing.

Volume 2, Section 1 contains an alphabetical list of over 70,000 individuals serving as officers, directors, trustees, partners, and so on. It provides such data as principal business affiliations, business address, and residence address.

Volume 2, Section 2—Indices: Divided into seven subsections:

- *Section 1*—Explains the construction and use of the NAICS code numbers and lists these numbers by major groups and by alphabetical and numerical division of major groups.
- *Section 2*—Lists corporations under the six-digit NAICS codes, which are arranged in numerical order.
- *Section 3*—Lists companies geographically by states and by major cities.
- *Section 4*—Lists and cross-references subsidiaries, divisions, and affiliates in alphabetical sequence and links them to their ultimate parent company listed in Volume 1.
- *Section 5*—Lists the deaths of which publishers have been notified in the past year.
- *Section 6*—Lists individuals whose names appear in the Register for the first time.
- *Section 7*—Lists the companies appearing in the Register for the first time.

STANDARD & POOR'S ANALYST'S HANDBOOK

This source contains selected income account and balance sheet items and related ratios as applied to the Standard & Poor's industry group stock price indexes. The progress of a given company may possibly be compared with a composite of its industry groups. Brief monthly updates for selected industries supplement the annual editions of the handbook.

STANDARD & POOR'S STANDARD CORPORATION DESCRIPTIONS (CORPORATION RECORDS)

This source provides background information and detailed financial statistics on U.S. corporations, with extensive coverage for some corporations. The contents and the index are updated throughout the year.

AMERICA'S CORPORATE FAMILIES:® THE BILLION DOLLAR DIRECTORY®

The directory listings include approximately 11,000 U.S. ultimates and 80,000 of their domestic subsidiaries, divisions, and major branches. Corporate family listings are alphabetical, geographical, and by SIC classification. This annual directory provides a cross-reference index of divisions, subsidiaries, and ultimate parent companies, as well as such data as lines of business and telephone numbers of parent and subsidiary companies.

The directory is in two volumes. Volume I covers the ultimate parent companies. Volume II covers (1) alphabetic cross-references of ultimate parent companies, subsidiaries, divisions, and branches; (2) businesses geographically; and (3) businesses by industrial classification.

D&B® MILLION DOLLAR DIRECTORY®

This directory provides information on more than 160,000 U.S. companies. Company listings are shown alphabetically, geographically, and by SIC classification. Data include lines of business, accounting firm, stock ticker symbol, and names of officers. This directory includes companies with sales of $1 million, or 20+ employees.

DIRECTORY OF CORPORATE AFFILIATIONS™

This directory gives an in-depth view of companies and their divisions, subsidiaries, and affiliates. It contains an alphabetical index, geographical index, and SIC classifications. The parent company listing consists of address, telephone number, stock ticker symbol, stock exchange(s), approximate sales, number of employees, type of business, and top corporate officers.

THOMAS REGISTER OF AMERICAN MANUFACTURERS

This is a comprehensive reference for products and services (Volumes 1–14), company profiles (Volumes 15 & 16), and a catalog file.

MERGENT INDUSTRIAL MANUAL AND NEWS REPORTS

Published in two volumes, these manuals cover 2,000 industrial corporations listed on the New York and American stock exchanges. Extensive information is provided such as history, business, properties, subsidiaries, financial statements, and SIC codes.

SECURITY OWNER'S STOCK GUIDE

This monthly guide, published by Standard & Poor's, covers over 5,300 common and preferred stocks. It contains trading activity, price range, dividends, and so on, for companies traded on the New York Stock Exchange, American Stock Exchange, over the counter, and regional exchanges. The information is displayed with numerous abbreviations and notes, in order to fit concisely into one single line, for each publicly traded security.

STANDARD & POOR'S STATISTICAL SERVICE

Standard & Poor's Statistical Service includes comprehensive statistics on many industries such as agriculture, metals, building, and transportation. Many additional statistics are included such as price indexes and daily highs, lows, and closes for stock.

MERGENT DIVIDEND RECORD
STANDARD & POOR'S ANNUAL DIVIDEND RECORD

These dividend publications provide a dividend record of payments on virtually all publicly owned American and some foreign companies.

D&B REFERENCE BOOK OF CORPORATE MANAGEMENTS

The four volumes contain profile information on over 200,000 principal corporate officers in over 12,000 companies. The information includes the year of birth, education, military service, present business position, and previous positions. Names and titles of other officers, as well as names of directors who are not officers, are also provided.

COMPACT DISCLOSURE

This database of textual and financial information on approximately 12,000 public companies can be accessed by a menu-driven screen. The information is taken from annual and periodic reports filed by each company with the Securities and Exchange Commission. A full printout for a company is approximately 14 pages. It includes the major financial statements (annual and quarterly), many financial ratios for the prior three years, institutional holdings, ownership by insiders, president's letter, and financial notes.

A company can be accessed by keying its name or ticker symbol. In addition, the system can be searched by type of business (SIC), geographic area (state, city, ZIP Code, or telephone area code), stock price financial ratios, and much more.

LEXIS-NEXIS

This service provides accounting, legal, newspaper, and periodical information. Lexis-Nexis includes complete statement portions of annual reports for thousands of publicly traded companies. Many colleges of business, law schools, accounting firms, and law firms subscribe to this service.

The Users of Financial Statements

The financial statements are prepared for a group of diversified users. Users of financial data have their own objectives in analysis.

Management, an obvious user of financial data, must analyze the data from the viewpoints of both investors and creditors. Management must be concerned about the current position of the entity to meet its obligations, as well as the future earning prospects of the firm.

Management is interested in the financial structure of the entity in order to determine a proper mix of short-term debt, long-term debt, and equity from owners. Also of interest is the asset structure of the entity: the combination of cash, inventory, receivables, investments, and fixed assets.

Management must guide the entity toward sound short- and long-term financial policies and also earn a profit. For example, liquidity and profitability are competitive since the most highly liquid assets (cash and marketable securities) are usually the least profitable. It does the entity little good to be guided toward a maximum profitability goal if resources are not available to meet current obligations. The entity would soon find itself in bankruptcy as creditors cut off lines of credit and demand payment. Similarly, management must utilize resources properly to obtain a reasonable return.

The investing public, another category of users, is interested in specific types of analysis. Investors are concerned with the financial position of the entity and its ability to earn future profits. The investor uses an analysis of past trends and the current position of the entity to project the future prospects of the entity.

Credit grantors are interested in the financial statements of the entity. Pure credit grantors obtain a limited return from extending credit: a fixed rate of interest (as in the case of banks) or the profit on the merchandise or services provided (as in the case of suppliers). Since these rewards are limited and the possibility exists that the principal will not be repaid, credit grantors tend to be conservative in extending credit.

The same principle applies to suppliers that extend credit. If merchandise with a 20% markup is sold on credit, it takes five successful sales of the same amount to make up for one sale not collected. In addition, the creditor considers the cost of the funds when extending credit. Extending credit really amounts to financing the entity.

A difference exists between the objectives of short-term grantors of credit and those of long-term grantors. The short-term creditor can look primarily to current resources that appear on the financial statements in order to determine if credit should be extended. Long-term creditors must usually look to the future prospects of earnings in order to be repaid. For example, if bonds are issued that are to be repaid in 30 years, the current resources of the entity will not be an indication of its ability to meet this obligation. The repayment for this obligation will come from future earnings. Thus, the objectives of financial analysis by credit grantors will vary, based on such factors as the term of the credit and the purpose. Profitability of the entity may not be a major consideration, as long as the resources for repayment can be projected.

The financial structure of the entity is of interest to creditors because the amount of equity capital in relation to debt indicates the risk that the owners bear in relation to the creditors. The equity capital provides creditors with a cushion against loss. When this equity cushion is small, creditors are bearing the risk of the entity.

Many other parties are interested in analyzing financial statements. Unions that represent employees are interested in the ability of the entity to grant wage increases and fringe benefits, such as pension plans. The government also has an interest in analyzing financial statements for tax purposes and to ensure compliance with antitrust laws.

Summary

Financial analysis consists of the quantitative and qualitative aspects of measuring the relative financial position among firms and industries. Analysis can be done in different ways, depending on the type of firm or industry and the specific needs of the user. Financial statements will vary by size of firm and among industries.

The SIC and NAICS classification systems have been developed to promote comparability of firms. Determining a company's SIC and/or NAICS is a good starting point in researching a company, an industry, or a product.

The analysis of an entity's financial statements is more meaningful if the results are compared with industry averages and with results of competitors. At the same time, caution must be exercised in using industry averages and results of competitors.

Many library services are available that relate to individual companies, industries, and products. These sources can be a valuable aid in researching a firm.

Financial statements are prepared for a group of diversified users. These users have various needs and uses for the financial statements.

to the net

1. Go to the SEC Web site (http://www.sec.gov). Under "Filings & Forms (EDGAR)," click on "Search for Company Filings." Click on "Companies & Other Filers." Under Company Name, enter "Alexander & Baldwin" (or under Ticker Symbol, enter "ALEX"). Select the 10-K filed February 26, 2007. For the following partial consolidated statements of income, compute horizontal and vertical common-size analysis. Use December 31, 2004, for the base on the horizontal common-size analysis. Use total revenue for the vertical common-size analysis. Comment on the results.

	Years Ended December 31,		
	2006	2005	2004
Operating revenue:			
Ocean transportation			
Logistics services			
Property leasing			
Property sales			
Agribusiness			
Total revenue			

2. Go to the SEC Web site (http://www.sec.gov). Under "Filings & Forms (EDGAR)," click on "Search for Company Filings." Click on "Companies & Other Filers." Under Company Name, enter "Best Buy Co" (or under Ticker Symbol, enter "BBY"). Select the 10-K filed May 2, 2007. For the following partial consolidated statements of earnings, compute horizontal and vertical common-size analyses. Use February 26, 2005, for the base in the horizontal common-size analysis. Use revenue for the vertical common-size analysis. Comment on the results.

Consolidated Statements of Earnings			
	March 3, 2007	Feb. 25, 2006	Feb. 26, 2005
Revenue			
Cost of goods sold			
Gross profit			
Selling, general, and administrative expense			
Operating income			

3. Go to the SEC Web site (http://www.sec.gov). Under "Filings & Forms (EDGAR)," click on "Search for Company Filings." Click on "Companies & Other Filers." Under Company Name, enter "Amazoncom Inc" (or under Ticker Symbol, enter "AMZN"). Select the 10-K filed February 16, 2007. For the following partial consolidated balance sheets, compute horizontal and vertical common-size analyses. Use December 31, 2005, for the base in the horizontal common-size analysis. Use total liabilities and stockholders' equity for the vertical common-size analysis. Comment on the results.

	December 31,	
	2006	2005
Liabilities and stockholders' equity		
Total current liabilities		
Long-term debt		
Other long-term liabilities		
Stockholders' equity		
Common stock		
Treasury stock, at cost		
Additional paid-in capital		
Accumulated other comprehensive income (loss)		
Accumulated deficit		
Total stockholders' equity		
Total liabilities and stockholders' equity		

4. Go to the SEC Web site (http://www.sec.gov). Under "Filings & Forms (EDGAR)," click on "Search for Company Filings." Click on "Companies & Other Filers." Under Company Name, enter "Kroger Co" (or under Ticker Symbol, enter "KR"). Select the 10-K filed April 4, 2007. For the following partial consolidated statement of income, prepare a horizontal common-size analysis with change in dollars. Use the year ended January 28, 2005, as the base. Comment on the results.

Consolidated Statement of Income
Years Ended February 3, 2007, and
January 28, 2006
(In millions)

	Feb. 3, 2007 53 Weeks	Jan. 28, 2006 52 Weeks	Increase (Decrease) Dollars	Percent
Sales				
Merchandise costs, including advertising, warehousing, and transportation, excluding items shown separately below				
Operating, general and administrative				
Rent				
Depreciation and amortization				
Operating profit				

5. Go to the SEC Web site (http://www.sec.gov). Under "Filings & Forms (EDGAR)," click on "Search for Company Filings." Click on "Companies & Other Filers." Under Company Name, enter "Yahoo Inc." (or under Ticker Symbol, enter "YHOO"). Select the 10-K filed February 23, 2007. For the following partial consolidated statements of operations, prepare a horizontal common-size analysis with change in dollars. Use the year ended December 31, 2005, as the base. Comment on the results.

Consolidated Statements of Operations
Years Ended December 31, 2005, and December 31, 2006 (In thousands)

	Dec. 31, 2005	Dec. 31, 2006	Increase (Decrease) Dollars	Percent
Revenues				
Cost of revenues				
Gross profit				
Operating expenses:				
Sales and marketing				
Product development				
General and administrative				
Amortization of intangibles				
Total operating expense				
Income from operations				

Questions

Q 5-1. What is a ratio? How do ratios help to alleviate the problem of size differences among firms?

Q 5-2. What does each of the following categories of ratios attempt to measure? (a) liquidity; (b) long-term borrowing capacity; (c) profitability. Name a group of users who might be interested in each category.

Q 5-3. Brown Company earned 5.5% on sales in 2007. What further information would be needed to evaluate this result?

Q 5-4. Differentiate between absolute and percentage changes. Which is generally a better measure of change? Why?

Q 5-5. Differentiate between horizontal and vertical analysis. Using sales as a component for each type, give an example that explains the difference.

Q 5-6. What is trend analysis? Can it be used for ratios? For absolute figures?

Q 5-7. Suppose you are comparing two firms within an industry. One is large and the other is small. Will relative or absolute numbers be of more value in each case? What kinds of statistics can help evaluate relative size?

Q 5-8. Are managers the only users of financial reports? Discuss.

Q 5-9. Briefly describe how each of these groups might use financial reports: managers, investors, and creditors.

Q 5-10. Refer to Exhibits 5-3, 5-4, and 5-5 to answer the following questions:
a. For each of the firms illustrated, what is the single largest asset category? Does this seem typical of this type of firm?
b. Which of the three firms has the largest amount in current assets in relation to the amount in current liabilities? Does this seem logical? Explain.

Q 5-11.   Differentiate between the types of inventory typically held by a retailing firm and a manufacturing firm.

Q 5-12.   Sometimes manufacturing firms have only raw materials and finished goods listed on their balance sheets. This is true of Avon Products, a manufacturer of cosmetics, and it might be true of food canners also. Explain the absence of work in process.

Q 5-13.   Using these results for a given ratio, compute the median, upper quartile, and lower quartile. 14%, 13.5%, 13%, 11.8%, 10.5%, 9.5%, 9.3%, 9%, 7%.

Q 5-14.   You want profile information on the president of a company. Which reference book should be consulted?

Q 5-15.   Answer the following concerning the *Almanac of Business and Industrial Financial Ratios*:
   a. This service presents statistics for how many size categories of firms?
   b. Indicate some of the industries covered by this service.

Q 5-16.   Using *The Department of Commerce Financial Report* discussion in the text, answer the following:
   a. Could we determine the percentage of total sales income after income taxes that a particular firm had in relation to the total industry sales? Explain.
   b. Could we determine the percentage of total assets that a particular firm had in relation to the total industry? Explain.

Q 5-17.   a. What is the SIC number? How can it aid in the search of a company, industry, or product?
   b. What is the NAICS number? How can it aid in the search of a company, industry, or product?

Q 5-18.   You want to know if there have been any reported deaths of officers of a company you are researching. What library source will aid you in your search?

Q 5-19.   You want to compare the progress of a given company with a composite of that company's industry group for selected income statement and balance sheet items. Which library source will aid you?

Q 5-20.   You are considering buying the stock of a large publicly traded company. You need an opinion of timeliness of the industry and the company. Which publication could you use?

Q 5-21.   You want to know the trading activity (volume of its stock sold) for a company. Which service provides this information?

Q 5-22.   Indicate some sources that contain a dividend record of payments.

Q 5-23.   What source includes comprehensive statistics on many industries?

Q 5-24.   You would like to determine the principal business affiliations of the president of a company you are analyzing. Which reference service may have this information?

Q 5-25.   Indicate some sources that contain an appraisal of the outlook for particular industries.

Q 5-26.   What source contains a comprehensive reference for products and services, company profiles, and a catalog file?

Problems

P 5-1.   Best Buy Co., Inc.'s consolidated balance sheets from its 2007 annual report are presented in Exhibit 5-3.

Required   a. Using the balance sheets, prepare a vertical common-size analysis for 2007 and 2006. Use total assets as a base.
   b. Using the balance sheets, prepare a horizontal common-size analysis for 2007 and 2006. Use 2006 as the base.
   c. Comment on significant trends that appear in (a) and (b).

P 5-2. Best Buy Co., Inc.'s consolidated statements of earnings from its 2007 annual report are presented in Exhibit 5-3.

Required
a. Using the statement of earnings, prepare a vertical common-size analysis for 2007, 2006, and 2005. Use revenue as a base.
b. Using the statement of earnings, prepare a horizontal common-size analysis for 2007, 2006, and 2005. Use 2005 as the base.
c. Comment on significant trends that appear in (a) and (b).

P 5-3. The Kelly Services, Inc. and Subsidiaries balance sheets from its 2006 annual report are presented in Exhibit 5-4.

Required
a. Using the balance sheets, prepare a vertical common-size analysis for 2006 and 2005. Use total assets as a base.
b. Using the balance sheets, prepare a horizontal common-size analysis for 2006 and 2005. Use 2005 as the base.
c. Comment on significant trends that appear in (a) and (b).

P 5-4. The Kelly Services, Inc. and Subsidiaries statements of earnings from its 2006 annual report are presented in Exhibit 5-4.

Required
a. Using the statements of earnings, prepare a vertical common-size analysis for 2006, 2005, and 2004. Use revenues as the base.
b. Using the statements of earnings, prepare a horizontal common-size analysis for 2006, 2005, and 2004. Use 2004 as the base.
c. Comment on significant trends that appear in (a) and (b).

P 5-5.

| | | | Change Analysis | |
Item	Year 1	Year 2	Amount	Percent
1	—	3,000		
2	6,000	(4,000)		
3	(7,000)	4,000		
4	4,000	—		
5	8,000	10,000		

Required Determine the absolute change and the percentage for these items.

P 5-6.

| | | | Change Analysis | |
Item	Year 1	Year 2	Amount	Percent
1	4,000	—		
2	5,000	(3,000)		
3	(9,000)	2,000		
4	7,000	—		
5	—	15,000		

Required Determine the absolute change and the percentage for these items.

P 5-7.

Rapid Retail
Comparative Statements of Income

| | December 31 | | Increase (Decrease) | |
(In thousands of dollars)	2008	2007	Dollars	Percent
Net sales	$30,000	$28,000		
Cost of goods sold	20,000	19,500		
Gross profit	10,000	8,500		

(continued)

(In thousands of dollars)	December 31		Increase (Decrease)	
	2008	2007	Dollars	Percent
Selling, general and administrative expense	3,000	2,900		
Operating income	7,000	5,600		
Interest expense	100	80		
Income before taxes	6,900	5,520		
Income tax expense	2,000	1,600		
Net income	$ 4,900	$ 3,920		

Required
a. Complete the increase (decrease) in dollars and percent.
b. Comment on trends.

P 5-8.

Required   Answer the following multiple-choice questions:
a. Which of the following statements is incorrect?
    1. Ratios are fractions expressed in percent or times per year.
    2. A ratio can be computed from any pair of numbers.
    3. A very long list of meaningful ratios can be derived.
    4. There is one standard list of ratios.
    5. Comparison of income statement and balance sheet numbers, in the form of ratios, should not be done.
b. A figure from this year's statement is compared with a base selected from the current year.
    1. Vertical common-size statement
    2. Horizontal common-size statement
    3. Funds statement
    4. Absolute figures
    5. Balance sheet
c. Fremont Electronics has income of $1,000,000. Columbus Electronics has income of $2,000,000. Which of the following statements is a correct statement?
    1. Columbus Electronics is getting a higher return on assets employed.
    2. Columbus Electronics has higher profit margins than does Fremont Electronics.
    3. Fremont Electronics could be more profitable than Columbus Electronics in relation to resources employed.
    4. No comparison can be made between Fremont Electronics and Columbus Electronics.
    5. Fremont Electronics is not making good use of its resources.
d. Industry ratios should *not* be considered as absolute norms for a given industry because of all but which of the following?
    1. The firms have different accounting methods.
    2. Many companies have varied product lines.
    3. Companies within the same industry may differ in their method of operations.
    4. The fiscal year-ends of the companies may differ.
    5. The financial services may be private independent firms.
e. Which of the following is a publication of the federal government for manufacturing, mining, and trade corporations?
    1. *Annual Statement Studies*
    2. *Standard & Poor's Industry Surveys*
    3. *Almanac of Business and Industrial Financial Ratios*
    4. *Industry Norms and Key Business Ratios*
    5. *The Department of Commerce Financial Report*
f. Which service represents a compilation of corporate tax return data?
    1. *Annual Statement Studies*
    2. *Standard & Poor's Industry Surveys*
    3. *Almanac of Business and Industrial Financial Ratios*
    4. *Industry Norms and Key Business Ratios*
    5. *The Department of Commerce Financial Report*

g. Which service includes over 800 different lines of business?
   1. *Annual Statement Studies*
   2. *Standard & Poor's Industry Surveys*
   3. *Almanac of Business and Industrial Financial Ratios*
   4. *Industry Norms and Key Business Ratios*
   5. *The Department of Commerce Financial Report*

h. Which analysis compares each amount with a base amount for a selected base year?
   1. Vertical common-size
   2. Horizontal common-size
   3. Funds statement
   4. Common-size statement
   5. None of these

i. Suppose you are comparing two firms in the coal industry. Which type of numbers would be most meaningful for statement analysis?
   1. Relative numbers would be most meaningful for both firms, especially for interfirm comparisons.
   2. Relative numbers are not meaningful.
   3. Absolute numbers would be most meaningful.
   4. Absolute numbers are not relevant.
   5. It is not meaningful to compare two firms.

j. Management is a user of financial analysis. Which of the following comments does *not* represent a fair statement as to the management perspective?
   1. Management is not interested in the view of investors.
   2. Management is interested in liquidity.
   3. Management is interested in profitability.
   4. Management is interested in the debt position.
   5. Management is interested in the financial structure of the entity.

Web Case

Thomson One *Business School Edition*

Please complete the Web case that covers material discussed in this chapter at academic.cengage.com/accounting/Gibson. You'll be using Thomson One Business School Edition, a powerful tool, that combines a full range of fundamental financial information, earnings estimates, market data, and source documents for 500 publicly traded companies.

Chapter 6

Liquidity of Short-Term Assets; Related Debt-Paying Ability

An entity's ability to maintain its short-term debt-paying ability is important to all users of financial statements. If the entity cannot maintain a short-term debt-paying ability, it will not be able to maintain a long-term debt-paying ability, nor will it be able to satisfy its stockholders. Even a very profitable entity will find itself bankrupt if it fails to meet its obligations to short-term creditors. The ability to pay current obligations when due is also related to the cash-generating ability of the firm. This will be discussed in Chapter 10.

When analyzing the short-term debt-paying ability of the firm, we find a close relationship between the current assets and the current liabilities. Generally, the current liabilities will be paid with cash generated from the current assets. As previously indicated, the profitability of the firm does not determine the short-term debt-paying ability. In other words, using accrual accounting, the entity may report very high profits but may not have the ability to pay its current bills because it lacks available funds. If the entity reports a loss, it may still be able to pay short-term obligations.

This chapter suggests procedures for analyzing short-term assets and the short-term debt-paying ability of an entity. The procedures require an understanding of current assets, current liabilities, and the notes to financial statements.

This chapter also includes a detailed discussion of four very important assets—cash, marketable securities, accounts receivable, and inventory. Accounts receivable and inventory, two critical assets, often substantially influence the liquidity and profitability of a firm.

Chapters 6 through 10 will extensively use the 2007 financial statements of Nike, Inc. (Nike) to illustrate the technique of financial analysis. This will aid readers in viewing financial analysis as a whole. The Nike, Inc. 2007 financial statements are presented following Chapter 10. With the Nike statements is an analysis that summarizes and expands on the Nike analysis in Chapters 6 through 10.

Current Assets, Current Liabilities, and the Operating Cycle

Current assets (1) are in the form of cash, (2) will be realized in cash, or (3) conserve the use of cash *within the operating cycle of a business or one year, whichever is longer.*[1]

The five categories of assets usually found in current assets, listed in their order of liquidity, include cash, marketable securities, receivables, inventories, and prepayments. Other assets may also be classified in current assets, such as assets held for sale. This chapter will examine in detail each type of current asset.

The **operating cycle** for a company is the time period between the acquisition of goods and the final cash realization resulting from sales and subsequent collections. For example, a food store purchases inventory and then sells the inventory for cash. The relatively short time that the inventory remains an asset of the food store represents a very short operating cycle. In another example, a car manufacturer purchases materials and then uses labor and overhead to convert these materials into a finished car. A dealer buys the car on credit and then pays the manufacturer. Compared to the food store, the car manufacturer has a much longer operating cycle, but it is still less than a year. Only a few businesses have an operating cycle longer than a year. For example, if a business is involved in selling resort property, the average time period that the property is held before sale, plus the average collection period, is typically longer than a year.

CASH

Cash is a medium of exchange that a bank will accept for deposit and a creditor will accept for payment. To be classified as a current asset, cash must be free from any restrictions that would prevent its deposit or use it to pay creditors classified as current. If restricted for specific short-term creditors, many firms still classify this cash under current assets, but they disclose the restrictions. Cash restricted for short-term creditors should be eliminated along with the related amount of short-term debt when determining the short-term debt-paying ability. Cash should be available to pay general short-term creditors to be considered as part of the firm's short-term debt-paying ability.

It has become common for banks to require a portion of any loan to remain on deposit in the bank for the duration of the loan period. These deposits, termed **compensating balances**, reduce the amount of cash available to the borrower to meet obligations, and they increase the borrower's effective interest rate.

Compensating balances against short-term borrowings are separately stated in the current asset section or noted. Compensating balances for long-term borrowings are separately stated as noncurrent assets under either investments or other assets.

The cash account on the balance sheet is usually entitled *cash, cash and equivalents*, or *cash and certificates of deposit*. The cash classification typically includes currency and unrestricted funds on deposit with a bank.

There are two major problems encountered when analyzing a current asset: determining a fair valuation for the asset and determining the liquidity of the asset. These problems apply to the cash asset only when it has been restricted. Thus, it is usually a simple matter to decide on the amount of cash to use when determining the short-term debt-paying ability of an entity.

MARKETABLE SECURITIES

The business entity has varying cash needs throughout the year. Because an inferred cost arises from keeping money available, management does not want to keep all of the entity's cash needs in the form of cash throughout the year. The available alternative turns some of the cash into productive use through short-term investments (marketable securities), which can be converted into cash as the need arises.

To qualify as a **marketable security**, the investment must be readily marketable, and it must be the intent of management to convert the investment to cash within the current operating cycle or one year, whichever is longer. The key element of this test is **managerial intent**.

It is to management's advantage to show investments under marketable securities, instead of long-term investments, because this classification improves the liquidity appearance of the firm. When the same securities are carried as marketable securities year after year, they are likely held for a business purpose. For example, the other company may be a major supplier or customer of the firm being analyzed. The firm would not want to sell these securities to pay short-term creditors. Therefore, to be conservative, it is better to reclassify them as investments for analysis purposes.

Investments classified as marketable securities should be temporary. Examples of marketable securities include treasury bills, short-term notes of corporations, government bonds, corporate bonds, preferred stock, and common stock. Investments in preferred stock and common stock are referred to as *marketable equity securities*.

Debt and equity securities are to be carried at fair value. An exception is that debt securities can be carried at amortized cost if classified as held-to-maturity securities, but these debt securities would be classified under investments (not classified under current assets).[2]

A security's liquidity must be determined in order for it to be classified as a marketable security. The analyst must assume that securities classified as marketable securities are readily marketable.

Exhibit 6-1 presents the marketable securities on the 2007 annual report of Nike, Inc. It discloses the detail of the marketable securities account. Many companies do not disclose this detail.

Exhibit 6-1	NIKE, INC.*

Marketable Securities (Short-Term Investments)

NIKE, INC.
CONSOLIDATED BALANCE SHEETS

	May 31,	
ASSETS	**2007**	**2006**
Current Assets:		
Cash and cash equivalents	$1,856.7	$ 954.2
Short-term investments	990.3	1,348.8
Accounts receivable, net	2,494.7	2,382.9
Inventories (Note 2)	2,121.9	2,076.7
Deferred income taxes (Note 8)	219.7	203.3
Prepaid expenses and other current assets	393.2	380.1
Total current assets	$8,076.5	$7,346.0

Note 1—Summary of Significant Accounting Policies (in Part)

Short-Term Investments

Short-term investments consist of highly liquid investments, primarily U.S. Treasury debt securities, with maturities over three months from the date of purchase. Debt securities which the Company has the ability and positive intent to hold to maturity are carried at amortized cost. Available-for-sale debt securities are recorded at fair value with any net unrealized gains and losses reported, net of tax, in other comprehensive income. Realized gains or losses are determined based on the specific identification method. The Company holds no investments considered to be trading securities. Amortized cost of both available-for-sale and held-to-maturity debt securities approximates fair market value due to their short maturities. Substantially all short-term investments held at May 31, 2007 have remaining maturities of 180 days or less. Included in interest (income) expense, net for the years ended May 31, 2007, 2006, and 2005, was interest income of $116.9 million, $87.3 million and $34.9 million, respectively, related to short-term investments and cash equivalents.

*"Our principal business activity is the design, development and worldwide marketing of high quality footwear, apparel, equipment, and accessory products." 10-K

RECEIVABLES

An entity usually has a number of claims to future inflows of cash. These claims are usually classified as accounts receivable and notes receivable on the financial statements. The primary claim that most entities have comes from the selling of merchandise or services on account to customers, referred to as *trade receivables*, with the customer promising to pay within a limited period of time, such as 30 days. Other claims may be from sources such as loans to employees or a federal tax refund.

Claims from customers, usually in the form of accounts receivable, neither bear interest nor involve claims against specific resources of the customer. In some cases, however, the customer signs a note instead of being granted the privilege of having an open account. Usually, the interest-bearing note will be for a longer period of time than an account receivable. In some cases, a customer who does not pay an account receivable when due signs a *note receivable* in place of the account receivable.

The common characteristic of receivables is that the company expects to receive cash some time in the future. This causes two valuation problems. First, a period of time must pass before the receivable can be collected, so the entity incurs costs for the use of these funds. Second, collection might not be made.

The valuation problem from waiting to collect is *ignored in the valuation of receivables and of notes classified as current assets* because of the short waiting period and the immaterial difference in value. The waiting period problem is not ignored if the receivable or note is long term and classified as an investment. The stipulated rate of interest is presumed to be fair, except when:

1. No interest is stated.
2. The stated rate of interest is clearly unreasonable.
3. The face value of the note is materially different from the cash sales price of the property, goods, or services, or the market value of the note at the date of the transaction.[3]

Under the condition that the face amount of the note does not represent the fair value of the consideration exchanged, *the note is recorded as a present value amount on the date of the original transaction.* The note is recorded at less than (or more than) the face amount, taking into consideration the time value of money. The difference between the recorded amount and the face amount is subsequently amortized as interest income (note receivable) or as interest expense (note payable).

The second problem in valuing receivables or notes is that collection may not be made. Usually, an allowance provides for estimated uncollectible accounts. Estimated losses must be accrued against income, and the impairment of the asset must be recognized (or liability recorded) under the following conditions:

1. Information available prior to the issuance of the financial statements indicates that it is probable that an asset has been impaired, or a liability has been incurred at the date of the financial statements.
2. The amount of the loss can be reasonably estimated.[4]

Both of these conditions are normally met with respect to the uncollectibility of receivables, and the amount subject to being uncollectible is usually material. Thus, in most cases, the company must estimate bad debt expense and indicate the impairment of the receivable. The expense is placed on the income statement, and the impairment of the receivable is disclosed by the use of an account, allowance for doubtful accounts, which is subtracted from the gross receivable account. Later, a specific customer's account, identified as being uncollectible, is charged against allowance for doubtful accounts and the gross receivable account on the balance sheet. (This does not mean that the firm will stop efforts to collect.)

It is difficult for the firm to estimate the collectibility of any individual receivable, but when it considers all of the receivables in setting up the allowance, the total estimate should be reasonably accurate. The problem of collection applies to each type of receivable, including notes. The company normally provides for only one allowance account as a matter of convenience, but it considers possible collection problems with all types of receivables and notes when determining the allowance account.

The impairment of receivables may come from causes other than uncollectibility, such as cash discounts allowed, sales returns, and allowances given. Usually, the company considers all of the causes that impair receivables in allowance for doubtful accounts, rather than setting up a separate allowance account for each cause.

Nike presented its receivable account for May 31, 2007, and 2006, as follows:

	2007	2006
Accounts receivable, net	$2,494,700,000	$2,382,900,000

This indicates that net receivables were $2,494,700,000 at May 31, 2007, and $2,382,900,000 at May 31, 2006, after subtracting allowances for doubtful accounts.

Note 1. Summary of Significant Accounting Policies (in Part)

Allowance for Uncollectible Accounts Receivable

Accounts receivable consists principally of amounts receivable from customers. We make ongoing estimates relating to the collectibility of our accounts receivable and maintain an allowance for estimated losses resulting from the inability of our customers to make required payments. In determining the amount of the allowance, we consider our historical level of credit losses and make judgments about the creditworthiness of significant customers based on ongoing credit evaluations. Accounts receivable with anticipated collection dates greater than twelve months from the balance sheet date and related allowances are considered non-current and recorded in other assets. The allowance for uncollectible accounts receivable was $71.5 million and $67.6 million at May 31, 2007 and 2006, respectively, of which $33.3 million and $29.2 million was recorded in other assets.

Using this note, the allowance for uncollectible accounts receivable presented with accounts receivable, net can be computed as follows:

	2007	2006
Total allowance for uncollectible accounts	$71,500,000	$67,600,000
Loss:		
Recorded in other assets	(33,300,000)	(29,200,000)
Presented with accounts receivable	$38,200,000	$38,400,000

The use of the allowance for doubtful accounts approach results in the bad debt expense being charged to the period of sale, thus matching this expense with its related revenue. It also results in the recognition of the impairment of the asset. The later charge-off of a specified account receivable does not influence the income statement or net receivables on the balance sheet. The charge-off reduces accounts receivable and allowance for doubtful accounts.

When both conditions specified are not met, or the receivables are immaterial, the entity recognizes bad debt expense using the direct write-off method. With this method, bad debt expense is recognized when a specific customer's account is identified as being uncollectible. At this time, the bad debt expense is recognized on the income statement, and gross accounts receivable is decreased on the balance sheet. This method recognizes the bad debt expense in the same period for both the income statement and the tax return.

The direct write-off method frequently results in the bad debt expense being recognized in the year subsequent to the sale, and thus does not result in a proper matching of expense with revenue. This method reports gross receivables, which does not recognize the impairment of the asset from uncollectibility.

Some companies have trade receivables and installment receivables. Installment receivables will usually be for a relatively long period of time. Installment receivables due within a year are classified under current assets. Installment receivables due after a year are classified below current assets.

Installment receivables classified under current assets are normally much longer than the typical trade receivables. The analyst should make special note of this when making comparisons with competitors. For example, a retail company that has substantial installment receivables is not comparable to a retail company that does not have installment receivables. Installment receivables are usually considered to be of lower quality than other receivables because of the length of time needed to collect the installment receivables. More importantly, the company with installment receivables should have high standards when granting credit and should closely monitor its receivables.

Exhibit 6-2 indicates the disclosure by CA, Inc. and Subsidiaries.

Exhibit	6-2	CA, INC. AND SUBSIDIARIES*

Installment Receivables

Consolidated Balance Sheets (in Part)

	March 31,	
(Dollars in millions)	2007	2006
Assets		
Current Assets		
Cash and cash equivalents	$ 2,275	$ 1,831
Marketable securities	5	34
Trade and installment accounts receivable, net	390	552
Deferred income taxes	360	271
Other current assets	71	50
Total Current Assets	3,101	2,738
Installment accounts receivable, due after one year, net	331	449
Property and Equipment		
Land and buildings	233	488
Equipment, furnitures and improvements	1,158	1,066
	1,391	1,554
Accumulated depreciation and amortization	(922)	(920)
Total Property and Equipment, net	469	634
Purchased software products, net accumulated amortization		
of $4,600 and $4,299, respectively	203	461
Goodwill	5,345	5,308
Federal and state income taxes receivable—noncurrent	39	38
Deferred income taxes	328	142
Other noncurrent assets	769	750
Total Assets	$10,585	$10,520

Note 6. Trade and Installment Accounts Receivable

Note: A detailed descriptive note was included with the statements.

*"CA, Inc. is one of the world's largest independent providers of information technology (IT) management software." 10-K

Customer concentration can be an important consideration in the quality of receivables. When a large portion of receivables is from a few customers, the firm can be highly dependent on those customers. Nike's Form 10-K disclosed that "during the years ended May 31, 2007, 2006, and 2005, revenues derived from Foot Locker, Inc., represented 10%, 10%, and 11% of the company's consolidated revenues, respectively."

The liquidity of the trade receivables for a company can be examined by making *two computations. The first computation* determines the number of days' sales in receivables at the end of the accounting period, and *the second computation* determines the accounts receivable turnover. The turnover figure can be computed to show the number of times per year receivables turn over or to show how many days on the average it takes to collect the receivables.

Days' Sales in Receivables

The number of days' sales in receivables relates the amount of the accounts receivable to the average daily sales on account. For this computation, the accounts receivable amount should include trade notes receivable. Other receivables not related to sales on account should not be included in this computation. Compute the days' sales in receivables as follows:

$$\text{Days' Sales in Receivables} = \frac{\text{Gross Receivables}}{\text{Net Sales/365}}$$

This formula divides the number of days in a year into net sales on account and then divides the resulting figure into gross receivables. Exhibit 6-3 presents this computation for Nike at the end of 2007 and 2006. The decrease in days' sales in receivables from 59.10 days at the end of 2006 to 56.63 days at the end of 2007 indicates an improvement in the control of receivables.

Exhibit	6-3	NIKE, INC.		
	Days' Sales in Receivables			
	Years Ended May 31, 2007 and 2006			
(In millions)			**2007**	**2006**
Accounts receivable, net			$ 2,494.7	$ 2,382.9
Allowance for uncollectible accounts			38.2	38.4
Gross receivables (net plus allowance) [A]			2,532.9	2,421.3
Net sales			16,325.9	14,954.9
Average daily sales on account (net sales on account divided by 365) [B]			44.73	40.97
Days' sales in receivables [A ÷ B]			56.63 days	59.10 days

An internal analyst compares days' sales in receivables with the company's credit terms as an indication of how efficiently the company manages its receivables. For example, if the credit term is 30 days, days' sales in receivables should not be materially over 30 days. If days' sales in receivables are materially more than the credit terms, the company has a collection problem. An effort should be made to keep the days' sales in receivables close to the credit terms.

Consider the effect on the quality of receivables from a change in the *credit terms*. Shortening the credit terms indicates that there will be less risk in the collection of future receivables, and a lengthening of the credit terms indicates a greater risk. Credit term information is readily available for internal analysis and may be available in notes.

Right of return privileges can also be important to the quality of receivables. Liberal right of return privileges can be a negative factor in the quality of receivables and on sales that have already been recorded. Pay particular attention to any change in the right of return privileges. Right of return privileges can readily be determined for internal analysis, and this information should be available in a note if considered to be material.

The net sales figure includes collectible and uncollectible accounts. The uncollectible accounts *would not exist* if there were an accurate way, prior to sale, of determining which credit customers would not pay. Firms make an effort to determine credit standing when they approve a customer for credit, but this process does not eliminate uncollectible accounts. Since the net sales figure includes both collectible and uncollectible accounts (gross sales), the comparable receivables figure should include gross receivables, rather than the net receivables figure that remains after the allowance for doubtful accounts is deducted.

The days' sales in receivables gives an indication of the length of time that the receivables have been outstanding at the end of the year. *The indication can be misleading if sales are seasonal and/or the company uses a natural business year.* If the company uses a natural business year for its accounting period, the days' sales in receivables will tend to be understated because the actual sales per day at the end of the year will be low when compared to the average sales per day for the year. The understatement of days' sales in receivables can also be explained by the fact that gross receivables will tend to be below average at that time of year.

The following is an example of how days' sales in receivables will tend to be understated when a company uses a natural business year:

Average sales per day for the entire year	$ 2,000
Sales per day at the end of the natural business year	1,000
Gross receivables at the end of the year	100,000

Days' sales in receivables based on the formula:

$$\frac{\$100,000}{\$2,000} = 50 \text{ days}$$

Days' sales in receivables based on sales per day at the end of the natural business year:

$$\frac{\$100,000}{\$1,000} = 100 \text{ days}$$

The liquidity of a company that uses a natural business year tends to be overstated. However, the only positive way to know if a company uses a natural business year is through research. The information may not be readily available.

It is unlikely that a company that has a seasonal business will close the accounting year during peak activity. At the peak of the business cycle, company personnel are busy and receivables are likely to be at their highest levels. If a company closed during peak activity, the days' sales in receivables would tend to be overstated and the liquidity understated.

The length of time that the receivables have been outstanding gives an indication of their collectibility. The days' sales in receivables should be compared for several years. A comparison should also be made between the days' sales in receivables for a particular company and comparable figures for other firms in the industry and industry averages. This type of comparison can be made when doing either internal or external analysis.

Assuming that the days' sales in receivables computation is *not* distorted because of a seasonal business and/or the company's use of a natural business year, consider the following reasons to explain why the days' sales in receivables appears to be abnormally high:

1. Sales volume expands materially late in the year.
2. Receivables are uncollectible and should have been written off.
3. The company seasonally dates invoices. (An example would be a toy manufacturer that ships in August with the receivable due at the end of December.)
4. A large portion of receivables are on the installment basis.

Assuming that the distortion is *not* from a seasonal situation or the company's use of a natural business year, the following should be considered as possible reasons why the days' sales in receivables appears to be abnormally low:

1. Sales volume decreases materially late in the year.
2. A material amount of sales are on a cash basis.
3. The company has a factoring arrangement in which a material amount of the receivables is sold. (With a factoring arrangement, the receivables are sold to an outside party.)

When doing external analysis, many of the reasons why the days' sales in receivables is abnormally high or low cannot be determined without access to internal information.

Accounts Receivable Turnover

Another computation, accounts receivable turnover, indicates the liquidity of the receivables. Compute the accounts receivable turnover measured in times per year as follows:

$$\text{Accounts Receivable Turnover} = \frac{\text{Net Sales}}{\text{Average Gross Receivables}}$$

Exhibit 6-4 presents this computation for Nike at the end of 2007 and 2006. The turnover of receivables increased between 2006 and 2007 from 6.28 times per year to 6.59 times per year. For Nike, this would be a positive trend.

Computing the average gross receivables based on beginning-of-year and end-of-year receivables can be misleading if the business has seasonal fluctuations or if the company uses a natural business year. To avoid problems of seasonal fluctuations or of comparing a company that uses a natural business year with one that uses a calendar year, the monthly balances (or even

Exhibit	6-4	NIKE, INC.

Accounts Receivable Turnover

(In millions)	Years Ended May 31, 2007 and 2006	
	2007	**2006**
Net sales [A]	$16,325.9	$14,954.9
End-of-year receivables, net	2,494.7	2,382.9
Beginning-of-year receivables, net	2,382.9	2,262.1
Allowance for doubtful accounts:		
End of 2007 $38.2		
End of 2006 $38.4*		
End of 2005 $80.4*		
Ending gross receivables (net plus allowance)	2,532.9	2,421.3
Beginning gross receivables (net plus allowance)	2,421.3	2,342.5
Average gross receivables [B]	2,477.1	2,381.9
Accounts receivables turnover [A ÷ B]	6.59 times	6.28 times

Note: Based on the May 31, 2007, disclosure relating to allowance for uncollectible accounts receivable, it is likely that some of the allowance for uncollectible accounts receivable at the end of May 31, 2005, relates to other assets.

The accounts receivable, net, for May 31, 2006, is disclosed as $2,382,900,000 on the May 31, 2007, statement. It is disclosed as $2,395,900,000 on the May 31, 2006, statement.

These items would have an immaterial impact on the accounts receivable turnover and would not change the trend.

weekly balances) of accounts receivable should be used in the computation. This is feasible when performing internal analysis, but not when performing external analysis. In the latter case, quarterly figures can be used to help eliminate these problems. If these problems cannot be eliminated, companies not on the same basis should not be compared. The company with the natural business year tends to overstate its accounts receivable turnover, thus overstating its liquidity.

Accounts Receivable Turnover in Days

The accounts receivable turnover can be expressed in terms of days instead of times per year. Turnover in number of days also gives a comparison with the number of days' sales in the ending receivables. The accounts receivable turnover in days also results in an answer directly related to the firm's credit terms. Compute the accounts receivable turnover in days as follows:

$$\text{Accounts Receivable Turnover in Days} = \frac{\text{Average Gross Receivables}}{\text{Net Sales/365}}$$

This formula is the same as that for determining number of days' sales in receivables, except that the accounts receivable turnover in days is computed using the average gross receivables. Exhibit 6-5 presents the computation for Nike at the end of 2007 and 2006.

Exhibit	6-5	NIKE, INC.

Accounts Receivable Turnover in Days

(In millions)	Years Ended May 31, 2007 and 2006	
	2007	**2006**
Net sales	$16,325.9	$14,954.9
Average gross receivables [A]	2,477.1	2,381.9
Sales per day (net sales divided by 365) [B]	44.73	40.97
Accounts receivable turnover in days [A ÷ B]	55.38 days	58.14 days

Accounts receivable turnover in days decreased from 58.14 days in 2006 to 55.38 days in 2007. This would represent a positive trend.

The accounts receivable turnover in times per year and days can both be computed by alternative formulas, using Nike's 2007 figures, as follows:

1. Accounts Receivable Turnover in Times per Year

$$\frac{365}{\text{Accounts Receivable Turnover in Days}} = \frac{365}{55.38} = 6.59 \text{ Times per Year}$$

2. Accounts Receivable Turnover in Days

$$\frac{365}{\text{Accounts Receivable Turnover in Times per Year}} = \frac{365}{6.59 \text{ Times per Year}} = 55.39 \text{ Days}$$

The answers obtained for both accounts receivable turnover in number of times per year and accounts receivable turnover in days, using the alternative formulas, may differ slightly from the answers obtained with the previous formulas. The difference is due to rounding.

Credit Sales versus Cash Sales

A difficulty in computing receivables' liquidity is the problem of credit sales versus cash sales. Net sales includes both credit sales and cash sales. To have a realistic indication of the liquidity of receivables, only the credit sales should be included in the computations. If cash sales are included, the liquidity will be overstated.

The internal analyst determines the credit sales figure and eliminates the problem of credit sales versus cash sales. The external analyst should be aware of this problem, and not be misled by the liquidity figures. The distinction between cash sales and credit sales is not usually a major problem for the external analyst because certain types of businesses tend to sell only on cash terms, and others sell only on credit terms. For example, a manufacturer usually sells only on credit terms. Some businesses, such as a retail department store, have a mixture of credit sales and cash sales.

In cases of mixed sales, the proportion of credit and cash sales tends to stay rather constant. Therefore, the liquidity figures are comparable (but overstated), enabling the reader to compare figures from period to period as well as figures of similar companies.

INVENTORIES

Inventory is often the most significant asset in determining the short-term debt-paying ability of an entity. Often, the inventory account is more than half of the total current assets. Because of the significance of inventories, a special effort should be made to analyze properly this important area.

To be classified as inventory, the asset should be for sale in the ordinary course of business, or used or consumed in the production of goods. A trading concern purchases merchandise in a form to sell to customers. Inventories of a trading concern, whether wholesale or retail, usually appear in one inventory account (Merchandise Inventory). A manufacturing concern produces goods to be sold. Inventories of a manufacturing concern are normally classified in three distinct inventory accounts: inventory available to use in production (raw materials inventory), inventory in production (work in process inventory), and inventory completed (finished goods inventory).

Usually, the determination of the inventory figures is much more difficult in a manufacturing concern than in a trading concern. The manufacturing concern deals with materials, labor, and overhead when determining the inventory figures, while the trading concern only deals with purchased merchandise. The overhead portion of the work in process inventory and the finished goods inventory is often a problem when determining a manufacturer's inventory. The overhead consists of all the costs of the factory other than direct materials and direct labor. From an analysis viewpoint, however, many of the problems of determining the proper inventory value are solved before the entity publishes financial statements.

Inventory is particularly sensitive to changes in business activity, so management must keep inventory in balance with business activity. Failure to do so leads to excessive costs (such as storage cost), production disruptions, and employee layoffs. For example, it is difficult for automobile manufacturers to balance inventories with business activities. When sales decline rapidly, the industry has difficulty adjusting production and the resulting inventory to match the decline. Manufacturers have to use customer incentives, such as price rebates, to get the large inventory buildup back to a manageable level. When business activity increases, inventory shortages can lead to overtime costs. The increase in activity can also lead to cash shortages because of the length of time necessary to acquire inventory, sell the merchandise, and collect receivables.

Inventory quantities and costs may be accounted for using either the **perpetual** or **periodic** system. Using the perpetual system, the company maintains a continuous record of physical quantities in its inventory. When the perpetual system includes costs (versus quantities only), then the company updates its inventory and cost of goods sold continually as purchases and sales take place. (The inventory needs to be verified by a physical count at least once a year.)

Using the periodic system, physical counts are taken periodically, which should be at least once a year. The cost of the ending inventory is determined by attaching costs to the physical quantities on hand based on the cost flow assumption used. The cost of goods sold is calculated by subtracting the ending inventory from the cost of goods available for sale.

Inventory Cost

The most critical problem that many entities face is determining which cost to use, since the cost prices have usually varied over time. If it were practical to determine the specific cost of an item, this would be a good cost figure to use. It would also substantially reduce inventory valuation problems. In practice, because of the different types of inventory items and the constant flow of these items, it is not practical to determine the specific costs. Exceptions to this are large items and/or expensive items. For example, it would be practical to determine the specific cost of a new car in the dealer's showroom or the specific cost of an expensive diamond in a jewelry store. When specific costs are used, this is referred to as the **specific identification** method.

Because the cost of specific items is not usually practical to determine and because other things are considered (such as the income result), companies typically use a cost flow assumption. The most common cost flow assumptions are first-in, first-out (FIFO), last-in, first-out (LIFO), or some average computation. These assumptions can produce substantially different results because of changing prices.

The **FIFO method** assumes that the first inventory acquired is the first sold. This means that the cost of goods sold account consists of beginning inventory and the earliest items purchased. The latest items purchased remain in inventory. These latest costs are fairly representative of the current costs to replace the inventory. If the inventory flows slowly (low turnover), or if there has been substantial inflation, even FIFO may not produce an inventory figure for the balance sheet representative of the replacement cost. Part of the inventory cost of a manufacturing concern consists of overhead, some of which may represent costs from several years prior, such as depreciation on the plant and equipment. Often, the costs transferred to cost of goods sold under FIFO are low in relation to current costs, so current costs are not matched against current revenue. During a time of inflation, the resulting profit is overstated. To the extent that inventory does not represent replacement cost, an understatement of the inventory cost occurs.

The **LIFO method** assumes that the costs of the latest items bought or produced are matched against current sales. This assumption usually materially improves the matching of current costs against current revenue, so the resulting profit figure is usually fairly realistic. The first items (and oldest costs) in inventory can materially distort the reported inventory figure in comparison with its replacement cost. A firm that has been on LIFO for many years may have some inventory costs that go back 20 years or more. Because of inflation, the resulting inventory figure will not reflect current replacement costs. LIFO accounting was started in the United States. It is now accepted in a few other countries.

Averaging methods lump the costs to determine a midpoint. An average cost computation for inventories results in an inventory amount and a cost of goods sold amount somewhere between FIFO and LIFO. During times of inflation, the resulting inventory is more than LIFO and less than FIFO. The resulting cost of goods sold is less than LIFO and more than FIFO.

Exhibit 6-6 summarizes the inventory methods used by the 600 companies surveyed for *Accounting Trends & Techniques*. The table covers the years 2005, 2004, 2003, and 2002. (Notice that the number of companies in the table does not add up to 600 because many companies use more than one method.) Exhibit 6-6 indicates that the most popular inventory methods are FIFO and LIFO. It is perceived that LIFO requires more cost to administer than FIFO. LIFO is not as popular during times of relatively low inflation. During times of relatively high inflation, LIFO becomes more popular because LIFO matches the latest costs against revenue. LIFO results in tax benefits because of the matching of recent higher costs against revenue.

| Exhibit | 6-6 | INVENTORY COST DETERMINATION |

		Number of Companies			
		2005	**2004**	**2003**	**2002**
Methods:					
First-in, first-out (FIFO)		385	386	384	380
Last-in, first-out (LIFO)		229	239	251	255
Average cost		155	169	167	165
Other		30	27	31	28
Use of LIFO:					
All inventories		16	20	26	17
50% or more of inventories		113	108	120	121
Less than 50% of inventories		76	85	77	88
Not determinable		24	26	28	29
Companies using LIFO		229	239	251	255

Source: *Accounting Trends & Techniques,* copyright © 2006 by American Institute of Certified Public Accountants, Inc., p. ATT-SEC 1.31. Reprinted with permission.

Exhibit 6-6 includes a summary of companies that use LIFO for all inventories, 50% or more of inventories, less than 50% of inventories, and not determinable. This summary indicates that only a small percentage of companies that use LIFO use it for all of their inventories.

For the following illustration, the periodic system is used with the inventory count at the end of the year. The same answer would result for FIFO and specific identification under either the perpetual or periodic system. A different answer would result for LIFO or average cost, depending on whether a perpetual or periodic system is used.

To illustrate the major costing methods for determining which costs apply to the units remaining in inventory at the end of the year and which costs are allocated to cost of goods sold, consider the following:

Date	Description	Number of Units	Cost per Unit	Total Cost
January 1	Beginning inventory	200	$ 6	$ 1,200
March 1	Purchase	1,200	7	8,400
July 1	Purchase	300	9	2,700
October 1	Purchase	400	11	4,400
		2,100		$16,700

A physical inventory count on December 31 indicates 800 units on hand. There were 2,100 units available during the year, and 800 remained at the end of the year; therefore, 1,300 units were sold.

Four cost assumptions will be used to illustrate the determination of the ending inventory costs and the related cost of goods sold: *first-in, first-out (FIFO), last-in, first-out (LIFO), average cost,* and *specific identification.*

First-In, First-Out Method (FIFO)

The cost of ending inventory is found by attaching cost to the physical quantities on hand, based on the FIFO cost flow assumption. The cost of goods sold is calculated by subtracting the ending inventory cost from the cost of goods available for sale.

		Number of Units	Cost per Unit		Inventory Cost	Cost of Goods Sold
October 1	Purchase	400	@	$11	$4,400	
July 1	Purchase	300	@	9	2,700	
March 1	Purchase	100	@	7	700	
Ending inventory		800			$7,800	
Cost of goods sold ($16,700 − $7,800)						$8,900

Last-In, First-Out Method (LIFO)

The cost of the ending inventory is found by attaching costs to the physical quantities on hand, based on the LIFO cost flow assumption. The cost of goods sold is calculated by subtracting the ending inventory cost from the cost of goods available for sale.

		Number of Units	Cost per Unit		Inventory Cost	Cost of Goods Sold
January 1	Beginning inventory	200	@	$6	$1,200	
March 1	Purchase	600	@	7	4,200	
Ending inventory		800			$5,400	
Cost of goods sold ($16,700 − $5,400)						$11,300

Average Cost

There are several ways to compute the average cost. The weighted average divides the total cost by the total units to determine the average cost per unit. The average cost per unit is multiplied by the inventory quantity to determine inventory cost. The cost of goods sold is calculated by subtracting the ending inventory cost from the cost of goods available for sale.

	Inventory Cost	Cost of Goods Sold
Total cost $\frac{\$16,700}{2,100}$ = $7.95 Total units		
Ending inventory (800 × $7.95)	$6,360	
Cost of goods sold ($16,700 − $6,360)		$10,340

Specific Identification

With the specific identification method, the items in inventory are identified as coming from specific purchases. For this example, assume that the 800 items in inventory can be identified with the March 1 purchase. The cost of goods sold is calculated by subtracting the ending inventory cost from the cost of goods available for sale.

	Inventory Cost	Cost of Goods Sold
Ending inventory (800 × $7.00)	$5,600	
Cost of goods sold ($16,700 − $5,600)		$11,100

The difference in results for inventory cost and cost of goods sold from using different inventory methods may be material or immaterial. The major impact on the results usually comes from the rate of inflation. In general, the higher the inflation rate, the greater the differences between the inventory methods.

Because the inventory amounts can be substantially different under the various cost flow assumptions, the analyst should be cautious when comparing the liquidity of firms that have different inventory cost flow assumptions. Caution is particularly necessary when one of the firms is using the LIFO method because LIFO may prove meaningless with regard to the firm's short-term debt-paying ability. If two firms that have different cost flow assumptions need to be compared, this problem should be kept in mind to avoid being misled by the indicated short-term debt-paying ability.

Since the resulting inventory amount will not be equal to the cost of replacing the inventory, regardless of the cost method, another problem needs to be considered when determining the short-term debt-paying ability of the firm: the inventory must be sold for more than cost in order to realize a profit. To the extent that the inventory is sold for more than cost, the short-term debt-paying ability has been understated. However, the extent of the understatement is materially reduced by several factors. One, the firm will incur substantial selling and administrative costs in addition to the inventory cost, thereby reducing the understatement of liquidity to the resulting net profit. Two, the replacement cost of the inventory usually exceeds the reported inventory cost, even if FIFO is used. Therefore, more funds will be required to replace the inventory sold. This will reduce the future short-term debt-paying ability of the firm. Also, since accountants support the conservatism concept, they would rather have a slight understatement of the short-term debt-paying ability of the firm than an overstatement.

The impact on the entity of the different inventory methods must be understood. Since the extremes in inventory costing are LIFO and FIFO, the following summarizes these methods. This summary assumes that the entity faces a period of inflation. The conclusions arrived at in this summary would be reversed if the entity faces a deflationary period.

1. LIFO generally results in a lower profit than does FIFO, as a result of a higher cost of goods sold. This difference can be substantial.

2. Generally, reported profit under LIFO is closer to reality than profit reported under FIFO because the cost of goods sold is closer to replacement cost under LIFO. This is the case under both inflationary and deflationary conditions.

3. FIFO reports a higher inventory ending balance (closer to replacement cost). However, this figure falls short of true replacement cost.

4. The cash flow under LIFO is greater than the cash flow under FIFO because of the difference in tax liability between the two methods, an important reason why a company selects LIFO.

5. Some companies use a periodic inventory system, which updates the inventory in the general ledger once a year. Purchases made late in the year become part of the cost of goods sold under LIFO. If prices have increased during the period, the cost of goods sold will increase and profits will decrease. It is important that accountants inform management that profits will be lower if substantial purchases of inventory are made near the end of the year, and a periodic inventory system is used.

6. A company using LIFO could face a severe tax problem and a severe cash problem if sales reduce or eliminate the amount of inventory normally carried. The reduction in inventory would result in older costs being matched against current sales. This distorts profits on the high side. Because of the high reported profit, income taxes would increase. When the firm needs to replenish the inventory, it has to use additional cash. These problems can be reduced by planning and close supervision of production and purchases. A method called dollar-value LIFO is now frequently used by companies that use LIFO. The dollar-value LIFO method uses price indexes related to the inventory instead of units and unit costs. With dollar-value LIFO, inventory each period is determined for pools of inventory dollars. (See an intermediate accounting book for a detailed explanation of dollar-value LIFO.)

7. LIFO would probably not be used for inventory that has a high turnover rate because there would be an immaterial difference in the results between LIFO and FIFO.

8. LIFO results in a lower profit figure than does FIFO, the result of a higher cost of goods sold.

A firm using LIFO must disclose a LIFO reserve account, usually in a note to the financial statement. Usually, the amount disclosed must be added to inventory to approximate the inventory at FIFO. An inventory at FIFO is usually a reasonable approximation of the current replacement cost of the inventory.

Nike uses the FIFO inventory method. The Gorman-Rupp Company will be used to illustrate LIFO. "The principal products of the Company are pumps and fluid control products." 10-K

Summary of major accounting policies indicates the following in its 2006 annual report:

Consolidated Balance Sheets (in Part)

Inventories	December 31,	
	2006	2005
Raw materials and in-process	$22,423,000	$29,187,000
Finished parts	23,491,000	21,883,000
Finished products	4,385,000	1,333,000
	$50,299,000	$52,403,000

Notes to Consolidated Financial Statements (in Part)

Note A—Summary of Major Accounting Policies (in Part)

Inventories

"Inventories are stated at the lower of cost or market. The costs for approximately 92% and 94% of inventories at December 31, 2006 and 2005, respectively, are determined using the last-in, first-out (LIFO) method, with the remainder determined using the first-in, first-out method. Cost is comprised of materials, labor and an appropriate proportion of fixed and variable overheads, on an absorption costing basis."

Note C—Inventories

"The excess of replacement cost over LIFO cost is approximately $41,904,000 and $38,221,000 at December 31, 2006 and 2005, respectively. Replacement cost approximates current cost. Reserves for excess and obsolete inventory totaled $2,408,000 and $2,847,000 at December 31, 2006 and 2005 respectively."

The approximate current costs of the Gorman-Rupp inventory at December 31, 2006 and 2005 follow.

	2006	2005
Balance per balance sheet	$50,299,000	$52,403,000
Additional amount in note	41,904,000	38,221,000
Approximate current costs	$92,203,000	$90,624,000

Lower-of-Cost-or-Market Rule

We have reviewed the inventory cost-based measurements of FIFO, LIFO, average, and specific identification. These cost-based measurements are all considered to be historical cost approaches. The accounting profession decided that a "departure from the cost basis of inventory pricing is required when the utility of the goods is no longer as great as its cost." Utility of the goods has been measured through market values. When the market value of inventory falls below cost, it is necessary to write the inventory down to the lower market value. This is known as the lower-of-cost-or-market (LCM) rule. Market is defined in terms of current replacement cost, either by purchase or manufacture.

    Following the LCM rule, inventories can be written down below cost but never up above cost. The LCM rule provides for the recognition of the loss in utility during the period in which the loss occurs. The LCM rule is consistent with both the matching and the conservatism assumptions.

    The LCM rule is used by many countries other than the United States. As indicated, market is defined in the United States in terms of current replacement cost. Market in other countries may be defined differently, such as "net realizable value."

Liquidity of Inventory

The analysis of the liquidity of the inventories can be approached in a manner similar to that taken to analyze the liquidity of accounts receivable. One computation determines the *number of days' sales in inventory* at the end of the accounting period, another computation determines the *inventory turnover in times per year*, and a third determines the *inventory turnover in days*.

Days' Sales in Inventory

The number of days' sales in inventory ratio relates the amount of the ending inventory to the average daily cost of goods sold. All of the inventory accounts should be included in the computation. The computation gives an indication of the length of time that it will take to use up the inventory through sales. This can be misleading if sales are seasonal or if the company uses a natural business year.

If the company uses a natural business year for its accounting period, the number of days' sales in inventory will tend to be understated because the average daily cost of goods sold will be at a low point at this time of year. If the days' sales in inventory is understated, the liquidity of the inventory is overstated. The same caution should be observed here as was suggested for determining the liquidity of receivables, when one company uses a natural business year and the other uses a calendar year.

If the company closes its year during peak activity, the number of days' sales in inventory would tend to be overstated and the liquidity would be understated. As indicated with receivables, no good business reason exists for closing the year when activities are at a peak, so this situation should rarely occur.

Compute the number of days' sales in inventory as follows:

$$\text{Days' Sales in Inventory} = \frac{\text{Ending Inventory}}{\text{Cost of Goods Sold}/365}$$

The formula divides the number of days in a year into the cost of goods sold, and then divides the resulting figure into the ending inventory. Exhibit 6-7 presents the number of days' sales in inventory for Nike for May 31, 2007, and May 31, 2006. The number of days' sales in inventory has decreased from 90.57 days at the end of 2006 to 84.50 days at the end of 2007. This represents a positive trend.

Exhibit 6-7	NIKE, INC.		
Days' Sales in Inventory			
	Years Ended May 31, 2007 and 2006		
(In millions)		**2007**	**2006**
Inventories, end of year [A]		$2,121.9	$2,076.7
Cost of goods sold		9,165.4	8,367.9
Average daily cost of goods sold (cost of goods sold divided by 365) [B]		25.11	22.93
Number of days' sales in inventory [A ÷ B]		84.50 days	90.57 days

If sales are approximately constant, then the lower the number of days' sales in inventory, the better the inventory control. An inventory buildup can be burdensome if business volume decreases. However, it can be good if business volume expands, since the increased inventory would be available for customers.

The days' sales in inventory estimates the number of days that it will take to sell the current inventory. For several reasons, this estimate may not be very accurate. The cost of goods sold figure is based on last year's sales, divided by the number of days in a year. Sales next year may not be at the same pace as last year. Also, the ending inventory figure may not be representative of the quantity of inventory actually on hand, especially if using LIFO.

A seasonal situation, with inventory unusually low or high at the end of the year, would also result in an unrealistic days' sales in inventory computation. Also, a natural business year with low inventory at the end of the year would result in an unrealistic days' sales in inventory. Therefore, the resulting answer should be taken as a rough estimate, but it helps when comparing periods or similar companies.

The number of days' sales in inventory could become too low, resulting in lost sales. A good knowledge of the industry and the company is required to determine if the number of days' sales in inventory is too low.

In some cases, not only will the cost of goods sold not be reported separately, but the figure reported will not be a close approximation of the cost of goods sold. This, of course, presents a problem for the external analyst. In such cases, use net sales in place of the cost of goods sold. The result will not be a realistic number of days' sales in inventory, but it can be useful in comparing periods within one firm and in comparing one firm with another. Using net sales produces a much lower number of days' sales in inventory, which materially overstates the liquidity of the ending inventory. Therefore, only the trend determined from comparing one period with another and one firm with other firms should be taken seriously (not actual absolute figures). When you suspect that the days' sales in inventory computation does not result in a reasonable answer, consider using this ratio only to indicate a trend.

If the dollar figures for inventory and/or the cost of goods sold are not reasonable, the ratios calculated with these figures may be distorted. These distortions can be eliminated to some extent by using quantities rather than dollars in the computation. The use of quantities in the computation may work very well for single products or groups of similar products. It does not work very well for a large diversified inventory because of possible changes in the mix of the inventory. Also, using quantities rather than dollars will not be feasible when using externally published statements.

An example of the use of quantities, instead of dollars, follows:

Ending inventory   50 units
Cost of goods sold   500 units

$$\text{Days' sales in inventory} = \frac{50}{500/365} = 36.50 \text{ days}$$

Inventory Turnover

Inventory turnover indicates the liquidity of the inventory. This computation is similar to the accounts receivable turnover computation.

The inventory turnover formula follows:

$$\text{Inventory Turnover} = \frac{\text{Cost of Goods Sold}}{\text{Average Inventory}}$$

Exhibit 6-8 presents the inventory turnover using the 2007 and 2006 figures for Nike. For Nike, the inventory turnover increased from 4.30 to 4.37.

Computing the average inventory based on the beginning-of-year and end-of-year inventories can be misleading if the company has seasonal fluctuations or if the company uses a natural business year. The solution to the problem is similar to that used when computing the receivables turnover—that is, use the monthly (or even weekly) balances of inventory. Monthly estimates of inventory are available for internal analysis, but not for external analysis.

| **Exhibit** | **6-8** | NIKE, INC. |

| Merchandise Inventory Turnover | | |

	Years Ended May 31, 2007 and 2006	
(In millions)	**2007**	**2006**
Cost of goods sold [A]	$9,165.4	$8,367.9
Inventories:		
Beginning of year	2,076.7	1,811.1
End of year	2,121.9	2,076.7
Total	4,198.6	3,887.8
Average inventory [B]	2,099.3	1,943.9
Merchandise inventory turnover [A ÷ B]	4.37 times per year	4.30 times per year

Quarterly figures may be available for external analysis. If adequate information is not available, avoid comparing a company on a natural business year with a company on a calendar year. The company with the natural business year tends to overstate inventory turnover and therefore the liquidity of its inventory.

Over time, the difference between the inventory turnover for a firm that uses LIFO and one that uses a method that results in a higher inventory figure can become very material. The LIFO firm will have a much lower inventory and therefore a much higher turnover. Also, it may not be reasonable to compare firms in different industries.

When you suspect that the inventory turnover computation does not result in a reasonable answer because of unrealistic inventory and/or cost of goods sold dollar figures, perform the computation using quantities rather than dollars. As with the days' sales in inventory, this alternative is feasible only when performing internal analysis. (It may not be feasible even for internal analysis because of product line changes.)

Inventory Turnover in Days

The inventory turnover figure can be expressed in number of days instead of times per year. This is comparable to the computation that expressed accounts receivable turnover in days. Compute the inventory turnover in days as follows:

$$\text{Inventory Turnover in Days} = \frac{\text{Average Inventory}}{\text{Cost of Goods Sold}/365}$$

This is the same formula for determining the days' sales in inventory, except that it uses the average inventory. Exhibit 6-9 uses the 2007 and 2006 Nike data to compute the inventory turnover in days. There was a slight decrease in inventory turnover in days for Nike in 2007. This represents an unfavorable trend.

Exhibit 6-9	NIKE, INC.

Inventory Turnover in Days

Years Ended May 31, 2007 and 2006

(In millions)	2007	2006
Cost of goods sold	$9,165.4	$8,367.9
Average inventory [A]	2,099.3	1,943.9
Sales of inventory per day		
(cost of goods sold divided by 365) [B]	25.11	22.93
Inventory turnover in days [A ÷ B]	83.60 days	84.78 days

The inventory turnover in days can be used to compute the inventory turnover per year, as follows:

$$\frac{365}{\text{Inventory Turnover in Days}} = \text{Inventory Turnover per Year}$$

Using the 2007 Nike data, the inventory turnover is as follows:

$$\frac{365}{\text{Inventory Turnover in Days}} = \frac{365}{83.60} = 4.37 \text{ times per year}$$

Operating Cycle

The operating cycle represents the period of time elapsing between the acquisition of goods and the final cash realization resulting from sales and subsequent collections. An approximation of the operating cycle can be determined from the receivables liquidity figures and the inventory liquidity figures. Compute the operating cycle as follows:

$$\text{Operating Cycle} = \frac{\text{Accounts Receivable}}{\text{Turnover in Days}} + \frac{\text{Inventory Turnover}}{\text{in Days}}$$

Chapter 6 *Liquidity of Short-Term Assets; Related Debt-Paying Ability*   219

Exhibit 6-10 uses the 2007 and 2006 Nike data to compute the operating cycle. For Nike, the operating cycle decreased, which is a positive trend.

The estimate of the operating cycle is not realistic if the accounts receivable turnover in days and the inventory turnover in days are not realistic. Remember that the accounts receivable turnover in days and the inventory turnover in days are understated, and thus the liquidity overstated, if the company uses a natural business year and computed the averages based on beginning-of-year and end-of-year data. It should also be remembered that the inventory turnover in days is understated, and the liquidity of the inventory overstated, if the company uses LIFO inventory. Also note that accounts receivable turnover in days is understated, and liquidity of receivables overstated, if the sales figures used included cash and credit sales.

Exhibit 6-10	NIKE, INC.		
	Operating Cycle		
	Years Ended May 31, 2007 and 2006		
		2007	2006
	Accounts receivable turnover in days [A]	55.38	58.14
	Inventory turnover in days [B]	83.60	84.78
	Operating cycle [A + B]	138.98	142.92

The operating cycle should be helpful when comparing a firm from period to period and when comparing a firm with similar companies. This would be the case, even if understated or overstated, as long as the figures in the computation are comparable.

Related to the operating cycle figure is a computation that indicates how long it will take to realize cash from the ending inventory. This computation consists of combining the number of days' sales in ending receivables and the number of days' sales in ending inventory. The 2007 Nike data produced a days' sales in ending receivables of 56.63 days and a days' sales in ending inventory of 84.50 days, for a total of 141.13 days. In this case, there is an increase, considering the year-end numbers. Therefore, the receivables and inventory at the end of the year are higher than the receivables and inventory carried during the year. This indicates less liquidity at the end of the year than during the year.

PREPAYMENTS

Prepayments consist of unexpired costs for which payment has been made. These current assets are expected to be consumed within the operating cycle or one year, whichever is longer. Prepayments normally represent an immaterial portion of the current assets. Therefore, they have little influence on the short-term debt-paying ability of the firm.

Since prepayments have been paid for and will not generate cash in the future, they differ from other current assets. Prepayments relate to the short-term debt-paying ability of the entity because they conserve the use of cash.

Because of the nature of prepayments, the problems of valuation and liquidity are handled in a simple manner. Valuation is taken as the cost that has been paid. Since a prepayment is a current asset that has been paid for in a relatively short period before the balance sheet date, the cost paid fairly represents the cash used for the prepayment. Except in rare circumstances, a prepayment will not result in a receipt of cash; therefore, no liquidity computation is needed. An example of a circumstance where cash is received would be an insurance policy canceled early. No liquidity computation is possible, even in this case.

OTHER CURRENT ASSETS

Current assets other than cash, marketable securities, receivables, inventories, and prepayments may be listed under current assets. These other current assets may be very material in any one year and, unless they are recurring, may distort the firm's liquidity.

These assets will, in management's opinion, be realized in cash or conserve the use of cash within the operating cycle of the business or one year, whichever is longer. Examples of other current assets include property held for sale and advances or deposits, often explained in a note.

CURRENT LIABILITIES

Current liabilities are "obligations whose liquidation is reasonably expected to require the use of existing resources properly classifiable as current assets or the creation of other current liabilities."[5] Thus, the definition of current liabilities correlates with the definition of current assets.

Typical items found in current liabilities include accounts payable, notes payable, accrued wages, accrued taxes, collections received in advance, and current portions of long-term liabilities. The 2007 Nike annual report listed current liabilities as follows:

	(In millions)
Current liabilities:	
Current portion of long-term debt	$ 30.5
Notes payable	100.8
Accounts payable	1,040.3
Accrued liabilities	1,303.4
Income taxes payable	109.0
Total current liabilities	$2,584.0

For a current liability, liquidity is not a problem, and the valuation problem is immaterial and is disregarded. Theoretically, the valuation of a current liability should be the present value of the required future outlay of money. Since the difference between the present value and the amount that will be paid in the future is immaterial, the current liability is carried at its face value.

Current Assets Compared with Current Liabilities

A comparison of current assets with current liabilities gives an indication of the short-term debt-paying ability of the entity. Several comparisons can be made to determine this ability:

1. Working capital
2. Current ratio
3. Acid-test ratio
4. Cash ratio

WORKING CAPITAL

The working capital of a business is an indication of the short-run solvency of the business. Compute working capital as follows:

Working Capital = Current Assets − Current Liabilities

Exhibit 6-11 presents the working capital for Nike at the end of 2007 and 2006. Nike had $5,492,500,000 in working capital in 2007 and $4,733,600,000 in working capital in 2006.

Exhibit 6-11	NIKE, INC.		
Working Capital			
	Years Ended May 31, 2007 and 2006		
(In millions)		**2007**	**2006**
Current assets [A]		$8,076.5	$7,346.0
Current liabilities [B]		2,584.0	2,612.4
Working capital [A − B]		$5,492.5	$4,733.6

These figures tend to be understated because some of the current assets, such as inventory, may be understated, based on the book figures.

The inventory as reported may be much less than its replacement cost. The difference between the reported inventory amount and the replacement amount is normally material when the firm is using LIFO inventory. The difference may also be material when using one of the other cost methods.

The current working capital amount should be compared with past amounts to determine if working capital is reasonable. Because the relative size of a firm may be expanding or contracting, comparing working capital of one firm with that of another firm is usually meaningless because of their size differences. If the working capital appears to be out of line, find the reasons by analyzing the individual current asset and current liability accounts.

CURRENT RATIO

Another indicator, the current ratio, determines short-term debt-paying ability and is computed as follows:

$$\text{Current Ratio} = \frac{\text{Current Assets}}{\text{Current Liabilities}}$$

Exhibit 6-12 presents the current ratio for Nike at the end of 2007 and 2006. For Nike, the current ratio was 3.13 at the end of 2007 and 2.81 at the end of 2006. This indicates a positive trend considering liquidity.

Exhibit 6-12	NIKE, INC.	
Current Ratio		
Years Ended May 31, 2007 and 2006		
(In millions)	**2007**	**2006**
Current assets [A]	$8,076.5	$7,346.0
Current liabilities [B]	2,584.0	2,612.4
Current ratio [A ÷ B]	3.13	2.81

For many years, the guideline for the minimum current ratio has been 2.00. Until the mid-1960s, the typical firm successfully maintained a current ratio of 2.00 or better. Since that time, the current ratio of many firms has declined to a point below the 2.00 guideline. Currently, many firms are not successful in staying above a current ratio of 2.00. This indicates a decline in the liquidity of many firms. It also could indicate better control of receivables and/or inventory.

A comparison with industry averages should be made to determine the typical current ratio for similar firms. In some industries, a current ratio substantially below 2.00 is adequate, while other industries require a much larger ratio. In general, the shorter the operating cycle, the lower the current ratio. The longer the operating cycle, the higher the current ratio.

A comparison of the firm's current ratio with prior periods, and a comparison with industry averages, will help to determine if the ratio is high or low. These comparisons do not indicate why it is high or low. Possible reasons can be found from an analysis of the individual current asset and current liability accounts. Often, the major reasons for the current ratio being out of line will be found in a detailed analysis of accounts receivable and inventory.

The current ratio is considered to be more indicative of the short-term debt-paying ability than the working capital. Working capital only determines the absolute difference between the current assets and current liabilities. The current ratio shows the relationship between the size of the current assets and the size of the current liabilities, making it feasible to compare the current ratio, for example, between IBM and Intel. A comparison of the working capital of these two firms would be meaningless because IBM is a larger firm than Intel.

LIFO inventory can cause major problems with the current ratio because of the understatement of inventory. The result is an understated current ratio. Extreme caution should be exercised when comparing a firm that uses LIFO and a firm that uses some other costing method.

Before computing the current ratio, the analyst should compute the accounts receivable turnover and the merchandise inventory turnover. These computations enable the analyst to formulate an opinion as to whether liquidity problems exist with receivables and/or inventory. An opinion as to the quality of receivables and inventory should influence the analyst's opinion of the current ratio. If liquidity problems exist with receivables and/or inventory, the current ratio needs to be much higher.

ACID-TEST RATIO (QUICK RATIO)

The current ratio evaluates an enterprise's overall liquidity position, considering current assets and current liabilities. At times, it is desirable to access a more immediate position than that indicated by the current ratio. The acid-test (or quick) ratio relates the most liquid assets to current liabilities.

Inventory is removed from current assets when computing the acid-test ratio. Some of the reasons for removing inventory are that inventory may be slow-moving or possibly obsolete, and parts of the inventory may have been pledged to specific creditors. For example, a winery's inventory requires considerable time for aging and, therefore, a considerable time before sale. To include the wine inventory in the acid-test computation would overstate the liquidity. A valuation problem with inventory also exists because it is stated at a cost figure that may be materially different from a fair current valuation.

Compute the acid-test ratio as follows:

$$\text{Acid-Test Ratio} = \frac{\text{Current Assets} - \text{Inventory}}{\text{Current Liabilities}}$$

Exhibit 6-13 presents the acid-test ratio for Nike at the end of 2007 and 2006. For Nike, the acid-test ratio was 2.30 at the end of 2007 and 2.02 at the end of 2006. This represents a positive trend.

Exhibit 6-13 NIKE, INC.		
Acid-Test Ratio		
Years Ended May 31, 2007 and 2006		
(In millions)	**2007**	**2006**
Current assets	$8,076.5	$7,346.0
Less: Ending inventory	2,121.9	2,076.7
Remaining current assets [A]	$5,954.6	$5,269.3
Current liabilities [B]	$2,584.0	$2,612.4
Acid-test ratio [A ÷ B]	2.30	2.02

It may also be desirable to exclude some other items from current assets that may not represent current cash flow, such as prepaid and miscellaneous items. Compute the more conservative acid-test ratio as follows:

$$\text{Acid-Test Ratio} = \frac{\text{Cash Equivalents} + \text{Marketable Securities} + \text{Net Receivables}}{\text{Current Liabilities}}$$

Usually, a very immaterial difference occurs between the acid-test ratios computed under the first method and this second method. Frequently, the only difference is the inclusion of prepayments in the first computation.

Exhibit 6-14 presents the conservative acid-test ratio for Nike at the end of 2007 and 2006. This approach resulted in an acid-test ratio of 2.07 at the end of 2007 and 1.79 at the end of 2006.

Exhibit	**6-14**	NIKE, INC.		

Acid-Test Ratio (Conservative Approach)

	Years Ended May 31, 2007 and 2006	
(In millions)	**2007**	**2006**
Cash, including short-term investments	$2,847.0	$2,303.0
Net receivables	2,494.7	2,382.9
Total quick assets [A]	$5,341.7	$4,685.9
Current liabilities [B]	$2,584.0	$2,612.4
Acid-test ratio [A ÷ B]	2.07	1.79

From this point on in this book, the more conservative computations will be used for the acid-test ratio. When a company needs to view liquidity with only inventory removed, the alternative computation should be used.

For many years, the guideline for the minimum acid-test ratio was 1.00. A comparison should be made with the firm's past acid-test ratios and with major competitors and the industry averages. Some industries find that a ratio less than 1.00 is adequate, while others need a ratio greater than 1.00. For example, a grocery store may sell only for cash and not have receivables. This type of business can have an acid-test ratio substantially below the 1.00 guideline and still have adequate liquidity.

Before computing the acid-test ratio, compute the accounts receivable turnover. An opinion as to the quality of receivables should help the analyst form an opinion of the acid-test ratio.

There has been a major decline in the liquidity of companies in the United States, as measured by the current ratio and the acid-test ratio. Exhibit 6-15 shows the dramatically reduced

Exhibit	**6-15**	TRENDS IN CURRENT RATIO AND ACID-TEST RATIO

All U.S. Manufacturing Companies, 1964–2006

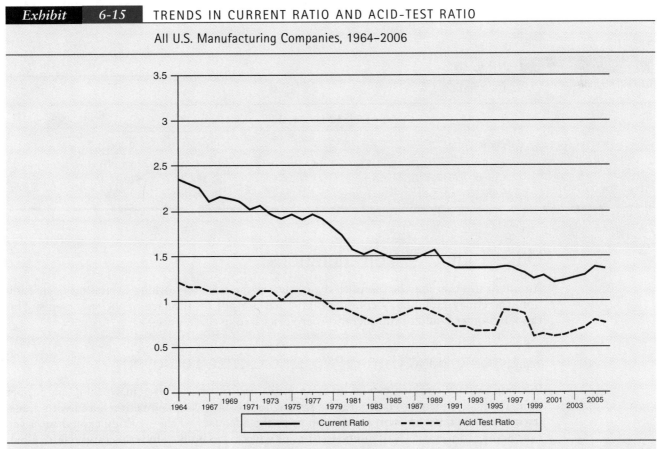

Source: Quarterly financial reports of manufacturing, mining and trading, Department of Commerce Washington D.C.; government.

liquidity of U.S. companies. Reduced liquidity leads to more bankruptcies and greater risk for creditors and investors.

CASH RATIO

Sometimes an analyst needs to view the liquidity of a firm from an extremely conservative point of view. For example, the company may have pledged its receivables and its inventory, or the analyst suspects severe liquidity problems with inventory and receivables. The best indicator of the company's short-run liquidity may be the cash ratio. Compute the cash ratio as follows:

$$\text{Cash Ratio} = \frac{\text{Cash Equivalents} + \text{Marketable Securities}}{\text{Current Liabilities}}$$

The analyst seldom gives the cash ratio much weight when evaluating the liquidity of a firm because it is not realistic to expect a firm to have enough cash equivalents and marketable securities to cover current liabilities. If the firm must depend on cash equivalents and marketable securities for its liquidity, its solvency may be impaired.

Analysts should consider the cash ratio of companies that have naturally slow-moving inventories and receivables and companies that are highly speculative. For example, a land development company in Florida may sell lots paid for over a number of years on the installment basis, or the success of a new company may be in doubt.

The cash ratio indicates the immediate liquidity of the firm. A high cash ratio indicates that the firm is not using its cash to its best advantage; cash should be put to work in the operations of the company. Detailed knowledge of the firm is required, however, before drawing a definite conclusion. Management may have plans for the cash, such as a building expansion program. A cash ratio that is too low could indicate an immediate problem with paying bills.

Exhibit 6-16 presents this ratio for Nike at the end of 2007 and 2006. For Nike, the cash ratio was 1.10 at the end of 2007 and 0.88 at the end of 2006. Nike's cash ratio increased materially at the end of 2007 in relation to the end of 2006.

Exhibit	6-16	NIKE, INC.

Cash Ratio

Years Ended May 31, 2007 and 2006

(In millions)	2007	2006
Cash, including short-term investments [A]	$2,847.0	$2,303.0
Current liabilities [B]	$2,584.0	$2,612.4
Cash ratio [A ÷ B]	1.10	0.88

Other Liquidity Considerations

Another ratio that may be useful to the analyst is the sales to working capital ratio. In addition, there may be liquidity considerations that are not on the face of the statements. This ratio and other liquidity considerations are discussed in this section.

SALES TO WORKING CAPITAL (WORKING CAPITAL TURNOVER)

Relating sales to working capital gives an indication of the turnover in working capital per year. The analyst needs to compare this ratio with the past, with competitors, and with industry averages in order to form an opinion as to the adequacy of the working capital turnover. Like many ratios, no rules of thumb exist as to what it should be. Since this ratio relates a balance sheet number (working capital) to an income statement number (sales), a problem exists if the balance sheet number is not representative of the year. To avoid this problem, use the average monthly working capital figure when available. Compute the working capital turnover as follows:

$$\text{Sales to Working Capital} = \frac{\text{Sales}}{\text{Average Working Capital}}$$

A low working capital turnover ratio tentatively indicates an unprofitable use of working capital. In other words, sales are not adequate in relation to the available working capital. A high ratio tentatively indicates that the firm is undercapitalized (overtrading). An undercapitalized firm is particularly susceptible to liquidity problems when a major adverse change in business conditions occurs.

Exhibit 6-17 presents this ratio for Nike at the end of 2007 and 2006. The sales to working capital ratio decreased from 2006 to 2007. (Working capital in 2007 was higher in relation to sales than it was in 2006.) This tentatively indicates a slightly less profitable use of working capital in 2007 in relation to 2006.

Exhibit 6-17	NIKE, INC.		
	Sales to Working Capital		
	Years Ended May 31, 2007 and 2006		
(In millions)		**2007**	**2006**
Net sales [A]		$16,325.9	$14,954.9
Working capital at beginning of year		4,733.6	4,351.9
Working capital at end of year		5,492.2	4,733.6
Average working capital [B]		5,112.9	4,542.8
Sales to working capital [A ÷ B]		3.19 times per year	3.29 times per year

LIQUIDITY CONSIDERATIONS NOT ON THE FACE OF THE STATEMENTS

A firm may have a better liquidity position than indicated by the face of the financial statements. The following paragraphs present several examples:

1. Unused bank credit lines would be a positive addition to liquidity. They are frequently disclosed in notes.

2. A firm may have some long-term assets that could be converted to cash quickly. This would add to the firm's liquidity. Extreme caution is advised if there is any reliance on long-term assets for liquidity. For one thing, the long-term assets are usually needed in operations. Second, even excess long-term assets may not be easily converted into cash in a short period of time. An exception might be investments, depending on the nature of the investments.

3. A firm may be in a very good long-term debt position and therefore have the capability to issue debt or stock. Thus, the firm could relieve a severe liquidity problem in a reasonable amount of time.

A firm may not be in as good a position of liquidity as indicated by the ratios, as the following examples show:

1. A firm may have notes discounted on which the other party has full recourse against the firm. Discounted notes should be disclosed in a note. (A company that discounts a customer note receivable is in essence selling the note to the bank with recourse.)

2. A firm may have major contingent liabilities that have not been recorded, such as a disputed tax claim. Unrecorded contingencies that are material are disclosed in a note.

3. A firm may have guaranteed a bank note for another company. This would be disclosed in a note.

Summary

The ratios related to the liquidity of short-term assets and the short-term debt-paying ability follow:

$$\text{Days' Sales in Receivables} = \frac{\text{Gross Receivables}}{\text{Net Sales/365}}$$

$$\text{Accounts Receivable Turnover} = \frac{\text{Net Sales}}{\text{Average Gross Receivables}}$$

$$\text{Accounts Receivable Turnover in Days} = \frac{\text{Average Gross Receivables}}{\text{Net Sales/365}}$$

$$\text{Days' Sales in Inventory} = \frac{\text{Ending Inventory}}{\text{Cost of Goods Sold/365}}$$

$$\text{Inventory Turnover} = \frac{\text{Cost of Goods Sold}}{\text{Average Inventory}}$$

$$\text{Inventory Turnover in Days} = \frac{\text{Average Inventory}}{\text{Cost of Goods Sold/365}}$$

$$\text{Operating Cycle} = \frac{\text{Accounts Receivable}}{\text{Turnover in Days}} + \frac{\text{Inventory Turnover}}{\text{in Days}}$$

$$\text{Working Capital} = \text{Current Assets} - \text{Current Liabilities}$$

$$\text{Current Ratio} = \frac{\text{Current Assets}}{\text{Current Liabilities}}$$

$$\text{Acid-Test Ratio} = \frac{\text{Cash Equivalents} + \text{Marketable Securities} + \text{Net Receivables}}{\text{Current Liabilities}}$$

$$\text{Cash Ratio} = \frac{\text{Cash Equivalents} + \text{Marketable Securities}}{\text{Current Liabilities}}$$

$$\text{Sales to Working Capital} = \frac{\text{Sales}}{\text{Average Working Capital}}$$

to the net

1. Go to the SEC Web site (http://www.sec.gov). Under "Filings & Forms (EDGAR)," click on "Search for Company Filings." Click on "Companies & Other Filers."

    a. Under Company Name, enter "JLG Industries Inc" (or under Ticker Symbol, enter "JLG"). Select the 10-K filed October 2, 2006.

       1. Determine the SIC.

       2. Copy the first sentence in the "Item 1. Business" section.

       3. Compute the current ratio for July 31, 2006 and 2005.

    b. Under Company Name, enter "Kroger Co" (or under Ticker Symbol, enter "KR"). In the Form Type box, enter "10–K." Select the 10-K filed April 4, 2007.

       1. Determine the SIC.

       2. Copy the first sentence in the "Item 1. Business" section.

       3. Compute the current ratio for February 3, 2007, and January 28, 2006.

    c. Consider the nature of the business of these companies. Comment on why JLG has a higher current ratio than Kroger Co.

2. Go to the SEC Web site (http://www.sec.gov). Under "Filings & Forms (EDGAR)," click on "Search for Company Filings." Click on "Companies & Other Filers." Under Company Name, enter "Kroger Co" (or under Ticker Symbol, enter "KR"). Select the 10-K filed April 4, 2007.

   a. Determine the SIC.

   b. Copy the first sentence in the "Item 1. Business" section.

   c. Determine the net inventory balances at February 3, 2007.

   d. Determine the replacement cost of inventory at February 3, 2007.

   e. Comment on why the inventory balance is lower than replacement cost.

3. Go to the SEC Web site (http://www.sec.gov). Under "Filings & Forms (EDGAR)," click on "Search for Company Filings." Click on "Companies & Other Filers." Under Company Name, enter "Dynatronics Corp" (or under Ticker Symbol, enter "DYNT"). Select the 10-K SB filed September 28, 2006.

   a. Copy the first paragraph in the "Item 1. Business" section.

   b. What is the net receivable at June 30, 2006?

   c. What is the gross receivable at June 30, 2006?

   d. Describe the inventory method.

4. Go to the SEC Web site (http://www.sec.gov). Under "Filings & Forms (EDGAR)," click on "Search for Company Filings." Click on "Companies & Other Filers." Under Company Name, enter "Tribune Co" (or under Ticker Symbol, enter "TRB"). Select the 10-K filed February 26, 2007.

   a. Determine the SIC.

   b. Copy the first two sentences in the "Item 1. Business" section.

   c. What is the net receivable at December 31, 2006?

   d. What is the gross receivable at December 31, 2006?

   e. Why the relative low amount in inventories in relation to total current assets?

   f. 1. Compute working capital at December 31, 2006.
      2. Compute the current ratio at December 31, 2006.

   g. What account in current assets is specific to this industry? Why is some of this account listed under other assets? What is the related account under current liabilities? What is the related account under other noncurrent liabilities?

5. Go to the SEC Web site (http://www.sec.gov). Under "Filings & Forms (EDGAR)," click on "Search for Company Filings." Click on "Companies & Other Filers." Under Company Name, enter "Dell Inc" (or under Ticker Symbol, enter "DELL"). Select the 10-K filed March 15, 2006.

   a. Determine the SIC.

   b. Copy the first sentence in the "Item 1. Business" section.

   c. Speculate why inventories are relatively low in relation to accounts receivable, net.

   d. Speculate why accounts receivable, net is relatively low in relation to accounts payable.

   e. Speculate why the amounts in cash and cash equivalents and short-term investments are large in relation to total current assets.

Questions

Q 6-1.   It is proposed at a stockholders' meeting that the firm slow its rate of payments on accounts payable in order to make more funds available for operations. It is contended that this procedure will enable the firm to expand inventory, which will in turn enable the firm to generate more sales. Comment on this proposal.

Q 6-2.   Jones Wholesale Company has been one of the fastest growing wholesale firms in the United States for the last five years in terms of sales and profits. The firm has maintained a current ratio above the average for the wholesale industry. Mr. Jones has asked you to explain possible reasons why the firm is having difficulty meeting its payroll and its accounts payable. What would you tell Mr. Jones?

Q 6-3.   What is the reason for separating current assets from the rest of the assets found on the balance sheet?

Q 6-4.   Define the operating cycle.

Q 6-5.   Define current assets.

Q 6-6.   List the major categories of items usually found in current assets.

Q 6-7.   Rachit Company has cash that has been frozen in a bank in Cuba. Should this cash be classified as a current asset? Discuss.

Q 6-8.   A. B. Smith Company has guaranteed a $1,000,000 bank note for Alender Company. How would this influence the liquidity ratios of A. B. Smith Company? How should this situation be considered?

Q 6-9.   Arrow Company has invested funds in a supplier to help ensure a steady supply of needed materials. Would this investment be classified as a marketable security (current asset)?

Q 6-10.   List the two computations that are used to determine the liquidity of receivables.

Q 6-11.   List the two computations that are used to determine the liquidity of inventory.

Q 6-12.   Would a company that uses a natural business year tend to overstate or understate the liquidity of its receivables? Explain.

Q 6-13.   T. Melcher Company uses the calendar year. Sales are at a peak during the holiday season, and T. Melcher Company extends 30-day credit terms to customers. Comment on the expected liquidity of its receivables, based on the days' sales in receivables and the accounts receivable turnover.

Q 6-14.   A company that uses a natural business year, or ends its year when business is at a peak, will tend to distort the liquidity of its receivables when end-of-year and beginning-of-year receivables are used in the computation. Explain how a company that uses a natural business year or ends its year when business is at a peak can eliminate the distortion in its liquidity computations.

Q 6-15.   If a company has substantial cash sales and credit sales, is there any meaning to the receivable liquidity computations that are based on gross sales?

Q 6-16.   Describe the difference in inventories between a firm that is a trading concern and a firm that is a manufacturing concern.

Q 6-17.   During times of inflation, which of the inventory costing methods listed below would give the most realistic valuation of inventory? Which method would give the least realistic valuation of inventory? Explain.
   a. LIFO
   b. Average
   c. FIFO

Q 6-18.   The number of days' sales in inventory relates the amount of the ending inventory to the average daily cost of goods sold. Explain why this computation may be misleading under the following conditions:
   a. The company uses a natural business year for its accounting period.
   b. The company closes the year when activities are at a peak.
   c. The company uses LIFO inventory, and inflation has been a problem for a number of years.

Q 6-19.   The days' sales in inventory is an estimate of the number of days that it will take to sell the current inventory.
   a. What is the ideal number of days' sales in inventory?
   b. In general, does a company want many days' sales in inventory?
   c. Can days' sales in inventory be too low?

Q 6-20.   Some firms do not report the cost of goods sold separately on their income statements. In such a case, how should you proceed to compute days' sales in inventory? Will this procedure produce a realistic days' sales in inventory?

Q 6-21.   One of the computations used to determine the liquidity of inventory determines the inventory turnover. In this computation, usually the average inventory is determined by using the beginning-of-the-year and the end-of-the-year inventory figures, but this computation can be misleading if the company has seasonal fluctuations or uses a natural business year. Suggest how to eliminate these distortions.

Q 6-22.   Explain the influence of the use of LIFO inventory on the inventory turnover.

Q 6-23.   Define working capital.

Q 6-24.   Define current liabilities.

Q 6-25.   Several comparisons can be made to determine the short-term debt-paying ability of an entity. Some of these are:
a. Working capital
b. Current ratio
c. Acid-test ratio
d. Cash ratio
    1. Define each of these terms.
    2. If the book figures are based on cost, will the results of the preceding computations tend to be understated or overstated? Explain.
    3. What figures should be used in order to avoid the problem referred to in (2)?

Q 6-26.   Discuss how to use working capital in analysis.

Q 6-27.   Both current assets and current liabilities are used in the computation of working capital and the current ratio, yet the current ratio is considered to be more indicative of the short-term debt-paying ability. Explain.

Q 6-28.   In determining the short-term liquidity of a firm, the current ratio is usually considered to be a better guide than the acid-test ratio, and the acid-test ratio is considered to be a better guide than the cash ratio. Discuss when the acid-test ratio would be preferred over the current ratio and when the cash ratio would be preferred over the acid-test ratio.

Q 6-29.   Discuss some benefits that may accrue to a firm from reducing its operating cycle. Suggest some ways that may be used to reduce a company's operating cycle.

Q 6-30.   Discuss why some firms have longer natural operating cycles than other firms.

Q 6-31.   Would a firm with a relatively long operating cycle tend to charge a higher markup on its inventory cost than a firm with a short operating cycle? Discuss.

Q 6-32.   Is the profitability of the entity considered to be of major importance in determining the short-term debt-paying ability? Discuss.

Q 6-33.   Does the allowance method for bad debts or the direct write-off method result in the fairest presentation of receivables on the balance sheet and the fairest matching of expenses against revenue?

Q 6-34.   When a firm faces an inflationary condition and the LIFO inventory method is based on a periodic basis, purchases late in the year can have a substantial influence on profits. Comment.

Q 6-35.   Why could a current asset such as Net Assets of Business Held for Sale distort a firm's liquidity, in terms of working capital or the current ratio?

Q 6-36.   Before computing the current ratio, the accounts receivable turnover and the inventory turnover should be computed. Why?

Q 6-37.   Before computing the acid-test ratio, compute the accounts receivable turnover. Comment.

Q 6-38.   Which inventory costing method results in the highest balance sheet amount for inventory? (Assume inflationary conditions.)

Q 6-39.   Indicate the single most important factor that motivates a company to select LIFO.

Q 6-40.   A relatively low sales to working capital ratio is a tentative indication of an efficient use of working capital. Comment. A relatively high sales to working capital ratio is a tentative indication that the firm is undercapitalized. Comment.

Q 6-41.   List three situations in which the liquidity position of the firm may be better than that indicated by the liquidity ratios.

Q 6-42.   List three situations in which the liquidity position of the firm may not be as good as that indicated by the liquidity ratios.

Q 6-43.   Indicate the objective of the sales to working capital ratio.

Q 6-44.   Why does LIFO result in a very unrealistic ending inventory figure in a period of rising prices?

Q 6-45.   The cost of inventory at the close of the calendar year of the first year of operation is $40,000, using LIFO inventory, resulting in a profit before tax of $100,000. If the FIFO inventory would have been $50,000, what would the reported profit before tax have been? If the average cost method would have resulted in an inventory of $45,000, what would the reported profit before tax have been? Should the inventory costing method be disclosed? Why?

Problems

P 6-1.   In this problem, compute the acid-test ratio as follows:

$$\frac{\text{Current Assets} - \text{Inventory}}{\text{Current Liabilities}}$$

Required   Determine the cost of sales of a firm with the financial data given below.

Current ratio	2.5
Quick ratio or acid-test	2.0
Current liabilities	$400,000
Inventory turnover	3 times

P 6-2.   Hawk Company wants to determine the liquidity of its receivables. It has supplied you with the following data regarding selected accounts for December 31, 2007, and 2006:

	2007	2006
Net sales	$1,180,178	$2,200,000
Receivables, less allowance for losses and discounts		
Beginning of year (allowance for losses and discounts, 2007—$12,300; 2006—$7,180)	240,360	230,180
End of year (allowance for losses and discounts, 2007—$11,180; 2006—$12,300)	220,385	240,360

Required   a. Compute the number of days' sales in receivables at December 31, 2007, and 2006.

b. Compute the accounts receivable turnover for 2007 and 2006. (Use year-end gross receivables.)

c. Comment on the liquidity of Hawk Company receivables.

P 6-3.   Mr. Williams, the owner of Williams Produce, wants to maintain control over accounts receivable. He understands that days' sales in receivables and accounts receivable turnover will give a good indication of how well receivables are being managed. Williams Produce does 60% of its business during June, July, and August. Mr. Williams provided the following pertinent data:

	For Year Ended December 31, 2007	For Year Ended July 31, 2007
Net sales	$800,000	$790,000
Receivables, less allowance for doubtful accounts		
Beginning of period (allowance January 1, $3,000; August 1, $4,000)	50,000	89,000
End of period (allowance December 31, $3,500; July 31, $4,100)	55,400	90,150

Required   a. Compute the days' sales in receivables for July 31, 2007, and December 31, 2007, based on the accompanying data.

b. Compute the accounts receivable turnover for the period ended July 31, 2007, and December 31, 2007. (Use year-end gross receivables.)

c. Comment on the results from (a) and (b).

P 6-4.   L. Solomon Company would like to compare its days' sales in receivables with that of a competitor, L. Konrath Company. Both companies have had similar sales results in the past, but L. Konrath Company has had better profit results. L. Solomon Company suspects that one reason for the better profit results is that L. Konrath Company did a better job of managing receivables. L. Solomon Company uses a calendar year that ends on December 31, while L. Konrath Company uses a fiscal year that ends on July 31. Information related to sales and receivables of the two companies follows:

	For Year Ended December 31, 20XX
L. Solomon Company	
Net sales	$1,800,000
Receivables, less allowance for doubtful accounts of $8,000	110,000

	For Year Ended July 31, 20XX
L. Konrath Company	
Net sales	$1,850,000
Receivables, less allowance for doubtful accounts of $4,000	60,000

Required   a. Compute the days' sales in receivables for both companies. (Use year-end gross receivables.)

b. Comment on the results.

P 6-5a.   P. Gibson Company has computed its accounts receivable turnover in days to be 36.

Required   Compute the accounts receivable turnover per year.

P 6-5b.   P. Gibson Company has computed its accounts receivable turnover per year to be 12.

Required   Compute the accounts receivable turnover in days.

P 6-5c.   P. Gibson Company has gross receivables at the end of the year of $280,000 and net sales for the year of $2,158,000.

Required   Compute the days' sales in receivables at the end of the year.

P 6-5d.   P. Gibson Company has net sales of $3,500,000 and average gross receivables of $324,000.

Required   Compute the accounts receivable turnover.

P 6-6.   J. Shaffer Company has an ending inventory of $360,500 and a cost of goods sold for the year of $2,100,000. It has used LIFO inventory for a number of years because of persistent inflation.

Required   a. Compute the days' sales in inventory.

b. Is J. Shaffer Company's days' sales in inventory as computed realistic in comparison with the actual days' sales in inventory?

c. Would the days' sales in inventory computed for J. Shaffer Company be a helpful guide?

P 6-7.   J. Szabo Company had an average inventory of $280,000 and a cost of goods sold of $1,250,000.

Required   Compute the following:

a. The inventory turnover in days

b. The inventory turnover

P 6-8. The inventory and sales data for this year for G. Rabbit Company are as follows:

	End of Year	Beginning of Year
Net sales	$3,150,000	
Gross receivables	180,000	$160,000
Inventory	480,000	390,000
Cost of goods sold	2,250,000	

Required Using the above data from G. Rabbit Company, compute the following:

a. The accounts receivable turnover in days
b. The inventory turnover in days
c. The operating cycle

P 6-9. Anna Banana Company would like to estimate how long it will take to realize cash from its ending inventory. For this purpose, the following data are submitted:

Accounts receivable, less allowance for doubtful accounts of $30,000	$ 560,000
Ending inventory	680,000
Net sales	4,350,000
Cost of goods sold	3,600,000

Required Estimate how long it will take to realize cash from the ending inventory.

P 6-10. Laura Badora Company has been using LIFO inventory. The company is required to disclose the replacement cost of its inventory and the replacement cost of its cost of goods sold on its annual statements. Selected data for the year ended 2007 are as follows:

Ending accounts receivable, less allowance for doubtful accounts of $25,000	$ 480,000
Ending inventory, LIFO (estimated replacement $900,000)	570,000
Net sales	3,650,000
Cost of goods sold (estimated replacement cost $3,150,000)	2,850,000

Required

a. Compute the days' sales in receivables.
b. Compute the days' sales in inventory, using the cost figure.
c. Compute the days' sales in inventory, using the replacement cost for the inventory and the cost of goods sold.
d. Should replacement cost of inventory and cost of goods sold be used, when possible, when computing days' sales in inventory? Discuss.

P 6-11. A partial balance sheet and income statement for King Corporation follow:

KING CORPORATION
Partial Balance Sheet
December 31, 2007

Assets	
Current assets:	
Cash	$ 33,493
Marketable securities	215,147
Trade receivables, less allowance of $6,000	255,000
Inventories, LIFO	523,000
Prepaid expenses	26,180
Total current assets	$1,052,820
Liabilities	
Current liabilities:	
Trade accounts payable	$ 103,689
Notes payable (primarily to banks) and commercial paper	210,381
Accrued expenses and other liabilities	120,602
Income taxes payable	3,120
Current maturities of long-term debt	22,050
Total current liabilities	$ 459,842

KING CORPORATION
Partial Income Statement
For Year Ended December 31, 2007

Net sales		$3,050,600
Miscellaneous income		45,060
		$3,095,660
Costs and expenses:		
Cost of sales	$2,185,100	
Selling, general, and administrative expenses	350,265	
Interest expense	45,600	
Income taxes	300,000	
		2,880,965
Net income		$ 214,695

Note: The trade receivables at December 31, 2006, were $280,000, net of an allowance of $8,000, for a gross receivables figure of $288,000. The inventory at December 31, 2006, was $565,000.

Required Compute the following:

a. Working capital
b. Current ratio
c. Acid-test ratio
d. Cash ratio
e. Days' sales in receivables

f. Accounts receivable turnover in days
g. Days' sales in inventory
h. Inventory turnover in days
i. Operating cycle

P 6-12. Individual transactions often have a significant impact on ratios. This problem will consider the direction of such an impact.

	Total Current Assets	Total Current Liabilities	Net Working Capital	Current Ratio
a. Cash is acquired through issuance of additional common stock.	_____	_____	_____	_____
b. Merchandise is sold for cash. (Assume a profit.)	_____	_____	_____	_____
c. A fixed asset is sold for more than book value.	_____	_____	_____	_____
d. Payment is made to trade creditors for previous purchases.	_____	_____	_____	_____
e. A cash dividend is declared and paid.	_____	_____	_____	_____
f. A stock dividend is declared and paid.	_____	_____	_____	_____
g. Cash is obtained through long-term bank loans.	_____	_____	_____	_____
h. A profitable firm increases its fixed assets depreciation allowance account.	_____	_____	_____	_____
i. Current operating expenses are paid.	_____	_____	_____	_____
j. Ten-year notes are issued to pay off accounts payable.	_____	_____	_____	_____
k. Accounts receivable are collected.	_____	_____	_____	_____
l. Equipment is purchased with short-term notes.	_____	_____	_____	_____
m. Merchandise is purchased on credit.	_____	_____	_____	_____
n. The estimated taxes payable are increased.	_____	_____	_____	_____
o. Marketable securities are sold below cost.	_____	_____	_____	_____

Required Indicate the effects of the previous transactions on each of the following: total current assets, total current liabilities, net working capital, and current ratio. Use + to indicate an increase, – to indicate a decrease, and 0 to indicate no effect. Assume an initial current ratio of more than 1 to 1.

P 6-13.   Current assets and current liabilities for companies D and E are summarized as follows:

	Company D	Company E
Current assets	$400,000	$900,000
Current liabilities	200,000	700,000
Working capital	$200,000	$200,000

Required   Evaluate the relative solvency of companies D and E.

P 6-14.   Current assets and current liabilities for companies R and T are summarized below.

	Company R	Company T
Current assets	$400,000	$800,000
Current liabilities	200,000	400,000
Working capital	$200,000	$400,000

Required   Evaluate the relative solvency of companies R and T.

P 6-15.   The following financial data were taken from the annual financial statements of Smith Corporation:

	2005	2006	2007
Current assets	$ 450,000	$ 400,000	$ 500,000
Current liabilities	390,000	300,000	340,000
Sales	1,450,000	1,500,000	1,400,000
Cost of goods sold	1,180,000	1,020,000	1,120,000
Inventory	280,000	200,000	250,000
Accounts receivable	120,000	110,000	105,000

Required   a. Based on these data, calculate the following for 2006 and 2007:
  1. Working capital
  2. Current ratio
  3. Acid-test ratio
  4. Accounts receivable turnover
  5. Merchandise inventory turnover
  6. Inventory turnover in days
b. Evaluate the results of your computations in regard to the short-term liquidity of the firm.

P 6-16.   Anne Elizabeth Corporation is engaged in the business of making toys. A high percentage of its products are sold to consumers during November and December. Therefore, retailers need to have the toys in stock prior to November. The corporation produces on a relatively stable basis during the year in order to retain its skilled employees and to minimize its investment in plant and equipment. The seasonal nature of its business requires a substantial capacity to store inventory.

   The gross receivables balance at April 30, 2006, was $75,000, and the inventory balance was $350,000 on this date. Sales for the year ended April 30, 2007, totaled $4,000,000, and the cost of goods sold totaled $1,800,000.

   Anne Elizabeth Corporation uses a natural business year that ends on April 30. Inventory and accounts receivable data are given in the following table for the year ended April 30, 2007:

Month	Month-End Balance	
	Gross Receivables	Inventory
May 2006	$ 60,000	$525,000
June 2006	40,000	650,000
July 2006	50,000	775,000
August 2006	60,000	900,000
September 2006	200,000	975,000
October 2006	800,000	700,000
November 2006	1,500,000	400,000
December 2006	1,800,000	25,000

Month	Gross Receivables	Inventory
January 2007	$1,000,000	$100,000
February 2007	600,000	150,000
March 2007	200,000	275,000
April 2007	50,000	400,000

Required   a. Using averages based on the year-end figures, compute the following:

  1. Accounts receivable turnover in days
  2. Accounts receivable turnover per year
  3. Inventory turnover in days
  4. Inventory turnover per year

  b. Using averages based on monthly figures, compute the following:

  1. Accounts receivable turnover in days
  2. Accounts receivable turnover per year
  3. Inventory turnover in days
  4. Inventory turnover per year

  c. Comment on the difference between the ratios computed in (a) and (b).
  d. Compute the days' sales in receivables.
  e. Compute the days' sales in inventory.
  f. How realistic are the days' sales in receivables and the days' sales in inventory that were computed in (d) and (e)?

P 6-17.   The following data relate to inventory for the year ended December 31, 2007:

Date	Description	Number of Units	Cost per Unit	Total Cost
January 1	Beginning inventory	400	$5.00	$ 2,000
March 1	Purchase	1,000	6.00	6,000
August 1	Purchase	200	7.00	1,400
November 1	Purchase	200	7.50	1,500
		1,800		$10,900

A physical inventory on December 31, 2007, indicates that 400 units are on hand and that they came from the March 1 purchase.

Required   Compute the cost of goods sold for the year ended December 31, 2007, and the ending inventory under the following cost assumptions:

  a. First-in, first-out (FIFO)
  b. Last-in, first-out (LIFO)
  c. Average cost (weighted average)
  d. Specific identification

P 6-18.   The following data relate to inventory for the year ended December 31, 2007. A physical inventory on December 31, 2007, indicates that 600 units are on hand and that they came from the July 1 purchase.

Date	Description	Number of Units	Cost per Unit	Total Cost
January 1	Beginning inventory	1,000	$4.00	$ 4,000
February 20	Purchase	800	4.50	3,600
April 1	Purchase	900	4.75	4,275
July 1	Purchase	700	5.00	3,500
October 22	Purchase	500	4.90	2,450
December 10	Purchase	500	5.00	2,500
		4,400		$20,325

Required   Compute the cost of goods sold for the year ended December 31, 2007, and the ending inventory under the following cost assumptions:

a. First-in, first-out (FIFO)
b. Last-in, first-out (LIFO)
c. Average cost (weighted average)
d. Specific identification

P 6-19.   J.A. Appliance Company has supplied you with the following data regarding working capital and sales for the years 2007, 2006, and 2005.

	2007	2006	2005
Working capital	$270,000	$260,000	$240,000
Sales	$650,000	$600,000	$500,000
Industry average for the ratio sales to working capital	4.10 times	4.05 times	4.00 times

Required   a. Compute the sales to working capital ratio for each year.
b. Comment on the sales to working capital ratio for J.A. Appliance in relation to the industry average and what this may indicate.

P 6-20.   Depoole Company manufactures industrial products and employs a calendar year for financial reporting purposes. Items (a) through (e) present several of Depoole's transactions during 2007. The total of cash equivalents, marketable securities, and net receivables exceeded total current liabilities both before and after each transaction described. Depoole has positive profits in 2007 and a credit balance throughout 2007 in its retained earnings account.

Required   Answer the following multiple-choice questions:

a. Payment of a trade account payable of $64,500 would
   1. Increase the current ratio, but the acid-test ratio would not be affected.
   2. Increase the acid-test ratio, but the current ratio would not be affected.
   3. Increase both the current and acid-test ratios.
   4. Decrease both the current and acid-test ratios.
   5. Have no effect on the current and acid-test ratios.

b. The purchase of raw materials for $85,000 on open account would
   1. Increase the current ratio.
   2. Decrease the current ratio.
   3. Increase net working capital.
   4. Decrease net working capital.
   5. Increase both the current ratio and net working capital.

c. The collection of a current accounts receivable of $29,000 would
   1. Increase the current ratio.
   2. Decrease the current ratio.
   3. Increase the acid-test ratio.
   4. Decrease the acid-test ratio.
   5. Not affect the current or acid-test ratios.

d. Obsolete inventory of $125,000 was written off during 2007. This would
   1. Decrease the acid-test ratio.
   2. Increase the acid-test ratio.
   3. Increase net working capital.
   4. Decrease the current ratio.
   5. Decrease both the current and acid-test ratios.

e. The early liquidation of a long-term note with cash would
   1. Affect the current ratio to a greater degree than the acid-test ratio.
   2. Affect the acid-test ratio to a greater degree than the current ratio.
   3. Affect the current and acid-test ratios to the same degree.
   4. Affect the current ratio, but not the acid-test ratio.
   5. Affect the acid-test ratio, but not the current ratio.

Source: Adapted from past CMA Examinations. Used by Permission of The Institute of Certified Management Accountants.

(CMA Adapted)

P 6-21.   Information from Greg Company's balance sheet follows:

Current assets:	
Cash	$ 2,100,000
Marketable securities	7,200,000
Accounts receivable	50,500,000
Inventories	65,000,000
Prepaid expenses	1,000,000
Total current assets	$125,800,000
Current liabilities:	
Notes payable	$ 1,400,000
Accounts payable	18,000,000
Accrued expenses	11,000,000
Income taxes payable	600,000
Payments due within one year on long-term debt	3,000,000
Total current liabilities	$ 34,000,000

Required   Answer the following multiple-choice questions:

a. What is the acid-test ratio for Greg Company?

   1. 1.60
   2. 1.76
   3. 1.90
   4. 2.20

b. What is the effect of the collection of accounts receivable on the current ratio and net working capital, respectively?

	Current Ratio	**Net Working Capital**
1.	No effect	No effect
2.	Increase	Increase
3.	Increase	No effect
4.	No effect	Increase

P 6-22.   The following data apply to items (a) and (b). Mr. Sparks, the owner of School Supplies, Inc., wants to maintain control over accounts receivable. He understands that accounts receivable turnover will give a good indication of how well receivables are being managed. School Supplies, Inc., does 70% of its business during June, July, and August. The terms of sale are 2/10, net/60.

Net sales for the year ended December 31, 2007, and receivables balances follow:

Net sales	$1,500,000
Receivables, less allowance for doubtful accounts of $8,000 at January 1, 2007	72,000
Receivables, less allowance for doubtful accounts of $10,000 at December 31, 2007	60,000

Required   Answer the following multiple-choice questions:

a. The average accounts receivable turnover calculated from the previous data is

   1. 20.0 times.
   2. 25.0 times.
   3. 22.7 times.
   4. 18.75 times.
   5. 20.8 times.

b. The average accounts receivable turnover computed for School Supplies, Inc., in item (a) is

   1. Representative for the entire year.
   2. Overstated.
   3. Understated.

Source: Adapted from past CMA Examinations. Used by Permission of The Institute of Certified Management Accountants.

(CMA Adapted)

P 6-23.   Items (a) through (d) are based on the following information:

SHARKEY CORPORATION
Selected Financial Data

	As of December 31,	
	2007	2006
Cash	$ 8,000	$ 60,000
Marketable securities	32,000	8,000
Accounts receivable	40,000	110,000
Inventory	80,000	140,000
Net property, plant, and equipment	240,000	280,000
Accounts payable	60,000	100,000
Short-term notes payable	30,000	50,000
Cash sales	1,500,000	1,400,000
Credit sales	600,000	900,000
Cost of goods sold	1,260,000	1,403,000

Required   Answer the following multiple-choice questions:

a. Sharkey's acid-test ratio as of December 31, 2007, is
    1. 0.63.
    2. 0.70.
    3. 0.89.
    4. 0.99.

b. Sharkey's receivables turnover for 2007 is
    1. 8 times.
    2. 6 times.
    3. 12 times.
    4. 14 times.

c. Sharkey's inventory turnover for 2007 is
    1. 11.45 times.
    2. 10.50 times.
    3. 9.85 times.
    4. 8.45 times.

d. Sharkey's current ratio at December 31, 2007, is
    1. 1.40.
    2. 2.60.
    3. 1.90.
    4. 1.78.

e. If current assets exceed current liabilities, payments to creditors made on the last day of the year will
    1. Decrease current ratio.
    2. Increase current ratio.
    3. Decrease working capital.
    4. Increase working capital.

P 6-24.

Required   Answer the following multiple-choice questions:

a. A company's current ratio is 2.2 to 1 and quick (acid-test) ratio is 1.0 to 1 at the beginning of the year. At the end of the year, the company has a current ratio of 2.5 to 1 and a quick ratio of 0.8 to 1. Which of the following could help explain the divergence in the ratios from the beginning to the end of the year?
    1. An increase in inventory levels during the current year
    2. An increase in credit sales in relationship to cash sales
    3. An increase in the use of trade payables during the current year

4. An increase in the collection rate of accounts receivable
5. The sale of marketable securities at a price below cost

b. If, just prior to a period of rising prices, a company changed its inventory measurement method from FIFO to LIFO, the effect in the next period would be to
   1. Increase both the current ratio and inventory turnover.
   2. Decrease both the current ratio and inventory turnover.
   3. Increase the current ratio and decrease inventory turnover.
   4. Decrease the current ratio and increase inventory turnover.
   5. Leave the current ratio and inventory turnover unchanged.

c. Selected year-end data for Bayer Company are as follows:

Current liabilities	$600,000
Acid-test ratio	2.5
Current ratio	3.0
Cost of sales	$500,000

Bayer Company's inventory turnover based on these year-end data is
1. 1.20.
2. 2.40.
3. 1.67.
4. Some amount other than those given.
5. Not determinable from the data given.

d. If a firm has a high current ratio but a low acid-test ratio, one can conclude that
   1. The firm has a large outstanding accounts receivable balance.
   2. The firm has a large investment in inventory.
   3. The firm has a large amount of current liabilities.
   4. The cash ratio is extremely high.
   5. The two ratios must be recalculated because both conditions cannot occur simultaneously.

e. Investment instruments used to invest temporarily idle cash balances should have which of the following characteristics?
   1. High expected return, low marketability, and a short term to maturity
   2. High expected return, readily marketable, and no maturity date
   3. Low default risk, low marketability, and a short term to maturity
   4. Low default risk, readily marketable, and a long term to maturity
   5. Low default risk, readily marketable, and a short term to maturity

f. The primary objective in the management of accounts receivable is
   1. To achieve a combination of sales volume, bad-debt experience, and receivables turnover that maximizes the profits of the corporation.
   2. To realize no bad debts because of the opportunity cost involved.
   3. To provide the treasurer of the corporation with sufficient cash to pay the company's bills on time.
   4. To coordinate the activities of manufacturing, marketing, and financing so that the corporation can maximize its profits.
   5. To allow the most liberal credit acceptance policy because increased sales mean increased profits.

g. A firm requires short-term funds to cover payroll expenses. These funds can come from
   1. Trade credit.
   2. Collections of receivables.
   3. Bank loans.
   4. Delayed payments of accounts payable.
   5. All of the above.

Source: Adapted from past CMA Examinations. Used by Permission of The Institute of Certified Management Accountants.

(CMA Adapted)

P 6-25.   Consecutive five-year balance sheets and income statements of Anne Gibson Corporation follow:

Anne Gibson Corporation
Balance Sheet
December 31, 2003 through December 31, 2007

(Dollars in thousands)	2007	2006	2005	2004	2003
Assets:					
Current assets					
Cash	$ 47,200	$ 46,000	$ 45,000	$ 44,000	$ 43,000
Marketable securities	2,000	2,500	3,000	3,000	3,000
Accounts receivable, less allowance of $1,000, December 31, 2007; $900, December 31, 2006; $900, December 31, 2005; $800, December 31, 2004; $1,200, December 31, 2003	131,000	128,000	127,000	126,000	125,000
Inventories	122,000	124,000	126,000	127,000	125,000
Prepaid expenses	3,000	2,500	2,000	1,000	1,000
Total current assets	305,200	303,000	303,000	301,000	297,000
Property, plant and equipment, net	240,000	239,000	238,000	237,500	234,000
Other assets	10,000	8,000	7,000	6,500	7,000
Total assets	$555,200	$550,000	$548,000	$545,000	$538,000
Liabilities and stockholders' equity:					
Current liabilities					
Accounts payable	$ 72,000	$ 73,000	$ 75,000	$ 76,000	$ 78,500
Accrued compensation	26,000	25,000	25,500	26,000	26,000
Income taxes	11,500	12,000	13,000	12,500	11,000
Total current liabilities	109,500	110,000	113,500	114,500	115,500
Long-term debt	68,000	60,000	58,000	60,000	62,000
Deferred income taxes	25,000	24,000	23,000	22,000	21,000
Stockholders' equity	352,700	356,000	353,500	348,500	339,500
Total liabilities and stockholders' equity	$555,200	$550,000	$548,000	$545,000	$538,000

Anne Gibson Corporation
Statement of Earnings
For Years Ended December 31, 2003–2007

(In thousands, except per share)	2007	2006	2005	2004	2003
Net sales	$880,000	$910,000	$840,000	$825,000	$820,000
Cost of goods sold	740,000	760,000	704,000	695,000	692,000
Gross profit	140,000	150,000	136,000	130,000	128,000
Selling and administrative expense	53,000	52,000	50,000	49,800	49,000
Interest expense	6,700	5,900	5,800	5,900	6,000
Earnings from continuing operations before income taxes	80,300	92,100	80,200	74,300	73,000
Income taxes	26,000	27,500	28,000	23,000	22,500
Net earnings	$ 54,300	$ 64,600	$ 52,200	$ 51,300	$ 50,500
Earnings per share	$1.40	$1.65	$1.38	$1.36	$1.33

Required   a. Using year-end balance sheet figures, compute the following for the maximum number of years, based on the available data:

1. Days' sales in receivables
2. Accounts receivable turnover
3. Accounts receivable turnover in days
4. Days' sales in inventory
5. Inventory turnover

    6. Inventory turnover in days

    7. Operating cycle

    8. Working capital

    9. Current ratio

  10. Acid-test ratio

  11. Cash ratio

  12. Sales to working capital

b. Using average balance sheet figures, as suggested in the chapter, compute the following for the maximum number of years, based on the available data:

    1. Days' sales in receivables

    2. Accounts receivable turnover

    3. Accounts receivable turnover in days

    4. Days' sales in inventory

    5. Inventory turnover

    6. Inventory turnover in days

    7. Operating cycle

    8. Working capital

    9. Current ratio

  10. Acid-test ratio

  11. Cash ratio

  12. Sales to working capital

c. Comment on trends indicated in short-term liquidity.

Source: Materials identified as CFA Examination I, June 4, 1988, June 6, 1987, and June 6, 1988 are reproduced with permission from the Association for Investment Management and Research and the Institute of Chartered Financial Analysts.

Case 6-1

STEEL MAN

AK STEEL HOLDING CORPORATION*
CONSOLIDATED BALANCE SHEETS

December 31, 2006 and 2005
(dollars in millions, except per share amounts)

	2006	2005
ASSETS		
Current Assets		
Cash and cash equivalents	$ 519.4	$ 519.6
Accounts receivable, net	696.8	570.0
Inventories, net	857.6	808.4
Deferred tax asset	437.4	323.2
Other current assets	36.3	25.2
Total Current Assets	2,547.5	2,246.4
Property, Plant and Equipment	5,021.5	4,985.6
Less accumulated depreciation	(2,888.1)	(2,728.1)
Property, plant and equipment, net	2,133.4	2,257.5
Other Assets:		
Investment in AFSG	55.6	55.6
Other investments	70.4	62.4
Goodwill	37.1	37.1
Other intangible assets	0.3	40.2
Deferred tax asset	647.1	752.5
Other	26.2	36.2
TOTAL ASSETS	$ 5,517.6	$ 5,487.9

*"AK Holding is a fully-integrated producer of flat-rolled carbon, stainless and electrical steels and tubular products through its wholly-owned subsidiary, AK Steel Corporation." 10-K

(continued)

STEEL MAN (Continued)

	2006	2005
LIABILITIES AND STOCKHOLDERS' EQUITY		
Current Liabilities:		
Accounts payable	$ 567.1	$ 450.0
Accrued liabilities	207.4	216.4
Current portion of pension and other postretirement		
benefit obligations	157.0	237.0
Total Current Liabilities	931.5	903.4
Non-current Liabilities:		
Long-term debt	1,115.2	1,114.9
Pension and other postretirement benefit obligations	2,927.6	3,115.6
Other liabilities	126.3	133.5
Total Non-current Liabilities	4,169.1	4,364.0
TOTAL LIABILITIES	5,100.6	5,267.4
Stockholders' Equity:		
Preferred stock, authorized 25,000,000 shares	—	—
Common stock, authorized 200,000,000 shares of $.01		
par value each; issued 2006, 119,025,234 shares;		
2005, 118,415,233 shares; outstanding 2006, 110,324,847		
shares; 2005, 109,806,200 shares	1.2	1.2
Additional paid-in capital	1,841.4	1,832.1
Treasury stock, common shares at cost, 2006,		
8,700,387; 2005, 8,609,033 shares	(124.4)	(123.6)
Accumulated deficit	(1,296.1)	(1,308.1)
Accumulated other comprehensive loss	(5.1)	(181.1)
TOTAL STOCKHOLDERS' EQUITY	417.0	220.5
TOTAL LIABILITIES AND STOCKHOLDERS' EQUITY	$ 5,517.6	$ 5,487.9

NOTES TO CONSOLIDATED FINANCIAL STATEMENTS (in Part)

1. **Summary of Significant Accounting Policies (in Part)**

   Inventories—Inventories are valued at the lower of cost or market. The cost of the majority of inventories is measured on the last in, first out ("LIFO") method. Other inventories are measured principally at average cost and consist mostly of foreign inventories and certain raw materials.

	2006	2005
Inventories on LIFO:		
Finished and semi-finished	$925.2	$776.3
Raw materials and supplies	411.9	344.4
Adjustment to state inventories at LIFO value	(507.9)	(351.7)
Total	829.2	769.0
Other inventories	28.4	39.4
Total inventories	$857.6	$808.4

Required
a. What is the working capital at the end of 2006?

b. What is the balance in the LIFO reserve account at the end of 2006? Describe this account.

c. If the LIFO reserve account was added to the inventory at LIFO, what would be the resulting inventory number at the end of 2006? Which inventory amount do you consider to be more realistic?

d. Does the use of LIFO or FIFO produce higher, lower, or the same income during (1) price increases; (2) price decreases; and (3) constant prices? (Assume no decrease or increase in inventory quantity.)

e. Does the use of LIFO or FIFO produce higher, lower, or the same amount of cash flow during (1) price increases; (2) price decreases; and (3) constant costs? Answer the question for both pretax cash flows and after-tax cash flows. (Assume no decrease or increase in inventory quantity.)

f. Assume that the company purchased inventory on the last day of the year, beginning inventory equaled ending inventory, and inventory records for the

(continued)

Case		STEEL MAN (Continued)
6-1		

item purchases were maintained periodically on the LIFO basis. Would that purchase be included on the income statement or the balance sheet at year-end?

g. Explain how liquidation of LIFO layers generates income.

Case		RISING PRICES, A TIME TO SWITCH OFF LIFO?
6-2		

The following information was taken directly from the annual report of a firm that wishes to remain anonymous. (The dates have been changed.)

Financial Summary

Effects of LIFO Accounting

For a number of years, the corporation has used the last-in, first-out (LIFO) method of accounting for its steel inventories. In periods of extended inflation, coupled with uncertain supplies of raw materials from foreign sources, and rapid increases and fluctuations in prices of raw materials such as nickel and chrome nickel scrap, earnings can be affected unrealistically for any given year.

Because of these factors, the corporation will apply to the Internal Revenue Service for permission to discontinue using the LIFO method of accounting for valuing those inventories for which this method has been used. If such application is granted, the LIFO reserve at December 31, 2007, of $12,300,000 would be eliminated, which would require a provision for income taxes of approximately $6,150,000. The corporation will also seek permission to pay the increased taxes over a 10-year period. If the corporation had not used the LIFO method of accounting during 2006, net earnings for the year would have been increased by approximately $1,500,000.

The 2007 annual report also disclosed the following:

		2007	2006
1.	Sales and revenues	$536,467,782	$487,886,449
2.	Earnings per common share	$3.44	$3.58

Required

a. The corporation indicates that earnings can be affected unrealistically by rapid increases and fluctuations in prices when using LIFO. Comment.

b. How much taxes will need to be paid on past earnings from the switch from LIFO? How will the switch from LIFO influence taxes in the future?

c. How will a switch from LIFO affect 2007 profits?

d. How will a switch from LIFO affect future profits?

e. How will a switch from LIFO affect 2007 cash flow?

f. How will a switch from LIFO affect future cash flow?

g. Speculate on the real reason that the corporation wishes to switch from LIFO.

Case		IMAGING INNOVATOR
6-3		

Eastman Kodak Company*
CONSOLIDATED STATEMENT OF OPERATIONS (in Part)

	For the Year Ended December 31,		
(In millions, except per share data)	**2006**	**2005**	**2004**
Net sales	$13,274	$14,268	$13,517
Cost of goods sold	9,906	10,650	9,601
Gross profit	3,368	3,618	3,916

*"Eastman Kodak Company... is the world's foremost imaging innovator, providing leading products and services to the photographic, graphic communications and healthcare markets." 10-K

(continued)

IMAGING INNOVATOR (Continued)

	For the Year Ended December 31,		
	2006	2005	2004
Selling, general and administrative expenses	2,389	2,668	2,491
Research and development costs	710	892	836
Restructuring costs and other	471	690	695
Loss from continuing operations before interest, other income (charges), net and income taxes	(202)	(632)	(106)
Interest expense	262	211	168
Other income (charges), net	118	44	161
Loss from continuing operations before income taxes	(346)	(799)	(113)
Provision (benefit) for income taxes	254	555	(182)
(Loss) earnings from continuing operations	$(600)	$(1,354)	$ 69
(Loss) earnings from discontinued operations, net of income taxes	$ (1)	$ 150	$ 475
Loss from cumulative effect of accounting change, net of income taxes	$ —	$ (57)	$ —
NET (LOSS) EARNINGS	$(601)	$(1,261)	$ 544

Eastman Kodak Company
CONSOLIDATED STATEMENT OF FINANCIAL POSITION

	At December 31,	
(In millions, except share and per share data)	2006	2005
ASSETS		
CURRENT ASSETS		
Cash and cash equivalents	$ 1,469	$ 1,665
Receivables, net	2,669	2,760
Inventories, net	1,202	1,455
Deferred income taxes	108	100
Other current assets	109	116
Total current assets	5,557	6,096
Property, plant and equipment, net	2,842	3,778
Goodwill	2,196	2,141
Other long-term assets	3,725	3,221
TOTAL ASSETS	$14,320	$15,236
LIABILITIES AND SHAREHOLDERS' EQUITY		
CURRENT LIABILITIES		
Accounts payable and other current liabilities	$ 4,143	$ 4,187
Short-term borrowings	64	819
Accrued income and other taxes	764	483
Total current liabilities	4,971	5,489
Long-term debt, net of current portion	2,714	2,764
Pension and other postretirement liabilities	3,964	3,476
Other long-term liabilities	1,283	1,225
Total liabilities	12,932	12,954
Commitments and Contingencies (Note 11)		
SHAREHOLDERS' EQUITY		
Common stock, $2.50 par value, 950,000,000 shares authorized; 391,292,760 shares issued as of December 31, 2006 and 2005; 287,333,123 and 287,223,323 shares outstanding as of December 31, 2006 and 2005	978	978
Additional paid in capital	881	867
Retained earnings	5,967	6,717
Accumulated other comprehensive loss	(635)	(467)
	7,191	8,095

(continued)

IMAGING INNOVATOR (Continued)

	At December 31,	
	2006	2005
Treasury stock, at cost 103,959,637 shares as of December 31, 2006 and 104,069,437 shares as of December 31, 2005	5,803	5,813
Total shareholders' equity	1,388	2,282
TOTAL LIABILITIES AND SHAREHOLDERS' EQUITY	$14,320	$15,236

Notes to Financial Statements (in Part)

NOTE 2: RECEIVABLES, NET

(In millions)	2006	2005
Trade receivables	$2,304	$2,447
Miscellaneous receivables	365	313
Total (net of allowances of $157 and $162 as of December 31, 2006 and 2005, respectively)	$2,669	$2,760

Of the total trade receivable amounts of $2,304 million and $2,447 million as of December 31, 2006 and 2005, respectively, approximately $344 million and $374 million, respectively, are expected to be settled through customer deductions in lieu of cash payments. Such deductions represent rebates owed to the customer and are included in accounts payable and other current liabilities in the accompanying Consolidated Statement of Financial Position at each respective balance sheet date.

NOTE 8: ACCOUNTS PAYABLE AND OTHER CURRENT LIABILITIES

(In millions)	2006	2005
Accounts payable	$1,003	$ 996
Accrued employment-related liabilities	876	950
Accrued advertising and promotional expenses	596	683
Deferred revenue	496	350
Accrued restructuring liabilities	263	309
Other	909	899
Total	$4,143	$4,187

The other component above consists of other miscellaneous current liabilities that, individually, are less than 5% of the total current liabilities component within the Consolidated Statement of Financial Position, and therefore, have been aggregated in accordance with Regulation S-X.

NOTE 9: SHORT-TERM BORROWINGS AND LONG-TERM DEBT

SHORT-TERM BORROWINGS

The Company's short-term borrowings at December 31, 2006 and 2005 were as follows:

(In millions)	2006	2005
Current portion of long-term debt	$17	$706
Short-term bank borrowings	47	113
Total	$64	$819

The weighted-average interest rates for short-term bank borrowings outstanding at December 31, 2006 and 2005 were 9.84% and 5.82%, respectively.

As of December 31, 2006, the Company and its subsidiaries, on a consolidated basis, maintained $1,110 million in committed bank lines of credit and $616 million in uncommitted bank lines of credit to ensure continued access to short-term borrowing capacity.

Required   a. Based on these data, calculate the following for 2006 and 2005:
1. Days' sales in receivables (use trade receivables)
2. Accounts receivable turnover (use gross trade receivables at year-end)

(continued)

Case	
6-3	

IMAGING INNOVATOR (Continued)

      3. Days' sales in inventory
      4. Inventory turnover (use year-end inventory)
      5. Working capital
      6. Current ratio
      7. Acid-test ratio
  b. Comment on each ratio individually.
  c. Why are portions of long-term debt included in short-term borrowings?
  d. 1. How do committed bank lines of credit influence liquidity?
      2. How do uncommitted bank lines of credit influence liquidity?
  e. Prepare a vertical common-size analysis for the balance sheets using 2006 and 2005 (use total assets as the base).
  f. Comment on the vertical common-size analysis.
  g. Comment on the apparent total liquidity.

Case	
6-4	

DIVERSIFIED TECHNOLOGY

Consolidated Statement of Income (in Part)

3M Company and Subsidiaries*
Years ended December 31

(Millions, except per share amounts)	2006	2005	2004
Net sales	$22,923	$21,167	$20,011
Operating expenses			
Cost of sales	11,713	10,408	10,002
Selling, general and administrative expenses	5,066	4,631	4,437
Research, development and related expenses	1,522	1,274	1,246
Gain on sale of pharmaceuticals business	(1,074)	—	—
Total	17,227	16,313	15,685
Operating income	5,696	4,854	4,326
Interest expense and income			
Interest expense	122	82	69
Interest income	(51)	(56)	(46)
Total	71	26	23
Income before income taxes, minority interest and cumulative effect of accounting change	5,625	4,828	4,303
Provision for income taxes	1,723	1,627	1,400
Minority interest	51	55	62
Income before cumulative effect of accounting change	3,851	3,146	2,841
Cumulative effect of accounting change	—	(35)	—
Net income	$ 3,851	$ 3,111	$ 2,841

Consolidated Balance Sheet

3M Company and Subsidiaries
At December 31

(Dollars in millions, except per share amount)	2006	2005
Assets		
Current assets		
Cash and cash equivalents	$ 1,447	$ 1,072
Marketable securities—current	471	—
Accounts receivable—net of allowances of $71 and $73	3,102	2,838

*"3M is a diversified technology company with a global presence in the following businesses; industrial and transportation; health care; display and graphics; consumer and office; safety; security and protection services; and electro and communications." 10-K

(continued)

Case 6-4	DIVERSIFIED TECHNOLOGY (Continued)		

	2006	2005
Inventories		
Finished goods	1,235	1,050
Work in process	795	706
Raw materials and supplies	571	406
Total inventories	2,601	2,162
Other current assets	1,325	1,043
Total current assets	8,946	7,115
Marketable securities—non-current	166	—
Investments	314	272
Property, plant and equipment	17,017	16,127
Less: Accumulated depreciation	(11,110)	(10,534)
Property, plant and equipment, net	5,907	5,593
Goodwill	4,082	3,530
Intangible assets, net	708	486
Prepaid pension and postretirement benefits	395	2,905
Other assets	776	640
Total assets	$21,294	$20,541
Liabilities and Stockholders' Equity		
Current liabilities		
Short-term borrowings and current portion of long-term debt	$ 2,506	$ 1,072
Accounts payable	1,402	1,256
Accrued payroll	520	469
Accrued income taxes	1,134	989
Other current liabilities	1,761	1,452
Total current liabilities	7,323	5,238
Long-term debt	1,047	1,309
Other liabilities	2,965	3,599
Total liabilities	$11,335	$10,146
Commitments and contingencies (Note 13)		
Stockholders' equity		
Common stock, par value $.01 per share	9	9
Shares outstanding—2006: 734,362,802		
Shares outstanding—2005: 754,538,387		
Additional paid-in capital	2,484	2,225
Retained earnings	17,933	15,715
Treasury stock	(8,456)	(6,965)
Unearned compensation	(138)	(178)
Accumulated other comprehensive income (loss)	(1,873)	(411)
Stockholders' equity—net	9,959	10,395
Total liabilities and stockholders' equity	$21,294	$20,541

Notes to Consolidated Financial Statements (in Part)

Note 1. Significant Accounting Policies (in Part)

Cash and Cash Equivalents: Cash and cash equivalents consist of cash and temporary investments with maturities of three months or less when purchased.

Accounts Receivable and Allowances: Trade accounts receivable are recorded at the invoices amount and do not bear interest. The Company maintains allowances for bad debts, cash discounts, product returns and various other items. The allowance for doubtful accounts and product returns is based on the best estimate of the amount of probable credit losses in existing accounts receivable and anticipated sales returns. The Company determines the allowances based on historical write-off experience by industry and regional economic data and historic sales returns. The Company reviews the allowance for doubtful accounts monthly. The Company does not have any off-balance-sheet credit exposure related to its customers.

Inventories: Inventories are stated at the lower of cost or market, with cost generally determined on a first-in, first-out basis.

(continued)

Case 6-4

DIVERSIFIED TECHNOLOGY (Continued)

Required   a. Based on these data, calculate the following for 2006 and 2005:
1. Days' sales in receivables
2. Accounts receivable turnover (gross receivables at year-end)
3. Days' sales in inventory
4. Inventory turnover (use inventory at year-end)
5. Working capital
6. Current ratio
7. Acid-test ratio

b. Comment on each ratio individually.

c. Prepare a vertical common-size analysis for the balance sheets using 2006 and 2005 (use total assets as the base).

d. Comment on the vertical common-size analysis.

e. Comment on the apparent total liquidity.

Case 6-5

BOOMING RETAIL

The Grand retail firm reported the following financial data for the past several years:

	Year				
(Amounts in 000s)	5	4	3	2	1
Sales	$1,254,131	$1,210,918	$1,096,152	$979,458	$920,797
Net accounts receivable	419,731	368,267	312,776	72,450	230,427

The Grand retail firm had a decentralized credit operation allowing each store to administer its credit operation. Many stores provided installment plans allowing the customer up to 36 months to pay. Gross profits on installment sales were reflected in the financial statements in the period when the sales were made.

Required   a. Using Year 1 as the base, prepare horizontal common-size analysis for sales and net accounts receivable.

b. Compute the accounts receivable turnover for Years 2–5. (Use net accounts receivable.)

c. Would financial control of accounts receivable be more important with installment sales than with sales on 30-day credit? Comment.

d. Comment on what is apparently happening at The Grand retail firm.

Note: Data from an actual retail company.

Case 6-6

GREETING

AMERICAN GREETINGS CORPORATION*
CONSOLIDATED STATEMENT OF INCOME (in Part)
Years ended February 28, 2007, 2006 and 2005
(Thousands of dollars except share and per share amounts)

	2007	2006	2005
Net Sales	$1,744,603	$1,875,104	$1,871,246
Costs and expenses:			
Material, labor and other production costs	826,791	846,958	890,906
Selling, distribution and marketing	627,906	631,943	642,718
Administrative and general	251,089	242,727	249,227
Goodwill impairment	—	43,153	—

*"Founded in 1906, American Greetings operates predominantly in a single industry; the design, manufacture and sale of everyday and seasonal greeting cards and other social expression products." 10-K

(continued)

Case 6-6

GREETING (Continued)

	2007	2006	2005
Interest expense	34,986	35,124	79,397
Other income—net	(65,530)	(64,676)	(96,038)
	1,675,242	1,735,229	1,766,210
Income from continuing operations before income tax expense	69,361	139,875	105,036
Income tax expense	26,096	48,879	37,329
Income from continuing operations	43,265	90,996	67,707
(Loss) income from discontinued operations, net of tax	(887)	(6,620)	27,572
Net income	$ 42,378	$ 84,376	$ 95,279

CONSOLIDATED STATEMENT OF FINANCIAL POSITION
February 28, 2007 and 2006
(Thousands of dollars except share and per share amounts)

	2006	2005
ASSETS		
CURRENT ASSETS		
Cash and cash equivalents	$ 144,713	$ 213,613
Short-term investments	—	208,740
Trade accounts receivable, net	103,992	139,384
Inventories	182,618	213,109
Deferred and refundable income taxes	135,379	153,282
Assets of business held for sale	5,199	24,903
Prepaid expenses and other	227,380	212,814
Total current assets	799,281	1,165,845
GOODWILL	224,105	200,763
OTHER ASSETS	416,887	548,514
DEFERRED INCOME TAXES	52,869	—
PROPERTY, PLANT AND EQUIPMENT—NET	285,072	303,840
	$1,778,214	$2,218,962
LIABILITIES AND SHAREHOLDERS' EQUITY		
CURRENT LIABILITIES		
Debt due within one year	$ —	$ 174,792
Accounts payable	118,204	123,757
Accrued liabilities	80,389	73,532
Accrued compensation and benefits	61,192	68,864
Income taxes	26,385	17,240
Liabilities of businesses held for sale	1,932	3,627
Other current liabilities	84,898	97,270
Total current liabilities	373,000	559,082
LONG-TERM DEBT	223,915	300,516
OTHER LIABILITIES	162,410	116,554
DEFERRED INCOME TAXES	6,315	22,785
SHAREHOLDERS' EQUITY		
Common shares—par value $1 per share:		
Class A—79,301,976 shares issued less 28,462,579 treasury shares in 2007 and 78,942,962 shares issued less 22,812,601 treasury shares in 2006	50,839	56,130
Class B—6,066,092 shares issued less 1,782,695 treasury shares in 2007 and 6,066,092 shares issued less 1,848,344 treasury shares in 2006	4,283	4,218
Capital in excess of par value	414,859	398,505
Treasury stock	(710,414	(676,436)
Accumulated other comprehensive (loss) income	(1,013	9,823
Retained earnings	1,254,020	1,427,785
Total shareholders' equity	1,012,574	1,220,025
	$1,778,214	$2,218,962

(continued)

Notes to Consolidated Financial Statements (in Part)

Note 1. Significant Accounting Policies (in Part)

Cash Equivalents: The Corporation considers all highly liquid instruments purchased with a maturity of less than three months to be cash equivalents.

Short-Term Investments: The Corporation invests in auction rate securities, which are highly liquid, variable-rate debt securities associated with bond offerings. While the underlying security has a long-term nominal maturity, the interest rate is reset through Dutch auctions that are typically held every 7, 28, or 35 days, creating short-term liquidity for the Corporation. The securities trade at par and are callable at par on any interest payment date at the option of the issuer. Interest is paid at the end of each auction period. The investments are classified as available-for-sale and are recorded at cost, which approximates market value.

Allowance for Doubtful Accounts: The Corporation evaluates the collectibility of its accounts receivable based on a combination of factors. In circumstances where the Corporation is aware of a customer's inability to meet its financial obligations (evidenced by such events as bankruptcy or insolvency proceedings), a specific allowance for bad debts against amounts due is recorded to reduce the receivable to the amount the Corporation reasonably expects will be collected. In addition, the Corporation recognized allowances for bad debts based on estimates developed by using standard quantitative measures incorporating historical write-offs and current economic conditions. See Note 6 for further information.

Customer Allowances and Discounts: The Corporation offers certain of its customers allowances and discounts including cooperative advertising, rebates, marketing allowances and various other allowances and discounts. These amounts are recorded as a reduction of gross accounts receivable and are recognized as reductions of net sales when earned. These amounts are earned by the customer as product is purchased from the Corporation and recorded based on the terms of individual customer contracts. See Note 6 for further information.

Financial Instruments: The carrying values of the Corporation's financial instruments approximate their fair market values, other than the fair value of the Corporation's publicly-traded debt. See Note 11 for further discussion. The Corporation has no derivative financial instruments as of February 28, 2007.

Concentration of Credit Risks: The Corporation sells primarily to customers in the retail trade, including those in the mass merchandise, drug store, supermarket and other channels of distribution. These customers are located throughout the United States, Canada, the United Kingdom, Australia, New Zealand and Mexico. Net sales from continuing operations to the Corporation's five largest customers accounted for approximately 37%, 35% and 33% of net sales in 2007, 2006 and 2005, respectively. Net sales to Wal-Mart Stores, Inc. and it subsidiaries accounted for approximately 17%, 16% and 15% of net sales from continuing operations in 2007, 2006 and 2005, respectively.

The Corporation conducts business based on periodic evaluations of its customers' financial condition and generally does not require collateral to secure their obligation to the Corporation. While the competitiveness of the retail industry presents an inherent uncertainty, the Corporation does not believe a significant risk of loss from a concentration of credit exists.

Inventories: Finished products, work in process and raw materials inventories are carried at the lower of cost or market. The last-in, first-out (LIFO) cost method is used for certain domestic inventories, which approximate 65% and 55% of the total pre-LIFO consolidated inventories in 2007 and 2006, respectively. Foreign inventories and the remaining domestic inventories principally use the first-in, first-out (FIFO) method except for display material and factory supplies which are carried at average cost. See Note 7 for further information.

In November 2004, the Financial Accounting Standards Board (the "FASB") issued Statement of Financial Accounting Standards ("SFAS") No. 151 ("SFAS 151"), "Inventory Costs – an

(continued)

GREETING (Continued)

amendment of ARB No. 43, Chapter 4." SFAS 151 seeks to clarify the accounting for abnormal amounts of idle facility expense, freight, handling costs and wasted material (spoilage) in the determination of inventory carrying costs. The statement required such costs to be treated as a current period expense. SFAS 151 also establishes the concept of "normal capacity" and requires the allocation of fixed production overhead to inventory based on the normal capacity of the production facilities. Any unallocated overhead would be treated as a current period expense in the period incurred. This statement was effective for fiscal years beginning after July 15, 2005. The adoption of SFAS 151, effective March 1, 2006, did not significantly impact the Corporation's consolidated financial statements.

NOTE 6—TRADE ACCOUNTS RECEIVABLE, NET

Trade accounts receivable are reported net of certain allowances and discounts. The most significant of these are as follows:

	February 28, 2007	February 28, 2006
Allowances for seasonal sales returns	$ 62,567	$ 71,590
Allowance for doubtful accounts	6,350	8,075
Allowance for cooperative advertising and marketing funds	24,048	21,658
Allowance for rebates	40,053	51,597
	$133,018	$153,280

NOTE 7—INVENTORIES

	February 28, 2007	February 28, 2006
Raw materials	$ 17,590	$ 19,806
Work in process	11,315	15,399
Finished products	207,676	235,657
	236,581	270,862
Less LIFO reserve	79,145	79,403
	157,436	191,459
Display material and factory supplies	25,182	21,650
	$182,618	$213,109

There were no material LIFO liquidations in 2007, 2006 or 2005.

Required
a. Based on these data, calculate the following for 2007 and 2006:
   1. Days' sales in receivables
   2. Accounts receivable turnover (gross receivables at year-end)
   3. Days' sales in inventory
   4. Inventory turnover (use inventory at year-end)
   5. Working capital
   6. Current ratio
   7. Acid-test ratio
b. Comment on each ratio individually.
c. Describe the short-term investments.
d. 1. Describe the individual allowance consideration.
   2. Are some of these allowance considerations normal for most companies?
e. What would be the inventory balance at February 28, 2007, if the LIFO reserve were removed?
f. The inventory balance was $182,618,000 at February 28, 2007, and $213,109,000 at February 28, 2006. The LIFO reserve was $79,145,000 at February 28, 2007, and $79,403,000 at February 28, 2006. There were no material LIFO liquidations in 2007, 2006, or 2005. Does it appear that there could be a material LIFO liquidation subsequent to February 28, 2007? Comment.
g. Comment on the apparent total liquidity.

EAT AT MY RESTAURANT—LIQUIDITY REVIEW

With this case, we review the liquidity of several restaurant companies. The restaurant companies reviewed and the year-end dates are as follows:

1. **Yum Brands, Inc. (December 30, 2006; December 30, 2005)**
   "Yum consists of six operating segments; KFC, Pizza Hut, Taco Bell, LJS/A&W, Yum Restaurants International . . . and YUM Restaurants China." 10-K

2. **Panera Bread (December 26, 2006; December 27, 2005)**
   "As of December 26, 2006 we operated directly and through area development agreements with 41 franchise groups, bakery cafes under Panera Bread® and Saint Louis Bread® names." 10-K

3. **Starbucks (October 1, 2006; October 2, 2005)**
   "Starbucks purchases and roasts high-quality whole bean coffees and sells them, along with fresh, rich-brewed coffees, Italian-style espresso beverages, cold blended beverages, a variety of complementary food items, coffee-related accessories and equipment, a selection of premium teas and a line of compact discs, primarily through Company-operated retail stores." 10-K

	Yum Brands, Inc.		Panera Bread		Starbucks	
Data Reviewed	2006	2005	2006	2005	2006	2005
Current ratio	0.52	0.53	1.16	1.18	0.79	0.99
Acid test	0.32	0.27	0.83	0.91	0.35	0.41

Required
a. For each company, indicate the trend in liquidity.
b. Give your opinion as to the relative liquidity of each of these companies. How would you rank these companies?

Thomson One *Business School Edition*

Please complete the Web case that covers material discussed in this chapter at academic.cengage .com/accounting/Gibson. You'll be using Thomson One Business School Edition, a powerful tool, that combines a full range of fundamental financial information, earnings estimates, market data, and source documents for 500 publicly traded companies.

Endnotes

1. *Accounting Research Bulletin No. 43,* "Restatement and Revision of Accounting Research Bulletins," 1953, Chapter 3, Section A, par. 4.
2. *Statement of Financial Accounting Standards No. 115,* "Accounting for Certain Investments in Debt and Equity Securities" (Norwalk, Conn.: Financial Accounting Standards Board, 1993).
3. *Opinions of the Accounting Principles Board No. 21,* "Interest on Receivables and Payables" (New York: American Institute of Certified Public Accountants, 1971), par. 11.
4. *Statement of Financial Accounting Standards No. 5,* "Accounting for Contingencies" (Stamford, Conn.: Financial Accounting Standards Board, 1975), par. 8.
5. Committee on Accounting Procedure, American Institute of Certified Public Accountants, "Accounting Research and Terminology Bulletins" (New York: American Institute of Certified Public Accountants, 1961), p. 21.

Chapter 7

Long-Term Debt-Paying Ability

This chapter covers two approaches to viewing a firm's long-term debt-paying ability. One approach views the firm's ability to carry the debt as indicated by the income statement, and the other considers the firm's ability to carry debt as indicated by the balance sheet.

In the long run, a relationship exists between the reported income resulting from the use of accrual accounting and the ability of the firm to meet its long-term obligations. Although the reported income does not agree with the cash available in the short run, the revenue and expense items eventually do result in cash movements. Because of the close relationship between the reported income and the ability of the firm to meet its long-run obligations, the entity's profitability is an important factor when determining long-term debt-paying ability.

In addition to the profitability of the firm, the amount of debt in relation to the size of the firm should be analyzed. This analysis indicates the amount of funds provided by outsiders in relation to those provided by owners of the firm. If a high proportion of the resources has been provided by outsiders, the risks of the business have been substantially shifted to the outsiders. A large proportion of debt in the capital structure increases the risk of not meeting the principal or interest obligation because the company may not generate adequate funds to meet these obligations.

Income Statement Consideration when Determining Long-Term Debt-Paying Ability

The firm's ability to carry debt, as indicated by the income statement, can be viewed by considering the times interest earned and the fixed charge coverage. These ratios are now reviewed.

TIMES INTEREST EARNED

The times interest earned ratio indicates a firm's long-term debt-paying ability from the income statement view. If the times interest earned is adequate, little danger exists that the firm will not be able to meet its interest obligation. If the firm has good coverage of the interest obligation, it should also be able to refinance the principal when it comes due. In effect, the funds will probably never be required to pay off the principal if the company has a good record of covering the interest expense. A relatively high, stable coverage of interest over the years indicates a good record. A low, fluctuating coverage from year to year indicates a poor record.

Companies that maintain a good record can finance a relatively high proportion of debt in relation to stockholders' equity and, at the same time, obtain funds at favorable rates. Utility companies have traditionally been examples of companies that have a high debt structure, in relation to stockholders' equity. They accomplished this because of their relatively high, stable coverage of interest over the years. This stability evolved in an industry with a regulated profit and a relatively stable demand. During the 1970s, 1980s, and 1990s, utilities experienced a severe strain on their profits, as rate increases did not keep pace with inflation. In addition, the demand was not as predictable as in prior years. The strain on profits and the uncertainty of demand influenced investors to demand higher interest rates from utilities than had been previously required in relation to other companies.

A company issues debt obligations to obtain funds at an interest rate less than the earnings from these funds. This is called **trading on the equity or leverage.** With a high interest rate, the added risk exists that the company will not be able to earn more on the funds than the interest cost on them.

Compute times interest earned as follows:

$$\text{Times Interest Earned} = \frac{\text{Recurring Earnings, Excluding Interest Expense, Tax Expense, Equity Earnings, and Minority Earnings}}{\text{Interest Expense, Including Capitalized Interest}}$$

The income statement contains several figures that might be used in this analysis. In general, the primary analysis of the firm's ability to carry the debt as indicated by the income statement should include only income expected to occur in subsequent periods. Thus, the following nonrecurring items should be excluded:

1. Discontinued operations
2. Extraordinary items

In addition to these nonrecurring items, additional items that should be excluded for the times interest earned computation include:

1. **Interest expense.** This is added back to net income because the interest coverage would be understated by one if interest expense were deducted before computing times interest earned.
2. **Income tax expense.** Income taxes are computed after deducting interest expense, so they do not affect the safety of the interest payments.
3. **Equity earnings (losses) of nonconsolidated subsidiaries.** These are excluded because they are not available to cover interest payments, except to the extent that they are accompanied by cash dividends.
4. **Minority income (loss).** This adjustment at the bottom of the income statement should be excluded; use income before minority interest. Minority income (loss) results from consolidating a firm in which a company has control but less than 100% ownership. All of the interest expense of the firm consolidated is included in the consolidated income statement. Therefore, all of the income of the firm consolidated should be considered in the coverage.

Capitalization of interest results in interest being added to a fixed asset instead of expensed. The interest capitalized should be included with the total interest expense in the denominator of the times interest earned ratio because it is part of the interest payment. The capitalized interest must be added to the interest expense disclosed on the income statement or in notes.

An example of capitalized interest would be interest during the current year on a bond issued to build a factory. As long as the factory is under construction, this interest would be added to the asset account, Construction in Process, on the balance sheet. This interest does not appear on the income statement, but it is as much of a commitment as the interest expense deducted on the income statement.

When the factory is completed, the annual interest on the bond issued to build the factory will be expensed. When expensed, interest appears on the income statement.

Capitalized interest is usually disclosed in a note. Some firms describe the capitalized interest on the face of the income statement.

Exhibit 7-1 shows the computation for times interest earned for the years 2007 and 2006. These are very high numbers and the coverage increased in 2007.

To evaluate the adequacy of coverage, the times interest earned ratio should be computed for a period of three to five years and compared to competitors and the industry average. Computing interest earned for three to five years provides insight on the stability of the interest coverage. Because the firm needs to cover interest in the bad years as well as the good years, the lowest times interest earned in the period is used as the primary indication of the interest coverage. A cyclical firm may have a very high times interest earned ratio in highly profitable years, but interest may not be covered in low profit years.

Exhibit 7-1	NIKE, INC.		
	Times Interest Earned		
		Years Ended May 31, 2007 and 2006	
(In millions)		**2007**	**2006**
Income before income taxes		$ 2,199.90	$ 2,141.60
Plus: Interest expense		49.70*	50.50*
Adjusted income [A]		$ 2,249.60	$ 2,192.10
Interest expense		$ 49.70*	$ 50.50*
Capitalized interest		**	**
Total interest expense [B]		$ 49.70	$ 50.50
Times interest earned [A ÷ B]		45.26 times per year	43.41 times per year

*Interest expense includes both expensed and capitalized.

**Per Note 3—Property, Plant and Equipment
"Capitalized interest was not material for the years ended May 31, 2007, 2006 and 2005." 10-K

Interest coverage on long-term debt is sometimes computed separately from the normal times interest earned. For this purpose only, use the interest on long-term debt, thus focusing on the long-term interest coverage. Since times interest earned indicates long-term debt-paying ability, this revised computation helps focus on the long-term position. For external analysis, it is usually not practical to compute times interest coverage on long-term debt because of the lack of data. However, this computation can be made for internal analysis.

In the long run, a firm must have the funds to meet all of its expenses. In the short run, a firm can often meet its interest obligations even when the times interest earned is less than 1.00. Some of the expenses, such as depreciation expense, amortization expense, and depletion expense, do not require funds in the short run. The airline industry has had several bad periods when the times interest earned was less than 1.00, but it was able to maintain the interest payments.

To get a better indication of a firm's ability to cover interest payments in the short run, the noncash expenses such as depreciation, depletion, and amortization can be added back to the numerator of the times interest earned ratio. The resulting ratio, which is less conservative, gives a type of cash basis times interest earned useful for evaluating the firm in the short run.

FIXED CHARGE COVERAGE

The **fixed charge coverage ratio**, an extension of the times interest earned ratio, also indicates a firm's long-term debt-paying ability from the income statement view. The fixed charge coverage ratio indicates a firm's ability to cover fixed charges. It is computed as follows:

$$\text{Fixed Charge Coverage} = \frac{\substack{\text{Recurring Earnings, Excluding Interest Expense,} \\ \text{Tax Expense, Equity Earnings, and Minority} \\ \text{Earnings + Interest Portion of Rentals}}}{\substack{\text{Interest Expense, Including Capitalized Interest} \\ \text{+ Interest Portion of Rentals}}}$$

A difference of opinion occurs in practice as to what should be included in the fixed charges. When assets are leased, the lessee classifies leases as either capital leases or operating leases. The lessee treats a capital lease as an acquisition and includes the leased asset in fixed assets and the related obligation in liabilities. Part of the lease payment is considered to be interest expense. Therefore, the interest expense on the income statement includes interest related to capital leases.

A portion of operating lease payments is an item frequently included in addition to interest expense. Operating leases are not on the balance sheet, but they are reflected on the income statement in the rent expense. An operating lease for a relatively long term is a type of long-term financing, so part of the lease payment is really interest. When a portion of operating lease payments is included in fixed charges, it is an effort to recognize the true total interest that the firm pays.

SEC reporting may require a more conservative computation than the times interest earned ratio in order to determine the firm's long-term debt-paying ability. The SEC refers to its ratio as the **ratio of earnings to fixed charges**. The major difference between the times interest earned computation and the ratio of earnings to fixed charges is that the latter computation includes a portion of the operating leases.

Usually, one-third of the operating leases' rental charges is included in the fixed charges because this is an approximation of the proportion of lease payment that is interest. The SEC does not accept the one-third approximation automatically, but requires a more specific estimate of the interest portion based on the terms of the lease. Individuals interested in a company's ratio of earnings to fixed charges can find this ratio on the face of the income statement included with the SEC registration statement (Form S-7) when debt securities are registered.

The same adjusted earnings figure is used in the fixed charge coverage ratio as is used for the times interest earned ratio, except that the interest portion of operating leases (rentals) is added to the adjusted earnings for the fixed charge coverage ratio. The interest portion of operating leases is added to the adjusted earnings because it was previously deducted on the income statement as rental charges.

Nike, under Note 14—Commitments and Contingencies, disclosed the following:

> *The Company leases space for certain of its offices, warehouses and retail stores under leases expiring from one to twenty-seven years after May 31, 2007. Rent expense was $285.2 million, $252.0 million and $232.6 million for the years ended May 31, 2007, 2006 and 2005, respectively. Amounts of minimum future annual rental commitments under non-cancelable operating leases in each of the five years ending May 31, 2008 through 2012 are $260.9 million, $219.9 million, $183.3 million, $156.7 million, $128.4 million, respectively, and $587.0 million in later years.*

Exhibit 7-2 shows the fixed charge coverage for Nike for 2007 and 2006, with the interest portion of rentals considered. This figure, more conservative than the times interest earned, is still very good for Nike.

Among the other items sometimes considered as fixed charges are depreciation, depletion and amortization, debt principal payments, and pension payments. Substantial preferred dividends may also be included, or a separate ratio may be computed to consider preferred dividends. The more items considered as fixed charges, the more conservative the ratio. The trend is usually similar to that found for the times interest earned ratio.

Balance Sheet Consideration when Determining Long-Term Debt-Paying Ability

The firm's ability to carry debt, as indicated by the balance sheet, can be viewed by considering the debt ratio and the debt/equity ratio. These ratios are now reviewed.

DEBT RATIO

The debt ratio indicates the firm's long-term debt-paying ability. It is computed as follows:

$$\text{Debt Ratio} = \frac{\text{Total Liabilities}}{\text{Total Assets}}$$

Exhibit	7-2	NIKE, INC.

Fixed Charge Coverage

Years Ended May 31, 2007 and 2006

(In millions)	2007	2006
Income before income taxes	$ 2,199.90	$ 2,141.60
Plus: Interest expense	49.70*	50.50*
Interest portion of rentals	95.07	84.00
Earnings adjusted [A]	$ 2,344.67	$ 2,276.10
Interest expense	$ 49.70*	$ 50.50*
Capitalized interest	**	**
Interest portion of rentals	95.07	84.00
Adjusted interest [B]	$ 144.77	$ 134.50
Fixed charge coverage [A ÷ B]	16.20 times per year	16.92 times per year

*Interest expense includes both expensed and capitalized.

**Per Note 3—Property, Plant and Equipment
"Capitalized interest was not material for the years ended May 31, 2007, 2006 and 2005." 10-K

Total liabilities includes short-term liabilities, reserves, deferred tax liabilities, minority shareholders' interests, redeemable preferred stock, and any other noncurrent liability. It does not include stockholders' equity.

The debt ratio indicates the percentage of assets financed by creditors, and it helps to determine how well creditors are protected in case of insolvency. If creditors are not well protected, the company is not in a position to issue additional long-term debt. From the perspective of long-term debt-paying ability, the lower this ratio, the better the company's position.

Exhibit 7-3 shows the debt ratio for Nike for May 31, 2007, and May 31, 2006. The exhibit indicates that substantially less than one-half of the Nike assets were financed by outsiders in both 2007 and 2006. This debt ratio is a conservative computation because all of the liabilities and near liabilities have been included. At the same time, the assets are understated because no adjustments have been made for assets that have a fair market value greater than book value.

The debt ratio should be compared with competitors and industry averages. Industries that have stable earnings can handle more debt than industries that have cyclical earnings. This comparison can be misleading if one firm has substantial hidden assets, or liabilities that other firms do not (such as substantial land carried at historical cost).

Exhibit	7-3	NIKE, INC.

Debt Ratio

Years Ended May 31, 2007 and 2006

(In millions)	2007	2006
Total liabilities compiled:		
Current liabilities	$ 2,584.0	$2,612.4
Long-term debt	409.9	410.7
Deferred income taxes and other liabilities	668.7	561.0
Redeemable preferred stock	0.3	0.3
Total liabilities [A]	$ 3,662.9	$3,584.4
Total assets [B]	$10,688.3	$9,869.6
Debt ratio [A ÷ B]	34.27%	36.32%

In practice, substantial disagreement occurs on the details of the formula to compute the debt ratio. Some of the disagreement revolves around whether short-term liabilities should be included. Some firms exclude short-term liabilities because they are not long-term sources of funds and are, therefore, not a valid indication of the firm's long-term debt position. Other firms include short-term liabilities because these liabilities become part of the total source of outside funds in the long run. For example, individual accounts payable are relatively short term, but accounts payable in total becomes a rather permanent part of the entire sources of funds. This book takes a conservative position that includes the short-term liabilities in the debt ratio.

Another issue involves whether certain other items should be included in liabilities. Under current GAAP, some liabilities clearly represent a commitment to pay out funds in the future, whereas other items may never result in a future payment. Items that present particular problems as to a future payment of funds include reserves, deferred taxes, minority shareholders' interests, and redeemable preferred stock. Each of these items will be reviewed in the sections that follow.

Reserves

The reserve accounts classified under liabilities (some short-term and some long-term) result from an expense charge to the income statement and an equal increase in the reserve account on the balance sheet. These reserve accounts do not represent definite commitments to pay out funds in the future, but they are estimates of funds that will be paid out.

Reserve accounts are used infrequently in U.S. financial reporting. It is thought that they provide too much discretion in determining the amount of the reserve and the related impact on reported income. When the reserve account is increased, income is reduced. When the reserve account is decreased, income is increased. Reserve accounts are popular in some other countries like Germany. This book takes a conservative position that includes the reserves in liabilities in the debt ratio.

Deferred Taxes (Interperiod Tax Allocation)

In the United States, a firm may recognize certain income and expense items in one period for the financial statements and in another period for the federal tax return. This can result in financial statement income in any one period that is substantially different from tax return income. For many other countries, this is not the case. For example, there are few timing differences in Germany, and there are no timing differences in Japan. For these countries, deferred taxes are not a substantial issue or are not an issue at all. In the United States, taxes payable based on the tax return can be substantially different from income tax expense based on financial statement income. Current GAAP directs that the tax expense for the financial statements be based on the tax-related items on the financial statements. Taxes payable are based on the actual current taxes payable, determined by the tax return. (The Internal Revenue Code specifies the procedures for determining taxable income.) The tax expense for the financial statements often does not agree with the taxes payable. The difference between tax expense and taxes payable is recorded as deferred income taxes. The concept that results in deferred income taxes is called interperiod tax allocation.

As an illustration of deferred taxes, consider the following facts related to machinery purchase for $100,000:

Three-year write-off for tax purposes:	
1st year	$ 25,000
2nd year	38,000
3rd year	37,000
	$100,000
Five-year write-off for financial statements:	
1st year	$ 20,000
2nd year	20,000
3rd year	20,000
4th year	20,000
5th year	20,000
	$100,000

For both tax and financial statement purposes, $100,000 was written off for the equipment. The write-off on the tax return was three years, while the write-off on the financial statements was five years. The faster write-off on the tax return resulted in lower taxable income than the income reported on the income statement during the first three years. During the last two years, the income statement income was lower than the tax return income.

In addition to temporary differences, the tax liability can be influenced by an **operating loss carryback** and/or **operating loss carryforward**. The tax code allows a corporation reporting an operating loss for income tax purposes in the current year to carry this loss back and forward to offset reported taxable income. The company may first carry an operating loss back two years in sequential order, starting with the earliest of the two years. If the taxable income for the past two years is not enough to offset the operating loss, then the remaining loss is sequentially carried forward 20 years and offset against future taxable income.

A company can elect to forgo a carryback and, instead, only carry forward an operating loss. A company would not normally forgo a carryback because an operating loss carryback results in a definite and immediate income tax refund. A carryforward will reduce income taxes payable in future years to the extent of earned taxable income. A company could possibly benefit from forgoing a carryback if prospects in future years are good and an increase in the tax rate is anticipated.

Interperiod tax allocation should be used for all temporary differences. A temporary difference between the tax basis of an asset or a liability and its reported amount in the financial statements will result in taxable or deductible amounts in future years when the reported amount of the asset or liability is recovered or settled, respectively.

A corporation usually reports deferred taxes in two classifications: a net current amount and a net noncurrent amount. The net current amount could result in a current asset or a current liability being reported. The net noncurrent amount could result in a noncurrent asset or a noncurrent liability being reported.

Classification as current or noncurrent is usually based on the classification of the asset or liability responsible for the temporary difference. For example, a deferred tax liability resulting from the excess of tax depreciation over financial reporting depreciation would be reported as a noncurrent liability. This is because the temporary difference is related to noncurrent assets (fixed assets).

When a deferred tax asset or liability is not related to an asset or a liability, the deferred tax asset or liability is classified according to the expected reversal date of the temporary difference. For example, a deferred tax amount resulting from an operating loss carryforward would be classified based on the expected reversal date of the temporary difference.

There should be a valuation allowance against a deferred tax asset if sufficient uncertainty exists about a corporation's future taxable income. A valuation allowance reduces the deferred tax asset to its expected realizable amount. At the time that the valuation allowance is recognized, tax expense is increased.

A more likely than not criterion is used to measure uncertainty. If more likely than not a deferred asset will not be realized, a valuation allowance would be required.

Nike discloses deferred taxes in current assets, long-term assets, and long-term liabilities. For many firms, the long-term liability, deferred taxes, has grown to a substantial amount, which often increases each year. This occurs because of the growth in the temporary differences that cause the timing difference. The Nike amount increased substantially in 2007 for the long-term asset and the long-term liability.

Deferred taxes must be accounted for, using the liability method, which focuses on the balance sheet. Deferred taxes are recorded at amounts at which they will be settled when underlying temporary differences reverse. Deferred taxes are adjusted for tax rate changes. A change in tax rates can result in a material adjustment to the deferred account and can substantially influence income in the year of the tax rate change.

Some individuals disagree with the concept of deferred taxes (interperiod tax allocation). It is uncertain that the deferred tax will be paid. If it will be paid (received), it is uncertain when it will be paid (or received). The deferred tax accounts are, therefore, often referred to as **soft accounts**.

Because of the uncertainty over whether (and when) a deferred tax liability (asset) will be paid (received), some individuals elect to exclude deferred tax liabilities and assets when performing analysis. This is inconsistent with GAAP, which recognize deferred taxes.

Some revenue and expense items, referred to as **permanent differences**, never go on the tax return, but do go on the income statement. Examples would be premiums on life insurance and life insurance proceeds. Federal tax law does not allow these items to be included in expense and revenue, respectively. These items never influence either the tax expense or the tax liability, so they never influence the deferred tax accounts.

Minority Shareholders' Interest

The account, minority shareholders' interest, results when the firm has consolidated another company of which it owns less than 100%. The proportion of the consolidated company that is not owned appears on the balance sheet just above stockholders' equity.

Some firms exclude the minority shareholders' interest when computing debt ratios because this amount does not represent a commitment to pay funds to outsiders. Other firms include the minority shareholders' interest when computing debt ratios because these funds came from outsiders and are part of the total funds that the firm uses. This book takes the conservative position of including minority shareholders' interest in the primary computation of debt ratios. To review minority shareholders' interest, refer to the section of Chapter 3 on minority interest.

Redeemable Preferred Stock

Redeemable preferred stock is subject to mandatory redemption requirements or has a redemption feature outside the control of the issuer. Some redeemable preferred stock agreements require the firm to purchase certain amounts of the preferred stock on the open market. The Securities and Exchange Commission dictates that redeemable preferred stock not be disclosed under stockholders' equity.

The nature of redeemable preferred stock leaves open to judgment how it should be handled when computing debt ratios. One view excludes it from debt and includes it in stockholders' equity, on the grounds that it does not represent a normal debt relationship. A conservative position includes it as debt when computing the debt ratios. This book uses the conservative approach and includes redeemable preferred stock in debt for the primary computation of debt ratios. For a more detailed review, refer to the section of Chapter 3 that describes redeemable preferred stock.

DEBT/EQUITY RATIO

The **debt/equity ratio** is another computation that determines the entity's long-term debt-paying ability. This computation compares the total debt with the total shareholders' equity. The debt/equity ratio also helps determine how well creditors are protected in case of insolvency. From the perspective of long-term debt-paying ability, the lower this ratio is, the better the company's debt position.

In this book, the computation of the debt/equity ratio is conservative because all of the liabilities and near liabilities are included, and the stockholders' equity is understated to the extent that assets have a value greater than book value. This ratio should also be compared with industry averages and competitors. Compute the debt/equity ratio as follows:

$$\text{Debt/Equity Ratio} = \frac{\text{Total Liabilities}}{\text{Shareholders' Equity}}$$

Exhibit 7-4 shows the debt/equity ratio for Nike for May 31, 2007, and May 31, 2006. Using a conservative approach to computing debt/equity, Exhibit 7-4 indicates the debt/equity ratio was 52.14% at the end of 2007, down from 57.03% at the end of 2006.

The debt ratio and the debt/equity ratio have the same objectives. Therefore, these ratios are alternatives to each other if computed in the manner recommended here. Because some financial services may be reporting the debt ratio and others may be reporting the debt/equity ratio, the reader should be familiar with both.

As indicated previously, a problem exists with the lack of uniformity in the way some ratios are computed. This especially occurs with the debt ratio and the debt/equity ratio.

Exhibit 7-4	NIKE, INC.		
Debt/Equity Ratio			

	Years Ended May 31, 2007 and 2006		
(In millions)		**2007**	**2006**
Total liabilities [Exhibit 7-3] [A]		$3,662.9	$3,584.4
Shareholders' equity [B]		$7,025.4	$6,285.2
Debt/equity ratio [A ÷ B]		52.14%	57.03%

When comparing the debt ratio and the debt/equity ratio with industry ratios, try to determine how the industry ratios were computed. A reasonable comparison may not be possible because the financial sources sometimes do not indicate what elements of debt the computations include.

DEBT TO TANGIBLE NET WORTH RATIO

The debt to tangible net worth ratio also determines the entity's long-term debt-paying ability. This ratio also indicates how well creditors are protected in case of the firm's insolvency. As with the debt ratio and the debt/equity ratio, from the perspective of long-term debt-paying ability, it is better to have a lower ratio.

The debt to tangible net worth ratio is a more conservative ratio than either the debt ratio or the debt/equity ratio. It eliminates intangible assets, such as goodwill, trademarks, patents, and copyrights, because they do not provide resources to pay creditors—a very conservative position. Compute the debt to tangible net worth ratio as follows:

$$\text{Debt to Tangible Net Worth Ratio} = \frac{\text{Total Liabilities}}{\text{Shareholders' Equity} - \text{Intangible Assets}}$$

In this book, the computation of the debt to tangible net worth ratio is conservative. All of the liabilities and near liabilities are included, and the stockholders' equity is understated to the extent that assets have a value greater than book value.

Exhibit 7-5 shows the debt to tangible net worth ratios for Nike for May 31, 2007, and May 31, 2006. This is a conservative view of the debt-paying ability. There was a substantial improvement in 2007.

Exhibit 7-5	NIKE, INC.		
Debt to Tangible Net Worth Ratio			

	Years Ended May 31, 2007 and 2006		
(In millions)		**2007**	**2006**
Total liabilities [Exhibit 7-3] [A]		$3,662.9	$3,584.4
Shareholders' equity		$7,025.4	$6,285.2
Less: Intangible assets		(540.7)	(536.3)
Adjusted shareholders' equity [B]		$6,484.7	$5,748.9
Debt to tangible net worth ratio [A ÷ B]		56.49%	62.35%

OTHER LONG-TERM DEBT-PAYING ABILITY RATIOS

A number of additional ratios indicate perspective on the long-term debt-paying ability of a firm. This section describes some of these ratios.

The **current debt/net worth ratio** indicates a relationship between current liabilities and funds contributed by shareholders. The higher the proportion of funds provided by current liabilities, the greater the risk.

Another ratio, the **total capitalization ratio**, compares long-term debt to total capitalization. Total capitalization consists of long-term debt, preferred stock, and common stockholders' equity. The lower the ratio, the lower the risk.

Another ratio, the **fixed asset/equity ratio**, indicates the extent to which shareholders have provided funds in relation to fixed assets. Some firms subtract intangibles from shareholders' equity to obtain tangible net worth. This results in a more conservative ratio. The higher the fixed assets in relation to equity, the greater the risk.

Exhibit 7-6 indicates the trend in current liabilities, total liabilities, and owners' equity of firms in the United States between 1964 and 2006. It shows that there has been a major shift in the capital structure of firms, toward a higher proportion of debt in relation to total assets. This indicates a substantial increase in risk as management more frequently faces debt coming due. It also indicates that short-term debt is a permanent part of the financial structure of firms. This supports the decision to include short-term liabilities in the ratios determining long-term debt-paying ability (debt ratio, debt/equity ratio, and debt to tangible net worth ratio).

Exhibit	7-6	TRENDS IN CURRENT LIABILITIES, LONG-TERM LIABILITIES, AND OWNERS' EQUITY 1964–2006

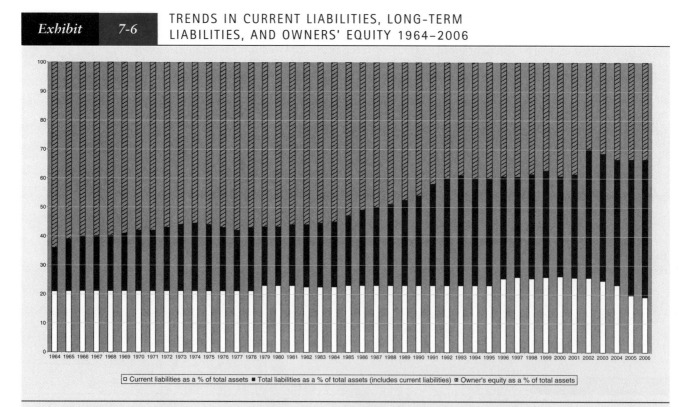

☐ Current liabilities as a % of total assets   ■ Total liabilities as a % of total assets (includes current liabilities)   ▨ Owner's equity as a % of total assets

Source: Quarterly Financial Reports of Manufacturing, Mining & Trading, Department of Commerce. Washington, DC: Government Printing Office.

Special Items That Influence a Firm's Long-Term Debt-Paying Ability

A number of special items influence a firm's long-term debt-paying ability. These items are now reviewed.

LONG-TERM ASSETS VERSUS LONG-TERM DEBT

The specific assets of the firm are important if the firm becomes unprofitable and the assets are sold. Therefore, consider the assets of the firm when determining the long-term debt-paying ability. The assets are insurance should the firm become unprofitable. The ability to analyze the assets, in relation to the long-term debt-paying ability, is limited, based on the information reported in the published financial statements. The statements do not extensively disclose market or liquidation values; they disclose only unrecovered cost for many items. The market value figure reported for some investments has been an exception.

A review of the financial statements is often of value if the firm liquidates or decides to reduce the scope of its operations. Examples of assets that may have substantial value would be land, timberlands, and investments.

When Penn Central Company went bankrupt, it had substantial debt and operating losses. Yet because of assets that had substantial market values, creditors were repaid. In other cases, creditors receive nothing or only nominal amounts when a firm goes bankrupt.

Substantial assets that have a potential value higher than the book figures may also indicate an earnings potential that will be realized later. For example, knowing that a railroad owns land that contains millions or billions of tons of coal could indicate substantial profit potential, even if the coal is not economical to mine at the present time. In future years, as the price of competitive products such as oil and gas increases, the coal may become economical to mine. This happened in the United States in the late 1970s. Several railroads that owned millions or billions of tons of unmined coal found that the coal became very valuable as the price of oil and gas increased.

LONG-TERM LEASING

Earlier, this chapter explained the influence of long-term leasing in relation to the income statement. Now we will consider the influence of long-term leasing from the balance sheet perspective.

First, review some points made previously. The lessee classifies leases as either capital leases or operating leases. A capital lease is handled as if the lessee acquired the asset. The leased asset is classified as a fixed asset, and the related obligation is included in liabilities. Operating leases are not reflected on the balance sheet but in a note and on the income statement as rent expense.

Operating leases for a relatively long term (a type of long-term financing) should be considered in a supplemental manner as to their influence on the debt structure of the firms. Capital leases have already been considered in the debt ratios computed because the capital leases were part of the total assets and also part of the total liabilities on the balance sheet.

The capitalized asset amount will not agree with the capitalized liability amount because the liability is reduced by payments and the asset is reduced by depreciation taken. Usually, a company depreciates capital leases faster than payments are made. This would result in the capitalized asset amount being lower than the related capitalized liability amount. On the original date of the capital lease, the capitalized asset amount and the capitalized liability amount are the same.

The Nike note relating to long-term leases indicates the minimum future rentals under operating leases for years subsequent to May 31, 2007. These figures do not include an amount for any possible contingent rentals because they are not practicable to estimate.

Note 14—Commitments and Contingencies

The Company leases space for certain of its offices, warehouses and retail stores under leases expiring from one to twenty-seven years after May 31, 2007. Rent expense was $285.2 million, $252.0 million and $232.6, million for the years ended May 31, 2007, 2006 and 2005, respectively. Amounts of minimum future annual rental commitments under non-cancelable operating leases in each of the five years ending May 31, 2008 through 2012 are $260.9 million, $219.9 million, $183.3 million, $156.7 million, $128.4 million, respectively, and $587.0 million in later years.

If these leases had been capitalized, the amount added to fixed assets and the amount added to liabilities would be the same at the time of the initial entry. As indicated previously, the amounts would not be the same, subsequently, because the asset is depreciated at some selected rate, while the liability is reduced as payments are made. When incorporating the operating leases into the debt ratios, use the liability amount and assume that the asset and the liability amount would be the same since no realistic way exists to compute the difference.

It would not be realistic to include the total future rentals that relate to operating leases in the lease commitments note ($1,536.2 million) because part of the commitment would be an interest consideration. Earlier, this chapter indicated that some firms estimate that one-third of the operating lease commitment is for interest. With a one-third estimate for interest, two-thirds is estimated for principal. For Nike, this amount is $1,024.13 million ($1,536.2 × 2/3). This amount can be added to fixed assets and long-term liabilities in order to obtain a supplemental view of the debt ratios that relate to the balance sheet. Exhibit 7-7 shows the adjusted debt ratio and debt/ equity ratio for Nike at May 31, 2007; this increases the debt position by a substantial amount.

Exhibit 7-7	NIKE, INC.	
Adjusted Debt Ratio and Debt/Equity Ratio Considering Operating Leases		
(In millions)		**May 31, 2007**
Adjusted debt ratio:		
Unadjusted total liabilities [Exhibit 7-3]		$ 3,662.90
Plus: Estimated for operating leases ($1,536.2 × 2/3)		1,024.13
Adjusted liabilities [A]		$ 4,687.03
Unadjusted total assets		$10,688.30
Plus: Estimated for operating leases		1,024.13
Adjusted assets [B]		$11,712.43
Adjusted debt ratio [A ÷ B]		40.02%
Unadjusted debt ratio [Exhibit 7-3]		34.27%
Adjusted debt/equity:		
Adjusted liabilities (above) [A]		$ 4,687.03
Shareholders' equity [B]		7,025.40
Adjusted debt/equity [A ÷ B]		66.72%
Unadjusted debt/equity [Exhibit 7-4]		52.14%

PENSION PLANS

The Employee Retirement Income Security Act (ERISA) became law in 1974 and substantially influenced the administration of pension plans, while elevating their liability status for the firm. This act includes provisions requiring minimum funding of plans, minimum rights to employees upon termination of their employment, and the creation of a special federal agency, the Pension Benefit Guaranty Corporation (PBGC), to help fund employee benefits when pension plans are terminated. The PBGC receives a fee for every employee covered by a pension plan subject to the PBGC. The PBGC has the right to impose a lien against a covered firm of 30% of the firm's net worth. This lien has the status of a tax lien and, therefore, ranks high among creditor claims. In practice, the PBGC has been reluctant to impose this lien except when a firm is in bankruptcy proceedings. This has resulted in the PBGC receiving a relatively small amount of assets when it has imposed the lien.

An important provision in a pension plan is the vesting provision. An employee vested in the pension plan is eligible to receive some pension benefits at retirement, regardless of whether the employee continues working for the employer. ERISA has had a major impact on reducing the vesting time. The original ERISA has been amended several times to increase the responsibility of firms regarding their pension plans.

In 1980, Congress passed the Multiemployer Pension Plan Amendment Act. Multiemployer pension plans are plans maintained jointly by two or more unrelated employers. This act provides for significant increased employer obligations for multiemployer pension plans and makes the PBGC coverage mandatory for multiemployer plans.

When a firm has a multiemployer pension plan, it normally covers union employees. Such a firm usually has other pension plans that cover nonunion employees. When disclosing a multiemployer pension plan, the firm normally includes the cost of the plan with the cost of the other pension plans. It is usually not practical to isolate the cost of these plans because of commingling. These plans operate usually on a pay-as-you-go basis, so no liability arises unless a payment has not been made. A potential significant liability arises if the company withdraws from the multiemployer plan. Unfortunately, the amount of this liability often cannot be ascertained from the pension note.

Albertson's, Inc. included the following comment in its February 2, 2006 annual report (in millions):

Multi-Employer Plans

The Company contributes to various multi-employer pension plans under industry-wide collective bargaining agreements, primarily for defined benefit pension plans. These plans generally provide retirement benefits to participants based on their service to contributing employers. The Company contributed $130, $115 and $92 to these plans in the years 2005, 2004 and 2003, respectively. Based on available information, the Company believes that some of the multi-employer plans to which it contributes are under-funded. Company contributions to these plans are likely to continue to increase in the near term. However, the amount of any increase or decrease in contributions will depend on a variety of factors, including the results of the Company's collective bargaining efforts, return on the assets held in the plans, actions taken by trustees who manage the plans and the potential payment of a withdrawal liability if the Company chooses to exit a market or another employer withdraws from a plan without provision for their share of pension liability. Many recently completed labor negotiations have positively affected the Company's future contributions to these plans.

Defined Contribution Plan

A company-sponsored pension plan is either a defined contribution plan or a defined benefit plan. A defined contribution plan defines the contributions of the company to the pension plan. Once this defined contribution is paid, the company has no further obligation to the pension plan. This type of plan shifts the risk to the employee as to whether the pension funds will grow to provide for a reasonable pension payment upon retirement. With this type of plan, which gained popularity during the 1980s, there is no problem of estimating the company's pension liability or pension expense. Thus, defined contribution plans do not present major financial reporting problems.

A 401(k) is a type of defined contribution plan. These plans may or may not require a company's contribution. They may provide for an employee's contribution. When a company makes a required contribution, this ends any pension liability.

For firms with defined contribution plans, try to grasp the significance by doing the following:

1. For a three-year period, compare pension expense with operating revenue. This will indicate the materiality of pension expense in relation to operating revenue and the trend.
2. For a three-year period, compare pension expense with income before income taxes. This will indicate the materiality of pension expense in relation to income and the trend.
3. Note any balance sheet items. (There will usually not be a balance sheet item because the firm is paying on a pay-as-you-go basis.)

Nike does not have a defined contribution plan, but it does have a 401(k) employee savings plan. We can approach analysis of this plan in a manner similar to the analysis of a defined contribution pension plan. Note 12 (benefit plans) explains the following:

The Company has various 401(k) employee savings plans available to U.S.-based employees. The Company matches a portion of employee contributions with common stock or cash. Company contributions to the savings plans were $24.9 million, $22.5 million, and $20.3 million for the years ended May 31, 2007, 2006 and 2005, respectively, and are included in selling and administrative expenses.

Thus, the savings plan expenses as a percentage of revenues 0.15%, 0.15%, and 0.15% in 2007, 2006, and 2005, respectively. Savings plans appear to be immaterial. No balance sheet items are disclosed.

Defined Benefit Plan

A defined benefit plan defines the benefits to be received by the participants in the plan. For example, the plan may call for the participant to receive 40% of his or her average pay for the three years before retirement. This type of plan leaves the company with the risk of having insufficient funds in the pension fund to meet the defined benefit. This type of plan was the predominant type of plan prior to the 1980s. Most companies still have a defined benefit plan, partly because of the difficulties involved in switching to a defined contribution plan. Some companies have terminated their defined benefit plan by funding the obligations of the plan and starting a defined contribution plan. In some cases, this has resulted in millions of dollars being transferred to the company from the pension plan after the defined benefit plan obligations have been met. The U.S. Congress added an excise tax on "reversions" in 1990. This excise tax can be as high as 50%. This has substantially slowed down the "reversions."

A number of assumptions about future events must be made regarding a defined benefit plan. Some of these assumptions that relate to the future are interest rates, employee turnover, mortality rates, compensation, and pension benefits set by law. Assumptions about future events contribute materially to the financial reporting problems in the pension area. Two firms with the same plan may make significantly different assumptions, resulting in major differences in pension expense and liability.

There are many technical terms associated with defined benefit plans. A description of all of these terms is beyond the scope of this book.

For firms with defined benefit plans, try to grasp the significance by doing the following:

1. For a three-year period, compare pension expense with operating revenue. This will indicate the materiality of pension expense in relation to operating revenue and the trend.
2. For a three-year period, compare pension expense with income before income taxes. This will indicate the materiality of pension expense in relation to income and the trend.
3. Compare the benefit obligations with the value of plan assets. This can indicate significant underfunding or overfunding. Underfunding represents a potential liability. Overfunding represents an opportunity to reduce future pension expense. Overfunding can also be used to reduce related costs, such as disability benefits, retiree health costs, and staff downsizings. Overfunding can also be used to take credits to the income statement.
4. Note the net balance sheet liability (asset) recognized.

Exhibit 7-8 shows selected items from the Vulcan Materials Company pension note. It also includes selected items from the statement of earnings and the balance sheet.

We note that the Vulcan Materials Company pension plans are defined benefit plans. Observe the following relating to the Vulcan Materials Company plans:

1. Pension expense (cost) in relation to operating revenue:

	2006	2005	2004
Pension cost [A]	$9,278,000	$12,183,000	$9,688,000
Operating revenue [B]	$3,342,475,000	$2,895,327,000	$2,454,335,000
Pension expense/ operating revenue [A ÷ B]	0.28%	0.42%	0.39%

Note: Pension cost decreased materially between 2005 and 2006, and it is not material.

2. Pension expense (cost) in relation to earnings from continuing operations before income taxes:

	2006	2005	2004
Pension cost [A]	$9,278,000	$12,183,000	$9,688,000
Earnings from continuing operations before income taxes [B]	$703,461,000	$480,237,000	$375,566,000
Pension expense (cost)/earnings from continuing operations before income taxes [A ÷ B]	1.32%	2.54%	2.58%

Note: Pension cost decreased materially between 2005 and 2006, and it is not material.

Exhibit	7-8	VULCAN MATERIALS COMPANY*

Pension Benefits—Defined Benefit Pension Plans

Consolidated Statements of Earnings (in Part)
Amounts in thousands

For the years ended December 31	2006	2005	2004
Amounts in thousands			
Net sales	$3,041,093	$2,614,965	$2,213,160
Delivery revenues	301,382	280,362	241,175
Total revenues	$3,342,475	$2,895,327	$2,454,335
Earnings from continuing operations before income taxes	$ 703,461	$ 480,237	$ 375,566

Consolidated Balance Sheets (in Part)
Amounts in thousands

	2006	2005	2004
Total current assets	$ 731,379	$1,164,722	$1,417,959
Total assets	3,424,225	3,588,884	3,665,133
Total current liabilities	493,687	579,014	426,689
Total liabilities	1,423,114	1,462,343	1,651,158
Total shareholders' equity	2,001,111	2,126,541	2,013,975

Note 10: Benefit Plans (in Part)
Amounts in thousands

	2006	2005	2004
Benefit obligation at end of year	$579,641	$535,686	$524,332
Fair value of assets at end of year	611,184	557,036	519,550
Funded status	$ 31,543	$ 21,350	$ 4,782

Amounts Recognized in the Consolidated Balance Sheets and Net Periodic Pension Cost
Amounts in thousands

	2006	2005	2004
Noncurrent assets (2006)/prepaid benefit cost (2005 and 2004)	$ 68,517	$ 61,703	$ 56,639
Current liabilities	(1,584)		
Noncurrent liabilities (2006)/accrued benefit liability (2005 and 2004)	(35,390)	(30,918)	(34,851)
Intangible assets	N/A	396	1,206
Accumulated other comprehensive loss	N/A	3,584	2,020
Net amount recognized	$ 31,543	$ 34,765	$ 25,014
Net periodic pension benefit cost	$ 9,278	$ 12,183	$ 9,688

*"Our business consists of the production, distribution and sale of construction aggregates and other construction materials and related services." 10-K

3. Comparison of benefit obligation with fair value of assets at end of year:

	2006	2005
Benefit obligation	$579,641,000	$535,686,000
Fair value of assets	611,184,000	557,036,000
Fair value of assets over benefit obligation	$ 31,543,000	$ 21,350,000

Note: Fair value of assets is over benefit obligation.

4. Amounts recognized in the consolidated balance sheets:

	2006	2005	2004
Noncurrent assets (2006)/ prepaid benefit cost (2005 and 2004)	$68,517,000	$61,703,000	$56,639,000
Current liabilities	(1,584,000)		
Noncurrent liabilities (2006)/ accrued benefit liability (2005 and 2004)	(35,390,000)	(30,918,000)	(34,851,000)
Intangible assets	N/A	396,000	1,206,000
Accumulated other comprehensive loss	N/A	3,584,000	2,020,000
Net amount recognized	$31,543,000	$34,765,000	$25,014,000

Note: There is not a significant balance sheet presence. The asset recognition is materially more than the liability recognized.

POSTRETIREMENT BENEFITS OTHER THAN PENSIONS

Some benefits other than pensions, such as medical insurance and life insurance contracts, accrue to employees upon retirement. These benefits can be substantial. Many firms have obligations in the millions of dollars. Prior to 1993, most firms did not have these obligations funded; therefore, for these firms, a potential for a significant liability existed.

Beginning in 1993, firms were required to accrue, or set up a reserve for, future postretirement benefits other than pensions (rather than deduct these costs when paid). Firms can usually spread the catch-up accrual costs over 20 years or take the charge in one lump sum. The amount involved is frequently material, so this choice can represent a major problem when comparing financial results of two or more firms. For some firms, the catch-up charge for medical insurance was so material that it resulted in a deficit in retained earnings or even a deficit to the entire stockholders' equity section.

Many firms reduce costs by changing their plans to limit health care benefits to retirees to a maximum fixed amount. This type of plan, in contrast to open-ended medical benefits, could materially reduce the firm's health care costs for retirees. Review the notes closely to determine how the firm records health care costs for retirees.

For firms with postretirement benefits other than pensions, you should try to grasp the significance using the same basic approach as was used for defined benefit plans for pensions.

Exhibit 7-9 shows selected items from the Vulcan Materials Company postretirement benefits other than pensions. It also includes selected items from the statement of earnings and the balance sheet.

Observe the following relating to the Vulcan Materials Company postretirement plans.

1. Expense (cost) in relation to operating revenue:

	2006	2005	2004
Net periodic postretirement benefit cost [A]	$8,687,000	$10,396,000	$10,930,000
Total revenues [B]	$3,342,475,000	$2,895,327,000	$2,454,335,000
Net periodic postretirement benefit cost/total revenues [A ÷ B]	0.26%	0.36%	0.45%

Note: Postretirement cost has decreased materially and is not material.

2. Expense (cost) in relation to income before taxes:

	2006	2005	2004
Net periodic postretirement benefit cost [A]	$8,687,000	$10,396,000	$10,930,000
Earnings from continuing operations before income taxes [B]	$703,461,000	$480,237,000	$375,566,000
Net periodic postretirement benefit cost/ earnings from continuing operations before income taxes [A ÷ B]	1.23%	2.16%	2.91%

Note: Postretirement cost has decreased materially and is not material.

Exhibit	7-9	VULCAN MATERIALS COMPANY*

Postretirement Plans

Consolidated Statements of Earnings (in Part)
Amounts in thousands

For the years ended December 31	2006	2005	2004
Amounts in thousands			
Net sales	$3,041,093	$2,614,965	$2,213,160
Delivery revenues	301,382	280,362	241,175
Total revenues	$3,342,475	$2,895,327	$2,454,335
Earnings from continuing operations before income taxes	$ 703,461	$ 480,237	$ 375,566

Consolidated Balance Sheets (in Part)
Amounts in thousands

	2006	2005	2004
Total current assets	$ 731,379	$1,164,722	$1,417,959
Total assets	3,424,225	3,588,884	3,665,133
Total current liabilities	493,687	579,014	426,689
Total liabilities	1,423,114	1,462,343	1,651,158
Total shareholders' equity	2,001,111	2,126,541	2,013,975

Note 10: Benefit Plans (in Part)
Postretirement Plans (in Part)
Amounts in thousands

	2006	2005	2004
Benefit obligation at end of year	$ 90,805	$ 89,735	$ 100,878
Fair value of assets at end of year	—	—	—
Funded status	$(90,805)	$(89,735)	$(100,878)

Amounts Recognized in the Consolidated Balance Sheets
Postretirement Plans and Net Periodic Postretirement Benefit Cost
Amounts in thousands

	2006	2005	2004
Current liabilities	$ (5,497)	$ (5,555)	$ —
Noncurrent liabilities (2006)/accrued postretirement benefits (2005 and 2004)	(85,308)	(69,537)	(70,646)
Net amount recognized	$(90,805)	$(75,092)	$(70,646)
Net periodic postretirement benefit cost	$ 8,687	$ 10,396	$ 10,930

*"Our business consists of the production, distribution and sale of construction aggregates and other construction materials and related services."   10-K

---

3. Comparison of benefit obligations with the fair value of the plan assets:

	2006	2005	2004
Benefit obligation	$90,805,000	$89,735,000	$100,878,000
Fair value of assets	—	—	—
Excess of obligations over plan assets	$90,805,000	$89,735,000	$100,878,000

Note: Benefit obligation is not funded. Comparing 2006 benefit obligation with total liabilities results in 6.38%. Some would consider this to be material, but we noted that pension benefits had fair value of assets to be greater than benefit obligation. These considered together would likely be considered immaterial.

4.   Amounts recognized in the consolidated balance sheet:

	2006	2005	2004
Current liabilities	$ 5,497,000	$ 5,555,000	$ —
Noncurrent liabilities 2006/accrued postretirement benefits (2005 and 2004)	85,308,000	69,537,000	70,646,000
Net amount recognized	$90,805,000	$75,092,000	$70,646,000

Note: Many would not consider this to be material, but it is increasing.

JOINT VENTURES

A joint venture is an association of two or more businesses established for a special purpose. Some joint ventures are in the form of partnerships or other unincorporated forms of business. Others are in the form of corporations jointly owned by two or more other firms.

The accounting principles for joint ventures are flexible because of their many forms. The typical problem concerns whether a joint venture should be carried as an investment or consolidated. Some joint ventures are very significant in relation to the parent firm. There is typically a question as to whether the parent firm has control or only significant influence. When the parent firm has control, it usually consolidates joint ventures by using a pro rata share. Other joint ventures are usually carried in an investment account by using the equity method. In either case, disclosure of significant information often appears in a note.

When a firm enters into a joint venture, it frequently makes commitments such as guaranteeing a bank loan for the joint venture or a long-term contract to purchase materials with the joint venture. This type of action can give the company significant potential liabilities or commitments that do not appear on the face of the balance sheet. This potential problem exists with all joint ventures, including those that have been consolidated. To be aware of these significant potential liabilities or commitments, read the note that relates to the joint venture. Then consider this information in relation to the additional liabilities or commitments to which the joint venture may commit the firm.

Exhibit 7–10 details a joint venture of EarthLink, Inc.

Exhibit   7-10   EARTHLINK, INC.*

Joint Ventures (2006 Annual Report)

EarthLink, Inc.
Notes to Consolidated Financial Statements (in Part)

4. Investments (in Part)

Investment in Equity Affiliate

In March 2005, the Company completed the formation of a joint venture with SK Telecom, HELIO, to market and sell wireless voice and data services in the U.S. EarthLink and SK Telecom each have an equal voting and economic ownership interest in HELIO. Upon formation, the Company invested $43.0 million of cash and contributed non-cash assets valued at $40.0 million, including 27,000 wireless customers, contractual arrangements and agreements to prospectively market HELIO's services. The non-cash assets contributed were recorded by the Company as an additional investment of $0.5 million based on the Company's carrying value of the assets. The Company recorded its initial investment at $43.5 million, reflecting the cash invested plus the carrying value of assets contributed. In addition, the Company paid HELIO to assume $0.9 million of net liabilities associated with wireless customers and related operations. The Company recorded no gain or loss in

*"EarthLink, Inc. is a total communications provider, providing integrated communication services and related value-added services to individual consumers and business customers utilizing Internet Protocol, or IP, based technologies." 10-K

| Exhibit | 7-10 | EARTHLINK, INC. (Continued) |

March 2005 associated with the contribution of non-cash assets, the transfer of net liabilities, or the associated payment to HELIO to assume the net liabilities upon completing the formation of HELIO.

Pursuant to the HELIO Contribution and Formation Agreement, the Company contributed $122.0 million of cash and non-cash assets during 2005, $78.5 million during 2006 and is committed to invest an additional $19.5 million of cash in HELIO during 2007, which includes $13.5 million that was contributed in February 2007. During 2006, HELIO received minority investments, which reduced EarthLink's and SK Telecom's economic ownership interest in HELIO from 50 percent at formation to approximately 48 percent as of December 31, 2006. However, EarthLink's and SK Telecom's voting interest remains the same.

The Company accounts for its investment in HELIO under the equity method of accounting because the Company can exert significant influence over HELIO's operating and financial policies. As a result, the Company records its proportionate share of HELIO's net loss in its Consolidated Statement of Operations. The Company is amortizing the difference between the book value and fair value of non-cash assets contributed to HELIO over their estimated useful lives. The amortization increases the carrying value of the Company's investment and decreases the net losses of equity affiliate included in the Consolidated Statement of Operations. During the years ended December 31, 2005 and 2006, the Company recorded $15.6 million and $84.8 million, respectively, of net losses of equity affiliate related to its HELIO investment, which is net of amortization of basis differences and certain other equity method accounting adjustments.

The following is summarized statement of operations information of HELIO for the years ended December 31, 2005 and 2006:

	Year Ended December 31,	
	2005	2006
	(In thousands)	
Revenues	$ 16,365	$ 46,580
Operating loss	(45,658)	(201,266)
Net loss	(42,023)	(191,755)

The following is summarized balance sheet information of HELIO as of December 31, 2005 and 2006:

	As of December 31,	
	2005	2006
	(In thousands)	
Current assets	$164,377	$189,661
Long-term assets	59,570	75,309
Current liabilities	17,912	78,889
Long-term liabilities	2,394	4,853

CONTINGENCIES

A **contingency** is an existing condition, situation, or set of circumstances involving uncertainty as to possible gain or loss to an enterprise that will ultimately be resolved when one or more future events occur or fail to occur.[1]

A contingency is characterized by an existing condition, uncertainty as to the ultimate effect, and its resolution depending on one or more future events. A loss contingency should be accrued if two conditions are met:[2]

1. Information prior to issuance of the financial statements indicates that it is *probable* that an asset has been impaired or a liability has been incurred at the date of the financial statements.

2. The amount of the loss can be *reasonably estimated.*

If a contingency loss meets one, but not both, of the criteria for recording and is, therefore, not accrued, disclosure by note is made when it is at *least reasonably possible* that there has been an impairment of assets or that a liability has been incurred. Examples of contingencies include warranty obligations and collectibility of receivables. If the firm guarantees the indebtedness of others, the contingency is usually disclosed in a note.

When examining financial statements, a note that describes contingencies should be closely reviewed for possible significant liabilities not disclosed on the face of the balance sheet.

The following covers gain contingencies:

1. Contingencies that might result in gains usually are not reflected in the accounts, since to do so might be to recognize revenue prior to its realization.
2. Adequate disclosure shall be made of contingencies that might result in gains, but care shall be exercised to avoid misleading implications as to the likelihood of realization.[3]

The notes of the firm should be reviewed for gain contingencies. Exhibit 7–11 details gain contingencies for Manitowoc Company, Inc.

Exhibit	7-11	MANITOWOC COMPANY, INC.*

Gain Contingencies (2006 Annual Report)

The company has been in negotiations with one of its Marine segment customers to recover certain cost overruns that resulted primarily from specification inadequacies, change orders, cumulative disruption and constructive acceleration associated with a particular contract. During the third quarter of 2005, due to the fact that these negotiations were not successful within a timeframe satisfactory to the company, the company filed a lawsuit seeking recovery of these cost overruns from the customer. The customer filed a counter claim against the company in the fourth quarter of 2005. During the fourth quarter of 2005, the company established a reserve of $10.2 million to reflect the inherent uncertainties in litigation of this type. The $10.2 million reserve is recorded in cost of sales of the Marine segment in the Consolidated Statements of Operations for the year ended December 31, 2005. If the company is successful in its recovery of costs as a result of this lawsuit or negotiations, the favorable impact on its Consolidated Statements of Operations and Cash Flows in a future period could be material.

*"We are a diversified industrial manufacturer in three principal markets: Cranes and Related Products (Crane); Foodservice Equipment (Foodservice) and Marine." 10-K

FINANCIAL INSTRUMENTS WITH OFF-BALANCE-SHEET RISK AND FINANCIAL INSTRUMENTS WITH CONCENTRATIONS OF CREDIT RISK

Credit and market risk for all financial instruments with off-balance-sheet risk require the following disclosure:

1. The face or contract amount.
2. The nature and terms including, at a minimum, a discussion of credit and market risk, cash requirements, and accounting policies.[4]

Disclosure is also required of the following regarding financial instruments with off-balance-sheet credit risk:

1. The amount of accounting loss the entity would incur if any party failed completely to perform according to the terms of the contract and the collateral or other security, if any, proved worthless.
2. The entity's policy of requiring collateral and a brief description of the collateral it currently holds.[5]

Accounting loss represents the worst-case loss if everything related to a contract went wrong. This includes the possibility that a loss may occur from the failure of another party to perform according to the terms of a contract, as well as the possibility that changes in market prices may make a financial instrument less valuable or more troublesome.

In addition to requiring disclosure of matters relating to off-balance-sheet financial instruments, disclosure is required of credit risk concentration. This disclosure includes information on the extent of risk from exposures to individuals or groups of counterparties in the same industry or region. The activity, region, or economic characteristic that identifies a concentration requires a narrative description. The provision of requiring disclosure of credit risk concentration can be particularly significant to small companies. Examples are a retail store whose receivables are substantially with local residents and a local bank with a loan portfolio concentrated with debtors dependent on the local tourist business.

Exhibit 7-12 presents financial instruments with off-balance-sheet risk and financial instruments with concentrations of credit risk for Nordson Corporation as disclosed in its 2006 annual report.

Exhibit 7-12   NORDSON CORPORATION*

Off-Balance-Sheet Risk and Concentrations of Credit Risk (2006 Annual Report)

Note 11—Financial Instruments (in Part) (In thousands)

The Company enters into foreign currency forward contracts, which are derivative financial instruments, to reduce the risk of foreign currency exposures resulting from receivables, payables, intercompany receivables, intercompany payables and loans denominated in foreign currencies. The maturities of these contracts are usually less than 90 days. Forward contracts are marked to market each accounting period, and the resulting gains or losses are included in other income (expense) in the Consolidated Statement of Income. A gain of $2,534 was recognized from changes in fair value of these contracts for the year ended October 31, 2006. A loss of $2,573 and a gain of $807 were recognized from changes in fair value of these contracts for the years ended October 30, 2005 and October 31, 2004, respectively.

At October 31, 2006, the Company had outstanding forward exchange contracts that mature at various dates through January 2007. The following table summarizes, by currency, the Company's forward exchange contracts:

	Sell		Buy	
October 31, 2006 contract amounts	Notional Amount	Fair Market Value	Notional Amount	Fair Market Value
Euro	$ 7,835	$ 7,877	$ 77,824	$ 78,500
British pound	755	763	9,987	10,132
Japanese yen	2,573	2,565	18,204	18,313
Others	3,419	3,429	12,285	12,444
Total	$14,582	$14,634	$118,300	$119,389

	Sell		Buy	
October 31, 2005 contract amounts	Notional Amount	Fair Market Value	Notional Amount	Fair Market Value
Euro	$ 6,259	$ 6,095	$ 68,505	$ 67,486
British pound	1,087	1,058	8,553	8,388
Japanese yen	2,513	2,422	17,526	17,049
Others	2,803	2,771	12,343	12,194
Total	$12,662	$12,346	$106,927	$105,117

*"Nordson Corporation is one of the world's leading producers of precision dispensing equipment that applies adhesives, sealants and coatings to a broad range of consumer and industrial products during manufacturing operations, helping customers meet quality, productivity and environmental targets." 10-K

DISCLOSURES ABOUT FAIR VALUE OF FINANCIAL INSTRUMENTS

Disclosure is required about the fair value of financial instruments. This includes financial instruments recognized and not recognized in the balance sheet (both assets and liabilities). When estimating fair value is not practicable, then descriptive information pertinent to estimating fair value should be disclosed.

The disclosure about fair value of financial instruments can be either in the body of the financial statements or in the notes.[6] This disclosure could possibly indicate significant opportunity or additional risk to the company. For example, long-term debt disclosed at a fair value above the carrying amount increases the potential for a loss.

Exhibit 7-13 presents the fair value of financial instruments for Northrop Grumman, as disclosed in its 2006 annual report.

Exhibit   7-13   NORTHROP GRUMMAN*

Fair Value of Financial Instruments (2006 Annual Report)

Note 11—Fair Value of Financial Instruments (in Part) (In millions)

Carrying amounts and the related estimated fair values of the company's financial instruments at December 31 are as follows:

$ in millions	2006		2005	
	Carrying Amount	Fair Value	Carrying Amount	Fair Value
Cash and cash equivalents	$ 1,015	$ 1,015	$ 1,605	$ 1,605
Investments in marketable securities	208	208	180	180
Cash surrender value of life insurance policies	290	290	256	256
Investment in TRW Auto			97	257
Short-term notes payable	(95)	(95)	(50)	(50)
Long-term debt	(4,067)	(4,562)	(5,095)	(5,682)
Mandatorily redeemable preferred stock	(350)	(459)	(350)	(445)
Interest rate swaps	(8)	(8)	(7)	(7)
Foreign currency forward contracts			(2)	(2)

*"Northrop Grumman Corporation . . . is an integrated enterprise consisting of some 25 formerly separate businesses that cover the entire defense spectrum, from undersea to outer space and into cyberspace." 10-K

Summary

This chapter covered two approaches to a firm's long-term debt-paying ability. One approach considers the firm's ability to carry debt as indicated by the income statement, and the other approach views it as indicated by the balance sheet. The ratios related to debt include the following:

$$\text{Times Interest Earned} = \frac{\text{Recurring Earnings, Excluding Interest Expense, Tax Expense, Equity Earnings, and Minority Earnings}}{\text{Interest Expense, Including Capitalized Interest}}$$

$$\text{Fixed Charge Coverage} = \frac{\text{Recurring Earnings, Excluding Interest Expense, Tax Expense, Equity Earnings, and Minority Earnings} + \text{Interest Portion of Rentals}}{\text{Interest Expense, Including Capitalized Interest} + \text{Interest Portion of Rentals}}$$

$$\text{Debt Ratio} = \frac{\text{Total Liabilities}}{\text{Total Assets}}$$

$$\text{Debt/Equity Ratio} = \frac{\text{Total Liabilities}}{\text{Shareholders' Equity}}$$

$$\text{Debt to Tangible Net Worth Ratio} = \frac{\text{Total Liabilities}}{\text{Shareholders' Equity} - \text{Intangible Assets}}$$

to the net

1. Go to the SEC Web site (http://www.sec.gov). Under "Filings & Forms (EDGAR)," click on "Search for Company Filings." Click on "Companies & Other Filers." Under Company Name, enter "Walt Disney" (or under Ticker Symbol, enter "DIS"). In the Form Type box, enter "10-K." Select the 10-K submitted November 22, 2006.

   a. Determine the standard industrial classification (SIC).

   b. Copy the first sentence in the "Item 1. Business" section.

   c. Comment on legal proceedings related to Winnie the Pooh.

   d. Item 9—Changes and Disagreements with Accountants on Accounting and Financial Disclosure. Comment on these disclosures or lack of disclosures.

   e. Note 3—Significant Acquisitions and Dispositions and Restructuring and Impairment Changes. Describe the acquisition of Pixar.

   f. Item 11—Executive Compensation table (*Hint*: You may need to go to a report other than the 10-K.) Locate where the Executive Compensation Table is disclosed.

2. Go to the SEC Web site (http://www.sec.gov). Under "Filings & Forms (EDGAR)", click on "Search for Company Filings." Click on "Companies & Other Filers." Under Company Name, enter "Goodyear Tire" (or under Ticker Symbol, enter "GT"). In the Form Type box, enter "10-K." Select the 10-K submitted February 16, 2007.

   a. Determine the total cost of pension, and other postretirement benefit (Note 13) for the year ended December 31, 2006. How material is the cost in relation to net sales? How material is this cost in relation to (loss) income before income taxes and cumulative effect of accounting change?

   b. Determine the total benefit obligation at December 31, 2006. Determine the total in plan assets at December 31, 2006. Determine the total net funded status at December 31, 2006. Compare the total net funded status

with total liabilities at December 31, 2006. Comment on the significance of the net funded status with total liabilities.

   c. Determine the total amounts recognized in the balance sheets at December 31, 2006, for pension, and other postretirement benefits. How significant is the amount recognized in relation to total liabilities at December 31, 2006? How significant is the amount recognized in relation to total net funded status at December 31, 2006?

3. Go to the SEC Web site (http://www.sec.gov). Under "Filings & Forms (EDGAR)," click on "Search for Company Filings." Click on "Companies & Other Filers." Under Company Name, enter "Flowers Foods Inc" (or under Ticker Symbol, enter "FLO"). Select the 10-K submitted February 28, 2007.

   a. Compute the times interest earned ratio for the fiscal year ended December 30, 2006.

   b. Compute the debt ratio for the year ended December 30, 2006.

   c. Compute the operating cash flow/total debt for the year ended December 30, 2006.

   d. Comment on the above ratios.

4. Go to the SEC Web site (http://www.sec.gov). Under "Filings & Forms (EDGAR)," click on "Search for Company Filings." Click on "Companies & Other Filers." Under Company Name, enter "Amazon Com Inc" (or under Ticker Symbol enter "AMZN"). Select the 10-K submitted February 16, 2007.

   a. Compute the times interest earned ratio for the fiscal year ended December 31, 2004; December 31, 2005; and December 31, 2006.

   b. Compute the debt ratio for the fiscal year ended December 31, 2005; and December 31, 2006.

   c. Compute the operating cash flow/total debt for the fiscal year ended December 31, 2005; and December 31, 2006.

   d. Comment on the above ratios.

Questions

Q 7-1.   Is profitability important to a firm's long-term debt-paying ability? Discuss.

Q 7-2.   List the two approaches to examining a firm's long-term debt-paying ability. Discuss why each of these approaches gives an important view of a firm's ability to carry debt.

Q 7-3.   What type of times interest earned ratio would be desirable? What type would not be desirable?

Q 7-4.   Would you expect an auto manufacturer to finance a relatively high proportion of its long-term funds from debt? Discuss.

Q 7-5.   Would you expect a telephone company to have a high debt ratio? Discuss.

Q 7-6.   Why should capitalized interest be added to interest expense when computing times interest earned?

Q 7-7.   Discuss how noncash charges for depreciation, depletion, and amortization can be used to obtain a short-run view of times interest earned.

Q 7-8.   Why is it difficult to determine the value of assets?

Q 7-9.   Is it feasible to get a precise measurement of the funds that could be available from long-term assets to pay long-term debts? Discuss.

Q 7-10.   One of the ratios used to indicate long-term debt-paying ability compares total liabilities to total assets. What is the intent of this ratio? How precise is this ratio in achieving its intent?

Q 7-11.   For a given firm, would you expect the debt ratio to be as high as the debt/equity ratio? Explain.

Q 7-12.   Explain how the debt/equity ratio indicates the same relative long-term debt-paying ability as does the debt ratio, only in a different form.

Q 7-13.   Why is it important to compare long-term debt ratios of a given firm with industry averages?

Q 7-14.   How should lessees account for operating leases? Capital leases? Include both income statement and balance sheet accounts.

Q 7-15.   A firm with substantial leased assets that have not been capitalized may be overstating its long-term debt-paying ability. Explain.

Q 7-16.   Capital leases that have not been capitalized will decrease the times interest earned ratio. Comment.

Q 7-17.   Indicate the status of pension liabilities under the Employee Retirement Income Security Act.

Q 7-18.   Why is the vesting provision an important provision of a pension plan? How has the Employee Retirement Income Security Act influenced vesting periods?

Q 7-19.   Indicate the risk to a company if it withdraws from a multiemployer pension plan or if the multiemployer pension plan is terminated.

Q 7-20.   Operating leases are not reflected on the balance sheet, but they are reflected on the income statement in the rent expense. Comment on why an interest expense figure that relates to long-term operating leases should be considered when determining a fixed charge coverage.

Q 7-21.   What portion of net worth can the federal government require a company to use to pay for pension obligations?

Q 7-22.   Consider the debt ratio. Explain a position for including short-term liabilities in the debt ratio. Explain a position for excluding short-term liabilities from the debt ratio. Which of these approaches would be more conservative?

Q 7-23.   Consider the accounts of bonds payable and reserve for rebuilding furnaces. Explain how one of these accounts could be considered a firm liability and the other could be considered a soft liability.

Q 7-24.   Explain why deferred taxes that are disclosed as long-term liabilities may not result in actual cash outlays in the future.

Q 7-25.   A firm has a high current debt/net worth ratio in relation to prior years, competitors, and the industry. Comment on what this tentatively indicates.

Q 7-26.   Comment on the implications of relying on a greater proportion of short-term debt in relation to long-term debt.

Q 7-27.   When a firm guarantees a bank loan for a joint venture that it participates in and the joint venture is handled as an investment, then the overall potential debt position will not be obvious from the face of the balance sheet. Comment.

Q 7-28.   When examining financial statements, a note that describes contingencies should be reviewed closely for possible significant liabilities that are not disclosed on the face of the balance sheet. Comment.

Q 7-29.   There is a chance that a company may be in a position to have large sums transferred from the pension fund to the company. Comment.

Q 7-30.   Indicate why comparing firms for postretirement benefits other than pensions can be difficult.

Q 7-31.   Speculate on why the disclosure of the concentrations of credit risk is potentially important to the users of financial reports.

Q 7-32.   Comment on the significance of disclosing off-balance-sheet risk of accounting loss.

Q 7-33.   Comment on the significance of disclosing the fair value of financial instruments.

Problems

P 7-1.   Consider the following operating figures:

Net sales	$1,079,143
Cost and deductions:	
Cost of sales	792,755
Selling and administration	264,566
Interest expense, net	4,311
Income taxes	5,059
	1,066,691
	$ 12,452

Note: Depreciation expense totals $40,000.

Required   a. Compute the times interest earned.
           b. Compute the cash basis times interest earned.

P 7-2.   Jones Petro Company reports the following consolidated statement of income:

Operating revenues	$2,989
Costs and expenses:	
Cost of rentals and royalties	543
Cost of sales	314
Selling, service, administrative, and general expense	1,424
Total costs and expenses	2,281
Operating income	708
Other income	27
Other deductions (interest)	60
Income before income taxes	675

(continued)

Income taxes	309
Income before outside shareholders' interests	366
Outside shareholders' interests	66
Net income	$ 300

Note: Depreciation expense totals $200; operating lease payments total $150; and preferred dividends total $50. Assume that 1/3 of operating lease payments is for interest.

Required

a. Compute the times interest earned.

b. Compute the fixed charge coverage.

P 7-3.   Sherwill's statement of consolidated income is as follows:

Net sales	$658
Other income	8
	666
Costs and expenses:	
Cost of products sold	418
Selling, general, and administrative expenses	196
Interest	16
	630
Income before income taxes and extraordinary charges	36
Income taxes	18
Income before extraordinary charge	18
Extraordinary charge—losses on tornado damage (net)	4
Net income	$ 14

Note: Depreciation expense totals $200; operating lease payments total $150; and preferred dividends total $50. Assume that 1/3 of operating lease payments is for interest.

Required

a. Compute the times interest earned.

b. Compute the fixed charge coverage.

P 7-4.   Kaufman Company's balance sheet follows.

Assets

Current assets	
Cash	$ 13,445
Short-term investments—at cost (approximate market)	5,239
Trade accounts receivable, less allowance of $1,590	88,337
Inventories—at lower of cost (average method) or market:	
Finished merchandise	113,879
Work in process, raw materials and supplies	47,036
	160,915
Prepaid expenses	8,221
Total current assets	276,157
Other assets:	
Receivables, advances, and other assets	4,473
Intangibles	2,324
Total other assets	6,797
Property, plant, and equipment:	
Land	5,981
Buildings	78,908
Machinery and equipment	162,425
	247,314
Less allowances for depreciation	106,067
Net property, plant, and equipment	141,247
Total assets	$424,201

Liabilities and Shareholders' Equity

Current liabilities:	
Notes payable	$ 2,817
Trade accounts payable	23,720
Pension, interest, and other accruals	33,219

Taxes, other than income taxes	4,736
Income taxes	3,409
Total current liabilities	67,901
Long-term debt, 12% debentures	86,235
Deferred income taxes	8,768
Minority interest in subsidiaries	12,075
Total liabilities	174,979
Stockholders' equity:	
Serial preferred	9,154
Common $5.25 par value	33,540
Additional paid-in capital	3,506
Retained earnings	203,712
	249,912
Less cost of common shares in treasury	690
Total shareholders' equity	249,222
Total liabilities and shareholders' equity	$424,201

Required
a. Compute the debt ratio.
b. Compute the debt/equity ratio.
c. Compute the ratio of total debt to tangible net worth.
d. Comment on the amount of debt that Kaufman Company has.

P 7-5. Individual transactions often have a significant impact on ratios. This problem will consider the direction of such an impact.

Ratio Transaction	Times Interest Earned	Debt Ratio	Debt/ Equity Ratio	Debt to Tangible Net Worth
a. Purchase of buildings financed by mortgage.	___	___	___	___
b. Purchase of inventory on short-term loan at 1% over prime rate.	___	___	___	___
c. Declaration and payment of cash dividend.	___	___	___	___
d. Declaration and payment of stock dividend.	___	___	___	___
e. Firm increases profits by cutting cost of sales.	___	___	___	___
f. Appropriation of retained earnings.	___	___	___	___
g. Sale of common stock.	___	___	___	___
h. Repayment of long-term bank loan.	___	___	___	___
i. Conversion of bonds to common stock outstanding.	___	___	___	___
j. Sale of inventory at greater than cost.	___	___	___	___

Required Indicate the effect of each of the transactions on the ratios listed. Use + to indicate an increase, − to indicate a decrease, and 0 to indicate no effect. Assume an initial times interest earned of more than 1, and a debt ratio, debt/equity ratio, and a total debt to tangible net worth of less than 1.

P 7-6. Mr. Parks has asked you to advise him on the long-term debt-paying ability of Arodex Company. He provides you with the following ratios:

	2007	2006	2005
Times interest earned	8.2	6.0	5.5
Debt ratio	40%	39%	40%
Debt to tangible net worth	80%	81%	81%

Required
a. Give the implications and the limitations of each item separately and then the collective influence that could be drawn from them about Arodex Company's long-term debt position.
b. What warnings should you offer Mr. Parks about the limitations of ratio analysis for the purpose stated here?

P 7-7. For the year ended June 30, 2007, A.E.G. Enterprises presented the financial statements shown on page 280.

Early in the new fiscal year, the officers of the firm formalized a substantial expansion plan. The plan will increase fixed assets by $190,000,000. In addition, extra inventory will be needed to support expanded production. The increase in inventory is purported to be $10,000,000.

The firm's investment bankers have suggested the following three alternative financing plans:

Plan A: Sell preferred stock at par.

Plan B: Sell common stock at $10 per share.

Plan C: Sell long-term bonds, due in 20 years, at par ($1,000), with a stated interest rate of 16%.

A.E.G. ENTERPRISES
Balance Sheet for June 30, 2007 (in thousands)

Assets

Current assets:

Cash	$ 50,000	
Accounts receivable	60,000	
Inventory	106,000	
Total current assets		$216,000
Property, plant, and equipment	$504,000	
Less: Accumulated depreciation	140,000	364,000
Patents and other intangible assets		20,000
Total assets		$600,000

Liabilities and Stockholders' Equity

Current liabilities:

Accounts payable	$ 46,000	
Taxes payable	15,000	
Other current liabilities	32,000	
Total current liabilities		$ 93,000
Long-term debt		100,000

Stockholders' equity:

Preferred stock ($100 par, 10% cumulative, 500,000 shares authorized and issued)	50,000
Common stock ($1 par, 200,000,000 shares authorized, 100,000,000 issued)	100,000
Premium on common stock	120,000
Retained earnings	137,000
Total liabilities and stockholders' equity	$600,000

A.E.G. ENTERPRISES
Income Statement
For the Year Ended June 30, 2007
(in thousands except earnings per share)

Sales		$936,000
Cost of sales		671,000
Gross profit		$265,000
Operating expenses:		
Selling	$62,000	
General	41,000	103,000
Operating income		$162,000
Other items:		
Interest expense		20,000
Earnings before provision for income tax		$142,000
Provision for income tax		56,800
Net income		$ 85,200
Earnings per share		$ 0.83

Required

a. For the year ended June 30, 2007, compute:

   1. Times interest earned

   2. Debt ratio

   3. Debt/equity ratio

   4. Debt to tangible net worth ratio

b. Assuming the same financial results and statement balances, except for the increased assets and financing, compute the same ratios as in (a) under each financing alternative. Do not attempt to adjust retained earnings for the next year's profits.

c. Changes in earnings and number of shares will give the following earnings per share: Plan A—0.73, Plan B—0.69, and Plan C—0.73. Based on the information given, discuss the advantages and disadvantages of each alternative.

d. Why does the 10% preferred stock cost the company more than the 16% bonds?

P 7-8.   The consolidated statement of earnings of Anonymous Corporation for the year ended December 31, 2007, is as follows:

Net sales	$1,550,010,000
Other income, net	10,898,000
	1,560,908,000
Costs and expenses:	
Cost of goods sold	1,237,403,000
Depreciation and amortization	32,229,000
Selling, general, and administrative	178,850,000
Interest	37,646,000
	1,486,128,000
Earnings from continuing operations before income taxes and equity earnings	74,780,000
Income taxes	37,394,000
Earnings from continuing operations before equity earnings	37,386,000
Equity in net earnings of unconsolidated subsidiaries and affiliated companies	27,749,000
Earnings from continuing operations	65,135,000
Earnings (losses) from discontinued operations, net of applicable income taxes	6,392,000
Net earnings	$ 71,527,000

Required   a. Compute the times interest earned for 2007.
            b. Compute the times interest earned for 2007, including the equity income in the coverage.
            c. What is the impact of including equity earnings from the coverage? Why should equity income be excluded from the times interest earned coverage?

P 7-9.   Allen Company and Barker Company are competitors in the same industry. Selected financial data from their 2007 statements follow.

Balance Sheet
December 31, 2007

	Allen Company	Barker Company
Cash	$ 10,000	$ 35,000
Accounts receivable	45,000	120,000
Inventory	70,000	190,000
Investments	40,000	100,000
Intangibles	11,000	20,000
Property, plant, and equipment	180,000	520,000
Total assets	$356,000	$985,000
Accounts payable	$ 60,000	$165,000
Bonds payable	100,000	410,000
Preferred stock, $1 par	50,000	30,000
Common stock, $10 par	100,000	280,000
Retained earnings	46,000	100,000
Total liabilities and capital	$356,000	$985,000

Income Statement
For the Year Ended December 31, 2007

	Allen Company	Barker Company
Sales	$1,050,000	$2,800,000
Cost of goods sold	725,000	2,050,000
Selling and administrative expenses	230,000	580,000
Interest expense	10,000	32,000
Income taxes	42,000	65,000
Net income	$ 43,000	$ 73,000

Industry Averages:

Times interest earned	7.2 times
Debt ratio	40.3%
Debt/equity	66.6%
Debt to tangible net worth	72.7%

Required   a. Compute the following ratios for each company:
  1. Times interest earned
  2. Debt ratio
  3. Debt/equity ratio
  4. Debt to tangible net worth
  b. Is Barker Company in a position to take on additional long-term debt? Explain.
  c. Which company has the better long-term debt position? Explain.

P 7-10.   Consecutive five-year balance sheets and income statements of Laura Gibson Corporation are shown below and on the following page.

Required   a. Compute the following for the years ended December 31, 2003–2007:
  1. Times interest earned
  2. Fixed charge coverage
  3. Debt ratio
  4. Debt/equity ratio
  5. Debt to tangible net worth
  b. Comment on the debt position and the trends indicated in the long-term debt-paying ability.

Laura Gibson Corporation
Balance Sheets
December 31, 2003 through December 31, 2007

(Dollars in thousands)	2007	2006	2005	2004	2003
Assets					
Current assets:					
Cash	$ 27,000	$ 26,000	$ 25,800	$ 25,500	$ 25,000
Accounts receivable, net	135,000	132,000	130,000	129,000	128,000
Inventories	128,000	130,000	134,000	132,000	126,000
Total current assets	290,000	288,000	289,800	286,500	279,000
Property, plant, and equipment, net	250,000	248,000	247,000	246,000	243,000
Intangibles	20,000	18,000	17,000	16,000	15,000
Total assets	$560,000	$554,000	$553,800	$548,500	$537,000
Liabilities and stockholders' equity					
Current liabilities:					
Accounts payable	$ 75,000	$ 76,000	$ 76,500	$ 77,000	$ 78,000
Income taxes	13,000	13,500	14,000	13,000	13,500
Total current liabilities	88,000	89,500	90,500	90,000	91,500
Long-term debt	170,000	168,000	165,000	164,000	262,000
Stockholders' equity	302,000	296,500	298,300	294,500	183,500
Total liabilities and stockholders' equity	$560,000	$554,000	$553,800	$548,500	$537,000

Laura Gibson Corporation
Statement of Earnings
For the Years Ended December 31, 2003–2007

(In thousands, except per share)	2007	2006	2005	2004	2003
Net sales	$920,000	$950,000	$910,000	$850,000	$800,000
Cost of goods sold	640,000	648,000	624,000	580,000	552,000
Gross margin	280,000	302,000	286,000	270,000	248,000
Selling and administrative expense	156,000	157,000	154,000	150,000	147,000
Interest expense	17,000	16,000	15,000	14,500	23,000

	2007	2006	2005	2004	2003
Earnings from continuing operations before income taxes	$107,000	$129,000	$117,000	$105,500	$ 78,000
Income taxes	36,300	43,200	39,800	35,800	26,500
Earnings from continuing operations	70,700	85,800	77,200	69,700	51,500
Discontinued operating earnings (loss), net of taxes:					
From operations	(1,400)	1,300	1,400	1,450	1,600
On disposal	(900)	—	—	—	—
Earnings (loss) from discontinued operation	(2,300)	1,300	1,400	1,450	1,600
Net earnings	$ 68,400	$ 87,100	$ 78,600	$ 71,150	$ 53,100
Earnings (loss) per share:					
Continuing operations	$ 1.53	$ 1.69	$ 1.46	$ 1.37	$ 1.25
Discontinued operations	(0.03)	0.01	0.01	0.01	0.01
Net earnings per share	$ 1.50	$ 1.70	$ 1.47	$ 1.38	$ 1.26

Note: Operating lease payments were as follows: 2007, $30,000; 2006, $27,000; 2005, $28,500; 2004, $30,000; 2003, $27,000 (dollars in thousands).

P 7-11.

Required   Answer the following multiple-choice questions:

a. Which of the following ratios can be used as a guide to a firm's ability to carry debt from an income perspective?
   1. Debt ratio
   2. Debt to tangible net worth
   3. Debt/equity
   4. Times interest earned
   5. Current ratio

b. There is disagreement on all but which of the following items as to whether it should be considered a liability in the debt ratio?
   1. Short-term liabilities
   2. Reserve accounts
   3. Deferred taxes
   4. Minority shareholders' interest
   5. Preferred stock

c. A firm may have substantial liabilities that are not disclosed on the face of the balance sheet from all but which of the following?
   1. Leases
   2. Pension plans
   3. Joint ventures
   4. Contingencies
   5. Bonds payable

d. In computing the debt ratio, which of the following is subtracted in the denominator?
   1. Copyrights
   2. Trademarks
   3. Patents
   4. Marketable securities
   5. None of the above

e. All but which of these ratios are considered to be debt ratios?
   1. Times interest earned
   2. Debt ratio
   3. Debt/equity
   4. Fixed charge ratio
   5. Current ratio

f. Which of the following statements is false?
  1. The debt to tangible net worth ratio is more conservative than the debt ratio.
  2. The debt to tangible net worth ratio is more conservative than the debt/equity ratio.
  3. Times interest earned indicates an income statement view of debt.
  4. The debt/equity ratio indicates an income statement view of debt.
  5. The debt ratio indicates a balance sheet view of debt.

g. Sneider Company has long-term debt of $500,000, while Abbott Company has long-term debt of $50,000. Which of the following statements best represents an analysis of the long-term debt position of these two firms?
  1. Sneider Company's times interest earned should be lower than Abbott Company's.
  2. Abbott Company's times interest earned should be lower than Sneider Company's.
  3. Abbott Company has a better long-term borrowing ability than does Sneider Company.
  4. Sneider Company has a better long-term borrowing ability than does Abbott Company.
  5. None of the above

h. A times interest earned ratio of 0.20 to 1 means
  1. That the firm will default on its interest payment.
  2. That net income is less than the interest expense (including capitalized interest).
  3. That cash flow exceeds the net income.
  4. That the firm should reduce its debt.
  5. None of the above

i. In computing debt to tangible net worth, which of the following is *not* subtracted in the denominator?
  1. Patents
  2. Goodwill
  3. Land
  4. Bonds payable
  5. Both 3 and 4

j. The ratio fixed charge coverage
  1. Is a cash flow indication of debt-paying ability.
  2. Is an income statement indication of debt-paying ability.
  3. Is a balance sheet indication of debt-paying ability.
  4. Will usually be higher than the times interest earned ratio.
  5. None of the above

k. Under the Employee Retirement Income Security Act, a company can be liable for its pension plan up to
  1. 30% of its net worth.
  2. 30% of pension liabilities.
  3. 30% of liabilities.
  4. 40% of its net worth.
  5. None of the above

l. Which of the following statements is correct?
  1. Capitalized interest should be included with interest expense when computing times interest earned.
  2. A ratio that indicates a firm's long-term debt-paying ability from the balance sheet view is the times interest earned.
  3. Some of the items on the income statement that are excluded in order to compute times interest earned are interest expense, income taxes, and interest income.
  4. Usually, the highest times interest coverage in the most recent five-year period is used as the primary indication of the interest coverage.
  5. None of the above

m. Which of these items does *not* represent a definite commitment to pay out funds in the future?
  1. Notes payable
  2. Bonds payable
  3. Minority shareholders' interests
  4. Wages payable
  5. None of the above

Case 7-1

EXPENSING INTEREST NOW AND LATER

JOHNSON & JOHNSON AND SUBSIDIARIES*
CONSOLIDATED STATEMENTS OF EARNINGS
(Dollars in Millions Except Per Share Figures) (Note1)

	2006	2005	2004
Sales to customers	$53,324	$50,514	$47,348
Cost of products sold	15,057	14,010	13,474
Gross profit	38,267	36,504	33,874
Selling, marketing and administrative expenses	17,433	17,211	16,174
Research expense	7,125	6,462	5,344
Purchased in-process research and development (Note 17)	559	362	18
Interest income	(829)	(487)	(195)
Interest expense, net of portion capitalized (Note 3)	63	54	187
Other (income) expense, net	(671)	(214)	15
	23,680	23,388	21,543
Earnings before provision for taxes on income	14,587	13,116	12,331
Provision for taxes on income (Note 8)	3,534	3,056	4,151
Net earnings	$11,053	$10,060	$ 8,180
Basic net earnings per share (Notes 1 and 19)	$ 3.76	$ 3.38	$ 2.76
Diluted net earnings per share (Notes 1 and 19)	$ 3.73	$ 3.35	$ 2.74

3. Property, Plant and Equipment

At the end of 2006 and 2005, property, plant and equipment at cost and accumulated depreciation were:

	Dollars in Millions	
	2006	2005
Land and land improvements	$ 611	$ 502
Buildings and building equipment	7,347	5,875
Machinery and equipment	13,108	10,835
Construction in progress	2,962	2,504
	24,028	19,716
Less accumulated depreciation	10,984	8,886
	$13,044	$10,830

The company capitalizes interest expense as part of the cost of construction of facilities and equipment. Interest expense capitalized in 2006, 2005 and 2004 was $118 million, $111 million and $316 million, respectively.

Depreciation expense, including the amortization of capitalized interest in 2006, 2005 and 2004 was $1.6 billion, $1.5 billion and $1.5 billion, respectively.

Upon retirement or other disposal of property, plant and equipment, the cost and related amount of accumulated depreciation or amortization are eliminated from the asset and accumulated depreciation accounts, respectively. The difference, if any, between the net asset value and the proceeds is recorded in earnings.

Required
a. What is the amount of gross interest expense for 2006, 2005, and 2004?
b. What is the interest reported on the income statement for 2006, 2005, and 2004?

*"Johnson & Johnson and its subsidiaries have approximately 122,200 employees worldwide engaged in the research and development, manufacture and sale of a broad range of products in the health care field." 10-K

(continued)

EXPENSING INTEREST NOW AND LATER (Continued)

c. What was the interest added to cost of property, plant and equipment during 2006, 2005, and 2004?

d. When is capitalized interest recognized as an expense? Describe.

e. What was the effect on income from capitalizing interest? Describe.

f. Compute times interest earned for 2006, 2005, and 2004. Comment on the absolute amounts and the trend.

CONSIDERATION OF LEASES

Steelcase*
Consolidated Statements of Income
(In millions, except share data)

	Year Ended		
	February 25, 2005	February 27, 2004 (as restated)	February 28, 2003 (as restated)
Revenue	$2,613.8	$2,345.6	$2,529.9
Cost of sales	1,859.9	1,688.0	1,785.3
Restructuring costs	8.2	42.3	16.5
Gross profit	745.7	615.3	728.1
Operating expenses	722.3	678.5	745.6
Restructuring costs	5.2	11.2	44.7
Operating income (loss)	18.2	(74.4)	(62.2)
Interest expense	(20.9)	(18.5)	(20.9)
Other income (expense), net	7.7	—	16.4
Income (loss) from continuing operations before income tax benefit	5.0	(92.9)	(66.7)
Income tax benefit	(6.7)	(50.9)	(25.1)
Income (loss) from continuing operations	11.7	(42.0)	(41.6)
Income from discontinued operations, net of income taxes	—	2.4	4.7
Gain on sale of net assets of discontinued operations, net of income taxes	1.0	20.0	—
Income (loss) from before cumulative effect of accounting change, net of income taxes	12.7	(19.6)	(36.9)
Cumulative effect of accounting change, net of income taxes	—	(4.2)	(229.9)
Net income (loss)	$ 12.7	$ (23.8)	$ (266.8)
Basic and diluted per share data:			
Income (loss) from continuing operations	$ 0.08	$ (0.28)	$ (0.28)
Income and gain on sale of discontinued operations	0.01	0.15	0.03
Cumulative effect of accounting change	—	(0.03)	(1.56)
Earnings (loss)	$ 0.09	$ (0.16)	$ (1.81)
Dividends declared per common share	$ 0.24	$ 0.24	$ 0.24

*"Steelcase is the world's leading designer, marketer and manufacturer of office furniture and complimentary products and services. . . . " 10-K

(continued)

CONSIDERATION OF LEASES (Continued)

Steelcase
Consolidated Balance Sheets
(In millions, except share data)

	February 25, 2005	February 27, 2004 (as restated)
Assets		
Current assets:		
Cash and cash equivalents	$ 216.6	$ 182.2
Short-term investments	131.6	80.4
Accounts receivable, net of allowances of $41.6 and $44.4	378.1	363.2
Inventories	132.9	114.4
Deferred income taxes	90.2	101.7
Other current assets	107.9	103.8
Total current assets	1,057.3	945.7
Property and equipment, net	606.0	713.8
Company owned life insurance	186.1	177.9
Deferred income taxes	148.0	117.7
Goodwill	210.2	210.2
Other intangible assets, net of accumulated amortization of $40.1 and $36.0	79.8	88.1
Other assets	77.2	106.0
Total assets	$2,364.6	$2,359.4
Liabilities and Shareholders' Equity		
Current liabilities:		
Accounts payable	$ 175.9	$ 162.8
Short-term borrowings and current portion of long-term debt	67.6	34.4
Accrued expenses:		
Employee compensation	123.3	91.3
Employee benefit plan obligations	31.7	33.9
Workers' compensation claims	29.1	27.4
Income taxes payable	22.5	34.3
Product warranties	20.9	20.9
Other	138.5	139.7
Total current liabilities	609.5	544.7
Long-term liabilities:		
Long-term debt less current maturities	258.1	319.6
Employee benefit plan obligations	249.7	243.7
Other long-term liabilities	50.7	46.6
Total long-term liabilities	558.5	609.9
Total liabilities	1,168.0	1,154.6
Shareholders' equity:		
Preferred Stock—no par value; 50,000,000 shares authorized, none issues and outstanding	—	—
Class A Common Stock—no par value; 475,000,000 shares authorized, 61,084,925 and 49,544,049 issues and outstanding	162.5	123.2
Class B Convertible Common Stock—no par value; 475,000,000 shares authorized, 87,490,230 and 98,435,538 issued and outstanding	134.9	166.6
Additional paid in capital	1.3	0.2
Accumulated other comprehensive loss	(33.1)	(40.8)
Deferred compensation—restricted stock	(3.1)	(1.4)
Retained earnings	934.1	957.0
Total shareholders' equity	1,196.6	1,204.8
Total liabilities and shareholders' equity	$2,364.6	$2,359.4

Notes to Consolidated Financial Statements (in Part)

We lease certain sales offices, showrooms and equipment under non-cancelable operating leases that expire at various dates through 2020. During the normal course of business, we have entered into several sale-leaseback arrangements for certain equipment and facilities. In

(continued)

CONSIDERATION OF LEASES (Continued)

accordance with GAAP, these leases are accounted for as operating leases and any gains from the sale of the original properties were recorded as deferred gains and are amortized over the lease term. The deferred gains are included as a component of *Other Long-term Liabilities,* and amounted to $25.2 as of February 25, 2005, and $27.2 as of February 27, 2004.

**Minimum Annual Rental Commitments
Under Non-cancelable Operating Leases**

Year Ending February	Amount
2006	$ 52.1
2007	41.0
2008	35.1
2009	30.1
2010	27.0
Thereafter	105.9
	$291.2

Rent expense under all operating leases was $57.9 for 2005, $57.2 for 2004, and $58.5 for 2003, as restated.

Required
    a. Compute the following for 2005 and 2004:
        1. Times interest earned
        2. Fixed change coverage
        3. Debt ratio
        4. Debt/equity ratio
    b. Compute the debt ratio, considering operating leases.
    c. Give your opinion regarding the significance of considering operating leases in the debt ratio.

HOW MAY I HELP YOU?*

Consolidated Balance Sheets (in Part)

	January 31,	
(Amounts in millions except per share data)	2005	2004
Assets		
Property under capital lease:		
Property under capital lease	$ 4,997	$ 4,286
Less accumulated amortization	1,838	1,673
Property under capital lease, net	$ 3,159	$ 2,613
Liabilities		
Current liabilities:		
Commercial paper	$ 3,812	$ 3,267
Accounts payable	21,671	19,425
Accrued liabilities	12,155	10,671
Accrued income taxes	1,281	1,377
Long-term debt due within one year	3,759	2,904
Obligations under capital leases due within one year	210	196
Total current liabilities	$42,888	$37,840
Long-term debt	20,087	17,102
Long-term obligations under capital leases	3,582	2,997
Deferred income taxes and other	2,947	2,359
Minority interest	1,323	1,484

Required
    a. Observe that accumulated amortization is deducted from property under capital lease. Why is this described as amortization instead of depreciation?
    b. Why do the assets under capital leases not equal the liabilities under capital leases?

*"Wal-Mart Stores, Inc. operates retail stores in various formats around the world." 10-K

LOCKOUT

The Celtics Basketball Holdings, L.P. and Subsidiary included the following note in its 1998 annual report:

Note G—Commitments and Contingencies (in Part)

National Basketball Association ("NBA") players, including those that play for the Boston Celtics, are covered by a collective bargaining agreement between the NBA and the NBA Players Association (the "NBPA") that was to be in effect through June 30, 2001 (the "Collective Bargaining Agreement"). Under the terms of the Collective Bargaining Agreement, the NBA had the right to terminate the Collective Bargaining Agreement after the 1997–98 season if it was determined that the aggregate salaries and benefits paid by all NBA teams for the 1997–98 season exceeded 51.8% of projected Basketball Related Income, as defined in the Collective Bargaining Agreement ("BRI"). Effective June 30, 1998, the Board of Governors of the NBA voted to exercise that right and reopen the Collective Bargaining Agreement, as it had been determined that the aggregate salaries and benefits paid by the NBA teams for the 1997–98 season would exceed 51.8% of projected BRI. Effective July 1, 1998, the NBA commenced a lockout of NBA players in support of its attempt to reach a new collective bargaining agreement. The NBA and the NBPA have been engaged in negotiations regarding a new collective bargaining agreement, but as of September 18, 1998, no agreement has been reached. In the event that the lockout extends into the 1998–99 season, NBA teams, including the Boston Celtics, will refund amounts paid by season ticket holders (plus interest) for any games that are canceled as a result of the lockout. In addition, as a result of the lockout, NBA teams have not made any payments due to players with respect to the 1998–99 season. The NBPA has disputed the NBA's position on this matter, and both the NBA and the NBPA have presented their cases to an independent arbitrator, who will make his ruling no later than the middle of October 1998. As of September 18, 1998, the arbitrator has not ruled on this matter.

Although the ultimate outcome of this matter cannot be determined at this time, any loss of games as a result of the absence of a collective bargaining agreement or the continuation of the lockout will have a material adverse effect on the Partnership's financial condition and its results of operations. Further, if NBA teams, including the Boston Celtics, are required to honor the player contracts for the 1998–99 season and beyond without agreeing to a new collective bargaining agreement or without ending the lockout, which would result in the loss of games, the Partnership's financial condition and results of operations will be materially and adversely affected.

The Partnership has employment agreements with officers, coaches and players of the basketball team (Celtics Basketball). Certain of the contracts provide for guaranteed payments which must be paid even if the employee is injured or terminated. Amounts required to be paid under such contracts in effect as of September 18, 1998, including option years and $8,100,000 included in accrued expenses at June 30, 1998, but excluding deferred compensation commitments disclosed in Note E—Deferred Compensation, are as follows:

Years ending June 30, 1999	$32,715,000
2000	33,828,000
2001	27,284,000
2002	20,860,000
2003	19,585,000
2004 and thereafter	10,800,000

Commitments for the year ended June 30, 1999, include payments due to players under contracts for the 1998–99 season in the amount of $18,801,000, which are currently not being paid as a result of the lockout described above.

(continued)

LOCKOUT (Continued)

Celtics Basketball maintains disability and life insurance policies on most of its key players. The level of insurance coverage maintained is based on management's determination of the insurance proceeds which would be required to meet its guaranteed obligations in the event of permanent or total disability of its key players.

Required   Discuss how to incorporate the contingency note into an analysis of Celtics Basketball Holdings, L.P. and Subsidiary.

MANY EMPLOYERS*

Multi-Employer Pension Plans

Safeway participates in various multi-employer retirement plans, covering substantially all Company employees not covered under the Company's non-contributory retirement plans, pursuant to agreements between the Company and various unions. These plans are generally defined benefit plans; however, in many cases, specific benefit levels are not negotiated with or known by the employer-contributors. Contributions of $253.8 million in 2006, $234.5 million in 2005 and $196.8 million in 2004 were made and charged to expense. The increase from the 2005 contributions was largely due to the expiration of a pension holiday.

Required   a.   What were the contributions to multiemployer pension plans for 2006, 2005, and 2004? Comment on the trend.
              b.   Determine the total liability for multiemployer pension plans at the end of 2006.
              c.   What control does Safeway, Inc., have over multiemployer pension plans?

*"Safeway, Inc. is one of the largest food and drug retailers in North America, with 1,761 stores at year-end 2006." 10-K

POSTRETIREMENT COMMITMENTS*

Retirement Restoration Plan

The Retirement Restoration Plan provides death benefits and supplemental income payments for senior executives after retirement. The Company recognized expense of $5.2 million in 2006, $6.4 million in 2005 and $7.1 million in 2004. The aggregate projected benefit obligation of the Retirement Restoration Plan was approximately $57.0 million at year-end 2006 and $72.8 million at year-end 2005.

Postretirement Benefits Other than Pensions

In addition to the Company's retirement plans and the Retirement Restoration Plan benefits, the Company sponsors plans that provide postretirement medical and life insurance benefits to certain employees. Retirees share a portion of the cost of the postretirement medical plans. Safeway pays all the costs of the life insurance plans. The plans are not funded.

The Company's accrued postretirement benefit obligation ("APBO") was $51.7 million at year-end 2006 and $50.3 million at year-end 2005. The APBO represents the actuarial present value of the benefits expected to be paid after retirement. Postretirement benefit expense was $5.5 million in 2006, $4.2 million in 2005 and $10.3 million in 2004.

*"Safeway, Inc. is one of the largest food and drug retailers in North America, with 1,761 stores at year-end 2006." 10-K

(continued)

Case 7-6	POSTRETIREMENT COMMITMENTS (Continued)

Required a. 1. Retirement Restoration Plan:
What was the recognized expense for 2006, 2005, and 2004?
2. Postretirement Benefits Other than Pension:
What was the benefit expense for 2006, 2005, and 2004?
b. 1. Retirement Restoration Plan:
What was the aggregate projected benefit obligation at the end of 2006 and 2005?
2. Postretirement Benefits Other than Pensions:
What was the postretirement benefit obligation at the end of 2006 and 2005?
c. How much is funded for these plans at the end of 2006?

Case 7-7	PLAY IT SAFE

Safeway Inc.* presented the following consolidated statements of income and partial pension note with its 2006 annual report.

SAFEWAY INC. AND SUBSIDIARIES
Consolidated Statements of Operations (in Part)
(In millions, except per-share amounts)

	52 Weeks 2006	52 Weeks 2005	52 Weeks 2004
Sales and other revenue	$ 40,185.0	$ 38,416.0	$ 35,822.9
Cost of products sold	(28,604.0)	(27,303.1)	(25,227.6)
Gross profit	11,581.0	11,112.9	10,595.3
Operating and administrative expense	(9,981.2)	(9,898.2)	(9,422.5)
Operating profit	1,599.8	1,214.7	1,172.8
Interest expense	(396.1)	(402.6)	(411.2)
Other income, net	36.3	36.9	32.3
Income before income taxes	1,240.0	849.0	793.9
Income taxes	(369.4)	(287.9)	(233.7)
Net income	$ 870.6	$ 561.1	$ 560.2

* * * * *

SAFEWAY INC. AND SUBSIDIARIES
Consolidated Balance Sheets (in Part)
(In millions, except per-share amounts)

	Year-End 2006	Year-End 2005
Total current assets	$ 3,565.7	$ 3,702.4
Total assets	16,273.8	15,756.9
Total current liabilities	4,601.4	4,263.9
Total liabilities	10,606.9	10,837.2
Total stockholders' equity	5,666.9	4,919.7

* * * * *

Note I: Employee Benefit Plans and Collective Bargaining Agreements (in Part)

Retirement Plans The Company maintains defined benefit, non-contributory retirement plans for substantially all of its employees not participating in multi-employer pension plans.

Safeway's adoption of SFAS No. 158 required the Company to recognize the funded status of its retirement plans on its consolidated balance sheet beginning as of fiscal 2006 year end. Under SFAS No. 158, the benefit obligation for pension plans was measured as the projected benefit obligation. The benefit obligation for postretirement benefit plans was measured as the accumulated benefit obligation.

*"Safeway Inc. is one of the largest food and drug retailers in North America, with 1,761 stores at year-end 2006." 10-K

(continued)

The following tables provide a reconciliation of the changes in the retirement plans' benefit obligation and fair value of assets over the two-year period ended December 30, 2006 and a statement of the funded status as of year-end 2006 and 2005 (in millions):

	2006	2005
Change in projected benefit obligation:		
Beginning balance	$2,110.1	$2,005.5
Service cost	101.1	108.0
Interest cost	129.3	125.5
Plan amendments	29.7	57.0
Actuarial gain	(40.0)	(99.2)
Benefit payments	(143.8)	(107.9)
Currency translation adjustment	(4.8)	21.2
Ending balance	$2,181.6	$2,110.1

	2006	2005
Change in fair value of plan assets		
Beginning balance	$2,102.8	$2,029.7
Actual return on plan assets	235.1	146.6
Employer contributions	25.0	16.7
Benefit payments	(143.8)	(107.9)
Currency translation adjustment	(4.4)	17.7
Ending balance	$2,214.7	$2,102.8

	2006	2005
Funded status:		
Fair value of plan assets	$ 2,214.7	$ 2,102.8
Projected benefit obligation	(2,181.6)	(2,110.1)
Funded status	33.1	(7.3)
Amounts not yet recognized		
Adjustment for difference in book and tax basis of assets	N/A	(165.1)
Unamortized prior service cost	N/A	130.9
Unrecognized actuarial loss	N/A	265.8
Additional minimum liability adjustment	N/A	(44.9)
Net amount recognized in financial position	$ 33.1	$ 179.4
Components of net amount recognized in financial position:		
Prepaid pension costs	137.3	179.4
Other accrued liabilities (current liability)	(1.3)	—
Pension and postretirement benefit obligations (non-current liability)	(102.9)	—
	$ 33.1	$ 179.4
Amounts recognized in accumulated other comprehensive income as a result of adoption of SFAS No. 158 consist of:		
Net actuarial loss	179.2	N/A
Prior service cost	124.9	N/A
Transition obligation	5.6	N/A
Difference in the book and tax basis of assets	(165.1)	N/A
Deferred taxes	(47.9)	N/A
Total	$ 96.7	$ N/A

N/A (Not Applicable): The adoption of SFAS No. 158 resulted in recognition of previously unrecognized net actuarial loss and prior service cost on our consolidated financial position. Overall, the prepaid asset was adjusted and a liability recognized through an adjustment to other comprehensive income.

Safeway expects approximately $5.8 million of the net actuarial loss, $22.8 million of the prior service cost and $1.4 million of the transition obligation to be recognized as a component of net periodic benefit cost in 2007.

(continued)

Case 7-7   PLAY IT SAFE (Continued)

Underfunded plans

Year-end information for plans with accumulated benefit obligations in excess of plan assets (in millions):

	2006	2005
Funded status:		
Fair value of plan assets	$ 567.9	$ 517.2
Projected benefit obligation	(672.1)	(616.6)
Funded status	$(104.2)	$ (99.4)

The following table provides the components of 2006, 2005 and 2004 net pension expense for the retirement plans (in millions):

	2006	2005	2004
Estimated return on assets	$191.2	$ 167.8	$ 154.0
Service cost	(101.1)	(108.0)	(109.9)
Interest cost	(129.3)	(125.5)	(107.8)
Amortization of prior service cost	(22.4)	(16.8)	(16.6)
Amortization of unrecognized losses	(21.5)	(33.1)	(32.6)
Net pension expense	$ (83.1)	$(115.6)	$(112.9)

Prior service costs are amortized on a straight-line basis over the average remaining service period of active participants. Actuarial gains and losses are amortized over the average remaining service life of active participants when the accumulation of such gains and losses exceeds 10% of the greater of the projected benefit obligation and the fair value of plan assets. The Company uses its fiscal year-end date as the measurement date for its plans. The accumulated benefit obligation for all Safeway plans was $2,011.4 million at year-end 2006 and $1,881.5 million at year-end 2005.

* * * * *

Safeway expects to contribute approximately $31.8 million to its defined benefit pension plan trusts in 2007.

* * * * *

Collective Bargaining Agreements   At year-end 2006, Safeway had more than 207,000 full and part-time employees. Approximately 80% of Safeway's employees in the United States and Canada are covered by collective bargaining agreements negotiated with union locals affiliated with one of 10 different international unions. There are approximately 400 such agreements, typically having three-year terms, with some agreements having terms up to five years. Accordingly, Safeway renegotiates a significant number of these agreements every year.

Required
a. For the defined benefit, noncontributory retirement plans, compare pension expense (cost) with operating revenue for 2006, 2005, and 2004. Comment.
b. For the defined benefit, noncontributory retirement plans, compare pension expense (cost) with income before income taxes for 2006, 2005, and 2004. Comment.
c. For the defined benefit, noncontributory retirement plans, compare the benefit obligations with the value of plan assets at the end of 2006 and 2005. Comment.
d. Are all of Safeway's defined benefit, noncontributory retirement plans overfunded or underfunded? Comment.
e. Are the components of net amount recognized in financial position (related to defined benefit, noncontributory retirement plans) material in relation to the total balance sheet amounts? Comment.

PRINTERS

TRANSACT TECHNOLOGIES INCORPORATED*
Notes to Consolidated Financial Statements (in Part)

9. RETIREMENT SAVINGS PLAN

On April 11, 1997, we established the TransAct Technologies Retirement Savings Plan [the "401(k) Plan"], a defined contribution plan under Section 401(k) of the Internal Revenue Code. All full-time employees are eligible to participate in the 401(k) Plan at the beginning of the calendar quarter immediately following their date of hire. We match employees' contributions at a rate of 50% of employees' contributions up to the first 6% of the employees' compensation contributed to the 401(k) Plan. Our matching contributions were $249,000, $225,000 and $201,000 in 2006, 2005 and 2004, respectively.

TRANSACT TECHNOLOGIES INCORPORATED
CONSOLIDATED STATEMENTS OF INCOME (in Part)
(In thousands, except per share data)

| | Year Ended December 31, | | |
	2006	2005	2004
Net sales	$64,328	$51,091	$59,847
Income before income taxes	6,033	329	8,437

Required
    a. In general, what type of retirement savings plan does TransAct Technologies have?
    b. Give your opinion as to the materiality of the pension plan.
    c. Give your opinion as to the control of pension expense.

*"TransAct Technologies Incorporated . . . designs, develops, assembles, markets and services world-class transaction printers under the Epic™ and Ithaca® brand names." 10-K

FAIR VALUE OF FINANCIAL INSTRUMENTS

MSC Software Corporation*
Notes to Consolidated Financial Statements (in Part)

Note 1—Nature of Operations and Summary of Significant Accounting Policies (in Part)

Fair Value of Financial Instruments—At December 31, 2004, 2005 and 2006, the Company's financial instruments included cash and cash equivalents, trade receivables, marketable securities, accounts payable, notes payable to shareholders, subordinated notes payable and subordinated convertible notes. The carrying amount of cash and cash equivalents, trade receivables and accounts payable approximates fair value due to the short-term maturities of these instruments. The estimated fair value of marketable equity investments, debt securities and subordinated convertible notes were determined based on quoted market prices at year-end. The estimated fair value of the notes payable to shareholders and subordinated notes payable was determined based on the present value of their future cash flows using a discount rate that approximates the Company's current borrowing rate.

*"We are a leader in the development, marketing and support of enterprise simulation solutions, including simulation software and related services." 10-K

(continued)

Case	FAIR VALUE OF FINANCIAL INSTRUMENTS (Continued)
7-9	

The carrying amounts and estimated fair values of the Company's financial instruments as of December 31, 2005 and 2006 are as follows (in thousands):

	2005		2006	
	Carrying Amount	Estimated Fair Value	Carrying Amount	Estimated Fair Value
Financial Instrument Assets:				
Equity Investments	$ 12,820	$ 12,820	$14,123	$14,123
Pledged Securities	6,074	5,974	—	—
Investments Held in Supplemental				
Retirement Plan	828	828	1,082	1,082
Financial Instrument Liabilities:				
Subordinated Notes Payable, including				
Current Portion	(7,375)	(7,926)	(7,556)	(5,238)
Subordinated Convertible Debentures	(100,000)	(199,000)	—	—

Required   Give your opinion as to the fair value of financial instruments in relation to carrying amount.

Case	EAT AT MY RESTAURANT—DEBT VIEW
7-10	

With this case, we review the debt of several restaurant companies. The restaurant companies reviewed and the year-end dates are as follows:

1. **Yum Brands, Inc. (December 30, 2006; December 30, 2005)**
    "Yum Brands consist of six operating segments; KFC, Pizza Hut, Taco Bell, LJS/A&W, Yum Restaurants International . . ., and Yum Restaurants China." 10-K

2. **Panera Bread (December 26, 2006; December 27, 2005)**
    "As of December 26, 2006, we operated directly and through area development agreements with 41 franchise groups, bakery-cafes under Panera Bread® and Saint Louis Bread® names." 10-K

3. **Starbucks (October 1, 2006; October 2, 2005)**
    "Starbucks purchases and roasts high-quality whole bean coffees and sells them, along with fresh, rich-brewed coffees, Italian-style espresso beverages, cold blended beverages, a variety of complementary food items, coffee-related accessories and equipment, a selection of premium teas and a line of compact discs, primarily through company-operated retail stores." 10-K

	Yums Brands, Inc.		Panera Bread		Starbucks	
Data Reviewed	2006	2005	2006	2005	2006	2005
Times interest earned	8.19	9.08	1,008.35	1,644.56	73.94	554.61
Fixed charge coverage						
(times per year)	4.55	4.79	7.06	8.44	5.56	6.13
Debt ratio (%)	77.38	75.00	26.71	27.58	49.68	40.51
Debt/equity ratio (%)	342.10	300.07	36.45	38.07	98.74	68.10
Debt to tangible net						
worth ratio (%)	1,148.60	748.36	43.41	45.51	108.45	72.54

Required   a. Comment on the times interest earned for each company.
           b. Comment on the relative times interest earned between the companies.
           c. Comment on the fixed charge coverage for each company.
           d. Comment on the relative fixed charge coverage for each company.

(continued)

EAT AT MY RESTAURANT—DEBT VIEW (Continued)

e. Comment on the relative times interest earned vs. the fixed charge coverage. Why is the times interest earned materially higher than the fixed charge coverage?

f. Why is the debt/equity materially more than the debt ratio?

g. Considering the debt ratio, comment on the relative debt position of these companies.

h. Why is the debt to tangible net worth ratio materially higher than the debt/equity ratio?

Thomson One *Business School Edition*

Please complete the Web case that covers material discussed in this chapter at academic.cengage .com/accounting/Gibson. You'll be using Thomson One Business School Edition, a powerful tool, that combines a full range of fundamental financial information, earnings estimates, market data, and source documents for 500 publicly traded companies.

Endnotes

1. *Statement of Financial Accounting Standards No. 5,* "Accounting for Contingencies" (Stamford, Conn.: Financial Accounting Standards Board, 1975), par. 1.

2. *Statement of Financial Accounting Standards No. 5,* par. 8.

3. *Statement of Financial Accounting Standards No. 5,* par. 17.

4. *Statement of Financial Accounting Standards No. 105,* "Disclosure of Information About Financial Instruments with Off-Balance-Sheet Risk and Financial Instruments with Concentrations of Credit Risk" (Stamford, Conn.: Financial Accounting Standards Board, 1990), par. 17.

5. *Statement of Financial Accounting Standards No. 105,* par. 18.

6. *Statement of Financial Accounting Standards No. 107,* "Disclosure About Fair Value of Financial Instruments" (Stamford, Conn.: Financial Accounting Standards Board, 1991), par. 10.

Chapter 8

Profitability

Profitability is the ability of the firm to generate earnings. Analysis of profit is of vital concern to stockholders since they derive revenue in the form of dividends. Further, increased profits can cause a rise in market price, leading to capital gains. Profits are also important to creditors because profits are one source of funds for debt coverage. Management uses profit as a performance measure.

In profitability analysis, absolute figures are less meaningful than earnings measured as a percentage of a number of bases: the productive assets, the owners' and creditors' capital employed, and sales.

Profitability Measures

The income statement contains several figures that might be used in profitability analysis. In general, the primary financial analysis of profit ratios should include only the types of income arising from the normal operations of the business. This excludes the following:

1. Discontinued operations
2. Extraordinary items

Exhibit 4-3 in Chapter 4 illustrates an income statement with these items. Review this section on special income statement items in Chapter 4 before continuing with the discussion of profitability. Equity in earnings of nonconsolidated subsidiaries and the minority share of earnings are also important to the analysis of profitability. Chapter 4 covers these items, and Exhibits 4-5 and 4-9 illustrate the concepts.

Trend analysis should also consider only income arising from the normal operations of the business. An illustration will help justify this reasoning. XYZ Corporation had net income of $100,000 in Year 1 and $150,000 in Year 2. Year 2, however, included an extraordinary gain of $60,000. In reality, XYZ suffered a drop in profit from operating income.

NET PROFIT MARGIN

A commonly used profit measure is return on sales, often termed net profit margin. If a company reports that it earned 6% last year, this statistic usually means that its profit was 6% of sales. Calculate net profit margin as follows:

$$\text{Net Profit Margin} = \frac{\begin{array}{c}\text{Net Income Before Minority Share of Earnings,}\\ \text{Equity Income and Nonrecurring Items}\end{array}}{\text{Net Sales}}$$

This ratio gives a measure of net income dollars generated by each dollar of sales. While it is desirable for this ratio to be high, competitive forces within an industry, economic conditions, use of debt financing, and operating characteristics such as high fixed costs will cause the net profit margin to vary between and within industries.

Exhibit 8-1 shows the net profit margin using the 2007 and 2006 figures for Nike. This analysis shows that Nike's net profit margin declined moderately, but would still be considered high.

Exhibit	8-1	NIKE, INC.		

Net Profit Margin			

Years Ended May 31, 2007 and 2006		
(In millions)	**2007**	**2006**
Net income [A]	$ 1,491.5	$ 1,392.0
Net sales [B]	$16,325.9	$14,954.9
Net profit margin [A ÷ B]	9.14%	9.31%

Several refinements to the net profit margin ratio can make it more accurate than the ratio computation in this book. Numerator refinements include removing "other income" and "other expense" items from net income. These items do not relate to net sales (denominator). Therefore, they can cause a distortion in the net profit margin.

This book does not adjust the net profit margin ratio for these items because this often requires an advanced understanding of financial statements beyond the level intended. Also, this chapter covers operating income margin, operating asset turnover, and return on operating assets. These ratios provide a look at the firm's operations.

When working the problems in this book, do not remove "other income" or "other expense" when computing the net profit margin unless otherwise instructed by the problem. In other analyses, if you elect to refine a net profit margin computation by removing "other income" or "other expense" items from net income, remove them net of the firm's tax rate. This is a reasonable approximation of the tax effect.

If you do not refine a net profit margin computation for "other income" and "other expense" items, at least observe whether the company has a net "other income" or a net "other expense." A net "other income" distorts the net profit margin on the high side, while a net "other expense" distorts the profit margin on the low side.

The Nike statement can be used to illustrate the removal of items that do not relate to net sales. Exhibit 8-2 shows the net profit margin computed with these items removed for 2007 and 2006. The adjusted computation results in the 2007 net profit margin being decreased by 0.29% and the 2006 net profit margin being decreased by 0.14%. Both of these decreases are likely to be considered immaterial, but the 2007 decrease was over twice the 2006 decrease. The trend between 2006 and 2007 was negative, and this negative trend increased with the revised computation.

TOTAL ASSET TURNOVER

Total asset turnover measures the activity of the assets and the ability of the firm to generate sales through the use of the assets. Compute total asset turnover as follows:

$$\text{Total Asset Turnover} = \frac{\text{Net Sales}}{\text{Average Total Assets}}$$

Exhibit 8-3 shows total asset turnover for Nike for 2007 and 2006. The total asset turnover decreased from 1.60 to 1.59. This decrease would be considered to be immaterial.

The total asset turnover computation has refinements that relate to assets (denominator) but do not relate to net sales (numerator). Examples would be the exclusion of investments

| Exhibit | 8-2 | NIKE, INC. |

Net Profit Margin (Revised Computation)

Years Ended May 31, 2007 and 2006

(In millions)	2007	2006
Net income	$1,491.5	$1,392.0
Tax rate:		
Provision for income taxes [A]	708.4	749.6
Income before income taxes [B]	2,199.9	2,141.6
Tax rate [A ÷ B]*	32.20%	35.00%
Items not related to net sales:		
Interest (income) expense, net	(67.2)	(36.8)
Other (income) expense, net	(0.9)	4.4
Net (income) expense not related to net sales	(68.1)	(32.4)
Net (income) expense not related to net sales × (1 − Tax rate)	(46.17)	(21.06)
Net income minus net of tax items not related to net sales [C]	1,445.33	1,370.94
Net sales [D]	16,325.9	14,954.9
Adjusted net profit margin [C ÷ D]	8.85%	9.17%

*The tax rate could also be determined from the income tax note.

| Exhibit | 8-3 | NIKE, INC. |

Total Asset Turnover

Years Ended May 31, 2007 and 2006

(In millions)	2007	2006
Net sales [A]	$16,325.9	$14,954.9
Average total assets:		
Beginning of year	$ 9,869.6	$ 8,793.6
End of year	10,688.3	9,869.6
Total	$20,557.9	$18,663.2
Average [B]	$10,279.0	$ 9,331.6
Total asset turnover [A ÷ B]	1.59 times	1.60 times

and construction in progress. This book does not make these refinements. This chapter covers operating income margin, operating asset turnover, and return on operating assets.

If the refinements are not made, observe the investment account, Construction in Progress, and other assets that do not relate to net sales. The presence of these accounts distorts the total asset turnover on the low side. (Actual turnover is better than the computation indicates.)

RETURN ON ASSETS

Return on assets measures the firm's ability to utilize its assets to create profits by comparing profits with the assets that generate the profits. Compute the **return on assets** as follows:

$$\text{Return on Assets} = \frac{\text{Net Income Before Minority Share of Earnings and Nonrecurring Items}}{\text{Average Total Assets}}$$

Exhibit 8-4 shows the 2007 and 2006 return on assets for Nike. The return on total assets for Nike decreased moderately in 2007.

Theoretically, the best average would be based on month-end figures, which are not available to the outside user. Computing an average based on beginning and ending figures provides

Exhibit	8-4	NIKE, INC.		

Return on Assets

Years Ended May 31, 2007 and 2006

(In millions)	2007	2006
Net income [A]	$ 1,491.5	$1,392.0
Average total assets [B]	$10,279.0	$9,331.6
Return on assets [A ÷ B]	14.51%	14.92%

a rough approximation that does not consider the timing of interim changes in assets. Such changes might be related to seasonal factors.

However, even a simple average based on beginning and ending amounts requires two figures. Ratios for two years require three years of balance sheet data. Since an annual report only contains two balance sheets, obtaining the data for averages may be a problem. If so, ending balance sheet figures may be used consistently instead of averages for ratio analysis. Similar comments could be made about other ratios that utilize balance sheet figures.

DuPont Return on Assets

The net profit margin, the total asset turnover, and the return on assets are usually reviewed together because of the direct influence that the net profit margin and the total asset turnover have on return on assets. This book reviews these ratios together. When these ratios are reviewed together, it is called the DuPont return on assets.

The rate of return on assets can be broken down into two component ratios: the net profit margin and the total asset turnover. These ratios allow for improved analysis of changes in the return on assets percentage. E. I. DuPont de Nemours and Company developed this method of separating the rate of return ratio into its component parts. Compute the DuPont return on assets as follows:

$$\frac{\text{Net Income Before Minority Share of Earnings and Nonrecurring Items}}{\text{Average Total Assets}} = \frac{\text{Net Income Before Minority Share of Earnings and Nonrecurring Items}}{\text{Net Sales}} \times \frac{\text{Net Sales}}{\text{Average Total Assets}}$$

Exhibit 8-5 shows the DuPont return on assets for Nike for 2007 and 2006. Separating the ratio into the two elements allows for discussion of the causes for the increase in the percentage of return on assets. Exhibit 8-5 indicates that Nike's return on assets decreased primarily because of a decrease in net profit margin. The decrease in return on assets was slightly caused by the very slight decrease in total asset turnover.

Exhibit	8-5	NIKE, INC.		

DuPont Return on Assets

Years Ended May 31, 2007 and 2006

	Return on Assets*	=	Net Profit Margin	×	Total Asset Turnover
2007	14.51%	=	9.14%	×	1.59
2006	14.92%	=	9.31%	×	1.60

*There are some minor differences due to rounding.

INTERPRETATION THROUGH DUPONT ANALYSIS

The following examples help to illustrate the use of this analysis:

Example 1

	Return on Assets	=	Net Profit Margin	×	Total Asset Turnover
Year 1	10%	=	5%	×	2.0
Year 2	10%	=	4%	×	2.5

Example 1 shows how a more efficient use of assets can offset rising costs such as labor or materials.

Example 2

	Return on Assets	=	Net Profit Margin	×	Total Asset Turnover
Firm A					
Year 1	10%	=	4.0%	×	2.5
Year 2	8%	=	4.0%	×	2.0
Firm B					
Year 1	10%	=	4.0%	×	2.5
Year 2	8%	=	3.2%	×	2.5

Example 2 shows how a trend in return on assets can be better explained through the breakdown into two ratios. The two firms have identical returns on assets. Further analysis shows that Firm A suffers from a slowdown in asset turnover. It is generating fewer sales for the assets invested. Firm B suffers from a reduction in the net profit margin. It is generating less profit per dollar of sales.

VARIATION IN COMPUTATION OF DUPONT RATIOS CONSIDERING ONLY OPERATING ACCOUNTS

It is often argued that only operating assets should be considered in the return on asset calculation. Operating assets exclude construction in progress, long-term investments, intangibles, and the other assets category from total assets. Similarly, operating income—the profit generated by manufacturing, merchandising, or service functions—that equals net sales less the cost of sales and operating expenses should also be used instead of net income.

The DuPont analysis, considering only operating accounts, requires a computation of operating income and operating assets. Exhibit 8-6 shows the computations of operating income and operating assets for Nike. This includes operating income for 2007 and 2006 and operating assets for 2007, 2006, and 2005.

The operating ratios may give significantly different results from net earnings ratios if a firm has large amounts of nonoperating assets. For example, if a firm has heavy investments in unconsolidated subsidiaries, and if these subsidiaries pay large dividends, then other income may be a large portion of net earnings. The profit picture may not be as good if these earnings from other sources are eliminated by analyzing operating ratios. Since earnings from investments are not derived from the primary business, the lower profit figures that represent normal earnings will typically be more meaningful.

OPERATING INCOME MARGIN

The operating income margin includes only operating income in the numerator. Compute the operating income margin as follows:

$$\text{Operating Income Margin} = \frac{\text{Operating Income}}{\text{Net Sales}}$$

Exhibit 8-7 indicates the operating income margin for Nike in 2007 and 2006. It shows a substantial decrease in 2007 in the operating income margin percentage.

Exhibit	8-6	NIKE, INC.

Operating Income and Operating Assets

Years Ended May 31, 2007 and 2006

(In millions)	2007	2006	
Operating income:			
Net sales [A]	$16,325.9	$14,954.9	
Operating expenses:			
Cost of products sold	$ 9,165.4	$ 8,367.9	
Selling, general and administrative	5,028.7	4,477.8	
Total operating expenses [B]	$14,194.1	$12,845.7	
Operating income [A – B]	$ 2,131.8	$ 2,109.2	
	2007	**2006**	**2005**
Operating assets:			
Total assets [A]	$10,688.3	$9,869.6	$8,793.6
Less: Construction in progress, identifiable intangible assets, net, goodwill, deferred income taxes and other assets [B]	1,027.9	947.3	909.8
Operating assets [A – B]	$ 9,660.4	$8,922.3	$7,883.8

Exhibit	8-7	NIKE, INC.

Operating Income Margin

Years Ended May 31, 2007 and 2006

(In millions)	2007	2006
Operating income [A]	$ 2,131.8	$ 2,109.2
Net sales [B]	$16,325.9	$14,954.9
Operating income margin [A ÷ B]	13.06%	14.10%

OPERATING ASSET TURNOVER

This ratio measures the ability of operating assets to generate sales dollars. Compute operating asset turnover as follows:

$$\text{Operating Asset Turnover} = \frac{\text{Net Sales}}{\text{Average Operating Assets}}$$

Exhibit 8-8 shows the operating asset turnover for Nike in 2007 and 2006. It indicates a slight decrease from 2006 to 2007. This slight decrease is similar to the slight decrease in total asset turnover.

RETURN ON OPERATING ASSETS

Adjusting for nonoperating items results in the following formula for **return on operating assets:**

$$\text{Return on Operating Assets} = \frac{\text{Operating Income}}{\text{Average Operating Assets}}$$

Exhibit 8-9 shows the return on operating assets for Nike for 2007 and 2006. It indicates a decrease in the return on operating assets from 2006 to 2007.

Exhibit 8-8	NIKE, INC.

Operating Asset Turnover

Years Ended May 31, 2007 and 2006

(In millions)	2007	2006
Net sales [A]	$16,325.9	$14,954.9
Average operating assets:		
Beginning of year	$ 8,922.3	$ 7,883.8
End of year	9,660.4	8,922.3
Total [B]	$18,582.7	$16,806.1
Average [B ÷ 2] = [C]	$ 9,291.4	$ 8,403.5
Operating asset turnover [A ÷ C]	1.76 times per year	1.78 times per year

Exhibit 8-9	NIKE, INC.

Return on Operating Assets

Years Ended May 31, 2007 and 2006

(In millions)	2007	2006
Operating income [A]	$2,131.8	$2,109.2
Average operating assets [B]	$9,291.4	$8,403.1
Return on operating assets [A ÷ B]	22.94%	25.10%

The return on operating assets can be viewed in terms of the DuPont analysis that follows:

$$\text{DuPont Return on Operating Assets} = \frac{\text{Operating Income Margin}}{} \times \frac{\text{Operating Asset Turnover}}{}$$

Exhibit 8-10 indicates the DuPont return on operating assets for Nike for 2007 and 2006. This figure supports the conclusion that a substantial decrease in operating income margin and a slight decrease in operating asset turnover resulted in a substantial decrease in return on operating assets.

Exhibit 8-10	NIKE, INC.

DuPont Analysis with Operating Accounts

Years Ended May 31, 2007 and 2006

	Return on Operating Assets*	=	Operating Income Margin	×	Operating Asset Turnover
2007	22.94%	=	13.06%	×	1.76
2006	25.10%	=	14.10%	×	1.78

*There are some differences due to rounding.

SALES TO FIXED ASSETS

This ratio measures the firm's ability to make productive use of its property, plant, and equipment by generating sales dollars. Since construction in progress does not contribute to current sales, it should be excluded from net fixed assets. This ratio may not be meaningful because of old fixed assets or a labor-intensive industry. In these cases, the ratio is substantially higher because of the low fixed asset base. Compute the **sales to fixed assets** as follows:

$$\text{Sales to Fixed Assets} = \frac{\text{Net Sales}}{\text{Average Net Fixed Assets}}$$
$$\text{(Exclude Construction in Progress)}$$

Exhibit 8-11 shows the sales to fixed assets for Nike for 2007 and 2006. It increased substantially between 2006 and 2007. Sales increases more than kept up with net fixed assets increases.

Exhibit	8-11	NIKE, INC.

Sales to Fixed Assets (Exclude Construction in Progress)

Years Ended May 31, 2007 and 2006

(In millions)	2007	2006
Net sales [A]	$16,325.9	$14,954.9
Net fixed assets: (Exclude Construction in Progress)		
Beginning of year	$ 1,576.3	$ 1,532.7
End of year	1,583.9	1,576.3
Total [B]	$ 3,160.2	$ 3,109.0
Average [B ÷ 2] = [C]	$ 1,580.1	$ 1,554.5
Sales to fixed assets [A ÷ C]	10.33 times per year	9.62 times per year

RETURN ON INVESTMENT (ROI)

The **return on investment (ROI)** applies to ratios measuring the income earned on the invested capital. These types of measures are widely used to evaluate enterprise performance. Since return on investment is a type of return on capital, this ratio measures the ability of the firm to reward those who provide long-term funds and to attract providers of future funds. Compute the return on investment as follows:

$$\text{Return on Investment} = \frac{\begin{array}{c}\text{Net Income Before Minority Share of}\\ \text{Earnings and Nonrecurring Items +}\\ \text{[(Interest Expense)} \times (1 - \text{Tax Rate})]\end{array}}{\text{Average (Long-Term Liabilities + Equity)}}$$

This ratio evaluates the earnings performance of the firm without regard to the way the investment is financed. It measures the earnings on investment and indicates how well the firm utilizes its asset base. Exhibit 8-12 shows the return on investment for Nike for 2007 and 2006. This ratio decreased slightly between 2006 and 2007.

RETURN ON TOTAL EQUITY

The **return on total equity** measures the return to both common and preferred stockholders. Compute the return on total equity as follows:

$$\text{Return on Total Equity} = \frac{\begin{array}{c}\text{Net Income Before Nonrecurring Items} -\\ \text{Dividends on Redeemable Preferred Stock}\end{array}}{\text{Average Total Equity}}$$

Preferred stock subject to mandatory redemption is termed **redeemable preferred stock**. The SEC requires that redeemable preferred stock be categorized separately from other equity securities because the shares must be redeemed in a manner similar to the repayment of debt. Most companies do not have redeemable preferred stock. For those firms that do, the redeemable preferred is excluded from total equity and considered part of debt. Similarly, the dividends must be deducted from income. They have not been deducted on the income

Exhibit	8-12	NIKE, INC.

Return on Investment

Years Ended May 31, 2007 and 2006

(In millions)	2007	2006
Interest expense [A]*	$ 49.7	$ 50.5
Net income	$ 1,491.5	$ 1,392.0
Tax rate (see note 8 in 10-K)	32.2%	35.0%
1 – Tax rate [B]	67.8%	65.0%
(Interest expense*) × (1 – Tax rate) [A × B]	$ 33.70	$ 32.83
Net income + [(Interest expense*) × (1 – Tax rate)] [C]	$1,525.20	$1,424.83
Long-term liabilities and stockholders' equity		
Beginning of year:		
Long-term liabilities	$ 972.0	$ 1,150.2
Total stockholders' equity	6,285.2	5,644.2
End of year:		
Long-term liabilities	1,078.9	972.0
Total stockholders' equity	7,025.4	6,285.2
Total [D]	$15,361.5	$14,051.6
Average [D ÷ 2] = [E]	$ 7,680.8	$ 7,025.8
Return on investment [C ÷ E]	19.86%	20.28%

*Nike did not disclose interest expense. Used cash paid during the year for interest, net of capitalized interest.

statement, despite the similarity to debt and interest, because they are still dividends and payable only if declared.

Exhibit 8-13 shows the return on total equity for Nike for 2007 and 2006. It decreased moderately from 23.34% to 22.41%.

Exhibit	8-13	NIKE, INC.

Return on Total Equity

Years Ended May 31, 2007 and 2006

(In millions)	2007	2006
Net income	$ 1,491.50	$ 1,392.00
Less: Redeemable preferred dividends	0.03	0.03
Adjusted income [A]	$ 1,491.47	$ 1,391.97
Total equity:		
Beginning of year	$ 6,285.20	$ 5,644.20
End of year	7,025.40	6,285.20
Total equity [B]	$13,310.60	$11,929.40
Average [B ÷ 2] = [C]	$ 6,655.30	$ 5,964.70
Return on total equity [A ÷ C]	22.41%	23.34%

RETURN ON COMMON EQUITY

This ratio measures the return to the common stockholder, the residual owner. Compute the **return on common equity** as follows:

$$\text{Return on Common Equity} = \frac{\text{Net Income Before Nonrecurring Items} - \text{Preferred Dividends}}{\text{Average Common Equity}}$$

The net income appears on the income statement. The preferred dividends appear most commonly on the statement of stockholders' equity. Common equity includes common capital stock and retained earnings less common treasury stock. This amount equals total equity minus the preferred capital and any minority interest included in the equity section.

Exhibit 8-14 shows the return on common equity for Nike for 2007 and 2006. Nike's return on common equity is the same as its return on total equity.

Exhibit	8-14	NIKE, INC.

Return on Common Equity

Years Ended May 31, 2007 and 2006

(In millions)	2007	2006
Net income	$ 1,491.50	$ 1,392.00
Less: Redeemable preferred dividends	0.03	0.03
Adjusted income [A]	$ 1,491.47	$ 1,391.97
Total common equity:		
Beginning of year	$ 6,285.20	$ 5,644.20
End of year	7,025.40	6,285.20
Total [B]	$13,310.60	$11,929.40
Average common equity [B ÷ 2] = [C]	$ 6,655.30	$ 5,964.70
Return on common equity [A ÷ C]	22.41%	23.34%

THE RELATIONSHIP BETWEEN PROFITABILITY RATIOS

Technically, a ratio with a profit figure in the numerator and some type of "supplier of funds" figure in the denominator is a type of return on investment. Another frequently used measure is a variation of the return on total assets. Compute this return on total assets variation as follows:

$$\text{Return on Total Assets Variation} = \frac{\text{Net Income} + \text{Interest Expense}}{\text{Average Total Assets}}$$

This ratio includes the return to all suppliers of funds, both long- and short-term, by both creditors and investors. It differs from the return on assets ratio previously discussed because it adds back the interest. It differs from the return on investment in that it does not adjust interest for the income tax effect, it includes short-term funds, and it uses the average investment. It will not be discussed or utilized further here because it does not lend itself to DuPont analysis.

Rates of return have been calculated on a variety of bases. The interrelationship between these ratios is of importance in understanding the return to the suppliers of funds. Exhibit 8-15 displays a comparison of profitability measures for Nike.

The return on assets measures the return to all providers of funds since total assets equal total liabilities and equity. This ratio will usually be the lowest since it includes all of the assets.

Exhibit	8-15	NIKE, INC.

Comparison of Profitability Measures

Years Ended May 31, 2007 and 2006

	2007	2006
Return on assets	14.51%	14.92%
Return on investment	19.86%	20.28%
Return on total equity	22.41%	23.34%
Return on common equity	22.41%	23.34%

The return on investment measures the return to long-term suppliers of funds, and it is usually higher than the return on assets because of the relatively low amount paid for short-term funds. This is especially true of accounts payable.

The rate of return on total equity will usually be higher than the return on investment because the rate of return on equity measures return only to the stockholders. A profitable use of long-term sources of funds from creditors provides a higher return to stockholders than the return on investment. In other words, the profits made on long-term funds from creditors were greater than the interest paid for the use of the funds.

Common stockholders absorb the greatest degree of risk and, therefore, usually earn the highest return. For the return on common equity to be the highest, the return on funds obtained from preferred stockholders must be more than the funds paid to the preferred stockholders.

GROSS PROFIT MARGIN

Gross profit equals the difference between net sales revenue and the cost of goods sold. The cost of goods sold is the beginning inventory plus purchases minus the ending inventory. It is the cost of the product sold during the period. Changes in the cost of goods sold, which represents such a large expense for merchandising and manufacturing firms, can have a substantial impact on the profit for the period. Comparing gross profit to net sales is termed the **gross profit margin**. Compute the gross profit margin as follows:

$$\text{Gross Profit Margin} = \frac{\text{Gross Profit}}{\text{Net Sales}}$$

This ratio should then be compared with industry data or analyzed by trend analysis. Exhibit 8-16 illustrates trend analysis. In this illustration, the gross profit margin has declined substantially over the three-year period. This could be attributable to a number of factors:

1. The cost of buying inventory has increased more rapidly than have selling prices.
2. Selling prices have declined due to competition.
3. The mix of goods has changed to include more products with lower margins.
4. Theft is occurring. If sales are not recorded, the cost of goods sold figure in relation to the sales figure is very high. If inventory is being stolen, the ending inventory will be low and the cost of goods sold will be high.

Exhibit	8-16	EXAMPLE GROSS PROFIT MARGIN

Years Ended May 31, 2007, 2006, and 2005

	2007	2006	2005
Net sales [B]	$5,000,000	$4,500,000	$4,000,000
Less: Cost of goods sold	3,500,000	2,925,000	2,200,000
Gross profit [A]	$1,500,000	$1,575,000	$1,800,000
Gross profit margin [A ÷ B]	30.00%	35.00%	45.00%

Gross profit margin analysis helps a number of users. Managers budget gross profit levels into their predictions of profitability. Gross profit margins are also used in cost control. Estimations utilizing gross profit margins can determine inventory levels for interim statements in the merchandising industries. Gross profit margins can also be used to estimate inventory involved in insured losses. In addition, gross profit measures are used by auditors and the Internal Revenue Service to judge the accuracy of accounting systems.

Gross profit margin analysis requires an income statement in multiple-step format. Otherwise, the gross profit must be computed, which is the case with Nike. Exhibit 8-17 presents Nike's gross profit margin, which decreased between 2005 and 2006 and between 2006 and 2007. This represents a slight decrease in profitability. This slight decrease is from very high numbers.

Exhibit	8-17	NIKE, INC.

Gross Profit Margin

Years Ended May 31, 2007, 2006, and 2005

(In millions)	2007	2006	2005
Net sales [B]	$16,325.9	$14,954.9	$13,739.7
Less: Cost of products sold	9,165.4	8,367.9	7,624.3
Gross profit [A]	$ 7,160.5	$ 6,587.0	$ 6,115.4
Gross profit margin [A ÷ B]	43.86%	44.05%	44.51%

Trends in Profitability

Exhibit 8-18 shows profitability trends for manufacturing for the period 1965–2006. Operating profit compared with net sales declined substantially over this period. Net income compared with net sales fluctuated substantially. Notice the material decline in this ratio in 1992 and 2001 and the substantial increase in this ratio for 2002, 2003, 2004, and 2006.

Exhibit	8-18	TRENDS IN PROFITABILITY

United States Manufacturing

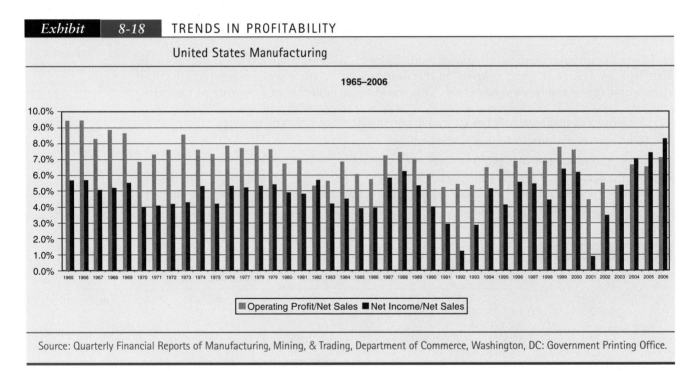

1965–2006

■ Operating Profit/Net Sales   ■ Net Income/Net Sales

Source: Quarterly Financial Reports of Manufacturing, Mining, & Trading, Department of Commerce, Washington, DC: Government Printing Office.

Segment Reporting

A public business enterprise reports financial and descriptive information about reportable operating segments. Operating segments are segments about which separate financial information is available that is evaluated by the chief operating decision maker in deciding how to allocate resources and in assessing performance. It requires information about the countries in which the firm earns revenues and holds assets, and about major customers.

Descriptive information must be disclosed about the way the operating segments were determined. Disclosure is required for products and services by the operating segments. Disclosure is also required about the differences between the measurements used in reporting segment information and those used in the firm's general-purpose financial information.

Segment data can be analyzed both in terms of trends and ratios. Vertical and horizontal common-size analyses can be used for trends. Examples of ratios would be relating profits to sales or identifiable assets.

Segment trends would be of interest to management and investors. The maximum benefits from this type of analysis come when analyzing a nonintegrated company in terms of product lines, especially with segments of relatively similar size.

Nike reported operating segments and related information in Note 17. Note 17 is partially included in Exhibit 8-19. These data should be reviewed, and consideration should be given to using vertical and horizontal analyses and to computing ratios that appear meaningful. This type of review is illustrated in Exhibits 8-20 and 8-21 on pages 310 and 311.

| Exhibit | 8-19 | NIKE, INC. |

Segment Information

Note 17 Operating Segments and Related Information (in Part)

| | Year Ended May 31, | | |
| | 2007 | 2006 | 2005 |
	(In millions)		
Net Revenue			
United States	$ 6,107.1	$ 5,722.5	$ 5,129.3
Europe, Middle East and Africa	4,723.3	4,326.6	4,281.6
Asia Pacific	2,283.4	2,053.8	1,897.3
Americas	952.5	904.9	695.8
Other	2,259.6	1,947.1	1,735.7
	$16,325.9	$14,954.9	$13,739.7
Pretax Income			
United States	$ 1,300.3	$ 1,244.5	$ 1,127.9
Europe, Middle East and Africa	1,000.7	960.7	917.5
Asia Pacific	483.7	412.5	399.8
Americas	187.4	172.6	116.5
Other	303.7	153.6	154.8
Corporate	(1,075.9)	(802.3)	(856.7)
	$ 2,199.9	$ 2,141.6	$ 1,859.8
Additions to Long-Lived Assets			
United States	$ 67.3	$ 59.8	$ 54.8
Europe, Middle East and Africa	94.9	73.6	38.8
Asia Pacific	20.7	16.8	22.0
Americas	5.3	6.9	6.8
Other	36.0	33.2	31.3
Corporate	89.3	143.4	103.4
	$ 313.5	$ 333.7	$ 257.1
Property, Plant and Equipment, net			
United States	$ 232.7	$ 219.3	$ 216.0
Europe, Middle East and Africa	325.4	266.6	230.0
Asia Pacific	326.1	354.8	380.4
Americas	16.9	17.0	15.7
Other	103.6	98.2	93.4
Corporate	673.6	701.8	670.3
	$ 1,678.3	$ 1,657.7	$ 1,605.8

Exhibit 8-20 presents some Nike information in vertical common-size analysis. Net revenue, pretax income, additions to long-lived assets, and property, plant and equipment, net, are included. Based on this analysis, the United States is the dominant segment, followed by the segment of Europe, Middle East, and Africa. The proportion of revenue coming from the United States has been reasonably steady. The relatively small Americas segment had a substantial increase as did the Other segment.

Pretax income increased materially in the Americas and Other segments.

Corporate represented a substantial proportion of additions to long-lived assets and property, plant and equipment, net. The Europe, Middle East and Africa segment had a material increase in additions to long-lived assets and property, plant and equipment, net.

Exhibit	8-20	NIKE, INC.

Segment Information
Vertical Common-Size Analysis*

	Year Ended May 31,		
	2007	**2006**	**2005**
Net Revenue			
United States	37.4%	38.3%	37.3%
Europe, Middle East, and Africa	28.9	28.9	31.2
Asia Pacific	14.0	13.7	13.8
Americas	5.8	6.1	5.1
Other	13.8	13.0	12.6
	100.0%	100.0%	100.0%
Pretax Income			
United States	59.1%	58.1%	60.6%
Europe, Middle East, and Africa	45.5	44.9	49.3
Asia Pacific	22.0	19.3	21.5
Americas	8.5	8.1	6.3
Other	13.8	7.2	8.3
Corporate	(48.9)	(37.5)	(46.1)
	100.0%	100.0%	100.0%
Additions to Long-Lived Assets			
United States	21.5%	17.9%	21.3%
Europe, Middle East, and Africa	30.3	22.1	15.1
Asia Pacific	6.6	5.0	8.6
Americas	1.7	2.1	2.6
Other	11.5	9.9	12.2
Corporate	28.5	43.0	40.2
	100.0%	100.0%	100.0%
Property, Plant and Equipment, net			
United States	13.9%	13.2%	13.5%
Europe, Middle East, and Africa	19.4	16.1	14.3
Asia Pacific	19.4	21.4	23.7
Americas	1.0	1.0	1.0
Other	6.2	5.9	5.8
Corporate	40.1	42.3	41.7
	100.0%	100.0%	100.0%

*There are some rounding differences.

A review of Exhibit 8-21 (Segment Information—Ratio Analysis) indicates that Americas and Other had material increases when relating pretax income to net revenue. The Europe, Middle East, and Africa segment materially increased when relating additions to long-lived assets to property, plant and equipment, net.

Revenues by Major Product Lines

Exhibit 8-22 shows revenues by major product lines presented by Nike. Revenues by Major Product Lines—Horizontal Common-Size Analysis is presented in Exhibit 8-23. Footwear is the dominate segment representing over half the revenues. The fastest growth was experienced in the Other segment.

Gains and Losses from Prior Period Adjustments

Prior period adjustments result from certain changes in accounting principles, the realization of income tax benefits of preacquisition operating loss carryforwards of purchased subsidiaries, a change in accounting entity, and corrections of errors in prior periods. Prior period adjustments are charged to retained earnings.

Exhibit	8-21	NIKE, INC.

Segment Information—Ratio Analysis

	Years Ended May 31,		
	2007	2006	2005
Pretax income to net revenue:			
United States	21.3%	21.7%	22.0%
Europe, Middle East, and Africa	21.2	22.2	21.4
Asia Pacific	21.2	20.1	21.1
Americas	19.7	19.1	16.7
Other	13.4	7.9	8.9
Additions to long-lived assets to property, plant and equipment, net:			
United States	28.9%	27.3%	25.4%
Europe, Middle East, and Africa	29.2	27.6	16.9
Asia Pacific	6.3	4.7	5.8
Americas	31.4	40.6	43.3
Other	34.7	33.8	33.5
Corporate	13.3	20.4	15.4

Exhibit	8-22	NIKE, INC.

**Segment Information
Revenues by Major Product Lines (Note 17—in Part)**

Revenues by Major Product Lines. Revenues to external customers for NIKE brand products are attributable to sales of footwear, apparel and equipment. Other revenues to external customers primarily include external sales by Cole Haan Holdings Incorporated, Converse Inc., Exeter Brands Group LLC (beginning August 11, 2004), Hurley International LLC, NIKE Bauer Hockey Corp., and NIKE Golf.

	Year Ended May 31,		
(In millions)	2007	2006	2005
Footwear	$ 8,514.0	$ 7,965.9	$ 7,299.7
Apparel	4,576.5	4,168.0	3,879.4
Equipment	975.8	873.9	824.9
Other	2,259.6	1,947.1	1,735.7
	$16,325.9	$14,954.9	$13,739.7

Exhibit	8-23	NIKE, INC.

**Segment Information
Revenues by Major Product Lines (Prepared from Note 17—in Part)
Horizontal Common-Size Analysis**

	Year Ended May 31,		
	2007	2006	2005
Footwear	116.6%	109.1%	100.0%
Apparel	118.0	107.4	100.0
Equipment	118.3	106.0	100.0
Other	130.2	112.2	100.0

These items are a type of gain or loss but they never go through the income statement. They are not recognized on the income statement. If material, they should be considered in analysis. Current period ratios would not be revised because these items relate to prior periods.

A review of the retained earnings account presented in the statement of stockholders' equity will reveal prior period adjustments.

Exhibit 8-24 presents a prior period adjustment of Kohl's Corporation.

Exhibit 8-24	KOHL'S CORPORATION*

Prior Period Adjustment

Kohl's Corporation included this information in its financial statements for the year ended January 28, 2006.

Note: In addition to the notes, the Consolidated Statement of Changes in Shareholders' Equity disclosed the cumulative effect of restatement in prior years.

Notes to Consolidated Financial Statements (in Part)

1. Summary of Accounting Policies (in Part)

Stock Options

In December 2004, the Financial Accounting Standards Board (FASB) issued Statement of Financial Accounting Standards (SFAS) No. 123 (revised 2004) (SFAS No. 123R), "Share Based Payment," which is a revision of SFAS No. 123, "Accounting for Stock-Based Compensation." SFAS No. 123R supersedes Accounting Principles Board (APB) Opinion No. 25, "Accounting for Stock Issued to Employees," and amends SFAS No. 95, "Statement of Cash Flows." Generally, the approach in SFAS No. 123R is similar to the approach described in SFAS No. 123. However, SFAS No. 123R requires all share-based payments to employees, including grants of employee stock options, to be recognized in the income statement based on their fair values.

Effective January 30, 2005, the Company adopted the fair value recognition provisions of SFAS No. 123R using the "modified retrospective" method, which requires the prior period financial statements to be restated to recognize the compensation cost in the amounts previously reported in the pro forma footnote disclosures. See Note 2 for the effect of the adoption on the fiscal 2004 and 2003 results.

2. Restatement of Financial Statements (in Part)

Effective January 30, 2005, the Company adopted the fair value recognition provisions of SFAS No. 123R using the "modified retrospective" method, which requires the prior period financial statements to be restated to recognize compensation cost in the amounts previously reported in the pro forma footnotes.

Below is a summary of the effects of the restatement on the Company's consolidated balance sheet as of January 29, 2005, as well as the effects of these changes on the Company's consolidated statements of income and consolidated statements of cash flows for fiscal years 2004 and 2003. The cumulative effect of the restatement relating to fiscal years 1995 through 2002 is an increase in paid-in capital of $167.0 million, an increase in deferred income taxes of $52.3 million and an increase in selling, general and administrative expenses (S,G&A) of $185.9 million. As a result, retained earnings at January 31, 2004 decreased by $114.7 million.

Note: This note also included detail of adjustments to consolidated balance sheets, consolidated statement of income, and consolidated statement of cash flows.

---

*"The Company operates family-oriented specialty department stores that feature quality, exclusive and national brand merchandise priced to provide value to customers." 10-K

Comprehensive Income

Chapter 4 explained that the categories within accumulated other income are: (1) foreign currency translation adjustments, (2) unrealized holding gains and losses on available-for-sale marketable securities, (3) changes to stockholders' equity resulting from additional minimum pension liability adjustments, and (4) unrealized gains and losses from derivative instruments. Chapter 4 also explained that there is considerable flexibility in reporting comprehensive income. One format uses a single income statement to report net income and comprehensive income. The second format reports comprehensive income in a separate statement of financial activity. The third format reports comprehensive income within the statement of changes in stockholders' equity.

Review the reporting of comprehensive income to determine which items are reported. Nike presents comprehensive income within the statement of changes in stockholders' equity. The two comprehensive income items reported by Nike are foreign currency translation adjustments and adjustment for fair value of hedge derivatives.

Note that comprehensive income includes items not in net income. Our traditional profitability analysis includes items that related to net income. This excludes other comprehensive income items. Ratios in which you may want to consider including comprehensive income are: (1) return on assets, (2) return on investment, (3) return on total equity, and (4) return on common equity. For some firms, these ratios will change substantially. Exhibit 8-25 presents these ratios for Nike. For Nike, there was a moderate increase for these profitability ratios.

Exhibit	8-25	NIKE, INC.	

Selected Ratios Considering Comprehensive Income		
Year Ended May 31, 2007		
	2007	
	Prior Computation	Including Comprehensive Income
Return on assets	14.51%	15.17%
Return on investment	19.86%	20.74%
Return on total equity	22.41%	23.43%
Return on common equity	22.41%	23.43%

Pro Forma Financial Information

Pro forma financial information is a hypothetical or projected amount. Synonymous with "what if" analysis, pro forma data indicate what would have happened under specified circumstances.

Used properly, pro forma financial information makes a positive contribution to financial reporting—for example, what would be the net income if additional shares were issued?

Used improperly, pro forma financial information can be a negative contribution to financial reporting. For example, releasing pro forma earnings can be misleading if not explained.

It became popular in the United States for companies to release pro forma earnings at approximately the time that financial results were released that used GAAP. Typically, how the company arrived at the pro forma earnings was not adequately disclosed. It was inferred that this was the better number for investors to follow. Many investors did make decisions based on the pro forma earnings as opposed to the GAAP earnings.

The Sarbanes-Oxley Act required the Commission (SEC) to adopt rules requiring that if a company publicly discloses non-GAAP financial measures or includes them in a Commission filing:

1. the company must reconcile those non-GAAP financial measures to a company's financial condition and results of operations under GAAP.

2. that any public disclosure of a non-GAAP financial measure not contain an untrue statement of a material fact or omit to state a material fact necessary in order to make the non-GAAP financial measure, in light of circumstances under which it is presented, not misleading.[1]

A June 2004 article in *Accounting Horizons* compared S&P Companies' own reported earnings data (pro forma) with U.S. GAAP net income, 1990–2003. In each year, the pro forma earnings were higher. In some years, the pro forma earnings were materially more than the U.S. GAAP net income.[2]

The Wall Street Journal made the following comment in a September 2003 article:

> "*If you thought the Sarbanes-Oxley Act, that sweeping package of overhauls adopted in response to U.S. corporate scandals, got rid of the "pro forma"-like tactics by which companies were able to make their earnings look better, you thought wrong.*"[3]

One example in the article was "Sanmina-SCI Corp., which strips restructuring costs out of its GAAP earnings to help reach its pro forma earnings—and has done so every quarter for the past 2 1/2 years. 'Restructuring' costs might seem to imply a one-time event, but Sanmina has stripped out restructuring costs in each of its last 10 quarters, back to 2001."[4]

Interim Reports

Interim reports are an additional source of information on profitability. These are reports that cover fiscal periods of less than one year. The SEC requires that limited financial data be provided on Form 10-Q. The SEC also requires that these companies disclose certain quarterly information in notes to the annual report.

The same reporting principles used for annual reports should be employed for interim reports, with the intent that the interim reporting be an integral part of the annual report. For interim financial reports, timeliness of data offsets lack of detail. Some data included are:

1. Income statement amounts:
    a. Sales or gross revenues
    b. Provision for income taxes
    c. Extraordinary items and tax effect
    d. Cumulative effect of an accounting change
    e. Net income
2. Earnings per share
3. Seasonal information
4. Significant changes in income tax provision or estimate
5. Disposal of segments of business and unusual items material to the period
6. Contingent items
7. Changes in accounting principles or estimates
8. Significant changes in financial position

Interim reports contain more estimates in the financial data than in the annual reports. Interim reports are also unaudited. For these reasons, they are less reliable than annual reports.

Income tax expense is an example of a figure that can require considerable judgment and estimation for the interim period. The objective with the interim income tax expense is to use an annual effective tax rate, which may require considerable estimation. Some reasons for this are foreign tax credits and the tax effect of losses in an interim period.

Interim statements must disclose the seasonal nature of the activities of the firm. It is also recommended that firms that are seasonal in nature supplement their interim report by including information for 12-month periods ended at the interim date for the current and preceding years.

Interim statements can help the analyst determine trends and identify trouble areas before the year-end report is available. The information obtained (such as a lower profit margin) may indicate that trouble is brewing.

Nike included a section called "Selected Quarterly Financial Data" in its annual report. It indicates that the fourth quarter has the highest volume and is most profitable. This would be the months of March, April, and May. Revenue was up in each quarter compared with 2006. Net income was down in the first quarter compared with 2006. Net income was up in the second quarter, third quarter, and fourth quarter in relation to 2006.

Summary

Profitability is the ability of a firm to generate earnings. It is measured relative to a number of bases, such as assets, sales, and investment.

The ratios related to profitability covered in this chapter follow:

$$\text{Net Profit Margin} = \frac{\text{Net Income Before Minority Share of Earnings, Equity Income and Nonrecurring Items}}{\text{Net Sales}}$$

$$\text{Total Asset Turnover} = \frac{\text{Net Sales}}{\text{Average Total Assets}}$$

$$\text{Return on Assets} = \frac{\text{Net Income Before Minority Share of Earnings and Nonrecurring Items}}{\text{Average Total Assets}}$$

$$\frac{\text{Net Income Before Minority Share of Earnings and Nonrecurring Items}}{\text{Average Total Assets}} = \frac{\text{Net Income Before Minority Share of Earnings and Nonrecurring Items}}{\text{Net Sales}} \times \frac{\text{Net Sales}}{\text{Average Total Assets}}$$

$$\text{Operating Income Margin} = \frac{\text{Operating Income}}{\text{Net Sales}}$$

$$\text{Operating Asset Turnover} = \frac{\text{Net Sales}}{\text{Average Operating Assets}}$$

$$\text{Return on Operating Assets} = \frac{\text{Operating Income}}{\text{Average Operating Assets}}$$

$$\text{DuPont Return on Operating Assets} = \text{Operating Income Margin} \times \text{Operating Asset Turnover}$$

$$\text{Sales to Fixed Assets} = \frac{\text{Net Sales}}{\text{Average Net Fixed Assets (Exclude Construction in Progress)}}$$

$$\text{Return on Investment} = \frac{\text{Net Income Before Minority Share of Earnings and Nonrecurring Items} + [(\text{Interest Expense}) \times (1 - \text{Tax Rate})]}{\text{Average (Long-Term Liabilities} + \text{Equity)}}$$

$$\text{Return on Total Equity} = \frac{\text{Net Income Before Nonrecurring Items} - \text{Dividends on Redeemable Preferred Stock}}{\text{Average Total Equity}}$$

$$\text{Return on Common Equity} = \frac{\text{Net Income Before Nonrecurring Items} - \text{Preferred Dividends}}{\text{Average Common Equity}}$$

$$\text{Gross Profit Margin} = \frac{\text{Gross Profit}}{\text{Net Sales}}$$

1. Go to the SEC Web site (http://www.sec.gov). Under "Filings & Forms (EDGAR)," click on "Search for Company Filings." Click on "Companies & Other Filers." Under Company Name, enter "Google Inc." (or under Ticker Symbol, enter "GOOG"). Select the 10-K filed March 1, 2007.

   a. Determine the standard industrial classification.

   b. Copy the first sentence in the "Item 1. Business Overview" section.

   c. Prepare a horizontal common-size analysis for the following (use 2004 as the base):

	2004	2005	2006
Revenue			
Income from operations			
Net income			

   d. Comment on the trends in (c).

2. Go to the SEC Web site (http://www.sec.gov). Under "Filings & Forms (EDGAR)," click on "Search for Company Filings." Click on "Companies & Other Filers." Under Company Name, enter "Flowers Foods Inc" (or under Ticker Symbol, enter "FLO"). Select the 10-K filed February 28, 2007.

   a. Determine the standard industrial classification.

   b. Copy the first sentence in "Item 1. Business," the Company.

   c. Complete this schedule:

   Flowers Foods, Inc. and Subsidiaries
   Consolidated Statements of Income (in Part)

	For the 52 Weeks Ended		
(Amounts in thousands)	December 30, 2006	December 31, 2005	January 1, 2005
Sales			
Materials, supplies, labor and other production costs (exclusive of depreciation and amortization shown separately below)			
Selling, marketing and administrative expenses			
Depreciation and amortization			
Asset impairment			
Income from operations			

   d. Complete the schedule in (c) using horizontal common-size analysis. Use January 1, 2005, as the base.

   e. Comment on the comparability of these years.

   f. Comment on the trends observed in (c) and (d).

3. a. Go to the SEC Web site (http://www.sec.gov). Under "Filings & Forms (EDGAR)," click on "Search for Company Filings." Click on "Companies & Other Filers." Under Company Name, enter "Intel Corp" (or under Ticker Symbol, enter "INTC"). Select the 10-K filed February 26, 2007.

   1. Determine the standard industrial classification.

   2. Copy the first sentence in the "Industry" subsection from the "Item 1. Business" section.

   3. Complete the following schedule:

   Intel Corporation
   Consolidated Statements of Income (in Part)
   Three Years Ended December 30, 2006

(In millions)	2006[1]	2005	2004
Net revenue			
Cost of sales			
Gross margin			
Operating income			

   (1) Cost of sales and operating expenses for the year ended, December 31, 2006, include share-based compensation.

   b. Go to the SEC Web site (http://www.sec.gov). Under "Filings & Forms (EDGAR)," click on "Search for Company Filings." Click on "Companies & Other Filers." Under Company Name, enter "Advanced Micro Devices Inc" (or under Ticker Symbol, enter "AMD"). Select the 10-K filed March 1, 2007.

   1. Determine the standard industrial classification.

   2. Copy the first sentence in the "General" subsection from the "Item 1. Business" section.

   3. Complete the following schedule:

   Advanced Micro Devices, Inc.
   Consolidated Statements of Operations (in Part)
   Three Years Ended December 31, 2006

(In thousands)	2006	2005	2004
Total net revenue			
Cost of sales			
Gross margin			
Operating income (loss)			

   c. Which firm appears to have performed better? Comment.

4. a. Go to the SEC Web site (http://www.sec.gov). Under "Filings & Forms (EDGAR)," click on "Search for Company Filings." Click on "Companies & Other Filers." Under Company Name, enter "Ford Motor Company" (or under Ticker Symbol, enter "F"). Select the 10-K filed February 28, 2007.

   1. Determine the standard industrial classification.

2. Complete the following schedule:

Ford Motor Company and Subsidiaries
Consolidated Statement of Income (in Part)
For the Years Ended December 31,
2006, 2005 and 2004
(In millions)

	2006	2005	2004
Automotive:			
Sales			
Total costs and expenses			
Operating income (loss)			
Financial services			
Revenues			
Total costs and expenses			
Income/(loss) before income taxes—financial services			

3. Comment on the trends for automotive and financial services.

b. Go to the SEC Web site (http://www.sec.gov). Under "Filings & Forms (EDGAR)," click on "Search for Company Filings." Click on "Companies & Other Filers." Under Company Name, enter "General Motors Corp" (or under Ticker Symbol, enter "GM"). Select the 10-K filed March 15, 2007.

1. Determine the standard industrial classification.

2. Complete the following schedule:

General Motors Corporation and Subsidiaries
Consolidated Statement of Operations
(Dollars in millions, except per share amounts)

	2006	2005	2004
Net sales and revenues			
Automotive sales			
Financial services and insurance revenues			
Total net sales and revenues			
Cost and expenses			
Automotive cost of sales			
Selling, general, and administrative expenses			
Interest expense			
Provisions for credit and insurance losses related to financing and insurance operations			
Other expenses			
Total costs and expenses			
Operating loss			

3. Comment on trends for automotive sales and financial services and insurance revenues.

c. Which firm appears to have performed better? Comment.

Questions

Q 8-1. Profits might be compared to sales, assets, or stockholders' equity. Why might all three bases be used? Will trends in these ratios always move in the same direction?

Q 8-2. What is the advantage of segregating extraordinary items in the income statement?

Q 8-3. If profits as a percent of sales decline, what can be said about expenses?

Q 8-4. Would you expect the profit margin in a quality jewelry store to differ from that of a grocery store? Comment.

Q 8-5. The ratio return on assets has net income in the numerator and total assets in the denominator. Explain how each part of the ratio could cause return on assets to fall.

Q 8-6. What is DuPont analysis, and how does it aid in financial analysis?

Q 8-7. How does operating income differ from net income? How do operating assets differ from total assets? What is the advantage in removing nonoperating items from the DuPont analysis?

Q 8-8. Why are equity earnings usually greater than cash flow generated from the investment? How can these equity earnings distort profitability analysis?

Q 8-9. Explain how return on assets could decline, given an increase in net profit margin.

Q 8-10. How is return on investment different from return on total equity? How does return on total equity differ from return on common equity?

Q 8-11.   What is return on investment? What are some of the types of measures for return on investment? Why is the following ratio preferred?

$$\frac{\text{Net Income Before Minority Share of Earnings and Nonrecurring Items} + [(\text{Interest Expense}) \times (1 - \text{Tax Rate})]}{\text{Average (Long-Term Debt} + \text{Equity)}}$$

Why is the interest multiplied by (1 − Tax Rate)?

Q 8-12.   G. Herrich Company and Thomas, Inc., are department stores. For the current year, they reported a net income after tax of $400,000 and $600,000, respectively. Is Thomas, Inc., a more profitable company than G. Herrich Company? Discuss.

Q 8-13.   Since interim reports are not audited, they are not meaningful. Comment.

Q 8-14.   Speculate on why accounting standards do not mandate full financial statements in interim reports.

Q 8-15.   Why may comprehensive income fluctuate substantially more than net income?

Q 8-16.   Why can pro forma financial information be misleading?

Problems

P 8-1.   Ahl Enterprise lists the following data for 2007 and 2006:

	2007	2006
Net income	$ 52,500	$ 40,000
Net sales	1,050,000	1,000,000
Average total assets	230,000	200,000
Average common equity	170,000	160,000

Required   Calculate the net profit margin, return on assets, total asset turnover, and return on common equity for both years. Comment on the results. (For return on assets and total asset turnover, use end-of-year total assets; for return on common equity, use end-of-year common equity.)

P 8-2.   Income statement data for Starr Canning Corporation are as follows:

	2007	2006
Sales	$1,400,000	$1,200,000
Cost of goods sold	850,000	730,000
Selling expenses	205,000	240,000
General expenses	140,000	100,000
Income tax expense	82,000	50,000

Required   a. Prepare an income statement in comparative form, stating each item for both years as a percent of sales (vertical common-size analysis).

b. Comment on the findings in (a).

P 8-3.   The balance sheet for Schultz Bone Company at December 31, 2007, had the following account balances:

Total current liabilities (non-interest-bearing)	$450,000
Bonds payable, 6% (issued in 1982; due in 2013)	750,000
Preferred stock, 5%, $100 par	300,000
Common stock, $10 par	750,000
Premium on common stock	150,000
Retained earnings	600,000

Income before income tax was $200,000, and income taxes were $80,000 for the current year.

Required   Calculate each of the following:
a. Return on assets (using ending assets)
b. Return on total equity (using ending total equity)
c. Return on common equity (using ending common equity)
d. Times interest earned

P 8-4.   Revenue and expense data for Vent Molded Plastics and for the plastics industry as a whole follow:

	Vent Molded Plastics	Plastics Industry
Sales	$462,000	100.3%
Sales returns	4,500	0.3
Cost of goods sold	330,000	67.1
Selling expenses	43,000	10.1
General expenses	32,000	7.9
Other income	1,800	0.4
Other expense	7,000	1.3
Income tax	22,000	5.5

Required   Convert the dollar figures for Vent Molded Plastics into percentages based on net sales. Compare these with the industry average, and comment on your findings.

P 8-5.   Day Ko Incorporated presented the following comparative income statements for 2007 and 2006:

	For the Years Ended	
	2007	2006
Net sales	$1,589,150	$1,294,966
Other income	22,334	20,822
	1,611,484	1,315,788
Costs and expenses:		
Material and manufacturing costs of products sold	651,390	466,250
Research and development	135,314	113,100
General and selling	526,680	446,110
Interest	18,768	11,522
Other	15,570	7,306
	1,347,722	1,044,288
Earnings before income taxes and minority equity	263,762	271,500
Provision for income taxes	114,502	121,740
Earnings before minority equity	149,260	149,760
Minority equity in earnings	11,056	12,650
Net earnings	$ 138,204	$ 137,110

Other relevant financial information follows:

	For the Years Ended	
	2007	2006
Average common shares issued	29,580	29,480
Total long-term debt	$ 209,128	$ 212,702
Total stockholders' equity (all common)	810,292	720,530
Total assets	1,437,636	1,182,110
Operating assets	1,411,686	1,159,666
Dividends per share	1.96	1.86
Stock price (December 31)	$53^3/_4$	$76^1/_8$

Required   a. How did 2007 net sales compare to 2006?
b. How did 2007 net earnings compare to 2006?
c. Calculate the following for 2007 and 2006:
1. Net profit margin
2. Return on assets (using ending assets)
3. Total asset turnover (using ending assets)
4. DuPont analysis
5. Operating income margin
6. Return on operating assets (using ending assets)

7. Operating asset turnover (using ending assets)
8. DuPont analysis with operating ratios
9. Return on investment (using ending liabilities and equity)
10. Return on equity (using ending common equity)
d. Based on the previous computations, summarize the trend in profitability for this firm.

P 8-6.   Dorex, Inc., presented the following comparative income statements for 2007, 2006, and 2005:

| | For the Years Ended | | |
	2007	2006	2005
Net sales	$1,600,000	$1,300,000	$1,200,000
Other income	22,100	21,500	21,000
	1,622,100	1,321,500	1,221,000
Costs and expenses:			
Material and manufacturing costs of products sold	740,000	624,000	576,000
Research and development	90,000	78,000	71,400
General and selling	600,000	500,500	465,000
Interest	19,000	18,200	17,040
Other	14,000	13,650	13,800
	$1,463,000	$1,234,350	$1,143,240

| | For the Years Ended | | |
	2007	2006	2005
Earnings before income taxes and minority equity	$159,100	$87,150	$77,760
Provision for income taxes	62,049	35,731	32,659
Earnings before minority equity	97,051	51,419	45,101
Minority equity in earnings	10,200	8,500	8,100
Net earnings	86,851	42,919	37,001

| | For the Years Ended | | |
	2007	2006	2005
Other relevant financial information:			
Average common shares issued	29,610	29,100	28,800
Average long-term debt	$ 211,100	$ 121,800	$ 214,000
Average stockholders' equity (all common)	811,200	790,100	770,000
Average total assets	1,440,600	1,220,000	1,180,000
Average operating assets	1,390,200	1,160,000	1,090,000

Required   a. Calculate the following for 2007, 2006, and 2005:
1. Net profit margin
2. Return on assets
3. Total asset turnover
4. DuPont analysis
5. Operating income margin
6. Return on operating assets
7. Operating asset turnover
8. DuPont analysis with operating ratios
9. Return on investment
10. Return on total equity
b. Based on the previous computations, summarize the trend in profitability for this firm.

P 8-7.   Selected financial data for Squid Company are as follows:

	2007	2006	2005
Summary of operations:			
Net sales	$1,002,100	$980,500	$900,000
Cost of products sold	520,500	514,762	477,000
Selling, administrative, and general expenses	170,200	167,665	155,700
Nonoperating income	9,192	8,860	6,500

	2007	2006	2005
Interest expense	14,620	12,100	11,250
Earnings before income taxes	287,588	277,113	249,550
Provision for income taxes	116,473	113,616	105,560
Net earnings	171,115	163,497	143,990
Financial information:			
Working capital	$ 190,400	$189,000	$180,000
Average property, plant, and equipment	302,500	281,000	173,000
Average total assets	839,000	770,000	765,000
Average long-term debt	120,000	112,000	101,000
Average stockholders' equity	406,000	369,500	342,000

Required

a. Compute the following for 2007, 2006, and 2005:
   1. Net profit margin
   2. Return on assets
   3. Total asset turnover
   4. DuPont analysis
   5. Return on investment
   6. Return on total equity
   7. Sales to fixed assets

b. Discuss your findings in (a).

P 8-8. D. H. Muller Company presented the following income statement in its 2007 annual report:

(Dollars in thousands except per-share amounts)	For the Years Ended		
	2007	2006	2005
Net sales	$297,580	$256,360	$242,150
Cost of sales	206,000	176,300	165,970
Gross profit	91,580	80,060	76,180
Selling, administrative, and other expenses	65,200	57,200	56,000
Operating earnings	26,380	22,860	20,180
Interest expense	(5,990)	(5,100)	(4,000)
Other deductions, net	(320)	(1,100)	(800)
Earnings before income taxes, minority interests, and extraordinary items	20,070	16,660	15,380
Income taxes	(8,028)	(6,830)	(6,229)
Net earnings of subsidiaries applicable to minority interests	(700)	(670)	(668)
Earnings before extraordinary items	11,342	9,160	8,483
Extraordinary items:			
Gain on sale of investment, net of federal and state income taxes of $520	—	1,050	—
Loss due to damages to South American facilities, net of minority interest of $430	—	(1,600)	—
Net earnings	$ 11,342	$ 8,610	$ 8,483
Earnings per common share:			
Earnings before extraordinary items	$2.20	$ 1.82	$1.65
Extraordinary items	—	(0.06)	—
Net earnings	$2.20	$ 1.76	$1.65

The asset side of the balance sheet is summarized as follows:

(Dollars in thousands)	2007	2006	2005
Current assets	$ 89,800	$ 84,500	$ 83,100
Property, plant, and equipment	45,850	40,300	39,800
Other assets (including investments, deposits, deferred charges, and intangibles)	10,110	12,200	13,100
Total assets	$145,760	$137,000	$136,000

Required   a. Based on these data, compute the following for 2007, 2006, and 2005:
             1. Net profit margin
             2. Return on assets (using total assets)
             3. Total asset turnover (using total assets)
             4. DuPont analysis
             5. Operating income margin
             6. Return on operating assets (using end-of-year operating assets)
             7. Operating asset turnover (using end-of-year operating assets)
             8. DuPont analysis with operating ratios
             9. Gross profit margin
             b. Discuss your findings.

P 8-9.   The following financial information is for A. Galler Company for 2007, 2006, and 2005:

	2007	2006	2005
Income before interest	$4,400,000	$4,000,000	$3,300,000
Interest expense	800,000	600,000	550,000
Income before tax	3,600,000	3,400,000	2,750,000
Tax	1,500,000	1,450,000	1,050,000
Net income	$2,100,000	$1,950,000	$1,700,000

	2007	2006	2005
Current liabilities	$ 2,600,000	$2,300,000	$2,200,000
Long-term debt	7,000,000	6,200,000	5,800,000
Preferred stock (14%)	100,000	100,000	100,000
Common equity	$10,000,000	9,000,000	8,300,000

Required   a. For 2007, 2006, and 2005, determine the following:
             1. Return on assets (using end-of-year total assets)
             2. Return on investment (using end-of-year long-term liabilities and equity)
             3. Return on total equity (using ending total equity)
             4. Return on common equity (using ending common equity)
             b. Discuss the trend in these profit figures.
             c. Discuss the benefit from the use of long-term debt and preferred stock.

P 8-10.   Dexall Company recently had a fire in its store. Management must determine the inventory loss for the insurance company. Since the firm did not have perpetual inventory records, the insurance company has suggested that it might accept an estimate using the gross profit test. The beginning inventory, as determined from the last financial statements, was $10,000. Purchase invoices indicate purchases of $100,000. Credit and cash sales during the period were $120,000. Last year, the gross profit for the firm was 40%, which was also the industry average.

Required   a. Based on these data, estimate the inventory loss.
             b. If the industry average gross profit was 50%, why might the insurance company be leery of the estimated loss?

P 8-11.   Transactions affect various financial statement amounts.

	Net Profit	Retained Earnings	Total Stockholders' Equity
a. A stock dividend is declared and paid.			
b. Merchandise is purchased on credit.			
c. Marketable securities are sold above cost.			
d. Accounts receivable are collected.			
e. A cash dividend is declared and paid.			
f. Treasury stock is purchased and recorded at cost.			
g. Treasury stock is sold above cost.			
h. Common stock is sold.			
i. A fixed asset is sold for less than book value.			
j. Bonds are converted into common stock.			

Required   Indicate the effects of the previous transactions on each of the following: net profit, retained earnings, total stockholders' equity. Use + to indicate an increase, − to indicate a decrease, and 0 to indicate no effect.

P 8-12.   Consecutive five-year balance sheets and income statements of Mary Lou Szabo Corporation are as follows:

MARY LOU SZABO CORPORATION
Balance Sheets
December 31, 2003, through December 31, 2007

(Dollars in thousands)	2007	2006	2005	2004	2003
Assets					
Current assets:					
Cash	$ 24,000	$ 25,000	$ 26,000	$ 24,000	$ 26,000
Accounts receivable, net	120,000	122,000	128,000	129,000	130,000
Inventories	135,000	138,000	141,000	140,000	137,000
Total current assets	279,000	285,000	295,000	293,000	293,000
Property, plant and equipment, net	500,000	491,000	485,000	479,000	470,000
Goodwill	80,000	85,000	90,000	95,000	100,000
Total assets	$859,000	$861,000	$870,000	$867,000	$863,000
Liabilities and Stockholders' Equity					
Current liabilities:					
Accounts payable	$180,000	$181,000	$181,500	$183,000	$184,000
Income taxes	14,000	14,500	14,000	12,000	12,500
Total current liabilities	194,000	195,500	195,500	195,000	196,500
Long-term debt	65,000	67,500	79,500	82,000	107,500
Redeemable preferred stock	80,000	80,000	80,000	80,000	—
Total liabilities	339,000	343,000	355,000	357,000	304,000
Stockholders' equity:					
Preferred stock	70,000	70,000	70,000	70,000	120,000
Common stock	350,000	350,000	350,000	350,000	350,000
Paid-in capital in excess of par, common stock	15,000	15,000	15,000	15,000	15,000
Retained earnings	85,000	83,000	80,000	75,000	74,000
Total stockholders' equity	520,000	518,000	515,000	510,000	559,000
Total liabilities and stockholders' equity	$859,000	$861,000	$870,000	$867,000	$863,000

MARY LOU SZABO CORPORATION
Statement of Earnings
Years Ended December 31, 2003–2007

(Dollars in thousands)	2007	2006	2005	2004	2003
Net sales	$980,000	$960,000	$940,000	$900,000	$880,000
Cost of goods sold	625,000	616,000	607,000	580,000	566,000
Gross profit	355,000	344,000	333,000	320,000	314,000
Selling and administrative expense	(240,000)	(239,000)	(238,000)	(239,000)	(235,000)
Interest expense	(6,500)	(6,700)	(8,000)	(8,100)	(11,000)
Earnings from continuing operations before income taxes	108,500	98,300	87,000	72,900	68,000
Income taxes	35,800	33,400	29,200	21,700	23,100
Earnings from continuing operations	72,700	64,900	57,800	51,200	44,900
Extraordinary loss, net of taxes	—	—	—	—	(30,000)
Net earnings	$ 72,700	$ 64,900	$ 57,800	$ 51,200	$ 14,900
Earnings (loss) per share:					
Continuing operations	$ 2.00	$ 1.80	$ 1.62	$ 1.46	$ 1.28
Extraordinary loss	—	—	—	—	(0.85)
Net earnings per share	$ 2.00	$ 1.80	$ 1.62	$ 1.46	$ 0.43

Note: Dividends on preferred stock were as follows:

Redeemable preferred stock	Preferred stock	
2004–2007 $6,400	2004–2007	$ 6,300
	2003	10,800

Required   a. Compute the following for the years ended December 31, 2003–2007:
   1. Net profit margin
   2. Total asset turnover
   3. Return on assets
   4. DuPont return on assets
   5. Operating income margin
   6. Operating asset turnover
   7. Return on operating assets
   8. DuPont return on operating assets
   9. Sales to fixed assets
   10. Return on investment
   11. Return on total equity
   12. Return on common equity
   13. Gross profit margin

Note: For ratios that call for using average balance sheet figures, compute the rate using average balance sheet figures and year-end balance sheet figures.

   b. Briefly comment on profitability and trends indicated in profitability. Also comment on the difference in results between using the average balance sheet figures and year-end figures.

P 8-13.

Required   Answer the following multiple-choice questions:
   a. Which of the following is *not* considered to be a nonrecurring item?
   1. Discontinued operations
   2. Extraordinary items
   3. Cumulative effect of change in accounting principle
   4. Interest expense
   5. None of the above
   b. Ideally, which of these ratios will indicate the highest return for an individual firm?
   1. Return on assets
   2. Return on assets variation
   3. Return on investments
   4. Return on total equity
   5. Return on common equity
   c. If a firm's gross profit has declined substantially, this could be attributed to all but which of the following reasons?
   1. The cost of buying inventory has increased more rapidly than selling prices.
   2. Selling prices have declined due to competition.
   3. Selling prices have increased due to competition.
   4. The mix of goods has changed to include more products with lower margins.
   5. Theft is occurring.
   d. Gross profit analysis could be of value for all but which of the following?
   1. Projections of profitability
   2. Estimating administrative expenses
   3. Inventory for interim statements
   4. Estimating inventory for insurance claims
   5. Replacing the physical taking of inventory on an annual basis
   e. Total asset turnover measures
   1. Net income dollars generated by each dollar of sales.
   2. The ability of the firm to generate sales through the use of the assets.
   3. The firm's ability to make productive use of its property, plant, and equipment through generation of profits.
   4. The relationship between the income earned on the capital invested.
   5. Return to the common shareholders.

f. Equity earnings can represent a problem in analyzing profitability because
    1. Equity earnings may not be related to cash flow.
    2. Equity earnings are extraordinary.
    3. Equity earnings are unusual.
    4. Equity earnings are not from operations.
    5. Equity earnings are equal to dividends received.

g. Which of the following is *not* a type of operating asset?
    1. Intangibles   4. Inventory
    2. Receivables   5. Building
    3. Land

h. Earnings based on percent of holdings by outside owners of consolidated subsidiaries are termed
    1. Equity earnings.   4. Minority earnings.
    2. Earnings of subsidiaries.   5. None of the above.
    3. Investment income.

i. Net profit margin × total asset turnover measures
    1. DuPont return on assets.
    2. Return on investment.
    3. Return on stockholders' equity.
    4. Return on common equity.
    5. None of the above.

j. Return on assets cannot rise under which of the following circumstances?

	Net profit margin	Total asset turnover
1.	Decline	Rise
2.	Rise	Decline
3.	Rise	Rise
4.	Decline	Decline
5.	The ratio could rise under all of the above.	

k. A reason that equity earnings create a problem in analyzing profitability is because
    1. Equity earnings are nonrecurring.
    2. Equity earnings are extraordinary.
    3. Equity earnings are usually less than the related cash flow.
    4. Equity earnings relate to operations.
    5. None of the above.

l. Which of the following ratios will usually have the highest percent?
    1. Return on investment
    2. Return on total equity
    3. Return on common equity
    4. Return on total assets
    5. There is not enough information to tell.

m. Which of the following ratios will usually have the lowest percent?
    1. Return on investment
    2. Return on total equity
    3. Return on common equity
    4. Return on total assets
    5. There is not enough information to tell.

n. Which of the following items will be reported on the income statement as part of net income?
    1. Prior period adjustment
    2. Unrealized decline in market value of investments
    3. Foreign currency translation
    4. Gain from selling land
    5. None of the above

o. Minority share of earnings is
   1. The total earnings of unconsolidated subsidiaries.
   2. Earnings based on the percent of holdings by the parent of unconsolidated subsidiaries.
   3. Total earnings of unconsolidated subsidiaries.
   4. Earnings based on the percent of holdings by outside owners of unconsolidated subsidiaries.
   5. None of the above.
p. Which of the following could cause return on assets to decline when net profit margin is increasing?
   1. Purchase of land at year-end
   2. Increase in book value
   3. A stock dividend
   4. Increased turnover of operating assets
   5. None of the above

Case	JEFF'S SELF-SERVICE STATION
8-1	

John Dearden and his wife, Patricia, have been taking an annual vacation to Stowe, Vermont, each summer. They like the area very much and would like to retire someday in this vicinity. While in Stowe during the summer, they notice a "for sale" sign in front of a self-service station. John is 55 and is no longer satisfied with commuting to work in New York City. He decides to inquire about the asking price of the station. He is aware that Stowe is considered a good vacation area during the entire year, especially when the ski season is in progress.

On inquiry, John determines that the asking price of the station is $70,000, which includes two pumps, a small building, and 1/8 acre of land.

John asks to see some financial statements and is shown profit and loss statements for 2007 and 2006 that have been prepared for tax purposes by a local accountant.

JEFF'S SELF-SERVICE STATION
Statement of Earnings
For the Years Ended December 31, 2007 and 2006

	2007	2006
Revenue	$185,060	$175,180
Expenses:		
Cost of goods sold	160,180	153,280
Depreciation (a)	1,000	1,000
Real estate and property taxes	1,100	1,050
Repairs and maintenance	1,470	1,200
Other expenses	680	725
Total expenses	164,430	157,255
Profit	$ 20,630	$ 17,925

(a) Building and equipment cost	$30,000
Original estimated life	30 years
Depreciation per year	$1,000

John is also given an appraiser's report on the property. The land is appraised at $50,000, and the equipment and building are valued at $20,000. The equipment and building are estimated to have a useful life of 10 years.

The station has been operated by Jeff Szabo without additional help. He estimates that if help were hired to operate the station, it would cost $10,000 per year. John anticipates that he will be able to operate the station without additional help. John intends to incorporate. The anticipated tax rate is 50%.

Required   a. Determine the indicated return on investment if John Dearden purchases the station. Include only financial data that will be recorded on the books. Consider 2007 and 2006 to be representative years for revenue and expenses.

(continued)

JEFF'S SELF-SERVICE STATION (Continued)

    b. Determine the indicated return on investment if help were hired to operate the station.

    c. Why is there a difference between the rates of return in (a) and (b)? Discuss.

    d. Determine the cash flow for 2008 if John serves as the manager and 2008 turns out to be the same as 2007. Do not include the cost of the hired help. No inventory is on hand at the date of purchase, but an inventory of $10,000 is on hand at the end of the year. There are no receivables or liabilities.

    e. Indicate some other considerations that should be analyzed.

    f. Should John purchase the station?

WORKING ON THE RAILROAD

Segment Reporting

Genesee & Wyoming Inc.*
Notes to Consolidated Financial Statements (in Part)

17. Business Segment and Geographic Area Information (in Part)

Geographic Data

	For the Years Ended December 31,					
	2006		**2005**		**2004**	
Operating revenues:						
United States	$348,608	72.8%	$299,440	77.7%	$226,521	74.6%
Canada	55,555	11.6%	50,960	13.2%	44,008	14.5%
Australia	46,520	9.7%	—	0.0%	—	0.0%
Mexico	28,163	5.9%	34,989	9.1%	33,255	10.9%
Total operating revenues	$478,846	100.0%	$385,389	100.0%	$303,784	100.0%

	December 31,			
	2006		**2005**	
Long-lived assets located in:				
United States	$602,238	80.3%	$734,636	86.3%
Canada	104,807	14.0%	71,726	8.4%
Australia	36,364	4.8%	—	0.0%
Mexico	6,736	0.9%	45,140	5.3%
Total long-lived assets	$750,145	100.0%	$851,502	100.0%

Required

    a. Prepare horizontal common-size analysis for operating revenues. Comment on the results.

    b. Prepare horizontal common-size analysis for long-lived assets. Comment on the results.

    c. Comment on the vertical common-size analysis for operating revenues.

    d. Comment on the vertical common-size analysis for long-lived assets.

    e. Comment on the absolute numbers for operating revenues.

    f. Comment on the absolute numbers for long-lived assets.

*"We are a leading owner and operator of short line and regional freight railroads in the United States, Australia, Canada, and Mexico and own a minority interest in a railroad in Bolivia." 10-K

THE STORY OF STARBUCKS—IN SEGMENTS

Starbucks Corporation*

Starbucks presented the following in its 2006 annual report:

Notes to Consolidated Financial Statements (in Part)

Note 19: Segment Reporting (in Part)

Segment information is prepared on the same basis that the Company's management reviews financial information for operational decision making purposes. Beginning in the fiscal fourth quarter of 2006, the Company increased its reporting segments from two to three to include a Global CPG segment in addition to the United States and International segments. This additional operating segment reflects the culmination of internal management realignments in fiscal 2006, and the successful development and launch of certain branded products in the United States and internationally, commencing in fiscal 2005 and continuing throughout fiscal 2006. Additionally, with the 100% acquisition of the Company's operations in Hawaii in fiscal 2006 and the shift in internal management of this market to the United States, these operations have been moved from the International segment into the United States segment. Segment information for all prior periods presented has been revised to reflect these changes.

United States

The Company's United States operations ("United States") represent 83% of total Company-operated retail revenues, 57% of total specialty revenues and 79% of total net revenues. United States operations sell coffee and other beverages, whole bean coffees, complementary food, coffee brewing equipment and merchandise primarily through Company-operated retail stores. Specialty Operations within the United States include licensed retail stores, foodservice accounts and other initiatives related to the Company's core business.

International

The Company's International operations ("International") represent the remaining 17% of Company-operated retail revenues and 18% of total specialty revenues as well as 17% of total net revenues. International operations sell coffee and other beverages, whole bean coffees, complementary food, coffee brewing equipment and merchandise through Company-operated retail stores in the United Kingdom, Canada, Thailand, Australia, Germany, China, Singapore, Puerto Rico, Chile and Ireland. Specialty Operations in International primarily include retail store licensing operations in more than 25 countries and foodservice accounts in Canada and the United Kingdom. The Company's International operations are in various early stages of development that require a more extensive support organization, relative to the current levels of revenue and operating income, than in the United States.

Global Consumer Products Group

The Company's CPG segment represents 25% of total specialty revenues and 4% of total net revenues. CPG operations sell a selection of whole bean and ground coffees as well as a selection of premium Tazo® teas through licensing arrangements with Kraft and other grocery and warehouse club stores in United States and international markets. CPG operations also produce and sell ready-to-drink beverages which include, among others, bottled Frappuccino® coffee drinks and Starbucks DoubleShot® espresso drinks, and Starbucks® superpremium ice creams, through its joint venuture partnerships and Starbucks™ Coffee and Cream Liqueurs through a marketing and distribution agreement. Through other manufacturing, distribution and co-packing agreements, the Company produces and sells ready-to-drink products in international locations.

*"Starbucks purchases and roasts high-quality whole bean coffees and sells them, along with fresh, rich-brewed coffees, Italian-style espresso beverages, cold blended beverages, a variety of complementary food items, coffee-related accessories and equipment, a selection of premium teas and a line of compact discs, primarily through company-operated retail stores." 10-K

(continued)

The accounting policies of the operating segments are the same as those described in the summary of significant accounting policies in Note 1. Operating income represents earnings before "Interest and other income, net" and "Income taxes." Allocations of portions of corporate overhead, interest or income taxes to the segments are not significant. Identifiable assets by segment are those assets used in the Company's operations in each segment. Unallocated corporate assets include cash and investments, unallocated assets of the corporate headquarters and roasting facilities, deferred taxes and certain other intangibles. Management evaluates performance of segments based on net revenues and operating expenses.

The table below represents information by operating segment for the fiscal years noted (*in thousands*):

	United States	International	Global CPG	Unallocated Corporate[1]	Total
Fiscal 2006					
Net Revenues:					
Company-operated retail	$5,495,240	$1,087,858	$ —	$ —	$6,583,098
Specialty:					
Licensing	369,155	186,050	305,471	—	860,676
Foodservice and other	314,162	29,006	—	—	343,168
Total specialty	683,317	215,056	305,471	—	1,203,844
Total net revenues	6,178,557	1,302,914	305,471	—	7,786,942
Earnings/(loss) before income taxes	957,631	109,494	166,918	(327,800)	906,243
Depreciation and amortization	284,625	66,800	108	35,678	387,211
Income from equity investees	151	34,370	59,416	—	93,937
Equity method investments	—	163,566	41,438	—	205,004
Identifiable assets	1,996,295	746,398	94,160	1,592,088	4,428,941
Net impairment and disposition losses	9,395	10,084	—	143	19,622
Net capital expenditures	545,074	112,054	286	113,816	771,230

(1) Unallocated corporate includes certain general and administrative expenses, related depreciation and amortization expenses and amounts included in "Interest and other income, net" on the consolidated statements of earnings.

Note: Fiscal 2005 and fiscal 2004 are not presented with the case.

The tables below represent information by geographic area (*in thousands*):

FISCAL YEAR ENDED	Oct. 1, 2006	Oct. 2, 2005	Oct. 3, 2004
Net revenues from external customers:			
United States	$6,478,142	$5,346,967	$4,501,288
Foreign countries	1,308,800	1,022,333	792,959
Total	$7,786,942	$6,369,300	$5,294,247

No customer accounts for 10% or more of the Company's revenues. Revenues from foreign countries are based on the geographic location of the customers and consist primarily of revenues from the United Kingdom and Canada, which together account for approximately 75% of foreign net revenues.

FISCAL YEAR ENDED	Oct. 1, 2006	Oct. 2, 2005	Oct. 3, 2004
Long-lived assets:			
United States	$2,446,126	$1,914,846	$1,739,638
Foreign countries	453,027	389,513	299,740
Total	$2,899,153	$2,304,359	$2,039,378

(continued)

THE STORY OF STARBUCKS—IN SEGMENTS (Continued)

Required

a. For fiscal 2006, prepare a vertical common-size analysis for net revenues using total net revenues as the base.

b. For fiscal year ended, net revenues from external customers, prepare a horizontal common-size analysis using October 3, 2004, as the base.

c. For fiscal year ended, long-lived assets, prepare a horizontal common-size analysis using October 3, 2004, as the base.

d. Comment on the results in (a), (b), and (c).

SCOREBOARDS, ELECTRONIC DISPLAYS, ETC.

Daktronics* included this statement in its 2005 annual report:

	Years Ended		
	April 30, 2005	**May 1, 2004**	**May 3, 2003**
Net sales	$230,346	$209,907	$177,764
Cost of goods sold	157,137	137,436	118,633
Gross profit	73,209	72,471	59,131
Operating expenses:			
Selling	32,840	27,305	24,966
General and administrative	10,434	9,510	7,422
Product design and development	10,499	8,126	6,918
	53,773	44,941	39,306
Operating income	19,436	27,530	19,825
Nonoperating income (expense):			
Interest income	1,453	1,014	694
Interest expense	(211)	(478)	(897)
Other income (expense), net	768	586	974
Income before income taxes and minority interest	21,446	28,652	20,596
Income tax expense	5,786	10,907	8,107
Income before minority interest	15,660	17,745	12,489
Minority interest in income of subsidiary	—	(18)	(31)
Net income	$ 15,660	$ 17,727	$ 12,458
Earnings per share:			
Basic	$ 0.83	$ 0.95	$ 0.68
Diluted	$ 0.78	$ 0.89	$ 0.64

Daktronics, Inc. and Subsidiaries
Consolidated Balance Sheets
(In thousands, except share data)

Assets	April 30, 2005	May 1, 2004
Current Assets:		
Cash and cash equivalents	$ 15,961	$ 12,255
Marketable securities	8,105	4,001
Accounts receivable, less allowance for doubtful accounts	23,762	28,686

*"We are the world's leading supplier of electronic scoreboards, large electronic display systems, marketing services, digital messaging solutions and related software and services for sports, commercial and transportation applications." 10-K

(continued)

SCOREBOARDS, ELECTRONIC DISPLAYS, ETC. (Continued)

	April 30, 2005	May 1, 2004
Current maturities of long-term receivables	5,196	3,771
Inventories	24,612	16,604
Costs and estimated earnings in excess of billings	15,301	12,862
Prepaid expenses and other	1,725	905
Deferred income taxes	5,076	4,375
Income taxes receivable	1,812	813
Rental equipment available for sale	2,733	2,706
Total current assets	104,283	86,978
Property and equipment, net	31,053	25,096
Advertising rights, net	1,722	1,415
Long-term receivables, less current maturities	9,900	10,267
Goodwill	2,621	1,411
Intangible and other assets	1,101	920
Deferred income taxes	782	149
	$151,462	$126,236

Liabilities and Shareholders' Equity

Current Liabilities:

Notes payable, bank	$ 79	$ 214
Accounts payable	17,121	12,586
Accrued expenses and warranty obligations	10,973	9,911
Current maturities of long-term debt	909	1,181
Current maturities of long-term marketing obligations	304	115
Billings in excess of costs and estimated earnings	5,463	6,761
Customer deposits	4,164	2,829
Deferred maintenance revenue	2,983	1,700
Total current liabilities	41,996	35,297
Long-term debt, less current maturities	171	1,148
Long-term marketing obligations, less current maturities	595	350
Deferred income	1,357	1,134
Deferred income taxes	3,433	2,043
	5,556	4,675

Shareholders' Equity:

Common stock, no par value, authorized 60,000,000 shares; 19,165,369 and 18,886,492 shares issued at April 30, 2005 and May 1, 2004, respectively	17,739	16,406
Additional paid-in capital	2,684	2,274
Retained earnings	83,337	67,677
Treasury stock, at cost, 19,680 shares	(9)	(9)
Accumulated other comprehensive income (loss)	159	(84)
	103,910	86,264
	$151,462	$126,236

Required   a. Compute the following for 2005 and 2004:

1. Net profit margin
2. Total asset turnover (use year-end assets)
3. Return on assets (use year-end assets)
4. Operating income margin
5. Return on operating assets (use year-end assets)
6. Sales to fixed assets (use year-end fixed assets)
7. Return on investment (use year-end balance sheet accounts)
8. Return on total equity (use year-end equity)
9. Return on common equity (use year-end common equity)
10. Gross profit margin

b. Comment on the trends in (a).

YAHOO! SERVICES

YAHOO! INC.
Consolidated Statements of Operations
(In thousands, except per share amounts)

	Years Ended December 31,		
	2002	2003	2004
Revenues	$ 953,067	$1,625,097	$3,574,517
Cost of revenues	162,881	358,103	1,298,559
Gross profit	790,186	1,266,994	2,275,958
Operating expenses:			
Sales and marketing	429,968	530,613	778,029
Product development	141,766	207,285	368,760
General and administrative	100,676	157,027	262,602
Stock compensation expense*	8,402	22,029	32,290
Amortization of intangibles	21,186	54,374	145,696
Total operating expenses	701,998	971,328	1,587,377
Income from operations	88,188	295,666	688,581
Other income, net	69,287	47,506	496,443
Income before income taxes, earnings in equity interests, minority interests and cumulative effect of accounting change	157,475	343,172	1,185,024
Provision for income taxes	(71,290)	(147,024)	(437,966)
Earnings in equity interests	22,301	47,652	94,991
Minority interests in operations of consolidated subsidiaries	(1,551)	(5,921)	(2,496)
Net income before cumulative effect of accounting change	106,935	237,879	839,553
Cumulative effect of accounting change	(64,120)	—	—
Net income	$ 42,815	$ 237,879	$ 839,553
Net income per share—basic			
Net income per share before cumulative effect of accounting change	$ 0.09	$ 0.19	$ 0.62
Cumulative effect of accounting change per share	(0.05)	—	—
Net income per share—basic	$ 0.04	$ 0.19	$ 0.62
Net income per share—diluted			
Net income per share before cumulative effect of accounting change	$ 0.09	$ 0.18	$ 0.58
Cumulative effect of accounting change per share	(0.05)	—	—
Net income per share—diluted	$ 0.04	$ 0.18	$ 0.58
Shares used in per share calculation—basic	1,187,677	1,233,480	1,353,439
Shares used in per share calculation—diluted	1,220,120	1,310,796	1,452,499
*Stock compensation expense by function:			
Sales and marketing	$ 1,424	$ 5,785	$ 9,620
Product development	1,702	10,526	12,010
General and administrative	5,276	5,718	10,660
Total stock compensation expense	$ 8,402	$ 22,029	$ 32,290

YAHOO! INC.
Consolidated Balance Sheets
(In thousands, except par values)

	December 31,	
Assets	2003	2004
Current assets:		
Cash and cash equivalents	$ 415,892	$ 823,723
Marketable debt securities	893,625	1,875,964

"Yahoo! Inc., together with its consolidated subsidiaries, . . . is a leading global internet brand and one of the most trafficked internet destinations worldwide. . . ." 10-K

(continued)

YAHOO! SERVICES (Continued)

	December 31,	
	2003	2004
Marketable equity securities	—	812,288
Accounts receivable, net of allowance of $31,961 and $34,215, respectively	282,415	479,993
Prepaid expenses and other current assets	129,777	98,507
Total current assets	1,721,709	4,090,475
Long-term marketable debt securities	1,256,698	1,042,575
Property and equipment, net	449,512	531,696
Goodwill	1,805,561	2,550,957
Intangible assets, net	445,640	480,666
Other assets	252,534	481,832
Total assets	$5,931,654	$9,178,201

Liabilities and Stockholders' Equity

Current liabilities:		
Accounts payable	$ 31,890	$ 48,205
Accrued expenses and other current liabilities	483,628	853,115
Deferred revenue	192,278	279,387
Total current liabilities	707,796	1,180,707
Long-term deferred revenue	—	65,875
Long-term debt	750,000	750,000
Other long-term liabilities	72,890	35,907
Commitments and contingencies (Note 13)		
Minority interests in consolidated subsidiaries	37,478	44,266
Stockholders' equity:		
Preferred Stock, $0.001 par value; 10,000 shares authorized; none issued or outstanding	—	—
Common Stock, $0.001 par value; 10,000,000 shares authorized; 1,321,408 and 1,383,584 issued and outstanding, respectively	1,354	1,416
Additional paid-in capital	4,340,514	5,682,884
Deferred stock-based compensation	(52,374)	(28,541)
Treasury stock	(159,988)	(159,988)
Retained earnings	230,386	1,069,939
Accumulated other comprehensive income	3,598	535,736
Total stockholders' equity	4,363,490	7,101,446
Total liabilities and stockholders' equity	$5,931,654	$9,178,201

The accompanying notes are an integral part of these consolidated financial statements.

Required   a. Compute the following for 2004 and 2003:

1. Net profit margin
2. Total asset turnover (use year-end total assets)
3. Return on assets (use year-end total assets)
4. Operating income margin
5. Return on operating assets (use year-end operating assets)
6. Sales to fixed assets (use year-end fixed assets)
7. Return on investment (use year-end long-term liabilities & equity)
8. Return on total equity (use year-end total equity)
9. Gross profit margin

b. Comment on the trends in (a).

c. 1. Prepare a horizontal common-size consolidated statement of operations for 2002–2004. Use 2002 as the base.
2. Comment on the results in (1).

EAT AT MY RESTAURANT—PROFITABILITY VIEW

With this case, we review the profitability of several restaurant companies. The restaurant companies reviewed and the year-end dates are as follows:

1. **Yum Brands, Inc. (December 30, 2006; December 30, 2005)**
   "Yum consists of six operating segments: KFC, Pizza Hut, Taco Bell, LSS/A&W, Yum Restaurants International . . . and Yum Restaurants China." 10-K

2. **Panera Bread (December 26, 2006; December 27, 2005)**
   "As of December 26, 2006, we operated directly and through area development agreements with 41 franchise groups, bakery-cafes under the Panera Bread® and Saint Louis Bread® names." 10-K

3. **Starbucks (October 1, 2006; October 2, 2005)**
   "Starbucks purchases and roasts high-quality whole bean coffees and sells them, along with fresh, rich-brewed coffees, Italian-style espresso beverages, cold blended beverages, a variety of complementary food items, coffee-related accessories and equipment, a selection of premium teas and a line of compact discs, primarily through company-operated retail stores." 10-K

Data Reviewed	Yum Brands, Inc.		Panera Bread		Starbucks	
	2006	2005	2006	2005	2006	2005
Net profit margin	8.62%	8.15%	7.10%	8.15%	6.26%	6.56%
Return on assets	13.56%	13.26%	12.01%	13.69%	14.64%	14.33%
Return on total equity	57.10%	50.07%	16.47%	18.69%	26.93%	21.68%

Required
a. Comment on the net profit margin for these companies. Consider absolute amounts and trend.
b. Comment on the return on assets for these companies. Consider absolute amounts and trend.
c. Comment on the return on total equity for these companies. Consider absolute amounts and trend.
d. Comment on the relative profitability of these companies.

Thomson One *Business School Edition*

Please complete the Web case that covers material discussed in this chapter at academic.cengage.com/accounting/Gibson. You'll be using Thomson One Business School Edition, a powerful tool, that combines a full range of fundamental financial information, earnings estimates, market data, and source documents for 500 publicly traded companies.

Endnotes

1. Release No. 33-8176, January 22, 2003, Conditions for Use of Non-GAAP Financial Measures Release Nos.: 34-47226; FR-65. http://www.sec.gov, "Regulatory Actions, Final Rule Releases."
2. Richard Barker, "Reporting Financial Performance," *Accounting Horizons* (June 2004), p. 159.
3. Michael Rapoport, "Pro Forma Proves a Hard Habit to Break on Earning Reports," *The Wall Street Journal* (September 18, 2003), p. B38.
4. Ibid., p. B38.

Chapter 9

For the Investor

Certain types of analysis particularly concern investors. While this chapter is not intended as a comprehensive guide to investment analysis, it will introduce certain types of analysis useful to the investor. In addition to the analysis covered in this chapter, an investor would also be interested in the liquidity, debt, and profitability ratios covered in prior chapters.

Leverage and Its Effects on Earnings

The use of debt, called *financial leverage*, has a significant impact on earnings. The existence of fixed operating costs, called *operating leverage*, also affects earnings. The higher the percentage of fixed operating costs, the greater the variation in income as a result of a variation in sales (revenue).

This book does not compute a ratio for operating leverage because it cannot be readily computed from published financial statements. This book does compute financial leverage because it is readily computed from published financial statements.

The expense of debt financing is interest, a fixed charge dependent on the amount of financial principal and the rate of interest. Interest is a contractual obligation created by the borrowing agreement. In contrast to dividends, interest must be paid regardless of whether the firm is in a highly profitable period. An advantage of interest over dividends is its tax deductibility. Because the interest is subtracted to calculate taxable income, income tax expense is reduced.

DEFINITION OF FINANCIAL LEVERAGE AND MAGNIFICATION EFFECTS

The use of financing with a fixed charge (such as interest) is termed **financial leverage**. Financial leverage is successful if the firm earns more on the borrowed funds than it pays to use them. It is not successful if the firm earns less on the borrowed funds than it pays to use them. Using financial leverage results in a fixed financing charge that can materially affect the earnings available to the common shareholders.

Exhibit 9-1 illustrates financial leverage and its magnification effects. In this illustration, earnings before interest and tax for Dowell Company are $1,000,000. Further, the firm has interest expense of $200,000 and a tax rate of 40%. The statement illustrates the effect of

| Exhibit | 9-1 | DOWELL COMPANY |

Financial Leverage—Partial Income Statement to Illustrate Magnification Effects

	Base Year Figures	20% Decrease in Earnings Before Interest and Tax	10% Increase in Earnings Before Interest and Tax
Earnings before interest and tax	$1,000,000	$ 800,000	$1,100,000
Interest	(200,000)	(200,000)	(200,000)
Earnings before tax	800,000	600,000	900,000
Income tax (40%)	(320,000)	(240,000)	(360,000)
Net income	$ 480,000	$ 360,000	$ 540,000
Percentage change in net income [A]		25.0%	12.5%
Percentage change in earnings before interest and tax [B]		20.0%	10.0%
Degree of financial leverage [A ÷ B]		1.25	1.25

leverage on the return to the common stockholder. At earnings before interest and tax (EBIT) of $1,000,000, the net income is $480,000. If EBIT increases by 10% to $1,100,000, as in the exhibit, the net income rises by 12.5%. This magnification is caused by the fixed nature of interest expense. While earnings available to pay interest rise, interest remains the same, thus leaving more for the residual owners. Note that since the tax rate remains the same, earnings before tax change at the same rate as earnings after tax. Hence, this analysis could be made with either profit figure.

If financial leverage is used, a rise in EBIT will cause an even greater rise in net income, and a decrease in EBIT will cause an even greater decrease in net income. Looking again at the statement for Dowell Company in Exhibit 9-1, when EBIT declined 20%, net income dropped from $480,000 to $360,000—a decline of $120,000, or 25%, based on the original $480,000. The use of financial leverage, termed trading on the equity, is only successful if the rate of earnings on borrowed funds exceeds the fixed charges.

COMPUTATION OF THE DEGREE OF FINANCIAL LEVERAGE

The degree of financial leverage is the multiplication factor by which the net income changes as compared to the change in EBIT. One way of computing it follows:

$$\frac{\% \text{ Change Net Income}}{\% \text{ Change EBIT}}$$

For Dowell Company:

$$\frac{12.5\%}{10.0\%} = 1.25, = \frac{25.0\%}{20.0\%} = 1.25$$

The degree of financial leverage is 1.25. From a base EBIT of $1,000,000, any change in EBIT will be accompanied by 1.25 times that change in net income. If net income before interest and tax rises 4%, earnings to the stockholder will rise 5%. If net income before interest and tax falls 8%, earnings to the stockholder will decline 10%. The degree of financial leverage (DFL) can be computed more easily as follows:

$$\text{Degree of Financial Leverage} = \frac{\text{Earnings Before Interest and Tax}}{\text{Earnings Before Tax}}$$

Again referring to Dowell Company:

$$\frac{\text{Degree of Financial Leverage at Earnings}}{\text{Before Interest and Tax on } \$1,000,000} = \frac{\$1,000,000}{\$800,000} = 1.25$$

Note that the degree of financial leverage represents a particular base level of income. The degree of financial leverage may differ for other levels of income or fixed charges.

The degree of financial leverage formula will not work precisely when the income statement includes any of the following items:

1. Minority share of earnings
2. Equity income
3. Nonrecurring items
   a. Discontinued operations
   b. Extraordinary items

When any of these items are included, they should be eliminated from the numerator and denominator. The all-inclusive formula follows:

$$\text{Degree of Financial Leverage} = \frac{\text{Earnings Before Interest, Tax, Minority Share of Earnings, Equity Income, and Nonrecurring Items}}{\text{Earnings Before Tax, Minority Share of Earnings, Equity Income, and Nonrecurring Items}}$$

This formula results in the ratio by which earnings before interest, tax, minority share of earnings, equity income, and nonrecurring items will change in relation to a change in earnings before tax, minority share of earnings, equity income, and nonrecurring items. In other words, it eliminates the minority share of earnings, equity income, and nonrecurring items from the degree of financial leverage.

Exhibit 9-2 shows the degree of financial leverage for 2007 and 2006 for Nike. The degree of financial leverage is 1.02 for 2007 and 1.02 for 2006. This is a very low degree of financial leverage. Therefore, the financial leverage at the end of 2007 indicates that as earnings before interest changes, net income will change by 1.02 times that amount. If earnings before interest increases, the financial leverage will be favorable. If earnings before interest decreases, the financial leverage will be unfavorable. In periods of relatively low interest rates or declining interest rates, financial leverage looks more favorable than in periods of high interest rates or increasing interest rates. (*Note:* Essentially, Nike has minor financial leverage in 2007 and 2006.)

Exhibit 9-2	NIKE, INC.		
	Degree of Financial Leverage		
	Base Years 2007 and 2006		
(In millions)		**2007**	**2006**
Income before income taxes [B]		$2,199.9	$2,141.6
Interest		49.7	50.5
Earnings before interest and tax [A]		$2,249.6	$2,192.1
Degree of financial leverage [A ÷ B]		1.02	1.02

SUMMARY OF FINANCIAL LEVERAGE

Two things are important in looking at financial leverage as part of financial analysis. First, how high is the degree of financial leverage? This is a type of risk (or opportunity) measurement from the viewpoint of the stockholder. The higher the degree of financial leverage, the greater the multiplication factor. Second, does the financial leverage work for or against the owners?

Earnings per Common Share

Earnings per share—the amount of income earned on a share of common stock during an accounting period—applies only to common stock and to corporate income statements. Nonpublic companies, because of cost-benefit considerations, do not have to report earnings per share. Because earnings per share receives much attention from the financial community, investors, and potential investors, it will be described in some detail.

Fortunately, we do not need to compute earnings per share. A company is required to present it at the bottom of the income statement. Per-share amounts for discontinued operations and extraordinary items must be presented on the face of the income statement or in the notes to the financial statements. Earnings per share for recurring items is the most significant for primary analysis.

Computing earnings per share initially involves net income, preferred stock dividends declared and accumulated, and the weighted average number of shares outstanding, as follows:

$$\text{Earnings per Share} = \frac{\text{Net Income} - \text{Preferred Dividends}}{\substack{\text{Weighted Average Number of} \\ \text{Common Shares Outstanding}}}$$

Since earnings pertain to an entire period, they should be related to the common shares outstanding during the period. Thus, the denominator of the equation is the weighted average number of common shares outstanding.

To illustrate, assume that a corporation had 10,000 shares of common stock outstanding at the beginning of the year. On July 1, it issued 2,000 shares, and on October 1, it issued another 3,000 shares. The weighted average number of shares outstanding would be computed as follows:

Months Shares Are Outstanding	Shares Outstanding	×	Fraction of Year Outstanding	=	Weighted Average
January–June	10,000		6/12		5,000
July–September	12,000		3/12		3,000
October–December	15,000		3/12		3,750
					11,750

When the common shares outstanding increase as a result of a stock dividend or stock split, retroactive recognition must be given to these events for all comparative earnings per share presentations. Stock dividends and stock splits do not provide the firm with more funds; they only change the number of outstanding shares. Earnings per share should be related to the outstanding common stock after the stock dividend or stock split. In the weighted average common shares illustration, if we assume that a 2-for-1 stock split took place on December 31, the denominator of the earnings per share computation becomes 23,500 (11,750 × 2). The denominator of prior years' earnings per share computations would also be doubled. If we assume that net income is $100,000 and preferred dividends total $10,000 in this illustration, then the earnings per common share would be $3.83 [($100,000 − $10,000)/23,500].

The current earnings per share guidelines call for the presentation of basic earnings per share and diluted earnings per share. Basic earnings per share is computed by dividing net income less preferred dividends by the weighted average number of shares of common stock outstanding during the period. Diluted earnings per share is computed by dividing net income less preferred dividends by the weighted average number of shares of common stock outstanding plus the dilutive effect of potentially dilutive securities. Potentially dilutive securities are convertible securities, warrants, options, or other rights that upon conversion or exercise could in the aggregate dilute earnings per common share.

Exhibit 9-3 presents the earnings per share of Nike for the years 2005, 2006, and 2007. There was a material increase in earnings per share.

Exhibit	9-3	NIKE, INC.		

Earnings per Share

Years Ended May 31, 2007, 2006, and 2005

	2007	2006	2005
Basic earnings per common share	$2.96	$2.69	$2.31
Diluted earnings per common share	$2.93	$2.64	$2.24

Price/Earnings Ratio

The price/earnings (P/E) ratio expresses the relationship between the market price of a share of common stock and that stock's current earnings per share. Compute the P/E ratio as follows:

$$\text{Price/Earnings Ratio} = \frac{\text{Market Price per Share}}{\substack{\text{Diluted Earnings per Share,} \\ \text{Before Nonrecurring Items}}}$$

Using diluted earnings per share results in a higher price/earnings ratio, a conservative computation of the ratio. Ideally, the P/E ratio should be computed using diluted earnings per share for continuing earnings per share. This gives an indication of what is being paid for a dollar of recurring earnings.

P/E ratios are available from many sources, such as *The Wall Street Journal* and *Standard & Poor's Industry Surveys*. Exhibit 9-4 shows the P/E ratio for Nike for 2007 and 2006. The P/E ratio was 19.37 at the end of 2007 and 15.21 at the end of 2006. This indicates that the stock has been selling for about 19 times earnings. You can get a perspective on this ratio by comparing it to competitors, average P/E for the industry, and an average for all of the stocks on an exchange, such as the New York Stock Exchange. These averages will vary greatly over several years.

Exhibit	9-4	NIKE, INC.		

Price/Earnings Ratio

May 31, 2007 and 2006

	2007	2006
Market price per common share (May 31, close) [A]	$56.75	$40.16
Diluted earnings per share before nonrecurring items [B]	$ 2.93	$ 2.64
Price/earnings ratio [A ÷ B]	19.37	15.21

Investors view the P/E ratio as a gauge of future earning power of the firm. Companies with high growth opportunities generally have high P/E ratios; firms with low growth tend to have lower P/E ratios. However, investors may be wrong in their estimates of growth potential. One fundamental of investing is to be wiser than the market. An example would be buying a stock that has a relatively low P/E ratio when the prospects for the company are much better than reflected in the P/E ratio.

P/E ratios do not have any meaning when a firm has abnormally low profits in relation to the asset base or when a firm has losses. The P/E ratio in these cases would be abnormally high or negative.

Percentage of Earnings Retained

The proportion of current earnings retained for internal growth is computed as follows:

$$\text{Percentage of Earnings Retained} = \frac{\text{Net Income Before Nonrecurring Items} - \text{All Dividends}}{\text{Net Income Before Nonrecurring Items}}$$

The percentage of earnings retained is better for trend analysis if nonrecurring items are removed. This indicates what is being retained of recurring earnings. Determine dividends from the statement of cash flows.

A problem occurs because the percentage of earnings retained implies that earnings represent a cash pool for paying dividends. Under accrual accounting, earnings do not represent a cash pool. Operating cash flow compared with cash dividends gives a better indication of the cash from operations and the dividends paid. Chapter 10 introduces this ratio.

Many firms have a policy on the percentage of earnings that they want retained—for example, between 60% and 75%. In general, new firms, growing firms, and firms perceived as growth firms will have a relatively high percentage of earnings retained. Many new firms, growing firms, and firms perceived as growing firms do not pay dividends.

In the *Almanac of Business and Industrial Financial Ratios*, the percentage of earnings retained is called the *ratio of retained earnings to net income*. The phrase *retained earnings* as used in the ratio in the *Almanac* is a misnomer. Retained earnings in this ratio does not mean accumulated profits, but rather that portion of income retained in a single year. Hence, this ratio has two different names.

Exhibit 9-5 shows the percentage of earnings retained by Nike, using 2007 and 2006 figures. Nike retains a substantial proportion of its profits for internal use. The percentage of earnings retained has been consistent [2001 (78.01%); 2002 (80.71%); 2003 (81.38%); 2004 (81.05%); 2005 (80.46%); 2006 (79.10%); 2007 (76.96%)].

Exhibit 9-5	NIKE, INC.		
Percentage of Earnings Retained			
Years Ended May 31, 2007 and 2006			
(In millions)		**2007**	**2006**
Net income before nonrecurring items [B]		$1,491.5	$1,392.0
Less: Dividends		(343.7)	(290.9)
Earnings retained [A]		$1,147.8	$1,101.1
Percentage of earnings retained [A ÷ B]		76.96%	79.10%

Dividend Payout

The dividend payout ratio measures the portion of current earnings per common share being paid out in dividends. Compute the dividend payout ratio as follows:

$$\text{Dividend Payout} = \frac{\text{Dividends per Common Share}}{\text{Diluted Earnings per Share Before Nonrecurring Items}}$$

Earnings per share are diluted in the formula because this is the most conservative viewpoint. Ideally, diluted earnings per share should not include nonrecurring items since directors normally look at recurring earnings to develop a stable dividend policy.

The dividend payout ratio has a similar problem as the percentage of earnings retained. Investors may assume that dividend payout implies that earnings per share represent cash. Under accrual accounting, earnings per share do not represent a cash pool.

Most firms hesitate to decrease dividends since this tends to have adverse effects on the market price of the company's stock. No rule of thumb exists for a correct payout ratio. Some stockholders prefer high dividends; others prefer to have the firm reinvest the earnings in hopes of higher capital gains. In the latter case, the payout ratio would be a relatively smaller percentage.

Exhibit 9-6 presents Nike's 2007 and 2006 dividend payout ratios, which increased from 22.35% in 2006 to 24.23% in 2007. These are conservative payout ratios. Often, to attract the type of stockholder who looks favorably on a low dividend payout ratio, a company must have a good return on common equity. The dividend payout has been fairly consistent, but did turn up in recent years [2001 (22.22%); 2002 (19.51%); 2003 (19.49%); 2004 (21.08%); 2005 (21.21%); 2006 (22.35%); 2007 (24.23%)].

Exhibit 9-6	NIKE, INC.		
	Dividend Payout		
	Years Ended May 31, 2007 and 2006		
		2007	2006
	Dividends per share [A]	$0.71	$0.59
	Diluted earnings per share before nonrecurring items [B]	$2.93	$2.64
	Dividend payout ratio [A ÷ B]	24.23%	22.35%

Industry averages of dividend payout ratios are available in *Standard & Poor's Industry Surveys*. Although no correct payout exists, even within an industry, the outlook for the industry often makes the bulk of the ratios in a particular industry similar.

In general, new firms, growing firms, and firms perceived as growth firms have a relatively low dividend payout. Nike would be considered a growing firm.

Dividend Yield

The dividend yield indicates the relationship between the dividends per common share and the market price per common share. Compute the dividend yield as follows:

$$\text{Dividend Yield} = \frac{\text{Dividends per Common Share}}{\text{Market Price per Common Share}}$$

For this ratio, multiply the fourth quarter dividend declared by 4. This indicates the current dividend rate. Exhibit 9-7 shows the dividend yield for Nike for 2007 and 2006. The dividend yield has been relatively low.

Exhibit 9-7	NIKE, INC.		
	Dividend Yield		
	May 31, 2007 and 2006		
		2007	2006
	Dividends per share [A]	$ 0.71	$ 0.59
	Market price per share [B]	$56.75	$40.16
	Dividend yield [A ÷ B]	1.25%	1.47%

Since total earnings from securities include both dividends and price appreciation, no rule of thumb exists for dividend yield. The yield depends on the firm's dividend policy and the market price. If the firm successfully invests the money not distributed as dividends, the price should rise. If the firm holds the dividends at low amounts to allow for reinvestment of profits, the dividend yield is likely to be low. A low dividend yield satisfies many investors if the company has a record of above average return on common equity. Investors that want current income prefer a high dividend yield.

Investors are likely very satisfied with the dividend yield of Nike. Dividend yield decreased from 1.47% in 2006 to 1.25% in 2007. During this period, the market price increased from $40.16 to $56.75.

Book Value per Share

A figure frequently published in annual reports is book value per share, which indicates the amount of stockholders' equity that relates to each share of outstanding common stock. The formula for book value per share follows:

$$\text{Book Value per Share} = \frac{\text{Total Stockholders' Equity} - \text{Preferred Stock Equity}}{\text{Number of Common Shares Outstanding}}$$

Preferred stock equity should be stated at liquidation price, if other than book, because the preferred stockholders would be paid this value in the event of liquidation. Liquidation value is sometimes difficult to locate in an annual report. If this value cannot be found, the book figure that relates to preferred stock may be used in place of liquidation value. Exhibit 9-8 shows the book value per share for Nike for 2007 and 2006. The book value increased from $12.28 in 2006 to $14.00 in 2007.

Exhibit 9-8	NIKE, INC.		
	Book Value per Share		
	May 31, 2007 and 2006		
(In millions)		**2007**	**2006**
Shareholders' equity		$7,025.4	$6,285.2
Less: Preferred stock*		—	—
Adjusted shareholders' equity [A]		$7,025.4	$6,285.2
Shares outstanding [B]		501.7	512.0
Book value per share [A ÷ B]		$ 14.00	$ 12.28

*Redeemable preferred stock classified above shareholders' equity.

The market price of the securities usually does not approximate the book value. These historical dollars reflect past unrecovered cost of the assets. The market value of the stock, however, reflects the potential of the firm as seen by the investor. For example, land will be valued at cost, and this asset value will be reflected in the book value. If the asset were purchased several years ago and is now worth substantially more, however, the market value of the stock may recognize this potential.

Book value is of limited use to the investment analyst since it is based on the book numbers. When market value is below book value, investors view the company as lacking potential. A market value above book value indicates that investors view the company as having enough potential to be worth more than the book numbers. Note that Nike was selling materially above book value (Market 2007, $56.75).

When investors are pessimistic about the prospects for stocks, the stocks sell below book value. On the other hand, when investors are optimistic about stock prospects, the stocks sell above book value. There have been times when the majority of stocks sold below book value. There have also been times when the majority of stocks sold at a multiple of 5 or 6 times book value.

Stock Options (Stock-Based Compensation)

Corporations frequently provide stock options (or other stock-based compensation) for employees and officers of the company. Setting aside shares for options (or other stock-based compensation) is very popular in the United States.

Stock Appreciation Rights

Some firms grant key employees stock appreciation rights instead of stock options or in addition to stock options. Stock appreciation rights give the employee the right to receive compensation in cash or stock (or a combination of these) at some future date, based on the difference between the market price of the stock at the date of exercise over a preestablished price.

The accounting for stock appreciation rights directs that the compensation expense recognized each period be based on the difference between the quoted market value at the end of each period and the option price. This compensation expense is then reduced by previously recognized compensation expense on the stock appreciation right. For example, assume that the option price is $10.00 and the market value is $15.00 at the end of the first period of the stock appreciation right. Compensation expense would be recognized at $5.00 ($15.00 − $10.00) per share included in the plan. If 100,000 shares are in the plan, then the expense to be charged to the income statement would be $500,000 ($5.00 × 100,000 shares). If the market value is $12.00 at the end of the second period of the stock appreciation right, expenses are reduced by $3.00 per share. This is because the total compensation expense for the two years is $2.00 ($12.00 − $10.00). Since $5.00 of expense was recognized in the first year, $3.00 of negative compensation is considered in the second year in order to total $2.00 of expense. With 100,000 shares, the reduction to expenses in the second year would be $300,000 ($3.00 × 100,000 shares). Thus, stock appreciation rights can have a material influence on income, dictated by changing stock prices.

A company with outstanding stock appreciation rights describes them in a note to the financial statements. If the number of shares is known, a possible future influence on income can be computed, based on assumptions made regarding future market prices. For example, if the note discloses that the firm has 50,000 shares of stock appreciation rights outstanding, and the stock market price was $10.00 at the end of the year, the analyst can assume a market price at the end of next year and compute the compensation expense for next year. With these facts and an assumed market price of $15.00 at the end of next year, the compensation expense for next year can be computed to be $250,000 [($15.00 − $10.00) × 50,000 shares]. This potential charge to earnings should be considered as the stock is evaluated as a potential investment.

Stock appreciation rights tied to the future market price of the stock can represent a material potential drain on the company. Even a relatively small number of stock appreciation rights outstanding could be material. This should be considered by existing and potential stockholders. Some firms have placed limits on the potential appreciation in order to control the cost of appreciation rights.

Forbes reported the following in a May 17, 1999, article, "Safe Haven."

> *According to the Company's latest filing with the SEC, both the Daimler-Benz and the Chrysler compensation systems disappeared when the merger was consummated. The Daimler bonus and the Chrysler option plan was replaced with performance-based stock appreciation rights.*

The General Electric Company 2001 annual report indicated that "at year-end 2001, there were 131 thousand SARs outstanding at an average exercise price of $7.68." The General Electric Company stock price during 2001 ranged from a low of $28.25 to a high of $52.90.

Apparently, stock appreciation rights were not outstanding as of May 31, 2007, for Nike.

Summary

This chapter has reviewed certain types of analysis that particularly concern investors. Ratios relevant to this analysis include the following:

$$\text{Degree of Financial Leverage} = \frac{\text{Earnings Before Interest and Tax}}{\text{Earnings Before Tax}}$$

A basic understanding of stock option accounting (or other stock-based compensation) is needed in order to assess the disclosure of a company.

In December 2004, the FASB issued SFAS No. 123, revised (R), which is a revision of SFAS No. 123, "Accounting for Stock-Based Compensation." Prior to SFAS No. 123 (R), a company could elect to present the effect of stock-based compensation expense in the body of the income statement or in the notes. Under SFAS No. 123 (R), the effect of stock-based compensation must be presented in the income statement (disclosure detail can be in the notes).

The Securities and Exchange Commission accepted SFAS No. 123 (R), except for the compliance dates. In April 2005, the Commission issued revised compliance dates. The Commission rule allows companies to implement SFAS No. 123 (R) at the beginning of their fiscal year, instead of the next reporting period, that begins after June 15, 2005, or December 15, 2005, for small business issuers.

SFAS No. 123 (R) resulted in greater international comparability in the accounting for share-based transactions. In February 2004, the International Accounting Standards Board (IASB) issued a reporting standard that requires all entities to recognize an expense for all employee services received in share-based payment transactions, using a fair-value-based method that is similar in most respects to the fair-value-based method established in SFAS No. 123 (R).

SFAS No. 123 (R) essentially carried forward the reporting of noncompensatory plans. A noncompensatory plan attempts to raise capital or encourage widespread ownership of the corporation's stock among officers and employees. Because the officers and employees purchase the stock at only a slight discount (usually 5% or less) from the market price, there is not a substantial dilution of the position of existing stockholders or a substantial compensation issue. For those plans, no compensation expense is recognized when these options are exercised, and the shares are issued slightly below the market price.

Two terms that are particularly important to understanding SFAS No. 123 (R) are *grant date* and *vested*. The grant date is the date at which an employer and an employee reach a mutual understanding of the key terms and conditions of a share-based payment award. The employer becomes contingently obligated on the grant date to issue equity instruments or transfer assets to an employee who renders the requisite service.[1] A share-based payment award becomes vested at the date that the employee's right to receive or retain shares, other instruments, or cash under the award is no longer contingent on satisfaction of either a service condition or a performance condition.[2]

Key provisions of SFAS No. 123 (R) are as follows:

1. It requires a public entity to measure the cost of employee services received in exchange for an award of equity instruments based on the grant-date fair value of the award.

2. The option expense will be recognized over the period during which an employee is required to provide service in exchange for the award (usually the vesting period).

3. A public entity will initially measure the cost of employee services received in exchange for an award of liability instruments based on its current fair value.

4. The notes to financial statements of both public and nonpublic entities will disclose information to assist users of financial information to understand the nature of share-based payment transactions and the effects of these transactions on the financial statements.

Warren E. Buffett, one of the world's richest persons and likely the world's most famous investor, has been critical of firms not recognizing option expense in the body of the income statement. His view is that option expense needs to be considered when evaluating the performance of a company.

When stock prices decline, is there a value to holding stock options? A decline in stock prices could make the existing stock options worthless. But many companies rewrite the options with a lower price when the stock declines. Thus, for the holders of the options, it becomes a situation of "tails I win, heads I win." Buffett tells the following story relating to stock options:

> *"A gorgeous woman slinks up to a CEO at a party and through moist lips purrs, 'I'll do anything—anything—you want. Just tell me what you would like.' With no hesitation, he replies, 'Reprice my options.'"*[3]

Nike disclosed $147.7, $11.8, and $4.9 (in millions) in total stock-based compensation for the years ended May 31, 2007, 2006, and 2005, respectively (see Exhibit 9-9). There also

A basic understanding of stock option accounting (or other stock-based compensation) is needed in order to assess the disclosure of a company.

In December 2004, the FASB issued SFAS No. 123, revised (R), which is a revision of SFAS No. 123, "Accounting for Stock-Based Compensation." Prior to SFAS No. 123 (R), a company could elect to present the effect of stock-based compensation expense in the body of the income statement or in the notes. Under SFAS No. 123 (R), the effect of stock-based compensation must be presented in the income statement (disclosure detail can be in the notes).

The Securities and Exchange Commission accepted SFAS No. 123 (R), except for the compliance dates. In April 2005, the Commission issued revised compliance dates. The Commission rule allows companies to implement SFAS No. 123 (R) at the beginning of their fiscal year, instead of the next reporting period, that begins after June 15, 2005, or December 15, 2005, for small business issuers.

SFAS No. 123 (R) resulted in greater international comparability in the accounting for share-based transactions. In February 2004, the International Accounting Standards Board (IASB) issued a reporting standard that requires all entities to recognize an expense for all employee services received in share-based payment transactions, using a fair-value-based method that is similar in most respects to the fair-value-based method established in SFAS No. 123 (R).

SFAS No. 123 (R) essentially carried forward the reporting of noncompensatory plans. A noncompensatory plan attempts to raise capital or encourage widespread ownership of the corporation's stock among officers and employees. Because the officers and employees purchase the stock at only a slight discount (usually 5% or less) from the market price, there is not a substantial dilution of the position of existing stockholders or a substantial compensation issue. For those plans, no compensation expense is recognized when these options are exercised, and the shares are issued slightly below the market price.

Two terms that are particularly important to understanding SFAS No. 123 (R) are *grant date* and *vested*. The **grant date** is the date at which an employer and an employee reach a mutual understanding of the key terms and conditions of a share-based payment award. The employer becomes contingently obligated on the grant date to issue equity instruments or transfer assets to an employee who renders the requisite service.[1] A share-based payment award becomes **vested** at the date that the employee's right to receive or retain shares, other instruments, or cash under the award is no longer contingent on satisfaction of either a service condition or a performance condition.[2]

Key provisions of SFAS No. 123 (R) are as follows:

1. It requires a public entity to measure the cost of employee services received in exchange for an award of equity instruments based on the grant-date fair value of the award.

2. The option expense will be recognized over the period during which an employee is required to provide service in exchange for the award (usually the vesting period).

3. A public entity will initially measure the cost of employee services received in exchange for an award of liability instruments based on its current fair value.

4. The notes to financial statements of both public and nonpublic entities will disclose information to assist users of financial information to understand the nature of share-based payment transactions and the effects of these transactions on the financial statements.

Warren E. Buffett, one of the world's richest persons and likely the world's most famous investor, has been critical of firms not recognizing option expense in the body of the income statement. His view is that option expense needs to be considered when evaluating the performance of a company.

When stock prices decline, is there a value to holding stock options? A decline in stock prices could make the existing stock options worthless. But many companies rewrite the options with a lower price when the stock declines. Thus, for the holders of the options, it becomes a situation of "tails I win, heads I win." Buffett tells the following story relating to stock options:

> "*A gorgeous woman slinks up to a CEO at a party and through moist lips purrs, 'I'll do anything—anything—you want. Just tell me what you would like.' With no hesitation, he replies, 'Reprice my options.'*"[3]

Nike disclosed $147.7, $11.8, and $4.9 (in millions) in total stock-based compensation for the years ended May 31, 2007, 2006, and 2005, respectively (see Exhibit 9-9). There also

Exhibit	9-9	NIKE, INC.

Stock-Based Compensation Expense

Note 10—Common Stock (in Part)

The following table summarizes the Company's total stock-based compensation expense recognized in selling and administrative expense:

	Year Ended May 31,		
	2007	2006	2005
	(In millions)		
Stock options	$134.9	$ 0.3	$1.0
ESPPs	7.0	—	—
Restricted stock[1]	5.8	11.5	3.9
Total stock-based compensation expense	$147.7	$11.8	$4.9

[1]The expense related to restricted stock awards was included in selling and administrative expense in prior years and was not affected by the adoption of FAS 123R.

During the years ended May 31, 2007, 2006 and 2005, the Company also granted shares of stock under the Long-Term Incentive Plan ("LTIP"), adopted by the Board of Directors and approved by shareholders in September 1997. The LTIP provides for the issuance of up to 2.0 million shares of Class B Common Stock. Under the LTIP, awards are made to certain executives in their choice of either cash or stock, based on performance targets established over three-year time periods. Once performance targets are achieved, cash or shares of stock are issued. The shares are immediately vested upon grant. The value of the shares is established by the market price on the date of issuance. Under the LTIP, 3,000, 6,000 and 8,000 shares with a price of $38.84, $40.79 and $34.85, respectively, were issued during the years ended May 31, 2007, 2006 and 2005 for the plan years ended May 31, 2006, 2005 and 2004, respectively. The Company recognized nominal expense related to the shares issued during the years ended May 31, 2007 and 2006, and $0.1 million during the year ended May 31, 2005. The Company recognized $30.0 million, $21.7 million and $22.1 million of selling and administrative expense related to the cash awards during the years ended May 31, 2007, 2006 and 2005, respectively. During the year ended May 31, 2007, LTIP participants agreed to amend their grant agreements to eliminate the ability to receive payments in shares of stock, so shares of stock are no longer awarded. Beginning with the plan year ended May 31, 2007, cash will be awarded if performance targets are achieved.

Note 1—Summary of Significant Accounting Policies (in Part)

The following table summarizes the effects of applying FAS 123R during the year ended May 31, 2007. The resulting stock-based compensation expense primarily relates to stock options.

(in millions, except per share data)	
Addition to selling and administrative expense	$141.9
Reduction to income tax expense	(45.2)
Reduction to net income[1]	$ 96.7
Reduction to earnings per share:	
Basic	$ 0.19
Diluted	$ 0.18

[1]In accordance with FAS 123R, stock-based compensation expense reported during the year ended May 31, 2007, includes $24.2 million, net of tax, or $0.04 per diluted share, of accelerated stock-based compensation.

Exhibit	9-9	NIKE, INC. (Continued)

Comment added by author as follows: The Note 1 reduction to net income does not include the $5.8 million for restricted stock for year ended May 31, 2007. Including the restricted stock expense, net of tax results in an additional reduction to net income for the year ended May 31, 2007 of $3.95 million [$5.8 × (1 − tax rate) or $5.8 × (1 − 31.85%)].

Summary

Reduction to net income disclosed in note 1	$ 96.70 million
Reduction related to restricted stock	3.95
Total reduction to net income	$100.65

appeared to be a nominal amount of stock-based compensation under a long-term incentive plan (LTIP) for May 31, 2007, 2006, and 2005.

Note 10 (in Exhibit 9-9) states that: "During the year ended May 31, 2007, LTIP participants agreed to amend their grant agreements to eliminate the ability to receive payments in shares of stock, so shares of stock are no longer awarded. Beginning with the plan year ended May 31, 2007, cash will be awarded if performance targets are achieved."

The impact of option expense can be substantial, resulting in lower net income and earnings per share. It can have a particularly material impact on high-tech companies that are rewarding employees with substantial stock-based compensation.

To assist in determining the materiality of options, use the following ratio:

$$\text{Materiality of Options} = \frac{\begin{array}{c}\text{Net Income Before}\\\text{Nonrecurring Items Not}\\\text{Including Option Expense}\end{array} - \begin{array}{c}\text{Net Income Before}\\\text{Nonrecurring Items}\\\text{Including Option Expense}\end{array}}{\begin{array}{c}\text{Net Income Before Nonrecurring Items Not}\\\text{Including Option Expense}\end{array}}$$

Using data from Exhibits 9-5 and 9-9 for Nike, the materiality of options is computed for 2007 as follows:

$$\text{Materiality of Options} = \frac{(\$1,491.50 + \$100.65) - \$1,491.50}{(\$1,491.50 + \$100.65)}$$
$$= 6.32\%$$

For Nike, the impact of option expense appears to be moderate.

Restricted Stock

In July 2003, Microsoft Corporation announced that it would stop issuing stock options to employees and instead give them restricted stock. This was a defining event in the popularity of restricted stock and the reduction in stock option plans. With restricted stock, employees cannot sell their shares until a certain amount of time passes, and employees may have to forfeit their shares if they leave before vesting. Often, a portion of the shares vest each year for three, four, or five years. For some restricted stock, an employee forfeits the shares if certain financial targets are not met. With restricted stock, the expense is booked by companies in a manner similar to the new requirement for expensing options. Some employees prefer restricted stock over options because they receive actual shares of stock. Usually, the employee receives dividends. This may occur before the stock has vested.

Traditionally, restricted stock was only awarded to top executives, possibly along with options. In anticipation of a standard requiring expensing of options, firms started to issue restricted stock to a broad group of employees instead of options, sometimes in conjunction with options.

For Nike, as shown in Exhibit 9-9, restricted stock was included in the total stock-based compensation expense.

Stock Appreciation Rights

Some firms grant key employees stock appreciation rights instead of stock options or in addition to stock options. Stock appreciation rights give the employee the right to receive compensation in cash or stock (or a combination of these) at some future date, based on the difference between the market price of the stock at the date of exercise over a preestablished price.

The accounting for stock appreciation rights directs that the compensation expense recognized each period be based on the difference between the quoted market value at the end of each period and the option price. This compensation expense is then reduced by previously recognized compensation expense on the stock appreciation right. For example, assume that the option price is $10.00 and the market value is $15.00 at the end of the first period of the stock appreciation right. Compensation expense would be recognized at $5.00 ($15.00 − $10.00) per share included in the plan. If 100,000 shares are in the plan, then the expense to be charged to the income statement would be $500,000 ($5.00 × 100,000 shares). If the market value is $12.00 at the end of the second period of the stock appreciation right, expenses are reduced by $3.00 per share. This is because the total compensation expense for the two years is $2.00 ($12.00 − $10.00). Since $5.00 of expense was recognized in the first year, $3.00 of negative compensation is considered in the second year in order to total $2.00 of expense. With 100,000 shares, the reduction to expenses in the second year would be $300,000 ($3.00 × 100,000 shares). Thus, stock appreciation rights can have a material influence on income, dictated by changing stock prices.

A company with outstanding stock appreciation rights describes them in a note to the financial statements. If the number of shares is known, a possible future influence on income can be computed, based on assumptions made regarding future market prices. For example, if the note discloses that the firm has 50,000 shares of stock appreciation rights outstanding, and the stock market price was $10.00 at the end of the year, the analyst can assume a market price at the end of next year and compute the compensation expense for next year. With these facts and an assumed market price of $15.00 at the end of next year, the compensation expense for next year can be computed to be $250,000 [($15.00 − $10.00) × 50,000 shares]. This potential charge to earnings should be considered as the stock is evaluated as a potential investment.

Stock appreciation rights tied to the future market price of the stock can represent a material potential drain on the company. Even a relatively small number of stock appreciation rights outstanding could be material. This should be considered by existing and potential stockholders. Some firms have placed limits on the potential appreciation in order to control the cost of appreciation rights.

Forbes reported the following in a May 17, 1999, article, "Safe Haven."

> *According to the Company's latest filing with the SEC, both the Daimler-Benz and the Chrysler compensation systems disappeared when the merger was consummated. The Daimler bonus and the Chrysler option plan was replaced with performance-based stock appreciation rights.*

The General Electric Company 2001 annual report indicated that "at year-end 2001, there were 131 thousand SARs outstanding at an average exercise price of $7.68." The General Electric Company stock price during 2001 ranged from a low of $28.25 to a high of $52.90.

Apparently, stock appreciation rights were not outstanding as of May 31, 2007, for Nike.

Summary

This chapter has reviewed certain types of analysis that particularly concern investors. Ratios relevant to this analysis include the following:

$$\text{Degree of Financial Leverage} = \frac{\text{Earnings Before Interest and Tax}}{\text{Earnings Before Tax}}$$

$$\text{All-Inclusive Degree of Financial Leverage} = \frac{\text{Earnings Before Interest, Tax, Minority Share of Earnings, Equity Income, and Nonrecurring Items}}{\text{Earnings Before Tax, Minority Share of Earnings, Equity Income, and Nonrecurring Items}}$$

$$\text{Diluted Earnings per Common Share} = \frac{\text{Net Income} - \text{Preferred Dividends}}{\text{Weighted Average Number of Common Shares Outstanding}}$$

$$\text{Price/Earnings Ratio} = \frac{\text{Market Price per Share}}{\text{Diluted Earnings per Share, Before Nonrecurring Items}}$$

$$\text{Percentage of Earnings Retained} = \frac{\text{Net Income Before Nonrecurring Items} - \text{All Dividends}}{\text{Net Income Before Nonrecurring Items}}$$

$$\text{Dividend Payout} = \frac{\text{Dividends per Common Share}}{\text{Diluted Earnings per Share Before Nonrecurring Items}}$$

$$\text{Dividend Yield} = \frac{\text{Dividends per Common Share}}{\text{Market Price per Common Share}}$$

$$\text{Book Value per Share} = \frac{\text{Total Stockholders' Equity} - \text{Preferred Stock Equity}}{\text{Number of Common Shares Outstanding}}$$

$$\text{Materiality of Options} = \frac{\begin{array}{c}\text{Net Income Before} \\ \text{Nonrecurring Items} \\ \text{Not Including Option} \\ \text{Expense}\end{array} - \begin{array}{c}\text{Net Income Before} \\ \text{Nonrecurring Items} \\ \text{Including Option} \\ \text{Expense}\end{array}}{\begin{array}{c}\text{Net Income Before Nonrecurring Items} \\ \text{Not Including Option Expense}\end{array}}$$

to the net

1. Go to the SEC Web site (http://www.sec.gov). Under "Filings & Forms (EDGAR)," click on "Search for Company Filings." Click on "Companies & Other Filers." Under Company Name, enter "Belden" (or under Ticker Symbol, enter "BDC"). Select the 10-K submitted March 5, 2007. For the years ended 2006, 2005, and 2004, compute or find the following:

   a. Earnings per common share (basic and diluted).

   b. Price/earnings ratio.

   c. Percentage of earnings retained.

   d. Dividend payout.

   e. Dividend yield.

   Note:

   Market price—December 31

2006	$39.09
2005	$24.43
2004	$23.29

2. Go to the SEC Web site (http://www.sec.gov). Under "Filings & Forms (EDGAR)," click on "Search for Company Filings." Click on "Companies & Other Filers." Under Company Name, enter "Motorola Inc" (or under Ticker Symbol, enter "MOT"). Select the 10-K submitted February 28, 2007.

   Review the consolidated statements of operations for the years ended December 31, 2006, 2005, and 2004. In your opinion, what line item(s) makes it difficult to form an opinion on the results of Motorola, Inc.?

3. Go to the SEC Web site (http://www.sec.gov). Under "Filings & Forms (EDGAR)," click on "Search for Company Filings." Click on "Companies & Other Filers." Under Company Name, enter "Boeing Co" (or under Ticker Symbol, enter "BA"). Select the 10-K submitted February 16, 2007.

For the years ended December 31, 2006, 2005, and 2004, compute the following:

a. Earnings per common share.

b. Price/earnings ratio.

c. Percentage of earnings retained.

d. Dividend payout.

e. Dividend yield.

Note: Seldom does a firm include the year-end market price in its financial report. The year-end market price usually needs to be obtained from other sources.

4. Go to the SEC Web site (http://www.sec.gov). Under "Filings & Forms (EDGAR)," click on "Search for Company Filings." Click on "Companies & Other Filers." Under Company Name, enter "ICT Group Inc" (or under Ticker Symbol, enter "ICTG"). Select the 10-K

submitted March 9, 2007. For December 31, 2006, and 2005, find the following:

a. Total assets.

b. Shareholders' equity.

c. Common stock shares issued and outstanding.

d. Compute the total capitalization at December 31, 2006, and December 31, 2005.

e. Why is the total capitalization different than the total shareholders' equity?

Note:

Market price—December 31

2006	$31.59
2005	$16.95

Common Stock (in thousands)—December 31

2006	15,734 shares
2005	12,789 shares

Questions

Q 9-1.   Give a simple definition of *earnings per share*.

Q 9-2.   Assume that the corporation is a nonpublic company. Comment on the requirement for this firm to disclose earnings per share.

Q 9-3.   Keller & Fink, a partnership, engages in the wholesale fish market. How would this company disclose earnings per share?

Q 9-4.   Dividends on preferred stock total $5,000 for the current year. How would these dividends influence earnings per share?

Q 9-5.   The denominator of the earnings per share computation includes the weighted average number of common shares outstanding. Why use the weighted average instead of the year-end common shares outstanding?

Q 9-6.   Preferred dividends decreased this year because some preferred stock was retired. How would this influence the earnings per share computation this year?

Q 9-7.   Retroactive recognition is given to stock dividends and stock splits on common stock when computing earnings per share. Why?

Q 9-8.   Why do many firms try to maintain a stable percentage of earnings retained?

Q 9-9.   Define *financial leverage*. What is its effect on earnings? When is the use of financial leverage advantageous and disadvantageous?

Q 9-10.   Given a set level of earnings before interest and tax, how will a rise in interest rates affect the degree of financial leverage?

Q 9-11.   Why is the price/earnings ratio considered a gauge of future earning power?

Q 9-12.   Why does a relatively new firm often have a low dividend payout ratio? Why does a firm with a substantial growth record and/or substantial growth prospects often have a low dividend payout ratio?

Q 9-13. Why would an investor ever buy stock in a firm with a low dividend yield?

Q 9-14. Why is book value often meaningless? What improvements to financial statements would make it more meaningful?

Q 9-15. Why should an investor read the note concerning stock options? How might stock options affect profitability?

Q 9-16. Why can a relatively small number of stock appreciation rights prove to be a material drain on future earnings and cash of a company?

Q 9-17. Explain how outstanding stock appreciation rights could increase reported income in a particular year.

Problems

P 9-1. McDonald Company shows the following condensed income statement information for the current year:

Revenue from sales		$ 3,500,000
Cost of products sold		(1,700,000)
Gross profit		1,800,000
Operating expenses:		
Selling expenses	$425,000	
General expenses	350,000	(775,000)
Operating income		1,025,000
Other income		20,000
Interest		(70,000)
Operating income before income taxes		975,000
Taxes related to operations		(335,000)
Income from operations		640,000
Extraordinary loss (less applicable income taxes of $40,000)		(80,000)
Income before minority interest		560,000
Minority share of earnings		(50,000)
Net income		$ 510,000

Required Calculate the degree of financial leverage.

P 9-2. A firm has earnings before interest and tax of $1,000,000, interest of $200,000, and net income of $400,000 in Year 1.

Required
a. Calculate the degree of financial leverage in base Year 1.
b. If earnings before interest and tax increase by 10% in Year 2, what will be the new level of earnings, assuming the same tax rate as in Year 1?
c. If earnings before interest and tax decrease to $800,000 in Year 2, what will be the new level of earnings, assuming the same tax rate as in Year 1?

P 9-3. The following information was in the annual report of Rover Company:

	2007	2006	2005
Earnings per share	$1.12	$1.20	$1.27
Cash dividends per share (common)	$0.90	$0.85	$0.82
Market price per share	$12.80	$14.00	$16.30
Total common dividends	$21,700,000	$19,500,000	$18,360,000
Shares outstanding, end of year	24,280,000	23,100,000	22,500,000
Total assets	$1,280,100,000	$1,267,200,000	$1,260,400,000
Total liabilities	$800,400,000	$808,500,000	$799,200,000
Nonredeemable preferred stock	$15,300,000	$15,300,000	$15,300,000
Preferred dividends	$910,000	$910,000	$910,000
Net income	$31,200,000	$30,600,000	$29,800,000

Required   a. Based on these data, compute the following for 2007, 2006, and 2005:
              1. Percentage of earnings retained
              2. Price/earnings ratio
              3. Dividend payout
              4. Dividend yield
              5. Book value per share
            b. Discuss your findings from the viewpoint of a potential investor.

P 9-4.   The following data relate to Edger Company:

	2007	2006	2005
Earnings per share	$2.30	$3.40	$4.54
Dividends per share	$1.90	$1.90	$1.90
Market price, end of year	$41.25	$35.00	$29.00
Net income	$9,100,000	$13,300,000	$16,500,000
Total cash dividends	$6,080,000	$5,900,000	$6,050,000
Order backlog at year-end	$5,490,800,000	$4,150,200,000	$3,700,100,000
Net contracts awarded	$2,650,700,000	$1,800,450,000	$3,700,100,000

Note: The stock was selling at 120.5%, 108.0%, and 105.0% of book value in 2007, 2006, and 2005, respectively.

Required   a. Compute the following for 2007, 2006, and 2005:
              1. Percentage of earnings retained
              2. Price/earnings ratio
              3. Dividend payout
              4. Dividend yield
              5. Book value per share
            b. Comment on your results from (a). Include in your discussion the data on backlog and new contracts awarded.

P 9-5.   Dicker Company has the following pattern of financial data for Years 1 and 2:

	Year 1	Year 2
Net income	$40,000	$42,000
Preferred stock (5%)	$450,000	$550,000
Weighted average number of common shares outstanding	38,000	38,000

Required   Calculate earnings per share and comment on the trend.

P 9-6.   Assume the following facts for the current year:
              Common shares outstanding on January 1, 50,000 shares
              July 1, 2-for-1 stock split
              October 1, a stock issue of 10,000 shares

Required   Compute the denominator of the earnings per share computation for the current year.

P 9-7.   XYZ Corporation reported earnings per share of $2.00 in 2006. In 2007, XYZ Corporation reported earnings per share of $1.50. On July 1, 2007, and December 31, 2007, 2-for-1 stock splits were declared.

Required   Present the earnings per share for a two-year comparative income statement that includes 2007 and 2006.

P 9-8.   Cook Company shows the following condensed income statement information for the year ended December 31, 2007:

Income before extraordinary gain	$30,000
Plus: Extraordinary gain, net of tax expense of $2,000	5,000
Net income	$35,000

The company declared dividends of $3,000 on preferred stock and $5,000 on common stock. At the beginning of 2007, 20,000 shares of common stock were outstanding. On July 1, 2007, the company issued 1,000 additional common shares. The preferred stock is not convertible.

Required   a. Compute the earnings per share.
            b. How much of the earnings per share appears to be recurring?

P 9-9.   Assume the following facts for the current year:

Net income	$200,000
Common dividends	$20,000
Preferred dividends (The preferred stock is not convertible.)	$10,000
Common shares outstanding on January 1	20,000 shares
Common stock issued on July 1	5,000 shares
2-for-1 stock split on December 31	

Required   a. Compute the earnings per share for the current year.

b. Earnings per share in the prior year was $8.00. Use the earnings per share computed in (a) and present a two-year earnings per share comparison for the current year and the prior year.

P 9-10.   Smith and Jones, Inc., is primarily engaged in the worldwide production, processing, distribution, and marketing of food products. The following information is from its 2007 annual report:

	2007	2006
Earnings per share	$1.08	$1.14
Cash dividends per common share	$0.80	$0.76
Market price per common share	$12.94	$15.19
Common shares outstanding	25,380,000	25,316,000
Total assets	$1,264,086,000	$1,173,924,000
Total liabilities	$823,758,000	$742,499,000
Nonredeemable preferred stock	$16,600,000	$16,600,000
Preferred dividends	$4,567,000	$930,000
Net income	$32,094,000	$31,049,000

Required   a. Based on these data, compute the following for 2007 and 2006:
1. Percentage of earnings retained
2. Price/earnings ratio
3. Dividend payout
4. Dividend yield
5. Book value per share

b. Discuss your findings from the viewpoint of a potential investor.

P 9-11.   On December 31, 2007, Farley Camera, Inc., issues 5,000 stock appreciation rights to its president to entitle her to receive cash for the difference between the market price of its stock and a preestablished price of $20. The date of exercise is December 31, 2010, and the required service period is the entire three years. The market price fluctuates as follows: 12/31/08—$23.00; 12/31/09—$21.00; 12/31/10—$26.00. Farley Camera accrued the following compensation expense:

2008 $15,000   2009 $(10,000)   2010 $25,000

Required   a. What is the executive's main advantage of receiving stock appreciation rights over stock options?

b. In 2008, a $15,000 expense is recorded. What is the offsetting account?

c. What is the financial impact on the company of the exercise of the stock appreciation rights in 2010? How does this impact affect financial statement analysis?

P 9-12a.   A company has only common stock outstanding.

Required   Answer the following multiple-choice question. Total stockholders' equity minus preferred stock equity divided by the number of shares outstanding represents the
1. Return on equity.
2. Stated value per share.
3. Book value per share.
4. Price/earnings ratio.

P 9-12b.   Maple Corporation's stockholders' equity at June 30, 2007, consisted of the following:

Preferred stock, 10%, $50 par value; liquidating value, $55 per share; 20,000 shares issued and outstanding	$1,000,000
Common stock, $10 par value; 500,000 shares authorized; 150,000 shares issued and outstanding	1,500,000
Retained earnings	500,000

Required   Answer the following multiple-choice question. The book value per share of common stock is
1. $10.00.
2. $12.67.
3. $13.33.
4. $17.65.

P 9-13.   Consecutive five-year balance sheets and income statements of Donna Szabo Corporation are shown below and on the following page.

Required   a. Compute or determine the following for the years 2003–2007.
1. Degree of financial leverage
2. Earnings per common share
3. Price/earnings ratio
4. Percentage of earnings retained
5. Dividend payout
6. Dividend yield
7. Book value per share
8. Materiality of options (use stock options outstanding)
b. Comment from the perspective of an investor.

Donna Szabo Corporation
Balance Sheets
December 31, 2003 through December 31, 2007

(Dollars in thousands)	2007	2006	2005	2004	2003
Assets					
Current assets:					
Cash	$ 26,000	$ 27,000	$ 29,000	$ 28,000	$ 27,000
Accounts receivable, net	125,000	126,000	128,000	130,000	128,000
Inventories	140,000	143,000	145,000	146,000	144,000
Total current assets	291,000	296,000	302,000	304,000	299,000
Property, plant, and					
equipment, net	420,000	418,000	417,000	418,000	415,000
Total assets	$711,000	$714,000	$719,000	$722,000	$714,000
Liabilities and Stockholders' Equity					
Current liabilities:					
Accounts payable	$120,000	$122,000	$122,500	$124,000	$125,000
Income taxes	12,000	13,000	13,500	13,000	12,000
Total current liabilities	132,000	135,000	136,000	137,000	137,000
Long-term debt	90,000	65,000	67,000	68,000	69,000
Stockholders' equity:					
Preferred stock	49,000	76,000	80,000	82,000	75,000
Common stock	290,000	290,000	290,000	290,000	290,000
Paid-in capital in excess of par,					
common stock	70,000	70,000	70,000	70,000	70,000
Retained earnings	80,000	78,000	76,000	75,000	73,000
Total stockholders' equity	489,000	514,000	516,000	517,000	508,000
Total liabilities and					
stockholders' equity	$711,000	$714,000	$719,000	$722,000	$714,000

Donna Szabo Corporation
Statement of Earnings
Years Ended December 31, 2003–2007

(In thousands, except per share)	2007	2006	2005	2004	2003
Net sales	$ 890,000	$ 870,000	$ 850,000	$ 935,000	$ 920,000
Cost of goods sold	(540,000)	(530,700)	(522,750)	(579,000)	(570,000)
Gross profit	350,000	339,300	327,250	356,000	350,000
Selling and					
administrative expense	(230,000)	(225,000)	(220,000)	(225,000)	(224,000)
Interest expense	(9,500)	(6,600)	(6,800)	(6,900)	(7,000)

	2007	2006	2005	2004	2003
Earnings from continuing operations before income taxes	110,500	107,700	100,450	124,100	119,000
Income taxes	(33,000)	(33,300)	(32,100)	(30,400)	(37,400)
Earnings from continuing operations	77,500	74,400	68,350	93,700	81,600
Extraordinary gains, net of taxes	20,000	—	—	—	—
Net earnings	$ 97,500	$ 74,400	$ 68,350	$ 93,700	$ 81,600
Earnings per share:					
Continuing operations	$ 2.67	$ 2.57	$ 2.36	$ 3.23	$ 2.81
Extraordinary gain	0.69	—	—	—	—
Net earnings per share	$ 3.36	$ 2.57	$ 2.36	$ 3.23	$ 2.81

Note: Additional data:

1. Preferred stock dividends (in thousands):

2007	$3,920
2006	$6,100
2005	$6,400
2004	$6,600
2003	$6,000

2. Common shares outstanding, 29,000,000 (actual) (2003–2007)
3. Stock options outstanding, 1,000,000 (actual) (2003–2007)
4. Dividends per common share (actual):

2007	$3.16
2006	$2.29
2005	$2.10
2004	$2.93
2003	$2.80

5. Market price per common share (actual):

2007	$24.00
2006	$22.00
2005	$21.00
2004	$37.00
2003	$29.00

P 9-14.   Answer the following multiple-choice questions:

a. In 2005 and 2006, Zoret Company reported earnings per share of $0.80 and $1.00, respectively. In 2007, Zoret Company declared a 4-for-1 stock split. For the year 2007, Zoret Company reported earnings of $0.30 per share. The appropriate earnings per share presentation for a three-year comparative analysis that includes 2005, 2006, and 2007 would be

	2007	2006	2005
1.	$0.30	$0.25	$0.80
2.	$0.30	$4.00	$3.20
3.	$0.30	$0.25	$0.20
4.	$1.20	$0.25	$0.20
5.	$1.20	$4.00	$3.20

b. The degree of financial leverage for Zorro Company was 1.50 when EBIT was reported at $1,000,000. If EBIT goes to $2,000,000, the accompanying change in net income will be
   1. $2,500,000.
   2. $3,000,000.
   3. $2,000,000.
   4. $1,500,000.
   5. $1,000,000.

c. In 2008, Zello Company declared a 10% stock dividend. In 2007, earnings per share was $1.00. When the 2007 earnings per share is disclosed in the 2008 annual report, it will be disclosed at
   1. $1.00.
   2. $1.10.
   3. $1.20.
   4. $0.91.
   5. $0.81.

d. Which of the following ratios usually reflects investor's opinions of the future prospects for the firm?
   1. Dividend yield
   2. Book value per share
   3. Price/earnings ratio
   4. Earnings per share
   5. Dividend payout

e. Which of the following ratios gives a perspective on risk in the capital structure?
   1. Book value per share
   2. Dividend yield
   3. Dividend payout
   4. Degree of financial leverage
   5. Price/earnings ratio

f. The earnings per share ratio is computed for
   1. Convertible bonds.
   2. Redeemable preferred.
   3. Common stock.
   4. Nonredeemable preferred.
   5. None of the above.

g. Increasing financial leverage can be a risky strategy from the viewpoint of stockholders of companies having
   1. Steady and high profits.
   2. Low and falling profits.
   3. Relatively high and increasing profits.
   4. A low debt/equity ratio and relatively high profits.
   5. None of the above.

h. A firm has a degree of financial leverage of 1.3. If earnings before interest and tax increase by 10%, then net income
   1. Will increase by 13.0%.
   2. Will increase by 13.
   3. Will decrease by 13.0%.
   4. Will decrease by 13.
   5. None of the above.

i. The ratio that represents dividends per common share in relation to market price per common share is
   1. Dividend payout.
   2. Dividend yield.
   3. Price/earnings.
   4. Book value per share.
   5. Percentage of earnings retained.

j. Book value per share may not approximate market value per share because
   1. Investments may have a market value substantially above the original cost.
   2. Land may have substantially increased in value.
   3. Market value reflects future potential earning power.
   4. The firm owns patents that have substantial value.
   5. All of the above.

Casey's General Stores, Inc. and Subsidiaries
Consolidated Statements of Income
(In thousands, except share amounts)

	Years Ended April 30,		
	2005	**2004**	**2003**
Net sales	$2,809,420	$2,328,940	$2,117,293
Franchise revenue	1,065	1,669	2,451
	2,810,485	2,330,609	2,119,744
Cost of goods sold	2,352,580	1,908,807	1,709,387
Operating expenses	329,296	306,052	285,889
Depreciation and amortization	52,123	48,357	46,132
Interest, net (Note 2)	10,739	12,398	13,030
	2,744,738	2,275,614	2,054,438
Earnings from continuing operations before income taxes	65,747	54,995	65,306
Federal and state income taxes	23,215	17,098	24,294
Net earnings from continuing operations	42,532	37,897	41,012
Loss on discontinued operations, net of tax benefit of $3,154, $647 and $714	5,779	1,431	1,206
Net earnings	$ 36,753	$ 36,466	$ 39,806
Basic			
Earnings from continuing operations	$ 0.85	$ 0.76	$ 0.83
Loss on discontinued operations, net of tax benefit	0.12	0.03	0.03
Net earnings per common share	$ 0.73	$ 0.73	$ 0.80
Diluted			
Earnings from continuing operations	$ 0.85	$ 0.76	$ 0.82
Loss on discontinued operations, net of tax benefit	0.12	0.03	0.02
Net earnings per common share	$ 0.73	$ 0.73	$ 0.80

Note: Payments of cash dividends were as follows:

2005	$9,771
2004	6,479
2003	4,963

Casey's General Stores, Inc. and Subsidiaries
Consolidated Balance Sheets
(In thousands, except share amounts)

	April 30,	
	2005	**2004**
Assets		
Current assets		
Cash and cash equivalents	$ 49,051	$ 45,887
Receivables	7,481	5,751
Inventories (Note 1)	75,392	77,895
Prepaid expenses (Note 5)	4,579	6,392
Income taxes receivable	5,927	10,882
Total current assets	142,430	146,807

"Casey's General Stores, Inc. (Casey's) and its wholly owned subsidiaries . . . operate convenience stores under the name 'Casey's General Store' in 9 Midwest states, primarily Iowa, Missouri, and Illinois. The stores carry a broad selection of food (including freshly prepared foods such as pizza, donuts, and sandwiches), beverages, tobacco products, health and beauty aids, automotive products, and other nonfood items." 10-K

(continued)

CASEY'S (Continued)

	2005	2004
Other assets, net of amortization	$ 5,567	$ 1,154
Property and equipment, at cost		
Land	196,840	180,040
Buildings and leasehold improvements	429,056	409,320
Machinery and equipment	537,026	498,152
Leasehold interest in property and equipment (Note 6)	7,187	9,082
	1,170,109	1,096,594
Less accumulated depreciation and amortization	447,197	409,969
Net property and equipment	722,912	686,625
Total assets	$ 870,909	$ 834,586
Liabilities and Shareholders' Equity		
Current liabilities		
Current maturities of long-term debt (Note 2)	$ 27,636	$ 28,345
Accounts payable	100,640	83,388
Accrued expenses		
Property taxes	10,483	8,591
Other (Note 9)	31,368	25,516
Total current liabilities	170,127	145,840
Long-term debt, net of current maturities (Note 2)	123,064	144,158
Deferred income taxes (Note 5)	102,039	99,159
Deferred compensation (Note 7)	6,542	5,635
Total liabilities	401,772	394,792
Shareholders' equity (Note 3)		
Preferred stock, no par value, none issued	—	—
Common stock, no par value, 50,189,812		
and 50,015,862 shares issued and outstanding		
at April 30, 2005 and 2004, respectively	46,516	44,155
Retained earnings	422,621	395,639
Total shareholders' equity	469,137	439,794
Total liabilities and shareholders' equity	$ 870,909	$ 834,586

Required   a. 1. How many shares of common stock had been issued as of April 30, 2005?

                2. How many shares of common stock were outstanding at April 30, 2005?

                3. Which share number is used to compute earnings per share?

        b. When computing the price/earnings ratio, should the basic or diluted earnings per share be used? Why?

        c. Which earnings number would analysts put more emphasis on—net earnings from continuing operations or net earnings?

        d. Compute the book value for 2005 and 2004.

        e. Compute the dividend payout for 2005, 2004, and 2003.

MET-PRO SPLIT

In its financial statements for the year ended January 31, 2003, Met-Pro disclosed the following:

Net income	$5,888,379
Earnings per share:	
Basic	$0.95
Diluted	$0.95

"Met-Pro . . . manufactures and sells product recovery/pollution control equipment for purification of air and liquids, and fluid handling equipment for corrosive, abrasive, and high temperature liquids." 10-K

(continued)

Case 9-2

MET-PRO SPLIT (Continued)

Common stock:

  $0.10 par value

  18,000,000 shares authorized

  7,226,303 shares issued

  1,009,934 shares held in treasury

  Treasury stock at cost $12,036,835

On September 17, 2003, the Board of Directors declared a four-for-three split, effected in the form of a stock distribution, payable on October 15, 2003, to shareholders of record on October 1, 2003. The Company retained the current par value of $0.10 per share for all common shares.

Required a. For the following items, indicate the amount disclosed on the January 31, 2004, statements for the year ended January 31, 2003.

   1. Net income

   2. Earnings per share

    a. Basic

    b. Diluted

   3. Common stock

    a. Par value

    b. Shares authorized

    c. Shares issued

Case 9-3

STOCK-BASED COMPENSATION

Part 1. The Kroger Co.*

Consolidated Statements of Operations (in Part)
Years Ended February 3, 2007, January 28, 2006 and January 29, 2005

(In millions, except per share amounts)	2006	2005	2004
Net earnings (loss)	$1,115	$ 958	$ (104)
Net earnings (loss) per basic common share	$ 1.56	$1.32	$(0.14)
Average number of common shares used in basic calculation	715	724	736
Net earnings (loss) per diluted common share	$ 1.54	$1.31	$(0.14)
Average number of common shares used in diluted calculation	723	731	736

Notes to Consolidated Financial Statements (in Part)

1. Accounting Policies (in Part)

Effective January 29, 2006, the Company adopted the fair value recognition provisions of SFAS No. 123(R), *Share-Based Payment*, using the modified prospective transition method and, therefore, has not restated results for prior periods. Under this method, the Company recognizes compensation expense for all share-based payments granted after January 29, 2006, as well as all share-based payments granted prior to, but not yet vested as of January 29, 2006, in accordance with SFAS No. 123(R). Under the fair value recognition provisions of SFAS No. 123(R),

---

*"As of February 3, 2007, the Company was one of the largest retailers in the United States based on annual sales. The Company also manufactures and processes some of the food for sale in its supermarkets." 10-K

(continued)

the Company recognizes share-based compensation expense, net of an estimated forfeiture rate, over the requisite service period of the award. Prior to the adoption of SFAS No. 123(R), the Company accounted for share-based payments under Accounting Principles Board Opinion No. 25, *Accounting for Stock Issued to Employees*, ("APB No. 25") and the disclosure of provisions of SFAS No. 123. The Company also elected the alternative transition method for calculating windfall tax benefits available as of the adoption of SFAS No. 123(R). For further information regarding the adoption of SFAS No. 123(R), see Note 10 to the Consolidated Financial Statements.

10. Stock Option Plans (in Part)

Under SFAS No. 123(R), the Company records expense for restricted stock awards in an amount equal to the fair market value of the underlying stock on the grant date of the award, over the period the awards lapse.

Total stock compensation recognized in 2006 was $72. This included $50 for stock options and $22 for restricted shares. A total of $18 of the restricted stock expense was attributable to the wider distribution of restricted shares incorporated into the first quarter 2006 grant of share-based awards, and the remaining $4 of restricted stock expense related to previously issued restricted stock awards. The incremental compensation expense attributable to the adoption of SFAS No. 123(R) in 2006 was $68, pre-tax, or $43 and $0.06 per basic and diluted share, after tax. Stock compensation cost recognized in 2005, related entirely to restricted stock grants, was $7, pre-tax. These costs were recognized as operating, general and administrative expense in the Company's Consolidated Statements of Operations. The cumulative effect of applying a forfeiture rate to unvested restricted shares at January 29, 2006, was not material.

Part 2. The Boeing Company

THE BOEING COMPANY*
Consolidated Statements of Operations (in Part)
Dollars in millions, except per share data

Year ended December 31,	2006	2005	2004
Earnings before income taxes	$3,194	$2,819	$1,960
Income tax expense	(988)	(257)	(140)
Net earnings from continuing operations	2,206	2,562	1,820
Income from discontinued operations, net of taxes of $6			10
Net gain\(loss) on disposal of discontinued operations, net of taxes of $5, $(5) and $24	9	(7)	42
Cumulative effect of accounting change, net of taxes of $10		17	
Net earnings	$2,215	$2,572	$1,872
Basic earnings per share from continuing operations	$ 2.88	$ 3.26	$ 2.27
Income from discontinued operations, net of taxes			0.01
Net gain\(loss) on disposal of discontinued operations, net of taxes	0.01	(0.02)	0.05
Cumulative effect of accounting change, net of taxes		0.03	
Basic earnings per share	$ 2.89	$ 3.27	$ 2.33
Diluted earnings per share from continuing operations	$ 2.84	$ 3.19	$ 2.24
Income from discontinued operations, net of taxes			0.01
Net gain\(loss) on disposal of discontinued operations, net of taxes	0.01	(0.01)	0.05
Cumulative effect of accounting change, net of taxes		0.02	
Diluted earnings per share	$ 2.85	$ 3.20	$ 2.30

*"The Boeing Company, together with its subsidiaries . . . is one of the world's major aerospace firms." 10-K

(continued)

Notes to Consolidated Financial Statements (in Part)
(Dollars in millions, except per share data)

Note 1 Summary of Significant Accounting Policies (in Part)

Share-based compensation

Our primary types of share-based compensation consist of Performance Shares, ShareValue Trust distributions, stock options, and other stock unit awards.

   In 2005, we adopted the provisions of SFAS No. 123 (Revised 2004), Share-Based Payment [SFAS No. 123(R)] using the modified prospective method. Prior to 2005, we used a fair value based method of accounting for share-based compensation provided to our employees in accordance with SFAS No. 123. (See note 16)

Note 16—Share-Based Compensation and Other Compensation Arrangements (in Part)

Share-based plans expense is primarily included in general and administrative expense since it is incentive compensation issued primarily to our executives. The share-based plans expense and related income tax benefit follow:

	2006	2005	2004
Performance Shares	$473	$ 723	$449
Stock options, other	173	234	132
ShareValue Trust	97	79	74
Share-based plans expense	$743	$1,036	$655
Income tax benefit	$291	$ 322	$238

Part 3. Google, Inc.

Google, Inc.*
CONSOLIDATED STATEMENTS OF INCOME
(In thousands, except per share amounts)

	Years Ended December 31,		
	2004	2005	2006
Revenues	$3,189,223	$6,138,560	$10,604,917
Costs and expenses:			
Cost of revenues (including stock-based compensation expense of $11,314, $5,579, $17,629)**	1,468,967	2,577,088	4,225,027
Research and development (including stock-based compensation expense of $169,532, $115,532, $287,485)**	395,164	599,510	1,228,589
Sales and marketing (including stock-based compensation expense of $49,449, $28,411, $59,389)**	295,749	468,152	849,518
General and administrative (including stock-based compensation expense of $48,451, $51,187, $93,597)**	188,151	386,532	751,787
Contribution to Google Foundation	—	90,000	—
Non-recurring portion of settlement dispute with Yahoo	201,000	—	—
Total costs and expenses	2,549,031	4,121,282	7,054,921
Income from operations	640,192	2,017,278	3,549,996
Interest income and other, net	10,042	124,399	461,044

*"Google is a global technology leader focused on improving the ways people connect with information." 10-K

**Stock-based compensation recognized in the years ended December 31, 2004, and 2005, accounted for under Accounting Principles Board Opinion No. 25, *Accounting for Stock Issued to Employees*, has been reclassified to these expense lines to conform with the presentation for the year ended December 31, 2006. As discussed in Note 1 of the accompanying notes, stock-based compensation for the year end December 31, 2006, is presented in conformity with Financial Accounting Standards Board Statement of Financial Accounting Standards No. 123 (as revised), *Share-Based Payment*.

(continued)

STOCK-BASED COMPENSATION (Continued)

	2004	2005	2006
Income before income taxes	650,234	2,141,677	4,011,040
Provision for income taxes	251,115	676,280	933,594
Net income	$ 399,119	$1,465,397	$ 3,077,446
Net income per share of Class A and Class B common stock:			
Basic	$ 2.07	$ 5.31	$ 10.21
Diluted	$ 1.46	$ 5.02	$ 9.94

Required   a. Considering the nature of the industries in which these firms operate, would you expect a difference in the use of stock-based compensation?

b. Because of the implementation of SFAS No. 123(R), only comment on the materiality of stock-based compensation for 2006 for each company.

BIG BOY

Selected data from the 2007 annual report of Frisch's Restaurants, Inc. follow:

FRISCH'S RESTAURANTS, INC. AND SUBSIDIARIES*
CONSOLIDATED BALANCE SHEET
May 29, 2007 and May 30, 2006

ASSETS

	2007	2006
Current Assets		
Cash	$ 321,200	$ 815,346
Trade and other receivables	1,405,892	1,538,024
Inventories	6,376,059	4,791,898
Prepaid expenses and sundry deposits	984,132	2,795,444
Prepaid and deferred income taxes	1,930,701	2,122,544
Total current assets	11,017,984	12,063,256
Property and Equipment		
Land and improvements	64,518,917	60,691,775
Buildings	85,805,775	84,830,307
Equipment and fixtures	87,948,798	89,151,961
Leasehold improvements and buildings on leased land	29,153,070	28,171,132
Capitalized leases	5,054,200	5,257,019
Construction in progress	7,435,071	2,211,659
	279,915,831	270,313,853
Less accumulated depreciation and amortization	120,629,146	115,943,839
Net property and equipment	159,286,685	154,370,014
Other Assets		
Goodwill	740,644	740,644
Other intangible assets	1,216,620	1,383,729
Investments in land	2,249,890	2,272,405
Property held for sale	1,470,920	805,784
Other	3,275,811	3,646,989
Total other assets	8,953,885	8,849,551
Total assets	$179,258,554	$175,282,821

*"The registrant, Frisch's Restaurants, Inc. . . . is a regional company that operates full service family-style restaurants under the name "Frisch's Big Boy." The Company also operates grill buffet style restaurants under the "Golden Corral" pursuant to certain licensing agreements." 10-K

(continued)

BIG BOY (Continued)

FRISCH'S RESTAURANTS, INC. AND SUBSIDIARIES
CONSOLIDATED BALANCE SHEET
May 29, 2007 and May 30, 2006
LIABILITIES AND SHAREHOLDERS' EQUITY

	2007	2006
Current Liabilities		
Long-term obligations due within one year		
Long-term debt	$ 11,774,604	$ 8,926,194
Obligations under capitalized leases	2,480,419	388,222
Self insurance	716,443	856,962
Accounts payable	12,353,968	10,330,378
Accrued expenses	9,235,002	9,639,747
Income taxes	290,010	441,045
Total current liabilities	36,850,446	30,582,548
Long-Term Obligations		
Long-term debt	25,009,540	30,991,636
Obligations under capitalized leases	880,451	3,125,742
Self insurance	1,133,606	1,549,499
Deferred income taxes	3,457,714	4,496,802
Deferred compensation and other	4,057,022	3,855,158
Total long-term obligations	34,538,333	44,018,837
Commitments		
Shareholders' Equity		
Capital stock		
Preferred stock—authorized, 3,000,000 shares		
without par value; none issued	—	—
Common stock—authorized, 12,000,000 shares		
without par value; issued 7,568,680 and 7,521,930		
shares—stated value—$1	7,568,680	7,521,930
Additional contributed capital	63,838,824	62,531,311
	71,407,504	70,053,241
Accumulated other comprehensive loss	(1,214,704)	—
Retained earnings	70,448,512	63,420,622
	69,233,808	63,420,622
Less cost of treasury stock (2,445,764 and		
2,447,323 shares)	(32,771,537)	(32,792,427)
Total shareholders' equity	107,869,775	100,681,436
Total liabilities and shareholders' equity	$179,258,554	$175,282,821

FRISCH'S RESTAURANTS, INC. AND SUBSIDIARIES
CONSOLIDATED STATEMENT OF EARNINGS
Three years ended May 29, 2007

	2007	2006*	2005
Sales	$289,934,367	$290,967,866	$279,247,122
Cost of sales			
Food and paper	101,401,056	102,105,847	98,569,774
Payroll and related	95,500,491	96,097,853	92,351,759
Other operating costs	64,043,426	64,337,677	57,800,494
	260,944,973	262,541,377	248,722,027
Gross profit	28,989,394	28,426,489	30,525,095
Administrative and advertising	14,301,277	13,976,020	13,928,712
Franchise fees and other revenue	(1,253,398)	(1,249,771)	(1,351,967)
Gains on sale of assets	(250,069)	(567,987)	(86,921)
Operating profit	16,191,584	16,268,227	18,035,271

*Fiscal year 2006 contained 366 days. The other years presented contained 364 days.

(continued)

Case 9-4   BIG BOY (Continued)

	2007	2006*	2005
Other expense (income)			
Interest expense	2,672,171	2,771,342	2,820,449
Life insurance benefits in excess of cash surrender value	—	—	(4,440,000)
Earnings before income taxes	13,519,413	13,496,885	19,654,822
Income taxes			
Current			
Federal	5,482,285	4,616,461	4,226,844
Less tax credits	(782,886)	(601,779)	(785,855)
State and municipal	657,528	579,205	757,698
Deferred	(1,105,070)	(256,767)	715,310
Total income taxes	4,251,857	4,337,120	4,913,997
NET EARNINGS	$ 9,267,556	$ 9,159,765	$ 14,740,825
Earnings per share (EPS) of common stock:			
Basic net earnings per share	$ 1.82	$ 1.81	$ 2.92
Diluted net earnings per share	$ 1.78	$ 1.78	$ 2.86

Other selected data:

		Year Ended	
		May 29, 2007	May 30, 2006
1.	Market price per common share	$ 31.95	$ 25.70
2.	Dividends paid in total	$2,239,666	$2,229,327
3.	Dividends paid per share	$ 0.44	$ 0.44

Required   a. Compute the following for 2007 and 2006:
1. Degree of financial leverage
2. Price/earnings ratio
3. Percentage of earnings retained
4. Dividend yield
5. Book value per share
b. Comment on the ratios computed under (a).
c. 1. Identify special items on the income statement for each of the years 2007, 2006, and 2005.
2. What would be the net earnings for 2007, 2006, and 2005, with the special item(s) removed?
d. 1. Prepare a vertical common-size analysis for 2007, 2006, and 2005 for gross profit and operating profit. Use sales as the base.
2. Comment on (1).

Case 9-5   NEWS, NEWS, NEWS

The Gannett Co., Inc.,* presented this selected financial data with its 2006 annual report.

SELECTED FINANCIAL DATA (in Part)

In thousands of dollars, except per share amounts	2006	2005	2004	2003	2002
Net operating revenues					
Newspaper advertising	$ 5,370,453	$ 5,161,208	$ 4,835,335	$ 4,322,951	$ 4,051,361
Newspaper circulation	1,306,549	1,264,031	1,218,486	1,192,873	1,161,778

*"Gannett Co., Inc. is a leading international news and information company." 10-K

(continued)

Case 9-5   NEWS, NEWS, NEWS (Continued)

	2006	2005	2004	2003	2002
Broadcasting	854,821	736,452	821,543	719,884	771,303
All other	501,531	437,248	408,298	380,326	345,547
Total	8,033,354	7,598,939	7,283,662	6,616,034	6,329,989
Operating expenses					
Cost and expenses	5,758,347	5,276,502	4,930,052	4,440,987	4,219,308
Depreciation	242,781	251,130	229,500	220,314	212,220
Amortization of intangible assets	33,989	23,236	11,634	8,271	7,327
Total	6,035,117	5,550,868	5,171,186	4,669,572	4,438,855
Operating income	1,998,237	2,048,071	2,112,476	1,946,462	1,891,134
Non-operating (expense) income					
Interest expense	(288,040)	(210,625)	(140,647)	(139,271)	(146,359)
Other	9,285	(19,591)	(11,646)	(1,434)	(15,422)
Income before income taxes	1,719,482	1,817,855	1,960,183	1,805,757	1,729,353
Provision for income taxes	558,700	606,600	664,800	616,000	591,000
Income from continuing operations	$ 1,160,782	$ 1,211,255	$ 1,295,383	$ 1,189,757	$ 1,138,353
Income from continuing operations:					
per basic/diluted share	$4.91/$4.90	$4.94/$4.92	$4.89/$4.84	$4.41/$4.38	$4.27/$4.23
Other selected financial data					
Dividends declared per share	$ 1.20	$ 1.12	$ 1.04	$ .98	$ .94

Other:

Market price per share:

December 31, 2006	$60.46
December 25, 2005	$61.09
December 26, 2004	$80.69

Total dividends paid:
(In thousands of dollars)

2006	$280,008
2005	$272,885
2004	$273,028

Dividends declared per share:

2006	$1.20
2005	$1.12
2004	$1.04

Fiscal year:

The company's fiscal year ends on the last Sunday of the calendar year. The company's 2006 fiscal year ended on December 31, 2006, and encompassed a 53-week period. The company's 2005, 2004, 2003, and 2002 fiscal year encompassed 52-week periods.

Required

a. 1. For net operating revenues, prepare a horizontal common-size analysis for 2002–2006. Use 2002 as the base.
   2. Comment on the results in (1).

b. 1. For net operating revenues, prepare a vertical common-size analysis for 2002–2006. Use total net operating revenues as the base.
   2. Comment on the results in (1).

c. 1. For operating expenses, prepare a horizontal common-size analysis for 2002–2006. Use 2002 as the base.
   2. Comment on the results in (1).

d. 1. For operating expenses, prepare a vertical common-size analysis for 2002–2006. Use total operating expenses as the base.
   2. Comment on the results in (1).

e. Based on these data, compute the following for 2004–2006:
   1. Degree of financial leverage

   $$\frac{\text{Earnings Before Interest and Tax}}{\text{Earnings Before Tax}}$$

   2. Price/earnings ratio
   3. Dividend yield

f. Comment on the ratios in (e).

EAT AT MY RESTAURANT—INVESTOR VIEW

With this case, we review the investor view of several restaurant companies. The restaurant companies reviewed and the year-end date are as follows:

1. **Yum Brands, Inc. (December 30, 2006; December 30, 2005)**
   "Yum consists of six operating segments: KFC, Pizza Hut, Taco Bell, LJS/A&W, Yum Restaurants International . . . and Yum Restaurants China." 10-K

2. **Panera Bread (December 26, 2006; December 27, 2005)**
   "As of December 26, 2006, we operated directly and through area development agreements with 41 franchisee groups, bakery-cafes under Panera Bread® and Saint Louis Bread® names." 10-K

3. **Starbucks (October 1, 2006; October 2, 2005)**
   "Starbucks purchases and roasts high-quality whole bean coffees and sells them, along with fresh, rich-brewed coffees, Italian-style espresso beverages, cold blended beverages, a variety of complementary foods items, coffee-related accessories and equipment, a selection of premium teas and a line of compact discs, primarily through company-operated retail stores." 10-K

Data Reviewed	Yum Brands, Inc. 2006	Yum Brands, Inc. 2005	Panera Bread 2006	Panera Bread 2005	Starbucks 2006	Starbucks 2005
All-inclusive degree of financial leverage	1.14	1.12	1.00	1.00	1.01	1.00
Diluted earnings per share before nonrecurring items	$2.92	$2.55	$1.84	$1.65	$.73	$.61
Percentage of earnings retained	82.52%	83.86%	100.00%	100.00%	100.00%	100.00%
Dividend yield	1.47%	.95%	0	0	0	0
Price/earnings ratio	20.09	18.38	30.15	40.67	46.64	82.13
Market price per share	$58.65	$46.88	$55.47	$67.11	$34.05	$50.10

Required

a. Comment on all data reviewed for each individual company for 2005 and 2006.

b. Comment on each ratio comparing these companies.

c. Based on the above, which firm would you select?

Thomson One *Business School Edition*

Please complete the Web case that covers material covered in this chapter at academic.cengage.com/accounting/Gibson. You'll be using Thomson One Business School Edition, a powerful tool, that combines a full range of fundamental financial information, earnings estimates, market data, and source documents for 500 publicly traded companies.

Endnotes

1. FASB No. 123 (revised 2004), Glossary, Grant date.
2. Ibid., Glossary, Vest, Vesting, or Vested.
3. Copyrighted material—reproduced with permission of the author.

Chapter 10

Statement of Cash Flows

Considering the importance of cash, it is not surprising that the statement of cash flows has become one of the primary financial statements. The statement of cash flows gives managers, equity analysts, commercial lenders, and investment bankers a thorough explanation of the changes that occurred in the firm's cash balances.

The statement of cash flows provides an explanation of the changes that occurred in the firm's cash balances for a specific period. Cash is considered to be the lifeblood of the firm. Understanding the flow of cash is critical to having a handle on the pulse of the firm.

Quote the Banker, "Watch Cash Flow"

Once upon a midnight dreary as I pondered weak and weary
Over many a quaint and curious volume of accounting lore,
Seeking gimmicks (without scruple) to squeeze through some new tax loophole,
Suddenly I heard a knock upon my door,
*   Only this, and nothing more.*

Then I felt a queasy tingling and I heard the cash a-jingling
As a fearsome banker entered whom I'd often seen before.
His face was money-green and in his eyes there could be seen
Dollar-signs that seemed to glitter as he reckoned up the score.
*   "Cash flow," the banker said, and nothing more.*

I had always thought it fine to show a jet black bottom line,
But the banker sounded a resounding, "No,
Your receivables are high, mounting upward toward the sky;
Write-offs loom. What matters is cash flow."
*   He repeated, "Watch cash flow."*

Then I tried to tell the story of our lovely inventory
Which, though large, is full of most delightful stuff.
But the banker saw its growth, and with a mighty oath
He waved his arms and shouted, "Stop! Enough!
*   Pay the interest, and don't give me any guff!"*

Next I looked for non-cash items which could add ad infinitum
To replace the ever-outward flow of cash,
But to keep my statement black I'd held depreciation back,
And my banker said that I'd done something rash.
     He quivered, and his teeth began to gnash.

When I asked him for a loan, he responded, with a groan,
That the interest rate would be just prime plus eight,
And to guarantee my purity he'd insist on some security—
All my assets plus the scalp upon my pate.
     Only this, a standard rate.

Though my bottom line is black, I am flat upon my back.
My cash flows out and customers pay slow.
The growth of my receivables is almost unbelievable;
The result is certain—unremitting woe!
And I hear the banker utter an ominous low mutter,
     "Watch cash flow."

—Herbert S. Bailey
Reprinted with permission.

Basic Elements of the Statement of Cash Flows

The statement of cash flows is prepared using a concept of cash that includes not only cash itself but also short-term, highly liquid investments. This is referred to as the "cash and cash equivalent" focus. The category cash and cash equivalents includes cash on hand, cash on deposit, and investments in short-term, highly liquid investments. The cash flow statement analysis explains the change in these focus accounts by examining all the accounts on the balance sheet other than the focus accounts.

Management may use the statement of cash flows to determine dividend policy, cash generated by operations, and investing and financing policy. Outsiders, such as creditors or investors, may use it to determine such things as the firm's ability to increase dividends, its ability to pay debt with cash from operations, and the percentage of cash from operations in relation to the cash from financing.

The statement of cash flows must report all transactions affecting cash flow. A company will occasionally have investing and/or financing activities that have no direct effect on cash flow. For example, a company may acquire land in exchange for common stock. This is an investing transaction (acquiring the land) and a financing transaction (issuing the common stock). The conversion of long-term bonds into common stock involves two financing activities with no effect on cash flow. Since transactions such as these will have future effects on cash flows, these transactions are to be disclosed in a separate schedule presented with the statement of cash flows.

The statement of cash flows classifies cash receipts and cash payments into operating, investing, and financing activities.[1] In brief, operating activities involve income statement items. Investing activities generally result from changes in long-term asset items. Financing activities generally relate to long-term liability and stockholders' equity items. A description of these activities and typical cash flows are as follows:

1. **Operating activities.** Operating activities include all transactions and other events that are not investing or financing activities. Cash flows from operating activities are generally the cash effects of transactions and other events that enter into the determination of net income.
   Typical cash inflows:
      From sale of goods or services
      From return on loans (interest)
      From return on equity securities (dividends)

Typical cash outflows:
>   Payments for acquisitions of inventory
>   Payments to employees
>   Payments to governments (taxes)
>   Payments of interest expense
>   Payments to suppliers for other expenses

2. **Investing activities.** Investing activities include lending money and collecting on those loans and acquiring and selling investments and productive long-term assets.
>   Typical cash inflows:
>   From receipts from loans collected
>   From sales of debt or equity securities of other corporations
>   From sale of property, plant, and equipment
>   Typical cash outflows:
>   Loans to other entities
>   Purchase of debt or equity securities of other entities
>   Purchase of property, plant, and equipment

3. **Financing activities.** Financing activities include cash flows relating to liability and owners' equity.
>   Typical cash inflows:
>   From sale of equity securities
>   From sale of bonds, mortgages, notes, and other short- or long-term borrowings
>   Typical cash outflows:
>   Payment of dividends
>   Reacquisition of the firm's capital stock
>   Payment of amounts borrowed

The statement of cash flows presents cash flows from operating activities first, followed by investing activities and then financing activities. The individual inflows and outflows from investing and financing activities are presented separately. The operating activities section can be presented using the *direct method* or the *indirect method.* (The indirect method is sometimes referred to as the *reconciliation method.*) The direct method essentially presents the income statement on a cash basis, instead of an accrual basis. The indirect method adjusts net income for items that affected net income but did not affect cash.

SFAS No. 95 encouraged enterprises to use the direct method to present cash flows from operating activities. However, if a company uses the direct method, the standard requires a reconciliation of net income to net cash provided by operating activities in a separate schedule. If a firm uses the indirect method, it must make a separate disclosure of interest paid and income taxes paid during the period. Exhibit 10-1 presents skeleton formats of a statement of cash flows using the direct method and the indirect method.

| Exhibit   10-1 | JONES COMPANY EXAMPLE |

Statement of Cash Flows—Comparison of Presentation of Direct Method and Indirect Method (Operating Activities) For Year Ended December 31, 20XX

Direct Method

Cash flows from operating activities:	
Cash received from customers	$ 370,000
Cash paid to suppliers and employees	(310,000)
Interest received	10,000
Interest paid (net of amount capitalized)	(4,000)
Income taxes paid	(15,000)
Net cash provided by operations	51,000

(continued)

Exhibit	10-1	JONES COMPANY EXAMPLE (Continued)

Cash flows from investing activities:	
Capital expenditures	(30,000)
Proceeds from property, plant, and equipment disposals	6,000
Net cash used in investing activities	(24,000)
Cash flows from financing activities:	
Net proceeds from repayment of commercial paper	(4,000)
Proceeds from issuance of long-term debt	6,000
Dividends paid	(5,000)
Net cash used in financing activities	(3,000)
Net increase in cash and cash equivalents	24,000
Cash and cash equivalents at beginning of period	8,000
Cash and cash equivalents at end of period	$ 32,000
Reconciliation of net earnings to cash provided by operating activities:	
Net earnings	$ 40,000
Provision for depreciation	6,000
Provision for allowance for doubtful accounts	1,000
Deferred income taxes	1,000
Loss on property, plant, and equipment disposals	2,000
Changes in operating assets and liabilities:	
Receivables increase	(2,000)
Inventories increase	(4,000)
Accounts payable increase	5,000
Accrued income taxes increase	2,000
Net cash provided by operating activities	$ 51,000
Supplemental schedule of noncash investing and financing activities:	
Land acquired (investing) by issuing bonds (financing)	$ 10,000

Indirect Method

Operating activities:	
Net earnings	$ 40,000
Provision for depreciation	6,000
Provision for allowance for doubtful accounts	1,000
Deferred income taxes	1,000
Loss on property, plant, and equipment disposals	2,000
Changes in operating assets and liabilities:	
Receivables increase	(2,000)
Inventories increase	(4,000)
Accounts payable increase	5,000
Accrued income taxes increase	2,000
Net cash provided by operating activities	$ 51,000
Cash flows from investing activities:	
Capital expenditures	(30,000)
Proceeds from property, plant, and equipment disposals	6,000
Net cash used in investing activities	(24,000)
Cash flows from financing activities:	
Net proceeds from repayment of commercial paper	(4,000)
Proceeds from issuance of long-term debt	6,000
Dividends paid	(5,000)
Net cash used in financing activities	(3,000)
Net increase in cash and cash equivalents	24,000
Cash and cash equivalents at beginning of period	8,000
Cash and cash equivalents at end of period	$ 32,000
Supplemental disclosure of cash flow information:	
Interest paid	$ 500
Income taxes paid	10,000
Supplemental schedule of noncash investing and financing activities:	
Land acquired (investing) and issuing bonds (financing)	$ 10,000

The 1986 SFAS Exposure Draft, "Statement of Cash Flows," indicates that:

The principal advantage of the direct method is that it shows the operating cash receipts and payments. Knowledge of where operating cash flows came from and how cash was used in past periods may be useful in estimating future cash flows. The indirect method of reporting has the advantage of focusing on the differences between income and cash flow from operating activities.[2]

The statement of cash flows has now been a required financial statement for approximately 20 years. The financial community is in agreement as to the importance of this statement. Unfortunately, the statement of cash flows has not proven as useful as was expected by many. A major reason for this is the failure to require the direct method of presenting operating activities. Many ratios relating to the cash flow have been developed by companies, financial services, articles, and books. There is little agreement on what ratios to compute and how to compute these ratios. Also, the direct method allows for analysis that cannot be done with the indirect method.

Exhibit 10-2 on page 370 presents the 2007 Nike statement of cash flows. This statement presents cash from operations, using the indirect method. The statement closely follows the standard format.

In addition to reviewing the flow of funds on a yearly basis, reviewing a flow of funds for a three-year period may be helpful. This can be accomplished by adding a total column to the statement that represents the total of each item for the three-year period. This has been done for Nike in Exhibit 10-2.

Some observations on the 2007 Nike statement of cash flows, considering the three-year period ended May 31, 2007, follow:

1. Cash provided by operations was the major source of cash. This operating cash flow more than offset the cash outflow for investing activities and the outflow for financing activities.
2. Cash flow from operations related to net income and depreciation represented substantially all of the cash flow from operations.
3. Cash used for additions to property, plant and equipment represented approximately 60% of the total cash used for investing activities.
4. Cash used for repurchase of common stock represented approximately 88% of the total cash used for financing activities. Possibly some of the repurchase of stock was related to the proceeds from exercise of stock options and other stock issuances. One of the reasons for expensing stock options is that typically a company will repurchase stock and then issue stock with the exercise of options.

Exhibit 10-3 on page 371 presents the 2007 cash flow statement of Tech Data Corporation, with a total column for the three-year period. This firm presented the cash flows from operating activities using the direct method. Note the following with regard to the direct method in Exhibit 10-3.

1. Net cash provided by operations represented the major source of cash.
2. Expenditures for property and equipment represented the major outflow under investing activities.
3. Proceeds from issuance of convertible debentures, net of expenses represented the major inflow from financing activities.
4. Principal payments on long-term debt represented the major outflow of funds under financing activities.

Note the following with regard to the indirect method in Exhibit 10-3. [The indirect method represents "Reconciliation of net (loss) income to net cash (used in) provided by operating activities".]

1. Net income plus depreciation and amortization expense make up approximately 73% of the cash flow (remember that net income does not represent cash flow, and depreciation and amortization expense are not cash flow items).
2. Notice how changes in operating assets and liabilities make up approximately 74% of net cash provided by operating activities.

Exhibit	10-2	NIKE, INC.

Consolidated Statements of Cash Flows, with Three-Year Total (total column added)

NIKE, INC.
CONSOLIDATED STATEMENT OF CASH FLOWS

	Total	Year ended May 31, 2007	2006	2005
		(In millions)		
Cash provided (used) by operations:				
Net income	$ 4,095.1	$ 1,491.5	$ 1,392.0	$ 1,211.6
Income charges not affecting cash:				
Depreciation	808.9	269.7	282.0	257.2
Deferred income taxes	29.4	34.1	(26.0)	21.3
Stock-based compensation (Notes 1 and 10)	164.4	147.7	11.8	4.9
Amortization and other	23.2	0.5	(2.9)	25.6
Income tax benefit from exercise of stock options	117.3	—	54.2	63.1
Changes in certain working capital components and other assets and liabilities:				
Increase in accounts receivable	(218.2)	(39.6)	(85.1)	(93.5)
Increase in inventories	(353.1)	(49.5)	(200.3)	(103.3)
(Increase) decrease in prepaid expenses and other current assets	(26.6)	(60.8)	(37.2)	71.4
Increase in accounts payable, accrued liabilities and income taxes payable	476.9	85.1	279.4	112.4
Cash provided by operations	5,117.3	1,878.7	1,667.9	1,570.7
Cash provided (used) by investing activities:				
Purchase of short-term investments	(6,280.7)	(2,133.8)	(2,619.7)	(1,527.2)
Maturities of short-term investments	5,717.9	2,516.2	1,709.8	1,491.9
Additions to property, plant and equipment	(904.3)	(313.5)	(333.7)	(257.1)
Disposals of property, plant and equipment	37.1	28.3	1.6	7.2
Increase in other assets, net of other liabilities	(66.9)	(4.3)	(34.6)	(28.0)
Acquisition of subsidiary, net of cash acquired	(47.2)	—	—	(47.2)
Cash provided (used) by investing activities	(1,544.1)	92.9	(1,276.6)	(360.4)
Cash provided (used) by financing activities:				
Proceeds from issuance of long-term debt	41.8	41.8	—	—
Reductions in long-term debt, including current portion	(270.9)	(255.7)	(6.0)	(9.2)
Increase (decrease) in notes payable	(47.3)	52.6	(18.2)	(81.7)
Proceeds from exercise of stock options and other stock issuances	775.0	322.9	225.3	226.8
Excess tax benefits from share-based payment arrangements	55.8	55.8	—	—
Repurchase of common stock	(2,302.5)	(985.2)	(761.1)	(556.2)
Dividends—common and preferred	(871.3)	(343.7)	(290.9)	(236.7)
Cash used by financing activities	(2,619.4)	(1,111.5)	(850.9)	(657.0)
Effect of exchange rate changes	74.9	42.4	25.7	6.8
Net increase (decrease) in cash and equivalents	1,028.7	902.5	(433.9)	560.1
Cash and equivalents, beginning of year	828.0	954.2	1,388.1	828.0
Cash and equivalents, end of year	$ 1,856.7	$ 1,856.7	$ 954.2	$ 1,388.1
Supplemental disclosure of cash flow information:				
Cash paid during the year for:				
Interest, net of capitalized interest	$ 148.1	$ 60.0	$ 54.2	$ 33.9
Income taxes	1,939.0	601.1	752.6	585.3
Dividends declared and not paid	237.6	92.9	79.4	65.3

Exhibit 10-4 on page 372 restates the 2007 cash flows for Tech Data Corporation, viewing inflows and outflows separately. Some observations regarding Exhibit 10-4 follow:

1. Approximately 98% of the total inflows came from operations.
2. Approximately 99% of total cash outflows related to operations.

| Exhibit | 10-3 | TECH DATA CORPORATION* |

TECH DATA CORPORATION AND SUBSIDIARIES
CONSOLIDATED STATEMENT OF CASH FLOWS,
(In thousands)
with Three-Year Total (total column added)

	Three-Year Total	2007	2006	2005
Cash flows from operating activities:				
Cash received from customers	$61,436,056	$ 21,185,902	$ 20,504,871	$ 19,745,283
Cash paid to suppliers and employees	60,824,453	(21,091,764)	(20,160,865)	(19,571,824)
Interest paid, net	(66,829)	(26,910)	(21,082)	(18,837)
Income taxes paid	(194,378)	(81,216)	(65,485)	(47,677)
Net cash (used in) provided by operating activities	350,396	(13,988)	257,439	106,945
Cash flows from investing activities:				
Proceeds from sale of business	16,500	16,500	—	—
Proceeds from sale of property and equipment	17,862	3,563	9,169	5,130
Expenditures for property and equipment	(99,516)	(31,667)	(41,973)	(25,876)
Software and software development costs	(48,740)	(12,062)	(18,779)	(17,899)
Net cash used in investing activities	(113,894)	(23,666)	(51,583)	(38,645)
Cash flows from financing activities:				
Proceeds from the issuance of common stock and reissuance of treasury stock	74,602	25,183	16,686	32,733
Cash paid for purchase of treasury stock	(207,120)	(80,093)	(127,027)	—
Proceeds from issuance of convertible debentures, net of expenses	342,554	342,554	—	—
Net (repayments) borrowings on revolving credit loans	(9,613)	(164,824)	166,530	(11,319)
Principal payments on long-term debt	(302,452)	(1,611)	(291,627)	(9,214)
Excess tax benefit from stock-based compensation	544	544	—	—
Net cash provided by (used in) financing activities	(101,485)	121,753	(235,438)	12,200
Effect of exchange rate changes on cash and cash equivalents	21,188	24,242	(8,809)	5,755
Net increase (decrease) in cash and cash equivalents	156,205	108,341	(38,391)	86,255
Cash and cash equivalents at beginning of year	108,801	156,665	195,056	108,801
Cash and cash equivalents at end of year	$ 265,006	$ 265,006	156,665	195,056
Reconciliation of net (loss) income to net cash (used in) provided by operating activities:				
Net (loss) income	$ 92,065	$ (96,981)	$ 26,586	$ 162,460
Adjustments to reconcile net (loss) income to net cash (used in) provided by operating activities:				
Goodwill impairment	$ 136,093	$ 136,093	$ —	$ —
Gain on sale of discontinued operations, net of tax	(3,834)	(3,834)	—	—
Gain on sale of land	(3,563)	(3,563)	—	—
Depreciation and amortization	162,496	53,280	53,744	55,472
Provision for losses on accounts receivable	47,095	27,655	6,172	13,268
Stock-based compensation expense	7,973	7,973	—	—
Deferred income taxes	27,146	4,296	26,466	(3,616)
Excess tax benefit from stock-based compensation	(544)	(544)	—	—
Changes in operating assets and liabilities:				
Accounts receivable	(319,195)	(242,305)	(32,585)	(44,305)
Inventories	(177,504)	25,806	(83,311)	(119,999)
Prepaid expenses and other assets	(23,479)	5,636	3,078	(32,193)
Accounts payable	292,638	21,985	214,804	55,849
Accrued expenses and other liabilities	113,009	50,515	42,485	20,009
Total adjustments	258,331	82,993	230,853	(55,515)
Net cash (used in) provided by operating activities	$ 350,396	$ (13,988)	$ 257,439	$ 106,945

*"Tech Data Corporation . . . is a leading distributor of information technology ("IT") products, logistics management and other value-added services worldwide." 10-K

Exhibit	10-4	TECH DATA CORPORATION

Year Ended January 31, 2007

(In thousands)

	Inflows	Outflows	Percent Inflow	Percent Outflow
Cash flows from operating activities:				
Cash received from customers	$21,185,902		98.09	
Cash paid to suppliers and employees		$21,091,764		98.15
Interest paid, net		26,910		.12
Income taxes paid		81,216		.38
Net cash (used in) provided by operating activities	21,185,902	21,199,890	98.09	98.65
Cash flows from investing activities:				
Proceeds from sale of business	16,500		.08	
Proceeds from sale of property and equipment	3,563		.01	
Expenditures for property and equipment		31,667		.15
Software and software development costs		12,062		.05
Net cash used in investing activities	20,063	43,729	.09	.20
Cash flows from financing activities:				
Proceeds from the issuance of common stock and reissuance of treasury stock	25,183		.12	
Cash paid for purchase of treasury stock		80,093		.37
Proceeds from issuance of convertible debentures, net of expenses	342,554		1.59	
Net (repayments) borrowings on revaluing credit loans		164,824		.77
Principal payments on long-term debt		1,611		.01
Excess tax benefit from stock-based compensation	544		.00	
Net cash provided by (used in) financing activities	368,281	246,528	1.71	1.15
Effect of exchange rate changes on cash and cash equivalents	24,242	—	.11	—
Changes on cash:				
Total cash inflows (outflows)	21,598,488	$21,490,147	100.00	100.00
Total cash outflow	21,490,147			
Net increase in cash	$ 108,341			

3. No significant inflows or outflows came from investing activities.

4. No significant inflows or outflows came from financing activities. The largest inflow was 1.59% from proceeds from issuance of convertible debentures, net of expenses.

Financial Ratios and the Statement of Cash Flows

Financial ratios that relate to the statement of cash flows were slow in being developed. This was related to several factors. For one thing, most financial ratios traditionally related an income statement item(s) to a balance sheet item(s). This became the normal way of approaching financial analysis, and the statement of cash flows did not become a required statement until 1987. Thus, it took a while for analysts to become familiar with the statement.

Ratios have now been developed that relate to the cash flow statement. Some of these ratios are as follows:

1. Operating cash flow/current maturities of long-term debt and current notes payable
2. Operating cash flow/total debt
3. Operating cash flow per share
4. Operating cash flow/cash dividends

OPERATING CASH FLOW/CURRENT MATURITIES OF LONG-TERM DEBT AND CURRENT NOTES PAYABLE

The operating cash flow/current maturities of long-term debt and current notes payable is a ratio that indicates a firm's ability to meet its current maturities of debt. The higher this ratio, the better the firm's ability to meet its current maturities of debt. The higher this ratio, the better the firm's liquidity. This ratio relates to the liquidity ratios discussed in Chapter 6.

The formula for this ratio is as follows:

$$\frac{\text{Operating Cash Flow}}{\text{Current Maturities of Long-Term Debt and Current Notes Payable}}$$

It is computed for Nike for 2007 and 2006 in Exhibit 10-5. For Nike, this ratio substantially improved in 2007. Both years represent material coverage.

Exhibit 10-5	NIKE, INC.		
	Operating Cash Flow/Current Maturities of Long-Term Debt and Current Notes Payable		
	Years Ended May 31, 2007 and 2006		
(In millions)		**2007**	**2006**
Operating cash flow [A]		$1,878.7	$1,667.9
Current maturities of long-term debt and current notes payable [B]		$ 131.3	$ 298.7
Operating cash flow/current maturities of long-term debt and current notes payable [A ÷ B]		14.31 times	5.58 times

OPERATING CASH FLOW/TOTAL DEBT

The operating cash flow/total debt indicates a firm's ability to cover total debt with the yearly operating cash flow. The higher the ratio, the better the firm's ability to carry its total debt. From a debt standpoint, this is considered to be important. It relates to the debt ratios presented in Chapter 7. It is a type of income view of debt, except that operating cash flow is the perspective instead of an income figure.

The operating cash flow is the same cash flow amount that is used for the operating cash flow/current maturities of long-term debt and current notes payable. The total debt figure is the same total debt amount that was computed in Chapter 7 for the debt ratio and the debt/equity ratio. For the primary computation of the operating cash flow/total debt ratio, all possible balance sheet debt items are included, as was done for the debt ratio and the debt/equity ratio. This is the more conservative approach to computing the ratio. In practice, many firms are more selective in what is included in debt. Some include only short-term liabilities and long-term items, such as bonds payable. The formula for operating cash flow/total debt is as follows:

$$\frac{\text{Operating Cash Flow}}{\text{Total Debt}}$$

The operating cash flow/total debt ratio is computed in Exhibit 10-6 for Nike for the years ended May 31, 2007, and 2006. It indicates that cash flow is significant in relation to total debt in both years.

Exhibit	10-6	NIKE, INC.

Operating Cash Flow/Total Debt

Years Ended May 31, 2007 and 2006

(In millions)	2007	2006
Operating cash flow [A]	$1,878.7	$1,667.9
Total debt [B]	$3,662.9	$3,584.4
Operating cash flow/total debt [A ÷ B]	51.29%	46.53%

OPERATING CASH FLOW PER SHARE

Operating cash flow per share indicates the funds flow per common share outstanding. It is usually substantially higher than earnings per share because depreciation has not been deducted.

In the short run, operating cash flow per share is a better indication of a firm's ability to make capital expenditure decisions and pay dividends than is earnings per share. This ratio should not be viewed as a substitute for earnings per share in terms of a firm's profitability. For this reason, firms are prohibited from reporting cash flow per share on the face of the statement of cash flows or elsewhere in their financials. However, it is a complementary ratio that relates to the ratios of relevance to investors (discussed in Chapter 9).

The operating cash flow per share formula is as follows:

$$\frac{\text{Operating Cash Flow} - \text{Preferred Dividends}}{\text{Diluted Weighted Average Common Shares Outstanding}}$$

The operating cash flow amount is the same figure that was used in the two previous cash flow formulas in this chapter. For common shares outstanding, use the shares that were used for the purpose of computing earnings per share on the most diluted basis. This figure is available when doing internal analysis. It is also in a firm's 10-K annual report. Some companies disclose these shares in the annual report. This share number cannot be computed from information in the annual report, except for very simple situations.

When these share amounts are not available, use the outstanding shares of common stock. This will result in an approximation of the operating cash flow per share. The advantage of using the number of shares used for earnings per share is that this results in an amount that can be compared to earnings per share, and it avoids distortions.

Operating cash flow per share is computed for Nike for 2007 and 2006 in Exhibit 10-7. Operating cash flow per share was significantly more than earnings per share in both 2007 and 2006. Operating cash flow per share increased in 2007.

Exhibit	10-7	NIKE, INC.

Operating Cash Flow per Share

Years Ended May 31, 2007 and 2006

(In millions)	2007	2006
Operating cash flow	$1,878.7	$1,667.9
Less: Redeemable preferred dividends	0.3	0.3
Operating cash flow after preferred dividends [A]	$1,878.4	$1,667.6
Diluted weighted average common shares outstanding [B]	509.9	527.6
Operating cash flow per share [A ÷ B]	$ 3.68	$ 3.16

OPERATING CASH FLOW/CASH DIVIDENDS

The **operating cash flow/cash dividends** indicates a firm's ability to cover cash dividends with the yearly operating cash flow. The higher the ratio, the better the firm's ability to cover cash dividends. This ratio relates to the investor ratios discussed in Chapter 9.

The operating cash flow/cash dividends formula is as follows:

$$\frac{\text{Operating Cash Flow}}{\text{Cash Dividends}}$$

The operating cash flow amount is the same figure that was used in the three previous formulas in this chapter. Operating cash flow/cash dividends is computed for Nike for 2007 and 2006 in Exhibit 10-8. It indicates material coverage of cash dividends in both 2007 and 2006, although there was a decline in 2007.

Exhibit	10-8	NIKE, INC.

Operating Cash Flow/Cash Dividends		
Years Ended May 31, 2007 and 2006		
(In millions)	**2007**	**2006**
Operating cash flow [A]	$1,878.7	$1,667.9
Cash dividends [B]	$ 343.7	$ 290.9
Operating cash flow/cash dividends [A ÷ B]	5.47 times per year	5.73 times per year

Alternative Cash Flow

There is no standard definition of cash flow in the financial literature. Often, cash flow is used to mean net income plus depreciation expense. This definition of cash flow could be used to compute the cash flow amount for the formulas introduced in this chapter. However, this is a narrow definition of cash flow, and it is considered less useful than the net cash flow from operating activities.

Procedures for Development of the Statement of Cash Flows

Cash inflows and outflows are determined by analyzing all balance sheet accounts other than the cash and cash equivalent accounts. The following account balance changes indicate cash inflows:

1. Decreases in assets (e.g., the sale of land for cash)
2. Increases in liabilities (e.g., the issuance of long-term bonds)
3. Increases in stockholders' equity (e.g., the sale of common stock)

Cash outflows are indicated by the following account balance changes:

1. Increases in assets (e.g., the purchase of a building for cash)
2. Decreases in liabilities (e.g., retirement of long-term debt)
3. Decreases in stockholders' equity (e.g., the payment of a cash dividend)

Transactions within any individual account may result in both a source and a use of cash. For example, the land account may have increased, but analysis may indicate that there was both an acquisition and a disposal of land.

Exhibit 10-9 contains the data needed for preparing a statement of cash flows for ABC Company for the year ended December 31, 2007. These data will be used to illustrate the preparation of the statement of cash flows.

Three techniques may be used to prepare the statement of cash flows: (1) the visual method, (2) the T-account method, and (3) the worksheet method. The visual method can be used only when the financial information is not complicated. When the financial information is complicated, either the T-account method or the worksheet method must be used. This book illustrates only the visual method because of the emphasis on using financial accounting information, not on preparing financial statements. For an explanation of the T-account method and the worksheet method, consult an intermediate accounting textbook.

Following the steps in developing the statement of cash flows, first compute the change in cash and cash equivalents. For ABC Company, this is the increase of $600 in the cash account—the net increase in cash.

For the second step, compute the net change in each balance sheet account other than the cash account. The changes in the balance sheet accounts for ABC Company follow:

Assets:

Accounts receivable decrease	$ 100	Operating
Inventories increase	1,000	Operating
Land increase	9,500	Investing
Equipment increase	1,000	Investing
Accumulated depreciation increase (contra-asset—a change would be similar to a change in liabilities)	4,500	Operating

Liabilities:

Accounts payable decrease	1,100	Operating
Taxes payable increase	400	Operating
Bonds payable increase	5,000	Financing

Stockholders' equity:

Common stock increase	3,000	Financing
Retained earnings increase	200	*

*This is a combination of operating, financing, and investing activities.

For the third step, consider the changes in the balance sheet accounts along with the income statement for the current period and the supplementary information. The cash flows are segregated into cash flows from operating activities, cash flows from investing activities, and cash flows from financing activities. Noncash investing and/or financing activities should be shown in a separate schedule with the statement of cash flows.

To illustrate the direct and indirect methods of presenting operating activities, the ABC Company income statement is used, along with the relevant supplemental information and balance sheet accounts. For the direct approach, the income statement is adjusted to present the revenue and expense accounts on a cash basis. Exhibit 10-10 on page 378 illustrates the accrual basis income statement adjusted to a cash basis. Exhibit 10-11 on page 379 shows the statement of cash flows for ABC Company, using the direct approach for presenting cash flows from operations.

When the cash provided by operations is presented using the direct approach, the income statement accounts are usually described in terms of receipts or payments. For example, "sales" on the accrual basis income statement is usually described as "receipts from customers" when presented on a cash basis.

Exhibit 10-12 on page 380 shows the statement of cash flows for ABC Company, using the indirect approach. To compute cash flows from operations, we start with net income and add back or deduct adjustments necessary to change the income on an accrual basis to income on a cash basis, after eliminating gains or losses that relate to investing or financing activities.

Exhibit	10-9	ABC COMPANY

Financial Information for Statement of Cash Flows

Balance Sheet Information

Accounts	Balances December 31, 2006	Balances December 31, 2007	Category
Assets:			
Cash	$ 2,400	$ 3,000	Cash
Accounts receivable, net	4,000	3,900	Operating
Inventories	5,000	6,000	Operating
Total current assets	11,400	12,900	
Land	10,000	19,500	Investing
Equipment	72,000	73,000	Investing
Accumulated depreciation	(9,500)	(14,000)	Operating
Total assets	$83,900	$91,400	
Liabilities:			
Accounts payable	$ 4,000	$ 2,900	Operating
Taxes payable	1,600	2,000	Operating
Total current liabilities	5,600	4,900	
Bonds payable	35,000	40,000	Financing
Stockholders' Equity:			
Common stock, $10 par	36,000	39,000	Financing
Retained earnings	7,300	7,500	*
Total liabilities and stockholders' equity	$83,900	$91,400	

Income Statement Information
For the Year Ended December 31, 2007

		Category
Sales	$22,000	Operating
Operating expenses	17,500	Operating
Operating income	4,500	
Gain on sale of land	1,000	Investing
Income before tax expense	5,500	
Tax expense	2,000	Operating
Net income	$ 3,500	*

Supplemental Information	Category
(a) Dividends declared and paid are $3,300.	Financing
(b) Land was sold for $1,500.	Investing
(c) Equipment was purchased for $1,000.	Investing
(d) Bonds payable were retired for $5,000.	Financing
(e) Common stock was sold for $3,000.	Financing
(f) Operating expenses include depreciation expense of $4,500.	Operating
(g) The land account and the bonds payable account increased by $10,000 because of a noncash exchange.	Investing and Financing

*Retained earnings is decreased by cash dividends, $3,300 (financing), and increased by net income, $3,500. Net income can be a combination of operating, investing, and financing activities. In this exhibit, all of the net income relates to operating activities, except for the gain on sale of land (investing).

Exhibit	10-10	ABC COMPANY

Schedule of Change from Accrual Basis to Cash Basis Income Statement

	Accrual Basis	Adjustments*	Add (Subtract)	Cash Basis
Sales	$22,000	Decrease in receivables	100	$22,100
Operating expenses	17,500	Depreciation expense	(4,500)	
		Increase in inventories	1,000	
		Decrease in accounts payable	1,100	15,100
Operating income	4,500			7,000
Gain on sale of land	1,000	This gain is related to investing activities.	(1,000)	—
Income before tax expense	5,500			7,000
Tax expense	2,000	Increase in taxes payable	(400)	1,600
Net income	$ 3,500			$ 5,400

*Adjustments are for noncash flow items in the income statement, changes in balance sheet accounts related to cash flow from operations, and the removal of gains and losses on the income statement that are related to investing or financing activities.

The noncash flow items in the income statement are removed from the account. For example, depreciation expense may be in the cost of goods sold, and this expense would be removed from the cost of goods sold.

Changes in balance sheet accounts related to cash flow from operations are adjusted to the related income statement account as follows:

Revenue accounts	$ XXX
Add decreases in asset accounts and increases in liability accounts	+ XXX
Deduct increases in asset accounts and decreases in liability accounts	– XXX
Cash inflow	$ XXX
Expense accounts	
Add increases in asset accounts and decreases in liability accounts	+ XXX
Deduct decreases in asset accounts and increases in liability accounts	– XXX
Cash outflow	$ XXX

Notice on the ABC Company schedule of change from accrual basis to cash basis income statement (Exhibit 10-10) that the adjustments include noncash flow items on the income statement, changes in balance sheet accounts related to operations, and gains and losses on the income statement related to investing or financing activities.

For the indirect approach, follow these directions when adjusting the net income (or loss) to net cash flows from operating activities:

Net income (loss)	$ XXX
Noncash flow items:	
Add expense	+ XXX
Deduct revenues	– XXX
Changes in balance sheet accounts related to operations:*	
Add decreases in assets and increases in liabilities	+ XXX
Deduct increases in assets and decreases in liabilities	– XXX
Gains and losses on the income statement that are related to investing or financing activities:	
Add losses	+ XXX
Deduct gains	– XXX
Net cash provided by operating activities	$ XXX

*These are usually the current asset and current liability accounts.

The remaining changes in balance sheet accounts (other than those used to compute cash provided by operating activities) and the remaining supplemental information are used to determine the cash flows from investing activities and cash flows from financing activities. These accounts are also used to determine noncash investing and/or financing.

Exhibit	10-11	ABC COMPANY

Direct Approach for Presenting Cash Flows from Operations

Statement of Cash Flows
For the Year Ended December 31, 2007

Cash flows from operating activities:		
Receipts from customers	$ 22,100	
Payments to suppliers	(15,100)	
Income taxes paid	(1,600)	
Net cash provided by operating activities		$ 5,400
Cash flows from investing activities:		
Proceeds from sale of land	1,500	
Purchase of equipment	(1,000)	
Net cash provided by investing activities		500
Cash flows from financing activities:		
Dividends declared and paid	(3,300)	
Retirement of bonds payable	(5,000)	
Proceeds from common stock	3,000	
Net cash used for financing activities		(5,300)
Net increase in cash		$ 600
Reconciliation of net income to net cash provided by operating activities:		
Net income		$ 3,500
Adjustments to reconcile net income to net cash provided by operating activities:		
Decrease in accounts receivable		100
Depreciation expense		4,500
Increase in inventories		(1,000)
Decrease in accounts payable		(1,100)
Gain on sale of land		(1,000)
Increase in taxes payable		400
Net cash provided by operating activities		$ 5,400
Supplemental schedule of noncash investing and financing activities:		
Land acquired by issuing bonds		$10,000

Some observations on the ABC Company statement of cash flows follow:

1. Net cash provided by operating activities $5,400
2. Net cash provided by investing activities $500
3. Net cash used for financing activities $5,300
4. Net increase in cash $600

As previously indicated, when the operations section has been presented using the direct method, additional observations can be determined by preparing the statement of cash flows to present inflows and outflows separately. This has been done in Exhibit 10-13 on page 280. Some observations from the summary of cash flows in Exhibit 10-13 follow:

Inflows:

1. Receipts from customers represent approximately 83% of total cash inflow.
2. Proceeds from common stock sales approximate 11% of total cash inflow.
3. Proceeds from sales of land approximate 6% of total cash inflow.

Outflows:

1. Payments to suppliers represent approximately 58% of total cash outflow.
2. Retirement of bonds payable approximates 19% of total cash outflow.
3. Dividends paid approximate 13% of total cash outflow.

| Exhibit | 10-12 | ABC COMPANY |

Indirect Approach for Presenting Cash Flows from Operations

Statement of Cash Flows
For the Year Ended December 31, 2007

Cash flows from operating activities:		
Net income	$ 3,500	
Add (deduct) items not affecting operating activities:		
Depreciation expense	4,500	
Decrease in accounts receivable	100	
Increase in inventories	(1,000)	
Decrease in accounts payable	(1,100)	
Increase in taxes payable	400	
Gain on sale of land	(1,000)	
Net cash provided by operating activities		$ 5,400
Cash flows from investing activities:		
Proceeds from sale of land	1,500	
Purchase of equipment	(1,000)	
Net cash provided by investing activities		500
Cash flows from financing activities:		
Dividends declared and paid	(3,300)	
Retirement of bonds payable	(5,000)	
Proceeds from common stock	3,000	
Net cash used for financing activities		(5,300)
Net increase in cash		$ 600
Supplemental disclosure of cash flow information:		
Cash paid during the year for:		
Interest net of amount capitalized		$ 0
Income taxes		1,600
Supplemental schedule of noncash investing and financing activities:		
Land acquired by issuing bonds		$10,000

| Exhibit | 10-13 | ABC COMPANY |

Statement of Cash Flows
For the Year Ended December 31, 2007
(Inflows and Outflows, by Activity—Inflows Presented on Direct Basis)

	Inflows	Outflows	Inflow Percent	Outflow Percent
Operating activities:				
Receipts from customers	$22,100		83.1%	
Payments to suppliers		$15,100		58.1%
Income taxes paid		1,600		6.2
Cash flow from operating activities	22,100	16,700	83.1	64.3
Investing activities:				
Proceeds from sale of land	1,500		5.6	
Purchase of equipment		1,000		3.8
Cash flow from investing activities	1,500	1,000	5.6	3.8
Financing activities:				
Dividends declared and paid		3,300		12.7
Retirement of bonds payable		5,000		19.2
Proceeds from common stock	3,000		11.3	
Cash flow from financing activities	3,000	8,300	11.3	31.9
Total cash inflows/outflows	26,600	$26,000	100.0%	100.0%
Total cash outflows	26,000			
Net increase in cash	$ 600			

Summary

The statement of cash flows provides cash flow information that is critical for users to make informed decisions. The statement of cash flows should be reviewed for several time periods in order to determine the major sources of cash and the major uses of cash.

The ratios related to the statement of cash flows are the following:

$$\text{Operating Cash Flow/Current Maturities of Long-Term Debt and Current Notes Payable} = \frac{\text{Operating Cash Flow}}{\text{Current Maturities of Long-Term Debt and Current Notes Payable}}$$

$$\text{Operating Cash Flow/Total Debt} = \frac{\text{Operating Cash Flow}}{\text{Total Debt}}$$

$$\text{Operating Cash Flow per Share} = \frac{\text{Operating Cash Flow} - \text{Preferred Dividends}}{\text{Diluted Weighted Average Common Shares Outstanding}}$$

$$\text{Operating Cash Flow/Cash Dividends} = \frac{\text{Operating Cash Flow}}{\text{Cash Dividends}}$$

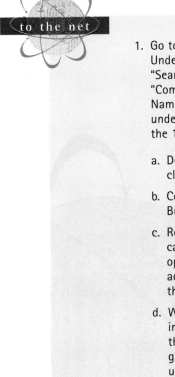

to the net

1. Go to the SEC Web site (http://www.sec.gov). Under "Filings & Forms (EDGAR)," click on "Search for Company Filings." Click on "Companies & Other Filers." Under Company Name, enter "Northrop Grumman Corp" (or under Ticker Symbol, enter "NOC"). Select the 10-K submitted February 21, 2007.

   a. Determine the standard industrial classification.

   b. Copy the first sentence in the "Item 1. Business" section.

   c. Review the consolidated statements of cash flows. Under what method are the operating activities presented? What advantage does this presentation have over the alternative presentation?

   d. Why are the noncash investing and financing activities presented at the bottom of the statement? Why would "consideration given for business purchased" be presented under noncash investing and financing activities?

2. Go to the SEC Web site (http://www.sec.gov). Under "Filings & Forms (EDGAR)," click on "Search for Company Filings." Click on "Companies & Other Filers." Under Company Name, enter "Dell Inc" (or under Ticker Symbol, enter "DELL"). Select the 10-K filed April 4, 2007.

   a. Describe this type of form.

   b. Describe the content of this filing.

   c. Could this type of situation present a challenge to multiple-year analysis?

3. Go to the SEC Web site (http://www.sec.gov). Under "Filings & Forms (EDGAR)," click on "Search for Company Filings." Click on "Companies & Other Filers." Under Company Name, enter "Molson Coors Brewing Co." (or under Ticker Symbol, enter "TAP"). Select the 10-K submitted March 1, 2007.

   a. Determine the standard industrial classification.

   b. Copy the first sentence in the "Item 1. Business" section.

c. Prepare the following ratios for December 31, 2006, and December 25, 2005:

1. Operating cash flow/current maturities of long-term debt and current notes payable.

2. Operating cash flow/total debt.

3. Operating cash flow per share.

4. Operating cash flow/cash dividends.

d. Comment on the results in (c).

4. Go to the SEC Web site (http://www.sec.gov). Under "Filings & Forms (EDGAR)," click on "Search for Company Filings." Click on "Companies & Other Filers." Under Company Name, enter "AnnTaylor Stores Corp" (or under Ticker Symbol, enter "ANN"). Select the 10-K submitted March 22, 2007.

a. Determine the standard industrial classification.

b. Copy the first sentence in the "General" subsection from the "Item 1. Business" section.

c. Determine the numbers for the following:

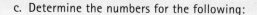

	Fiscal Year Ended		
	Feb. 3, 2007	Jan. 28, 2006	Jan. 29, 2005
Net sales			
Gross margin			
Operating income			
Net cash provided by operating activities			

d. Comment on the trends in (c).

e. Review the consolidated statements of cash flows.

1. Why is the depreciation and amortization added back to net income?

2. Why is the change in inventories subtracted from net income for the year ended February 3, 2007?

3. Why is the change in accounts payable and accrued expenses added to net income for the year ended February 3, 2007?

Questions

Q 10-1.   If a firm presents an income statement and a balance sheet, why is it necessary that a statement of cash flows also be presented?

Q 10-2.   Into what three categories are cash flows segregated on the statement of cash flows?

Q 10-3.   Using the descriptions of assets, liabilities, and stockholders' equity, summarize the changes to these accounts for cash inflows and changes to these accounts for cash outflows.

Q 10-4.   The land account may be used only to explain a use of cash, but not a source of cash. Comment.

Q 10-5.   Indicate the three techniques that may be used to complete the steps in developing the statement of cash flows.

Q 10-6.   There are two principal methods of presenting cash flow from operating activities—the direct method and the indirect method. Describe these two methods.

Q 10-7.   Depreciation expense, amortization of patents, and amortization of bond discount are examples of items that are added to net income when using the indirect method of presenting cash flows from operating activities. Amortization of premium on bonds and a reduction in deferred taxes are examples of items that are deducted from net income when using the indirect method of presenting cash flows from operating activities. Explain why these adjustments to net income are made to compute cash flows from operating activities.

Q 10-8.   What is the meaning of the term *cash* in the statement of cash flows?

Q 10-9.   What is the purpose of the statement of cash flows?

Q 10-10.   Why is it important to disclose certain noncash investing and financing transactions, such as exchanging common stock for land?

Q 10-11.   Would a write-off of uncollectible accounts against allowance for doubtful accounts be disclosed on a cash flow statement? Explain.

Q 10-12.   Fully depreciated equipment costing $60,000 was discarded, with no salvage value. What effect would this have on the statement of cash flows?

Q 10-13.   For the current year, a firm reported net income from operations of $20,000 on its income statement and an increase of $30,000 in cash from operations on the statement of cash flows. Explain some likely reasons for the greater increase in cash from operations than net income from operations.

Q 10-14.   A firm owed accounts payable of $150,000 at the beginning of the year and $250,000 at the end of the year. What influence will the $100,000 increase have on cash from operations?

Q 10-15.   A member of the board of directors is puzzled by the fact that the firm has had a very profitable year but does not have enough cash to pay its bills on time. Explain to the director how a firm can be profitable, yet not have enough cash to pay its bills and dividends.

Q 10-16.   Depreciation is often considered a major source of funds. Do you agree? Explain.

Q 10-17.   Pickerton started the year with $50,000 in accounts receivable. The firm ended the year with $20,000 in accounts receivable. How did this decrease influence cash from operations?

Q 10-18.   Aerco Company acquired equipment in exchange for $50,000 in common stock. Should this transaction be on the statement of cash flows?

Q 10-19.   Operating cash flow per share is a better indicator of profitability than is earnings per share. Do you agree? Explain.

Q 10-20.   Hornet Company had operating cash flow of $60,000 during a year in which it paid dividends of $11,000. What does this indicate about Hornet's dividend-paying ability?

Problems

P 10-1.   The following material relates to Darrow Company:

	Cash Flows Classification			Effect on Cash		Noncash
Data	Operating Activity	Investing Activity	Financing Activity	Increase	Decrease	Trans-actions
a. Net loss	_____	_____	_____	_____	_____	_____
b. Increase in inventory	_____	_____	_____	_____	_____	_____
c. Decrease in receivables	_____	_____	_____	_____	_____	_____
d. Increase in prepaid insurance	_____	_____	_____	_____	_____	_____
e. Issuance of common stock	_____	_____	_____	_____	_____	_____
f. Acquisition of land, using notes payable	_____	_____	_____	_____	_____	_____
g. Purchase of land, using cash	_____	_____	_____	_____	_____	_____
h. Paid cash dividend	_____	_____	_____	_____	_____	_____
i. Payment of income taxes	_____	_____	_____	_____	_____	_____
j. Retirement of bonds, using cash	_____	_____	_____	_____	_____	_____
k. Sale of equipment for cash	_____	_____	_____	_____	_____	_____

Required   Place an X in the appropriate columns for each of the situations.

P 10-2.

Data	Cash Flows Classification			Effect on Cash		Noncash Trans-actions
	Operating Activity	Investing Activity	Financing Activity	Increase	Decrease	
a. Net income	___	___	___	___	___	___
b. Paid cash dividend	___	___	___	___	___	___
c. Increase in receivables	___	___	___	___	___	___
d. Retirement of debt—paying cash	___	___	___	___	___	___
e. Purchase of treasury stock	___	___	___	___	___	___
f. Purchase of equipment	___	___	___	___	___	___
g. Sale of equipment	___	___	___	___	___	___
h. Decrease in inventory	___	___	___	___	___	___
i. Acquisition of land, using common stock	___	___	___	___	___	___
j. Retired bonds, using common stock	___	___	___	___	___	___
k. Decrease in accounts payable	___	___	___	___	___	___

Required   Place an X in the appropriate columns for each of the situations.

P 10-3.   BBB Company's balance sheet and income statement follow:

BBB COMPANY
Balance Sheet
December 31, 2007 and 2006

	December 31,	
	2007	2006
Assets		
Cash	$ 4,500	$ 4,000
Marketable securities	2,500	2,000
Accounts receivable	6,800	7,200
Inventories	7,500	8,000
Total current assets	21,300	21,200
Land	11,000	12,000
Equipment	24,000	20,500
Accumulated depreciation—equipment	(3,800)	(3,000)
Building	70,000	70,000
Accumulated depreciation—building	(14,000)	(12,000)
Total assets	$108,500	$108,700
Liabilities and Stockholders' Equity		
Accounts payable	$ 7,800	$ 7,000
Wages payable	1,050	1,000
Taxes payable	500	1,500
Total current liabilities	9,350	9,500
Bonds payable	30,000	30,000
Common stock, $10 par	32,000	30,000
Additional paid-in capital	21,000	19,200
Retained earnings	16,150	20,000
Total liabilities and stockholders' equity	$108,500	$108,700

BBB COMPANY
Income Statement
For Year Ended December 31, 2007

Sales		$38,000
Operating expenses:		
Depreciation expense	$ 2,800	
Other operating expenses	35,000	37,800
Operating income		200
Gain on sale of land		800
Income before tax expense		1,000
Tax expense		500
Net income		$ 500
Supplemental information:		
Dividends declared and paid	$ 4,350	
Land sold for cash	1,800	
Equipment purchased for cash	3,500	
Common stock sold for cash	3,800	

Required   a. Prepare a statement of cash flows for the year ended December 31, 2007. (Present the cash flows from operations, using the indirect method.)

b. Comment on the statement of cash flows.

P 10-4.   The income statement and other selected data for Frish Company follow:

FRISH COMPANY
Income Statement
For Year Ended December 31, 2007

Net sales	$640,000
Expenses:	
Cost of goods sold	360,000
Selling and administrative expense	43,000
Other expense	2,000
Total expenses	405,000
Income before income tax	235,000
Income tax	92,000
Net income	$143,000

Other data:
a. Cost of goods sold, including
   depreciation expense of $15,000
b. Selling and administrative expense, including
   depreciation expense of $5,000
c. Other expense, representing amortization
   of patent, $3,000, and amortization
   of bond premium, $1,000

d. Increase in accounts receivable	$ 27,000
e. Increase in accounts payable	15,000
f. Increase in inventories	35,000
g. Decrease in prepaid expenses	1,000
h. Increase in accrued liabilities	3,000
i. Decrease in income taxes payable	10,000

Required   a. Prepare a schedule of change from accrual basis to cash basis income statement.

b. Using the schedule of change from accrual basis to cash basis income statement computed in (a), present the cash provided by operations, using (1) the direct approach and (2) the indirect approach.

P 10-5.   The income statement and other selected data for Boyer Company follow:

BOYER COMPANY
Income Statement
For Year Ended December 31, 2007

Sales		$19,000
Operating expenses:		
Depreciation expense	$ 2,300	
Other operating expenses	12,000	14,300
Operating income		4,700

(continued)

Loss on sale of land	1,500
Income before tax expense	3,200
Tax expense	1,000
Net income	$ 2,200

Supplemental information:

a. Dividends declared and paid	$ 800
b. Land purchased	3,000
c. Land sold	500
d. Equipment purchased	2,000
e. Bonds payable retired	2,000
f. Common stock sold	1,400
g. Land acquired in exchange for common stock	3,000
h. Increase in accounts receivable	400
i. Increase in inventories	800
j. Increase in accounts payable	500
k. Decrease in income taxes payable	400

Required

a. Prepare a schedule of change from an accrual basis to a cash basis income statement.

b. Using the schedule of change from accrual basis to cash basis income statement computed in (a), present the cash provided by operations, using (1) the direct approach and (2) the indirect approach.

P 10-6.   Sampson Company's balance sheets for December 31, 2007 and 2006, as well as the income statement for the year ended December 31, 2007, are shown below.

SAMPSON COMPANY
Balance Sheet
December 31, 2007 and 2006

	2007	2006
Assets		
Cash	$ 38,000	$ 60,000
Net receivables	72,000	65,000
Inventory	98,000	85,000
Plant assets	195,000	180,000
Accumulated depreciation	(45,000)	(35,000)
Total assets	$358,000	$355,000
Liabilities and Stockholders' Equity		
Accounts payable	$ 85,000	$ 80,000
Accrued liabilities (related to cost of sales)	44,000	61,000
Mortgage payable	11,000	—
Common stock	180,000	174,000
Retained earnings	38,000	40,000
Total liabilities and stockholders' equity	$358,000	$355,000

SAMPSON COMPANY
Income Statement
For Year Ended December 31, 2007

Net sales	$145,000
Cost of sales	108,000
Gross profit	37,000
Other expenses	6,000
Profit before taxes	31,000
Tax expense	12,000
Net income	$ 19,000

Other data:

1. Dividends paid in cash during 2007 were $21,000.
2. Depreciation is included in the cost of sales.
3. The change in the accumulated depreciation account is the depreciation expense for the year.

Required

a. Prepare the statement of cash flows for the year ended December 31, 2007, using the indirect method for net cash flow from operating activities.

b. Prepare the statement of cash flows for the year ended December 31, 2007, using the direct method for net cash flow from operating activities.

c. Comment on significant items disclosed in the statement of cash flows.

P 10-7.   Arrowbell Company is a growing company. Two years ago, it decided to expand in order to increase its production capacity. The company anticipates that the expansion program can be completed in another two years. Financial information for Arrowbell is shown below and on the following page.

ARROWBELL COMPANY
Sales and Net Income

Year	Sales	Net Income
2003	$2,568,660	$145,800
2004	2,660,455	101,600
2005	2,550,180	52,650
2006	2,625,280	86,800
2007	3,680,650	151,490

ARROWBELL COMPANY
Balance Sheet
December 31, 2007 and 2006

	2007	2006
Assets		
Current assets:		
Cash	$ 250,480	$ 260,155
Accounts receivable (net)	760,950	690,550
Inventories at lower-of-cost-or-market	725,318	628,238
Prepaid expenses	18,555	20,250
Total current assets	1,755,303	1,599,193
Plant and equipment:		
Land, buildings, machinery, and equipment	3,150,165	2,646,070
Less: Accumulated depreciation	650,180	525,650
Net plant and equipment	2,499,985	2,120,420
Other assets:		
Cash surrender value of life insurance	20,650	18,180
Other	40,660	38,918
Total other assets	61,310	57,098
Total assets	$4,316,598	$3,776,711
Liabilities and Stockholders' Equity		
Current liabilities:		
Notes and mortgages payable, current portion	$ 915,180	$ 550,155
Accounts payable and accrued liabilities	1,160,111	851,080
Total current liabilities	2,075,291	1,401,235
Long-term notes and mortgages payable,		
less current portion above	550,000	775,659
Total liabilities	2,625,291	2,176,894
Stockholders' equity:		
Capital stock, par value $1.00; authorized,		
800,000; issued and outstanding,		
600,000 (2007 and 2006)	600,000	600,000
Paid in excess of par	890,000	890,000
Retained earnings	201,307	109,817
Total stockholders' equity	1,691,307	1,599,817
Total liabilities and stockholders' equity	$4,316,598	$3,776,711

ARROWBELL COMPANY
Statement of Cash Flows
For Years Ended December 31, 2007 and 2006

	2007	2006
Cash flows from operating activities:		
Net income	$ 151,490	$ 86,800
Noncash expenses, revenues, losses, and gains included in income:		
Depreciation	134,755	102,180
Increase in accounts receivable	(70,400)	(10,180)
Increase in inventories	(97,080)	(15,349)
Decrease in prepaid expenses in 2007, increase in 2006	1,695	(1,058)
Increase in accounts payable and accrued liabilities	309,031	15,265
Net cash provided by operating activities	429,491	177,658

(continued)

	2007	2006
Cash flows from investing activities:		
Proceeds from retirement of property, plant, and equipment	10,115	3,865
Purchases of property, plant, and equipment	(524,435)	(218,650)
Increase in cash surrender value of life insurance	(2,470)	(1,848)
Other	(1,742)	(1,630)
Net cash used for investing activities	(518,532)	(218,263)
Cash flows from financing activities:		
Retirement of long-term debt	(225,659)	(50,000)
Increase in notes and mortgages payable	365,025	159,155
Cash dividends	(60,000)	(60,000)
Net cash provided by financing activities	79,366	49,155
Net increase (decrease) in cash	$ (9,675)	$ 8,550

Required

a. Comment on the short-term debt position, including computations of current ratio, acid-test ratio, cash ratio, and operating cash flow/current maturities of long-term debt and current notes payable.

b. If you were a supplier to this company, what would you be concerned about?

c. Comment on the long-term debt position, including computations of the debt ratio, debt/equity, debt to tangible net worth, and operating cash flow/total debt. Review the statement of operating cash flows.

d. If you were a banker, what would you be concerned about if this company approached you for a long-term loan to continue its expansion program?

e. What should management consider doing at this point in regard to the company's expansion program?

P 10-8.   The balance sheet for December 31, 2007, income statement for the year ended December 31, 2007, and the statement of cash flows for the year ended December 31, 2007, of Bernett Company are shown below and on the following page.

The president of Bernett Company cannot understand why Bernett is having trouble paying current obligations. He notes that business has been very good, as sales have more than doubled, and the company achieved a profit of $69,000 in 2007.

BERNETT COMPANY
Balance Sheet
December 31, 2007 and 2006

	2007	2006
Assets		
Cash	$ 5,000	$ 28,000
Accounts receivable, net	92,000	70,000
Inventory	130,000	85,000
Prepaid expenses	4,000	6,000
Land	30,000	10,000
Building	170,000	30,000
Accumulated depreciation	(20,000)	(10,000)
Total assets	$411,000	$219,000
Liabilities and Stockholders' Equity		
Accounts payable	$ 49,000	$ 44,000
Income taxes payable	5,000	4,000
Accrued liabilities	6,000	5,000
Bonds payable (current $10,000 at 12/31/07)	175,000	20,000
Common stock	106,000	96,000
Retained earnings	70,000	50,000
Total liabilities and stockholders' equity	$411,000	$219,000

BERNETT COMPANY
Income Statement
For Year Ended December 31, 2007

Sales	$500,000
Less expenses:	
Cost of goods sold (includes depreciation of $4,000)	310,000
Selling and administrative expenses (includes depreciation of $6,000)	80,000
Interest expense	11,000
Total expenses	401,000

Income before taxes		99,000
Income tax expense		30,000
Net income		$ 69,000

BERNETT COMPANY
Statement of Cash Flows
For Year Ended December 31, 2007

Net cash flow from operating activities:		
Net income	$ 69,000	
Noncash expenses, revenues, losses, and gains included in income:		
Depreciation	10,000	
Increase in receivables	(22,000)	
Increase in inventory	(45,000)	
Decrease in prepaid expenses	2,000	
Increase in accounts payable	5,000	
Increase in income taxes payable	1,000	
Increase in accrued liabilities	1,000	
Net cash flow from operating activities		$ 21,000
Cash flows from investing activities:		
Increase in land	$ (20,000)	
Increase in buildings	(140,000)	
Net cash used by investing activities		(160,000)
Cash flows from financing activities:		
Bond payable increase	$ 155,000	
Common stock increase	10,000	
Cash dividends paid	(49,000)	
Net cash provided by financing activities		116,000
Net decrease in cash		$ (23,000)

Required

a. Comment on the statement of cash flows.

b. Compute the following liquidity ratios for 2007:
 1. Current ratio
 2. Acid-test ratio
 3. Operating cash flow/current maturities of long-term debt and current notes payable
 4. Cash ratio

c. Compute the following debt ratios for 2007:
 1. Times interest earned
 2. Debt ratio
 3. Operating cash flow/total debt

d. Compute the following profitability ratios for 2007:
 1. Return on assets (using average assets)
 2. Return on common equity (using average common equity)

e. Compute the following investor ratio for 2007: Operating cash flow/cash dividends.

f. Give your opinion as to the liquidity of Bernett.

g. Give your opinion as to the debt position of Bernett.

h. Give your opinion as to the profitability of Bernett.

i. Give your opinion as to the investor ratio.

j. Give your opinion of the alternatives Bernett has in order to ensure that it can pay bills as they come due.

P 10-9. Zaro Company's balance sheets for December 31, 2007 and 2006, income statement for the year ended December 31, 2007, and the statement of cash flows for the year ended December 31, 2007, follow:

ZARO COMPANY
Balance Sheet
December 31, 2007 and 2006

	2007	2006
Assets		
Cash	$ 30,000	$ 15,000
Accounts receivable, net	75,000	87,000
Inventory	90,000	105,000

(continued)

	2007	2006
Prepaid expenses	3,000	2,000
Land	25,000	25,000
Building and equipment	122,000	120,000
Accumulated depreciation	(92,000)	(80,000)
Total assets	$253,000	$274,000
Liabilities and Stockholders' Equity		
Accounts payable	$ 25,500	$ 32,000
Income taxes payable	2,500	3,000
Accrued liabilities	5,000	5,000
Bonds payable (current $20,000 at 12/31/07)	90,000	95,000
Common stock	85,000	85,000
Retained earnings	45,000	54,000
Total liabilities and stockholders' equity	$253,000	$274,000

ZARO COMPANY
Income Statement
For Year Ended December 31, 2007

Sales	$400,000
Less expense:	
Cost of goods sold (includes depreciation of $5,000)	$280,000
Selling and administrative expenses (includes depreciation expenses of $7,000)	78,000
Interest expense	8,000
Total expenses	$366,000
Income before taxes	34,000
Income tax expense	14,000
Net income	$ 20,000

ZARO COMPANY
Statement of Cash Flows
For Year Ended December 31, 2007

Net cash flow from operating activities:		
Net income	$ 20,000	
Noncash expenses, revenues, losses, and gains included in income:		
Depreciation	12,000	
Decrease in accounts receivable	12,000	
Decrease in inventory	15,000	
Increase in prepaid expenses	(1,000)	
Decrease in accounts payable	(6,500)	
Decrease in income taxes payable	(500)	
Net cash flow from operating activities		$ 51,000
Cash flows from investing activities:		
Increase in buildings and equipment	$ (2,000)	
Net cash used by investing activities		(2,000)
Cash flows from financing activities:		
Decrease in bonds payable	$ (5,000)	
Cash dividends paid	(29,000)	
Net cash used for financing activities		(34,000)
Net increase in cash		$ 15,000

The president of Zaro Company cannot understand how the company was able to pay cash dividends that were greater than net income and at the same time increase the cash balance. He notes that business was down slightly in 2007.

Required

a. Comment on the statement of cash flows.

b. Compute the following liquidity ratios for 2007:

 1. Current ratio
 2. Acid-test ratio
 3. Operating cash flow/current maturities of long-term debt and current notes payable
 4. Cash ratio

   c. Compute the following debt ratios for 2007:
     1. Times interest earned
     2. Debt ratio
   d. Compute the following profitability ratios for 2007:
     1. Return on assets (using average assets)
     2. Return on common equity (using average common equity)
   e. Give your opinion as to the liquidity of Zaro.
   f. Give your opinion as to the debt position of Zaro.
   g. Give your opinion as to the profitability of Zaro.
   h. Explain to the president how Zaro was able to pay cash dividends that were greater than net income and at the same time increase the cash balance.

P 10-10. The Ladies Store presented the following statement of cash flows for the year ended December 31, 2007:

THE LADIES STORE
Statement of Cash Flows
For Year Ended December 31, 2007

Cash received:	
From sales to customers	$150,000
From sales of bonds	100,000
From issuance of notes payable	40,000
From interest on bonds	5,000
Total cash received	295,000
Cash payments:	
For merchandise purchases	110,000
For purchase of truck	20,000
For purchase of investment	80,000
For purchase of equipment	45,000
For interest	2,000
For income taxes	15,000
Total cash payments	272,000
Net increase in cash	$ 23,000

Note: Depreciation expense was $15,000.

Required   a. Prepare a statement of cash flows in proper form.
        b. Comment on the major flows of cash.

P 10-11. Answer the following multiple-choice questions:
   a. Which of the following could lead to cash flow problems?
     1. Tightening of credit by suppliers
     2. Easing of credit by suppliers
     3. Reduction of inventory
     4. Improved quality of accounts receivable
     5. Selling of bonds
   b. Which of the following would not contribute to bankruptcy of a profitable firm?
     1. Substantial increase in inventory
     2. Substantial increase in receivables
     3. Substantial decrease in accounts payable
     4. Substantial decrease in notes payable
     5. Substantial decrease in receivables
   c. Which of the following current asset or current liability accounts is not included in the computation of cash flows from operating activities?
     1. Change in accounts receivable
     2. Change in inventory
     3. Change in accounts payable
     4. Change in accrued wages
     5. Change in notes payable to banks

d. Which of the following items is not included in the adjustment of net income to cash flows from operating activities?
    1. Increase in deferred taxes
    2. Amortization of goodwill
    3. Depreciation expense for the period
    4. Amortization of premium on bonds payable
    5. Proceeds from selling land
e. Which of the following represents an internal source of cash?
    1. Cash inflows from financing activities
    2. Cash inflows from investing activities
    3. Cash inflows from selling land
    4. Cash inflows from operating activities
    5. Cash inflows from issuing stock
f. How would revenue from services be classified?
    1. Investing inflow
    2. Investing outflow
    3. Operating inflow
    4. Operating outflow
    5. Financing outflow
g. What type of account is inventory?
    1. Investing
    2. Financing
    3. Operating
    4. Noncash
    5. Sometimes operating and sometimes investing
h. How would short-term investments in marketable securities be classified?
    1. Operating activities
    2. Financing activities
    3. Investing activities
    4. Noncash activities
    5. Cash and cash equivalents
i. Which of the following is *not* a typical cash flow under operating activities?
    1. Cash inflows from sale of goods or services
    2. Cash inflows from interest
    3. Cash outflows to employees
    4. Cash outflows to suppliers
    5. Cash inflows from sale of property, plant, and equipment
j. A transaction that will increase working capital is
    1. Purchase of marketable securities.
    2. Payment of accounts payable.
    3. Collection of accounts receivable.
    4. Sale of common stock.
    5. None of the above.
k. Working capital is defined as
    1. Current assets less current liabilities.
    2. Cash equivalent accounts less current liabilities.
    3. Current assets less notes payable.
    4. Total assets less current liabilities.
    5. Current assets less cash equivalent accounts.
l. Management should use the statement of cash flows for which of the following purposes?
    1. Determine the financial position
    2. Determine cash flow from investing activities
    3. Determine the balance in accounts payable
    4. Determine the balance in accounts receivable
    5. None of the above

m. The purchase of land by the issuance of bonds payable should be presented in a statement of cash flows in which of the following sections?

1. Cash flows from operating activities
2. Supplemental schedule of noncash investing and financing activities
3. Cash flows from investing activities
4. Cash flows from financing activities
5. None of the above

P 10-12.   Szabo Company presented the following data with its 2007 financial statements:

SZABO COMPANY
Statements of Cash Flows
For Years Ended December 31, 2007, 2006, and 2005

	2007	2006	2005
Increase (decrease) in cash:			
Cash flows from operating activities:			
Cash received from customers	$ 173,233	$ 176,446	$ 158,702
Cash paid to suppliers and employees	(150,668)	(157,073)	(144,060)
Interest received	132	105	89
Interest paid	(191)	(389)	(777)
Income taxes paid	(6,626)	(4,754)	(845)
Net cash provided by operations	15,880	14,335	13,109
Cash flows from investing activities:			
Capital expenditures	(8,988)	(5,387)	(6,781)
Proceeds from property, plant, and equipment disposals	1,215	114	123
Net cash used in investing activities	(7,773)	(5,273)	(6,658)
Cash flows from financing activities:			
Net increase (decrease) in short-term debt	—	5,100	7,200
Increase in long-term debt	4,100	3,700	5,200
Dividends paid	(6,050)	(8,200)	(8,000)
Purchase of common stock	(8,233)	(3,109)	(70)
Net cash used in financing activities	(10,183)	(2,509)	4,330
Net increase (decrease) in cash and cash equivalents	(2,076)	6,553	10,781
Cash and cash equivalents at beginning of year	24,885	18,332	7,551
Cash and cash equivalents at end of year	$ 22,809	$ 24,885	$ 18,332

Reconciliation of Net Income to Net Cash Provided by Operating Activities

	2007	2006	2005
Net income	$ 7,610	$ 3,242	$ 506
Provision for depreciation and amortization	12,000	9,700	9,000
Provision for losses on accounts receivable	170	163	140
Gain on property, plant, and equipment disposals	(2,000)	(1,120)	(1,500)
Changes in operating assets and liabilities:			
Accounts receivable	(2,000)	(1,750)	(1,600)
Inventories	(3,100)	(2,700)	(2,300)
Other assets	—	—	(57)
Accounts payable	—	5,100	7,200
Accrued income taxes	1,200	—	—
Deferred income taxes	2,000	1,700	1,720
Net cash provided by operating activities	$15,880	$14,335	$13,109

Required   a. Prepare a statement of cash flows with a three-year total column for 2005–2007.

b. Comment on significant trends you detect in the statement prepared in (a).

c. Prepare a statement of cash flows, with inflow/outflow for the year ended December 31, 2007.

d. Comment on significant trends you detect in the statement prepared in (c).

P 10-13.   Consider the following data for three different companies:

	($000 Omitted)		
	Owens	**Arrow**	**Alpha**
Net cash provided (used) by:			
Operating activities	$(2,000)	$2,700	$(3,000)
Investing activities	(6,000)	(600)	(400)
Financing activities	9,000	(400)	(2,600)
Net increase (decrease) in cash	$ 1,000	$1,700	$(6,000)

The patterns of cash flows for these firms differ. One firm is a growth firm that is expanding rapidly, another firm is in danger of bankruptcy, while another firm is an older firm that is expanding slowly.

Required   Select the growth firm, the firm in danger of bankruptcy, and the firm that is the older firm expanding slowly. Explain your selection.

P 10-14.   The following information was taken from the 2007 financial statements of Jones Corporation:

Accounts receivable, January 1, 2007	$ 30,000
Accounts receivable, December 31, 2007	40,000
Sales (all credit sales)	480,000

Note: No accounts receivable were written off or recovered during the year.

Required   a. Determine the cash collected from customers by Jones Corporation in 2007.
b. Comment on why cash collected from customers differed from sales.

P 10-15.   Webster Corporation's statement of cash flows for the year ended December 31, 2007, was prepared using the indirect method, and it included the following items:

Net income	$100,000
Noncash adjustments:	
Depreciation expense	20,000
Decrease in accounts receivable	8,000
Decrease in inventory	25,000
Increase in accounts payable	10,000
Net cash flows from operating activities	$163,000

Note: Webster Corporation reported revenues from customers of $150,000 in its 2007 income statement.

Required   a. What amount of cash did Webster receive from customers during the year ended December 31, 2007?
b. Did depreciation expense provide cash inflow? Comment.

Case	**STILL EXPANDING**
10-1	The data in this case come from the financial reports of Amazon.com, Inc.*

Selected Consolidated Balance Sheet Items

	December 31,		
(In millions)	2006	2005	2004
Total current assets	$3,373	$2,929	$2,539
Total assets	4,363	3,696	3,248
Total current liabilities	2,532	1,899	1,620
Long-term debt	1,247	1,480	1,855**
Other long-term liabilities	153	71	**
Total liabilities	3,932	3,450	3,475
Stockholders' equity***	431	246	(227)
Total liabilities and stockholders' equity	4,363	3,696	3,248

*"Amazon.com . . . today offers Earth's Biggest Selection. . . . We seek to be Earth's most customer-centric company, where customers can find and discover anything they might want to buy online, and endeavor to offer customers the lowest possible prices." 10-K

**Classified as "long-term debt and other"

***No preferred stock outstanding

(continued)

STILL EXPANDING (Continued)

AMAZON.COM, INC.
CONSOLIDATED STATEMENTS OF OPERATIONS
(in millions, except per share data)

	Year Ended December 31,		
	2006	2005	2004
Net sales	$10,711	$8,490	$6,921
Cost of sales	8,255	6,451	5,319
Gross profit	2,456	2,039	1,602
Operating expenses[1]:			
Fulfillment	937	745	601
Marketing	263	198	162
Technology and content	662	451	283
General and administrative	195	166	124
Other operating expense (income)	10	47	(8)
Total operating expense	2,067	1,607	1,162
Income from operations	389	432	440
Interest income	59	44	28
Interest expense	(78)	(92)	(107)
Other income (expense), net	(4)	2	(5)
Remeasurements and other	11	42	(1)
Total non-operating expense	(12)	(4)	(85)
Income before income taxes	377	428	355
Provision (benefit) for income taxes	187	95	(233)
Income before cumulative effect of change in accounting principle	190	333	588
Cumulative effect of change in accounting principle	—	26	—
Net income	$ 190	$ 359	$ 588
Basic earnings per share:			
Prior to cumulative effect of change in accounting principle	$ 0.46	$ 0.81	$ 1.45
Cumulative effect of change in accounting principle	—	0.06	—
	$ 0.46	$ 0.87	$ 1.45
Diluted earnings per share:			
Prior to cumulative effect of change in accounting principle	$ 0.45	$ 0.78	$ 1.39
Cumulative effect of change in accounting principle	—	0.06	—
	$ 0.45	$ 0.84	$ 1.39
Weighted average shares used in computation of earnings per share:			
Basic	416	412	406
Diluted	424	426	425
[1]Includes stock-based compensation as follows:			
Fulfillment	$24	$16	$10
Marketing	4	6	4
Technology and content	54	45	32
General and administrative	19	20	12

AMAZON.COM, INC.
CONSOLIDATED STATEMENTS OF CASH FLOWS
(in millions)

	Year Ended December 31,		
	2006	2005	2004
CASH AND CASH EQUIVALENTS, BEGINNING OF PERIOD	$1,013	$1,303	$1,102
OPERATING ACTIVITIES:			
Net income	190	359	588
Adjustments to reconcile net income to net cash from operating activities:			
Depreciation of fixed assets, including internal-use software and website development, and other amortization	205	121	76

(continued)

STILL EXPANDING (Continued)

	2006	2005	2004
Stock-based compensation	101	87	58
Other operating expense (income)	10	7	(8)
Gains on sales of marketable securities, net	(2)	(1)	(1)
Remeasurements and other	(6)	(37)	6
Deferred income taxes	22	70	(257)
Excess tax benefit on stock awards	(102)	(7)	—
Cumulative effect of change in accounting principle	—	(26)	—
Changes in operating assets and liabilities:			
Inventories	(282)	(104)	(169)
Accounts receivable, net and other current assets	(103)	(84)	(2)
Accounts payable	402	274	286
Accrued expenses and other liabilities	241	67	(14)
Additions to unearned revenue	206	156	110
Amortization of previously unearned revenue	(180)	(149)	(107)
Net cash provided by operating activities	702	733	566
INVESTING ACTIVITIES:			
Purchases of fixed assets, including internal-use software and website development	(216)	(204)	(89)
Acquisitions, net of cash acquired	(32)	(24)	(71)
Sales and maturities of marketable securities and other investments	1,845	836	1,427
Purchases of marketable securities and other investments	(1,930)	(1,386)	(1,584)
Net cash used in investing activities	(333)	(778)	(317)
FINANCING ACTIVITIES:			
Proceeds from exercises of stock options	35	59	60
Excess tax benefit on stock awards	102	7	—
Common stock repurchases	(252)	—	—
Proceeds from long-term debt and other	98	11	—
Repayments of long-term debt and capital lease obligations	(383)	(270)	(157)
Net cash used in financing activities	(400)	(193)	(97)
Foreign-currency effect on cash and cash equivalents	40	(52)	49
Net increase (decrease) in cash and cash equivalents	9	(290)	201
CASH AND CASH EQUIVALENTS, END OF PERIOD	$1,022	$1,013	$1,303
SUPPLEMENTAL CASH FLOW INFORMATION:			
Cash paid for interest	$ 86	$ 105	$ 108
Cash paid for income taxes	15	12	4
Fixed assets acquired under capital leases and other financing arrangements	69	6	1

Other: (Comments added by author)
1. There apparently was no capitalized interest during these years.
2. Stock market price:

Year Ended December 31,		
2006	2005	2004
$39.46	$47.15	$44.29

Required
a. Net cash provided by operating activities is materially higher than net income for 2006 and 2005 and less than net income for 2004. Comment on major reasons for this swing.
b. Why is fixed assets acquired under capital leases and other financing arrangements disclosed at the bottom of the statements of cash flows?
c. Compute the following ratios for 2006, 2005, and 2004:
   1. Operating cash flow/total debt
   2. Operating cash flow per share
   3. Operating cash flow/cash dividends
   4. Comment on the above ratios. Comment on the difference between operating cash flow per share and earnings per share.

(continued)

Case 10-1	STILL EXPANDING (Continued)

   d. Compute the following ratios for 2006, 2005, and 2004:
1. Working capital
2. Current ratio
3. Comment on the above ratios.

   e. Compute the following ratios for 2006, 2005, and 2004:
1. Times interest earned
2. Debt ratio
3. Comment on the above ratios.

   f. Compute the following ratios for 2006, 2005, and 2004:
1. Net profit margin
2. Operating income margin
3. Gross profit margin
4. Comment on the above ratios.

   g. Compute or note the following for 2006, 2005, and 2004:
1. All-inclusive degree of financial leverage
2. Diluted earnings per share
3. Price/earnings ratio
4. Comment on the above.

Case 10-2	DIRECT CASH FLOW

Arden Group, Inc. and Consolidated Subsidiaries*
Consolidated Statements of Cash Flows

(In thousands)	2006	2005	2004
Cash flows from operating activities:			
Cash received from customers	$ 482,645	$ 470,646	$ 503,553
Cash paid to suppliers and employees	(440,735)	(426,372)	(467,717)
Interest and dividends received	2,580	1,613	1,813
Interest paid	(125)	(155)	(184)
Income taxes paid	(17,645)	(12,653)	(26,046)
Net cash provided by operating activities	26,720	33,079	11,419
Cash flows from investing activities:			
Capital expenditures	(4,868)	(6,390)	(12,641)
Purchases of investments	(827)	(713)	(15,737)
Sales of investments	2,751	5,579	25,070
Proceeds from the sale of property, plant and equipment	215	52	54
Net cash used in investing activities	(2,729)	(1,472)	(3,254)
Cash flows from financing activities:			
Purchase and retirement of Company stock	(19,999)	(334)	0
Principal payments under capital lease obligations	(221)	(216)	(246)
Proceeds from exercise of stock options	0	0	58
Cash dividends paid	(3,267)	(3,382)	(70,911)
Net cash used in financing activities	(23,487)	(3,932)	(71,099)
Net increase (decrease) in cash and cash equivalents	504	27,675	(62,934)
Cash and cash equivalents at beginning of year	36,338	8,663	71,597
Cash and cash equivalents at end of year	$ 36,842	$ 36,338	$ 8,663

*"The Arden Group, Inc., presented this statement of cash flows in its 2006 annual report. "Arden Group, Inc. . . . is a holding company which conducts operations through its wholly-owned subsidiary, Arden-Mayfair, Inc. (Arden-Mayfair) and Arden-Mayfair's wholly-owned subsidiary, Gelson's Markets (Gelson's), which operates supermarkets in Southern California." 10-K

(continued)

DIRECT CASH FLOW (Continued)

(In thousands)	2006	2005	2004
Reconciliation of Net Income to Net Cash Provided by Operating Activities:			
Net income	$23,224	$19,851	$ 22,672
Adjustments to reconcile net income to net cash provided by operating activities:			
Depreciation and amortization	7,097	7,401	6,990
Provision for losses on accounts receivable	14	49	15
Deferred income taxes	(1,044)	(2,600)	849
Net (gain) loss from the disposal of property, plant and equipment	(191)	27	23
Realized gain on investments, net	(2)	(36)	(1,787)
Amortization of discount on investments	(6)	(62)	(196)
Stock appreciation rights compensation expense	3,671	946	3,658
Changes in assets and liabilities net of effects from noncash investing and financing activities:			
(Increase) decrease in assets:			
Accounts and notes receivable	(49)	270	713
Inventories	(735)	(381)	(1,768)
Other current assets	(316)	(549)	(236)
Other assets	(148)	(403)	307
Increase (decrease) in liabilities:			
Accounts payable, trade and other current liabilities	(2,859)	1,734	(11,761)
Federal and state income taxes payable	(705)	3,511	(11,434)
Deferred rent	274	924	399
Other liabilities	(1,505)	2,397	2,975
Net cash provided by operating activities	$26,720	$33,079	$ 11,419

Required

a. Prepare the statement of cash flows, with a total column for the three-year period. (Do not include reconciliation.)

b. Comment on significant cash flow items in the statement prepared in (a).

c. Prepare the statement of cash flows for 2006, with inflows separated from outflows. Present the data in dollars and percentages. Do not include reconciliation of net income to net cash provided by operating activities.

d. Comment on significant cash flow items on the statement prepared in (c).

GOOGLE IT*

Google, Inc.
CONSOLIDATED STATEMENTS OF CASH FLOWS
(In thousands)

	Year Ended December 31,		
	2004	2005	2006
Operating activities			
Net income	$ 399,199	$ 1,465,397	$ 3,077,446
Adjustments:			
Depreciation and amortization of property and equipment	128,523	256,812	494,430
Amortization of intangibles and other	19,950	37,000	77,509
In-process research and development	11,343	22,040	10,800
Stock-based compensation	278,746	200,709	458,100

*"Google is a global technology leader focused on improving the ways people connect with information." 10-K

(continued)

GOOGLE IT (Continued)

	Year Ended December 31,		
	2004	**2005**	**2006**
Excess tax benefits from stock-based award activity	191,570	433,724	(581,732)
Non-recurring portion of settlement of disputes with Yahoo	201,000	—	—
Other	—	—	1,674
Changes in assets and liabilities, net of effects of acquisitions:			
Accounts receivable	(156,928)	(372,290)	(624,012)
Income taxes, net	(125,227)	87,400	398,414
Prepaid revenue share, expenses and other assets	(99,779)	(51,663)	(289,157)
Accounts payable	(13,516)	80,631	95,402
Accrued expenses and other liabilities	86,374	166,764	291,533
Accrued revenue share	33,872	93,347	139,300
Deferred revenue	21,997	39,551	30,801
Net cash provided by operating activities	977,044	2,459,422	3,580,508
Investing activities			
Purchases of property and equipment	(318,995)	(838,217)	(1,902,798)
Purchase of marketable securities	(4,134,576)	(12,675,880)	(26,681,891)
Maturities and sales of marketable securities	2,611,078	10,257,214	23,107,132
Investments in non-marketable securities	—	—	(1,019,147)
Acquisitions, net of cash acquired and purchases of intangible and other assets	(58,863)	(101,310)	(402,446)
Net cash used in investing activities	(1,901,356)	(3,358,193)	(6,899,150)
Financing activities			
Net proceeds from stock-based award activity	12,001	85,026	321,117
Proceeds from exercise of warrants	21,944	—	—
Excess tax benefits from stock-based award activity	—	—	581,732
Net proceeds from public offerings	1,161,080	4,287,229	2,063,549
Payment of note receivable from officer/stockholder	4,300	—	—
Payments of principal on capital leases and equipment loans	(4,707)	(1,425)	—
Net cash provided by financing activities	1,194,618	4,370,830	2,966,398
Effect of exchange rate changes on cash and cash equivalents	7,572	(21,758)	19,741
Net increase (decrease) in cash and cash equivalents	277,878	3,450,301	(332,503)
Cash and cash equivalents at beginning of year	148,995	426,873	3,877,174
Cash and cash equivalents at end of year	$ 426,873	$ 3,877,174	$ 3,544,671
Supplemental disclosures of cash flow information			
Cash paid for interest	$ 709	$ 216	$ 257
Cash paid for taxes	$ 183,776	$ 153,628	$ 537,702
Acquisition related to activities:			
Issuance of equity in connection with acquisitions, net	$ 25,714	$ 22,407	$ 1,173,234

Required
a. 1. For net income and net cash provided by operating activities, perform a horizontal common-size analysis. Use 2004 as the base.

2. Comment.

b. Why is depreciation and amortization of property and equipment added back to net income?

c. Investing activities: Comment on the purchases of property and equipment. Does this indicate growth?

d. Acquisition related to activities: Issuance of equity in connection with acquisitions, net. Does this amount influence cash flow? Why is it listed at the bottom of the statement?

e. Considering the net cash provided by operating activities, why did Google have significant public offerings?

f. Identify items that indicate that Google is a growth company.

Case	
10-4	

THE RETAIL MOVER

This case represents an actual retail company. The dates and format have been changed.

Required
a. Compute and comment on the following for 2003, 2004, and 2007:
   1. Working capital
   2. Current ratio
b. Comment on the difference between net income and net cash outflow from operating activities for the year ended December 31, 2004, and December 31, 2007.
c. This company reported a loss of $177,340,000 for 2008. Reviewing the balance sheet data, speculate on major reasons for this loss.
d. Considering (a), (b), and (c), comment on the wisdom of the short-term bank loan in 2008. (Consider the company's perspective and the bank's perspective.)

a.

Selected Balance Sheet Data	December 31, 2004	December 31, 2003
Total current assets	$719,478,441	$628,408,895
Total current liabilities	458,999,682	366,718,656

The Retail Mover
Statement of Cash Flows
Year Ended December 31, 2004

Net cash flow from operating activities:	
Net income	$ 39,577,000
Noncash expenses, revenues, losses, and gains included in income:	
Increase in equity in Zeller's Limited	(2,777,000)
Depreciation and amortization	9,619,000
Net increase in reserves	74,000
Increase in deferred federal income taxes	232,000
Net increase in receivables	(51,463,995)
Net increase in inventories	(38,364,709)
Net increase in prepaid taxes, rents, etc.	(209,043)
Increase in accounts payable	9,828,348
Increase in salaries, wages, and bonuses	470,054
Increase in taxes withheld from employees' compensation	301,035
Decrease in taxes other than federal income taxes	(659,021)
Increase in federal income taxes payable	4,007,022
Increases in deferred credits, principally income taxes related to installment sales (short-term)	14,045,572
Rounding difference in working capital	520
Net cash outflow from operating activities	(15,319,217)
Cash flows from investing activities:	
Investment in properties, fixtures, and improvements	(16,141,000)
Investment in Zeller's Limited	(436,000)
Increase in sundry accounts (net)	(48,000)
Net cash outflow from investing activities	(16,625,000)
Cash flows from financing activities:	
Sales of common stock to employees	5,219,000
Dividends to stockholders	(20,821,000)
Purchase of treasury stock	(13,224,000)
Purchase of preferred stock for cancellation	(948,000)
Retirement of 4 3/4% sinking fund debentures	(1,538,000)
Increase in short-term notes payable	56,323,016
Increase in bank loans	7,965,000
Net cash inflow from financing activities	32,976,016
Net increase in cash and short-term securities	$ 1,031,799

(continued)

Case 10-4	THE RETAIL MOVER (Continued)

b.

Selected Balance Sheet Data	December 31, 2007
Total current assets	$1,044,689,000
Total current liabilities	661,058,000

The Retail Mover
Statement of Cash Flows
Year Ended December 31, 2007

Net cash flow from operating activities:	
Net income	$ 10,902,000
Noncash expenses, revenues, losses, and gains included in income:	
Undistributed equity in net earnings of unconsolidated subsidiaries	(3,570,000)
Depreciation and amortization of properties	13,579,000
Increase in deferred federal income taxes—noncurrent	2,723,000
Decrease in deferred contingent compensation and other liabilities	(498,000)
Net receivables increase	(52,737,000)
Merchandise inventories increase	(51,104,000)
Other current assets increase	(8,935,000)
Accounts payable for merchandise decrease	(2,781,000)
Salaries, wages, and bonuses decrease	(3,349,000)
Other accrued expenses increase	3,932,000
Taxes withheld from employees increase	2,217,000
Sales and other taxes increase	448,000
Federal income taxes payable decrease	(8,480,000)
Increase in deferred income taxes related to installment sales	4,449,000
Net cash flow from operating activities	(93,204,000)
Cash flows from investing activities:	
Investments on properties, fixtures, and improvements	(23,143,000)
Increase in other assets—net	(642,000)
Investment in Granjewel Jewelers & Distributors, Inc.	(5,700,000)
Net cash outflow from investing activities	(29,485,000)
Cash flows from financing activities:	
Increase in short-term notes payable to banks	100,000,000
Receipts from employees under stock purchase contracts	2,584,000
Short-term commercial notes	73,063,000
Cash dividends to stockholders	(21,122,000)
Decrease in long-term debt	(6,074,000)
Purchase of cumulative preferred stock, for cancellation	(618,000)
Purchase of treasury common stock	(136,000)
Bank loans decreased	(10,000,000)
Net cash inflow from financing activities	137,697,000
Net increase in cash	$ 15,008,000

c.

Income Statement Data related to 2007 and 2008 (in Part)

	2008	2007
Net earnings (loss)	$(177,340,000)	$10,902,000

Balance Sheet Data related to 2007 and 2008 (in Part)

	December 31, 2008	December 31, 2007
Assets		
Current assets:		
Cash notes	$ 79,642,000	$ 45,951,000
Customers' installment accounts receivable	518,387,000	602,305,000
Less:		
Allowance for doubtful accounts	(79,510,000)	(16,315,000)
Unearned credit insurance premiums	(1,386,000)	(4,923,000)
Deferred finance income	(37,523,000)	(59,748,000)
	399,968,000	521,319,000

(continued)

Case 10-4

THE RETAIL MOVER (Continued)

	December 31, 2008	December 31, 2007
Merchandise inventories	407,357,000	450,637,000
Other accounts receivable, refundable taxes, and claims	31,223,000	19,483,000
Prepaid expenses	6,591,000	7,299,000
Total current assets	$924,781,000	$1,044,689,000
Liabilities		
Current liabilities:		
Bank loans	$600,000,000	$ —
Short-term commercial notes	—	453,097,000
Current portion of long-term debt	995,000	
Accounts payable for merchandise	50,067,000	58,192,000
Salaries, wages, and bonuses	10,808,000	14,678,000
Other accrued expenses	49,095,000	14,172,000
Taxes withheld from employees	1,919,000	4,412,000
Sales and other taxes	17,322,000	13,429,000
Federal income taxes payable	17,700,000	—
Deferred income taxes related to installment sales	2,000,000	103,078,000
Total current liabilities	749,906,000	661,058,000
Other liabilities		
Long-term debt	216,341,000	220,336,000
Deferred federal income taxes	—	14,649,000
Deferred contingent compensation and other liabilities	2,183,000	4,196,000
Total other liabilities	218,524,000	239,181,000
Total liabilities	$968,430,000	$ 900,239,000

Case 10-5

NONCASH CHARGES

Owens Corning Fiberglass Corporation

For Immediate Release (February 6, 1992)

Owens Corning Takes $800 Million Non-Cash Charge to Accrue for Future Asbestos Claims

"This action demonstrates our desire to put the asbestos situation behind us," new chairman and CEO Glen H. Hiner says.

Toledo, Ohio, February 6, 1992—Owens Corning Fiberglass Corp. (NYSE:OCF) today announced that its results for the fourth quarter and year ended December 31, 1991, include a special non-cash charge of $800 million to accrue for the estimated uninsured cost of future asbestos claims the Company may receive through the balance of the decade. "This action demonstrates our desire to put the asbestos situation behind us," said Glen Hiner, Owens Corning's new chairman and chief executive officer. "After a thorough review of the situation with outside consultants, we believe this accrual will be sufficient to cover the company's uninsured costs for cases received until the year 2000. We will, of course, make adjustments to our reserves if that becomes appropriate, but this is our best estimate of these uninsured costs. With this action," Mr. Hiner continued, "everyone can now focus once again on the fundamental strengths of the Company. We generate considerable amounts of cash, our operating divisions are leaders in every market they serve throughout the world, and we have taken a number of steps in the last few years to strengthen our competitive position even further."

(continued)

NONCASH CHARGES (Continued)

Owens Corning Fiberglass Corporation
For Immediate Release (June 20, 1996)

Owens Corning Initiates Federal Lawsuit, Records
Post-1999 Asbestos Provisions and Announces Dividend

NEW YORK, New York, June 20, 1996—A Federal lawsuit aimed at fraudulent testing procedures for asbestos-related illnesses, involving tens of thousands of pending cases, was filed yesterday by Owens Corning. The Company also announced the quantification of liabilities related to post-1999 asbestos claims, the reinstatement of an annual dividend and a sales goal of $5 billion by 1999.

The specific announcements are as follows:

- A lawsuit, alleging falsified medical test results in tens of thousands of asbestos claims, was filed on June 19, 1996, in the U.S. District Court for the Eastern District of Louisiana against the owners and operators of three pulmonary function testing laboratories. Overall, a total of 40,000 cases may be impacted by the investigation for fraudulent testing procedures. The lawsuit is the subject of a separate press release also disseminated this morning.
- A net, after-tax charge of $545 million, or $9.56 per fully diluted share for asbestos claims—received after 1999—will be recorded in the second quarter of 1996, as detailed in a Form 8-K filed this morning with the SEC. Cash payments associated with this charge will begin after the year 2000 and will be spread over 15 years or more.
- The Board of Directors has approved an annual dividend policy of 25 cents per share and declared a quarterly dividend of 6-1/4 cents per share payable on October 15, 1996, to shareholders of record as of September 30, 1996.
- The company expects to reach its sales goal of $5 billion in 1999—a full year ahead of the original goal.

"The asbestos charge quantifies what we expect to be the cost to Owens Corning of post-1999 claims," stated Glen H. Hiner, chairman and chief executive officer. "We further believe that the present value of the Owens Corning asbestos liability, including the current charge, is less than the current discount in our stock price."

In addition to these developments, Owens Corning announced it is engaged in substantive discussions with 30 of the principal plaintiff law firms in an effort to obtain further resolution of its asbestos liability. These discussions have encompassed the possibility of global as well as individual law firm settlements.

"These meetings are by mutual consent," stated Hiner. "The discussions will continue and we expect to know by year end whether we can achieve further agreement. Plaintiff attorneys involved in the talks stated they will not serve any more non-malignancy claims on Owens Corning while negotiations continue."

In reference to the dividend, Hiner stated, "we were able to initiate this action because debt has been reduced to target levels and cash flow from operations will be in excess of internal funding requirements."

"We are delighted to be able to reward our shareholders with a dividend," said Hiner. "Reinstating the dividend has been a priority of mine since joining the company and I am pleased that we now are in a position to set the date."

The Toledo-based company had 1995 sales of $3.6 billion and employs 18,000 people in more than 30 countries.

(continued)

Owens Corning
Consolidated Statement of Cash Flows (in Part)
For the years ended December 31, 1997, 1996 and 1995

(In millions of dollars)	1997	1996	1995
Net Cash Flow from Operations			
Net income (loss)	$ 47	$(284)	$ 231
Reconciliation of net cash provided by operating activities:			
Noncash items:			
Provision for asbestos litigation claims (Note 22)	—	875	—
Cumulative effect of accounting change (Note 6)	15		—
Provision for depreciation and amortization	173	141	132
Provision (credit) for deferred income taxes (Note 11)	110	(258)	142
Other (Note 4)	49	(2)	(2)
(Increase) decrease in receivables (Note 13)	57	20	36
(Increase) decrease in inventories	60	(71)	(15)
Increase (decrease) in accounts payable and accrued liabilities	(60)	103	(50)
Disbursements (funding) of VEBA trust	19	45	(64)
Proceeds from insurance for asbestos litigation claims, excluding Fibreboard (Note 22)	97	101	251
Payments for asbestos litigation claims, excluding Fibreboard (Note 22)	(300)	(267)	(308)
Other	(136)	(68)	(68)
Net cash flow from operations	131	335	285

April 29, 1998

Owens Corning opened a new front in its battle to avoid being swamped by tens of thousands of damage claims filed by people who say they got sick from exposure to asbestos-containing insulation produced by the company. Owens Corning charged in U.S. District Court in Toledo, Ohio, that Allstate Insurance Co. is guilty of breach of contract by failing to provide coverage.

Owens Corning announced in March 1998 that it might have to spend more than expected to resolve asbestos claims because of growing damage awards to people with a severe form of asbestos-linked cancer called mesothelioma.

Required

a. In the long run, cash receipts from operations is equal to revenue from operations. Comment.

b. February 6, 1992—Owens Corning announced a special noncash charge of $800 million to accrue for the estimated uninsured cost of future asbestos claims the company may receive through the balance of the decade. How much will the non-cash charge reduce gross earnings in 1992? Over what period of time is the expected outflow?

c. June 20, 1996—Owens Corning announced a net, after-tax charge of $545 million for asbestos claims received after 1999. How much will this charge reduce net income in 1996? Over what period of time is the cash outflow expected?

d. Assume Owens Corning receives money related to the federal lawsuit alleging falsified medical tests. In what period will the cash inflow be recorded? When will the related revenue be recorded?

e. April 29, 1998—Owens Corning filed suit against Allstate Insurance Co. related to asbestos exposure coverage. What are the apparent implications if Owens Corning does not win the suit?

f. Owens Corning announced in March 1998 that it might have to spend more than expected to resolve asbestos claims. What does this imply as to future expenses and cash outflow related to asbestos claims?

g. Owens Corning, consolidated statement of cash flows, for the years ended December 31, 1997, 1996, and 1995.

   1. What year has a charge for asbestos litigation claims?

   2. What years have cash inflow from proceeds from insurance for asbestos litigation claims?

   3. What years have payments for asbestos litigation claims?

Case	SORRY—GIVE IT BACK*
10-6	

Owens Corning went into Chapter 11 bankruptcy in 2000. In October 2002, it claimed that it was insolvent for four years before filing for bankruptcy (1996–2000). Apparently, the major issue was asbestos cases.

Because of the insolvent condition, it claims dividends paid were invalid during the period 1996–2000. Owens Corning is only pursuing holders who received more than $100,000. This amounts to millions of dollars.

Required   Comment on implications to investors if firms in bankruptcy can claim dividends paid years after receipt.

*Source: Carrie Coolidge, "The Great Dividend Heist," *Forbes* (November 11, 2002), pp. 46–47.

Case	CASH MOVEMENTS AND PERIODIC INCOME DETERMINATION
10-7	

"The estimating of income, under conditions of uncertainty as well as of certainty, requires that the accountant trace carefully the relation between income flows and cash movements."

"While it is true that there may not be an equality between the amount of revenue and the amount of cash receipts for any period less than the duration of enterprise existence, receipts are the elements with which we construct all measures of revenue. A dollar is received at some time during the life of the enterprise for each dollar of revenue exhibited during the fiscal period. The sum of the annual revenues for all fiscal periods is equal to the amount of ultimate total revenue. There may be no equality between the amount of expense and the amount of cash disbursements for the fiscal period and yet the two sums are equal for the life of the enterprise. A dollar is disbursed at some time during the enterprise existence for each dollar exhibited as expense of the fiscal period."*

"The accountant's problem is essentially one of reconciling cash receipts with revenues and cash disbursements with expenses. That is, for every revenue recognized but not received in cash during the current period, an asset of equal value must be recorded (or a liability must be amortized); for every expense recognized but not paid in cash in the current period, a liability of equal value must be recognized but not paid in cash in the current period, a liability of equal value must be recognized (or an asset must be amortized)."

Required   a. Income determination is an exact science. Comment.
            b. Cash flow must be estimated. Comment.
            c. In the long run, cash receipts from operations is equal to revenue from operations. Comment.
            d. Assume that a firm has a negative cash flow from operations in the short run. How could this negative cash flow from operations be compensated for in the short run? Discuss.
            e. Assume that the reported operating income has been substantially more than the cash flow from operations for the past two years. Comment on what will need to happen to future cash flow from operations in order for the past reported income to hold up.

*Edward G. Nelson, "The Relationship between the Balance Sheet and the Profit and Loss Statement," *The Accounting Review*, Vol. XVIII (April 1942), p. 133.

Source: Excerpts from "Cash Movements and Periodic Income Determination," Reed K. Story, *The Accounting Review*, Vol. XXXV, No. 3 (July 1960), pp. 449–454.

| Case |
| 10-8 |

EAT AT MY RESTAURANT—CASH FLOW

With this case, we review the cash flow of several restaurant companies. The restaurant companies reviewed and their year-end dates are as follows:

1. Yum Brands, Inc. (December 30, 2006; December 30, 2005)
   "Yum consists of six operating segments: KFC, Pizza Hut, Taco Bell, LJS/A&W, Yum Restaurants International . . . and Yum Restaurants China." 10-K

2. Panera Bread (December 26, 2006; December 27, 2005)
   "As of December 26, 2006, we operated directly and through area development agreements with 41 franchisee groups, bakery-cafes under Panera Bread® and Saint Louis Bread® names." 10-K

3. Starbucks (October 1, 2006; October 2, 2005)
   "Starbucks purchases and roasts high-quality whole bean coffees and sells them, along with fresh, rich-brewed coffees, Italian-style espresso beverages, cold blended beverages, a variety of complementary foods items, coffee-related accessories and equipment, a selection of premium teas and a line of compact discs, primarily through company-operated retail stores." 10-K

	Yum Brands, Inc.		Panera Bread		Starbucks	
Data Reviewed	2006	2005	2006	2005	2006	2005
Net cash provided by operating activities	$1,302,000,000	$1,238,000,000	$104,895,000	$110,628,000	$1,131,633,000	$922,915,000
Net income	824,000,000	762,000,000	58,849,000	52,183,000	564,259,000	494,370,000
Operating cash flow/current maturities of long-term debt and current notes payable	5.74 times	5.87 times	No current maturities of long-term debt and current notes payable		1.61 times	3.32 times
Operating cash flow/total debt	26.48%	28.47%	72.37%	91.66%	51.43%	64.84%
Operating cash flow per share	$4.62	$4.15	$3.27	$3.50	$1.43	$1.13
Operating cash flow/cash dividends	9.04	10.07	No dividends		No dividends	

Required

a. Comment on the difference between net cash provided by operating activities and net income. Speculate on which number is likely to be the better indicator of long-term profitability.

b. Comment on the data reviewed for each firm.

c. Do any of these firms appear to have a cash flow problem? Comment.

| Web |
| Case |

Thomson One *Business School Edition*

Please complete the Web case that covers material discussed in this chapter at academic.cengage.com/accounting/Gibson. You'll be using Thomson One Business School Edition, a powerful tool, that combines a full range of fundamental financial information, earnings estimates, market data, and source documents for 500 publicly traded companies.

Endnotes

1. The effect of exchange rate changes on cash is presented separately at the bottom of the statement.
2. *Exposure Draft*, "Statement of Cash Flows" (Stamford, Conn.: Financial Accounting Standards Board, 1986), p. 21.

Summary Analysis Nike, Inc. (Includes 2007 Financial Statements on Form 10-K)

U sers must be able to apply and understand financial statement analysis. They must study ratio and trend analysis for meaning. This analysis is the difficult aspect of interpreting financial statements. Chapters 6 through 10 have illustrated the technique of calculating ratios for the analysis of Nike, Inc.

This summary analysis brings together the analysis in Chapters 6 through 10 relating to Nike. It adds information on a selected competitor and the industry. It also adds some common-size analysis.

Nike—Background Information

Bill Bowerman, head track coach, University of Oregon, teamed up with Philip Knight, a former student, to form Blue Ribbon Sports in 1964. Blue Ribbon Sports became Nike in 1972. The name "Nike" was chosen because Nike was the Greek goddess of victory.

Nike specialized in athletic footwear until 1979. In 1979, the Nike apparel line appeared. In 1996, the Nike equipment division formed.

By 1999, Nike was the world's largest supplier of athletic footwear and one of the world's largest suppliers of athletic apparel. Nike products are sold in over 160 countries. Nike and Adidas are possibly the only equipment, sports footwear, and apparel companies with the infrastructure to sell extensively worldwide.

Bill Bowerman retired from the board in June 1999 and passed away in December 1999. Philip Knight is the chairman of the board. He stepped down as chief executive officer at the end of 2004. Mark G. Parker is the chief executive officer and president. "Mr. Parker . . . has been president and chief executive officer and a director since January 2006. He has been employed by Nike since 1979 with primary responsibilities in product research, design and development, marketing, and brand management" (Proxy filed August 3, 2007).

MANAGEMENT'S DISCUSSION AND ANALYSIS OF FINANCIAL CONDITION AND RESULTS OF OPERATIONS (SEE 10-K, ITEM 7, IN PART)

Selected Highlights

- "Fiscal 2007 results were positively affected by a reduction in our effective tax rate of 2.8 percentage points as compared to fiscal 2006, primarily as a result of the European tax agreement the Company finalized in the second quarter of fiscal 2007."
- Future orders—"Worldwide futures and advance orders for footwear and apparel scheduled for delivery from June through November 2007 were nearly 12% higher than such orders reported for the comparable period of fiscal 2006."

Note: Item 7 of the Nike 10-K is approximately 24 pages. It is suggested that you read the 10-K, Item 7 before proceeding with this summary. After reviewing this summary, read the 10-K, Item 7 again. This will give you a very good understanding of Nike.

VERTICAL COMMON-SIZE STATEMENT OF INCOME (EXHIBIT 1)

Highlights

Gross margin was down slightly from 2005 to 2007. This was more than offset by an increase in interest (income) expense, net and a decrease in income taxes. The end result was a slight increase in net income.

Exhibit	1	NIKE, INC.

Vertical Common-Size Statement of Income

Consolidated Statements of Income

	Year Ended May 31,		
	2007	2006	2005
Revenues	100.0%	100.0%	100.0%
Cost of sales	56.1	56.0	55.5
Gross margin	43.9	44.0	44.5
Selling and administrative expense	30.8	29.9	30.7
Interest (income) expense, net	(0.4)	(0.2)	0.0
Other (income) expense, net	0.0	0.0	0.2
Income before income taxes	13.5	14.3	13.5
Income taxes	4.3	5.0	4.7
Net income	9.1	9.3	8.8

Note: There are some rounding differences.

HORIZONTAL COMMON-SIZE STATEMENT OF INCOME (EXHIBIT 2)

Highlights

- Material increase in revenues.
- Gross margin increased substantially less than revenues.
- Net income increase slightly more favorable than revenues increase.
- The majority of the net income increase was the result of the income tax decrease.

Exhibit	2	NIKE, INC.

Horizontal Common-Size Statement of Income

Consolidated Statements of Income

	Year Ended May 31,		
	2007	**2006**	**2005**
Revenues	121.0	108.8	100.0
Cost of sales	120.2	109.8	100.0
Gross margin	117.1	107.7	100.0
Selling and administrative expense	119.1	106.1	100.0
Interest (income) expense, net	N/A	N/A	100.0
Other (income) expense, net	N/A	N/A	100.0
Income before income taxes	118.3	115.2	100.0
Income taxes	109.3	115.6	100.0
Net income	123.1	114.9	100.0

THREE-YEAR COMPARISON (EXHIBIT 3)

The use of ratios can be very helpful in analysis, but caution must be exercised in drawing conclusions. Many potential problems were discussed in previous chapters. Keep these potential problems in mind when using ratios. Nike uses a year ended May 31 and has somewhat of a seasonal business. This could influence some of the ratios, particularly liquidity ratios.

Liquidity

- Days' sales in receivables decreased materially, which would be positive.
- Accounts receivable turnover increased materially, which would be positive.
- Accounts receivable turnover decreased materially, which would be positive.
- Days' sales in inventory decreased slightly, which would be positive.
- Merchandise inventory turnover decreased slightly, which would be negative.
- Inventory turnover increased slightly, which would be positive.
- Operating cycle decreased slightly, which would be positive.
- Working capital increased materially, which would be positive.
- Current ratio decreased slightly, which would be negative (this could be seen as positive because of the material improvement in receivables).
- Acid-test ratio increased slightly, which would be positive.
- Cash ratio increased materially, which would be positive.
- Sales to working capital decreased materially, which would be negative.
- Operating cash flow/current maturities of long-term debt and current notes payable decreased materially, which would be negative.

Summary—Liquidity

Some of the liquidity ratios improved and some declined. Receivables improved materially, which would be very positive. This resulted in an improved operating cycle. Working capital improved materially. The current ratio declined slightly, while the cash ratio improved materially. Sales to working capital and operating cash flow/current maturities of long-term debt and current notes payable declined materially.

Overall liquidity appears to be very good.

Long-Term Debt-Paying Ability

- Times interest earned decreased slightly from 2005, but it is still very good.
- Fixed charge coverage decreased slightly, but it is still very good.

Exhibit	3	NIKE, INC.

Three-Year Ratio Comparison

	Unit	2007	2006	2005
Liquidity:				
Days' sales in receivables	Days	56.63	59.10	62.23
Accounts receivable turnover	Times per year	6.59	6.28	6.03
Accounts receivable turnover	Days	55.38	58.14	60.55
Days' sales in inventory	Days	84.50	90.57	86.70
Merchandise inventory turnover	Times per year	4.37	4.30	4.41
Inventory turnover	Days	83.60	84.78	82.85
Operating cycle	Days	138.98	142.92	143.40
Working capital (in millions)		5,492.5	4,733.6	4,351.9
Current ratio	N/A	3.13	2.81	3.18
Acid-test ratio	N/A	2.07	1.79	2.04
Cash ratio	N/A	1.10	0.88	0.91
Sales to working capital	Times per year	3.19	3.29	3.50
Operating cash flow/current maturities of long-term debt and current notes payable	Times per year	14.31	5.58	20.67
Long-term debt-paying ability:				
Times interest earned	Times per year	45.26	43.41	47.85
Fixed charge coverage	Times per year	16.20	16.92	16.87
Debt ratio	%	34.27	36.32	35.81
Debt/equity	%	52.14	57.03	55.80
Debt to tangible net worth	%	56.49	62.35	61.72
Operating cash flow/total debt	%	51.29	46.53	49.87
Profitability:				
Net profit margin	%	9.14	9.31	8.82
Total asset turnover	Times per year	1.59	1.60	1.65
Return on assets	%	14.51	14.92	14.51
Operating income margin	%	13.06	14.10	13.78
Operating asset turnover	Times per year	1.76	1.78	1.84
Return on operating assets	%	22.94	25.10	25.31
Sales to fixed assets	Times per year	10.33	9.62	8.91
Return on investment	%	19.86	20.28	19.53
Return on total equity	%	22.41	23.34	23.24
Return on common equity	%	22.41	23.34	23.24
Gross profit margin	%	43.86	44.05	44.51
Investor analysis:				
Degree of financial leverage	N/A	1.02	1.02	1.02
Diluted earnings per share	$	2.93	2.64	2.24
Price/earnings ratio	N/A	19.37	15.21	18.35
Percentage of earnings retained	%	76.96	79.09	80.46
Dividend payout ratio	%	24.23	22.35	21.21
Dividend yield	%	1.25	1.47	1.16
Book value per share	$	14.00	12.28	10.81
Materiality of option compensation expense	%	6.32	5.52	5.29
Operating cash flow per share	$	3.68	3.16	2.91
Operating cash flow/cash dividends	Times per year	5.47	5.73	6.64
Year-end market price	$	56.75	40.16	41.10

- The debt ratio is very good, and it improved slightly.
- The debt/equity is very good, and it improved slightly.
- Debt to tangible net worth is very good, and it improved moderately.
- Operating cash flow/total debt is very good, and it improved slightly.

Summary—Long-Term Debt-Paying Ability

Some of the long-term debt-paying ratios improved and some declined. Times interest earned and the fixed charge coverage decreased slightly, but they are both very good. The debt ratio and the debt/equity improved slightly, and they both are very good. The debt to tangible net worth improved moderately, and it is very good. Operating cash flow/total debt improved slightly, and it is very good. The long-term debt-paying ability is very good.

Profitability

- Net profit margin is good and increased moderately in relation to 2005, but decreased slightly in 2007.
- Total asset turnover is good, but decreased slightly in both 2006 and 2007.
- Return on assets is very good and stayed the same in relation to 2005, and decreased slightly in relation to 2006.
- Operating income margin decreased moderately between 2005 and 2007, but appears to be good.
- Operating asset turnover is good, but declined in both 2006 and 2007.
- Return on operating assets is very good but decreased materially in 2007.
- Sales to fixed assets is good and increased substantially in both 2006 and 2007.
- Return on investment is very good, but decreased moderately in 2007 after increasing materially in 2006.
- Return on total equity is very good. It increased slightly in 2006 and decreased slightly in 2007.
- Return on common equity is very good. It increased slightly in 2006 and decreased slightly in 2007.
- Gross profit margin is very good, but it decreased slightly in 2006 and 2007.

Summary—Profitability

Profitability appears to be very good. Return on assets, return on investment, return on total equity, return on common equity, and gross profit margin contributed to this conclusion.

A number of ratios decreased in 2007, which we would want to monitor. These would be operating income margin, total asset turnover, return on assets, operating asset turnover, return on operating assets, return on total equity, return on common equity, and gross profit margin.

Investor Analysis

- Degree of financial leverage is practically nonexistent. This is good from a risk perspective, but financial leverage is only nominally contributing to profits.
- Diluted earnings per share increased materially each year. Very impressive.
- Price/earnings ratio increased slightly in relation to 2005, and materially in relation to 2006.
- Percentage of earnings retained decreased moderately.
- Dividend payout ratio increased materially.
- Dividend yield is relatively low.
- Book value per share increased materially.
- Materiality of option compensation expense increased materially in relation to 2005.
- Operating cash flow per share increased materially.
- Operating cash flow/cash dividends decreased materially.
- Year-end market price increased materially. This would be very positive.

Summary—Investor Analysis

In general, the investor analysis is very good. This is particularly influenced by the diluted earnings per share increase and the year-end market price increase.

Ratio Comparison with Selected Competitor (Exhibit 4)

Nike has substantial competition which is illustrated by the following comments in its 2007 10-K.

United States Market (in Part)

"In fiscal 2007, sales in the United States (including U.S. sales of Cole Haan, Converse, Exeter Brands Group, Hurley, NIKE Bauer Hockey and NIKE Golf) accounted for approximately 47 percent of total revenues, compared to 47 percent in fiscal 2006 and 45 percent in fiscal

Exhibit	4	NIKE, INC.

Ratio Comparison with Selected Competitor

Year Ended May 31, 2007 (Nike), Year Ended December 31, 2006 (Skechers U.S.A)

	Unit	Nike 2007	Skechers 2006
Liquidity:			
Days' sales in receivables	Days	56.63	57.02
Accounts receivable turnover	Times per year	6.59	7.30
Accounts receivable turnover	Days	55.38	49.98
Days' sales in inventory	Days	84.50	107.50
Merchandise inventory turnover	Times per year	4.37	4.05
Inventory turnover	Days	83.60	90.19
Operating cycle	Days	138.98	140.17
Working capital (in millions)		5,492.5	450.8
Current ratio	N/A	3.13	3.49
Acid-test ratio	N/A	2.07	1.38
Cash ratio	N/A	1.10	0.77
Sales to working capital	Times per year	3.19	3.42
Operating cash flow/current maturities of long-term debt and current notes payable	Times per year	14.31	45.21
Long-term debt-paying ability:			
Times interest earned	Times per year	45.26	12.79
Fixed charge coverage	Times per year	16.20	5.89
Debt ratio	%	34.27	39.07
Debt/equity	%	52.14	64.12
Debt to tangible net worth	%	56.49	64.21
Operating cash flow/total debt	%	51.29	9.04
Profitability:			
Net profit margin	%	9.14	5.89
Total asset turnover	Times per year	1.59	1.83
Return on assets	%	14.51	10.76
Operating income margin	%	13.06	9.00
Operating asset turnover	Times per year	1.76	1.85
Return on operating assets	%	22.94	16.61
Sales to fixed assets	Times per year	10.33	15.01
Return on investment	%	19.86	15.25
Return on total equity	%	22.41	17.91
Return on common equity	%	22.41	17.91
Gross profit margin	%	43.86	43.42
Investor analysis:			
Degree of financial leverage	N/A	1.02	1.08
Diluted earnings per share	$	2.93	1.59
Price/earnings ratio	N/A	19.37	20.95
Percentage of earnings retained	%	76.96	100.00
Dividend payout ratio	%	24.23	0.00
Dividend yield	%	1.25	0.00
Book value per share	$	14.00	10.73
Materiality of option compensation expense	%	6.32	2.25
Operating cash flow per share	$	3.68	0.56
Operating cash flow/cash dividends	Times per year	5.47	0.00
Year-end market price	$	56.75	33.31

2005. We sell to approximately 21,000 retail accounts in the United States. The NIKE brand domestic retail account base includes a mix of footwear stores, sporting goods stores, athletic specialty stores, department stores, skate, tennis and golf shops, and other retail accounts. During fiscal year 2007, our three largest customers accounted for approximately 29 percent of NIKE brand sales in the United States excluding sales from NIKE Bauer Hockey and NIKE Golf, and 24 percent of total sales in the United States."

International Markets (in Part)

"In fiscal 2007, non-U.S. sales (including non-U.S. sales of Cole Haan, Converse, Exeter Brands Group, Hurley, NIKE Bauer Hockey, and NIKE Golf) accounted for 53 percent of total revenues in fiscal 2007, compared to 53 percent in fiscal 2006 and 54 percent in fiscal 2005. We sell our products to retail accounts, through NIKE-owned retail stores, and through a mix of independent distributors and licensees around the world. We estimate that we sell to more than 25,000 retail accounts outside the United States, excluding sales by independent distributors and licensees. We operate 11 distribution centers in Europe, Asia, Australia, Africa and Canada. In many countries and regions, including Canada, Asia, some Latin American countries, and Europe, we have a futures ordering program for retailers similar to the United States futures program described above. NIKE's three largest customers outside of the U.S. accounted for approximately 9 percent of NIKE brand sales outside the United States excluding sales from NIKE Bauer Hockey and NIKE Golf, and approximately 9 percent of total non-U.S. sales."

Competition (in Part)

"The athletic footwear, apparel and equipment industry is keenly competitive in the United States and on a worldwide basis. We compete internationally with an increasing number of athletic and leisure shoe companies, athletic and leisure apparel companies, sports equipment companies, and large companies having diversified lines of athletic and leisure shoes, apparel and equipment, including Adidas, Puma, and others. The intense competition and the rapid changes in technology and consumer preferences in the markets for athletic and leisure footwear and apparel, and athletic equipment, constitute significant risk factors in our operations."

SELECTED COMPETITOR

Adidas has the closest resemblance to Nike. Adidas is a German company and statements using U.S. GAAP are not available for Adidas.

Using Thomson One, searching by SIC Code, Skechers U.S.A. Inc. is the closest competitor after Adidas. Nike has a SIC 3021/Rubber and Plastics footwear, while Skechers U.S.A. has a SIC 3140 footwear (no rubber).

Skechers U.S.A. describes its business in its December 31, 2006, 10-K as follows:

General (in Part)

"We design and market Skechers-branded contemporary footwear for men, women and children under several unique lines. Our footwear reflects a combination of style, quality and value that appeals to a broad range of consumers. In addition to Skechers-branded lines, we also offer nine uniquely branded designer, fashion and street-focused footwear lines for men, women and children. These lines are branded and marketed separately from Skechers and appeal to specific audiences. Our brands are sold through department stores, specialty stores, athletic retailers, and boutiques as well as our e-commerce website and our own retail stores. We operate 50 concept stores, 61 factory outlet stores and 33 warehouse outlet stores in the United States, and 10 concept stores and two factory outlets internationally. Our objective is to profitably grow our operations worldwide while leveraging our recognizable Skechers brand through our strong product lines, innovative advertising and diversified distribution channels."

Skechers U.S.A. is much smaller than Nike as indicated by revenue and assets.

Revenue:		
Nike	$16,325,900,000	(Year ended May 31, 2007)
Skechers U.S.A.	$1,205,368,000	(Year ended December 31, 2006)
Total Assets:		
Nike	$10,688,300,000	(Year ended May 31, 2007)
Skechers U.S.A.	$737,053,000	(Year ended December 31, 2006)

Again, caution must be exercised in drawing conclusions from the absolute numbers, ratios, and the analysis in general. Keep potential problems in mind when drawing conclusions. Some of the potential problems on this comparison are the different year-ends, somewhat seasonal nature of the business, and different size of firms. In this case, we would likely be particularly concerned about the different year-ends and different size of firms.

Liquidity

- In the receivables area, Skechers is ahead of Nike. Nike is slightly better off with days' sales in receivables, but substantially behind with times per year and accounts receivable turnover, days.
- In the inventory area, Nike appears to be ahead of Skechers. They do have somewhat different inventory methods, which could account for the difference.

  ### Skechers
  "Inventories, principally finished goods, are stated at the lower of cost (based on the first-in first-out method), or market."

  ### Nike
  "Inventories related to our wholesale operations are stated at lower of cost or market and valued on a first-in, first-out ("FIFO") or moving average cost basis. Inventories related to our retail operations are stated at the lower of average cost or market using the retail inventory method."

- Skechers has a slightly higher operating cycle, which favors Nike.
- Working capital cannot be compared. Nike is materially bigger than Skechers.
- Skechers' current ratio is materially higher than Nike's. This is not necessarily good because the Nike current ratio is very good, and Skechers possibly has too much inventory.
- Nike's acid-test ratio is materially better than Skechers'.
- Nike's cash ratio is materially better than Skechers'.
- Skechers' sales to working capital is substantially better than Nike's, even with the apparent high inventory.
- Skechers' operating cash flow/current maturities of long-term debt and current notes payable is materially better than Nike's, but Nike's is very good.

Summary—Liquidity

Nike appears to be in a better liquidity position. Important items were inventory, acid-test, and cash ratio. Skechers did better in the receivables area, which is important. Skechers did materially better than Nike in a number of areas, but these were areas where Nike had very good liquidity indicators. Some of these areas were current ratio, sales to working capital, and operating cash flow/current maturities of long-term debt and current notes payable.

An important item was inventory. Does Skechers have too much inventory? The somewhat different inventory methods cloud the inventory comparison.

Long-Term Debt-Paying Ability

- Nike has a materially better times interest earned and fixed charge coverage than Skechers, but the Skechers coverage is very good.
- Nike has a materially better debt ratio, debt/equity, and debt to tangible net worth. Skechers has good ratios in these areas.
- Nike has a materially better operating cash flow/total debt.

Summary—Long-Term Debt-Paying Ability

Nike's debt indicators appear to be materially better than Skechers. The Skechers' indicators are good.

Profitability

- Nike has a number of profitability indicators that are materially better than Skechers. Included here are net profit margin, return on assets, operating income margin, return on operating assets, return on investment, return on total equity, and return on common equity. Skechers has a number of profitability indicators that are better than Nike's. Indicators better for Skechers were total asset turnover, operating asset turnover, and sales to fixed assets.

Summary—Profitability

In general, Nike's profitability appears to be materially better than Skechers'.

Investor Analysis

- Neither company has a high degree of financial leverage, but Nike's is lower.
- Price/earnings ratio is slightly higher for Skechers. Take note that liquidity was better for Nike, long-term debt-paying ability was materially better for Nike, and profitability was materially better for Nike. Is the relatively high price/earnings ratio for Skechers justified?
- Skechers did not pay a dividend as indicated by percentage of earnings retained, dividend payout ratio, dividend yield, and operating cash flow/cash dividends. Nike paid a modest dividend.
- Nike had a materially higher option compensation expense percentage. This could be viewed as positive if it is tied to results and it achieved results.

Summary—Investor Analysis

The investor analysis appears to be much better for Nike than for Skechers U.S.A. Considering liquidity, long-term debt-paying ability, and profitability, we would expect Nike's price/earnings ratio to be higher than Skechers'. We find the price/earnings ratio of Skechers U.S.A. to be the higher ratio.

RATIO COMPARISON WITH INDUSTRY (EXHIBIT 5)

Comparison with the industry is frequently a problem as to the quality of the comparison. The companies in the industry will typically be using different accounting methods. An example would be costing of inventory, with some companies using LIFO, some using FIFO, and some using an average. Industry ratios frequently do not address issues such as income statement unusual or infrequent items, equity earnings, discontinued operations, extraordinary items, or minority earnings.

A problem with using industry data at a library is that commercial publications sometimes send the material to a library several months after general distribution. This brings a time issue to be considered. The U.S. Department of Commerce Quarterly Financial Report is online and represents relatively recent data. These data may be of limited or no use depending on the company that is being analyzed.

The industry ratios available are frequently of a broader industry coverage than the ideal. Nike is under SIC Rubber & Plastics Footwear (3021). Robert Morris Associates Annual Statement studies publishes some industry material using SIC 3052 Manufacturing Rubber and Plastics, Hose and Belting. Dun & Bradstreet Industry Norms & Key Business Ratios publishes SIC 30 Rubber & Plastics. The U.S. Department of Commerce publishes Quarterly Financial Report for manufacturing, mining and trade corporations. They have dropped SIC in favor of NAICS. They combine subsectors 315 and 316, apparel and leather products. For Nike, the NAICS is 316211, Rubber and Plastics Footwear Manufacturing.

In Nike's performance graph presented in the 2007 10-K, Nike compared its stock performance for the period May 2002–May 2007 with the S&P 500, Dow Jones U.S. Footwear, and S&P apparel, accessories and luxury goods. For stock performance, Nike most closely resembled Dow Jones U.S. Footwear. Both Nike and Dow Jones U.S. Footwear more than doubled their stock price during this period.

Although there are problems with using industry comparisons, the effort is usually beneficial. It is necessary to be cautious when drawing conclusions. You may want to review "Caution in Using Industry Averages" in Chapter 5.

Consider picking out four or five close competitors of the firm that you are analyzing and compute the industry average. This will likely result in a more meaningful comparison than using published industry data and more timely.

Liquidity

- Nike's receivables appear to be materially less liquid than the industry. Part of this can likely be explained by the May 31 year-end for Nike. The difference between the Nike ratios and the industry is so material that it is likely that most firms in the industry are using shorter credit terms. The Nike receivable ratios are in line with prior years.

| Exhibit | 5 | NIKE, INC. |

Ratio Comparison with Industry

Ratio	Unit	2007 Nike	Industry Ratio	Source
Liquidity:				
Days' sales in receivables	Days	56.63	40.28	DC
Accounts receivable turnover	Times per year	6.59	9.34	DC
Accounts receivable turnover	Days	55.38	39.09	DC
Days' sales in inventory	Days	84.50	Not available	
Merchandise inventory turnover	Times per year	4.37	5.2	RMA
Inventory turnover	Days	83.60	70.00	RMA
Operating cycle	Days	138.98	109.09	RMA & DC
Working capital (in millions)		5,492.5	N/A	
Current ratio	N/A	3.13	1.90	RMA
Acid-test ratio	N/A	2.07	0.90	RMA
Cash ratio	N/A	1.10	0.33	DC
Sales to working capital	Times per year	3.19	6.40	RMA
Operating cash flow/current maturities of long-term debt and notes payable	Times per year	14.31	Not available	
Long-term debt-paying ability:				
Times interest earned	Times per year	45.26	7.3	RMA
Fixed charge coverage	Times per year	16.20	Not available	
Debt ratio	%	34.27	53.20	RMA
Debt/equity	%	52.14	110.00	RMA
Debt to tangible net worth	%	56.49	Not available	
Operating cash flow/total debt	%	51.29	Not available	
Profitability:				
Net profit margin	%	9.14	8.29	DC
Total asset turnover	Times per year	1.59	0.96	DC
Return on assets	%	14.51	7.93	DC
Operating income margin	%	13.06	7.09	DC
Operating asset turnover	Times per year	1.76	1.83	DC
Return on operating assets	%	22.94	13.18	DC
Sales to fixed assets	Times per year	10.33	9.80	RMA
Return on investment	%	19.86	Not available	
Return on total equity	%	22.41	18.54	DC
Return on common equity	%	22.41	Not available	
Gross profit margin	%	43.86	27.7	RMA
Investor analysis:				
Degree of financial leverage	N/A	1.02	1.15	DC
Diluted earnings per share	$	2.93	N/A	
Price/earnings ratio	N/A	19.37	14.75	S&P
Percentage of earnings retained	%	76.96	65.33	DC
Dividend payout ratio	%	24.23	Not available	
Dividend yield	%	1.25	1.31	S&P
Book value per share	$	14.00	N/A	
Materiality of option compensation expense	%	6.32	Not available	
Operating cash flow per share	$	3.68	N/A	
Operating cash flow/cash dividends	Times per year	5.47	Not available	
Year-end market price	$	56.75	N/A	

Index: Industry statistics are directly from or computed from the following sources:

DC = U.S. Department of Commerce—Quarterly Financial Report for Manufacturing, Mining, and Trade Corporations

RMA = Robert Morris Associates, Annual Statement studies, SIC 3052, NAICS 326220

S&P = Standard and Poor's 500, The Outlook, 500 Composite

- Nike's inventory appears to be materially less liquid than the industry. Part of this can likely be explained by the May 31 year-end for Nike. Possibly, many firms in the industry are using a different inventory costing method than Nike uses. The Nike inventory ratios are in line with prior years.
- The operating cycle of Nike is materially longer than the operating cycle of the industry. This is the result of less liquid receivables and inventory.

- The current ratio and acid-test ratio are much better for Nike than for the industry. These would be influenced by less liquid receivables and inventory. They are also influenced by the materially better cash ratio of Nike.
- Sales to working capital is much better for the industry than for Nike.

Summary—Liquidity

We likely do not have good industry comparisons with Nike in the liquidity area. It is possible that Nike has substantially different policies in the receivables and inventory areas than the industry.

Long-Term Debt-Paying Ability

- Nike's time interest earned, debt ratio, and debt/equity are materially better than the industry.

Summary—Long-Term Debt-Paying Ability

Nike's long-term debt-paying ability appears to be materially better than the industry.

Profitability

All of the profitability ratios were materially better for Nike than the industry, except for operating asset turnover. Operating asset turnover was better for the industry.

Summary—Profitability

Nike had an outstanding profit year.

Investor Analysis

- The degree of financial leverage is much lower for Nike than for the industry.
- The price/earnings ratio is materially higher for Nike than the 500 Composite. This appears to be justified considering the outstanding profitability ratios for Nike.
- Nike retained a materially higher percentage of earnings than did the industry.
- The dividend yield was slightly lower for Nike.

Summary—Investor Analysis

Only a few comparisons were possible in the investor area. The comparisons are favorable toward Nike.

Other

Foot Locker, Inc., accounted for approximately 10% of global net sales of Nike during fiscal 2007. In a Form 8-K release, July 31, 2007, Foot Locker disclosed on July 30, 2007, that it issued a press release confirming the retention of Lehman Brothers as an advisor to work with the company to evaluate strategic alternatives. This press release further disclosed (1) merchandise inventory reduced through aggressive clearance strategy, (2) additional U.S. stores identified for potential early closure, (3) more aggressive store opening plans being developed for Foot Locker Europe, and (4) senior division management changes.

The happenings at Foot Locker could impact the profitability of Nike.

Exhibit 8-23, segment information, indicates that the Other segment had the best increase in revenues in percentage. This resulted in the Other segment having a material increase in pretax income to net revenue (Exhibit 8-21). The Other segment still had materially lower pretax income to net income in comparison with the other segments.

Summary

In general, the years 2005–2007 appear to be very good for Nike in terms of liquidity. The debt position appears to be very good. This appears to be the case from an income statement view and a balance sheet view. Profitability appears to be very good.

In the profitability area, there were slight declines in several areas. These areas included total asset turnover, operating asset turnover, return on equity, return on common equity, and gross profit margin. These areas need to be monitored closely.

Foot Locker, Inc., accounted for approximately 10% of global net sales for Nike during fiscal 2007. The developments at Foot Locker need to be monitored closely.

Nike 2007

The Nike 2007 financial statements and notes are presented along with the Nike Exhibit 12.1 which shows the computation of the ratio of earnings to total fixed charges. Exhibit 12.1 discloses the interest expense.

EXHIBIT 12.1 NIKE, INC. COMPUTATION OF RATIO OF EARNINGS TO FIXED CHARGES

	Year Ended May 31,		
	2007	2006	2005
	(In millions)		
Net income	$1,491.5	$1,392.0	$1,211.6
Income taxes	708.4	749.6	648.2
Income before income taxes	2,199.9	2,141.6	1,859.8
Add fixed charges			
Interest expense[1]	49.7	50.5	39.7
Interest component of leases[2]	95.1	84.0	77.5
Total fixed charges	144.8	134.5	117.2
Earnings before income taxes and fixed charges[3]	$2,344.7	$2,276.1	$1,977.0
Ratio of earnings to total fixed charges	16.2	16.9	16.9

[1] Interest expense includes interest both expensed and capitalized.

[2] Interest component of leases includes one-third of rental expense, which approximates the interest component of operating leases.

[3] Earnings before income taxes and fixed charges is exclusive of capitalized interest.

The 10-K can be located at http://www.sec.gov. Under "Filings & Forms (EDGAR)," select "Search for Company Filings." On the Search the EDGAR Database screen, select "Companies & Other Filers." Enter either the company name (Nike, Inc.) or the Ticker Symbol (NKE), check the Exclude button and click on "Find Companies." The form titles are in the left-hand column. Scroll down until you find the 10-K with a filing date of July 27, 2007. The 2007 proxy is filed as DEF 14A with a filing date of August 3, 2007. Click on the format that you prefer, html or text, to view the 10-K and proxy statements.

NIKE, INC.

CONSOLIDATED STATEMENTS OF INCOME

	Year Ended May 31,		
	2007	2006	2005
	(In millions, except per share data)		
Revenues	$16,325.9	$14,954.9	$13,739.7
Cost of sales	9,165.4	8,367.9	7,624.3
Gross margin	7,160.5	6,587.0	6,115.4
Selling and administrative expense	5,028.7	4,477.8	4,221.7
Interest (income) expense, net (Notes 1, 6 and 7)	(67.2)	(36.8)	4.8
Other (income) expense, net (Notes 5 and 16)	(0.9)	4.4	29.1
Income before income taxes	2,199.9	2,141.6	1,859.8
Income taxes (Note 8)	708.4	749.6	648.2
Net income	$ 1,491.5	$ 1,392.0	$ 1,211.6
Basic earnings per common share (Notes 1 and 11)	$ 2.96	$ 2.69	$ 2.31
Diluted earnings per common share (Notes 1 and 11)	$ 2.93	$ 2.64	$ 2.24
Dividends declared per common share	$ 0.71	$ 0.59	$ 0.475

The accompanying notes to consolidated financial statements are an integral part of this statement.

NIKE, INC.
CONSOLIDATED BALANCE SHEETS

	May 31,	
	2007	2006
	(In millions)	

ASSETS

Current assets:		
Cash and equivalents	$ 1,856.7	$ 954.2
Short-term investments	990.3	1,348.8
Accounts receivable, net	2,494.7	2,382.9
Inventories (Note 2)	2,121.9	2,076.7
Deferred income taxes (Note 8)	219.7	203.3
Prepaid expenses and other current assets	393.2	380.1
Total current assets	8,076.5	7,346.0
Property, plant and equipment, net (Note 3)	1,678.3	1,657.7
Identifiable intangible assets, net (Note 4)	409.9	405.5
Goodwill (Note 4)	130.8	130.8
Deferred income taxes and other assets (Note 8)	392.8	329.6
Total assets	$10,688.3	$9,869.6

LIABILITIES AND SHAREHOLDERS' EQUITY

Current liabilities:		
Current portion of long-term debt (Note 7)	$ 30.5	$ 255.3
Notes payable (Note 6)	100.8	43.4
Accounts payable (Note 6)	1,040.3	952.2
Accrued liabilities (Notes 5 and 16)	1,303.4	1,276.0
Income taxes payable	109.0	85.5
Total current liabilities	2,584.0	2,612.4
Long-term debt (Note 7)	409.9	410.7
Deferred income taxes and other liabilities (Note 8)	668.7	561.0
Commitments and contingencies (Notes 14 and 16)	—	—
Redeemable Preferred Stock (Note 9)	0.3	0.3
Shareholders' equity:		
Common stock at stated value (Note 10):		
Class A convertible — 117.6 and 127.8 shares outstanding	0.1	0.1
Class B — 384.1 and 384.2 shares outstanding	2.7	2.7
Capital in excess of stated value	1,960.0	1,447.3
Accumulated other comprehensive income (Note 13)	177.4	121.7
Retained earnings	4,885.2	4,713.4
Total shareholders' equity	7,025.4	6,285.2
Total liabilities and shareholders' equity	$10,688.3	$9,869.6

The accompanying notes to consolidated financial statements are an integral part of this statement.

NIKE, INC.

CONSOLIDATED STATEMENTS OF CASH FLOWS

	Year Ended May 31,		
	2007	2006	2005
		(In millions)	
Cash provided (used) by operations:			
Net income	$ 1,491.5	$ 1,392.0	$ 1,211.6
Income charges not affecting cash:			
Depreciation	269.7	282.0	257.2
Deferred income taxes	34.1	(26.0)	21.3
Stock-based compensation (Notes 1 and 10)	147.7	11.8	4.9
Amortization and other	0.5	(2.9)	25.6
Income tax benefit from exercise of stock options	—	54.2	63.1
Changes in certain working capital components and other assets and liabilities:			
Increase in accounts receivable	(39.6)	(85.1)	(93.5)
Increase in inventories	(49.5)	(200.3)	(103.3)
(Increase) decrease in prepaid expenses and other current assets	(60.8)	(37.2)	71.4
Increase in accounts payable, accrued liabilities and income taxes payable	85.1	279.4	112.4
Cash provided by operations	1,878.7	1,667.9	1,570.7
Cash provided (used) by investing activities:			
Purchases of short-term investments	(2,133.8)	(2,619.7)	(1,527.2)
Maturities of short-term investments	2,516.2	1,709.8	1,491.9
Additions to property, plant and equipment	(313.5)	(333.7)	(257.1)
Disposals of property, plant and equipment	28.3	1.6	7.2
Increase in other assets, net of other liabilities	(4.3)	(34.6)	(28.0)
Acquisition of subsidiary, net of cash acquired	—	—	(47.2)
Cash provided (used) by investing activities	92.9	(1,276.6)	(360.4)
Cash provided (used) by financing activities:			
Proceeds from issuance of long-term debt	41.8	—	—
Reductions in long-term debt, including current portion	(255.7)	(6.0)	(9.2)
Increase (decrease) in notes payable	52.6	(18.2)	(81.7)
Proceeds from exercise of stock options and other stock issuances	322.9	225.3	226.8
Excess tax benefits from share-based payment arrangements	55.8	—	—
Repurchase of common stock	(985.2)	(761.1)	(556.2)
Dividends — common and preferred	(343.7)	(290.9)	(236.7)
Cash used by financing activities	(1,111.5)	(850.9)	(657.0)
Effect of exchange rate changes	42.4	25.7	6.8
Net increase (decrease) in cash and equivalents	902.5	(433.9)	560.1
Cash and equivalents, beginning of year	954.2	1,388.1	828.0
Cash and equivalents, end of year	$ 1,856.7	$ 954.2	$ 1,388.1
Supplemental disclosure of cash flow information:			
Cash paid during the year for:			
Interest, net of capitalized interest	$ 60.0	$ 54.2	$ 33.9
Income taxes	601.1	752.6	585.3
Dividends declared and not paid	92.9	79.4	65.3

The accompanying notes to consolidated financial statements are an integral part of this statement.

52

NIKE, INC.

CONSOLIDATED STATEMENTS OF SHAREHOLDERS' EQUITY

	Common Stock				Capital in Excess of Stated Value	Accumulated Other Comprehensive Income (Loss)	Retained Earnings	Total
	Class A		Class B					
	Shares	Amount	Shares	Amount				
	(In millions, except per share data)							
Balance at May 31, 2004	155.2	$ 0.1	371.0	$ 2.7	$ 882.3	$ (86.3)	$ 3,982.9	$4,781.7
Stock options exercised			8.8		272.2			272.2
Conversion to Class B Common Stock	(11.4)		11.4					—
Repurchase of Class B Common Stock			(13.8)		(8.3)		(547.9)	(556.2)
Dividends on Common stock ($0.475 per share)							(249.4)	(249.4)
Issuance of shares to employees			1.0		21.9			21.9
Stock-based compensation (Note 10):					4.9			4.9
Forfeiture of shares from employees					(1.5)		(0.7)	(2.2)
Comprehensive income (Note 13):								
Net income							1,211.6	1,211.6
Other comprehensive income (net of tax expense of $40.2):								
Foreign currency translation						70.1		70.1
Adjustment for fair value of hedge derivatives						89.6		89.6
Comprehensive income						159.7	1,211.6	1,371.3
Balance at May 31, 2005	143.8	$ 0.1	378.4	$ 2.7	$ 1,171.5	$ 73.4	$ 4,396.5	$5,644.2
Stock options exercised			8.0		253.7			253.7
Conversion to Class B Common Stock	(16.0)		16.0					—
Repurchase of Class B Common Stock			(19.0)		(11.3)		(769.9)	(781.2)
Dividends on Common stock ($0.59 per share)							(304.9)	(304.9)
Issuance of shares to employees			1.0		26.9			26.9
Stock-based compensation (Note 10):					11.8			11.8
Forfeiture of shares from employees			(0.2)		(5.3)		(0.3)	(5.6)
Comprehensive income (Note 13):								
Net income							1,392.0	1,392.0
Other comprehensive income (net of tax benefit of $37.8):								
Foreign currency translation						87.1		87.1
Adjustment for fair value of hedge derivatives						(38.8)		(38.8)
Comprehensive income						48.3	1,392.0	1,440.3
Balance at May 31, 2006	127.8	$ 0.1	384.2	$ 2.7	$ 1,447.3	$ 121.7	$ 4,713.4	$6,285.2
Stock options exercised			10.7		349.7			349.7
Conversion to Class B Common Stock	(10.2)		10.2					—
Repurchase of Class B Common Stock			(22.1)		(13.2)		(962.0)	(975.2)
Dividends on Common stock ($0.71 per share)							(357.2)	(357.2)
Issuance of shares to employees			1.2		30.1			30.1
Stock-based compensation (Note 10):					147.7			147.7
Forfeiture of shares from employees			(0.1)		(1.6)		(0.5)	(2.1)
Comprehensive income (Note 13):								
Net income							1,491.5	1,491.5
Other comprehensive income (net of tax benefit of $0.5):								
Foreign currency translation						84.6		84.6
Adjustment for fair value of hedge derivatives						(16.7)		(16.7)
Comprehensive income						67.9	1,491.5	1,559.4
Adoption of FAS 158 (net of tax benefit of $5.4) (Note 12):						(12.2)		(12.2)
Balance at May 31, 2007	117.6	$ 0.1	384.1	$ 2.7	$ 1,960.0	$ 177.4	$ 4,885.2	$7,025.4

The accompanying notes to consolidated financial statements are an integral part of this statement.

53

NIKE, INC.

NOTES TO CONSOLIDATED FINANCIAL STATEMENTS

Note 1 — Summary of Significant Accounting Policies

Basis of Consolidation

The consolidated financial statements include the accounts of NIKE, Inc. and its subsidiaries (the "Company"). All significant intercompany transactions and balances have been eliminated.

Stock Split

On February 15, 2007 the Board of Directors declared a two-for-one stock split of the Company's Class A and Class B common shares, which was effected in the form of a 100% common stock dividend distributed on April 2, 2007. All references to share and per share amounts in the consolidated financial statements and accompanying notes to the consolidated financial statements have been retroactively restated to reflect the two-for-one stock split.

Recognition of Revenues

Wholesale revenues are recognized when the risks and rewards of ownership have passed to the customer, based on the terms of sale. This occurs upon shipment or upon receipt by the customer depending on the country of the sale and the agreement with the customer. Retail store revenues are recorded at the time of sale. Provisions for sales discounts, returns and miscellaneous claims from customers are made at the time of sale.

Shipping and Handling Costs

Shipping and handling costs are expensed as incurred and included in cost of sales.

Advertising and Promotion

Advertising production costs are expensed the first time the advertisement is run. Media (TV and print) placement costs are expensed in the month the advertising appears.

A significant amount of the Company's promotional expenses result from payments under endorsement contracts. Accounting for endorsement payments is based upon specific contract provisions. Generally, endorsement payments are expensed on a straight-line basis over the term of the contract after giving recognition to periodic performance compliance provisions of the contracts. Prepayments made under contracts are included in prepaid expenses or other assets depending on the period to which the prepayment applies.

Through cooperative advertising programs, the Company reimburses its retail customers for certain of their costs of advertising the Company's products. The Company records these costs in selling and administrative expense at the point in time when it is obligated to its customers for the costs, which is when the related revenues are recognized. This obligation may arise prior to the related advertisement being run.

Total advertising and promotion expenses were $1,912.4 million, $1,740.2 million, and $1,600.7 million for the years ended May 31, 2007, 2006 and 2005, respectively. Prepaid advertising and promotion expenses recorded in prepaid expenses and other assets totaled $253.0 million and $177.1 million at May 31, 2007 and 2006, respectively.

Cash and Equivalents

Cash and equivalents represent cash and short-term, highly liquid investments with maturities of three months or less at date of purchase. The carrying amounts reflected in the consolidated balance sheet for cash and equivalents approximate fair value.

NIKE, INC.

NOTES TO CONSOLIDATED FINANCIAL STATEMENTS — (Continued)

Short-term Investments

Short-term investments consist of highly liquid investments, primarily U.S. Treasury debt securities, with maturities over three months from the date of purchase. Debt securities which the Company has the ability and positive intent to hold to maturity are carried at amortized cost. Available-for-sale debt securities are recorded at fair value with any net unrealized gains and losses reported, net of tax, in other comprehensive income. Realized gains or losses are determined based on the specific identification method. The Company holds no investments considered to be trading securities. Amortized cost of both available-for-sale and held-to-maturity debt securities approximates fair market value due to their short maturities. Substantially all short-term investments held at May 31, 2007 have remaining maturities of 180 days or less. Included in interest (income) expense, net for the years ended May 31, 2007, 2006, and 2005, was interest income of $116.9 million, $87.3 million and $34.9 million, respectively, related to short-term investments and cash and equivalents.

Allowance for Uncollectible Accounts Receivable

Accounts receivable consists principally of amounts receivable from customers. We make ongoing estimates relating to the collectibility of our accounts receivable and maintain an allowance for estimated losses resulting from the inability of our customers to make required payments. In determining the amount of the allowance, we consider our historical level of credit losses and make judgments about the creditworthiness of significant customers based on ongoing credit evaluations. Accounts receivable with anticipated collection dates greater than twelve months from the balance sheet date and related allowances are considered non-current and recorded in other assets. The allowance for uncollectible accounts receivable was $71.5 million and $67.6 million at May 31, 2007 and 2006, respectively, of which $33.3 million and $29.2 million was recorded in other assets.

Inventory Valuation

Inventories related to our wholesale operations are stated at lower of cost or market and valued on a first-in, first-out ("FIFO") or moving average cost basis. Inventories related to our retail operations are stated at the lower of average cost or market using the retail inventory method. Under the retail inventory method, the valuation of inventories at cost is calculated by applying a cost-to-retail ratio to the retail value inventories. Permanent and point of sale markdowns, when recorded, reduce both the retail and cost components of inventory on hand so as to maintain the already established cost-to-retail relationship.

Property, Plant and Equipment and Depreciation

Property, plant and equipment are recorded at cost. Depreciation for financial reporting purposes is determined on a straight-line basis for buildings and leasehold improvements over 2 to 40 years and for machinery and equipment over 2 to 15 years. Computer software (including, in some cases, the cost of internal labor) is depreciated on a straight-line basis over 3 to 10 years.

Impairment of Long-Lived Assets

The Company estimates the future undiscounted cash flows to be derived from an asset to assess whether or not a potential impairment exists when events or circumstances indicate the carrying value of a long-lived asset may be impaired. If the carrying value exceeds the Company's estimate of future undiscounted cash flows, the Company then calculates the impairment as the excess of the carrying value of the asset over the Company's estimate of its fair market value.

55

NIKE, INC.

NOTES TO CONSOLIDATED FINANCIAL STATEMENTS — (Continued)

Identifiable Intangible Assets and Goodwill

Goodwill and intangible assets with indefinite lives are not amortized but instead are measured for impairment at least annually in the fourth quarter, or when events indicate that an impairment exists. As required by Statement of Financial Accounting Standards ("SFAS") No. 142, "Goodwill and other Intangible Assets" ("FAS 142"), in the Company's impairment test of goodwill, the Company compares the fair value of the applicable reporting unit to its carrying value. The Company estimates the fair value of its reporting units by using a combination of discounted cash flow analysis and comparisons with the market values of similar publicly traded companies. If the carrying value of the reporting unit exceeds the estimate of fair value, the Company calculates the impairment as the excess of the carrying value of goodwill over its implied fair value. In the impairment tests for indefinite-lived intangible assets, the Company compares the estimated fair value of the indefinite-lived intangible assets to the carrying value. The Company estimates the fair value of indefinite-lived intangible assets and trademarks using the relief from royalty approach, which is a standard form of discounted cash flow analysis used for the valuation of trademarks. If the carrying value exceeds the estimate of fair value, the Company calculates impairment as the excess of the carrying value over the estimate of fair value.

Intangible assets that are determined to have definite lives are amortized over their useful lives and are measured for impairment only when events or circumstances indicate the carrying value may be impaired.

Foreign Currency Translation and Foreign Currency Transactions

Adjustments resulting from translating foreign functional currency financial statements into U.S. dollars are included in the foreign currency translation adjustment, a component of accumulated other comprehensive income in shareholders' equity.

Transaction gains and losses generated by the effect of foreign exchange rates on recorded assets and liabilities denominated in a currency different from the functional currency of the applicable Company entity are recorded in other (income) expense, net, in the period in which they occur.

Accounting for Derivatives and Hedging Activities

The Company uses derivative financial instruments to limit exposure to changes in foreign currency exchange rates and interest rates. The Company accounts for derivatives pursuant to SFAS No. 133, "Accounting for Derivative Instruments and Hedging Activities," as amended and interpreted ("FAS 133"). FAS 133 establishes accounting and reporting standards for derivative instruments and requires that all derivatives be recorded at fair value on the balance sheet. Changes in the fair value of derivative financial instruments are either recognized in other comprehensive income (a component of shareholders' equity) or net income depending on whether the derivative is being used to hedge changes in cash flows or fair value.

See Note 16 for more information on the Company's Risk Management program and derivatives.

Stock-Based Compensation

On June 1, 2006, the Company adopted SFAS No. 123R "Share-Based Payment" ("FAS 123R") which requires the Company to record expense for stock-based compensation to employees using a fair value method. Under FAS 123R, the Company estimates the fair value of options granted under the NIKE, Inc. 1990 Stock Incentive Plan (the "1990 Plan") (see Note 10) and employees' purchase rights under the Employee Stock Purchase Plans ("ESPPs") using the Black-Scholes option pricing model. The Company recognizes this fair value, net of estimated forfeitures, as selling and administrative expense in the Consolidated Statements of Income over the vesting period using the straight-line method.

56

NIKE, INC.

NOTES TO CONSOLIDATED FINANCIAL STATEMENTS — (Continued)

The Company has adopted the modified prospective transition method prescribed by FAS 123R, which does not require the restatement of financial results for previous periods. In accordance with this transition method, the Company's Consolidated Statement of Income for the year ended May 31, 2007 includes (1) amortization of outstanding stock-based compensation granted prior to, but not vested, as of June 1, 2006, based on the fair value estimated in accordance with the original provisions of SFAS No. 123, "Accounting for Stock-Based Compensation" ("FAS 123") and (2) amortization of all stock-based awards granted subsequent to June 1, 2006, based on the fair value estimated in accordance with the provisions of FAS 123R.

The following table summarizes the effects of applying FAS 123R during the year ended May 31, 2007. The resulting stock-based compensation expense primarily relates to stock options.

(in millions, except per share data)	
Addition to selling and administrative expense	$141.9
Reduction to income tax expense	(45.2)
Reduction to net income[1]	$ 96.7
Reduction to earnings per share:	
Basic	$ 0.19
Diluted	$ 0.18

[1] In accordance with FAS 123R, stock-based compensation expense reported during the year ended May 31, 2007, includes $24.2 million, net of tax, or $0.04 per diluted share, of accelerated stock-based compensation expense recorded for employees eligible for accelerated stock option vesting upon retirement.

Prior to the adoption of FAS 123R, the Company used the intrinsic value method to account for stock options and ESPP shares in accordance with Accounting Principles Board Opinion No. 25, "Accounting for Stock Issued to Employees" as permitted by FAS 123. If the Company had instead accounted for stock options and ESPP shares issued to employees using the fair value method prescribed by FAS 123 during the years ended May 31, 2006 and 2005 the Company's pro forma net income and pro forma earnings per share would have been reported as follows:

	Year Ended May 31,	
	2006	2005
	(In millions, except per share data)	
Net income as reported	$ 1,392.0	$ 1,211.6
Add: Stock option expense included in reported net income, net of tax	0.2	0.6
Deduct: Total stock option and ESPP expense under fair value based method for all awards, net of tax[1]	(76.8)	(64.1)
Pro forma net income	$ 1,315.4	$ 1,148.1
Earnings per share:		
Basic — as reported	$ 2.69	$ 2.31
Basic — pro forma	2.54	2.19
Diluted — as reported	2.64	2.24
Diluted — pro forma	2.50	2.14

[1] Accelerated stock-based compensation expense for options subject to accelerated vesting due to employee retirement is not included in the pro forma figures shown above for the years ended May 31, 2006 and 2005. This disclosure reflects the expense of such options ratably over the stated vesting period or upon actual employee retirement. Had the Company recognized the fair value for such stock options on an accelerated

NIKE, INC.

NOTES TO CONSOLIDATED FINANCIAL STATEMENTS — (Continued)

basis in this pro forma disclosure, the Company would have recognized additional stock-based compensation expense of $17.5 million, net of tax, or $0.03 per diluted share for the year ended May 31, 2006 and $21.8 million, net of tax, or $0.04 per diluted share for the year ended May 31, 2005.

To calculate the excess tax benefits available for use in offsetting future tax shortfalls as of the date of implementation, the Company is following the alternative transition method discussed in FASB Staff Position No. 123R-3, "Transition Election Relating to Accounting for the Tax Effects of Share-Based Payment Awards."

See Note 10 for more information on the Company's stock programs.

Income Taxes

The Company accounts for income taxes using the asset and liability method. This approach requires the recognition of deferred tax assets and liabilities for the expected future tax consequences of temporary differences between the carrying amounts and the tax basis of assets and liabilities. United States income taxes are provided currently on financial statement earnings of non-U.S. subsidiaries that are expected to be repatriated. The Company determines annually the amount of undistributed non-U.S. earnings to invest indefinitely in its non-U.S. operations. See Note 8 for further discussion.

Earnings Per Share

Basic earnings per common share is calculated by dividing net income by the weighted average number of common shares outstanding during the year. Diluted earnings per common share is calculated by adjusting weighted average outstanding shares, assuming conversion of all potentially dilutive stock options and awards. See Note 11 for further discussion.

Management Estimates

The preparation of financial statements in conformity with generally accepted accounting principles requires management to make estimates, including estimates relating to assumptions that affect the reported amounts of assets and liabilities and disclosure of contingent assets and liabilities at the date of financial statements and the reported amounts of revenues and expenses during the reporting period. Actual results could differ from these estimates.

Reclassifications

Certain prior year amounts have been reclassified to conform to fiscal year 2007 presentation. These changes had no impact on previously reported results of operations or shareholders' equity.

Recently Issued Accounting Standards

In June 2006, the Financial Accounting Standards Board ("FASB") ratified the consensus reached on Emerging Issues Task Force ("EITF") Issue No. 06-3, "How Taxes Collected from Customers and Remitted to Governmental Authorities Should Be Presented in the Income Statement (That Is, Gross versus Net Presentation)" ("EITF 06-3"). EITF 06-3 requires disclosure of the method of accounting for the applicable assessed taxes and the amount of assessed taxes that are included in revenues if they are accounted for under the gross method. EITF 06-3 was adopted in the fourth quarter ended May 31, 2007; however, since the Company presents revenues net of any taxes collected from customers, no additional disclosures were required.

NIKE, INC.

NOTES TO CONSOLIDATED FINANCIAL STATEMENTS — (Continued)

In September 2006, the FASB issued SFAS No. 158, "Employers' Accounting for Defined Benefit Pension and Other Postretirement Plans" ("FAS 158"). FAS 158 requires employers to fully recognize the obligations associated with single-employer defined benefit pension, retiree healthcare and other postretirement plans in their financial statements. The Company adopted the provisions of FAS 158 in the fourth quarter ended May 31, 2007. See Note 12 for additional details.

In September 2006, the SEC staff issued Staff Accounting Bulletin No. 108, "Considering the Effects of Prior Year Misstatements when Quantifying Misstatements in Current Year Financial Statements" ("SAB 108"). SAB 108 requires public companies to quantify errors using both a balance sheet and income statement approach and evaluate whether either approach results in quantifying a misstatement as material, when all relevant quantitative and qualitative factors are considered. The adoption of SAB 108 at May 31, 2007 did not have a material impact on the Company's consolidated financial position or results of operations.

In June 2006, the FASB issued FASB Interpretation No. 48, "Accounting for Uncertainty in Income Taxes" ("FIN 48"). FIN 48 clarifies the accounting for uncertainty in income taxes recognized in the Company's financial statements in accordance with FASB Statement No. 109, "Accounting for Income Taxes". The provisions of FIN 48 are effective for the fiscal year beginning June 1, 2007. The Company has evaluated the impact of the provisions of FIN 48 and does not expect that the adoption will have a material impact on the Company's consolidated financial position or results of operations.

In June 2006, the FASB ratified the consensus reached on EITF Issue No. 06-2, "Accounting for Sabbatical Leave and Other Similar Benefits Pursuant to FASB Statement No. 43" ("EITF 06-2"). EITF 06-2 clarifies recognition guidance on the accrual of employees' rights to compensated absences under a sabbatical or other similar benefit arrangement. The provisions of EITF 06-2 are effective for the fiscal year beginning June 1, 2007 and will be applied through a cumulative effect adjustment to retained earnings. The Company has evaluated the provisions of EITF 06-2 and does not expect that the adoption will have a material impact on the Company's consolidated financial position or results of operations.

In September 2006, the FASB issued SFAS No. 157, "Fair Value Measurements" ("FAS 157"). FAS 157 defines fair value, establishes a framework for measuring fair value in accordance with generally accepted accounting principles, and expands disclosures about fair value measurements. The provisions of FAS 157 are effective for the fiscal year beginning June 1, 2008. The Company is currently evaluating the impact of the provisions of FAS 157.

In February 2007, the FASB issued SFAS No. 159, "The Fair Value Option for Financial Assets and Financial Liabilities — Including an Amendment of FASB Statement No. 115" ("FAS 159"). FAS 159 permits entities to choose to measure many financial instruments and certain other items at fair value. Unrealized gains and losses on items for which the fair value option has been elected will be recognized in earnings at each subsequent reporting date. The provisions of FAS 159 are effective for the fiscal year beginning June 1, 2008. The Company is currently evaluating the impact of the provisions of FAS 159.

Note 2 — Inventories

Inventory balances of $2,121.9 million and $2,076.7 million at May 31, 2007 and 2006, respectively, were substantially all finished goods.

NIKE, INC.

NOTES TO CONSOLIDATED FINANCIAL STATEMENTS — (Continued)

Note 3 — Property, Plant and Equipment

Property, plant and equipment includes the following:

	May 31,	
	2007	2006
	(In millions)	
Land	$ 193.8	$ 195.9
Buildings	840.9	842.6
Machinery and equipment	1,817.2	1,661.7
Leasehold improvements	672.8	626.7
Construction in process	94.4	81.4
	3,619.1	3,408.3
Less accumulated depreciation	1,940.8	1,750.6
	$1,678.3	$1,657.7

Capitalized interest was not material for the years ended May 31, 2007, 2006 and 2005.

Note 4 — Identifiable Intangible Assets and Goodwill:

The following table summarizes the Company's identifiable intangible assets and goodwill balances as of May 31, 2007 and May 31, 2006:

	May 31, 2007			May 31, 2006		
	Gross Carrying Amount	Accumulated Amortization	Net Carrying Amount	Gross Carrying Amount	Accumulated Amortization	Net Carrying Amount
	(In millions)					
Amortized intangible assets:						
Patents	$ 44.1	$ (12.3)	$ 31.8	$ 34.1	$ (10.5)	$ 23.6
Trademarks	49.8	(17.5)	32.3	46.4	(11.8)	34.6
Other	21.6	(17.3)	4.3	21.5	(15.7)	5.8
Total	$ 115.5	$ (47.1)	$ 68.4	$ 102.0	$ (38.0)	$ 64.0
Unamortized intangible assets — Trademarks			$ 341.5			$ 341.5
Total			$ 409.9			$ 405.5
Goodwill			$ 130.8			$ 130.8

Amortization expense of identifiable assets with definite lives, which is included in selling and administrative expense, was $9.9 million, $9.8 million and $9.3 million for the years ended May 31, 2007, 2006, and 2005, respectively. The estimated amortization expense for intangible assets subject to amortization for each of the years ending May 31, 2008 through May 31, 2012 is as follows: 2008: $9.7 million; 2009: $8.7 million; 2010: $8.2 million; 2011: $7.7 million; 2012: $6.9 million.

60

NIKE, INC.

NOTES TO CONSOLIDATED FINANCIAL STATEMENTS — (Continued)

Note 5 — Accrued Liabilities

Accrued liabilities include the following:

	May 31,	
	2007	2006
	(In millions)	
Compensation and benefits, excluding taxes	$ 451.6	$ 427.2
Endorser compensation	139.9	124.7
Taxes other than income taxes	133.4	115.1
Dividends payable	92.9	79.5
Fair value of derivatives	90.5	111.2
Import and logistics costs	81.4	63.3
Advertising and marketing	70.6	75.4
Converse arbitration[1]	—	51.9
Other[2]	243.1	227.7
	$1,303.4	$1,276.0

[1] The Converse arbitration relates to a charge taken during the fourth quarter ended May 31, 2006 as a result of a contract dispute between Converse and a former South American licensee. The dispute was settled during the first quarter ended August 31, 2006.

[2] Other consists of various accrued expenses and no individual item accounted for more than $50 million of the balance at May 31, 2007 or 2006.

Note 6 — Short-Term Borrowings and Credit Lines

Notes payable to banks and interest-bearing accounts payable to Sojitz Corporation of America ("Sojitz America") as of May 31, 2007 and 2006, are summarized below:

	May 31,				
	2007			2006	
	Borrowings	Interest Rate		Borrowings	Interest Rate
		(In millions)			
Notes payable:					
U.S. operations	$ 14.6	0.00%[1]		$ 21.0	0.00%[1]
Non-U.S. operations	86.2	9.85%		22.4	7.72%
	$ 100.8			$ 43.4	
Sojitz America	$ 44.6	6.09%		$ 69.7	5.83%

[1] Weighted average interest rate includes non-interest bearing overdrafts.

The carrying amounts reflected in the consolidated balance sheet for notes payable approximate fair value.

The Company purchases through Sojitz America certain athletic footwear, apparel and equipment it acquires from non-U.S. suppliers. These purchases are for the Company's operations outside of the United States, the Europe, Middle East, and Africa Region and Japan. Accounts payable to Sojitz America are generally due up to 60 days after shipment of goods from the foreign port. The interest rate on such accounts payable is the 60-day London Interbank Offered Rate ("LIBOR") as of the beginning of the month of the invoice date, plus 0.75%.

NIKE, INC.

NOTES TO CONSOLIDATED FINANCIAL STATEMENTS — (Continued)

The Company had no borrowings outstanding under its commercial paper program at May 31, 2007 and 2006.

In December 2006, the Company entered into a $1 billion multi-year credit facility that replaced the Company's previous $750 million facility. The facility matures in December 2011, and can be extended for one additional year on both the first and second anniversary date for a total extension of two years. Based on the Company's current long-term senior unsecured debt ratings, the interest rate charged on any outstanding borrowings would be the prevailing LIBOR plus 0.15%. The facility fee is 0.05% of the total commitment. Under this agreement, the Company must maintain, among other things, certain minimum specified financial ratios with which the Company was in compliance at May 31, 2007. No amounts were outstanding under these facilities as of May 31, 2007 or 2006.

In January 2007, one of the Company's Japanese subsidiaries entered into a 3.0 billion yen (approximately $24.7 million as of May 31, 2007) loan facility that replaced certain intercompany borrowings. The interest rate on the facility is based on the six-month Japanese Yen LIBOR plus a spread, resulting in an all-in rate of 0.805% at May 31, 2007. The facility expires December 31, 2007 unless both parties agree to an extension.

Note 7 — Long-Term Debt

Long-term debt includes the following:

	May 31,	
	2007	**2006**
	(In millions)	
5.5% Corporate Bond, payable August 15, 2006	$ —	$249.3
4.8% Corporate Bond, payable July 9, 2007	25.0	24.7
5.375% Corporate Bond, payable July 8, 2009	24.8	24.6
5.66% Corporate Bond, payable July 23, 2012	24.8	24.6
5.4% Corporate Bond, payable August 7, 2012	14.6	14.4
4.7% Corporate Bond, payable October 1, 2013	50.0	50.0
5.15% Corporate Bonds, payable October 15, 2015	99.6	98.2
4.3% Japanese yen note, payable June 26, 2011	86.4	93.8
1.5% Japanese yen note, payable February 14, 2012	41.1	—
2.6% Japanese yen note, maturing August 20, 2001 through November 20, 2020	51.2	59.7
2.0% Japanese yen note, maturing August 20, 2001 through November 20, 2020	22.9	26.6
Other	—	0.1
Total	440.4	666.0
Less current maturities	30.5	255.3
	$409.9	$410.7

The fair value of long-term debt is estimated using discounted cash flow analyses, based on the Company's incremental borrowing rates for similar types of borrowing arrangements. The fair value of the Company's long-term debt, including current portion, is approximately $443.2 million at May 31, 2007 and $674.0 million at May 31, 2006.

The Company had interest rate swap agreements with the same notional amount and maturity dates as the $250.0 million corporate bond that matured on August 15, 2006, whereby the Company received fixed interest payments at the same rate as the bond and paid variable interest payments based on the three-month LIBOR plus a spread. The interest rate payable on these swap agreements was approximately 6.6% at May 31, 2006.

NIKE, INC.

NOTES TO CONSOLIDATED FINANCIAL STATEMENTS — (Continued)

The Company has an effective shelf registration statement with the Securities and Exchange Commission for $1 billion of debt securities. The Company has a medium-term note program under the shelf registration ("medium-term note program") that allows the Company to issue up to $500 million in medium-term notes. The Company has issued $240 million in medium-term notes under this program. During the years ended May 31, 2007 and 2006, no notes were issued under the medium-term note program. The issued notes have coupon rates that range from 4.70% to 5.66%. The maturities range from July 9, 2007 to October 15, 2015. For each of these notes, except for the swap for the $50 million note maturing October 1, 2013, the Company has entered into interest rate swap agreements whereby the Company receives fixed interest payments at the same rate as the notes and pays variable interest payments based on the three-month or six-month LIBOR plus a spread. Each swap has the same notional amount and maturity date as the corresponding note. The swap for the $50 million note maturing October 1, 2013, expired October 2, 2006. At May 31, 2007, the interest rates payable on these swap agreements range from approximately 5.2% to 5.9%.

In June 1996, one of the Company's Japanese subsidiaries, NIKE Logistics YK, borrowed 10.5 billion Japanese yen in a private placement with a maturity of June 26, 2011. Interest is paid semi-annually. The agreement provides for early retirement after year ten.

In July 1999, NIKE Logistics YK assumed 13.0 billion in Japanese yen loans as part of its agreement to purchase a distribution center in Japan, which serves as collateral for the loans. These loans mature in equal quarterly installments during the period August 20, 2001 through November 20, 2020. Interest is also paid quarterly.

In February 2007, NIKE Logistics YK entered into a 5.0 billion yen (approximately $41.1 million at May 31, 2007) term loan maturing February 14, 2012 that replaces certain intercompany borrowings. The interest rate on the loan is approximately 1.5% and interest is paid semi-annually.

Amounts of long-term debt maturities in each of the years ending May 31, 2008 through 2012 are $30.5 million, $5.5 million, $30.5 million, $5.5 million and $133.0 million, respectively.

Note 8 — Income Taxes

Income before income taxes is as follows:

	Year Ended May 31,		
	2007	2006	2005
		(In millions)	
Income before income taxes:			
United States	$ 805.1	$ 838.6	$ 755.5
Foreign	1,394.8	1,303.0	1,104.3
	$2,199.9	$2,141.6	$1,859.8

NIKE, INC.

NOTES TO CONSOLIDATED FINANCIAL STATEMENTS — (Continued)

The provision for income taxes is as follows:

| | Year Ended May 31, | | |
	2007	2006	2005
		(In millions)	
Current:			
United States			
Federal	$352.6	$359.0	$279.6
State	59.6	60.6	50.7
Foreign	261.9	356.0	292.5
	674.1	775.6	622.8
Deferred:			
United States			
Federal	38.7	(4.2)	21.9
State	(4.8)	(6.8)	(5.3)
Foreign	0.4	(15.0)	8.8
	34.3	(26.0)	25.4
	$708.4	$749.6	$648.2

Deferred tax (assets) and liabilities are comprised of the following:

| | May 31, | |
	2007	2006
	(In millions)	
Deferred tax assets:		
Allowance for doubtful accounts	$ (12.4)	$ (10.9)
Inventories	(45.8)	(43.9)
Sales return reserves	(42.1)	(39.4)
Deferred compensation	(132.5)	(110.6)
Stock-based compensation	(30.3)	—
Reserves and accrued liabilities	(46.2)	(50.6)
Property, plant, and equipment	(16.3)	(28.6)
Foreign loss carryforwards	(37.5)	(29.2)
Foreign tax credit carryforwards	(3.4)	(9.5)
Hedges	(26.2)	(25.5)
Other	(33.0)	(29.1)
Total deferred tax assets	(425.7)	(377.3)
Valuation allowance	42.3	36.6
Total deferred tax assets after valuation allowance	(383.4)	(340.7)
Deferred tax liabilities:		
Undistributed earnings of foreign subsidiaries	232.6	135.3
Property, plant and equipment	66.1	91.4
Intangibles	97.2	96.8
Hedges	2.5	7.8
Other	17.8	12.5
Total deferred tax liabilities	416.2	343.8
Net deferred tax liability	$ 32.8	$ 3.1

64

NIKE, INC.

NOTES TO CONSOLIDATED FINANCIAL STATEMENTS — (Continued)

A reconciliation from the U.S. statutory federal income tax rate to the effective income tax rate follows:

	Year Ended May 31,		
	2007	**2006**	**2005**
Federal income tax rate	35.0%	35.0%	35.0%
State taxes, net of federal benefit	1.6	1.5	1.8
Foreign earnings	(4.1)	(1.5)	(2.8)
Other, net	(0.3)	—	0.9
Effective income tax rate	32.2%	35.0%	34.9%

The effective tax rate for the year ended May 31, 2007 of 32.2% has decreased from the fiscal 2006 effective tax rate of 35%. The decrease is primarily due to a European tax agreement entered into during the three months ended November 30, 2006. The Company recorded a retroactive benefit for the European tax agreement during the year ended May 31, 2007.

During the quarter ended November 30, 2005, the Company's CEO and Board of Directors approved a domestic reinvestment plan as required by the American Jobs Creation Act of 2004 (the "Act") to repatriate $500 million of foreign earnings in fiscal 2006. The Act created a temporary incentive for U.S. multinational corporations to repatriate accumulated income earned outside the U.S. by providing an 85% dividend received deduction for certain dividends from controlled foreign corporations. A $500 million repatriation was made during the quarter ended May 31, 2006 comprised of both foreign earnings for which U.S. taxes have previously been provided and foreign earnings that had been designated as permanently reinvested. Accordingly, the provisions made did not have a material impact on the Company's income tax expense or effective tax rate for the years ended May 31, 2007, 2006 and 2005.

The Company has indefinitely reinvested approximately $1,185.0 million of the cumulative undistributed earnings of certain foreign subsidiaries. Such earnings would be subject to U.S. taxation if repatriated to the U.S. The amount of unrecognized deferred tax liability associated with the permanently reinvested cumulative undistributed earnings was approximately $248.3 million as of May 31, 2007.

Deferred tax assets at May 31, 2007 and 2006 were reduced by a valuation allowance relating to tax benefits of certain foreign subsidiaries with operating losses where it is more likely than not that the deferred tax assets will not be realized.

During the years ended May 31, 2007, 2006, and 2005, income tax benefits attributable to employee stock-based compensation transactions of $56.6 million, $54.2 million, and $63.1 million, respectively, were allocated to shareholders' equity.

Note 9 — Redeemable Preferred Stock

Sojitz America is the sole owner of the Company's authorized Redeemable Preferred Stock, $1 par value, which is redeemable at the option of Sojitz America or the Company at par value aggregating $0.3 million. A cumulative dividend of $0.10 per share is payable annually on May 31 and no dividends may be declared or paid on the common stock of the Company unless dividends on the Redeemable Preferred Stock have been declared and paid in full. There have been no changes in the Redeemable Preferred Stock in the three years ended May 31, 2007, 2006 and 2005. As the holder of the Redeemable Preferred Stock, Sojitz America does not have general voting rights but does have the right to vote as a separate class on the sale of all or substantially all of the assets of the Company and its subsidiaries, on merger, consolidation, liquidation or dissolution of the Company or on the sale or assignment of the NIKE trademark for athletic footwear sold in the United States.

NIKE, INC.

NOTES TO CONSOLIDATED FINANCIAL STATEMENTS — (Continued)

Note 10 — Common Stock

The authorized number of shares of Class A Common Stock, no par value, and Class B Common Stock, no par value, are 350 million and 1.5 billion, respectively. Each share of Class A Common Stock is convertible into one share of Class B Common Stock. Voting rights of Class B Common Stock are limited in certain circumstances with respect to the election of directors.

In 1990, the Board of Directors adopted, and the shareholders approved, the NIKE, Inc. 1990 Stock Incentive Plan (the "1990 Plan"). The 1990 Plan provides for the issuance of up to 132 million previously unissued shares of Class B Common Stock in connection with stock options and other awards granted under the plan. The 1990 Plan authorizes the grant of non-statutory stock options, incentive stock options, stock appreciation rights, stock bonuses and the issuance and sale of restricted stock. The exercise price for non-statutory stock options, stock appreciation rights and the grant price of restricted stock may not be less than 75% of the fair market value of the underlying shares on the date of grant. The exercise price for incentive stock options may not be less than the fair market value of the underlying shares on the date of grant. A committee of the Board of Directors administers the 1990 Plan. The committee has the authority to determine the employees to whom awards will be made, the amount of the awards, and the other terms and conditions of the awards. The committee has granted substantially all stock options and restricted stock at 100% of the market price on the date of grant. Substantially all stock option grants outstanding under the 1990 plan were granted in the first quarter of each fiscal year, vest ratably over four years, and expire 10 years from the date of grant.

The weighted average fair value per share of the options granted during the years ended May 31, 2007, 2006 and 2005, as computed using the Black-Scholes pricing model, was $8.80, $9.68 and $13.95, respectively. The weighted average assumptions used to estimate these fair values are as follows:

	Year Ended May 31,		
	2007	**2006**	**2005**
Dividend yield	1.6%	1%	1%
Expected volatility	19%	21%	42%
Weighted average expected life (in years)	5.0	4.5	5.0
Risk-free interest rate	5.0%	4.0%	3.7%

For the years ended May 31, 2007 and 2006, the Company estimated the expected volatility based on the implied volatility in market traded options on the Company's common stock with a term greater than one year, along with other factors. For the year ended May 31, 2005, the Company estimated the expected volatility based on the historical volatility of the Company's common stock. The weighted average expected life of options is based on an analysis of historical and expected future exercise patterns. The interest rate is based on the U.S. Treasury (constant maturity) risk-free rate in effect at the date of grant for periods corresponding with the expected term of the options.

66

NIKE, INC.

NOTES TO CONSOLIDATED FINANCIAL STATEMENTS — (Continued)

The following summarizes the stock option transactions under the plan discussed above:

	Shares (In millions)	Weighted Average Option Price
Options outstanding May 31, 2004	37.6	$ 23.71
Exercised	(8.8)	23.17
Forfeited	(0.9)	26.33
Granted	10.8	36.96
Options outstanding May 31, 2005	38.7	27.49
Exercised	(8.0)	24.68
Forfeited	(1.8)	35.75
Granted	11.5	43.68
Options outstanding May 31, 2006	40.4	32.31
Exercised	(10.7)	27.55
Forfeited	(1.6)	37.17
Granted	11.6	39.54
Options outstanding May 31, 2007	39.7	$ 35.50
Options exercisable at May 31,		
2005	14.7	$ 23.01
2006	16.6	25.68
2007	15.3	29.52

The weighted average contractual life remaining for options outstanding and options exercisable at May 31, 2007 was 7.2 years and 5.4 years, respectively. The aggregate intrinsic value for options outstanding and exercisable at May 31, 2007 was $843.7 million and $417.0 million, respectively. The aggregate intrinsic value was the amount by which the market value of the underlying stock exceeded the exercise price of the options. The total intrinsic value of the options exercised during the years ended May 31, 2007, 2006 and 2005 was $204.9 million, $144.0 million and $145.7 million, respectively.

As of May 31, 2007, the Company had $132.4 million of unrecognized compensation costs from stock options, net of estimated forfeitures, to be recognized as selling and administrative expense over a weighted average period of 2.1 years.

In addition to the 1990 Plan, the Company gives employees the right to purchase shares at a discount to the market price under employee stock purchase plans ("ESPPs"). Employees are eligible to participate through payroll deductions up to 10% of their compensation. At the end of each six-month offering period, shares are purchased by the participants at 85% of the lower of the fair market value at the beginning or the ending of the offering period. During the years ended May 31, 2007, 2006 and 2005, employees purchased 0.8 million, 0.8 million and 0.6 million shares, respectively.

From time to time, the Company grants restricted stock and unrestricted stock to key employees under the 1990 Plan. The number of shares granted to employees during the years ended May 31, 2007, 2006 and 2005 were 345,000, 141,000 and 229,000 with weighted average prices of $39.38, $43.38 and $44.65, respectively. Recipients of restricted shares are entitled to cash dividends and to vote their respective shares throughout the period of restriction. The value of all of the granted shares was established by the market price on the date of grant.

NIKE, INC.

NOTES TO CONSOLIDATED FINANCIAL STATEMENTS — (Continued)

The following table summarizes the Company's total stock-based compensation expense recognized in selling and administrative expense:

| | Year Ended May 31, | | |
	2007	2006	2005
	(in millions)		
Stock options	$134.9	$ 0.3	$1.0
ESPPs	7.0	—	—
Restricted stock[1]	5.8	11.5	3.9
Total stock-based compensation expense	$147.7	$11.8	$4.9

[1] The expense related to restricted stock awards was included in selling and administrative expense in prior years and was not affected by the adoption of FAS 123R.

During the years ended May 31, 2007, 2006 and 2005, the Company also granted shares of stock under the Long-Term Incentive Plan ("LTIP"), adopted by the Board of Directors and approved by shareholders in September 1997. The LTIP provides for the issuance of up to 2.0 million shares of Class B Common Stock. Under the LTIP, awards are made to certain executives in their choice of either cash or stock, based on performance targets established over three-year time periods. Once performance targets are achieved, cash or shares of stock are issued. The shares are immediately vested upon grant. The value of the shares is established by the market price on the date of issuance. Under the LTIP, 3,000, 6,000 and 8,000 shares with a price of $38.84, $40.79 and $34.85, respectively, were issued during the years ended May 31, 2007, 2006 and 2005 for the plan years ended May 31, 2006, 2005 and 2004, respectively. The Company recognized nominal expense related to the shares issued during the years ended May 31, 2007 and 2006, and $0.1 million during the year ended May 31, 2005. The Company recognized $30.0 million, $21.7 million and $22.1 million of selling and administrative expense related to the cash awards during the years ended May 31, 2007, 2006 and 2005, respectively. During the year ended May 31, 2007, LTIP participants agreed to amend their grant agreements to eliminate the ability to receive payments in shares of stock, so shares of stock are no longer awarded. Beginning with the plan year ended May 31, 2007, cash will be awarded if performance targets are achieved.

Note 11 — Earnings Per Share

The following represents a reconciliation from basic earnings per share to diluted earnings per share. Options to purchase an additional 9.5 million, 11.3 million and 0.5 million shares of common stock were outstanding at May 31, 2007, 2006 and 2005, respectively, but were not included in the computation of diluted earnings per share because the options were antidilutive.

| | Year Ended May 31, | | |
	2007	2006	2005
	(In millions, except per share data)		
Determination of shares:			
Weighted average common shares outstanding	503.8	518.0	525.2
Assumed conversion of dilutive stock options and awards	6.1	9.6	15.4
Diluted weighted average common shares outstanding	509.9	527.6	540.6
Basic earnings per common share	$ 2.96	$ 2.69	$ 2.31
Diluted earnings per common share	$ 2.93	$ 2.64	$ 2.24

68

NIKE, INC.

NOTES TO CONSOLIDATED FINANCIAL STATEMENTS — (Continued)

Note 12 — Benefit Plans

The Company has a profit sharing plan available to most U.S.-based employees. The terms of the plan call for annual contributions by the Company as determined by the Board of Directors. A subsidiary of the Company also has a profit sharing plan available to its U.S.-based employees. The terms of the plan call for annual contributions as determined by the subsidiary's executive management. Contributions of $31.8 million, $33.2 million, and $29.1 million were made to the plans and are included in selling and administrative expenses in the consolidated financial statements for the years ended May 31, 2007, 2006 and 2005, respectively. The Company has various 401(k) employee savings plans available to U.S.-based employees. The Company matches a portion of employee contributions with common stock or cash. Company contributions to the savings plans were $24.9 million, $22.5 million, and $20.3 million for the years ended May 31, 2007, 2006 and 2005, respectively, and are included in selling and administrative expenses.

The Company has pension plans in various countries worldwide. The pension plans are only available to local employees and are generally government mandated. Upon adoption of FAS 158, "Employers' Accounting for Defined Benefit Pension and Other Postretirement Plans" on May 31, 2007, the Company recorded a liability of $17.6 million related to the unfunded pension liabilities of the plans.

Note 13 — Comprehensive Income

Comprehensive income is as follows:

	Year Ended May 31,		
	2007	**2006**	**2005**
		(In millions)	
Net income	$1,491.5	$1,392.0	$1,211.6
Other comprehensive income:			
Change in cumulative translation adjustment and other (net of tax (expense) benefit of ($5.4) in 2007, $19.7 in 2006, and $3.9 in 2005)	84.6	87.1	70.1
Changes due to cash flow hedging instruments (Note 16):			
Net loss on hedge derivatives (net of tax benefit of $9.5 in 2007, $2.8 in 2006 and $28.7 in 2005)	(38.1)	(5.6)	(54.0)
Reclassification to net income of previously deferred losses and (gains) related to hedge derivatives (net of tax expense (benefit) of ($3.6) in 2007, $15.3 in 2006 and ($72.8) in 2005)	21.4	(33.2)	143.6
Other comprehensive income	67.9	48.3	159.7
Total comprehensive income	$1,559.4	$1,440.3	$1,371.3

The components of accumulated other comprehensive income are as follows:

	May 31,	
	2007	**2006**
	(In millions)	
Cumulative translation adjustment and other[1]	$234.3	$161.9
Net deferred loss on hedge derivatives	(56.9)	(40.2)
	$177.4	$121.7

---

[1] Cumulative translation adjustment and other for the year ended May 31, 2007 includes a $12.2 million net-of-tax adjustment relating to the adoption of FAS 158. See Note 12 for additional details.

NIKE, INC.

NOTES TO CONSOLIDATED FINANCIAL STATEMENTS — (Continued)

Note 14 — Commitments and Contingencies

The Company leases space for certain of its offices, warehouses and retail stores under leases expiring from one to twenty-seven years after May 31, 2007. Rent expense was $285.2 million, $252.0 million and $232.6 million for the years ended May 31, 2007, 2006 and 2005, respectively. Amounts of minimum future annual rental commitments under non-cancelable operating leases in each of the five years ending May 31, 2008 through 2012 are $260.9 million, $219.9 million, $183.3 million, $156.7 million, $128.4 million, respectively, and $587.0 million in later years.

As of May 31, 2007 and 2006, the Company had letters of credit outstanding totaling $165.9 million and $347.6 million, respectively. These letters of credit were generally issued for the purchase of inventory.

In connection with various contracts and agreements, the Company provides routine indemnifications relating to the enforceability of intellectual property rights, coverage for legal issues that arise and other items that fall under the scope of FASB Interpretation No. 45, "Guarantor's Accounting and Disclosure Requirements for Guarantees, Including Indirect Guarantees of Indebtedness of Others." Currently, the Company has several such agreements in place. However, based on the Company's historical experience and the estimated probability of future loss, the Company has determined that the fair value of such indemnifications is not material to the Company's financial position or results of operations.

In the ordinary course of its business, the Company is involved in various legal proceedings involving contractual and employment relationships, product liability claims, trademark rights, and a variety of other matters. The Company does not believe there are any pending legal proceedings that will have a material impact on the Company's financial position or results of operations.

Note 15 — Acquisitions

In August 2004, the Company acquired 100% of the equity interests in Official Starter LLC and Official Starter Properties LLC (collectively "Official Starter"). The Exeter Brands Group LLC, a wholly-owned subsidiary of the Company, was formed soon thereafter to develop the Company's business in retail channels serving value-conscious consumers and to operate the Official Starter business. The acquisition was accounted for under the purchase method of accounting. The cash purchase price, including acquisition costs net of cash acquired, was $47.2 million. All assets and liabilities of Exeter Brands Group were initially recorded in the Company's Consolidated Balance Sheet based on their estimated fair values at the date of acquisition. The results of Exeter Brands Group's operations have been included in the consolidated financial statements since the date of acquisition as part of the Company's Other operating segment. The pro forma effect of the acquisition on the combined results of operations was not significant.

Note 16 — Risk Management and Derivatives

The Company is exposed to global market risks, including the effect of changes in foreign currency exchange rates and interest rates. The Company uses derivatives to manage financial exposures that occur in the normal course of business. The Company does not hold or issue derivatives for trading purposes.

The Company formally documents all relationships between hedging instruments and hedged items, as well as its risk-management objective and strategy for undertaking hedge transactions. This process includes linking all derivatives to either specific assets and liabilities on the balance sheet or specific firm commitments or forecasted transactions.

NIKE, INC.

NOTES TO CONSOLIDATED FINANCIAL STATEMENTS — (Continued)

Substantially all derivatives outstanding as of May 31, 2007 and 2006 are designated as either cash flow or fair value hedges. All derivatives are recognized on the balance sheet at their fair value. Unrealized gain positions are recorded as other current assets or other non-current assets, depending on the instrument's maturity date. Unrealized loss positions are recorded as accrued liabilities or other non-current liabilities. All changes in fair values of outstanding cash flow hedge derivatives, except the ineffective portion, are recorded in other comprehensive income, until net income is affected by the variability of cash flows of the hedged transaction. Fair value hedges are recorded in net income and are offset by the change in fair value of the underlying asset or liability being hedged.

Cash Flow Hedges

The purpose of the Company's foreign currency hedging activities is to protect the Company from the risk that the eventual cash flows resulting from transactions in foreign currencies, including revenues, product costs, selling and administrative expenses, investments in U.S. dollar-denominated available-for-sale debt securities and intercompany transactions, including intercompany borrowings, will be adversely affected by changes in exchange rates. It is the Company's policy to utilize derivatives to reduce foreign exchange risks where internal netting strategies cannot be effectively employed.

Derivatives used by the Company to hedge foreign currency exchange risks are forward exchange contracts and options. Hedged transactions are denominated primarily in euros, British pounds, Japanese yen, Korean won, Canadian dollars and Mexican pesos. The Company hedges up to 100% of anticipated exposures typically twelve months in advance, but has hedged as much as 32 months in advance. When intercompany loans are hedged, it is typically for their expected duration.

Substantially all foreign currency derivatives outstanding as of May 31, 2007 and 2006 qualify for and are designated as foreign-currency cash flow hedges, including those hedging foreign currency denominated firm commitments.

Changes in fair values of outstanding cash flow hedge derivatives, except the ineffective portion, are recorded in other comprehensive income, until net income is affected by the variability of cash flows of the hedged transaction. In most cases amounts recorded in other comprehensive income will be released to net income some time after the maturity of the related derivative. The consolidated statement of income classification of effective hedge results is the same as that of the underlying exposure. Results of hedges of revenue and product costs are recorded in revenue and cost of sales, respectively, when the underlying hedged transaction affects net income. Results of hedges of selling and administrative expense are recorded together with those costs when the related expense is recorded. Results of hedges of anticipated purchases and sales of U.S. dollar-denominated available-for-sale securities are recorded in other (income) expense, net when the securities are sold.

Results of hedges of anticipated intercompany transactions are recorded in other (income) expense, net when the transaction occurs. Hedges of recorded balance sheet positions are recorded in other (income) expense, net currently together with the transaction gain or loss from the hedged balance sheet position. Net foreign currency transaction gains and losses, which includes hedge results captured in revenues, cost of sales, selling and administrative expense and other (income) expense, net, were a $27.9 million loss, a $49.9 million gain, and a $217.8 million loss for the years ended May 31, 2007, 2006, and 2005, respectively.

Premiums paid on options are initially recorded as deferred charges. The Company assesses effectiveness on options based on the total cash flows method and records total changes in the options' fair value to other comprehensive income to the degree they are effective.

71

NIKE, INC.

NOTES TO CONSOLIDATED FINANCIAL STATEMENTS — (Continued)

As of May 31, 2007, $52.8 million of deferred net losses (net of tax) on both outstanding and matured derivatives accumulated in other comprehensive income are expected to be reclassified to net income during the next twelve months as a result of underlying hedged transactions also being recorded in net income. Actual amounts ultimately reclassified to net income are dependent on the exchange rates in effect when derivative contracts that are currently outstanding mature. As of May 31, 2007, the maximum term over which the Company is hedging exposures to the variability of cash flows for all forecasted and recorded transactions is 18 months.

The Company formally assesses, both at a hedge's inception and on an ongoing basis, whether the derivatives that are used in the hedging transaction have been highly effective in offsetting changes in the cash flows of hedged items and whether those derivatives may be expected to remain highly effective in future periods. When it is determined that a derivative is not, or has ceased to be, highly effective as a hedge, the Company discontinues hedge accounting prospectively.

The Company discontinues hedge accounting prospectively when (1) it determines that the derivative is no longer highly effective in offsetting changes in the cash flows of a hedged item (including hedged items such as firm commitments or forecasted transactions); (2) the derivative expires or is sold, terminated, or exercised; (3) it is no longer probable that the forecasted transaction will occur; or (4) management determines that designating the derivative as a hedging instrument is no longer appropriate.

When the Company discontinues hedge accounting because it is no longer probable that the forecasted transaction will occur in the originally expected period, the gain or loss on the derivative remains in accumulated other comprehensive income and is reclassified to net income when the forecasted transaction affects net income. However, if it is probable that a forecasted transaction will not occur by the end of the originally specified time period or within an additional two-month period of time thereafter, the gains and losses that were accumulated in other comprehensive income will be recognized immediately in net income. In all situations in which hedge accounting is discontinued and the derivative remains outstanding, the Company will carry the derivative at its fair value on the balance sheet, recognizing future changes in the fair value in other (income) expense, net. Any hedge ineffectiveness is recorded in other (income) expense, net. Effectiveness for cash flow hedges is assessed based on forward rates.

For each of the years ended May 31, 2007, 2006 and 2005, the Company recorded in other (income) expense, net an insignificant loss representing the total ineffectiveness of all derivatives. Net income for each of the years ended May 31, 2007, 2006 and 2005 was not materially affected due to discontinued hedge accounting.

Fair Value Hedges

The Company is also exposed to the risk of changes in the fair value of certain fixed-rate debt attributable to changes in interest rates. Derivatives currently used by the Company to hedge this risk are receive-fixed, pay-variable interest rate swaps.

Substantially all interest rate swap agreements are designated as fair value hedges of the related long-term debt and meet the shortcut method requirements under FAS 133. Accordingly, changes in the fair values of the interest rate swap agreements are exactly offset by changes in the fair value of the underlying long-term debt. No ineffectiveness has been recorded to net income related to interest rate swaps designated as fair value hedges for the years ended May 31, 2007, 2006 and 2005.

As discussed in Note 7, during the year ended May 31, 2004, the Company issued a $50 million medium-term note maturing October 1, 2013 and simultaneously entered into a receive-fixed, pay-variable interest rate swap with the same notional amount and fixed interest rate as the note. However, the swap expired

NIKE, INC.

NOTES TO CONSOLIDATED FINANCIAL STATEMENTS — (Continued)

October 2, 2006. This interest rate swap was not accounted for as a fair value hedge. Accordingly, changes in the fair value of the swap were recorded to net income each period as a component of other (income) expense, net. The change in the fair value of the swap was not material for the years ended May 31, 2007, 2006 and 2005.

In fiscal 2003, the Company entered into an interest rate swap agreement related to a Japanese yen denominated intercompany loan with one of the Company's Japanese subsidiaries. The Japanese subsidiary pays variable interest on the intercompany loan based on 3-month LIBOR plus a spread. Under the interest rate swap agreement, the subsidiary pays fixed interest payments at 0.8% and receives variable interest payments based on 3-month LIBOR plus a spread based on a notional amount of 8 billion Japanese yen. This interest rate swap is not accounted for as a fair value hedge. Accordingly, changes in the fair value of the swap are recorded to net income each period as a component of other (income) expense, net. The change in the fair value of the swap was not material for the years ended May 31, 2007, 2006 and 2005.

The fair values of all derivatives recorded on the consolidated balance sheet are as follows:

	May 31,	
	2007	2006
	(In millions)	
Unrealized Gains:		
Foreign currency exchange contracts and options	$ 43.5	$ 75.7
Interest rate swaps	0.5	0.9
Unrealized (Losses):		
Foreign currency exchange contracts and options	(90.6)	(122.2)
Interest rate swaps	(2.6)	(6.0)

Concentration of Credit Risk

The Company is exposed to credit-related losses in the event of non-performance by counterparties to hedging instruments. The counterparties to all derivative transactions are major financial institutions with investment grade credit ratings. However, this does not eliminate the Company's exposure to credit risk with these institutions. This credit risk is generally limited to the unrealized gains in such contracts should any of these counterparties fail to perform as contracted. To manage this risk, the Company has established strict counterparty credit guidelines that are continually monitored and reported to senior management according to prescribed guidelines. The Company utilizes a portfolio of financial institutions either headquartered or operating in the same countries the Company conducts its business. As a result of the above considerations, the Company considers the risk of counterparty default to be minimal.

In addition to hedging instruments, the Company is subject to concentrations of credit risk associated with cash and equivalents and accounts receivable. The Company places cash and equivalents with financial institutions with investment grade credit ratings and, by policy, limits the amount of credit exposure to any one financial institution. The Company considers its concentration risk related to accounts receivable to be mitigated by the Company's credit policy, the significance of outstanding balances owed by each individual customer at any point in time and the geographic dispersion of these customers.

Note 17 — Operating Segments and Related Information

Operating Segments.   The Company's operating segments are evidence of the structure of the Company's internal organization. The major segments are defined by geographic regions for operations participating in NIKE brand sales activity excluding NIKE Golf and NIKE Bauer Hockey. Each NIKE brand geographic segment operates predominantly in one industry: the design, production, marketing and selling of sports and fitness

73

NIKE, INC.

NOTES TO CONSOLIDATED FINANCIAL STATEMENTS — (Continued)

footwear, apparel, and equipment. The "Other" category shown below represents activities of Cole Haan, Converse, Exeter Brands Group (beginning August 11, 2004), Hurley, NIKE Bauer Hockey, and NIKE Golf, which are considered immaterial for individual disclosure based on the aggregation criteria in SFAS No. 131 "Disclosures about Segments of an Enterprise and Related Information".

Where applicable, "Corporate" represents items necessary to reconcile to the consolidated financial statements, which generally include corporate activity and corporate eliminations.

Net revenues as shown below represent sales to external customers for each segment. Intercompany revenues have been eliminated and are immaterial for separate disclosure. The Company evaluates performance of individual operating segments based on pre-tax income. On a consolidated basis, this amount represents income before income taxes as shown in the Consolidated Statements of Income. Reconciling items for pre-tax income represent corporate costs that are not allocated to the operating segments for management reporting including corporate activity, certain currency exchange rate gains and losses on transactions and intercompany eliminations for specific income statement items in the Consolidated Statements of Income.

Additions to long-lived assets as presented in the following table represent capital expenditures.

74

NIKE, INC.

NOTES TO CONSOLIDATED FINANCIAL STATEMENTS — (Continued)

Accounts receivable, inventories and property, plant and equipment for operating segments are regularly reviewed by management and are therefore provided below.

Certain prior year amounts have been reclassed to conform to fiscal 2007 presentation.

	Year Ended May 31,		
	2007	2006	2005
	(In millions)		
Net Revenue			
United States	$ 6,107.1	$ 5,722.5	$ 5,129.3
Europe, Middle East and Africa	4,723.3	4,326.6	4,281.6
Asia Pacific	2,283.4	2,053.8	1,897.3
Americas	952.5	904.9	695.8
Other	2,259.6	1,947.1	1,735.7
	$16,325.9	$14,954.9	$13,739.7
Pre-tax Income			
United States	$ 1,300.3	$ 1,244.5	$ 1,127.9
Europe, Middle East and Africa	1,000.7	960.7	917.5
Asia Pacific	483.7	412.5	399.8
Americas	187.4	172.6	116.5
Other	303.7	153.6	154.8
Corporate	(1,075.9)	(802.3)	(856.7)
	$ 2,199.9	$ 2,141.6	$ 1,859.8
Additions to Long-lived Assets			
United States	$ 67.3	$ 59.8	$ 54.8
Europe, Middle East and Africa	94.9	73.6	38.8
Asia Pacific	20.7	16.8	22.0
Americas	5.3	6.9	6.8
Other	36.0	33.2	31.3
Corporate	89.3	143.4	103.4
	$ 313.5	$ 333.7	$ 257.1
Depreciation			
United States	$ 45.4	$ 54.2	$ 49.0
Europe, Middle East and Africa	47.4	46.9	45.2
Asia Pacific	25.2	28.4	28.3
Americas	6.1	6.4	4.0
Other	28.2	29.0	28.5
Corporate	117.4	117.1	102.2
	$ 269.7	$ 282.0	$ 257.2

75

NIKE, INC.

NOTES TO CONSOLIDATED FINANCIAL STATEMENTS — (Continued)

	Year Ended May 31,		
	2007	2006	2005
	(In millions)		
Accounts Receivable, net			
United States	$ 806.8	$ 717.2	$ 627.0
Europe, Middle East and Africa	739.1	703.3	711.4
Asia Pacific	296.6	319.7	309.8
Americas	184.1	174.5	168.7
Other	404.9	410.0	394.0
Corporate	63.2	58.2	39.0
	$2,494.7	$2,382.9	$2,249.9
Inventories			
United States	$ 796.0	$ 725.9	$ 639.9
Europe, Middle East and Africa	554.5	590.1	496.5
Asia Pacific	214.1	238.3	228.9
Americas	132.0	147.6	96.8
Other	378.7	330.5	316.2
Corporate	46.6	44.3	32.8
	$2,121.9	$2,076.7	$1,811.1
Property, Plant and Equipment, net			
United States	$ 232.7	$ 219.3	$ 216.0
Europe, Middle East and Africa	325.4	266.6	230.0
Asia Pacific	326.1	354.8	380.4
Americas	16.9	17.0	15.7
Other	103.6	98.2	93.4
Corporate	673.6	701.8	670.3
	$1,678.3	$1,657.7	$1,605.8

Revenues by Major Product Lines.   Revenues to external customers for NIKE brand products are attributable to sales of footwear, apparel and equipment. Other revenues to external customers primarily include external sales by Cole Haan Holdings Incorporated, Converse Inc., Exeter Brands Group LLC (beginning August 11, 2004), Hurley International LLC, NIKE Bauer Hockey Corp., and NIKE Golf.

	Year Ended May 31,		
	2007	2006	2005
	(In millions)		
Footwear	$ 8,514.0	$ 7,965.9	$ 7,299.7
Apparel	4,576.5	4,168.0	3,879.4
Equipment	975.8	873.9	824.9
Other	2,259.6	1,947.1	1,735.7
	$16,325.9	$14,954.9	$13,739.7

Revenues and Long-Lived Assets by Geographic Area.   Geographical area information is similar to that shown previously under operating segments with the exception of the Other activity, which has been allocated to the geographical areas based on the location where the sales originated. Revenues derived in the United States were $7,593.7 million, $7,019.0 million, and $6,284.5 million, for the years ended May 31, 2007, 2006, and

76

NIKE, INC.

NOTES TO CONSOLIDATED FINANCIAL STATEMENTS — (Continued)

2005, respectively. The Company's largest concentrations of long-lived assets are in the United States and Japan. Long-lived assets attributable to operations in the United States, which are comprised of net property, plant & equipment were $991.3 million, $998.2 million, and $956.6 million at May 31, 2007, 2006, and 2005, respectively. Long-lived assets attributable to operations in Japan were $260.6 million, $296.3 million, and $321.0 million at May 31, 2007, 2006, and 2005, respectively.

Major Customers.   During the years ended May 31, 2007, 2006 and 2005, revenues derived from Foot Locker, Inc. represented 10 percent, 10 percent and 11 percent of the Company's consolidated revenues, respectively. Sales to this customer are included in all segments of the Company.

Chapter 11

Expanded Analysis

This chapter reviews special areas related to the usefulness of ratios and financial analyses. These special areas are as follows: (1) financial ratios as perceived by commercial loan departments, (2) financial ratios as perceived by corporate controllers, (3) financial ratios as perceived by certified public accountants, (4) financial ratios as perceived by chartered financial analysts, (5) financial ratios used in annual reports, (6) degree of conservatism and quality of earnings, (7) forecasting financial failure, (8) analytical review procedures, (9) management's use of analysis, (10) use of LIFO reserves, (11) graphing financial information, (12) management of earnings, (13) valuation.

Financial Ratios as Perceived by Commercial Loan Departments

Financial ratios can be used by a commercial loan department to aid the loan officers in deciding whether to grant a commercial loan and in maintaining control of a loan once it is granted.[1] In order to gain insights into how commercial loan departments view financial ratios, a questionnaire was sent to the commercial loan departments of the 100 largest banks in the United States. Usable responses were received from 44% of them.

A list of 59 financial ratios was drawn from financial literature, textbooks, and published industry data for this study. The study set three objectives: (1) the significance of each ratio, in the opinion of commercial loan officers, (2) how frequently each ratio is included in loan agreements, and (3) what a specific financial ratio primarily measures, in the opinion of commercial loan officers. For the primary measure, the choices were liquidity, long-term debt-paying ability, profitability, or other. Exhibit 11-1 lists the ratios included in this study.

MOST SIGNIFICANT RATIOS AND THEIR PRIMARY MEASURE

Exhibit 11-2 displays the 10 financial ratios given the highest significance rating by the commercial loan officers, as well as the primary measure of these ratios. The highest rating is a 9, and the lowest rating is a 0.

Most of the ratios given a high significance rating were regarded primarily as measures of liquidity or debt. Only 2 of the top 10 ratios measure profitability, 5 measure debt, and

Exhibit	11-1	RATIOS RATED BY COMMERCIAL LOAN OFFICERS

Ratio	Ratio
Cash ratio	Sales/fixed assets
Accounts receivable turnover in days	Sales/working capital
Accounts receivable turnover—times per year	Sales/net worth
Days' sales in receivables	Cash/sales
Quick ratio	Quick assets/sales
Inventory turnover in days	Current assets/sales
Inventory turnover—times per year	Return on assets:
Days' sales in inventory	before interest and tax
Current debt/inventory	before tax
Inventory/current assets	after tax
Inventory/working capital	Return on operating assets
Current ratio	Return on total invested:
Inventory/current assets	before tax
Inventory/working capital	after tax
Current ratio	Return on equity:
Net fixed assets/tangible net worth	before tax
Cash/total assets	after tax
Quick assets/total assets	Net profit margin:
Current assets/total assets	before tax
Retained earnings/total assets	after tax
Debt/equity ratio	Retained earnings/net income
Total debt as a % of net working capital	Cash flow/current maturities of
Total debt/total assets	long-term debt
Short-term debt as a % of total invested capital	Cash flow/total debt
Long-term debt as a % of total invested capital	Times interest earned
Funded debt/working capital	Fixed charge coverage
Total equity/total assets	Degree of operating leverage
Fixed assets/equity	Degree of financial leverage
Common equity as a % of total invested capital	Earnings per share
Current debt/net worth	Book value per share
Net worth at market value/total liabilities	Dividend payout ratio
Total asset turnover	Dividend yield
Sales/operating assets	Price/earnings ratio
	Stock price as a % of book value

Exhibit	11-2	COMMERCIAL LOAN DEPARTMENTS

Most Significant Ratios and Their Primary Measures

Ratio	Significance Rating	Primary Measure
Debt/equity	8.71	Debt
Current ratio	8.25	Liquidity
Cash flow/current maturities of long-term debt	8.08	Debt
Fixed charge coverage	7.58	Debt
Net profit margin after tax	7.56	Profitability
Times interest earned	7.50	Debt
Net profit margin before tax	7.43	Profitability
Degree of financial leverage	7.33	Debt
Inventory turnover in days	7.25	Liquidity
Accounts receivable turnover in days	7.08	Liquidity

3 measure liquidity. The two profitability ratios were two different computations of the net profit margin: (1) net profit margin after tax and (2) net profit margin before tax. Two of the top three ratios were measures of debt, and the other was a measure of liquidity. The debt/equity ratio was given the highest significance rating, with the current ratio second highest. We can assume that the financial ratios rated most significant by commercial loan officers would have the greatest influence on a loan decision.

RATIOS APPEARING MOST FREQUENTLY IN LOAN AGREEMENTS

A commercial bank may elect to include a ratio as part of a loan agreement. This would be a way of using ratios to control an outstanding loan. Exhibit 11-3 contains a list of the 10 financial ratios that appear most frequently in loan agreements, along with an indication of what each ratio primarily measures. For the two ratios that do not have a primary measure indicated, there was no majority opinion as to what the ratio primarily measured. Six of the ratios that appear most frequently in loan agreements primarily measure debt, two primarily measure liquidity, and none primarily measure profitability.

Exhibit 11-3	COMMERCIAL LOAN DEPARTMENTS

Ratios Appearing Most Frequently in Loan Agreements

Ratio	Percentage of Banks Including Ratio in 26% or More of Their Loan Agreements	Primary Measure
Debt/equity	92.5	Debt
Current ratio	90.0	Liquidity
Dividend payout ratio	70.0	*
Cash flow/current maturities of long-term debt	60.3	Debt
Fixed charge coverage	55.2	Debt
Times interest earned	52.6	Debt
Degree of financial leverage	44.7	Debt
Equity/assets	41.0	*
Cash flow/total debt	36.1	Debt
Quick ratio	33.3	Liquidity

*No majority primary measure indicated in this survey.

The two top ratios, debt/equity and current ratio, were given the highest significance rating. The dividend payout ratio was the third most likely ratio to appear in loan agreements, but it was not rated as a highly significant ratio. Logically, this ratio appears in loan agreements as a means of controlling outflow of cash for dividends.

Financial Ratios as Perceived by Corporate Controllers

To get the views of corporate controllers on important issues relating to financial ratios, a questionnaire was sent to the controllers of the companies included in the *Fortune 500* list of the largest industrials.[2] The study excluded companies 100% owned or controlled by another firm. The survey received a usable response rate of 19.42%. The questionnaire used the same ratios used for the commercial loan department survey. Three objectives of this study were the determination of: (1) the significance of a specific ratio as perceived by controllers, (2) which financial ratios are included as corporate objectives, and (3) the primary measure of each ratio.

MOST SIGNIFICANT RATIOS AND THEIR PRIMARY MEASURE

Exhibit 11-4 displays the 10 financial ratios given the highest significance rating by the corporate controllers, along with the primary measure of these ratios. The highest rating is a 9 and the lowest is a 0.

The financial executives gave the profitability ratios the highest significance ratings. The highest rated debt ratio was debt/equity, while the highest rated liquidity ratio was the current ratio. In comparing the responses of the commercial loan officers and the controllers,

| Exhibit | 11-4 | CORPORATE CONTROLLERS |

Most Significant Ratios and Their Primary Measures

Ratio	Significance Rating	Primary Measure
Earnings per share	8.19	Profitability
Return on equity after tax	7.83	Profitability
Net profit margin after tax	7.47	Profitability
Debt/equity ratio	7.46	Debt
Net profit margin before tax	7.41	Profitability
Return on total invested capital after tax	7.20	Profitability
Return on assets after tax	6.97	Profitability
Dividend payout ratio	6.83	Other*
Price/earnings ratio	6.81	Other*
Current ratio	6.71	Liquidity

*Primary measure indicated to be other than liquidity, debt, or profitability. The ratios rated this way tend to be related to stock analysis.

the controllers rate the profitability ratios as having the highest significance, while the commercial loan officers rate the debt and liquidity ratios highest.

KEY FINANCIAL RATIOS INCLUDED AS CORPORATE OBJECTIVES

Many firms have selected key financial ratios to be included as part of their corporate objectives. The next section of the survey was designed to determine what ratios the firms used in their corporate objectives. Exhibit 11-5 lists the 10 ratios most likely to be included in corporate objectives according to the controllers. Nine of the ratios included in Exhibit 11-5 were also included in Exhibit 11-4. One ratio, accounts receivable turnover in days, appears in the top 10 ratios in relation to corporate objectives but not in the top 10 significant ratios. One ratio, the price/earnings ratio, appears in the top 10 ratios in relation to significance but not in the top 10 ratios used for corporate objectives.

| Exhibit | 11-5 | RATIOS APPEARING IN CORPORATE OBJECTIVES AND THEIR PRIMARY MEASURES |

Ratio	Percentage of Firms Indicating That the Ratio Was Included in Corporate Objectives	Primary Measure
Earnings per share	80.6	Profitability
Debt/equity ratio	68.8	Debt
Return on equity after tax	68.5	Profitability
Current ratio	62.0	Liquidity
Net profit margin after tax	60.9	Profitability
Dividend payout ratio	54.3	Other
Return on total invested capital after tax	53.3	Profitability
Net profit margin before tax	52.2	Profitability
Accounts receivable turnover in days	47.3	Liquidity
Return on assets after tax	47.3	Profitability

Logically, there would be a high correlation between the ratios rated as highly significant and those included in corporate objectives. The debt/equity ratio and the current ratio are rated higher on the objectives list than on the significance list. This makes sense since a firm has to have some balance in its objectives between liquidity, debt, and profitability.

Financial Ratios as Perceived by Certified Public Accountants

A questionnaire was sent to one-third of the members of The Ohio Society of Certified Public Accountants who were registered as a partner in a CPA firm.[3] A total of 495 questionnaires were sent and the usable response rate was 18.8%.

This questionnaire used the same ratios as were used for the commercial loan department and corporate controllers. The specific objectives of this study were to determine the following from the viewpoint of the CPA:

1. The specific financial ratios that CPAs view primarily as a measure of liquidity, debt, and profitability.
2. The relative importance of the financial ratios viewed as a measure of liquidity, debt, or profitability.

Exhibit 11-6 displays the 10 financial ratios given the highest significance rating by the CPAs and the primary measure of these ratios. The highest rating is a 9 and the lowest is a 0.

Exhibit 11-6	CPAs	
Most Significant Ratios and Their Primary Measures		
Ratio	**Significance Rating**	**Primary Measure**
Current ratio	7.10	Liquidity
Accounts receivable turnover in days	6.94	Liquidity
After-tax return on equity	6.79	Profitability
Debt/equity ratio	6.78	Debt
Quick ratio (acid-test)	6.77	Liquidity
Net profit margin after tax	6.67	Profitability
Net profit margin before tax	6.63	Profitability
Return on assets after tax	6.39	Profitability
Return on total invested capital after tax	6.30	Profitability
Inventory turnover in days	6.09	Liquidity

The CPAs gave the highest significance rating to two liquidity ratios—the current ratio and the accounts receivable turnover in days. The highest rated profitability ratio was after-tax return on equity, and the highest rated debt ratio was debt/equity.

Financial Ratios as Perceived by Chartered Financial Analysts[4]

Exhibit 11-7 displays the 10 financial ratios given the highest significance rating by chartered financial analysts (CFAs) and the primary measure of these ratios. Again, the highest rating is a 9 and the lowest rating is a 0.

The surveyed CFAs gave the highest significance ratings to profitability ratios, with the exception of the price/earnings ratio. Return on equity after tax received the highest significance by a wide margin. Four of the next five most significant ratios were also profitability ratios—earnings per share, net profit margin after tax, return on equity before tax, and net profit margin before tax.

The price/earnings ratio—categorized by the analysts as an "other" measure—received the second highest significance rating. CFAs apparently view profitability and what is being paid for those profits before turning to liquidity and debt.

The two highest rated debt ratios were fixed charge coverage and times interest earned, rated seventh and tenth, respectively. Both of these ratios indicate a firm's ability to carry debt. The highest rated debt ratio relating to the balance sheet was the debt/equity ratio, rated as the eleventh most significant. Surprisingly, more significance was placed on debt ratios relating to the ability to carry debt than on those relating to the ability to meet debt obligations.

Exhibit	11-7	CHARTERED FINANCIAL ANALYSTS

Most Significant Ratios and Their Primary Measures

Ratio	Significance Rating	Primary Measure
Return on equity after tax	8.21	Profitability
Price/earnings ratio	7.65	*
Earnings per share	7.58	Profitability
Net profit margin after tax	7.52	Profitability
Return on equity before tax	7.41	Profitability
Net profit margin before tax	7.32	Profitability
Fixed charge coverage	7.22	Debt
Quick ratio (acid-test)	7.10	Liquidity
Return on assets after tax	7.06	Profitability
Times interest earned	7.06	Debt

*Primary measure indicated to be other than liquidity, debt, or profitability. The ratios rated this way tend to be related to stock analysis.

The highest rated liquidity ratio was the acid-test ratio, rated eighth. The second highest liquidity ratio was the current ratio, rated twentieth.[5]

Financial Ratios Used in Annual Reports

Financial ratios are used to interpret and explain financial statements.[6] Used properly, they can be effective tools in evaluating a company's liquidity, debt position, and profitability. Probably no tool is as effective in evaluating where a company has been financially and projecting its financial future as the proper use of financial ratios.

A firm can use its annual report effectively to relate financial data by the use of financial ratios. To determine how effectively firms use ratios to communicate financial data, the annual reports of 100 firms identified in the *Fortune 500* industrial companies were reviewed. The 100 firms represented the first 20 of each 100 in the *Fortune 500* list. The objective of this research project was to determine (1) which financial ratios were frequently reported in annual reports, (2) where the ratios were disclosed in the annual reports, and (3) what computational methodology was used to compute these ratios.

Exhibit 11-8 indicates the ratios disclosed most frequently in the annual reports reviewed and the section of the annual report where the ratios were located. The locations were the president's letter, management discussion, management highlights, financial review, and financial summary. In many cases, the same ratio was located in several sections, so the numbers under the sections in Exhibit 11-8 do not add up to the total number of annual reports where the ratio was included.

Seven ratios appeared more than 50% of the time in one section or another. These ratios and the number of times found were earnings per share (100), dividends per share (98), book value per share (84), working capital (81), return on equity (62), profit margin (58), and effective tax rate (50). The current ratio was found 47 times, and the next ratio in order of disclosure, the debt/capital ratio, appeared 23 times. From this listing, we can conclude that profitability ratios and ratios related to investing were the most popular. Exhibit 11-8 excludes ratios not disclosed at least five times.

Logically, profitability ratios and ratios related to investing were the most popular for inclusion in the annual report. Including ratios related to investing in the annual report makes sense because one of the annual report's major objectives is to inform stockholders.

A review of the methodology used indicated that wide differences of opinion exist on how some of the ratios should be computed. This is especially true of the debt ratios. The two debt ratios most frequently disclosed were the debt/capital ratio and the debt/equity ratio. This book does not cover the debt/capital ratio. It is similar to the debt/equity ratio, except that the denominator includes sources of capital, in addition to stockholders' equity.

The annual reports disclosed the debt/capital ratio 23 times and used 11 different formulas. One firm used average balance sheet amounts between the beginning and the end of the year, while 22 firms used ending balance sheet figures. The debt/equity ratio was disclosed 19 times,

| Exhibit | 11-8 | RATIOS DISCLOSED MOST FREQUENTLY IN ANNUAL REPORTS* |

	Number Included	President's Letter	Management Discussion	Management Highlights	Financial Review	Financial Summary
Earnings per share	100	66	5	98	45	93
Dividends per share	98	53	10	85	49	88
Book value per share	84	10	3	53	18	63
Working capital	81	1	1	50	23	67
Return on equity	62	28	3	21	23	37
Profit margin	58	10	3	21	23	35
Effective tax rate	50	2	1	2	46	6
Current ratio	47	3	1	16	12	34
Debt/capital	23	9	0	4	14	23
Return on capital	21	6	2	8	8	5
Debt/equity	19	5	0	3	8	8
Return on assets	13	4	1	2	5	10
Dividend payout	13	3	0	0	6	6
Gross profit	12	0	1	0	11	3
Pretax margin	10	2	0	3	6	6
Total asset turnover	7	1	0	0	4	4
Price/earnings ratio	7	0	0	0	1	6
Operating margin	7	1	0	2	6	1
Labor per hour	5	0	2	2	2	2

*Numbers represent both absolute numbers and percentages, since a review was made of the financial statements of 100 firms.

and 6 different formulas were used. All firms used the ending balance sheet accounts to compute the debt/equity ratio.

In general, no major effort is being made to explain financial results by the disclosure of financial ratios in annual reports. Several financial ratios that could be interpreted as important were not disclosed or were disclosed very infrequently. This is particularly important for ratios that cannot be reasonably computed by outsiders because of a lack of data such as accounts receivable turnover.

At present, no regulatory agency such as the SEC or the FASB accepts responsibility for determining either the content of financial ratios or the format of presentation for annual reports, except for the ratio earnings per share. Many practical and theoretical issues relate to the computation of financial ratios. As long as each firm can exercise its opinion as to the practical and theoretical issues, there will be a great divergence of opinion on how a particular ratio should be computed.

Degree of Conservatism and Quality of Earnings

A review of financial statements, including the notes, indicates their conservatism in regard to accounting policies. Accounting policies that result in the slowest reporting of income are the most conservative. When a firm has conservative accounting policies, it is said that its earnings are of high quality. This section reviews a number of areas that often indicate a firm's degree of conservatism in reporting income.

INVENTORY

Under inflationary conditions, the matching of current cost against the current revenue results in the lowest income for a period of time. The LIFO inventory method follows this procedure. FIFO, the least conservative method, uses the oldest costs and matches them against revenue. Other inventory methods fall somewhere between the results of LIFO and FIFO.

For a construction firm that has long-term contracts, the two principal accounting methods that relate to inventory are the completed-contract method and the percentage-of-completion method. The conservative completed-contract method recognizes all of the income when the contract is completed; the percentage-of-completion method recognizes income as work progresses on the contract.

Fixed Assets

Two accounting decisions related to fixed assets can have a significant influence on income: the method of depreciation and the period of time selected to depreciate an asset.

The conservative methods, sum-of-the-years'-digits and declining-balance, recognize a large amount of depreciation in the early years of the asset's life. The straight-line method, the least conservative method, recognizes depreciation in equal amounts over each year of the asset's life.

Sometimes a material difference in the asset's life used for depreciation occurs between firms. Comparing the lives used for depreciation for similar firms can be a clue as to how conservative the firms are in computing depreciation. The shorter the period of time used, the lower the income.

Intangible Assets

Intangible assets include goodwill, patents, and copyrights. Research and development (R&D) costs are a type of intangible asset, but they are expensed as incurred. The shorter the period of time used to recognize the cost of the intangible asset, the more conservative the accounting. (Goodwill is not amortized.)

Some firms spend very large sums on R&D, and others spend little or nothing. Because of the requirement that R&D costs be expensed in the period incurred, the income of a firm that does considerable research is reduced substantially in the period that the cost is incurred. This results in more conservative earnings.

Pensions

Two points relating to pensions should be examined when the firm has a defined benefit plan. One is the assumed discount rate used to compute the actuarial present value of the accumulated benefit obligation and the projected benefit obligation. The higher the interest rate used, the lower the present value of the liability and the lower the immediate pension cost. The other item is the rate of compensation increase used in computing the projected benefit obligations. If the rate is too low, the projected benefit obligation is too low. If the rate is too high, the projected benefit obligation is too high.

Forecasting Financial Failure

There have been many academic studies on the use of financial ratios to forecast financial failure. Basically, these studies try to isolate individual ratios or combinations of ratios that can be observed as trends that may forecast failure.

A reliable model that can be used to forecast financial failure can also be used by management to take preventive measures. Such a model can aid investors in selecting and disposing of stocks. Banks can use it to aid in lending decisions and in monitoring loans. Firms can use it in making credit decisions and in monitoring accounts receivable. In general, many sources can use such a model to improve the allocation and control of resources. A model that forecasts financial failure can also be valuable to an auditor. It can aid in the determination of audit procedures and in making a decision as to whether the firm will remain as a going concern.

Financial failure can be described in many ways. It can mean liquidation, deferment of payments to short-term creditors, deferment of payments of interest on bonds, deferment of payments of principal on bonds, or the omission of a preferred dividend. One of the problems in examining the literature on forecasting financial failure is that different authors use different criteria to indicate failure. When reviewing the literature, always determine the criteria used to define financial failure.

This book reviews two of the studies that deal with predicting financial failure. Based on the number of references to these two studies in the literature, they appear to be particularly significant on the subject of forecasting financial failure.

UNIVARIATE MODEL

William Beaver reported his univariate model in a study published in *The Accounting Review* in January 1968.[7] A univariate model uses a single variable. Such a model would use individual financial ratios to forecast financial failure. The Beaver study classified a firm as failed when any one of the following events occurred in the 1954–1964 period: bankruptcy, bond default, an overdrawn bank account, or nonpayment of a preferred stock dividend.

Beaver paired 79 failed firms with a similar number of successful firms drawn from *Moody's Industrial Manuals*. For each failed firm in the sample, a successful one was selected from the same industry. The Beaver study indicated that the following ratios were the best for forecasting financial failure (in the order of their predictive power):

1. Cash flow/total debt
2. Net income/total assets (return on assets)
3. Total debt/total assets (debt ratio)

Beaver speculated as to the reason for these results:

> My interpretation of the finding is that the cash flow, net income, and debt positions cannot be altered and represent permanent aspects of the firm. Because failure is too costly to all involved, the permanent, rather than the short-term, factors largely determine whether or not a firm will declare bankruptcy or default on a bond payment.[8]

Assuming that the ratios identified by Beaver are valid in forecasting financial failure, it would be wise to pay particular attention to trends in these ratios when following a firm. Beaver's reasoning for seeing these ratios as valid in forecasting financial failure appears to be very sound.

These three ratios for Nike for 2007 have been computed earlier. Cash flow/total debt was 51.29%, which appears to be very good. Net income/total assets (return on assets) was 14.51%, which appears to be very good. The debt ratio was 34.27%, which is very good. Thus, Nike appears to have minimal risk of financial failure.

The Beaver study also computed the mean values of 13 financial statement items for each year before failure. Several important relationships were indicated among the liquid asset items.[9]

1. Failed firms have less cash but more accounts receivable.
2. When cash and receivables are added together, as they are in quick assets and current assets, the differences between failed and successful firms is obscured because the cash and receivables differences are working in opposite directions.
3. Failed firms tend to have less inventory.

These results indicate that particular attention should be paid to three current assets when forecasting financial failure: cash, accounts receivable, and inventory. The analyst should be alert for low cash and inventory and high accounts receivable.

MULTIVARIATE MODEL

Edward I. Altman developed a multivariate model to predict bankruptcy.[10] His model uses five financial ratios weighted in order to maximize the predictive power of the model. The model produces an overall discriminant score, called a **Z score**. The Altman model is as follows:

$$Z = .012\ X_1 + .014\ X_2 + .033\ X_3 + .006\ X_4 + .010\ X_5$$

$$X_1 = \text{Working Capital/Total Assets}$$

This computation is a measure of the net liquid assets of the firm relative to the total capitalization.

$$X_2 = \text{Retained Earnings (balance sheet)/Total Assets}$$

This variable measures cumulative profitability over time.

$$X_3 = \text{Earnings Before Interest and Taxes/Total Assets}$$

This variable measures the productivity of the firm's assets, abstracting any tax or leverage factors.

$$X_4 = \text{Market Value of Equity/Book Value of Total Debt}$$

This variable measures how much the firm's assets can decline in value before the liabilities exceed the assets and the firm becomes insolvent. Equity is measured by the combined market value of all shares of stock, preferred and common, while debt includes both current and long-term debts.

$$X_5 = \text{Sales/Total Assets}$$

This variable measures the sales-generating ability of the firm's assets.

When computing the Z score, the ratios are expressed in absolute percentage terms. Thus, X_1 (working capital/total assets) of 25% is noted as 25.

The Altman model was developed using manufacturing companies whose asset size was between $1 million and $25 million. The original sample by Altman and the test samples used the period 1946–1965. The model's accuracy in predicting bankruptcies in more recent years (1970–1973) was reported in a 1974 article.[11] Not all of the companies included in the test were manufacturing companies, although the model was initially developed by using only manufacturing companies.

With the Altman model, the lower the Z score, the more likely that the firm will go bankrupt. By computing the Z score for a firm over several years, it can be determined if the firm is moving toward a more likely or less likely position in regard to bankruptcy. In a later study that covered the period 1970–1973, a Z score of 2.675 was established as a practical cutoff point. Firms that scored below 2.675 are assumed to have characteristics similar to those of past failures.[12] Current GAAP recognizes more liabilities than the GAAP used at the time of this study. Thus, we would expect firms to score somewhat less than in the time period 1970–1973. The Altman model is substantially less significant if there is no firm market value for the stock (preferred and common), because variable X_4 in the model requires that the market value of the stock be determined.

The Z score for Nike for 2007 follows:

$$
\begin{aligned}
Z = \ &.012 \ (\text{working capital/total assets}) \\
&+ .014 \ (\text{retained earnings [balance sheet]/total assets}) \\
&+ .033 \ (\text{earnings before interest and taxes/total assets}) \\
&+ .006 \ (\text{market value of equity/book value of total debt}) \\
&+ .010 \ (\text{sales/total assets})
\end{aligned}
$$

$$
\begin{aligned}
Z = \ &.012 \ (\$5,492,500,000)/\$10,688,300,000 \\
&+ .014 \ (\$4,885,200,000)/\$10,688,300,000 \\
&+ .033 \ (\$2,199,900,000 + \$49,700,000)/\$10,688,300,000 \\
&+ .006 \ (\$501,700,000 \times \$56.75)/\$3,662,900,000 \\
&+ .010 \ (\$16,325,900,000)/\$10,688,300,000
\end{aligned}
$$

$$
\begin{aligned}
Z = \ &.012 \ (51.39) \\
&+ .014 \ (45.71) \\
&+ .033 \ (21.05) \\
&+ .006 \ (777.29) \\
&+ .010 \ (152.75)
\end{aligned}
$$

$$Z = 8.14$$

The Z score for Nike for 2007 was 8.15. Considering that higher scores are better and that companies with scores below 2.675 are assumed to have characteristics similar to those of past failures, Nike is a very healthy company.

There are many academic studies on the use of ratios to forecast financial failure. These studies help substantiate that firms with weak ratios are more likely to go bankrupt than firms with strong ratios. Since no conclusive model has yet been developed, the best approach is probably an integrated one. As a supplemental measure, it may also be helpful to compute some of the ratios that appear useful in forecasting financial failure.

Analytical Review Procedures

Statement of Auditing Standards No. 23, "Analytical Review Procedures," provides guidance for the use of such procedures in audits. The objective of analytical review procedures is to isolate significant fluctuations and unusual items in operating statistics.

Analytical review procedures may be performed at various times, including the planning stage, during the audit itself, and near the completion of the audit. Some examples of analytical review procedures that may lead to special audit procedures follow.

1. Horizontal common-size analysis of the income statement may indicate that an item, such as selling expenses, is abnormally high for the period. This could lead to a close examination of the selling expenses.
2. Vertical common-size analysis of the income statement may indicate that cost of goods sold is out of line in relation to sales, in comparison with prior periods.
3. A comparison of accounts receivable turnover with the industry data may indicate that receivables are turning over much slower than is typical for the industry. This may indicate that receivables should be analyzed closely.
4. Cash flow in relation to debt may have declined significantly, indicating a materially reduced ability to cover debt from internal cash flow.
5. The acid-test ratio may have declined significantly, indicating a materially reduced ability to pay current liabilities with current assets less inventories.

When the auditor spots a significant trend in a statement or ratio, follow-up procedures should be performed to determine the reason. Such an investigation can lead to significant findings.

Management's Use of Analysis

Management can use financial ratios and common-size analysis as aids in many ways. Analysis can indicate the relative liquidity, debt, and profitability of a firm. Analysis can also indicate how investors perceive the firm and can help detect emerging problems and strengths in a firm. As indicated previously, financial ratios can also be used as part of the firm's corporate objectives. Using financial ratios in conjunction with the budgeting process can be particularly helpful. An objective of the budgeting process is the determination of the firm's game plan. The budget can consist of an overall comprehensive budget and many separate budgets, such as a production budget.

The comprehensive budget relating to financial statements indicates how a firm plans to get from one financial position (balance sheet) to another. The income statement details how the firm changed internally from one balance sheet position to another in terms of revenue and expenses. The statement of cash flows indicates how the firm's cash changed from one balance sheet to another.

A proposed comprehensive budget should be compared with financial ratios that have been agreed upon as part of the firm's corporate objectives. For example, if corporate objectives include a current ratio of 2:1, a debt equity of 40%, and a return on equity of 15%, then the proposed comprehensive budget should be compared with these corporate objectives before accepting the budget as the firm's overall game plan. If the proposed comprehensive budget will not result in the firm achieving its objectives, management should attempt to change the game plan in order to achieve its objectives. If management cannot change the proposed comprehensive budget satisfactorily to achieve the corporate objectives, they should know this when the comprehensive budget is accepted.

Use of LIFO Reserves

A firm that uses LIFO usually discloses a LIFO reserve account in a note on the face of the balance sheet. If a LIFO reserve account is not disclosed, there is usually some indication of an amount that approximates current cost. Nike uses first-in, first-out or moving average; therefore, it does not have a LIFO reserve. Therefore, Sherwin-Williams Company was selected to illustrate LIFO reserve analysis.

In its 2006 annual report, Sherwin-Williams Company disclosed that the excess of FIFO over LIFO was $226,818,000 and $187,425,000 for 2006 and 2005, respectively.

This information can be used for supplemental analysis of inventory and (in general) the analysis of liquidity, debt, and profitability. Supplemental analysis using this additional inventory information can be particularly significant when there is a substantial LIFO reserve and/or a substantial change in the reserve.

For Sherwin-Williams, an approximation of the increase or decrease in income if inventory is at approximate current acquisition costs could be computed by comparing the change in inventory, net of any tax effect. For 2006, compute the approximation of the income if the inventory were at approximate current acquisitions costs as follows:

		(in thousands)
2006 net income		$576,058
Net increase in inventory reserve:		
2006	$226,818	
2005	187,425	
(a)	$ 39,393	
(b) Effective tax rate (presented in Note 14—Income Taxes)	× 31.0%	
(c) Change in taxes [a × b]	$ 12,212	
(d) Net increase in income [a − b]		27,181
Estimated income if the inventory were presented at approximate current acquisitions costs		$603,239

Specific liquidity and debt ratios can be recomputed, taking into consideration the adjusted inventory figure. To make these computations, add the gross inventory reserve to the inventory disclosed in current assets. Add the approximate additional taxes to the current liabilities.

Estimate the additional tax figure by multiplying the gross LIFO reserve by the effective tax rate. This tax figure relates to the additional income that would have been reported in the current year and all prior years if the higher inventory amounts had been reported. The additional tax amount is a deferred tax amount that is added to current liabilities, to be conservative. The difference between the additional inventory amount and the additional tax amount is added to retained earnings because it represents the total prior influence on net income. The adjusted figures for Sherwin-Williams Company at the end of 2006 follow:

Inventory:	
As disclosed on the balance sheet	$ 825,179,000
Increase in inventory	226,818,000
	$1,051,997,000
Deferred current tax liability:	
Effective tax rate [31.0% × Increase in inventory ($226,818,000)]	$ 70,313,580
Retained earnings:	
As disclosed on the balance sheet	$3,485,564,000
Increase in retained earnings ($226,818,000 − $70,313,580)	156,504,420
	$3,642,068,420

An adjusted cost of goods sold can also be estimated, using the change in the inventory reserve. A net increase in the inventory reserve would reduce the cost of goods sold. A net decrease in inventory reserve would increase the cost of goods sold.

The adjusted liquidity, debt, and profitability ratios could possibly be considered to be more realistic than the unadjusted prior computations because of the use of current acquisition costs for inventory.

For many of the ratios, we cannot generalize about whether the ratio will improve or decline when the LIFO reserve is used. For example, if the current ratio is above 2.00, then it may not improve when the LIFO reserve is considered, especially if the firm has a high tax rate. When the current ratio and/or tax rate is low, then the current ratio will likely improve.

The Sherwin-Williams inventory disclosure on its December 31, 2006, annual report follows:

Consolidated Balance Sheets (in Part) (thousands of dollars) Inventories:	December 31, 2006
Finished goods	$707,196
Work in process and raw materials	117,983
	$825,179

NOTE 4—INVENTORIES

Inventories were stated at the lower of cost or market with cost determined principally on the last-in, first-out (LIFO) method. The following presents the effect on inventories, net income and net income per common share had the company used the first-in, first-out (FIFO) inventory valuation method adjusted for income taxes at the statutory rate and assuming no other adjustments.

Management believes that the use of LIFO results in a better matching of costs and revenues. This information is presented to enable the reader to make comparisons with companies using the FIFO method of inventory valuation.

	2006	2005	2004
Percentage of total inventories in LIFO	88%	89%	81%
Excess of FIFO over LIFO (in thousands)	$226,818	$187,425	$125,212
Decrease in net income due to LIFO (in thousands)	(24,033)	(40,855)	(18,580)
Decrease in net income per common share due to LIFO	(0.17)	(0.29)	(0.13)

Notice that Note 4 discloses a decrease in net income due to LIFO of $24,033 (in thousands), while our prior estimate was $27,181 (in thousands).

Graphing Financial Information

It has become popular to use graphs in annual reports to present financial information. Graphs make it easier to grasp key financial information. Graphs can be a better communication device than a written report or a tabular presentation because they communicate by means of pictures and, thus, create more immediate mental images.

There are many forms of graphs. Some popular forms used by accountants are line, column, bar, and pie graphs. These forms will be briefly described here, but a detailed description of those and other forms can be found in reference books and articles.[13]

The line graph uses a set of points connected by a line to show change over time. It is important for the vertical axis to start at zero and that it not be broken. Not starting the vertical axis at zero and/or breaking the vertical axis can result in a very misleading presentation. Exhibit 11-9 illustrates a line graph.

A column graph has vertical columns. As a line graph, it is important that the vertical axis start at zero and that it not be broken. A column graph is often the best form of graph for presenting accounting data. Exhibit 11-10 presents a column graph.

A bar graph is similar to a column graph, except that the bars are horizontal. Exhibit 11-11 on page 461 illustrates a bar graph.

A pie graph is divided into segments. This type of graph makes a comparison of the segments, which must add up to a total or to 100%. A pie graph can mislead if it creates an optical illusion. Also, some accounting data do not fit on a pie graph. Exhibit 11-12 on page 461 illustrates a pie graph.

| *Exhibit* | 11-9 | PFG—PERFORMANCE FOOD GROUP* |

Line Graph—Net Sales
2006 Annual Report

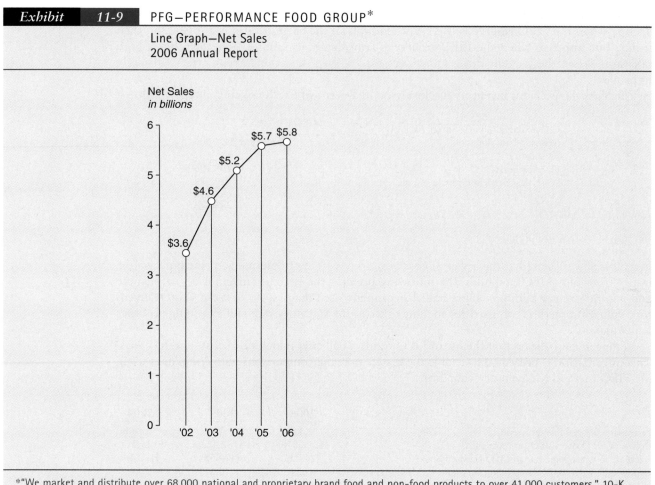

Net Sales
in billions

*"We market and distribute over 68,000 national and proprietary brand food and non-food products to over 41,000 customers." 10-K

| *Exhibit* | 11-10 | IDEX CORPORATION* |

Column Graph—Total Return to Shareholders
2006 Annual Report

Total Return to Shareholders
(Dollars Based on $100 Investment in 2001)

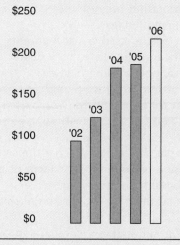

*"IDEX Corporation . . . is an applied solutions company specializing in fluid and metering technologies, health and science technologies, dispensing equipment and fire, safety and other diversified products." 10-K

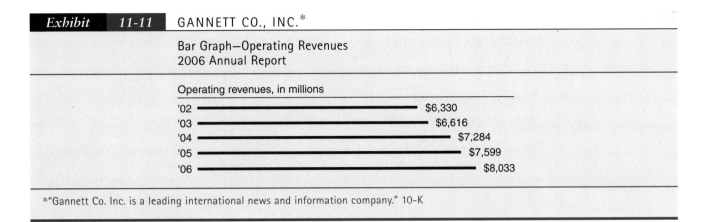

Exhibit 11-11 GANNETT CO., INC.*

Bar Graph—Operating Revenues
2006 Annual Report

Operating revenues, in millions

'02	$6,330
'03	$6,616
'04	$7,284
'05	$7,599
'06	$8,033

*"Gannett Co. Inc. is a leading international news and information company." 10-K

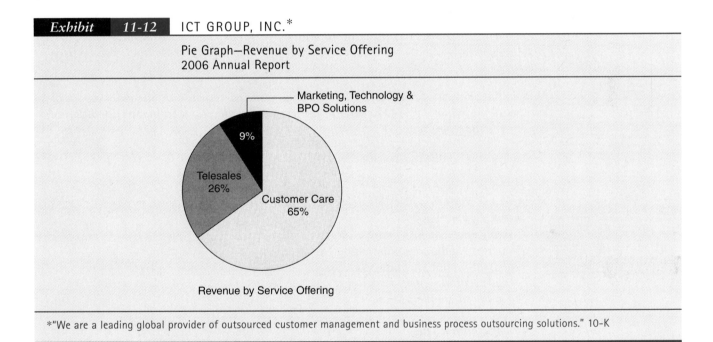

Exhibit 11-12 ICT GROUP, INC.*

Pie Graph—Revenue by Service Offering
2006 Annual Report

Marketing, Technology &
BPO Solutions
9%

Telesales
26%

Customer Care
65%

Revenue by Service Offering

*"We are a leading global provider of outsourced customer management and business process outsourcing solutions." 10-K

Management of Earnings

In Chapter 1, the cash basis is described as recognizing revenue when cash is received and recognizing expenses when cash is paid. It was indicated that the cash basis usually does not provide reasonable information about the earning capability of the entity in the short run. Because of the shortcomings of the cash basis, the accrual basis has been adopted for income reporting for most firms.

With the accrual basis, revenue is recognized when realized (realization concept), and expenses are recognized when incurred (matching concept). As indicated in Chapter 1, the use of the accrual basis complicates the accounting process, but the end result is more representative of an entity's financial condition than the cash basis. Without the accrual basis, accountants would not usually be able to make the time period assumption—that the entity can be accounted for with reasonable accuracy for a particular period of time.

Nike includes the following comment in its Management Discussion and Analysis of Financial Condition and Results of Operation in its 2007 annual report.

Critical Accounting Policies

Our previous discussion and analysis of our financial condition and results of operations are based upon our consolidated financial statements, which have been prepared in accordance with accounting principles generally accepted in the United States of America. The preparation of these financial statements requires us to make estimates and judgments that affect the reported amounts of assets, liabilities, revenues and expenses, and related disclosure of contingent assets and liabilities.

We believe that the estimates, assumptions and judgments involved in the accounting policies described below have the greatest potential impact on our financial statements, so we consider these to be our critical accounting policies. Because of the uncertainty inherent in these matters, actual results could differ from the estimates we use in applying the critical accounting policies. Certain of these critical accounting policies affect working capital account balances, including the policies for revenue recognition, the allowance for uncollectible accounts receivable, inventory reserves, and contingent payments under endorsements contracts. These policies require that we make estimates in the preparation of our financial statements as of a given date. However, since our business cycle is relatively short, actual results related to these estimates are generally known within the six-month period following the financial statement date. Thus, these policies generally affect only the timing of reported amounts across two to three fiscal quarters.

Within the context of these critical accounting policies, we are not currently aware of any reasonably likely events or circumstances that would result in materially different amounts being reported.

The accounting policies described in detail were the following:

- *Revenue recognition*
- *Allowance for uncollectible accounts receivable*
- *Inventory reserves*
- *Contingent payments under endorsement contracts*
- *Property, plant and equipment*
- *Goodwill and other intangible assets*
- *Hedge accounting for derivatives*
- *Stock-based compensation*
- *Taxes*
- *Other contingencies*

Thus, Nike describes the proper use of estimates and judgments to prepare its financial statements under generally accepted accounting principles.

Some firms have used estimates and judgments to improperly manipulate their financial statements. Other firms have deliberately made errors to manipulate their financial statements. This results in financial statements that are not a proper representation of financial condition and results of operations. This became a substantial problem during the 1990s. The former chairman of the Securities and Exchange Commission, Arthur Levitt, had this to say as part of his address entitled the "Numbers Game," at the New York University Center for Law and Business on September 28, 1998:

Increasingly, I have become concerned that the motivation to meet Wall Street earnings expectations may be overriding common sense business practices. Too many corporate managers, auditors, and analysts are participants in a game of nods and winks. In the zeal to satisfy consensus earnings estimates and project a smooth earnings path, wishful thinking may be winning the day over faithful representation.

As a result, I fear that we are witnessing an erosion in the quality of earnings, and therefore, the quality of financial reporting. Managing may be giving way to manipulations; integrity may be losing out to illusion.

Many in corporate America are just as frustrated and concerned about this trend as we, at the SEC, are. They know how difficult it is to hold the line on good practices when their competitors operate in the gray area between legitimacy and outright fraud.

A gray area where the Accounting is being perverted; where managers are cutting corners; and, where earnings reports reflect the desires of management rather than the underlying financial performance of the company.[14]

Thus, there was concern of the former chairman of the Securities and Exchange Commission and the financial community as to the apparent increase in the inappropriate management of earnings during the 1990s. We can speculate on why there was an increase in the improper management of earnings during the 1990s. Some of the reasons likely were (1) conviction that the capital markets would pay more for a stock that represented smooth earnings rather than peaks and valleys of earnings, (2) increase in the awarding of stock options as a means of compensation as opposed to cash, (3) substantial negative market reaction when a company would not meet its numbers, and (4) possibly an all-time high in greed.

The general public did not appear to be overly concerned with the increase in the improper management of earnings until the Enron situation developed in 2001. A possible reason for this was the substantial increase in stock prices during the 1990s. Starting in 2000, stock prices had substantial declines. These declines in stock prices likely influenced the general public to be concerned about the improper management of earnings.

There are many ways to improperly manage earnings. We don't know of all the possibilities. The ways that we do know would require a separate book to describe. We do know that revenue recognition is often involved in the manipulation of financial reports. The General Accounting Office, Congress's investigative arm, reported in an October 2002 report to the Senate Banking Committee that earnings restatements cost investors $100 billion in the prior five years. Earnings restatements rose by about 145% from 1997 through June 2002. Revenue-recognition issues arose in 38% of the cases studied.[15]

Revenue recognition often also involves inventory, accounts receivable, and cash flow. For example, early recognition of revenue could involve moving inventory from the balance sheet to cost of goods sold on the income statement, the booking of accounts receivable, and lack of cash flow. An understanding of financial reporting and analysis would help in detecting the problem.

Enron and WorldCom substantially influenced financial reporting in the United States. These cases crystallized views of the U.S. House and Senate that resulted in the Sarbanes-Oxley Act of 2002. Hopefully, the Sarbanes-Oxley Act leads to constructive improvement in financial reporting.

Enron was one of the largest corporations in the world. It announced in October 2001 that it was reducing after-tax net income by approximately $500 million and shareholders' equity by $1.2 billion. In November, it announced that it was restating reported net income for the years 1997–2000. In December 2001, Enron filed for bankruptcy.

There were many financial reporting issues in the Enron situation. Many of these issues were poorly disclosed or not disclosed. Some of the issues were accounting for investments in subsidiaries and special-purpose entities, sales of investments to special-purpose entities, revenue for fees, and fair value of investments.[16] The Enron financial statements, including the notes, were complicated and difficult to comprehend. The lesson here is if a reasonable understanding of financial reporting and analysis is not adequate to understand the financial report, then consider this when investing.

WorldCom announced in June 2002 that it had inflated profits by $3.8 billion over the previous five quarters. This was the largest corporate accounting fraud in history. Soon after this announcement, WorldCom declared bankruptcy.[17] In November 2002, a special bankruptcy court examiner reported that the improper accounting would exceed $7.2 billion.[18]

The WorldCom fraud was uncovered by three accountants working in the internal auditing department. Their findings were communicated to the audit committee of the board, and later the entire board was informed. The internal discovery and reporting of the fraud represents a positive aspect of the WorldCom fraud.[19]

The WorldCom problem apparently started in 2000 when business declined. Initially, WorldCom moved dollars from reserve accounts to hold up profits. When this was no longer sufficient, it then turned to shifting operating costs to capital accounts. Shifting operating costs (expenses on the income statement) to capital accounts (assets on the balance sheet) would make the company look more profitable in the short run. As capital expenditures, these costs would be depreciated in subsequent years. Apparently, WorldCom had planned a write-down. This would remove these accounts from the balance sheet. Hopefully, Wall Street would overlook the write-down when looking to the future.[20]

Although the WorldCom fraud was discovered by internal auditors, the Securities and Exchange Commission sent a "Request for Information" to WorldCom on March 7, 2002. The Securities and Exchange Commission apparently thought that the WorldCom profit figures were suspicious, considering that WorldCom's closest competitors, including AT&T Corp., were losing money throughout 2001. A lesson from WorldCom is that if the numbers look too good, that may be because they *are* too good.[21]

Many cases have been brought against companies and individuals for improper management of earnings since Enron and WorldCom. As of 2005, the largest company subsequent to Enron and WorldCom charged with improper management of earnings has been American International Group, Inc. (AIG). AIG is the world's biggest publicly traded seller of property-casualty insurance to businesses and the largest life insurer in the United States in terms of premiums.[22]

The SEC, the Justice Department, and the U.S. Attorney's office in New York City were all investigating AIG's accounting issues. New York's attorney general and insurance commissioner sued AIG and two former top executives accusing them of manipulating AIG's financial results.[23] The New York prosecutor's office presented evidence to a grand jury weighing criminal charges against individuals during the summer of 2005.[24]

On May 31, 2005, AIG restated its financial results for a five-year period. "The accounting adjustments tallied in the document slashed AIG's previously reported net income for 2004 by 12%, or $1.32 billion, to $9.73 billion, and reduced AIG's book value by $2.26 billion to $80.61 billion. Overall, the restatement reduced AIG's net income from 2000 through 2004 by $3.9 billion, or 10%."[25]

A United States Government Accountability Office (GAO) study dated July 2006 disclosed that "over the period of January 1, 2002 through September 30, 2005, the total number of restating companies (1,084) represents 16 percent of the average number of listed companies from 2002 to 2005, as compared to almost 8 percent during the 1997–2001 period."[26]

This study concluded that "a variety of factors appear to have contributed to the increased trend in restatements, including increased accountability requirements on the part of company executives; increased auditor and regulatory scrutiny . . . and a general unwillingness on the part of public companies to risk failing to restate regardless of the significance of the event."[27]

In an August 2006 correspondence, the GAO made this comment related to its July 2006 study: "Although there are many reasons for restatements, most restatements involve more routine reporting issues . . . and are not symptomatic of financial reporting fraud and/or accounting errors."[28]

It was noted in Chapter 4 that a FASB standard issued in May 2005 requires retrospective application to prior periods' financial statements of a voluntary change in accounting principle unless it is impracticable. This standard will contribute to additional retrospective application to prior periods.

The SEC issued Staff Bulletin No. 108 in September 2006 that requires retroactive revision of prior-period numbers presented in financial reporting. This relates to accounting for immaterial adjustments waived over time that become cumulatively material at a point in time. This bulletin will also contribute to additional retrospective application to prior periods.

Restatements have become a substantial problem when analyzing financial statements. Review companies that are being analyzed for restatements during the period of time that is being analyzed. Make a similar review for companies with which the company is being compared. It is impossible to guard against some unreliable industry data.

Valuation

Valuation is a process of estimating the value of a firm or some component of a firm. There are many approaches to valuation. Those approaches can be summarized as fundamental analysis and multiperiod discounted valuation approaches. In practice, a wide variety of valuation approaches are employed.

With fundamental analysis, the basic accounting measures are used to assess the firm's future operating cash flows or earnings. Fundamental analysis makes use of the financial statements. This approach considers items such as reported earnings, cash flow, and book value.

The multiperiod discounted valuation approach either projects earnings or cash flow and discounts these numbers to the present value (intrinsic value).

MULTIPLES

Fundamental valuation typically uses one or more multiples. Multiples frequently used are price-to-earnings (PE), price-to-book, price-to-operating cash flow, and price-to-sales. Perceived risk will reduce a multiple, while perceived growth will increase a multiple. When using a multiple approach, it is important to compare results with similar firms.

Multiples use conventional financial statements. For example, price-to-earnings (PE) uses earnings, price-to-book uses the book value, and price-to-operating cash flow uses operating cash flow, while price-to-sales uses sales. Often, the analysis would use several multiples.

The use of multiples and conventional financial reports is not well accepted by the traditional financial literature or many valuation books. However, ample evidence proves that the use of multiples is preferred by security analysts and fund managers.

MULTIPERIOD DISCOUNTED VALUATION MODELS

The financial literature and valuation books strongly support use of the multiperiod discounted valuation model either in terms of earnings or cash flow. Discounted cash flow is preferred.

Multiperiod Discounted Earnings Models

There are many multiperiod discounted earnings models. These models rely on accrual accounting to produce results that are closer to the firm's underlying economic performance in the short run than are cash flows.

The two most popular discounted earnings models appear to be (1) discounted abnormal earnings (DAE) and (2) residual income (RI).

Discounted Abnormal Earnings (DAE)

With this approach, the value of the firm's equity is the sum of its book value and discounted forecasts of abnormal earnings.

Residual Income (RI)

This approach discounts future expected earnings. The focus is on earnings as a periodic measure of shareholder wealth creation.

Multiperiod Discounted Cash Flow Models

There are many multiperiod discounted cash flow models. The three most popular seem to be (1) free cash flow (FCF), (2) dividend discount model (DDM), and (3) discounted cash flow (DCF).

Free Cash Flow (FCF)

The free cash flow model says that the intrinsic value (discounted free cash flow) equals the sum of the stream of expected free cash flows discounted to the present.

There are different definitions of free cash flow, but they are along these lines for common stock. Operating cash flows minus interest, minus cash outlays for operating capacity (buildings, equipment, etc.), minus repayments, minus preferred dividends.

Dividend Discount Model (DDM)

The dividend discount model discounts the projected dividend stream to present value. It considers only the dividend stream to common shareholders.

Discounted Cash Flow (DCF)

The discounted cash flow model involves a multiple-year forecast of cash flows. The forecasts are discounted at the firm's estimated cost of capital to arrive at an estimated present value.

What They Use

"Three recent studies have dealt with the issue of what models are actually used by analysts: Barker (1999), Demirakos et al. (2003) and Asquith et al. (2004). All these studies agree on the fact that multi-period discounted valuation models do not seem to play a significant role in analysts' normal valuation activity. Simple price-earnings multiples seem to be the predominant technique. Hence, any cost of equity capital discounted valuation model may not be an adequate representation of the reality of valuation."[29]

Let's review the three studies sited: Barker, Demirakos et al., and Asquith et al.

Barker

The Barker study states that the value of a share is given by the dividend discount model, but the actual determination of the share value is rarely based upon the direct estimation of the future dividends.[30]

Barker references prior studies of valuation models used by market participants which indicated that the strongest and most consistent finding in the behavioral literature is that the price-to-earnings is of primary importance.[31] A further finding was that discounted cash flow models are of little practical importance to investment decisions.[32]

The Barker study itself dealt with analysts and fund managers in the United Kingdom. The valuation models selected for study were price-earnings, dividend yield, price-cash flow (PCF), net asset value (NAV), sales/market capitalization, discounted cash flow, and dividend discount.[33] Analysts and fund managers were asked to rate the importance of these valuation models. Both groups picked the PE method as the preferred method of valuation. The PE, dividend yield, and price-cash flow were significantly more important than all other valuation models. (The discounted cash flow model and the dividend discount model were both of little practical importance.)[34]

The analysts were asked to rank the importance of selected financial ratios: the profit and loss account (ratios) were perceived to be of greater relevance than the balance sheet (ratios).[35]

For both the analysts and fund managers, "a consistent finding from these interviews was that valuation models are perceived to be important in the context of one another, and not just in isolation."[36] This also applied to financial ratios.

It was found that analysts anchor their process in accounting information combined with other sources that are considered relevant to the reliably foreseeable future.[37] This indicates the importance of financial reports.

Analysts and fund managers consider almost all information received directly from companies to be very important.[38] They both "perceive their own assessment of company management to be at the heart of investment decision-making."[39] If management makes the correct decisions, the firm will generate future cash flow streams.

Demirakos et al.

The Demirakos study examined the valuation practices of financial analysts at international investment banks. The firms consisted of 26 large U.K.-listed companies drawn from the beverages, electronics, and pharmaceuticals sectors.

Descriptive analysis "shows that almost all the sampled reports contain some form of valuation by reference to a multiple of earnings.[40] The attention given to PE models varies systematically across sectors in understandable ways."[41]

"The main message to emerge from this content analysis of financial analysts' reports is that analysts appear to tailor their valuation methodologies to the circumstances of the industry. PE models remain the mainstay of valuation practice, but other forms of analysis complement those as circumstances demand. In some cases, discounted cash flow (DCF) models are used and in others, more detailed analysis of price-to-sales multiples, growth options, or profitability analysis are used. Another finding is that use of the residual income valuation (RIV) model is extremely limited, but analysts frequently use accounting data in single-period comparative and hybrid models."[42]

Asquith et al.

The Asquith et al. study cataloged the complete contents of *Institutional Investor* All-American analyst reports and examined the market reactions to their release. This study found that analysts use market-to-book value as their asset multiple.[43] No information reported in this study indicated that discounted cash flow was used.

INTERNATIONAL ASPECTS

The Barker study dealt with analysts and fund managers in the United Kingdom. The Demirakos study examined the valuation practices of financial analysts at international investment banks. Twenty-six large U.K. firms were examined. The Asquith study examined the contents of *Institutional Investor* All-American analyst reports. Did the varied international aspects of these studies influence the results?

Marco Trombetta in his paper "Discussion of Implied Cost of Equity Capital in Earnings-Based Valuation: International Evidence" commented as follows:

"The kind of training that financial analysts are likely to receive around the world is probably fairly similar, especially if we focus on those countries with a significant important stock market. Moreover the globalization of capital markets and investment strategies calls into question the assumption that financial analysis is a national activity."[44]

VALUATION AS SEEN BY MANAGEMENT CONSULTANTS

This section comments on a book, *Valuation, Measuring, and Managing the Value of Companies,* that now is in the fourth edition. Because the three authors (Tom Copeland, Tim Koller, and Jack Murrin) are all current or former partners of McKinsey & Company, Inc. and co-leaders of its corporate finance practice, it reflects practice as viewed by consultants. Individuals interested in valuation from a firm's perspective would benefit from a review of this book.

FROM PAGE V

McKinsey & Company, Inc., is an international top management consulting firm. Founded in 1926, McKinsey advises leading companies around the world.

This book is from the perspective of creating value for the firm. The firm should be managed to increase its value. Its "premise is that the value of a company derives from its ability to generate cash flows and cash-flow-based returns on investment."[45]

Their position follows closely with the theory of valuation. Discounted cash flows provide a more reliable picture of a company's value than an earnings-multiple approach.[46] Discounted cash flows drive the value of a company.

The firm should focus on long-term cash flows rather than short-term cash flows. Short-term cash flows are easy to manipulate, such as delaying research.[47]

They examine mergers and acquisitions (M&A) and observe that the market is often unimpressed with the acquirers' deals. Through reviewing the results of academic studies of transactions involving public companies in mergers and acquisitions, it was observed that "shareholders of acquiring companies, on average, earned small returns that are not even statistically different from zero."[48] On the other hand, shareholders of acquired companies are often big winners "receiving on average a 20 percent premium in a friendly merger and a 35 percent premium in a hostile takeover."[49] Many acquisitions turn out badly because the purchaser paid too much.[50]

The authors observed that the acquirers overpaid for the following reasons:[51]

1. Overoptimistic appraisal of market potential
2. Overestimation of synergies
3. Poor due diligence
4. Overbidding

Dot.coms

The authors maintain that the correct way to value dot.coms is by using the classic discounted cash flow approach to valuating, reinforcing the continued importance of basic economics and finance.[52]

E-commerce firms have investments in customer acquisition which is expensed in the income statement. Thus, as more customers are acquired, the values balloon as the losses balloon.[53]

Amazon.com built a customer base and expanded its offerings. Amazon.com started with private equity financing and sold convertible preferred in 1996, which was converted to common in 1997.

Some data from the Amazon.com financial statements are given in Exhibit 11-13. Amazon.com had a market capitalization in the billions by the end of 2000, yet it had never made a profit.

Exhibit 11-13	SELECTED DATA FROM THE AMAZON.COM FINANCIAL STATEMENTS 1997–2000			
$ millions	**1997**	**1998**	**1999**	**2000**
Income statements:				
Sales	148	610	1,640	2,762
Operating loss	(33)	(109)	(606)	(864)
Net loss	(31)	(125)	(720)	(1,411)
Balance sheets:				
Current liabilities	44	162	739	975
Long-term debt	77	348	1,466	2,127
Stockholders' equity:				
Common stock	66	300	1,148	1,326
Accumulated deficit	(38)	(162)	(882)	(2,293)
Total	28	138	266	(967)
Total liabilities & stockholders' equity	149	648	2,471	2,135
Cash flow statements:				
Net cash provided (used) in operating activities	1	31	(91)	(130)
Proceeds from long-term debt	75	326	1,264	681
Proceeds of capital stock and exercise of stock options	53	14	64	45

According to the Copeland et al. approach to discounted cash flow for "high-growth companies like Amazon.com, don't be constrained by current performance. Instead of starting from the present—the usual practice in DCF valuations—start by thinking about what the industry and the company could look like when they evolve from today's very high-growth, unstable condition to a substantial, moderate growth rate in the future, and then extrapolate back to current performance."[54]

Copeland et al. also recommends a customer value analysis when valuing very high-growth companies. Five factors that drive the customer-value analysis of a retailer like Amazon.com are as follows:[55]

1. The average revenue per customer per year from purchases by its customers as well as revenues from advertisements on its site and from retailers that rent space on it to sell their own products.

2. The total number of customers.

3. The contribution margin per customer (before the cost of acquiring customers).

4. The average cost of acquiring a customer.

5. The customer churn rate (that is, the proportion of customers lost each year).

Any analysis should consider a company's ability to survive long enough for the projections to take place. Amazon.com was able to raise substantial capital prior to the dot.com crash in 2000. Apparently, Amazon.com raised more capital than needed in 1999 and 2000, which allowed it to operate on plan without making major adjustments because of inadequate capital. Note the proceeds from long-term debt: 1997 ($75,000,000), 1998 ($326,000,000), 1999 ($1,264,000,000), and 2000 ($681,000,000).

Summary

This chapter reviewed special areas related to financial statements. It was noted that commercial loan departments give a high significance rating to selected ratios that primarily measure liquidity or debt. The debt/equity ratio received the highest significance rating, and the current ratio was the second highest rated by the commercial loan officers. A commercial bank may elect to include a ratio as part of a loan agreement. The two ratios most likely to be included in a loan agreement are the debt/equity and the current ratio.

Financial executives give the profitability ratios the highest significance ratings. They rate earnings per share and return on investment the highest. Many firms have selected key financial ratios, such as profitability ratios, to be included as part of their corporate objectives.

Certified public accountants give the highest significance rating to two liquidity ratios: the current ratio and the accounts receivable turnover in days. The highest rated profitability ratio was the after-tax net profit margin, while the highest rated debt ratio was debt/equity.

A firm could use its annual report to relate financial data effectively by the use of financial ratios. In general, no major effort is being made to explain financial results by the disclosure of financial ratios in annual reports. A review of the methodology used to compute the ratios disclosed in annual reports indicated that wide differences of opinion exist on how many of the ratios should be computed.

A review of the financial statements, including the notes, indicates the conservatism of the statements in terms of accounting policies. When a firm has conservative accounting policies, it is said that its earnings are of high quality.

There have been many academic studies on the use of financial ratios to forecast financial failure. No conclusive model has yet been developed to forecast financial failure.

Auditors use financial analysis as part of their analytical review procedures. By using financial analysis, they can detect significant fluctuations and unusual items in operating statistics. This can result in a more efficient and effective audit.

Management can use financial analysis in many ways to manage a firm more effectively. A particularly effective use of financial analysis is to integrate ratios that have been accepted as corporate objectives into comprehensive budgeting.

It has become popular to use graphs in annual reports to present financial information. Graphs make it easier to grasp key financial information. Graphs can communicate better than a written report or a tabular presentation.

Many companies are restating their financial statements. This represents a substantial problem when analyzing financial statements.

The improper management of earnings has become a very hot topic. Hopefully, this improper manipulation of earnings is under control.

The objective with valuation is to determine a value for the firm's equity. In theory, the value of a company derives from its ability to generate cash flows and cash-flow-based returns on investment. Research indicates that multiperiod discounted valuation models do not seem to play a significant role in analysts' or fund managers' normal valuation activity. A simple price-earnings multiple seems to be predominant. The multiperiod discounted valuation models appear to play a significant role for a management consulting firm reviewed.

to the net

1. Go to the SEC Web site (http://www.sec.gov). Under "Filings & Forms (EDGAR)", click on "Search for Company Filings." Click on "Companies & Other Filers." Under Company Name, enter "Baldor Electric Company" (or under Ticker Symbol, enter "BEZ"). Select the 10-K filed February 28, 2007.

Determine:

a. The business description. Copy the first sentence.

b.

	December 30, 2006	December 31, 2005
Inventory balance		
Inventory reserve		

c. 2006 net income.

d. 2006 effective tax rate.

e. The approximate income for 2006 if inventory had been valued at approximate current cost.

2. Go to the SEC Web site (http://www.sec.gov). Under "Filings & Forms (EDGAR)," click on "Search for Company Filings." Click on "Companies & Other Filers." Under Company Name, enter "Omnova Solutions" (or under Ticker Symbol, enter "OMN"). Select the 10-K filed January 26, 2007.

　a. Determine the business description. Copy the second paragraph under introduction.

　b. What was the income (loss) from continuing operations for the years ended November 30, 2006, and 2005?

c. During 2006, LIFO inventory quantities were reduced. These reductions resulted in a liquidation of LIFO inventory quantities carried at lower cost prevailing in price years as compared with the cost of 2006.

Address the following:

1. Inventories valued using the LIFO method represented approximately what percentage of the total replacement cost of inventories at November 30, 2006?

2. During 2006, net LIFO inventory adjustments increased consolidated net income by how much?

3. During 2006, net LIFO inventory adjustments increased segment operating profit for Performance Chemicals and Decorative Products by how much, respectively?

Questions

Q 11-1. Commercial loan officers regard profitability financial ratios as very significant. Comment.

Q 11-2. Which two financial ratios do commercial loan officers regard as the most significant? Which two financial ratios appear most frequently in loan agreements?

Q 11-3. The commercial loan officers did not list the dividend payout ratio as a highly significant ratio, but they did indicate that the dividend payout ratio appeared frequently in loan agreements. Speculate on the reason for this apparent inconsistency.

Q 11-4. Corporate controllers regard profitability financial ratios as very significant. Comment.

Q 11-5. List the top five financial ratios included in corporate objectives according to the study reviewed in this book. Indicate what each of these ratios primarily measures.

Q 11-6. CPAs regard which two financial ratios as the most significant? The highest rated profitability ratio? The highest debt ratio?

Q 11-7. Financial ratios are used extensively in annual reports to interpret and explain financial statements. Comment.

Q 11-8. List the sections of annual reports where ratios are most frequently located, in order of use.

Q 11-9. According to a study of annual reports reviewed in this chapter, what type or types of financial ratios are most likely to be included in annual reports? Speculate on the probable reason for these ratios appearing in annual reports.

Q 11-10. The study of annual reports reviewed in this chapter showed that earnings per share was disclosed in every annual report. Why?

Q 11-11. The study of annual reports reviewed in this chapter indicated that wide differences of opinion exist on how many ratios should be computed. Comment.

Q 11-12.   What types of accounting policies are described as conservative?

Q 11-13.   Indicate which of the following accounting policies are conservative by placing an X under *Yes* or *No*. Assume inflationary conditions exist.

		Conservative	
		Yes	No
a.	LIFO inventory	_____	_____
b.	FIFO inventory	_____	_____
c.	Completed-contract method	_____	_____
d.	Percentage-of-completion method	_____	_____
e.	Accelerated depreciation method	_____	_____
f.	Straight-line depreciation method	_____	_____
g.	A relatively short estimated life for a fixed asset	_____	_____
h.	Short period for expensing intangibles	_____	_____
i.	Amortization of patent over five years	_____	_____
j.	High interest rate used to compute the present value of accumulated benefit obligation	_____	_____
k.	High rate of compensation increase used in computing the projected benefit obligation	_____	_____

Q 11-14.   All firms are required to expense R&D costs incurred each period. Some firms spend very large sums on R&D, while others spend little or nothing on this area. Why is it important to observe whether a firm has substantial or immaterial R&D expenses?

Q 11-15.   Indicate some possible uses of a reliable model that can be used to forecast financial failure.

Q 11-16.   Describe what is meant by a firm's *financial failure*.

Q 11-17.   According to the Beaver study, which ratios should be watched most closely, in order of their predictive power?

Q 11-18.   According to the Beaver study, three current asset accounts should be paid particular attention in order to forecast financial failure. List each of these accounts and indicate whether they should be abnormally high or low.

Q 11-19.   What does a Z score below 2.675 indicate, according to the Altman model?

Q 11-20.   Indicate a practical problem with computing a Z score for a closely held firm.

Q 11-21.   No conclusive model has been developed to forecast financial failure. This indicates that financial ratios are not helpful in forecasting financial failure. Comment.

Q 11-22.   You are the auditor of Piedmore Corporation. You determine that the accounts receivable turnover has been much slower this period than in prior periods and that it is also materially lower than the industry average. How might this situation affect your audit plan?

Q 11-23.   You are in charge of preparing a comprehensive budget for your firm. Indicate how financial ratios can help determine an acceptable, comprehensive budget.

Q 11-24.   List four popular forms of graphs used by accountants.

Q 11-25.   List two things that can make a line graph misleading.

Q 11-26.   Indicate two possible problems with a pie graph for accounting data.

Q 11-27.   The surveyed CFAs gave the highest significance rating to which type of financial ratio?

Q 11-28.   CFAs gave liquidity ratios a high significance rating. Comment.

Q 11-29.   Describe a proper management of earnings. Describe an improper management of earnings.

Q 11-30.   In valuation of stock equity, fundamental analysis makes extensive use of multiperiod discounted cash flow. Comment.

Q 11-31.   The use of multiples and conventional financial reports is not well accepted by the traditional financial literature or many valuation books. Comment.

Q 11-32.   Multiperiod discounted valuation models do not seem to play a significant role in analysts' normal valuation activity. Comment.

Q 11-33.   Comment on the importance of an assessment of company management when valuing a company from the perspective of analysts and fund managers.

Q 11-34.   We are interested in the future when valuing the stock equity of a company. Therefore, traditional financial statements are of little use in this endeavor. Comment.

Q 11-35.   It appears that most restatements are symptomatic of financial reporting fraud. Comment.

Problems

P 11-1.

Required   Answer the following multiple-choice questions:

a. Notes to financial statements are beneficial in meeting the disclosure requirements of financial reporting. The notes should not be used to
   1. Describe significant accounting policies.
   2. Describe depreciation methods employed by the company.
   3. Describe principles and methods peculiar to the industry in which the company operates when these principles and methods are predominately followed in that industry.
   4. Disclose the basis of consolidation for consolidated statements.
   5. Correct an improper presentation in the financial statements.

b. Which one of the following would be a source of funds under a cash concept of funds, but would not be listed as a source under the working capital concept?
   1. Sale of stock
   2. Sale of machinery
   3. Sale of treasury stock
   4. Collection of accounts receivable
   5. Proceeds from long-term bank borrowing

c. The concept of conservatism is often considered important in accounting. The application of this concept means that in the event some doubt occurs as to how a transaction should be recorded, it should be recorded so as to
   1. Understate income and overstate assets.
   2. Overstate income and overstate assets.
   3. Understate income and understate assets.
   4. Overstate income and understate assets.
   5. Overstate cash and overstate assets.

d. Early in a period in which sales were increasing at a modest rate and plant expansion and start-up costs were occurring at a rapid rate, a successful business would likely experience
   1. Increased profits and increased financing requirements because of an increasing cash shortage.
   2. Increased profits and decreased financing requirements because of an increasing cash surplus.
   3. Increased profits and no change in financing requirements.
   4. Decreased profits and increased financing requirements because of an increasing cash shortage.
   5. Decreased profits and decreased financing requirements because of an increasing cash surplus.

e. Which of the following ratios would best disclose effective management of working capital by a given firm relative to other firms in the same industry?
    1. A high rate of financial leverage relative to the industry average
    2. A high number of days' sales uncollected relative to the industry average
    3. A high turnover of net working capital relative to the industry average
    4. A high number of days' sales in inventory relative to the industry average
    5. A high proportion of fixed assets relative to the industry average

P 11-2.

Required   Answer the following multiple-choice questions:

a. If business conditions are stable, a decline in the number of days' sales outstanding from one year to the next (based on a company's accounts receivable at year-end) might indicate
    1. A stiffening of the company's credit policies.
    2. That the second year's sales were made at lower prices than the first year's sales.
    3. That a longer discount period and a more distant due date were extended to customers in the second year.
    4. A significant decrease in the volume of sales of the second year.
b. Trading on the equity (financial leverage) is likely to be a good financial strategy for stockholders of companies having
    1. Cyclical high and low amounts of reported earnings.
    2. Steady amounts of reported earnings.
    3. Volatile fluctuation in reported earnings over short periods of time.
    4. Steadily declining amounts of reported earnings.
c. The ratio of total cash, trade receivables, and marketable securities to current liabilities is
    1. The acid-test ratio.
    2. The current ratio.
    3. Significant if the result is 2-to-1 or below.
    4. Meaningless.
d. The times interest earned ratio is a primary measure of
    1. Liquidity.
    2. Long-term debt-paying ability.
    3. Activity.
    4. Profitability.
e. The calculation of the number of times bond interest is earned involves dividing
    1. Net income by annual bond interest expense.
    2. Net income plus income taxes by annual bond interest expense.
    3. Net income plus income taxes and bond interest expense by annual bond interest expense.
    4. Sinking fund earnings by annual bond interest expense.

P 11-3.

Required   Answer the following multiple-choice questions:

a. Which of the following would not be an example of the use of a multiple when valuing common equity?
    1. Multiperiod discounted earnings models
    2. Price-to-earnings (PE)
    3. Price-to-book
    4. Price-to-operating cash flow
b. The two most popular discounted earnings models appear to be
    1. Discounted abnormal earnings and residual income.
    2. Free cash flow and dividend discount model.
    3. Sales/market capitalization and price-earnings.
    4. Price-cash flow and dividend discount.

c. Shareholders of acquired companies are often big winners receiving on average a premium of what in a friendly merger?

1. 10%

2. 20%

3. 30%

4. 35%

d. Which of the following was not given as a reason for acquirers paying too much in an acquisition?

1. Overuse of conventional financial statements

2. Overbidding

3. Overoptimistic appraisal of market potential

4. Overestimation of synergies

e. Which of the following would likely be very useful when valuing a dot.com?

1. Discounted cash flow

2. Price-earnings

3. Net asset value

4. Dividend yield

P 11-4.   Thorpe Company is a wholesale distributor of professional equipment and supplies. The company's sales have averaged about $900,000 annually for the three-year period 2006–2008. The firm's total assets at the end of 2008 amounted to $850,000.

The president of Thorpe Company has asked the controller to prepare a report that summarizes the financial aspects of the company's operations for the past three years. This report will be presented to the board of directors at its next meeting.

In addition to comparative financial statements, the controller has decided to present a number of relevant financial ratios that can assist in the identification and interpretation of trends. At the request of the controller, the accounting staff has calculated the following ratios for the three-year period 2006–2008:

Ratio	2006	2007	2008
Current ratio	2.00	2.13	2.18
Acid-test (quick) ratio	1.20	1.10	0.97
Accounts receivable turnover	9.72	8.57	7.13
Inventory turnover	5.25	4.80	3.80
Percent of total debt to total assets	44.00%	41.00%	38.00%
Percent of long-term debt to total assets	25.00%	22.00%	19.00%
Sales to fixed assets (fixed asset turnover)	1.75	1.88	1.99
Sales as a percent of 2006 sales	100.00%	103.00%	106.00%
Gross profit percentage	40.0%	33.6%	38.5%
Net income to sales	7.8%	7.8%	8.0%
Return on total assets	8.5%	8.6%	8.7%
Return on stockholders' equity	15.1%	14.6%	14.1%

In preparing his report, the controller has decided first to examine the financial ratios independently of any other data to determine if the ratios themselves reveal any significant trends over the first three-year period.

Required   a. The current ratio is increasing, while the acid-test (quick) ratio is decreasing. Using the ratios provided, identify and explain the contributing factor(s) for this apparently divergent trend.

b. In terms of the ratios provided, what conclusion(s) can be drawn regarding the company's use of financial leverage during the 2006–2008 period?

c. Using the ratios provided, what conclusion(s) can be drawn regarding the company's net investment in plant and equipment?

(CMA Adapted)

Materials identified as CFA Examination 1, June 4, 1988, June 6, 1987, and June 6, 1988 are reproduced with permission from the Association for Investment Management and Research and the Institute of Chartered Financial Analysts.

P 11-5.   L. Konrath Company is considering extending credit to D. Hawk Company. L. Konrath estimated that sales to D. Hawk Company would amount to $2,000,000 each year. L. Konrath Company, a wholesaler, sells throughout the Midwest. D. Hawk Company, a retail chain operation, has a number of stores in the Midwest. L. Konrath Company has had a gross profit of approximately 60% in recent years and expects to have a similar gross profit on the D. Hawk Company order. The D. Hawk

Company order is approximately 15% of L. Konrath Company's present sales. Data from recent statements of D. Hawk Company follow:

(In millions)	2006	2007	2008
Assets			
Current assets:			
Cash	$ 2.6	$ 1.8	$ 1.6
Government securities (cost)	0.4	0.2	—
Accounts and notes receivable (net)	8.0	8.5	8.5
Inventories	2.8	3.2	2.8
Prepaid assets	0.7	0.6	0.6
Total current assets	14.5	14.3	13.5
Property, plant, and equipment (net)	4.3	5.4	5.9
Total assets	$18.8	$19.7	$19.4
Liabilities and Equities			
Current liabilities	$ 6.9	$ 8.5	$ 9.3
Long-term debt, 6%	3.0	2.0	1.0
Total liabilities	9.9	10.5	10.3
Shareholders' equity	8.9	9.2	9.1
Total liabilities and equities	$18.8	$19.7	$19.4
Income			
Net sales	$24.2	$24.5	$24.9
Cost of goods sold	16.9	17.2	18.0
Gross margin	7.3	7.3	6.9
Selling and administrative expenses	6.6	6.8	7.3
Earnings (loss) before taxes	0.7	0.5	(0.4)
Income taxes	0.3	0.2	(0.2)
Net income	$ 0.4	$ 0.3	$ (0.2)

Required

a. Calculate the following for D. Hawk Company for 2008:
   1. Rate of return on total assets
   2. Acid-test ratio
   3. Return on sales
   4. Current ratio
   5. Inventory turnover

b. As part of the analysis to determine whether L. Konrath should extend credit to D. Hawk, assume the ratios were calculated from D. Hawk Company statements. For each ratio, indicate whether it is a favorable, an unfavorable, or a neutral statistic in the decision to grant D. Hawk credit. Briefly explain your choice in each case.

Ratio	2006	2007	2008
Rate of return on total assets	1.96%	1.12%	(.87)%
Return on sales	1.69%	.99%	(.69)%
Acid-test ratio	1.73	1.36	1.19
Current ratio	2.39	1.92	1.67
Inventory turnover (times per year)	4.41	4.32	4.52
Equity relationships:			
Current liabilities	36.0%	43.0%	48.0%
Long-term liabilities	16.0	10.5	5.0
Shareholders' equity	48.0	46.5	47.0
	100.0%	100.0%	100.0%
Asset relationships:			
Current assets	77.0%	72.5%	69.5%
Property, plant, and equipment	23.0	27.5	30.5
	100.0%	100.0%	100.0%

c. Would you grant credit to D. Hawk Company? Support your answer with facts given in the problem.

d. What additional information, if any, would you want before making a final decision?

(CMA Adapted)

Materials identified as CFA Examination 1, June 4, 1988, June 6, 1987, and June 6, 1988 are reproduced with permission from the Association for Investment Management and Research and the Institute of Chartered Financial Analysts.

P 11-6.   Your company is considering the possible acquisition of Growth Inc. Financial statements of Growth Inc. follow:

GROWTH INC.
Balance Sheet
December 31, 2008 and 2007

	2008	2007
Assets		
Current assets:		
Cash	$ 64,346	$ 11,964
Accounts receivable, less allowance		
of $750 for doubtful accounts	99,021	83,575
Inventories, FIFO	63,414	74,890
Prepaid expenses	834	1,170
Total current assets	227,615	171,599
Investments and other assets	379	175
Property, plant, and equipment:		
Land and land improvements	6,990	6,400
Buildings	63,280	59,259
Machinery and equipment	182,000	156,000
	252,270	221,659
Less: Accumulated depreciation	110,000	98,000
Net property, plant, and equipment	142,270	123,659
Total assets	$370,264	$295,433
Liabilities and Stockholders' Equity		
Current liabilities:		
Accounts payable	$ 32,730	$ 26,850
Federal income taxes	5,300	4,800
Accrued liabilities	30,200	24,500
Current portion of long-term debt	5,500	5,500
Total current liabilities	73,730	61,650
Long-term debt	76,750	41,900
Other long-term liabilities	5,700	4,300
Deferred federal income taxes	16,000	12,000
Total liabilities	172,180	119,850
Stockholders' equity:		
Capital stock	44,000	43,500
Retained earnings	154,084	132,083
Total stockholders' equity	198,084	175,583
Total liabilities and stockholders' equity	$370,264	$295,433

GROWTH INC.
Statement of Income
Years Ended December 31, 2008, 2007 and 2006

	2008	2007	2006
Revenues	$578,530	$523,249	$556,549
Costs and expenses:			
Cost of products sold	495,651	457,527	482,358
Selling, general, and administrative	35,433	30,619	29,582
Interest and debt expense	4,308	3,951	2,630
	535,392	492,097	514,570
Income before income taxes	43,138	31,152	41,979
Provision for income taxes	20,120	12,680	17,400
Net income	$ 23,018	$ 18,472	$ 24,579
Net income per share	$ 2.27	$ 1.85	$ 2.43

Partial notes: Under the LIFO method, inventories have been reduced by approximately $35,300 and $41,100 at December 31, 2008 and 2007, respectively, from current cost, which would be reported under the first-in, first-out method.

The effective tax rates were 36.6%, 30.7%, and 31.4%, respectively, for the years ended December 31, 2008, 2007, and 2006.

Required   a. Compute the following for 2008, without considering the LIFO reserve:

Liquidity

1. Days' sales in inventory
2. Merchandise inventory turnover
3. Inventory turnover in days
4. Operating cycle
5. Working capital
6. Current ratio
7. Acid-test ratio
8. Cash ratio

Debt

1. Debt ratio
2. Debt/equity ratio
3. Times interest earned

Profitability

1. Net profit margin
2. Total asset turnover
3. Return on assets
4. Return on total equity

    b. Compute the ratios in part (a), considering the LIFO reserve.
    c. Comment on the apparent liquidity, debt, and profitability, considering both sets of ratios.

P 11-7.

Required   For each of the following numbered items, you are to select the lettered item(s) that indicate(s) its effect(s) on the corporation's statements. If more than one effect is applicable to a particular item, be sure to indicate *all* applicable letters. (Assume that the state statutes do not permit declaration of nonliquidating dividends except from earnings.)

Item	Effect
1. Declaration of a cash dividend due in one month on noncumulative preferred stock.	a. Reduces working capital
2. Declaration and payment of an ordinary stock dividend.	b. Increases working capital
3. Receipt of a cash dividend, not previously recorded, on stock of another corporation.	c. Reduces current ratio
	d. Increases current ratio
4. Passing of a dividend on cumulative preferred stocks.	e. Reduces the dollar amount of total capital stock
5. Receipt of preferred shares as a dividend on stock held as a temporary investment. This was not a regularly recurring dividend.	f. Increases the dollar amount of total capital stock
	g. Reduces total retained earnings
	h. Increases total retained earnings
6. Payment of dividend mentioned in (1).	i. Reduces equity per share of common stock
7. Issue of new common shares in a 5-for-1 stock split.	j. Reduces equity of each common stockholder

P 11-8.   Argo Sales Corporation has in recent years maintained the following relationships among the data on its financial statements:

Gross profit rate on net sales	40%
Net profit rate on net sales	10%
Rate of selling expenses to net sales	20%
Accounts receivable turnover	8 per year
Inventory turnover	6 per year
Acid-test ratio	2-to-1
Current ratio	3-to-1
Quick-asset composition: 8% cash, 32% marketable securities, 60% accounts receivable	
Asset turnover	2 per year
Ratio of total assets to intangible assets	20-to-1
Ratio of accumulated depreciation to cost of fixed assets	1-to-3
Ratio of accounts receivable to accounts payable	1.5-to-1
Ratio of working capital to stockholders' equity	1-to-1.6
Ratio of total debt to stockholders' equity	1-to-2

The corporation had a net income of $120,000 for 2008, which resulted in earnings of $5.20 per share of common stock. Additional information includes the following:

Capital stock authorized, issued (all in 2000), and outstanding:
  Common, $10 per share par value, issued at 10% premium.
  Preferred, 6% nonparticipating, $100 per share par value, issued at a 10% premium.
Market value per share of common at December 31, 2008: $78.
Preferred dividends paid in 2008: $3,000.
Times interest earned in 2008: 33.
The amounts of the following were the same at December 31, 2008, as at January 1, 2008: inventory, accounts receivable, 5% bonds payable—due 2017, and total stockholders' equity.
All purchases and sales were on account.

Required

a. Prepare in good form the condensed balance sheet and income statement for the year ending December 31, 2008, presenting the amounts you would expect to appear on Argo's financial statements (ignoring income taxes). Major captions appearing on Argo's balance sheet are current assets, fixed assets, intangible assets, current liabilities, long-term liabilities, and stockholders' equity. In addition to the accounts divulged in the problem, you should include accounts for prepaid expenses, accrued expenses, and administrative expenses. Supporting computations should be in good form.

b. Compute the following for 2008. (Show your computations.)
  1. Rate of return on stockholders' equity
  2. Price/earnings ratio for common stock
  3. Dividends paid per share of common stock
  4. Dividends paid per share of preferred stock
  5. Yield on common stock

(CMA Adapted)

Materials identified as CFA Examination 1, June 4, 1988, June 6, 1987, and June 6, 1988 are reproduced with permission from the Association for Investment Management and Research and the Institute of Chartered Financial Analysts.

P 11-9.   Warford Corporation was formed five years ago through a public subscription of common stock. Lucinda Street, who owns 15% of the common stock, was one of the organizers of Warford and is its current president. The company has been successful but currently is experiencing a shortage of funds. On June 10, Street approached Bell National Bank, asking for a 24-month extension on two $30,000 notes, which are due on June 30, 2008, and September 30, 2008. Another note of $7,000 is due on December 31, 2008, but Street expects no difficulty in paying this note on its due date. Street explained that Warford's cash flow problems are due primarily to the company's desire to finance a $300,000 plant expansion over the next two fiscal years through internally generated funds.

The commercial loan officer of Bell National Bank requested financial reports for the last two fiscal years. These reports follow:

WARFORD CORPORATION
Statement of Financial Position
March 31, 2007 and 2008

	2007	2008
Assets:		
Cash	$ 12,500	$ 16,400
Notes receivable	104,000	112,000
Accounts receivable (net)	68,500	81,600
Inventories (at cost)	50,000	80,000
Plant and equipment (net of depreciation)	646,000	680,000
Total assets	$881,000	$970,000
Liabilities and Owners' Equity:		
Accounts payable	$ 72,000	$ 69,000
Notes payable	54,500	67,000
Accrued liabilities	6,000	9,000
Common stock (60,000 shares, $10 par)	600,000	600,000
Retained earnings*	148,500	225,000
Total liabilities and owners' equity	$881,000	$970,000

*Cash dividends were paid at the rate of $1.00 per share in fiscal year 2007 and $1.25 per share in fiscal year 2008.

WARFORD CORPORATION
Income Statement
For the Fiscal Years Ended March 31, 2007 and 2008

	2007	2008
Sales	$2,700,000	$3,000,000
Cost of goods sold*	1,720,000	1,902,500
Gross profit	980,000	1,097,500
Operating expenses	780,000	845,000
Net income before taxes	200,000	252,500
Income taxes (40%)	80,000	101,000
Income after taxes	$ 120,000	$ 151,500

*Depreciation charges on the plant and equipment of $100,000 and $102,500 for fiscal years ended March 31, 2007 and 2008, respectively, are included in cost of goods sold.

Required

a. Calculate the following items for Warford Corporation:
1. Current ratio for fiscal years 2007 and 2008
2. Acid-test (quick) ratio for fiscal years 2007 and 2008
3. Inventory turnover for fiscal year 2008
4. Return on assets for fiscal years 2007 and 2008
5. Percentage change in sales, cost of goods sold, gross profit, and net income after taxes from fiscal year 2007 to 2008

b. Identify and explain what other financial reports and/or financial analyses might be helpful to the commercial loan officer of Bell National Bank in evaluating Street's request for a time extension on Warford's notes.

c. Assume that the percentage changes experienced in fiscal year 2008, as compared with fiscal year 2007 for sales, cost of goods sold, gross profit, and net income after taxes, will be repeated in each of the next two years. Is Warford's desire to finance the plant expansion from internally generated funds realistic? Explain.

d. Should Bell National Bank grant the extension on Warford's notes, considering Street's statement about financing the plant expansion through internally generated funds? Explain.

(CMA Adapted)

Materials identified as CFA Examination 1, June 4, 1988, June 6, 1987, and June 6, 1988 are reproduced with permission from the Association for Investment Management and Research and the Institute of Chartered Financial Analysts.

P 11-10. The following data apply to items (a) through (g):

JOHANSON COMPANY
Statement of Financial Position
December 31, 2007 and 2008

(In thousands)	2007	2008
Assets		
Current assets:		
Cash and temporary investments	$ 380	$ 400
Accounts receivable (net)	1,500	1,700
Inventories	2,120	2,200
Total current assets	4,000	4,300
Long-term assets:		
Land	500	500
Building and equipment (net)	4,000	4,700
Total long-term assets	4,500	5,200
Total assets	$8,500	$9,500
Liabilities and Equities		
Current liabilities:		
Accounts payable	$ 700	$1,400
Current portion of long-term debt	500	1,000
Total current liabilities	1,200	2,400
Long-term debt	4,000	3,000
Total liabilities	5,200	5,400
Stockholders' equity:		
Common stock	3,000	3,000
Retained earnings	300	1,100
Total stockholders' equity	3,300	4,100
Total liabilities and equities	$8,500	$9,500

JOHANSON COMPANY
Statement of Income and Retained Earnings
For the Year Ended December 31, 2008

(In thousands)

Net sales		$28,800
Less: Cost of goods sold	$15,120	
Selling expenses	7,180	
Administrative expenses	4,100	
Interest	400	
Income taxes	800	27,600
Net income		1,200
Retained earnings, January 1		300
Subtotal		1,500
Cash dividends declared and paid		400
Retained earnings, December 31		$ 1,100

Required   Answer the following multiple-choice questions:

a. The acid-test ratio for 2008 is
   1. 1.1-to-1.
   2. 0.9-to-1.
   3. 1.8-to-1.
   4. 0.2-to-1.
   5. 0.17-to-1.

b. The average number of days' sales outstanding in 2008 is
   1. 18 days.
   2. 360 days.
   3. 20 days.
   4. 4.4 days.
   5. 80 days.

c. The times interest earned ratio for 2008 is
   1. 3.0 times.
   2. 1.0 time.
   3. 72.0 times.
   4. 2.0 times.
   5. 6.0 times.

d. The asset turnover in 2008 is
   1. 3.2 times.
   2. 1.7 times.
   3. 0.4 time.
   4. 1.1 times.
   5. 0.13 time.

e. The inventory turnover in 2008 is
   1. 13.6 times.
   2. 12.5 times.
   3. 0.9 time.
   4. 7.0 times.
   5. 51.4 times.

f. The operating income margin in 2008 is
   1. 2.7%.
   2. 91.7%.
   3. 52.5%.
   4. 95.8%.
   5. 8.3%.

g. The dividend payout ratio in 2008 is
   1. 100%.
   2. 36%.
   3. 20%.
   4. 8.8%.
   5. 33.3%.

(CMA Adapted)

Materials identified as CFA Examination 1, June 4, 1988, June 6, 1987, and June 6, 1988 are reproduced with permission from the Association for Investment Management and Research and the Institute of Chartered Financial Analysts.

P 11-11.   The statement of financial position for Paragon Corporation at November 30, 2008, the end of its current fiscal year, follows. The market price of the company's common stock was $4 per share on November 30, 2008.

(In thousands)

Assets

Current assets:			
Cash		$ 6,000	
Accounts receivable	$ 7,000		
Less: Allowance for doubtful accounts	400	6,600	
Merchandise inventory		16,000	
Supplies on hand		400	
Prepaid expenses		1,000	
Total current assets			$30,000
Property, plant, and equipment:			
Land		27,500	
Building	$36,000		
Less: Accumulated depreciation	13,500	22,500	
Total property, plant, and equipment			50,000
Total assets			$80,000

Liabilities and Stockholders' Equity

Current liabilities:			
Accounts payable		$ 6,400	
Accrued interest payable		800	
Accrued income taxes payable		2,200	
Accrued wages payable		600	
Deposits received from customers		2,000	
Total current liabilities			$12,000
Long-term debt:			
Bonds payable—20-year, 8% convertible debentures due December 1, 2014 (Note 7)		20,000	
Less: Unamortized discount		200	19,800
Total liabilities			31,800
Stockholders' equity:			
Common stock—authorized 40,000,000 shares of $1 par value; 20,000,000 shares issued and outstanding		20,000	
Paid-in capital in excess of par value		12,200	
Total paid-in capital		32,200	
Retained earnings		16,000	
Total stockholders' equity			48,200
Total liabilities and stockholders' equity			$80,000

All items are to be considered independent of one another, and any transactions given in the items are to be considered the only transactions to affect Paragon Corporation during the just-completed current or coming fiscal year. Average balance sheet account balances are used in computing ratios involving income statement accounts. Ending balance sheet account balances are used in computing ratios involving only balance sheet items.

Required   Answer the following multiple-choice questions:

a. If Paragon paid back all of the deposits received from customers, its current ratio would be
   1. 2.50-to-1.00.
   2. 2.80-to-1.00.
   3. 2.33-to-1.00.
   4. 3.00-to-1.00.
   5. 2.29-to-1.00.

b. If Paragon paid back all of the deposits received from customers, its quick (acid-test) ratio would be
   1. 1.06-to-1.00.
   2. 1.00-to-1.00.
   3. 0.88-to-1.00.
   4. 1.26-to-1.00.
   5. 1.20-to-1.00.

c. A 2-for-1 common stock split by Paragon would
   1. Result in each $1,000 bond being convertible into 600 new shares of Paragon common stock.
   2. Decrease the retained earnings due to the capitalization of retained earnings.
   3. Not affect the number of common shares outstanding.
   4. Increase the total paid-in capital.
   5. Increase the total stockholders' equity.

d. Paragon Corporation's building is being depreciated using the straight-line method, salvage value of $6,000,000, and life of 20 years. The number of years the building has been depreciated by Paragon as of November 30, 2008, is
   1. 7.5 years.
   2. 12.5 years.
   3. 9.0 years.
   4. 15.0 years.
   5. None of these.

e. Paragon's book value per share of common stock as of November 30, 2008, is
   1. $4.00.
   2. $1.61.
   3. $1.00.
   4. $2.41.
   5. None of these.

f. If, during the current fiscal year ending November 30, 2008, Paragon had sales of $90,000,000 with a gross profit of 20% and an inventory turnover of five times per year, the merchandise inventory balance on December 1, 2007, was
   1. $14,400,000.
   2. $12,800,000.
   3. $18,000,000.
   4. $20,000,000.
   5. $16,000,000.

g. If Paragon has a payout ratio of 80% and declared and paid $4,000,000 of cash dividends during the current fiscal year ended November 30, 2008, the retained earnings balance on December 1, 2007, was
   1. $20,000,000.
   2. $17,000,000.
   3. $15,000,000.
   4. $11,000,000.
   5. None of these.

(CMA Adapted)

P 11-12. Calcor Company has been a wholesale distributor of automobile parts for domestic automakers for 20 years. Calcor has suffered through the recent slump in the domestic auto industry, and its performance has not rebounded to the levels of the industry as a whole.

Calcor's single-step income statement for the year ended November 30, 2008, follows:

CALCOR COMPANY
Income Statement
For the Year Ended November 30, 2008 (thousands omitted)

Net sales	$8,400
Expenses:	
Cost of goods sold	6,300
Selling expense	780
Administrative expense	900
Interest expense	140
Total	8,120
Income before income taxes	280
Income taxes	112
Net income	$ 168

Calcor's return on sales before interest and taxes was 5% in fiscal 2008 compared to the industry average of 9%. Calcor's turnover of average assets of four times per year and return on average assets before interest and taxes of 20% are both well below the industry average.

Joe Kuhn, president of Calcor, wishes to improve these ratios and raise them nearer to the industry averages. He established the following goals for Calcor Company for fiscal 2009:

Return on sales before interest and taxes	8%
Turnover of average assets	5 times per year
Return on average assets before interest and taxes	30%

For fiscal 2009, Kuhn and the rest of Calcor's management team are considering the following actions, which they expect will improve profitability and result in a 5% increase in unit sales:

1. Increase selling prices 10%.

2. Increase advertising by $420,000 and hold all other selling and administrative expenses at fiscal 2008 levels.

3. Improve customer service by increasing average current assets (inventory and accounts receivable) by a total of $300,000, and hold all other assets at fiscal 2008 levels.

4. Finance the additional assets at an annual interest rate of 10% and hold all other interest expense at fiscal 2008 levels.

5. Improve the quality of products carried; this will increase the units of goods sold by 4%.

6. Calcor's 2009 effective income tax rate is expected to be 40%—the same as in fiscal 2008.

Required a. Prepare a single-step pro forma income statement for Calcor Company for the year ended November 30, 2009, assuming that Calcor's planned actions would be carried out, and that the 5% increase in unit sales would be realized.

b. Calculate the following ratios for Calcor Company for the 2008–2009 fiscal year and state whether Kuhn's goal would be achieved:

1. Return on sales before interest and taxes

2. Turnover of average assets

3. Return on average assets before interest and taxes

c. Would it be possible for Calcor Company to achieve the first two of Kuhn's goals without achieving his third goal of a 30% return on average assets before interest and taxes? Explain your answer.

(CMA Adapted)

Materials identified as CFA Examination 1, June 4, 1988, June 6, 1987, and June 6, 1988 are reproduced with permission from the Association for Investment Management and Research and the Institute of Chartered Financial Analysts.

P 11-13.   The following data are for the A, B, and C Companies:

		Company	
Variables	A	B	C
Current assets	$150,000	$170,000	$180,000
Current liabilities	$60,000	$50,000	$30,000
Total assets	$300,000	$280,000	$250,000
Retained earnings	$80,000	$90,000	$60,000
Earnings before interest and taxes	$70,000	$60,000	$50,000
Market price per share	$20.00	$18.75	$16.50
Number of shares outstanding	9,000	9,000	9,000
Book value of total debt	$30,000	$50,000	$80,000
Sales	$430,000	$400,000	$200,000

Required   a. Compute the Z score for each company.

b. According to the Altman model, which of these firms is most likely to experience financial failure?

P 11-14.   General Company's financial statements for 2008 follow here and on the following pages:

GENERAL COMPANY
Statement of Income
Years Ended December 31, 2008, 2007, and 2006

	2008	2007	2006
Net sales	$860,000	$770,000	$690,000
Cost and expenses:			
Cost of products sold	730,000	630,000	580,000
Selling, general, and administrative	46,000	40,000	38,000
Interest and debt expense	4,000	3,900	6,500
	780,000	673,900	624,500
Income before income taxes	80,000	96,100	65,500
Provision for income taxes	33,000	24,000	21,000
Net income	$ 47,000	$ 72,100	$ 44,500
Net income per share	$ 2.67	$ 4.10	$ 2.54

GENERAL COMPANY
Statement of Cash Flows
Years Ended December 31, 2008, 2007, and 2006

	2008	2007	2006
Operating activities:			
Net income	$ 47,000	$ 72,100	$ 44,500
Adjustments to reconcile net income to net cash provided by operating activities:			
Depreciation and amortization	21,000	20,000	19,000
Deferred taxes	3,800	2,500	2,000
Increase in accounts receivable	(4,000)	(3,000)	(3,000)
Decrease (increase) in inventories	(3,000)	(2,500)	1,000
Decrease (increase) in prepaid expenses	(300)	(200)	100
Increase (decrease) in accounts payable	6,000	5,000	(1,000)
Increase (decrease) in income taxes	100	300	(100)
Increase (decrease) in accrued liabilities	6,000	3,000	(1,000)
Net cash provided by operating activities	76,600	97,200	61,500
Investing activities:			
Additions to property, plant, and equipment	(66,500)	$(84,400)	(52,500)
Financing activities:			
Payment on long-term debt	(1,000)	(2,000)	(1,500)
Issuance of other long-term liabilities	9,200	1,000	(1,000)
Issuance of capital stock	1,000	—	—
Dividend paid	(10,300)	(9,800)	(9,500)
Net cash used in financing activities	(1,100)	(10,800)	(12,000)
Increase (decrease) in cash	9,000	2,000	(3,000)
Cash at beginning of year	39,000	37,000	40,000
Cash at end of year	$ 48,000	$ 39,000	$ 37,000

GENERAL COMPANY
Balance Sheet
December 31, 2008

	2008	2007
Assets		
Current assets:		
Cash	$ 48,000	$ 39,000
Accounts receivable, less allowance for doubtful		
accounts of $2,000 in 2008 and $1,400 in 2009	125,000	121,000
Inventories	71,000	68,000
Prepaid expenses	2,500	2,200
Total current assets	246,500	230,200
Property, plant, and equipment:		
Land and land improvements	12,000	10,500
Buildings	98,000	89,000
Machinery and equipment	303,000	247,000
	413,000	346,500
Less: Accumulated depreciation	165,000	144,000
Net property, plant and equipment	248,000	202,500
Total assets	$494,500	$432,700
Liabilities and Stockholders' Equity		
Current liabilities:		
Accounts payable	$ 56,000	$ 50,000
Income taxes	3,700	3,600
Accrued liabilities	34,000	28,000
Total current liabilities	93,700	81,600
Long-term debt	63,000	64,000
Other long-term liabilities	16,000	6,800
Deferred federal income taxes	27,800	24,000
Total liabilities	200,500	176,400
Stockholders' equity:		
Capital stock	46,000	45,000
Retained earnings	248,000	211,300
Total stockholders' equity	294,000	256,300
Total liabilities and stockholders' equity	$494,500	$432,700

Note: The market price of the stock at the end of 2008 was $30.00 per share. There were 23,000 common shares outstanding at December 31, 2008.

Required

a. Compute the Z score of General Company at the end of 2008.
b. According to the Altman model, does the Z score of General Company indicate a high probability of financial failure?

P 11-15.

LIFO reserves: Rhodes Company
Reported year for analysis, 2008

2008 Net income as reported	$ 90,200,000
2008 Inventory reserve	50,000,000
2007 Inventory reserve	46,000,000
2008 Income taxes	55,000,000
2008 Income before income taxes	145,200,000

Required Compute the approximate income if inventory had been valued at approximate current cost.

P 11-16.

LIFO reserves: Lion Company
Reported year for analysis, 2007

2007 Net income as reported	$45,000,000
2007 Inventory reserve	20,000,000
2006 Inventory reserve	28,000,000
2007 Income taxes	14,000,000
2007 Income before income taxes	59,000,000

Required Compute the approximate income if inventory had been valued at approximate current cost.

P 11-17.   An airline presented this graph with its annual report.

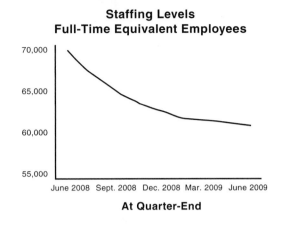

Required   Indicate the misleading feature in this graph.

Case 11-1

TIMBER, FOREST PRODUCTS, ETC.

Weyerhaeuser Company presented this comment in its 10-K for the fiscal year ended December 31, 2006.

OUR BUSINESS (in Part)

We are an integrated forest products company. We grow and harvest trees, build homes and make wood and paper products essential to everyday lives. Our goal is to do this safely, profitably and responsibly.

Our business has offices or operations in 18 countries and has customers worldwide. We manage 33 million acres of forests, and in 2006, we generated $21.9 billion in annual net sales and revenues.

Weyerhaeuser Company

CONSOLIDATED STATEMENT OF EARNINGS
(DOLLAR AMOUNTS IN MILLIONS EXCEPT PER-SHARE FIGURES)
FOR THE THREE-YEAR PERIOD ENDED DECEMBER 31, 2006

	2006	2005	2004
Net sales and revenues:			
Weyerhaeuser	$18,561	$19,131	$18,916
Real Estate and Related Assets	3,335	2,915	2,495
Total net sales and revenues	21,896	22,046	21,411
Costs and expenses:			
Weyerhaeuser:			
Costs of products sold	14,800	15,133	14,370
Depreciation, depletion and amortization	1,247	1,281	1,234
Selling expenses	492	455	474
General and administrative expenses	990	907	953
Research and development expenses	69	61	55
Charges for restructuring (Note 19)	22	21	39
Charges for closure of facilities (Note 20)	112	693	17
Impairment of goodwill (Note 8)	749	—	—
Refund of countervailing and anti-dumping deposits (Note 16)	(344)	—	—
Other operating costs (income), net (Note 18)	(133)	(44)	(231)
	18,004	18,507	16,911

(continued)

TIMBER, FOREST PRODUCTS, ETC. (Continued)

	2006	2005	2004
Real Estate and Related Assets:			
Costs and operating expenses	2,338	1,946	1,763
Depreciation and amortization	25	16	14
Selling expenses	180	152	126
General and administrative expenses	124	105	82
Other operating costs (income), net	(3)	(3)	(17)
Charge for impairment of long-lived assets	36	33	—
	2,700	2,249	1,968
Total costs and expenses	20,704	20,756	18,879
Operating income	1,192	1,290	2,532
Interest expense and other:			
Weyerhaeuser:			
Interest expense incurred	(615)	(739)	(838)
Less interest capitalized (Note 18)	84	59	9
Interest income and other (Notes 7 and 10)	70	214	24
Equity in income (loss) of affiliates (Note 7)	7	(6)	14
Real Estate and Related Assets:			
Interest expense incurred	(55)	(55)	(57)
Less interest capitalized	55	55	57
Interest income and other	30	12	31
Equity in income of unconsolidated entities (Note 7)	58	57	52
Earnings from continuing operations before income taxes	826	887	1,824
Income taxes (Note 15)	(471)	(318)	(609)
Earnings from continuing operations	355	569	1,215
Discontinued operations, net of income taxes (Note 22)	98	164	68
Net earnings	$ 453	$ 733	$ 1,283
Basic earnings per share (Note 3):			
Continuing operations	$ 1.45	$ 2.33	$ 5.16
Discontinued operations	0.40	0.67	0.29
Net earnings	$ 1.85	$ 3.00	$ 5.45
Diluted earnings per share (Note 3):			
Continuing operations	$ 1.44	$ 2.32	$ 5.14
Discontinued operations	0.40	0.66	0.29
Net earnings	$ 1.84	$ 2.98	$ 5.43
Dividends paid per share	$ 2.20	$ 1.90	$ 1.60

CONSOLIDATED BALANCE SHEET
(DOLLAR AMOUNTS IN MILLIONS, EXCEPT PER-SHARE FIGURES)

ASSETS

	DECEMBER 31, 2006	DECEMBER 25, 2005
Weyerhaeuser		
Current assets:		
Cash and cash equivalents	$ 223	$ 818
Receivables, less allowances of $17 and $15	1,569	1,707
Inventories (Note 4)	1,929	1,885
Prepaid expenses	400	414
Current assets of discontinued operations (Note 22)	—	52
Total current assets	4,121	4,876
Property and equipment, net (Note 5)	10,009	10,345
Construction in progress	407	527
Timber and timberlands at cost, less depletion charged to disposals	3,682	3,705
Investments in and advances to equity affiliates (Note 7)	499	486
Goodwill (Note 8)	2,203	2,982

(continued)

TIMBER, FOREST PRODUCTS, ETC. (Continued)

	DECEMBER 31, 2006	DECEMBER 25, 2005
Deferred pension and other assets (Note 9)	1,400	1,314
Restricted assets held by special purpose entities (Note 10)	917	916
Noncurrent assets of discontinued operations (Note 22)	—	171
	23,238	25,322
Real Estate and Related Assets		
Cash and cash equivalents	20	286
Receivables, less discounts and allowances of $4 and $3	144	42
Real estate in process of development and for sale (Note 6)	1,449	1,055
Land being processed for development	1,365	1,037
Investments in unconsolidated entities, less allowances of $11 and $4 (Note 7)	72	61
Other assets	423	296
Consolidated assets not owned (Note 10)	151	130
	3,624	2,907
Total assets	$26,862	$28,229
LIABILITIES AND SHAREHOLDERS' INTEREST		
Weyerhaeuser		
Current liabilities:		
Notes payable and commercial paper (Note 11)	$ 72	$ 3
Current maturities of long-term debt (Notes 13 and 14)	494	381
Accounts payable	1,048	1,227
Accrued liabilities (Note 12)	1,515	1,622
Current liabilities of discontinued operations (Note 22)	—	22
Total current liabilities	3,129	3,255
Long-term debt (Notes 13 and 14)	7,069	7,404
Deferred income taxes (Note 15)	3,691	4,032
Deferred pension, other postretirement benefits and other liabilities (Note 9)	1,796	1,591
Liabilities (nonrecourse to Weyerhaeuser) held by special purpose entities (Note 10)	765	764
Noncurrent liabilities of discontinued operations (Note 22)	—	3
Commitments and contingencies (Note 16)		
	16,450	17,049
Real Estate and Related Assets		
Notes payable and commercial paper (Note 11)	—	3
Long-term debt (Notes 13 and 14)	606	851
Other liabilities	606	417
Consolidated liabilities not owned (Note 10)	115	109
Commitments and contingencies (Note 16)		
	1,327	1,380
Total liabilities	17,777	18,429
Shareholders' interest (Note 17):		
Common shares: $1.25 par value; authorized 400,000,000 shares; issued and outstanding: 236,020,282 and 243,138,423 shares	295	304
Exchangeable shares: no par value; unlimited shares authorized; issued and held by nonaffiliates: 1,987,770 and 2,045,315 shares	135	139
Other capital	3,812	4,227
Retained earnings	4,755	4,840
Cumulative other comprehensive income	88	290
Total shareholders' interest	9,085	9,800
Total liabilities and shareholders' interest	$26,862	$28,229

(continued)

TIMBER, FOREST PRODUCTS, ETC. (Continued)

Notes to Consolidated Financial Statements (in Part)
For the three-year period ended December 31, 2006

Inventories

Inventories are stated at the lower of cost or market. Cost includes labor, materials and production overhead. The last-in, first-out (LIFO) method is used to cost more than half of domestic raw materials, in process and finished goods inventories. LIFO inventories were $710 million and $669 million at December 31, 2006, and December 25, 2005, respectively. The balance of domestic raw material and product inventories, all materials and supplies inventories, and all foreign inventories is costed at either the first-in, first-out (FIFO) or moving average cost methods. Had the FIFO method been used to cost all inventories, the amounts at which product inventories are stated would have been $262 million and $240 million greater at December 31, 2006, and December 25, 2005, respectively.

Required
a. Determine the change in net income for 2006 in comparison with the reported net income, if FIFO had been used for all inventory.
b. Compute the following for 2006, with no adjustments for LIFO reserve:
1. Days' sales in inventory
2. Working capital
3. Current ratio
4. Acid-test ratio
5. Debt ratio
c. Compute the measures in (b) considering the LIFO reserve (eliminate the LIFO reserve).
1. Days' sales in inventory
2. Working capital
3. Current ratio
4. Acid-test ratio
5. Debt ratio
d. Comment on the different results of the ratios computed in (b) and (c).

ACCOUNTING HOCUS-POCUS

This case is an excerpt from a presentation given by former Chairman Arthur Levitt, Securities and Exchange Commission, the "Numbers Game," to New York University Center for Law and Business, September 28, 1998.

Accounting Hocus-Pocus

Our accounting principles weren't meant to be a straitjacket. Accountants are wise enough to know they cannot anticipate every business structure or every new and innovative transaction, so they develop principles that allow for flexibility to adapt to changing circumstances. That's why the highest standards of objectivity, integrity and judgment can't be the exception. They must be the rule.

Flexibility in accounting allows it to keep pace with business innovations. Abuses such as earnings management occur when people exploit this pliancy. Trickery is employed to obscure actual financial volatility. This, in turn, masks the true consequences of management's decisions. These practices aren't limited to smaller companies struggling to gain investor interest. It's also happening in companies whose products we know and admire.

So what are these illusions? Five of the more popular ones I want to discuss today are "big bath" restructuring charges, creative acquisition accounting, "cookie jar reserves," "immaterial" misapplications of accounting principles and the premature recognition of revenue.

"Big-Bath" Charges

Let me first deal with "Big Bath" restructuring charges.

Companies remain competitive by regularly assessing the efficiency and profitability of their operations. Problems arise, however, when we see large charges associated with companies restructuring. These charges help companies "clean up" their balance sheet—giving them a so-called "big bath."

Why are companies tempted to overstate these charges? When earnings take a major hit, the theory goes Wall Street will look beyond a one-time loss and focus only on future earnings.

And if these charges are conservatively estimated with a little extra cushioning, that so-called conservative estimate is miraculously reborn as income when estimates change or future earnings fall short.

When a company decides to restructure, management and employees, investors and creditors, customers and suppliers all want to understand the expected effects. We need, of course, to ensure that financial reporting provides this information. But this should not lead to flushing all the associated costs—and maybe a little extra—through the financial statements.

Creative Acquisition Accounting

Let me turn now to the second gimmick.

In recent years, whole industries have been remade through consolidations, acquisitions and spin-offs. Some acquirers, particularly those using stock as an acquisition currency, have used this environment as an opportunity to engage in another form of "creative accounting." I call it "merger magic."

I am not talking tonight about the pooling versus purchase problem. Some companies have no choice but to use purchase accounting—which can result in lower future earnings. But that's a result some companies are unwilling to tolerate.

So what do they do? They classify an ever-growing portion of the acquisition price as "in-process" Research and Development, so—you guessed it—the amount can be written off in a "one-time" charge—removing any future earnings drag. Equally troubling is the creation of large liabilities for future operating expenses to protect future earnings—all under the mask of an acquisition.

Miscellaneous "Cookie Jar Reserves"

A third illusion played by some companies is using unrealistic assumptions to estimate liabilities for such items as sales returns, loan losses or warranty costs. In doing so, they stash accruals in cookie jars during the good times and reach into them when needed in the bad times.

I'm reminded of one U.S. company who took a large one-time loss to earnings to reimburse franchisees for equipment. That equipment, however, which included literally the kitchen sink, had yet to be bought. And, at the same time, they announced that future earnings would grow an impressive 15 percent per year.

"Materiality"

Let me turn now to the fourth gimmick—the abuse of materiality—a word that captures the attention of both attorneys and accountants. Materiality is another way we build flexibility into financial reporting. Using the logic of diminishing returns, some items may be so insignificant that they are not worth measuring and reporting with exact precision.

(continued)

Case	ACCOUNTING HOCUS-POCUS (Continued)
11-2	

But some companies misuse the concept of materiality. They intentionally record errors within a defined percentage ceiling. They then try to excuse that fib by arguing that the effect on the bottom line is too small to matter. If that's the case, why do they work so hard to create these errors? Maybe because the effect can matter, especially if it picks up that last penny of the consensus estimate. When either management or the outside auditors are questioned about these clear violations of GAAP, they answer sheepishly . . . "It doesn't matter. It's immaterial."

In markets where missing an earnings projection by a penny can result in a loss of millions of dollars in market capitalization, I have a hard time accepting that some of these so-called non-events simply don't matter.

Revenue Recognition

Lastly, companies try to boost earnings by manipulating the recognition of revenue. Think about a bottle of fine wine. You wouldn't pop the cork on that bottle before it was ready. But some companies are doing this with their revenue—recognizing it before a sale is complete, before the product is delivered to a customer, or at a time when the customer still has options to terminate, void or delay the sale.

Required

a. "Big Bath"—Comment on how a "Big Bath" would have enabled WorldCom to cover up its fraud.

b. Why would writing off "in-process" Research and Development be similar to a "Big Bath"?

c. How could a company use "allowance for doubtful accounts" as "Cookie Jar Reserves"?

d. Speculate on how a company could use "Materiality" or disregard or partially disregard a specific accounting standard.

Case	TURN A CHEEK
11-3	

June 1996, *New York Times* columnist Bob Herbert wrote a pair of opinion editorials accusing Nike Corp. of cruelly exploiting cheap Asian labor. Nike CEO Philip Knight replied in a letter to the editor, which the *Times* published. Some of the information in the Knight letter included that Nike has, on average, paid double the minimum wage as defined in countries where its products are produced under contract.[56]

In 1998, Marc Kasky, a resident of California, sued Nike alleging that the Knight letter violated California's consumer protection laws against deceptive advertising and unfair business practices.[57] In effect the position was that the *New York Times* editorials were under the First Amendment, but that the Nike reply was under the Fifth Amendment. The First Amendment covers freedom of speech, while the Fifth Amendment covers commercial speech.

The California Supreme Court ruled in May 2002 that the Nike reply had to be viewed under the Fifth Amendment. The Supreme Court stated it was "commercial speech because it is both more readily verifiable by its speaker and more hardy than noncommercial speech, can be effectively regulated to suppress false and actually or inherently misleading messages without undue risk of chilling public debate."[58]

Nike appealed the decision to the U.S. Supreme Court. The Supreme Court agreed to hear the case. In June 2003, the Supreme Court changed its mind and dismissed the matter on procedural grounds.[59] Usually, the justices consider cases only after the state courts render a final decision; here, the state court had only said the speech was a commercial speech and sent the case back down for further proceedings—likely including a trial on whether the statements were indeed misleading.[60]

(continued)

TURN A CHEEK (Continued)

A trial did not take place as Nike settled on September 2003, agreeing to pay $1.5 million over a three-year period to the Fair Labor Association, a Washington worker-rights group.[61]

Required
a. Write a position paper on why the Nike reply should be viewed under the First Amendment.
b. Write a position paper on why the Nike reply should be viewed under the Fifth Amendment.

Note: Good reference materials for this case are:

Roger Parloff, "Can We Talk," *Fortune* (September 2, 2002), pp. 102–104, 106, 108, 110.

Kasky v. Nike, Inc. Cite as 45 p. 3d 243 (Cal 2002).

Nike Web site http://www.Nike.com.

BOOKS GALORE

Case 11-4

Borders Group, Inc., presented this statement in its 10-K for the fiscal year ended February 3, 2007.

10-K Item 1—Business

General (in Part)

Borders Group, Inc., through its subsidiaries, Borders, Inc. ("Borders"), Walden Book Company, Inc. ("Waldenbooks"), Borders (UK) Limited, Borders Australia Pty Limited and others (individually and collectively, "the Company"), is the second largest operator of book, music and movie superstores and the largest operator of mail-based bookstores in the world based upon both sales and number of stores.

Borders Group, Inc., presented the following in its 10-K for the fiscal year ended February 3, 2007.

CONSOLIDATED STATEMENTS OF OPERATIONS
(dollars in millions except per share data)

	Fiscal Year Ended		
	Feb. 3, 2007	Jan. 28, 2006	Jan. 23, 2005
Sales	$4,063.9	$4,030.7	$3,879.5
Other revenue	49.6	48.5	51.9
Total revenue	$4,113.5	$4,079.2	$3,931.4
Cost of merchandise sold (includes occupancy)	3,065.2	2,939.5	2,812.4
Gross margin	1,048.3	1,139.7	1,119.0
Selling, general and administrative expenses	987.6	952.1	890.3
Pre-opening expense	11.3	7.6	4.8
Asset impairments and other writedowns	186.2	6.6	7.2
Operating income (loss)	(136.8)	173.4	216.7
Interest expense	32.4	14.3	9.1
Income (loss) before income tax	(169.2)	159.1	207.6
Income tax provision (benefit)	(17.9)	58.1	75.7
Net income (loss)	$ (151.3)	$ 101.0	$ 131.9
Earnings (loss) per common share data (Note 2)			
Diluted:			
Net income (Loss)	$ (2.44)	$ 1.42	1.69
Weighted-average common shares outstanding	61.9	71.1	77.9
Basic:			
Net income (loss)	$ (2.44)	$ 1.45	$ 1.72
Weighted-average common shares outstanding	61.9	69.8	76.6

(continued)

BOOKS GALORE (Continued)

CONSOLIDATED BALANCE SHEETS
(dollars in millions except share amounts)

	Fiscal Year Ended	
	Feb. 3, 2007	Jan. 28, 2006
Assets		
Current assets:		
Cash and cash equivalents	$ 120.4	$ 81.6
Merchandise inventories	1,452.0	1,405.9
Accounts receivable and other current assets	151.2	150.3
Total current assets	1,723.6	1,637.8
Property and equipment, net	707.7	703.9
Other assets	65.1	79.7
Deferred income taxes	76.7	26.3
Goodwill	40.3	124.5
Total assets	$2,613.4	$2,572.2
Liabilities, Minority Interest and Stockholders' Equity		
Current liabilities:		
Short-term borrowings and current portion of long-term debt	$ 542.6	$ 207.1
Trade accounts payable	631.4	660.3
Accrued payroll and other liabilities	333.1	293.4
Taxes, including income taxes	60.4	135.8
Deferred income taxes	28.4	14.5
Total current liabilities	1,595.9	1,311.1
Long-term debt	5.2	5.4
Other long-term liabilities	368.3	326.6
Commitments and contingencies (Note 9)	—	—
Total liabilities	1,969.4	1,643.1
Minority interest	2.0	1.3
Total liabilities and minority interest	1,971.4	1,644.4
Stockholders' equity:		
Common stock, 300,000,000 shares authorized; 58,476,306 and 64,149,397 shares issued and outstanding at February 3, 2007 and January 28, 2006, respectively	175.5	293.9
Accumulated other comprehensive income	28.5	19.4
Retained earnings	438.0	614.5
Total stockholders' equity	642.0	927.8
Total liabilities, minority interest and stockholders' equity	$2,613.4	$2,572.2

CONSOLIDATED STATEMENTS OF CASH FLOWS
(dollars in millions)

	Fiscal Year Ended		
	Feb. 3, 2007	Jan. 28, 2006	Jan. 23, 2005
Cash provided by (used for):			
Operations			
Net income (loss)	$(151.3)	$ 101.0	$ 131.9
Adjustments to reconcile net income (loss) to operating cash flows:			
Depreciation	130.0	121.5	112.9
Gain on deconsolidation of variable interest entities	—	—	(2.9)
Gain on sale of investments	(5.0)	(1.2)	—

(continued)

BOOKS GALORE (Continued)

	Fiscal Year Ended		
	Feb. 3, 2007	Jan. 28, 2006	Jan. 23, 2005
Loss on disposal of assets	6.8	5.3	2.4
Increase in minority interest	0.6	—	—
(Increase) decrease in deferred income taxes	(34.5)	(13.0)	12.6
Increase in other long-term assets	(1.3)	(3.9)	(6.7)
Increase in other long-term liabilities	29.8	29.4	13.3
Asset impairments and other writedowns	179.0	4.3	6.2
Cash provided by (used for) current assets and current liabilities:			
Increase in inventories	(33.4)	(105.0)	(63.8)
Increase in accounts receivable	(4.2)	(10.0)	(5.7)
(Increase) decrease in prepaid expenses	11.4	(24.0)	(9.9)
Increase (decrease) in accounts payable	(34.2)	48.1	13.8
Increase (decrease) in taxes payable	(75.8)	25.6	3.4
Increase (decrease) in accrued payroll and other liabilities	29.8	(8.2)	19.3
Net cash provided by operations	47.7	169.9	226.8
Investing			
Capital expenditures	(204.2)	(196.3)	(115.5)
Proceeds from sale of investments	21.6	105.2	118.0
Purchase of investments	—	—	(95.4)
Proceeds from sale-leaseback of assets	—	—	32.3
Acquisition	—	—	(31.2)
Net cash used for investing	(182.6)	(91.1)	(91.8)
Financing			
Net repayment of long-term debt	—	(0.1)	—
Net repayment of long-term capital lease obligations	(0.1)	(0.4)	(0.4)
Net funding from credit facility	317.3	23.3	7.2
Proceeds from the excess tax benefit of options exercised	4.3	—	—
Cash dividends paid	(25.2)	(25.5)	(25.1)
Issuance of common stock	26.0	27.6	44.8
Repurchase of common stock	(148.7)	(265.9)	(177.3)
Net cash provided by (used for) financing	173.6	(241.0)	(150.8)
Effect of exchange rates on cash and equivalents	0.1	(1.0)	(0.2)
Net increase (decrease) in cash and equivalents	38.8	(163.2)	(16.0)
Cash and equivalents at beginning of year	81.6	244.8	260.8
Cash and equivalents at end of year	$ 120.4	$ 81.6	$ 244.8
Supplemental cash flow disclosures:			
Interest paid	$ 34.0	$ 13.9	$ 8.5
Income taxes paid	$ 63.5	$ 55.0	$ 64.6

NOTES TO CONSOLIDATED FINANCIAL STATEMENTS (in Part)

(dollars in millions except per share data)

Note 1—Summary of Significant Accounting Policies (in Part)

Inventories: Merchandise inventories are valued on a first-in, first-out ("FIFO") basis at the lower of cost or market using the retail inventory method. The Company includes certain distribution and other expenses in its inventory costs, totaling $114.1 and $102.1 as of February 3, 2007, and January 28, 2006, respectively.

(continued)

Case	
11-4	**BOOKS GALORE** (Continued)

Other data provided for the case follow:

BORDERS GROUP, INC.
CONSOLIDATED BALANCE SHEET
(dollars in millions except share amounts)

	Fiscal Year Ended Jan. 23, 2005
Assets	
Current assets:	
Cash and cash equivalents	$ 244.8
Investments	95.4
Merchandise inventories	1,306.9
Accounts receivable and other current assets	118.3
Total current assets	1,765.4
Property and equipment, net	635.6
Other assets	84.8
Deferred income taxes	14.4
Goodwill	128.6
Total assets	$2,628.8
Liabilities, Minority Interest and Stockholders' Equity	
Current liabilities:	
Short-term borrowings and current portion of long-term debt	$ 141.2
Trade accounts payable	615.1
Accrued payroll and other liabilities	306.4
Taxes, including income taxes	118.3
Deferred income taxes	15.0
Total current liabilities	1,196.0
Long-term debt	55.8
Other long-term liabilities	286.7
Commitments and contingencies (Note 11)	—
Total liabilities	1,538.5
Minority interest	1.4
Total liabilities and minority interest	1,539.9
Stockholders' equity:	
Common stock, 200,000,000 shares authorized; 73,875,627	
shares issued and outstanding at January 23, 2005	525.1
Deferred compensation	(0.5)
Accumulated other comprehensive income	25.3
Retained earnings	539.0
Total stockholders' equity	1,088.9
Total liabilities, minority interest and stockholders' equity	$2,628.8

Required a. Compute the following liquidity ratios for 2007 and 2006:
  1. Days' sales in inventory
  2. Inventory turnover
  3. Working capital
  4. Current ratio
  5. Cash ratio
  6. Sales to working capital
  7. Operating cash flow/current maturities of long-term debt and current notes payable

  b. Compute the following long-term debt-paying ability for 2007 and 2006:
  1. Times interest earned
  2. Debt ratio
  3. Operating cash flow/total debt

(continued)

Case	BOOKS GALORE (Continued)
11-4	

    c. Compute the following profitability ratios for 2007 and 2006:
       1. Net profit margin
       2. Return on assets
       3. Return on total equity
       4. Gross profit margin
    d. Compute or obtain the following investor analysis:
       1. Degree of financial leverage
       2. Earnings per common share
       3. Operating cash flow/cash dividends
    e. Comment on the trend in net income (loss).
    f. Comment on the trend in net cash provided by operations.
    g. Using these ratios for 2007, comment using the Beaver Study on Possible Financial Failure.
       1. Cash flow/total debt
       2. Net income/total assets (return on assets)
       3. Total debt/total assets (debt ratio)

Case	VALUE—NIKE, INC.
11-5	

Selected data from Nike's financial statements for the period 2003–2007 follow:

Year Ended May 31,	2007	2006	2005	2004	2003
	(In millions except per share data and financial ratios)[1]				
Revenues	$16,325.9	$14,954.9	$13,739.7	$12,253.1	$10,697.0
Gross margin	7,160.5	6,587.0	6,115.4	5,251.7	4,383.4
Gross margin %	43.9%	44.0%	44.5%	42.9%	41.0%
Income before cumulative effect of accounting change	1,491.5	1,392.0	1,211.6	945.6	740.1
Cumulative effect of accounting change	—	—	—	—	266.1
Net income	1,491.5	1,392.0	1,211.6	945.6	474.0
Cash dividends declared per common share	0.71	0.59	0.475	0.37	0.27
Cash flow from operations	1,878.7	1,667.9	1,570.7	1,518.5	922.0
At May 31,					
Total assets	10,688.3	9,869.6	8,793.6	7,908.7	6,821.1
Long-term debt	409.9	410.7	687.3	682.4	531.6
Redeemable preferred stock	0.3	0.3	0.3	0.3	0.3
Shareholders' equity	7,025.4	6,285.2	5,644.2	4,781.7	3,990.7
Market capitalization	28,472.3	20,564.5	21,462.3	17,724.2	14,758.8
Financial ratios:					
Return on equity	22.4%	23.3%	23.2%	21.6%	18.9%
Return on assets	14.5%	14.9%	14.5%	12.8%	11.2%
Current ratio at May 31	3.1	2.8	3.2	2.7	2.4
Price/earnings ratio at May 31 (diluted before accounting change)	19.4	13.2	18.3	20.3	20.2

[1]All share and per share information has been restated to reflect the two-for-one stock split affected in the form of a 100% common stock dividend distributed on April 2, 2007.

Note: There are many approaches to valuing a company. The analysts would likely review a company using several approaches.

(continued)

Case	VALUE—NIKE, INC. (Continued)
11-5	

Required   a. Liquidity:

1. Review the summary analysis for Nike, Inc., from 2005–2007. Give your opinion of the liquidity position (refer back to Exhibit 3, Summary Analysis).
2. Review the current ratio in this case (2003–2007). Give your opinion of the liquidity position.
3. Review cash provided by operations (2003–2007). Give your opinion as to the trend.

b. Long-term debt-paying ability:

1. Review the summary analysis for Nike, Inc. From 2005–2007, give your opinion of the debt position (refer back to Exhibit 3, Summary Analysis).
2. Review the trend of long-term debt in relation to total assets (2003–2007). Give your opinion of the debt trend.

c. Profitability:

1. Review the summary analysis for Nike, Inc. from 2005–2007. Give your opinion of the profitability (refer back to Exhibit 3, Summary Analysis).
2. Review the trend in revenues (2003–2007). Comment on the trend.
3. Review the trend in gross margin (2003–2007). Comment on the trend.
4. Review the trend in gross margin % (2003–2007). Comment on the trend.

d. Investor analysis:

1. Review the absolute amount and trend in the price/earnings. Considering liquidity, debt, and profitability, is there a reasonable probability that the price/earnings may increase?
2. Comment on the trend in market capitalization (2003–2007) (Share price × number of outstanding shares).
3. Review dividends—common and preferred (2003–2007). Is there a likely chance that dividends will be increased during the year ended May 31, 2008?
4. Give your opinion of the stock price of Nike, Inc., on May 31, 2009. In practice, many things would be considered that are not presented in this case. Base your opinion on the summary analysis (2005–2007) and the data provided with this case.

e. Other:

1. This case has used a fundamental financial statement approach to valuing Nike. In your opinion, would an analyst likely use this type of approach for valuing Nike? Please comment.

Web	**Thomson One** *Business School Edition*
Case	

Please complete the Web case that covers material discussed in this chapter at academic .cengage.com/accounting/Gibson. You'll be using Thomson One Business School Edition, a powerful tool, that combines a full range of fundamental financial information, earnings estimates, market data, and source documents for 500 publicly traded companies.

Endnotes

1. C. H. Gibson, "Financial Ratios as Perceived by Commercial Loan Officers," *Akron Business and Economic Review* (Summer 1983), pp. 23–27.
2. The basis of the comments in this section is a study by Dr. Charles Gibson in 1981. The research was done under a grant from the Deloitte Haskins & Sells Foundation.

3. C. H. Gibson, "Ohio CPA's Perceptions of Financial Ratios," *The Ohio CPA Journal* (Autumn 1985), pp. 25–30. © 1985. Reprinted with permission of *The Ohio CPA Journal*.

4. C. H. Gibson, "How Chartered Financial Analysts View Financial Ratios," *Financial Analysts Journal* (May–June 1987), pp. 74–76.

5. Ibid.

6. C. H. Gibson, "Financial Ratios in Annual Reports," *The CPA Journal* (September 1982), pp. 18–29.

7. W. H. Beaver, "Alternative Accounting Measures as Predictors of Failure," *The Accounting Review* (January 1968), pp. 113–122.

8. Ibid., p. 117.

9. Ibid., p. 119.

10. E. I. Altman, "Financial Ratios, Discriminant Analysis and the Prediction of Corporate Bankruptcy," *Journal of Finance* (September 1968), pp. 589–609.

11. Edward I. Altman and Thomas P. McGough, "Evaluation of a Company as a Going Concern," *The Journal of Accountancy* (December 1974), pp. 50–57.

12. Ibid., p. 52.

13. Suggested reference sources:

Anker V. Andersen, "Graphing Financial Information: How Accountants Can Use Graphs to Communicate," *National Association of Accountants* (1983), p. 50.

Edward Bloches, Robert P. Moffie, and Robert W. Smud, "How Best to Communicate Numerical Data," *The Internal Auditor* (February 1985), pp. 38–42.

Deanna Qxender Burgess, "Graphical Sleight of Hand: How Can Auditors Spot Altered Exhibits that Appear in Annual Reports?" *Journal of Accountancy* (February 2002), pp. 45–50.

Charles H. Gibson and Nicholas Schroeder, "Improving Your Practice—Graphically," *The CPA Journal* (August 1990), pp. 28–37.

Johnny R. Johnson, Richard R. Rice, and Roger A. Roemmich, "Pictures That Lie: The Abuse of Graphs in Annual Reports," *Management Accounting* (October 1980), pp. 50–56.

Robert Lefferts, *How to Prepare Charts and Graphs for Effective Reports* (New York: Barnes & Noble Books, 1982), p. 166.

David Lynch and Steven Galen, "Got the Picture? CPAs Can Use Some Simple Principles to Create Effective Charts and Graphs for Financial Reports and Presentations," *Journal of Accountancy* (May 2002), pp. 183–187.

Calvin F. Schmid and Stanton E. Schmid, *Handbook of Graphic Presentation,* 2nd ed. (New York: Ronald Press, 1979), p. 308.

14. http://www.sec.gov.

15. "Restatements of Profits Prove Costly to Investors," *The Wall Street Journal* (October 24, 2002), p. D2.

16. George J. Benoton and Al L. Hartgraves, "Enron: What Happened and What We Can Learn from It," *Journal of Accounting and Public Policy* (August 2002), pp. 105–127.

17. Susan Pulliam and Deborah Solomon, "How Three Unlikely Sleuths Discovered Fraud at WorldCom," *The Wall Street Journal* (October 30, 2002), p. A6.

18. Jared Sandberg and Susan Pulliam, "Report by WorldCom Examiner Finds New Fraudulent Activities," *The Wall Street Journal* (November 5, 2002), p. 1.

19. Pulliam and Solomon, "How Three Unlikely Sleuths Discovered Fraud at WorldCom."

20. Ibid.

21. Ibid.

22. Theo Francis, "AIG Issues Report, and Caution," *The Wall Street Journal* (June 1, 2005), p. C1.

23. Ibid., p. C3.

24. Ibid.

25. Ibid.

26. Financial Restatements, July 2006, GAO-06-678, P4.

27. Ibid., p. 48.

28. United States Government Accountability Office, Washington D.C., Letter addressed to the Honorable Paul S. Sarbanes, Ranking Minority Member, Committee on Banking, Housing, and Urban Affairs, United States Senate, August 31, 2006. Enclosure I, pg. 5, GAO-06-1053a Financial Restatement Database.

29. Marco Trombetta, "Discussion of Implied Cost of Equity Capital in Earnings-Based Valuation: International Evidence," *Accounting and Business Research,* Volume 34, Number 4 (2004), p. 345.

30. Richard G. Barker, "The Role of Dividends in Valuation Models Used by Analysts and Fund Managers," *The European Accounting Review* (1999, 8:2), p. 195.

31. Ibid., p. 197.

32. Ibid.

33. Ibid., pp. 200–201.
34. Ibid., p. 200.
35. Ibid., p. 202.
36. Ibid.
37. Ibid., p. 204.
38. Ibid., p. 205.
39. Ibid., p. 214.
40. Efthimios G. Demirakos, Norman C. Strong, and Martin Walker, "What Valuation Models Do Analysts Use?," *Accounting Horizons*, Volume 18, Number 4 (December 2004), p. 229.
41. Ibid.
42. Ibid., p. 237.
43. Paul Asquith, Michael B. Mikhail, and Andrea S. Au, "Information Content of Equity Analyst Reports," *Journal of Financial Economics* (75, 2005), p. 278.
44. Marco Trombetta, p. 345.
45. Tom Copeland, Tim Koller, and Jack Murrin, *Valuation, Measuring, and Managing the Value of Companies,* Third Edition (New York: John Wiley & Sons, Inc., 2000), p. preface 1x.
46. Ibid., p. 62.
47. Ibid., p. 67.
48. Ibid., p. 113.
49. Ibid.
50. Ibid., p. 115.
51. Ibid., p. 116.
52. Ibid., p. 315.
53. Ibid.
54. Ibid., p. 317.
55. Ibid., p. 321.
56. Roger Parloff, "Can We Talk," *Fortune* (September 2, 2002), pp. 102–103.
57. Ibid., p. 103.
58. *Kasky v. Nike, Inc.* Cite as 45 p. 3d 243 (Cal 2002).
59. Eugene Valokh, "Nike and the Free-Speech Knot," *The Wall Street Journal* (June 30, 2003), p. A16.
60. Ibid.
61. Stephanie Kang, "Nike Settles Case with an Activist for $1.5 Million," *The Wall Street Journal* (September 15, 2003), p. 10.

Chapter 12

Special Industries: Banks, Utilities, Oil and Gas, Transportation, Insurance, Real Estate Companies

The preceding chapters covered material most applicable to manufacturing, retailing, wholesaling, and service industries. This chapter covers six specialized industries: banks, electric utilities, oil and gas, transportation, insurance, and real estate companies. The chapter notes the differences in statements and suggests changes or additions to analysis.

Banks

Banks operate under either a federal or state charter. National banks are required to submit uniform accounting statements to the Comptroller of the Currency. State banks are controlled by their state banking departments. In addition, the Federal Deposit Insurance Corporation and the Board of Governors of the Federal Reserve System receive financial and operating statements from all members of the Federal Reserve System. Member banks are required to keep reserves with their district Federal Reserve bank. State banking laws also dictate the geographical area within which a bank may function. The range runs from within one county to interstate.

Banking systems usually involve two types of structures: individual banks and bank holding companies. Bank holding companies consist of a parent that owns one or many banks. Additionally, the holding company may own bank-related financial services and nonfinancial subsidiaries. In financial report analysis, we must determine the extent of the business generated by banking services. In order for the specific industry ratios to be meaningful, a large proportion of the services should be bank related.

Exhibit 12-1 presents part of the 2006 annual report of National City. Located in Cleveland, Ohio, National City owns and operates commercial banks with offices in Ohio, Kentucky, Illinois, Indiana, Michigan, and Pennsylvania. National City is one of the largest financial holding companies in the United States.

BALANCE SHEET

The balance sheet of a commercial bank is sometimes termed the *report of condition*. Two significant differences exist between the traditional balance sheet and that of a bank. First, the accounts of banks may seem the opposite of those of other types of firms.

Exhibit 12-1 NATIONAL CITY*

Selected Data from 2006 Annual Report

CONSOLIDATED FINANCIAL STATEMENTS
Consolidated Balance Sheets

	December 31,	
(Dollars in Thousands, Except Per Share Amounts)	2006	2005
Assets		
Cash and demand balances due from banks	$ 3,521,153	$ 3,707,665
Federal funds sold and security resale agreements	1,551,350	301,260
Securities available for sale, at fair value	7,508,820	7,874,628
Other investments	6,317,779	2,108,622
Loans held for sale or securitization:		
Commercial	33,661	10,784
Commercial real estate	177,312	35,306
Residential real estate	9,327,783	9,192,282
Home equity lines of credit	2,888,512	—
Credit card	425,000	425,000
Student loans	638	3,758
Total loans held for sale or securitization	12,852,906	9,667,130
Portfolio loans:		
Commercial	31,052,021	27,571,913
Commercial construction	4,266,280	3,366,774
Commercial real estate	12,436,458	12,407,576
Residential real estate	24,775,632	32,822,947
Home equity lines of credit	14,594,782	21,438,690
Credit card and other unsecured lines of credit	3,006,789	2,611,679
Other consumer	5,360,110	5,819,144
Total portfolio loans	95,492,072	106,038,723
Allowance for loan losses	(1,131,175)	(1,094,047)
Net portfolio loans	94,360,897	104,944,676
Properties and equipment	1,402,150	1,328,903
Equipment leased to others	572,952	696,327
Other real estate owned	229,070	97,008
Mortgage servicing rights	2,094,387	2,115,715
Goodwill	3,815,911	3,313,109
Other intangible assets	183,648	168,353
Derivative assets	612,914	772,918
Accrued income and other assets	5,166,905	5,300,800
Total assets	**$140,190,842**	**$142,397,114**
Liabilities		
Deposits:		
Noninterest bearing	$ 17,537,278	$ 17,429,227
NOW and money market	30,335,531	28,304,007
Savings	1,881,444	2,147,022
Consumer time	23,620,821	20,527,784
Other	4,119,756	6,734,915
Foreign	9,738,760	8,843,036
Total deposits	87,233,590	83,985,991
Federal funds borrowed and security repurchase agreements	5,283,997	6,499,254
Borrowed funds	1,648,967	3,517,537
Long-term debt	25,406,971	30,496,093
Junior subordinated debentures owed to unconsolidated subsidiary trusts	948,705	473,523
Derivative liabilities	717,830	738,343
Accrued expenses and other liabilities	4,369,779	4,073,502
Total liabilities	**$125,609,839**	**$129,784,243**
Stockholders' Equity		
Preferred stock, no par value, $100 liquidation value per share, authorized 5,000,000 shares, 70,272 shares outstanding in 2006 and 2005	$ —	$ —

*"National City Corporation ... headquartered in Cleveland, Ohio, is one of the nation's largest financial holding companies. ... Our core businesses include commercial and retail banking, mortgage financing and servicing consumer finance and asset management." 10-K

| Exhibit | 12-1 | NATIONAL CITY (Continued) |

	December 31,	
	2006	**2005**
Common stock, par value $4 per share, 1,400,000,000 shares authorized, 632,381,603 and 615,047,663 outstanding shares at December 31, 2006 and 2005, respectively	2,529,527	2,460,191
Capital surplus	4,793,537	3,681,603
Retained earnings	7,328,853	6,459,212
Accumulated other comprehensive (loss) income	(70,914)	11,865
Total Stockholders' Equity	14,581,003	12,612,871
Total Liabilities and Stockholders' Equity	$140,190,842	$142,397,114

CONSOLIDATED FINANCIAL STATEMENTS
Consolidated Statements of Income

	For the Calendar Year		
	2006	**2005**	**2004**
Interest Income			
Loans	$8,351,493	$7,239,110	$5,560,221
Securities			
Taxable	385,807	342,797	338,724
Exempt from Federal income taxes	25,461	30,509	32,669
Dividends	2,906	8,857	5,906
Federal funds sold and security resale agreements	34,847	12,266	6,185
Other investments	133,248	98,280	82,298
Total interest income	8,933,762	7,731,819	6,026,003
Interest expense			
Deposits	2,420,316	1,604,601	896,131
Federal funds borrowed and security repurchase agreements	284,505	209,893	94,097
Borrowed funds	102,893	67,896	15,237
Long-term debt and capital securities	1,522,445	1,153,681	587,870
Total interest expense	4,330,159	3,036,071	1,593,335
Net Interest Income	4,603,603	4,695,748	4,432,668
Provision for Credit Losses	482,593	283,594	323,272
Net interest income after provision for credit losses	4,121,010	4,412,154	4,109,396
Noninterest Income			
Loan sale revenue	765,513	808,356	878,705
Loan servicing revenue	91,467	399,379	500,995
Deposit service charges	818,301	740,280	669,746
Trust and investment management fees	300,747	296,012	300,931
Leasing revenue	228,149	267,315	180,407
Other service fees	150,606	124,869	112,574
Insurance revenue	129,341	102,789	91,253
Brokerage revenue	157,823	159,433	145,869
Card-related fees	114,275	110,392	89,453
Gain on divestitures	983,940	16,001	790,506
Other	279,286	252,406	660,768
Total fees and other income	4,019,448	3,277,232	4,421,207
Securities (losses) gains, net	(483)	27,087	18,974
Total noninterest income	4,018,965	3,304,319	4,440,181
Noninterest Expense			
Salaries, benefits, and other personnel	2,603,554	2,560,250	2,362,949
Equipment	326,058	303,471	299,867
Net occupancy	297,949	315,647	254,006
Third-party services	352,343	332,391	350,298
Marketing and public relations	147,679	164,533	115,403
Leasing expense	165,067	178,969	125,685
Other	824,689	895,796	963,429
Total noninterest expense	4,717,339	4,751,057	4,471,637
Income before income tax expense	3,422,636	2,965,416	4,077,940
Income tax expense	1,122,800	980,187	1,298,006
Net income	$2,299,836	$1,985,229	$2,779,934

(continued)

Exhibit　12-1　NATIONAL CITY (Continued)

	For the Calendar Year		
	2006	2005	2004
Net Income Per Common Share			
Basic	$ 3.77	$ 3.13	$ 4.37
Diluted	3.72	3.09	4.31
Average Common Shares Outstanding			
Basic	609,316,070	633,431,660	635,450,188
Diluted	617,671,507	641,600,969	645,510,514
Dividends declared per common share	$ 1.52	$ 1.44	$ 1.34

Consolidated Statements of Changes in Stockholders' Equity (in Part)

(Dollars in Thousands, Except Per Share Amounts)	Preferred Stock	Common Stock	Capital Surplus	Retained Earnings	Accumulated Other Comprehensive Income (Loss)	Total
Balance, December 31, 2005	$ —	$2,460,191	$3,681,603	$6,459,212	$ 11,865	$12,612,871
Comprehensive income:						
Net income				2,299,836		2,299,836
Other comprehensive income, net of tax:						
Change in unrealized gains and losses on securities, net of reclassification adjustment for net losses included in net income					7,956	7,956
Change in unrealized gains and losses on derivative instruments used in cash flow hedging relationships, net of reclassification adjustment for net gains included in net income					(19,388)	(19,388)
Total comprehensive income						2,288,404
Cumulative effect of change in accounting for mortgage servicing assets				16,886		16,886
Cumulative effect of change in accounting for pension and other postretirement obligations					(71,347)	(71,347)
Common dividends declared, $1.52 per share				(931,828)		(931,828)
Preferred dividends declared, $24.26 per share				(1,704)		(1,704)
Issuance of 7,985,388 common shares under stock-based compensation plans		32,115	253,645			285,760
Issuance of 29,456,622 common shares pursuant to acquisition[1]		117,826	976,850			1,094,676
Repurchase of 20,151,100 common shares		(80,605)	(118,561)	(514,740)		(713,906)
Other				1,191		1,191
Balance, December 31, 2006	$ —	$2,529,527	$4,793,537	$7,328,853	$(70,914)	$14,581,003

[1]Includes fair value of stock options exchanged and other equity instruments issues, if applicable.

Checking accounts or demand deposits are liabilities to a bank, since it owes the customers money in these cases. Similarly, loans to customers are assets—receivables. Further, the balance sheet accounts are not subdivided into current and noncurrent accounts.

Some banks provide a very detailed disclosure of their assets and liabilities. Other banks provide only general disclosure. The quality of review that can be performed can be no better than the disclosure.

Representative assets of a bank may include cash on hand or due from other banks, investment securities, loans, bank premises, and equipment. Closely review the disclosure of a bank's assets. This review may indicate risk or opportunity. For example, a review of the assets may indicate that the bank has a substantial risk if interest rates increase. The general rule is that for 20-year fixed obligations, a gain or loss of 8% of principal arises when interest rates change by 1%. Thus, an investment of $100,000,000 in 20-year bonds would lose approximately $32,000,000 in principal if interest rates increased by 4%. A similar example would be a bank that holds long-term fixed-rate mortgages. The value of these mortgages could decline substantially if interest rates increased. Many bank annual reports do not disclose the amount of fixed-rate mortgages.

Review the stockholders' equity section of the balance sheet to determine if significant accumulated other comprehensive income (loss) exists. National City had accumulated comprehensive income of $11,865,000 at December 31, 2005, and a $70,914,000 loss at December 31, 2006. The major change in this account was a loss of $71,347,000 from a cumulative effect of change in accounting for pension and other postretirement obligations.

Subprime residential real estate loans became a major issue with financial institutions in 2007. There is no standard definition of subprime residential real estate loans. For these loans there is a perceived risk spread to other residential real estate loans.

National City includes a number of comments related to residential real estate in its 2006 annual report. Some of the comments follow:

1. "Residential Real Estate: The residential real estate category includes loans to consumers secured by residential real estate, including home equity installment loans and loans to residential real estate developers. The Corporations residential real estate lending policies require all loans to have viable repayment sources."

2. "Home Equity Lines of Credit: The home equity category consists mainly of revaluing lines of credit secured by residential real estate. Home equity lines of credit are generally governed by the same lending policies and subject to credit risk as described above for residential real estate loans."

3. "The Corporation sold its First Franklin nonconforming mortgage origination network on December 30, 2006."

4. "Residential real estate loan sale revenue for 2006 included losses associated with the decision to sell a $6.0 billion pool of nonconforming mortgage loans from portfolio. This pool was transferred to held for sale and approximately $3.9 billion was sold prior to year end."

Note that the balance sheet at December 31, 2006, indicated material declines in portfolio loans for residential real estate and home equity lines of credit. National City had substantially exited the residential real estate loan market before the subprime issue became a national issue in 2007.

In recent years, Less Developed Country (LDC) loans have become a national issue. In general, LDC loans are perceived as being more risky than domestic loans. National City apparently did not have international loans at the end of both 2006 and 2005.

As part of the review of assets, review the disclosure that describes related-party loans. Observe the materiality and the trend of these loans. National City apparently did not have material related-party transactions which would require disclosure.

Review the disclosure of allowance for loan losses. It may indicate a significant change and/or significant losses charged. National City disclosed net charge-offs of $442.0 million in 2006 and $380.0 million in 2005, respectively.

Review the disclosure of nonperforming assets. In general, nonperforming assets are those for which the bank is not receiving income or is receiving reduced income. The categories of nonperforming assets are nonaccrual loans, renegotiated loans, and other real estate. *Nonaccrual loans* are loans for which payments have fallen significantly behind, so that the bank has stopped accruing interest income on these loans. *Renegotiated loans* are loans that the bank has renegotiated with a customer because the customer has had trouble meeting the terms of the original loan. In addition to other factors, banks should consider renegotiated loans when they adjust the loan loss reserve.

Other real estate usually consists of real estate the bank has taken when it foreclosed on a loan. For example, the bank may have made a loan to a company for a hotel and accepted a mortgage on the hotel as collateral. If the bank must foreclose on the loan, it may take possession of the hotel. The bank would want to sell the hotel, but it may be necessary to hold and operate the hotel for a relatively long period of time before a buyer can be found.

The amount and trend of nonperforming assets should be observed closely. This can be an early indication of troubles to come. For example, a significant increase in nonperforming assets late in the year may have had an insignificant effect on the past year's profits, but it could indicate a significant negative influence on the future year's profits.

Part of the National City disclosure for nonperforming assets and delinquent loans follows:

Details of nonperforming assets follow:

Dollars in millions	**2006**	**2005**
Commercial	$124	$181
Commercial construction	38	20
Commercial real estate	111	114
Residential real estate	227	175
Total nonperforming loans	500	490
Other real estate owned (OREO)	229	97
Mortgage loans held for sale and other	3	9
Total nonperforming assets	$732	$596
Nonperforming assets as a percentage of price-end portfolio loans and other nonperforming assets.	.76%	.56%
Period-end total assets	.52	.42

National City had substantially higher percentages in 2003 and 2002. The trend between 2005 and 2006 is negative.

Typical liabilities of a bank include savings, time and demand deposits, loan obligations, and long-term debt. Closely review the disclosure of liabilities for favorable or unfavorable trends. For example, a decreasing amount in savings deposits would indicate that the bank is losing one of its cheapest sources of funds. Total deposits increased moderately in 2006, which would be positive. Total liabilities decreased moderately in 2006. The major reason for this was the decrease in long-term debt, which would be positive.

As part of the review of liabilities, look for a note that describes commitments and contingent liabilities. This note may reveal significant commitments and contingent liabilities. National City disclosed significant commitments at the end of 2006 and 2005. Commitments and contingent liabilities appear to have increased in 2006. Significant increases were in the areas of commitments to extend credit commercial and standby letters of credit. Very significant increases were in the areas of net commitments to sell mortgage loans and mortgage-backed securities, net commitments to sell commercial real estate loans, and commitments to fund civic and community investments.

The stockholders' equity of a bank resembles that of other types of firms, except that the total stockholders' equity is usually very low in relation to total assets. A general guide for many years was that a bank's stockholders' equity should be approximately 10% of total assets, but very few banks in recent years have had that much stockholders' equity. Currently, stockholders' equity of 6–7% would probably be considered favorable. National City had approximately 10.4% stockholders' equity at the end of 2006. In general, the lower the proportion of stockholders' equity in relation to total assets, the greater the risk of failure. A higher stockholders' equity in relation to total assets would probably improve safety, but the bank would perhaps be less profitable because of the additional capital requirement.

As part of the analysis of stockholders' equity, review the statement of stockholders' equity and the related notes for any significant changes. National City had significant increases from net income, issuance of common shares under stock-based compensation plans, and issuance of common shares pursuant to acquisition. Significant decreases were from common dividends declared and repurchase of common shares.

The current approach by bank regulators is not only to view the adequacy of stockholders' equity in relation to total assets, but also to view capital in relation to risk-adjusted assets. National City discloses that it "has a consistently maintained regulatory capital ratios at or above the 'well-capitalized' standards."

INCOME STATEMENT

A bank's principal revenue source is usually interest income from loans and investment securities. The principal expense is usually interest expense on deposits and other debt. The difference between interest income and interest expense is termed *net interest income* or *net interest margin.*

The net interest margin is important to the profitability of a bank. Usually, falling interest rates are positive for a bank's interest margin because the bank will be able to reduce the interest rate that it pays for deposits before the average rate of return earned on loans and investments declines. Increasing interest rates are usually negative for a bank's interest margin because the bank will need to increase the interest rate on deposits, which is usually done before rates on loans and investments are adjusted.

Bank income statements include a separate section for other income (noninterest income). Typical other income includes trust department fees, service charges on deposit accounts, trading account profits (losses), and securities transactions.

The importance of other income has substantially increased for banks. For example, service charges have increased in importance in recent years since many banks have set service charges at a level to make the service profitable. This has frequently been the result of improved cost analysis. In addition, banks have been adding nontraditional sources of income, such as mortgage banking, sales of mutual funds, sales of annuities, and computer services for other banks and financial institutions.

National City had net interest income after provision for credit losses of $4,121,010,000 and $4,412,154,000, respectively, for 2006 and 2005. The noninterest income increased from $3,277,232,000 in 2005 to $4,019,448,000 in 2006. The noninterest expense decreased slightly from $4,751,057,000 to $4,717,339,000.

RATIOS FOR BANKS

Because of the vastly different accounts and statement formats, few of the traditional ratios are appropriate for banks. Exceptions include return on assets, return on equity, and most of the investment-related ratios. The following sections present meaningful ratios for bank analysis, but this is not a comprehensive treatment. The investment firm of Keefe, Bruyette & Woods, Inc., in its *Bankbook Report on Performance*, lists 21 financial ratios. This is an excellent source of industry averages for banks.

Earning Assets to Total Assets

Earning assets includes loans, leases, investment securities, and money market assets. It excludes cash and nonearning deposits plus fixed assets. This ratio shows how well bank management puts bank assets to work. High-performance banks have a high ratio.

Banks typically present asset data on an average annual basis. National City provides a schedule of average balances in its annual report. This schedule is used for the average total assets in computing earning assets to total assets. Exhibit 12-2 presents National City's earning assets to total assets ratio, which has decreased very slightly between 2005 and 2006.

Exhibit 12-2 NATIONAL CITY		
Earning Assets to Total Assets 2006 and 2005		
(In millions of dollars)	**2006**	**2005**
Average earning assets [A]	$122,466	$125,153
Average total assets [B]	$138,678	$141,556
Earning assets to total assets [A ÷ B]	88.31%	88.41%

Interest Margin to Average Earning Assets

This is a key determinant of bank profitability, for it provides an indication of management's ability to control the spread between interest income and interest expense. Exhibit 12-3 presents this ratio for National City and indicates a slight increase in profitability.

Exhibit 12-3 NATIONAL CITY		
Interest Margin to Average Earning Assets		
For the Years Ended December 31, 2006 and 2005		
(In thousands of dollars)	**2006**	**2005**
Interest margin [A]	$4,603,603	$4,695,748
Average earning assets [B]	$122,466,000	$125,153,000
Interest margin to average earning assets [A ÷ B]	3.76%*	3.75%*
*The annual report has 3.75% and 3.74% for 2006 and 2005, respectively.		

Loan Loss Coverage Ratio

The loan loss coverage ratio, computed by dividing pretax income plus provision for loan losses by net charge-offs, helps determine the asset quality and the level of protection of loans. Exhibit 12-4 presents this ratio for National City. This ratio increased slightly in 2006.

Exhibit 12-4 NATIONAL CITY		
Loan Loss Coverage Ratio		
For the Years Ended December 31, 2006 and 2005		
(In thousands of dollars)	**2006**	**2005**
Pretax income	$3,422,636	$2,965,416
Provision for loan losses	489,000	300,000
[A]	$3,911,636	$3,265,416
Net charge-offs [B]	$ 442,000	$ 380,000
Loan loss coverage ratio [A ÷ B]	8.85 times	8.59 times

Equity Capital to Total Assets

This ratio, also called funds to total assets, measures the extent of equity ownership in the bank. This ownership provides the cushion against the risk of using debt and leverage. Exhibit 12-5 presents this ratio, computed by using average figures, for National City. This ratio increased in 2006 to 9.21% from 9.02% in 2005. Both of these ratios appear to be very good.

Exhibit 12-5 NATIONAL CITY		
Equity Capital to Total Assets		
For the Years Ended December 31, 2006 and 2005		
(In millions of dollars)	**2006**	**2005**
Average equity [A]	$12,779	$12,765
Average total assets [B]	$138,678	$141,556
Equity capital to total assets [A ÷ B]	9.21%	9.02%

Deposits Times Capital

The ratio of deposits times capital concerns both depositors and stockholders. To some extent, it is a type of debt/equity ratio, indicating a bank's debt position. More capital implies a greater margin of safety, while a larger deposit base gives a prospect of higher return to stockholders, since more money is available for investment purposes. Exhibit 12-6 presents this ratio for National City, based on average figures. Deposits times capital increased in 2006 to 5.22 from 5.05 in 2005.

Exhibit 12-6	NATIONAL CITY		
	Deposits Times Capital For the Years Ended December 31, 2006 and 2005		
(In millions of dollars)		**2006**	**2005**
Average deposits [A]		$66,646	$64,486
Average stockholders' equity [B]		$12,779	$12,765
Deposits times capital [A ÷ B]		5.22 times	5.05 times

Loans to Deposits

Average total loans to average deposits is a type of asset to liability ratio. Loans make up a large portion of the bank's assets, and its principal obligations are the deposits that can be withdrawn on request—within time limitations. This is a type of debt coverage ratio, and it measures the position of the bank with regard to taking risks. Exhibit 12-7 shows this ratio for National City. Loans to deposits decreased in 2006, indicating a decrease in risk from a debt standpoint.

Exhibit 12-7	NATIONAL CITY		
	Loans to Deposits For the Years Ended December 31, 2006 and 2005		
(In millions of dollars)		**2006**	**2005**
Average total loans [A]		$112,937	$116,365
Average deposits [B]		$66,646	$64,486
Loans to deposits [A ÷ B]		169.46%	180.45%

Regulated Utilities

Regulated utilities render a unique service on which the public depends. Regulated utilities are basically monopolies subject to government regulation, including rate regulation. In recent years, laws have been enacted that greatly reduce the monopoly aspect.

Uniformity of accounting is prescribed by the Federal Energy Regulatory Commission for interstate electric and gas companies and by the Federal Communications Commission for telephone and telegraph companies, as well as by state regulatory agencies.

This section includes comments on regulated utilities. In recent years, most utilities have added nonregulated businesses. In many cases, the nonregulated businesses have become more than the regulated businesses. These utilities usually do not present financial reports like a regulated utility, especially the form of the balance sheet. These balance sheets may appear like a normal balance sheet. The ratios introduced in this section may not be feasible to be computed for utilities with substantial nonregulated businesses.

FINANCIAL STATEMENTS

Balance sheets for utilities differ from business balance sheets mainly in the order that accounts for utilities are presented. Plant and equipment are the first assets listed, followed by investments and other assets, current assets, and deferred charges. Under liabilities and equity, the first section is capitalization. The capitalization section usually includes all sources of long-term capital, such as common stock, preferred stock, and long-term debt. The capitalization section is followed by current liabilities, and then deferred credits and other.

The income statement for utilities is set up by operating revenues, less operating expenses to arrive at net operating income. Net operating income is adjusted by other income (deductions) to arrive at income before interest charges. Interest charges are then deducted to arrive at income before income taxes.

Exhibit 12-8 presents a part of the 2006 annual report of Wisconsin Energy Corporation. Review Exhibit 12-8 to become familiar with the form of utility financial statements.

Inventories are not a problem for electric utilities. Traditionally, receivables have not been a problem because the services are essential and could be cut off for nonpayment and because often a prepayment is required of the customer. In recent years, receivables have been a problem for some utilities because some utility commissions have ruled that services could not be cut off during the winter.

Wisconsin Energy Corporation had $417,200,000 in materials, supplies, and inventories on December 31, 2006. It is partly a regulated and a nonregulated energy company.

A few accounts on the financial statements of a utility are particularly important to the understanding of the statements. On the balance sheet, many utilities have a construction work in progress account. Exhibit 12-8 discloses that Wisconsin Energy had construction work in progress of $992,400,000 and $596,600,000 in 2006 and 2005, respectively.

Utilities that have substantial construction work in progress are usually viewed as being more risky investments than utilities that do not. Most utility commissions allow no construction

Exhibit	12-8	WISCONSIN ENERGY CORPORATION*

Selected Financial Data

WISCONSIN ENERGY CORPORATION
CONSOLIDATED INCOME STATEMENTS (in Part)
Year Ended December 31

	2006	2005	2004
	(Millions of Dollars, Except Per Share Amounts)		
Operating Revenues	$3,996.4	$3,815.5	$3,406.1
Operating Expenses			
Fuel and purchased power	802.0	776.7	591.7
Cost of gas sold	1,018.3	1,047.3	890.9
Other operation and maintenance	1,183.7	1,007.9	986.7
Depreciation, decommissioning and amortization	326.4	332.0	319.5
Property and revenue taxes	97.5	88.7	87.3
Total Operating Expenses	3,427.9	3,252.6	2,876.1
Operating income	568.5	562.9	530.0
Equity in Earnings of Transmission Affiliate	38.6	34.6	30.1
Other Income and Deductions, net	53.1	28.7	(14.3)
Interest Expense	172.7	173.4	193.4
Income from Continuing Operations Before Income Taxes	487.5	452.8	352.4
Income Taxes	175.0	149.2	132.8
Income from Continuing Operations	312.5	303.6	219.6
Income from Discontinued Operations, Net of Tax	3.9	5.1	86.8
Net Income	$ 316.4	$ 308.7	$ 306.4

*"We conduct our operations primarily in two segments; a utility energy segment and a non-utility energy segment." 10-K

Exhibit	12-8	WISCONSIN ENERGY CORPORATION (Continued)

WISCONSIN ENERGY CORPORATION
CONSOLIDATED BALANCE SHEETS
December 31

Assets

	2006	2005
	(Millions of Dollars)	
Property, Plant and Equipment		
In service	$ 9,265.4	$ 8,849.6
Accumulated depreciation	(3,423.7)	(3,288.5)
	5,841.7	5,561.1
Construction work in progress	992.4	596.6
Leased facilities, net	87.5	93.2
Nuclear fuel, net	130.9	112.0
Net Property, Plant and Equipment	7,052.5	6,362.9
Investments		
Nuclear decommissioning trust fund	881.6	782.1
Equity investment in transmission affiliate	228.5	205.8
Other	54.7	92.1
Total Investments	1,164.8	1,080.0
Current Assets		
Cash and cash equivalents	37.0	73.2
Accounts receivable, net of allowance for doubtful accounts of $35.1 and $36.6	379.3	441.8
Accrued revenues	257.8	262.9
Materials, supplies and inventories	417.2	451.6
Prepayments and other	136.7	147.5
Total Current Assets	1,228.0	1,377.0
Deferred Charges and Other Assets		
Regulatory assets	1,091.0	1,025.6
Goodwill, net	441.9	441.9
Other	152.0	174.6
Total Deferred Charges and Other Assets	1,684.9	1,642.1
Total Assets	$11,130.2	$10,462.0

Capitalization and Liabilities

	2006	2005
	(Millions of Dollars)	
Capitalization		
Common equity	$2,889.0	$2,680.1
Preferred stock of subsidiary	30.4	30.4
Long-term debt	3,073.4	3,031.0
Total Capitalization	5,992.8	5,741.5
Current Liabilities		
Long-term debt due currently	296.7	496.0
Short-term debt	911.9	456.3
Accounts payable	404.5	418.1
Payroll and vacation accrued	79.3	75.2
Accrued taxes	56.6	31.0
Accrued interest	25.3	28.2
Other	113.7	142.0
Total Current Liabilities	1,888.0	1,646.8
Deferred Credits and Other Liabilities		
Regulatory liabilities	1,472.1	1,373.2
Asset retirement obligations	371.7	355.5
Deferred income taxes—long-term	572.9	593.7

(continued)

	2006	2005
	(Millions of Dollars)	
Accumulated deferred investment tax credits	52.0	56.3
Pension liability	195.9	274.4
Other long-term liabilities	584.8	420.6
Total Deferred Credits and Other Liabilities	3,249.4	3,073.7
Commitments and Contingencies (Note S)		
Total Capitalization and Liabilities	$11,130.2	$10,462.0

Summary of Significant Accounting Policies (in Part)

Allowance For Funds Used During Construction—Regulated: AFUDC is included in utility plant accounts and represents the cost of borrowed funds (AFUDC—Debt) used during plant construction and a return on stockholders' capital (AFUDC—Equity) used for construction purposes. AFUDC—debt is recorded as a reduction of interest expense and AFUDC—Equity is recorded in Other Income, net.

During 2006, Wisconsin Electric accrued AFUDC at a rate of 8.94%, as authorized by the PSCW. During 2005 and 2004, the authorized rate was 10.18%. Wisconsin Electric accrues AFUDC on all electric utility NO_{X9} SO_2 and particulates remediation projects. Wisconsin Electric's rates were set to provide a full return on electric safety and reliability projects so AFUDC is not accrued on these projects. Wisconsin Electric accrued AFUDC on 50% of the remaining electric, gas and steam projects in CWIP and rates were set assuming that 50% of the CWIP balances were included in rate base.

During 2006, Wisconsin Gas accrued AFUDC at a rate of 11.31%, as authorized by the PSCW. During 2005 and 2004, the authorized rate was 10.32%. Wisconsin Gas accrued AFUDC on specific large construction projects during 2005 and 2004. During 2006, Wisconsin Gas accrued AFUDC on 50% of CWIP balances.

Our regulated segment recorded the following AFUDC for the years ended December 31:

	2006	2005	2004
AFUDC—Debt	$ 5.2	$4.6	$1.5
AFUDC—Equity	$14.5	$9.2	$2.8

work in progress or only a small amount in the rate base. Therefore, the utility rates essentially do not reflect the construction work in progress.

The utility intends to have the additional property and plant considered in the rate base when the construction work is completed. However, the utility commission may not allow all of this property and plant in the rate base. If the commission rules that inefficiency caused part of the cost, it may disallow the cost. The commission may also disallow part of the cost on the grounds that the utility used bad judgment and provided for excess capacity. Costs disallowed are in effect charged to the stockholders, as future income will not include a return on disallowed cost. In the long run, everybody pays for inefficiency and excess capacity because disallowed costs are a risk that can drive the stock price down and interest rates up for the utility. This increases the cost of capital for the utility, which in turn may force utility rates up.

For the costs allowed, the risk exists that the utility commission will not allow a reasonable rate of return. It is important to observe what proportion of total property and plant is represented by construction work in progress. Also, be familiar with the political climate of the utility commission that will be ruling on the construction work in progress costs.

The income statement accounts—allowance for equity funds and allowance for borrowed funds used during construction—relate to construction work in progress costs on the balance sheet. Both of these accounts, sometimes jointly referred to as the allowance for funds used during construction, have been added to construction work in progress costs. Wisconsin Energy Corporation did not disclose these accounts separately on the income statement. It did describe them in a note.

The account allowance for equity funds used during construction represents an assumed rate of return on equity funds used for construction. The account allowance for borrowed funds used during construction represents the cost of borrowed funds that are used for construction.

By increasing the balance sheet account, Construction Work in Progress, for an assumed rate of return on equity funds, the utility builds into the cost base an amount for an assumed rate of return on equity funds. As explained previously, the utility commission may not accept this cost base. The costs that have been added into the cost base have also been added to income, through the allowance for equity funds. Sometimes the account allowance for equity funds used during construction represents a significant portion of the utility's net income.

The income statement account, Allowance for Borrowed Funds Used During Construction, charges to the balance sheet account, Construction in Progress, the interest on borrowed funds used for construction in progress. Thus, this interest is added to the cost base.

Utilities with substantial construction work in progress can have significant cash flow problems. Their reported net income can be substantially higher than the cash flow related to the income statement. Sometimes these utilities issue additional bonds and stocks to obtain funds to pay interest and dividends.

Exhibit 12-8 discloses that Wisconsin Energy had $992,400,000 construction work in progress at the end of 2006. Exhibit 12-8 also shows a relatively immaterial allowance for equity funds used during construction and allowance for borrowed funds used during construction throughout 2006.

Wisconsin Energy also had capitalized interest related to nonregulated energy. This nonregulated energy would be part of its construction work in progress.

RATIOS FOR REGULATED UTILITIES

Because of the vastly different accounts and statement formats, few of the traditional ratios are appropriate for regulated utilities. Exceptions are the return on assets, return on equity, debt/equity, and times interest earned. Investor-related ratios are also of value in analyzing utilities. For example, the cash flow per-share ratio can be a particularly important indicator of the utility's ability to maintain and increase dividends. Standard & Poor's *Industry Survey* is a good source for composite industry data on utilities.

The ratios reviewed here would often apply to the regulated and nonregulated as long as the nonregulated is associated with the utility business.

Operating Ratio

The operating ratio measures efficiency by comparing operating expenses to operating revenues. A profitable utility holds this ratio low. A vertical common-size analysis of the income statement will aid in conclusions regarding this ratio. Exhibit 12-9 presents the operating ratio for Wisconsin Energy. This ratio increased in 2006, thus having a negative influence on profitability.

Exhibit 12-9	WISCONSIN ENERGY CORPORATION		
	Operating Ratio For the Years Ended December 31, 2006 and 2005		
(In thousands of dollars)		**2006**	**2005**
Operating expenses [A]		$3,427,900	$3,252,600
Operating revenues [B]		$3,996,400	$3,815,500
Operating ratio [A ÷ B]		85.77%	85.25%

Funded Debt to Operating Property

A key ratio, the comparison of funded debt to net fixed operating property, is sometimes termed LTD (long-term debt) to *net property* because funded debt is long-term debt. Operating property consists of property and plant less the allowance for depreciation and any allowance for nuclear fuel amortization. Construction in progress is included since it has probably been substantially funded by debt. This ratio measures debt coverage and indicates how funds are supplied. It resembles debt to total assets, with only specialized debt and the specific assets that generate the profits to cover the debt charges. Exhibit 12-10 presents funded debt to operating property for Wisconsin Energy. This ratio decreased materially in 2006 indicating a less risky debt position.

Exhibit 12-10	WISCONSIN ENERGY CORPORATION		
	Funded Debt to Operating Property For the Years Ended December 31, 2006 and 2005		
(In thousands of dollars)		**2006**	**2005**
Funded debt* [A]		$3,370,100	$3,527,000
Operating property [B]**		$6,834,100	$6,157,700
Funded debt to operating property [A ÷ B]		49.31%	57.28%

*Included long-term debt and current maturities of long-term debt.
**Excluded leased facilities, net and nuclear fuel, net. From net property, plant and equipment.

Percent Earned on Operating Property

This ratio, sometimes termed *earnings on net property*, relates net earnings to the assets primarily intended to generate earnings—net property and plant. Exhibit 12-11 presents this ratio for Wisconsin Energy. Note that this ratio decreased in 2006, which is an unfavorable trend.

Exhibit 12-11	WISCONSIN ENERGY CORPORATION		
	Percent Earned on Operating Property For the Years Ended December 31, 2006 and 2005		
(In thousands of dollars)		**2006**	**2005**
Net income* [A]		$273,900	$269,000
Operating property** [B]		$6,060,100	$5,766,300
Percent earned on operating property [A ÷ B]		4.52%	4.67%

*Excluded discontinued operations and equity earnings.
**Excluded construction work in progress.

Operating Revenue to Operating Property

This ratio is basically an operating asset turnover ratio. In public utilities, the fixed plant is often much larger than the expected annual revenue, and this ratio will be less than 1. Exhibit 12-12 presents this ratio for Wisconsin Energy, which indicates a decrease in the operating revenue to operating property and represents an unfavorable trend.

Oil and Gas

Oil and gas companies' financial statements are affected significantly by the method they choose to account for costs associated with exploration and production. The method chosen

Exhibit 12-12	WISCONSIN ENERGY CORPORATION

Operating Revenue to Operating Property
For the Years Ended December 31, 2006 and 2005

(In thousands of dollars)	2006	2005
Operating revenues [A]	$3,996,400	$3,815,500
Operating property* [B]	$6,060,100	$5,766,300
Operating revenue to operating property [A ÷ B]	65.95%	66.17%

*Removed construction work in progress.

is some variation of the successful-efforts or full-costing methods, which will be explained along with their effects on the financial statements. The financial statements of oil and gas companies are also unique because they are required to disclose, in a note, supplementary information on oil and gas exploration, development, and production activities. This requirement will be explained in this section.

Cash flow is important to all companies, but particularly to oil and gas companies. Therefore, cash flow must be part of the analysis of an oil or a gas company. In addition, most of the traditional financial ratios apply to oil and gas companies. This section will not cover special ratios that relate to oil and gas companies.

The 2006 financial statements of ConocoPhillips will be used to illustrate oil and gas financial statements. ConocoPhillips is an integrated international energy company.

SUCCESSFUL-EFFORTS VERSUS FULL-COSTING METHODS

A variation of one of two costing methods is used by an oil or a gas company to account for exploration and production costs: the successful-efforts method and the full-costing method.

The successful-efforts method places only exploration and production costs of successful wells on the balance sheet under property, plant, and equipment. Exploration and production costs of unsuccessful (or dry) wells are expensed when it is determined that there is a dry hole. With the full-costing method, exploration and production costs of all the wells (successful and unsuccessful) are placed on the balance sheet under property, plant, and equipment.

Under both methods, exploration and production costs placed on the balance sheet are subsequently amortized as expense to the income statement. Amortization costs that relate to natural resources are called *depletion expense.*

The costing method used for exploration and production can have a very significant influence on the balance sheet and the income statement. Under both methods, exploration and production costs are eventually expensed, but a significant difference exists in the timing of the expense.

In theory, the successful-efforts method takes the position that a direct relationship exists between costs incurred and specific reserves discovered. These costs should be placed on the balance sheet. Costs associated with unsuccessful efforts are a period expense and should be charged to expense. In theory, the full-costing method takes the position that the drilling of all wells, successful and unsuccessful, is part of the process of finding successful wells. Therefore, all of the cost should be placed on the balance sheet.

In practice, the decision to use the successful-efforts method or the full-costing method is probably not significantly influenced by theory, but by practicalities. Most relatively small oil and gas companies select a variation of the full-costing method. This results in a much larger balance sheet. In the short run, it also usually results in higher reported profits. Small oil companies speculate that the larger balance sheet and the increased reported profits can be used to influence some banks and limited partners, which the small companies tend to use as sources of funds.

Large oil and gas companies tend to select a variation of the successful-efforts method. This results in a lower balance sheet amount and lower reported income in the short run. The large companies usually depend on bonds and stock as their primary sources of outside capital. Investors in bonds and stock are not likely to be influenced by the larger balance sheet and higher income that results from capitalizing dry wells.

The method used can have a significant influence on the balance sheet and the income statement. The successful-efforts method is more conservative. Review Exhibit 12-13 for a description of ConocoPhillips' method of accounting for exploration and production costs.

Exhibit	12-13	CONOCOPHILLIPS*

Note 1 to Consolidated Financial Statements (in Part)

Oil and Gas Exploration and Development—Oil and gas exploration and development costs are accounted for using the successful efforts method of accounting.

Property Acquisition Costs—Oil and gas leasehold acquisition costs are capitalized and included in the balance sheet caption properties, plants and equipment. Leasehold impairment is recognized based on exploratory experience and management's judgment. Upon discovery of commercial reserves, leasehold costs are transferred to proved properties.

Exploratory Costs—Geological and geophysical costs and the costs of carrying and retaining undeveloped properties are expensed as incurred. Exploratory well costs are capitalized, or "suspended," on the balance sheet pending further evaluation of whether economically recoverable reserves have been found. If economically recoverable reserves are not found, exploratory well costs are expensed as dry holes. If exploratory wells encounter potentially economic quantities of oil and gas, the well costs remain capitalized on the balance sheet as long as sufficient progress accessing the reserves and the economic and operating viability of the project is being made. For complex exploratory discoveries, it is not unusual to have exploratory wells remain suspended on the balance sheet for several years while we perform additional appraisal drilling and seismic work on the potential oil and gas field, or we seed government or co-venturer approval of development plans or seed environmental permitting. Once all required approval and permits have been obtained, the projects are moved into the development phase and the oil and gas reserves are designated as proved reserves.

Management reviews suspended well balances quarterly, continuously monitors the results of the additional appraisal drilling and seismic work, and expenses the suspended well costs as a dry hold when it judges that the potential field does not warrant further investment in the near term.

See Note 11—Properties, Plants and Equipment for additional information on suspended wells.

*"ConocoPhillips is an international, integrated energy company." 10-K

SUPPLEMENTARY INFORMATION ON OIL AND GAS EXPLORATION, DEVELOPMENT, AND PRODUCTION ACTIVITIES

As part of your review of an oil or a gas company, note the supplemental oil and gas information. Review Exhibit 12-14 for a brief summary of the supplementary information presented by ConocoPhillips.

CASH FLOW

Monitoring cash flow can be particularly important when following an oil or a gas company. The potential for a significant difference exists between the reported income and cash flow from operations. One reason is that large sums can be spent for exploration and development, years in advance of revenue from the found reserves. The other reason is that there can be significant

Exhibit	12-14	CONOCOPHILLIPS*

Oil and Gas Operations (Unaudited) (in Part)
2006 Annual Report

ConocoPhillips presented supplemental data (unaudited) using 20 pages in its 2006 annual report. Exhibit 12-14 represents only a small part of the disclosure.

Oil and Gas Operations (Unaudited)

In accordance with SFAS No. 69, "Disclosures about Oil and Gas Producing Activities," and regulations of the U.S. Securities and Exchange Commission (SEC), we are making certain supplemental disclosures about our oil and gas exploration and production operations. While this information was developed with reasonable care and disclosed in good faith, it is emphasized that some of the data is necessarily imprecise and represents only approximate amounts because of the subjective judgments involved in developing such information. Accordingly, this information may not necessarily represent our current financial condition or our expected future results.

The major headings to this disclosure follow:

- Proved Reserves Worldwide
- Results of Operations
- Statistics
- Costs Incurred
- Capitalized Costs
- Standardized Measure of Discounted Future Net Cash Flows Relating to Proved Oil and Gas Reserve Quantities

*"ConocoPhillips is an international, integrated energy company." 10-K

differences between when expenses are deducted on the financial statements and when they are deducted on the tax return. Therefore, observe the operating cash flow.

Cash from operating activities for a three-year period will be disclosed on the statement of cash flows. For ConocoPhillips, net cash provided by operating activities was $21,516,000,000, $17,628,000,000, and $11,959,000,000 for 2006, 2005, and 2004, respectively. Income from continuing operations was $15,550,000,000, $13,640,000,000, and $8,107,000,000 for 2006, 2005, and 2004, respectively.

Transportation

Three components of the transportation industry will be discussed: air carriers, railroads, and the motor carrier industry. The Civil Aeronautics Board, which requires the use of a uniform system of accounts and reporting, regulates interstate commercial aviation. The Interstate Commerce Commission, which also has control over a uniform system of accounts and reporting, regulates interstate railroads. The Interstate Commerce Commission also regulates interstate motor carriers whose principal business is transportation services.

FINANCIAL STATEMENTS

The balance sheet format for air carriers, railroads, and motor carriers resembles that for manufacturing or retailing firms. As in a heavy manufacturing firm, property and equipment make up a large portion of assets. Also, supplies and parts comprise the basic inventory items. The income statement format resembles that of a utility. The system of accounts provides for the grouping of all revenues and expenses in terms of both major natural objectives and functional activities. There is no cost of goods sold calculation; rather, there is operating income: revenue (categorized) minus operating expenses. In essence, the statements are a prescribed, categorized form of single-step income statement. They cannot be converted to multiple-step format.

RATIOS

Most of the traditional ratios also apply in the transportation field. Exceptions are inventory turnovers (because there is no cost of goods sold) and gross profit margin. The ratios discussed in the subsections that follow are especially suited to transportation. They are derived from the 2006 statement of income and balance sheet for Southwest Airlines Co., presented in Exhibit 12-15.

Exhibit	12-15	SOUTHWEST AIRLINES CO.*

Selected Financial Data

SOUTHWEST AIRLINES CO.
CONSOLIDATED BALANCE SHEET

	December 31,	
	2006	2005
	(In millions, except share data)	
ASSETS		
Current assets:		
Cash and cash equivalents	$ 1,390	$ 2,280
Short-term investments	369	251
Accounts and other receivables	241	258
Inventories of parts and supplies, at cost	181	150
Fuel derivative contracts	369	641
Prepaid expenses and other current assets	51	40
Total current assets	2,601	3,620
Property and equipment, at cost:		
Flight equipment	11,769	10,592
Ground property and equipment	1,356	1,256
Deposits on flight equipment purchase contracts	734	660
	13,859	12,508
Less allowance for depreciation and amortization	3,765	3,296
	10,094	9,212
Other assets	765	1,171
	$13,460	$14,003

LIABILITIES AND STOCKHOLDERS' EQUITY

Current assets:		
Accounts payable	$ 643	$ 524
Accrued liabilities	1,323	2,074
Air traffic liability	799	649
Current maturities of long-term debt	122	601
Total current liabilities	2,887	3,848
Long-term debt less current maturities	1,567	1,394
Deferred income taxes	2,104	1,681
Deferred gains from sale and leaseback of aircraft	120	136
Other deferred liabilities	333	269
Commitments and contingencies		
Stockholders' equity:		
Common stock, $1.00 par value: 2,000,000,000 shares authorized; 807,611,634 and 801,641,645 shares issued in 2006 and 2005, respectively	808	802
Capital in excess of par value	1,142	963
Retained earnings	4,307	4,018
Accumulated other comprehensive income	582	892
Treasury stock, at cost: 24,302,215 shares in 2006	(390)	—
Total stockholders' equity	6,449	6,675
	$13,460	$14,003

*"Southwest Airlines Co. is a major passenger airline that provides scheduled air transportation in the United States." 10-K

Exhibit	12-15	SOUTHWEST AIRLINES CO. (Continued)

SOUTHWEST AIRLINES CO.
CONSOLIDATED STATEMENT OF INCOME

	Years Ended December 31,		
	2006	2005	2004
	(In millions, except per share amounts)		
OPERATING REVENUES:			
Passenger	$8,750	$7,279	$6,280
Freight	134	133	117
Other	202	172	133
Total operating revenues	9,086	7,584	6,530
OPERATING EXPENSES:			
Salaries, wages, and benefits	3,052	2,782	2,578
Fuel and oil	2,138	1,341	1,000
Maintenance materials and repairs	468	446	472
Aircraft rentals	158	163	179
Landing fees and other rentals	495	454	408
Depreciation and amortization	515	469	431
Other operating expenses	1,326	1,204	1,058
Total operating expenses	8,152	6,859	6,126
OPERATING INCOME:	934	725	404
OTHER EXPENSES (INCOME):			
Interest expense	128	122	88
Capitalized interest	(51)	(39)	(39)
Interest income	(84)	(47)	(21)
Other (gains) losses, net	151	(90)	37
Total other expenses (income)	144	(54)	65
INCOME BEFORE INCOME TAXES	790	779	339
PROVISION FOR INCOME TAXES	291	295	124
NET INCOME	$ 499	$ 484	$ 215
NET INCOME PER SHARE, BASIC	$ .63	$ .61	$ .27
NET INCOME PER SHARE, DILUTED	$ .61	$ .60	$ .27

The traditional sources of industry averages cover transportation. The federal government accumulates numerous statistics for regulated industries, including transportation. An example is the Interstate Commerce Commission's *Annual Report* on transport statistics in the United States.

For the motor carrier industry, a particularly good source of industry data is the annual publication *Financial Analysis of the Motor Carrier Industry*, published by the American Trucking Association, Inc., 1616 P Street, NW, Washington, DC 20036. This publication includes an economic and industry overview, distribution of revenue by carrier type, and industry issues. It also includes definitions of terminology that relate to the motor carrier industry.

There are hundreds of motor carrier firms, most of which are relatively small. The American Trucking Association compiles data by composite carrier groups. For example, Group A includes composite data for several hundred general freight carriers with annual revenues of less than $5 million. One of the groups includes composite data for the publicly held carriers of general freight.

The very extensive composite data in the American Trucking Association publication include industry total dollars for the income statement and balance sheet. It also includes vertical common-size analyses for the income statement and the balance sheet. This publication also includes approximately 36 ratios and other analytical data, such as total tons.

Operating Ratio

The operating ratio is computed by comparing operating expenses to operating revenues. It measures cost and should be kept low, but external conditions, such as the level of business activity, may affect this ratio. Operating revenues vary from year to year because of differences in rates, classification of traffic, volume of traffic carried, and the distance traffic is transported. Operating expenses change because of variations in the price level, traffic carried, the type of service performed, and the effectiveness of operating and maintaining the properties. Common-size analysis of revenues and expenses is needed to explain changes in the operating ratio.

Exhibit 12-16 presents the operating ratio for Southwest Airlines Co. The operating ratio for Southwest Airlines decreased from 90.44% in 2005 to 89.72% in 2006. The operating ratio can dramatically affect the profitability of a carrier. This trend in the operating ratio is favorable for Southwest Airlines.

Exhibit	12-16	SOUTHWEST AIRLINES CO.

Operating Ratio
For the Years Ended December 31, 2006 and 2005

(In millions)	2006	2005
Operating expenses [A]	$8,152	$6,859
Operating revenues [B]	$9,086	$7,584
Operating ratio [A ÷ B]	89.72%	90.44%

Long-Term Debt to Operating Property

Because of the transportation companies' heavy investment in operating assets, such as equipment, the long-term ratios increase in importance. Long-term borrowing capacity is also a key consideration. The ratio of long-term debt to operating property ratio gives a measure of the sources of funds with which property is obtained. It also measures borrowing capacity. Operating property is defined as long-term property and equipment. Exhibit 12-17 presents this ratio for Southwest Airlines. For Southwest Airlines, the long-term debt to operating property ratio increased in 2006 to 15.52% from 15.13%. This represents a slight negative trend.

Exhibit	12-17	SOUTHWEST AIRLINES CO.

Long-Term Debt to Operating Property
For the Years Ended December 31, 2006 and 2005

(In millions)	2006	2005
Long-term debt less current maturities [A]	$1,567	$1,394
Operating property [B]	$10,094	$9,212
Long-term debt to operating property [A ÷ B]	15.52%	15.13%

Operating Revenue to Operating Property

This ratio measures turnover of operating assets. The objective is to generate as many dollars in revenue per dollar of property as possible. Exhibit 12-18 presents this ratio for Southwest Airlines. The operating revenue to operating property increased materially between 2005 and 2006.

Per-Mile, Per-Person, and Per-Ton Passenger Load Factors

For transportation companies, additional insight can be gained by looking at revenues and expenses on a per unit of usage basis. Examples would be per mile of line or per 10 miles for

Exhibit	12-18	SOUTHWEST AIRLINES CO.

Operating Revenue to Operating Property
For the Years Ended December 31, 2006 and 2005

(In millions)	2006	2005
Operating revenue [A]	$9,086	$7,584
Operating property [B]	$10,094	$9,212
Operating revenue to operating property [A ÷ B]	90.01%	82.33%

railroads, or a per passenger mile for air carriers. Although this type of disclosure is not required, it is often presented in highlights.

This type of disclosure is illustrated in Exhibit 12-19, which shows statistics for Southwest Airlines Co. Statistics in Exhibit 12-19 include revenue passengers carried, enplaned passengers, revenue passenger miles (RPMs), available seat miles (ASMs), load factor, average length of passenger haul, average stage length, trips flown, average passenger fare, passenger revenue yield per RPM, operating revenue yield per ASM, operating expenses per ASM, fuel cost per gallon, number of employees at year-end, and size of fleet at year-end.

Exhibit	12-19	SOUTHWEST AIRLINES CO.

Other Financial and Statistical Data
For the Years Ended December 31, 2002–2006

Item 6. Selected Financial Data (in Part)

The following financial information for the five years ended December 31, 2006, has been derived from the Company's Consolidated Financial Statements. This information should be read in conjunction with the Consolidated Financial Statements and related notes thereto included elsewhere herein.

	Years Ended December 31,				
	2006	**2005**	**2004**	**2003**	**2002**
Operating Data:					
Revenue passengers carried	83,814,823	77,693,875	70,902,773	65,673,945	63,045,988
Enplaned passengers	96,276,907	88,379,900	81,066,038	74,719,340	72,462,123
Revenue passenger miles (RPMs) (000s)	67,691,289	60,223,100	53,418,353	47,943,066	45,391,903
Available seat miles (ASMs) (000s)	92,663,023	85,172,795	76,861,296	71,790,425	68,886,546
Load factor[1]	73.1%	70.7%	69.5%	66.8%	65.9%
Average length of passenger haul (miles)	808	775	753	730	720
Average stage length (miles)	622	607	576	558	537
Trips flown	1,092,331	1,028,639	981,591	949,882	947,331
Average passenger fare	$104.40	$93.68	$88.57	$87.42	$84.72
Passenger revenue yield per RPM	12.93¢	12.09¢	11.76¢	11.97¢	11.77¢
Operating revenue yield per ASM	9.81¢	8.90¢	8.50¢	8.27¢	8.02¢
Operating expenses per ASM	8.80¢	8.05¢	7.97¢	7.74¢	7.52¢
Operating expenses per ASM, excluding fuel	6.49¢	6.48¢	6.67¢	6.59¢	6.41¢
Fuel cost per gallon (average)	$1.53	$1.03	$0.83	$0.72	$0.68
Number of employees at year-end	32,664	31,729	31,011	32,847	33,705
Size of fleet at year-end[2]	481	445	417	388	375

[1]Revenue passenger miles divided by available seat miles.

[2]Includes leased aircraft.

Insurance

Insurance companies provide two types of services. One is an identified contract service—mortality protection or loss protection. The second is investment management service.

There are basically four types of insurance organizations:

1. **Stock companies.** A stock company is a corporation organized to earn profits for its stockholders. The comments in this insurance section relate specifically to stock companies. Many of the comments are also valid for the other types of insurance organizations.
2. **Mutual companies.** A mutual company is an incorporated entity, without private ownership interest, operating for the benefit of its policyholders and their beneficiaries.
3. **Fraternal benefit societies.** A fraternal benefit society resembles a mutual insurance company in that, although incorporated, it does not have capital stock, and it operates for the benefit of its members and beneficiaries. Policyholders participate in the earnings of the society and the policies stipulate that the society has the power to assess them in case the legal reserves become impaired.
4. **Assessment companies.** An assessment company is an organized group with similar interests, such as a religious denomination.

The regulation of insurance companies started at the state level. Beginning in 1828, the state of New York required that annual reports be filed with the state controller. Subsequently, other states followed this precedent, and all 50 states have insurance departments that require annual statements of insurance companies. The reports are filed with the state insurance departments in accordance with statutory accounting practices (SAP). The National Association of Insurance Commissioners (NAIC), a voluntary association, has succeeded in achieving near uniformity among the states, so there are no significant differences in SAP among the states.[1]

Statutory accounting emphasizes the balance sheet. In its concern for protecting policyholders, statutory accounting focuses on the financial solvency of the insurance corporation. After the annual reports are filed with the individual state insurance departments, a testing process is conducted by the NAIC. This process is based on ratio calculations concerning the financial position of a company. If a company's ratio is outside the prescribed limit, the NAIC brings that to the attention of the state insurance department.

A.M. Best Company publishes *Best's Insurance Reports*, which are issued separately for life-health companies and property-casualty companies. *Best's Insurance Reports* evaluate the financial condition of more than 3,000 insurance companies. The majority of companies are assigned a Best's Rating, ranging from A+ (Superior) to C– (Fair). The other companies are classified as "Not Assigned." The "Not Assigned" category has 10 classifications to identify why a company has not been assigned a Best's Rating.

Some of the items included in Best's data include a balance sheet, summary of operations, operating ratios, profitability ratios, leverage ratios, and liquidity ratios. Most of the ratios are industry-specific. It is not practical to describe and explain them in this book. It should be noted that the financial data, including the ratios, are based on the data submitted to the state insurance departments and are thus based on SAP. Generally accepted accounting principles (GAAP) for insurance companies developed much later than SAP. The annual reports of insurance companies are based on GAAP.

The 1934 Securities and Exchange Act established national government regulation, in addition to the state regulation of insurance companies. Stock insurance companies with assets of $1 million and at least 500 stockholders must register with the SEC and file the required forms, such as the annual Form 10-K. Reports filed with the SEC must conform with GAAP.

Exhibit 12-20 contains the income statement and balance sheet from the 2006 annual report of The Chubb Corporation. These statements were prepared using GAAP. Review them to observe the unique nature of insurance company financial statements.

BALANCE SHEET UNDER GAAP

The balance sheet for an insurance company is not classified by current assets and current liabilities (nonclassified balance sheet). Instead, its basic sections are assets, liabilities, and shareholders' equity.

| Exhibit | 12-20 | THE CHUBB CORPORATION* |

2006 Annual Report
Selected Financial Data

THE CHUBB CORPORATION
Consolidated Statements of Income

	In Millions, Except for per Share Amounts Years Ended December 31,		
	2006	2005	2004
Revenues			
Premiums Earned	$11,958	$12,176	$11,636
Investment Income	1,580	1,408	1,256
Other Revenues	220	115	67
Realized Investment Gains	245	384	218
TOTAL REVENUES	14,003	14,083	13,177
Losses and Expenses			
Losses and Loss Expenses	6,574	7,813	7,321
Amortization of Deferred Policy Acquisition Costs	2,919	2,931	2,843
Other Insurance Operating Costs and Expenses	550	512	630
Investment Expenses	34	29	25
Other Expenses	207	161	111
Corporate Expenses	194	190	179
TOTAL LOSSES AND EXPENSES	10,478	11,636	11,109
INCOME BEFORE FEDERAL AND FOREIGN INCOME TAX	3,525	2,447	2,068
Federal and Foreign Income Tax	997	621	520
NET INCOME	$ 2,528	$ 1,826	$ 1,548
Net Income Per Share			
Basic	$ 6.13	$ 4.61	$ 4.08
Diluted	5.98	4.47	4.01

THE CHUBB CORPORATION
Consolidated Balance Sheets

	In Millions December 31,	
	2006	2005
Assets		
Invested Assets		
Short Term Investments	$ 2,254	$ 1,899
Fixed Maturities		
Held-to-Maturity—Tax Exempt (market $142 and $216)	135	205
Available-for-Sale		
Tax Exempt (cost $17,314 and $15,449)	17,613	15,750
Taxable (cost $14,310 and $14,515)	14,218	14,568
Equity Securities (cost $1,561 and $1,045)	1,957	1,169
Other Invested Assets	1,516	1,043
TOTAL INVESTED ASSETS	37,693	34,634
Cash	38	36
Securities Lending Collateral	2,620	2,077
Accrued Investment Income	411	391
Premiums Receivable	2,314	2,319
Reinsurance Recoverable on Unpaid Losses and Loss Expenses	2,594	3,769
Prepaid Reinsurance Premiums	354	244
Deferred Policy Acquisition Costs	1,480	1,445
Real Estate Assets	201	367
Investment in Partially Owned Company	—	260
Deferred Income Tax	591	623
Goodwill	467	467
Other Assets	1,514	1,429
TOTAL ASSETS	$50,277	$48,061

*"Chubb is a holding company for a family of property and casualty insurance companies known informally as the Chubb Group of Insurance Companies (the P & C Group)." 10-K

(continued)

| Exhibit | 12-20 | THE CHUBB CORPORATION (Continued) |

	In Millions December 31,	
	2006	2005
Liabilities		
Unpaid Losses and Loss Expenses	$22,293	$22,482
Unearned Premiums	6,546	6,361
Securities Lending Payable	2,620	2,077
Long Term Debt	2,466	2,467
Dividend Payable to Shareholders	104	90
Accrued Expenses and Other Liabilities	2,385	2,177
TOTAL LIABILITIES	36,414	35,654
Commitments and Contingent Liabilities (Notes 9 and 14)		
Shareholders' Equity		
Preferred Stock—Authorized 8,000,000 Shares; $1 Par Value;	—	—
Issued—None Common Stock—Authorized 1,200,000,000 Shares;		
$1 Par Value; Issued 411,276,940 and 420,864,596 Shares	411	210
Paid-In Surplus	1,539	2,364
Retained Earnings	11,711	9,600
Accumulated Other Comprehensive Income	202	368
Treasury Stock, at Cost—2,787,800 Shares in 2005	—	(135)
TOTAL SHAREHOLDERS' EQUITY	13,863	12,407
TOTAL LIABILITIES AND SHAREHOLDERS' EQUITY	$50,277	$48,061

ASSETS

The assets section starts with investments, a classification where most insurance companies maintain the majority of their assets. Many of the investments have a high degree of liquidity, so that prompt payment can be assured in the event of a catastrophic loss. The majority of the investments are typically in bonds, with stock investments being much lower. Real estate investments are usually present for both property-casualty insurance companies and for life insurance companies. Because liabilities are relatively short term for property-casualty companies, the investment in real estate for these companies is usually immaterial. For life insurance companies, the investment in real estate may be much greater than for property-casualty companies because of the generally longer-term nature and predictability of their liabilities.

For debt and equity investments, review the disclosure to determine if there are significant differences between the fair value and the cost or amortized cost. Also review the stockholders' equity section of the balance sheet to determine if there is significant unrealized appreciation of investments (gains or losses).

ASSETS—OTHER THAN INVESTMENTS

A number of asset accounts other than investments may be on an insurance company's balance sheet. Some of the typical accounts are described in the paragraphs that follow.

Real estate used in operations is reported at cost, less accumulated depreciation. Under SAP, real estate used in operations is expensed.

Deferred policy acquisition costs represent the cost of obtaining policies. Under GAAP, these costs are deferred and charged to expense over the premium-paying period. This is one of the major differences between GAAP reporting and SAP reporting. Under SAP reporting, these costs are charged to expense as they are incurred.

Goodwill is an intangible account resulting from acquiring other companies. The same account can be found on the balance sheet of companies other than insurance companies. Under GAAP, the goodwill account is accounted for as an asset. Under SAP, neither the goodwill account nor other intangibles are recognized.

Liabilities

Generally, the largest liability is for loss reserves. Reserving for losses involves estimating the ultimate value, considering the present value of the commitments. The quantification process is subject to a number of subjective estimates, including inflation, interest rates, and judicial interpretations. Mortality estimates are also important for life insurance companies. These reserve accounts should be adequate to pay policy claims under the terms of the insurance policies.

Another liability account found on an insurance company's balance sheet is policy and contract claims. This account represents claims that have accrued as of the balance sheet date. These claims are reported net of any portion that can be recovered.

Many other liability accounts, such as notes payable and income taxes payable, are found on an insurance company's balance sheet. These are typically reported in the same manner as other industries report them, except there is no current liability classification.

Stockholders' Equity

The stockholders' equity usually resembles the stockholders' equity section for companies in other industries. The account Accumulated Other Comprehensive Income can be particularly large for insurance companies. It will contain unrealized gains or losses that have not been recognized on the income statement.

For The Chubb Corporation, the details of the account Accumulated Other Comprehensive Income are in the consolidated statements of shareholders' equity (not shown in Exhibit 12-20). For The Chubb Corporation, the balance in Unrealized Appreciation of Investments is substantial.

INCOME STATEMENT UNDER GAAP

The manner of recognizing revenue on insurance contracts is unique for the insurance industry. In general, the duration of the contract governs the revenue recognition.

For contracts of short duration, revenue is ordinarily recognized over the period of the contract in proportion to the amount of insurance protection provided. When the risk differs significantly from the contract period, revenue is recognized over the period of risk in proportion to the amount of insurance protection.[2]

Policies relating to loss protection typically fall under the short-duration contract. An example would be casualty insurance in which the insurance company retains the right to cancel the contract at the end of the policy term.

For long-duration contracts, revenue is recognized when the premium is due from the policyholder. Examples would be whole-life contracts and single-premium life contracts.[3] Likewise, acquisition costs are capitalized and expensed in proportion to premium revenue.

Long-duration contracts that do not subject the insurance enterprise to significant risks arising from policyholder mortality or morbidity are referred to as *investment contracts*. Amounts received on these contracts are not to be reported as revenues but rather as liabilities and accounted for in the same way as interest-bearing instruments.[4] The contracts are regarded as investment contracts since they do not incorporate significant insurance risk. Interestingly, many of the life insurance policies currently being written are of this type.

With the investment contracts, premium payments are credited to the policyholder balance. The insurance company assesses charges against this balance for contract services and credits the balance for income earned. The insurer can adjust the schedule for contract services and the rate at which income is credited.

Investment contracts generally include an assessment against the policyholder on inception of the contract and an assessment when the contract is terminated. The inception fees are booked as recoveries of capitalized acquisition costs, and the termination fees are booked as revenue at the time of termination.

In addition to their insurance activities, insurance companies are substantially involved with investments. Realized gains and losses from investments are reported in operations in the period incurred.

RATIOS

As previously indicated, many of the ratios relating to insurance companies are industry-specific. An explanation of industry-specific ratios is beyond the scope of this book. The industry-specific ratios are frequently based on SAP financial reporting to the states, rather than the GAAP financial reporting that is used for the annual report and SEC requirements.

Ratios computed from the GAAP-based financial statements are often profitability- and investor-related. Examples of such ratios are return on common equity, price/earnings ratio, dividend payout, and dividend yield. These ratios are explained in other sections of this book.

Insurance companies tend to have a stock market price at a discount to the average market price (price/earnings ratio). This discount is typically 10 to 20%, but at times it is much more. There are likely many reasons for this relatively low market value. Insurance is a highly regulated industry that some perceive as having low growth prospects. It is also an industry with substantial competition. The regulation and the competition put pressure on the premiums that can be charged. The accounting environment likely also contributes to the relatively low market price for insurance company stocks. The existence of two sets of accounting principles, SAP and GAAP, contributes to the lack of understanding of insurance companies' financial statements. Also, many of the accounting standards are complex and industry-specific.

The nature of the insurance industry leads to standards that allow much subjectivity and possible manipulation of reported profit. For example, insurance companies are perceived to underreserve during tough years and overreserve during good years.

Insurance company financial fraud led to the April 2005 announcement from the Securities and Exchange Commission that it was increasing its enforcement of accounting rules. "The Securities and Exchange Commission, using its power as an enforcer of accounting rules, is asserting for the first time in decades a key role for federal officials overseeing the insurance industry."[5]

"The federal government's ability to regulate the insurance industry is still limited by law. The McCarran-Ferguson Act of 1945 gave primacy in regulating and taxing insurers for states. . . . Because of the law, even the SEC can only go so far with its accounting cudgel. Its mandate extends only to companies with publicly offered securities, while some of the largest U.S. insurers—including the biggest, State Farm—are either owned by policyholders or closely held."[6]

Real Estate Companies

Real estate companies typically construct and operate income-producing real properties. Examples of such properties are shopping centers, hotels, and office buildings. A typical project would involve selecting a site, arranging financing, arranging for long-term leases, construction, and subsequently operating and maintaining the property.

Real estate companies contend that conventional accounting—recognizing depreciation but not the underlying value of the property—misleads investors. In some cases, these companies have taken the drastic step of selling major parts or all of the companies' assets to realize greater benefits for stockholders. Some real estate companies have attempted to reflect value by disclosing current value in addition to the conventional accounting.

Summary

Financial statements vary among industries, and they are especially different for banks, utilities, transportation companies, and insurance companies. In each case, the accounting for these firms is subject to a uniform accounting system. Changes in analysis are necessitated by the differences in accounting presentation.

Oil and gas companies' financial statements are affected significantly by the method that they choose to account for costs associated with exploration and production. Another important aspect of the financial statements of oil and gas companies is the note requirement that relates to supplementary information on oil and gas exploration, development, and production activities. Cash flow is also particularly significant to oil and gas companies.

Real estate companies emphasize the underlying value of the property and earnings before depreciation and deferred taxes from operations.

Special industry ratios were reviewed in this chapter. The following ratios are helpful when analyzing a bank:

$$\text{Earning Assets to Total Assets} = \frac{\text{Average Earning Assets}}{\text{Average Total Assets}}$$

$$\text{Interest Margin to Average Earning Assets} = \frac{\text{Interest Margin}}{\text{Average Earning Assets}}$$

$$\text{Loan Loss Coverage Ratio} = \frac{\text{Pretax Income} + \text{Provision for Loan Losses}}{\text{Net Charge-Offs}}$$

$$\text{Equity Capital to Total Assets} = \frac{\text{Average Equity}}{\text{Average Total Assets}}$$

$$\text{Deposits Times Capital} = \frac{\text{Average Deposits}}{\text{Average Stockholders' Equity}}$$

$$\text{Loans to Deposits} = \frac{\text{Average Total Loans}}{\text{Average Deposits}}$$

The following ratios are helpful in analyzing utility performance:

$$\text{Operating Ratio} = \frac{\text{Operating Expense}}{\text{Operating Revenue}}$$

$$\text{Funded Debt to Operating Property} = \frac{\text{Funded Debt}}{\text{Operating Property}}$$

$$\text{Percent Earned on Operating Property} = \frac{\text{Net Income}}{\text{Operating Property}}$$

$$\text{Operating Revenue to Operating Property} = \frac{\text{Operating Revenue}}{\text{Operating Property}}$$

The ratios that follow are especially suited to transportation. Additional insight can be gained by looking at revenues and expenses on a per unit of usage basis.

$$\text{Operating Ratio} = \frac{\text{Operating Expense}}{\text{Operating Revenue}}$$

$$\text{Long-Term Debt to Operating Property} = \frac{\text{Long-Term Debt}}{\text{Operating Property}}$$

$$\text{Operating Revenue to Operating Property} = \frac{\text{Operating Revenue}}{\text{Operating Property}}$$

to the net

1. Go to the SEC Web site (http://www.sec.gov). Under "Filings & Forms (EDGAR)," click on "Search for Company Filings." Click on "Companies & Other Filers." Under Company Name, enter "Independent Bank Corp" (or under Ticker Symbol, enter "INDB"). Select the 10-K filed February 28, 2007.

   a. Copy the first sentence in the "Market Area and Competition" subsection from the "Item 1. Business" section.

   b. Comment on the trend found in "Table 5—Summary of Delinquency Information" and "Table 6—Nonperforming Assets" from the "Item 7. Management's Discussion and Analysis of Financial Condition and Results of Operation" section.

2. Go to the SEC Web site (http://www.sec.gov). Under "Filings & Forms (EDGAR)," click on "Search for Company Filings." Click on

"Companies & Other Filers." Under Company Name, enter "Columbia Bancorp" (or under Ticker Symbol, enter "CBBO"). Select the 10-K filed March 16, 2007.

a. Review the "General" subsection from the "Item 1. Description of Business" section and briefly describe what kind of business Columbia Bancorp is.

b. Go to "Note 4. Loans and Allowance for Loan Losses" found in the "Item 8. Financial Statements and Supplementary Data" section and answer the following:

1. Comment on the trend in total loan portfolio.

2. Comment on the trend in allowance for loan losses.

3. Comment on the trend in investment in impaired loans.

3. Go to the SEC Web site (http://www.sec.gov). Under "Filings & Forms (EDGAR)," click on "Search for Company Filings." Click on "Companies & Other Filers." Under Company Name, enter "Maine & Maritimes Corp" (or under Ticker Symbol, enter "MAM"). Select the 10-K filed March 16, 2007.

a. Determine the standard industrial classification.

b. Determine the Construction Work in Progress for December 31, 2006, and December 31, 2005.

c. Determine the Allowance for Equity Funds Used During Construction for the years ended December 31, 2006, 2005, and 2004.

d. Determine the Allowance for Borrowed Funds Used During Construction for the years ended December 31, 2006, 2005, and 2004.

e. Determine the Net Income From Continuing Operations for the years ended December 31, 2006, 2005, and 2004.

f. Does Allowance for Equity Funds and Borrowed Funds Used During Construction appear to be material?

4. Go to the SEC Web site (http://www.sec.gov). Under "Filings & Forms (EDGAR)," click on "Search for Company Filings." Click on "Companies & Other Filers." Under Company Name, enter "Cabot Oil & Gas Corp" (or under Ticker Symbol, enter "COG"). Select the 10-K filed February 28, 2007.

a. Determine the standard industrial classification.

b. Go to the "Reserves" subsection from the "Item 1. Business" section. Find the "Historical Reserves" table. Complete the following table for estimated proved reserves for the periods indicated:

	Natural Gas (Mmcf)	Oil & Liquids (Mbbl)	Total[1] (Mmcfe)
December 31, 2005			
Revision of Prior Estimates[2]			
Extensions, Discoveries and Other Additions			
Production			
Purchase of Reserves in Place			
Sales of Reserves in Place			
December 31, 2006			
Proved Developed Reserves			
December 31, 2003			
December 31, 2004			
December 31, 2005			
December 31, 2006			

[1]Includes natural gas and natural gas equivalents determined by using the ratio of Gmcf of natural gas to 1Bbl of crude oil, condensate or natural gas liquids.

[2]The majority of the revisions were the result of the decrease in the natural gas price on December 31, 2006, from the price on December 31, 2005.

c. Comment on the trend in reserves.

Questions

Q 12-1.   What are the main sources of revenue for banks?

Q 12-2.   Why are loans, which are usually liabilities, treated as assets for banks?

Q 12-3.   Why are savings accounts liabilities for banks?

Q 12-4.   Why are banks concerned with their loans/deposits ratios?

Q 12-5.   To what agencies and other users of financial statements must banks report?

Q 12-6.   Why must the user be cautious in analyzing bank holding companies?

Q 12-7.   What is usually the biggest expense item for a bank?

Q 12-8.   What does the ratio total deposits times capital measure?

Q 12-9.   What ratios are used to indicate profitability for banks?

Q 12-10.   Why are banks concerned about the percentage of earning assets to total assets?

Q 12-11.   What does the loan loss coverage ratio measure?

Q 12-12.   What type of ratio is deposits times capital?

Q 12-13.   Give an example of why a review of bank assets may indicate risk or opportunity of which you were not aware.

Q 12-14.   Why review the disclosure of the market value of investments versus the book amount of investments for banks?

Q 12-15.   Why review the disclosure of foreign loans for banks?

Q 12-16.   Why review the disclosure of allowance for loan losses for a bank?

Q 12-17.   Why review the disclosure of nonperforming assets for banks?

Q 12-18.   Why could a review of savings deposit balances be important when reviewing a bank's financial statements?

Q 12-19.   Why review the note that describes commitments and contingent liabilities for a bank?

Q 12-20.   Utilities are very highly leveraged. How is it that they are able to carry such high levels of debt?

Q 12-21.   How does demand for utilities differ from demand for other products or services?

Q 12-22.   Why are plant and equipment usually listed first for utilities?

Q 12-23.   Are inventory ratios meaningful for utilities? Why?

Q 12-24.   What does the funded debt to operating property ratio measure for a utility?

Q 12-25.   Is times interest earned meaningful for utilities? Why or why not?

Q 12-26.   Are current liabilities usually presented first in utility reporting? Comment.

Q 12-27.   For a utility, why review the account Construction Work in Progress?

Q 12-28.   For a utility, describe the income statement accounts, allowance for equity funds used during construction, and allowance for borrowed funds used during construction.

Q 12-29.   Differentiate between successful-efforts and full-costing accounting as applied to the oil and gas industry.

Q 12-30.   Some industries described in this chapter are controlled by federal regulatory agencies. How does this affect their accounting systems?

Q 12-31.   When reviewing the financial statements of oil and gas companies, why is it important to note the method of costing (expensing) exploration and production costs?

Q 12-32.   Oil and gas companies must disclose quantity estimates for proved oil and gas reserves and the major factors causing changes in these resource estimates. Briefly indicate why this disclosure can be significant.

Q 12-33.   For oil and gas companies, there is the potential for a significant difference between the reported income and cash flows from operations. Comment.

Q 12-34.   Is it more desirable to have the operating ratios increasing or decreasing for utilities and transportation companies?

Q 12-35.   What type of ratio is operating revenue to operating property? Will it exceed 1:1 for a utility?

Q 12-36.   What is the most important category of assets for transportation firms?

Q 12-37.   Briefly describe the revenue section of the income statement for a transportation firm.

Q 12-38.   In a transportation firm, what types of things will change operating revenues? Operating expenses?

Q 12-39.   If a transportation firm shows a rise in revenue per passenger mile, what does this rise imply?

Q 12-40.   How is the passenger load factor of a bus company related to profitability?

Q 12-41.   Explain how the publication *Financial Analysis of the Motor Carrier Industry* could be used to determine the percentage of total revenue a firm has in relation to similar trucking firms.

Q 12-42.   Annual reports filed with state insurance departments are in accordance with what accounting standards?

Q 12-43.   Annual reports that insurance companies issue to the public are in accordance with what accounting standards?

Q 12-44.   Why could an insurance company with substantial investments in real estate represent a risk?

Q 12-45.   For an insurance company, describe the difference between GAAP reporting and SAP reporting of deferred policy acquisition costs.

Q 12-46.   Briefly describe the difference between accounting for intangibles for an insurance company under GAAP and under SAP.

Q 12-47.   Briefly describe the unique aspects of revenue recognition for an insurance company.

Q 12-48.   Insurance industry-specific financial ratios are usually prepared from financial statements prepared under what standards?

Q 12-49.   Insurance companies tend to have a stock market price at a discount to the average market price (price/ earnings ratio). Indicate some perceived reasons for this relatively low price/earnings ratio.

Q 12-50.   Real estate companies contend that conventional accounting does not recognize the underlying value of the property and that this misleads investors. Discuss.

Problems

P 12-1.   The following are statistics from the annual report of McEttrick National Bank:

	2007	2006
Average loans	$16,000,000	$13,200,000
Average total assets	26,000,000	22,000,000
Average total deposits	24,000,000	20,000,000
Average total capital	1,850,000	1,600,000
Interest expenses	1,615,000	1,512,250
Interest income	1,750,000	1,650,000

Required   a. Calculate the total deposits times capital for each year.
            b. Calculate the loans to total deposits for each year.
            c. Calculate the capital funds to total assets for each year.
            d. Calculate the interest margin to average total assets for each year.
            e. Comment on any trends found in the calculations of (a) through (d).

P 12-2.   The following are statistics from the annual report of Dover Bank:

	2007	2006	2005
Average earning assets	$50,000,000	$45,000,000	$43,000,000
Average total assets	58,823,529	54,216,867	52,000,000
Income before securities transactions	530,000	453,000	420,000
Interest margin	2,550,000	2,200,000	2,020,000
Pretax income before securities transactions	562,000	480,500	440,000
Provision for loan losses	190,000	160,000	142,000
Net charge-offs	180,000	162,000	160,000
Average equity	4,117,600	3,524,000	3,120,000
Average net loans	32,500,000	26,000,000	22,500,000
Average deposits	52,500,000	42,500,000	37,857,000

Required   a. Calculate the following for 2007, 2006, and 2005:
   1. Earning assets to total assets
   2. Interest margin to average earning assets
   3. Loan loss coverage ratio
   4. Equity to total assets
   5. Deposits times capital
   6. Loans to deposits
   b. Comment on trends found in the ratios computed in (a).

P 12-3.   Super Power Company reported the following statistics in its statements of income:

	2007	2006
Electric revenues:		
Residential	$11,800,000	$10,000,000
Commercial and industrial	10,430,000	10,000,000
Other	600,000	500,000
	22,830,000	20,500,000
Operating expenses and taxes*	20,340,000	18,125,000
Operating income	2,490,000	2,375,000
Other income	200,000	195,000
Income before interest deductions	2,690,000	2,570,000
Interest deductions	1,200,000	1,000,000
Net income	$ 1,490,000	$ 1,570,000

*Includes taxes of $3,200,000 in 2007 and $3,000,000 in 2006.

Required   a. Calculate the operating ratio and comment on the results.
   b. Calculate the times interest earned and comment on the results.
   c. Perform a vertical common-size analysis of revenues, using total revenue as the base, and comment on the relative size of the component parts.

P 12-4.   The following statistics relate to Michgate, an electric utility:

	2007	2006	2005
(In thousands of dollars, except per share)			
Operating expenses	$ 850,600	$ 820,200	$ 780,000
Operating revenues	1,080,500	1,037,200	974,000
Earnings per share	3.00	2.90	2.60
Cash flow per share	3.40	3.25	2.30
Operating property	3,900,000	3,750,000	3,600,000
Funded debt (long-term)	1,500,000	1,480,000	1,470,000
Net income	280,000	260,000	230,000

Required   a. Calculate the following for 2007, 2006, and 2005:
   1. Operating ratio
   2. Funded debt to operating property
   3. Percent earned on operating property
   4. Operating revenue to operating property

b. Comment on trends found in the ratios computed in (a).

c. Comment on the trend between earnings per share and cash flow per share.

P 12-5. Local Airways had the following results in the last two years:

	2007	2006
Operating revenues	$624,000	$618,000
Operating expenses	$625,000	$617,000
Operating property	$365,000	$360,000
Long-term debt	$280,000	$270,000
Estimated passenger miles	7,340,000	7,600,000

Required Calculate the following for 2007 and 2006:

a. The operating ratio and comment on the trend.

b. The long-term debt to operating property ratio. What does this tell about debt use?

c. The operating revenue to operating property and comment on the trend.

d. The revenue per passenger mile. What has caused this trend?

P 12-6. Chihi Airways had the following results for the last three years:

	2007	2006	2005
(In thousands of dollars)			
Operating expenses	$1,550,000	$1,520,000	$1,480,000
Operating revenues	1,840,000	1,670,400	1,620,700
Long-term debt	910,000	900,500	895,000
Operating property	995,000	990,000	985,000
Passenger load factor	66.5%	59.0%	57.8%

Required a. Calculate the following for 2007, 2006, and 2005:

1. Operating ratio

2. Long-term debt to operating property

3. Operating revenue to operating property

b. Comment on trends found in the ratios computed in (a).

c. Comment on the passenger load factor.

P 12-7.

Required Answer the following multiple-choice questions related to insurance financial reporting:

a. Which of the following does not represent a basic type of insurance organization?

1. Stock companies

2. Bond companies

3. Mutual companies

4. Fraternal benefit societies

5. Assessment companies

b. Which of these statements is not correct?

1. The balance sheet is a classified balance sheet.

2. The assets section starts with investments.

3. The majority of the investments are typically in bonds.

4. For life insurance companies, the investment in real estate may be much greater than that for property-casualty companies.

5. Real estate investments are reported at cost less accumulated depreciation and an allowance for impairment in value.

c. Generally, the largest liability is for loss reserves. The quantification process is subject to a number of estimates. Which of the following would not be one of the estimates?

1. Investment gains/losses

2. Inflation rate

3. Interest rates

4. Judicial interpretations

5. Mortality estimates

d. The manner of recognizing revenue on insurance contracts is unique for the insurance industry. Which of the following statements is not true?

1. In general, the duration of the contract governs the revenue recognition.
2. When the risk differs significantly from the contract period, revenue is recognized over the period of risk in proportion to the amount of insurance protection.
3. For long-duration contracts, revenue is recognized when the premium is due from policyholders.
4. Realized gains and losses from investments are reported in operations in the period incurred.
5. For investment contracts, termination fees are booked as revenue over the period of the contract.

e. Which of the following statements is not true?

1. Statutory accounting has emphasized the balance sheet in its concern for protecting the policyholders by focusing on the financial solvency of the insurance corporation.
2. All 50 states have insurance departments that require annual statements of insurance companies. These annual reports are filed with the state insurance departments in accordance with statutory accounting practices (SAP).
3. After the annual reports are filed with the individual state insurance departments, a testing process is conducted by the NAIC. If a company's ratio is outside the prescribed limit, the NAIC brings that to the attention of the company.
4. A.M. Best Company publishes *Best's Insurance Reports*, which are published separately for life-health companies and property-casualty companies. The financial data, including the ratios, are based on the data submitted to the state insurance departments and are thus based on SAP.
5. Many stock insurance companies must register with the Securities and Exchange Commission and file the required forms, such as the annual Form 10-K. Reports filed with the SEC must conform with GAAP.

f. Insurance companies tend to have a stock market price at a discount to the average market price (price/earnings ratio). Which of the following is a likely reason for this relatively low market value?

1. Insurance is a highly regulated industry.
2. The insurance industry has substantial competition.
3. The accounting environment likely contributes to the relatively low market price for insurance company stocks.
4. The nature of the industry leads to standards that provide for much judgment and possible manipulation of reported profit.
5. All of the above.

P 12-8.

Required

Answer the following multiple-choice questions related to bank financial reporting:

a. All but which of the following would be a representative asset of a bank?

1. Investment securities
2. Loans
3. Equipment
4. Cash on hand
5. Savings accounts

b. All but which of the following would be considered an earning asset of a bank for the earning assets to total assets ratio?

1. Loans
2. Leases
3. Cash
4. Investment securities
5. Money market assets

c. The ratio for a bank that provides an indication of management's ability to control the spread between interest income and interest expense is the

1. Loan loss coverage ratio.
2. Earning assets to total assets.
3. Return on earning assets.
4. Interest margin to average total assets.
5. Equity capital to total assets.

d. All but which of the following would be a representative liability of a bank?
   1. Savings
   2. Demand deposits
   3. Cash on hand
   4. Long-term debt
   5. Time deposits

e. Typically, the largest expense for a bank will be
   1. Employer benefits.
   2. Occupancy expense.
   3. Salaries.
   4. Provision for loan losses.
   5. Interest expense.

f. The ratio that indicates the extent of equity ownership in a bank is the
   1. Interest margin to average total assets.
   2. Loss coverage ratio.
   3. Loans to deposits.
   4. Equity capital to total assets.
   5. Deposits times capital.

P 12-9.

Required   Answer the following multiple-choice questions:

a. A ratio that indicates how funds are supplied to a utility is
   1. Return on assets.
   2. Percent earned on operating property.
   3. Operating ratio.
   4. Funded debt to operating property.
   5. Operating revenue to operating property.

b. A ratio that relates net earnings to the assets primarily intended to generate earnings for a utility is
   1. Return on assets.
   2. Percent earned on operating property.
   3. Operating ratio.
   4. Funded debt to operating property.
   5. Operating revenue to operating property.

c. For a utility, the ratio that is basically an operating asset turnover ratio is
   1. Return on assets.
   2. Percent earned on operating property.
   3. Operating ratio.
   4. Funded debt to operating property.
   5. Operating revenue to operating property.

d. A ratio that indicates a measure of operating efficiency for a utility is
   1. Operating revenue to operating property.
   2. Funded debt to operating property.
   3. Operating ratio.
   4. Percent earned on operating property.
   5. Long-term debt to operating property.

e. For a transportation firm, which ratio gives a measure of the source of funds with which property is obtained?
   1. Operating ratio
   2. Operating revenue to operating property
   3. Long-term debt to operating property
   4. Per mile-per person-per ton
   5. Return on equity

f. Which ratio is a measure of turnover of operating assets for a transportation firm?
   1. Operating ratio
   2. Long-term debt to operating property
   3. Per mile-per person-per ton
   4. Return on investment
   5. Operating revenue to operating property

g. Which of these industries does not have a uniform system of accounts?
   1. Banks
   2. Utilities
   3. Transportation
   4. Oil and gas
   5. 1, 2, and 3

h. Which of the following has a balance sheet similar in format to a manufacturing firm?
   1. Banks
   2. Insurance companies
   3. Regulated utilities
   4. 1 and 2
   5. None of the above

Case 12-1	ALLOWANCE FOR FUNDS
	PG&E Corporation* Selected Financial Data

Note 1 Organization and Basis of Presentation (in Part)

PG&E Corporation
CONSOLIDATED STATEMENTS OF INCOME
(In millions, except per share amounts)

	Year Ended December 31,		
	2006	2005	2004
Operating Revenues			
Electric	$ 8,752	$ 7,927	$ 7,867
Natural gas	3,787	3,776	3,213
Total operating revenues	12,539	11,703	11,080
Operating Expenses			
Cost of electricity	2,922	2,410	2,770
Cost of natural gas	2,097	2,191	1,724
Operating and maintenance	3,703	3,397	2,871
Recognition of regulatory assets	—	—	(4,900)
Depreciation, amortization, and decommissioning	1,709	1,735	1,497
Total operating expenses	10,431	9,733	3,962
Operating Income	2,108	1,970	7,118
Interest income	188	80	63
Interest expense	(738)	(583)	(797)
Other expense, net	(13)	(19)	(98)
Income Before Income Taxes	1,545	1,448	6,286
Income tax provision	554	544	2,466
Income From Continuing Operations	991	904	3,820
Discontinued Operations			
Gain on disposal of NEGT (net of income tax benefit of $13 million in 2005 and income tax expense of $374 million in 2004)	—	13	684
Net Income	$ 991	$ 917	$ 4,504

*"PG&E Corporation is a holding company whose primary purpose is to hold interests in energy based businesses. PG&E conducts its business principally through Pacific Gas and Electric Company, or the Utility, a public utility operating in northern and central California. The Utility engages in the businesses of electricity and natural gas distribution, electricity generation, procurement and transmission, and natural gas procurement, transportation and storage." 10-K

(continued)

ALLOWANCE FOR FUNDS (Continued)

PG&E Corporation
CONSOLIDATED BALANCE SHEETS
(In millions)

	Balance at December 31,	
	2006	2005
Assets		
Current Assets		
Cash and cash equivalents	$ 456	$ 713
Restricted cash	1,415	1,546
Accounts receivable:		
Customers (net of allowance for doubtful accounts of $50 million in 2006 and $77 million in 2005)	2,343	2,422
Regulatory balancing accounts	607	727
Inventories:		
Gas stored underground and fuel oil	181	231
Materials and supplies	149	133
Income taxes receivables	—	21
Prepaid expenses and other	716	187
Total current assets	5,867	5,980
Property, Plant and Equipment		
Electric	24,036	22,482
Gas	9,115	8,794
Construction work in progress	1,047	738
Other	16	16
Total property, plant and equipment	34,214	32,030
Accumulated depreciation	(12,429)	(12,075)
Net property, plant and equipment	21,785	19,955
Other Noncurrent Assets		
Regulatory assets	4,902	5,578
Nuclear decommissioning funds	1,876	1,719
Other	373	842
Total other noncurrent assets	7,151	8,139
TOTAL ASSETS	$ 34,803	$ 34,074
LIABILITIES AND SHAREHOLDERS' EQUITY		
Current Liabilities		
Short-term borrowings	$ 759	$ 260
Long-term debt, classified as current	281	2
Rate reduction bonds, classified as current	290	290
Energy recovery bonds, classified as current	340	316
Accounts payable:		
Trade creditors	1,075	980
Disputed claims and customer refunds	1,709	1,733
Regulatory balancing accounts	1,030	840
Other	420	441
Interest payable	583	473
Income taxes payable	102	—
Deferred income taxes	148	181
Other	1,513	1,416
Total current liabilities	8,250	6,932
Noncurrent liabilities		
Long-term debt	6,697	6,976
Rate reduction bonds	—	290
Energy recovery bonds	1,936	2,276
Regulatory liabilities	3,392	3,506
Asset retirement obligations	1,466	1,587
Deferred income taxes	2,840	3,092
Deferred tax credits	106	112
Other	2,053	1,833
Total noncurrent liabilities	18,490	19,672

(continued)

ALLOWANCE FOR FUNDS (Continued)

	Balance at December 31,	
	2006	**2005**
Commitments and Contingencies (Notes 2, 4, 5, 6, 8, 9, 13, 15 and 17)		
Preferred Stock of Subsidiaries	252	252
Preferred Stock		
Preferred stock, no par value, 80,000,000 shares, $100 par value, 5,000,000 shares, non issued	—	—
Common Shareholders' Equity		
Common stock, no par value, authorized 800,000,000 shares, issued 372,803,521 common and 1,377,538 restricted shares in 2006 and issued 366,868,512 common and 1,399,990 restricted shares in 2005	5,877	5,827
Common stock held by subsidiary, at cost, 24,665,500	(718)	(718)
Unearned compensation	—	(22)
Reinvested earnings	2,671	2,139
Accumulated other comprehensive loss	(19)	(8)
Total common shareholders' equity	7,811	7,218
TOTAL LIABILITIES AND SHAREHOLDERS' EQUITY	$34,803	$34,074

Note 2 Summary of Significant Accounting Policies (in Part)

Property, Plant and Equipment

Property, plant and equipment are reported at their original cost. Original cost includes:

- Labor and materials;
- Construction overhead; and
- Allowance for funds used during construction, or AFUDC

AFUDC

AFUDC is the estimated cost of debt and equity used to finance regulated plant additions that can be recoded as part of the cost of construction projects. AFUDC is recoverable from customers through rates over the life of the related property once the property is placed in service. The Utility recorded AFUDC of approximately $47 million and $20 million related to equity and debt, respectively, during 2006, $37 million and $14 million related to equity and debt, respectively, during 2005, and $20 million and $12 million related to equity and debt, respectively, during 2004. PG&E Corporation on a stand-alone basis did not have any capitalized interest or AFUDC in 2006, 2005 and 2004.

Required   a. Describe AFUDC as used by PG&E.

b. How does capitalizing interest on borrowed funds affect income in the year of capitalization versus not capitalizing this interest? Explain.

c. Would net income tend to be higher than cash flow if there is substantial capitalization of interest on the borrowed funds during the current period?

d. How does capitalizing the allowance for equity funds used during construction affect income in the year of capitalization versus not capitalizing these charges?

e. Would net income tend to be higher than cash flow if there is substantial capitalization of the allowance for equity funds during construction for the current year?

f. Compute the following for the years 2006 and 2005. Comment on each.

   1. Operating ratio

   2. Funded debt to operating property

(continued)

3. Percent earned on operating property
4. Operating revenue to operating property
5. Times interest earned

g. Using the balances at December 31, 2006 and 2005, compute the percentage relationship between construction work in progress and net property, plant and equipment. Comment.

Case
12-2

RESULTS OF OPERATIONS FOR OIL AND GAS PRODUCING ACTIVITIES

Hess Corporation* included the information in this case as part of the Supplementary Oil and Gas Data. This case only represents a small portion of the Supplementary Oil and Gas Data.

Results of Operations for Oil and Gas Producing Activities

The results of operations shown below exclude non-oil and gas producing activities, including gains on sales of oil and gas properties, interest expense and gains and losses resulting from foreign exchange transactions. Therefore, these results are on a different basis than the net income from Exploration and Production operations reported in management's discussion and analysis of results of operations and in note 17, "Segment Information," in the notes to the financial statements.

For the Years Ended December 31	Total	United States	Europe	Africa	Asia and Other
			(Millions of dollars)		
2006					
Sales and other operating revenues					
Unaffiliated customers	$6,249	$ 957	$3,052	$1,637	$603
Intercompany	275	275	—	—	—
Total revenues	6,524	1,232	3,052	1,637	603
Costs and expenses					
Production expenses, including related taxes	1,250	221	631	284	114
Exploration expenses, including dry holes and lease impairment	552	353	39	117	43
General, administrative and other expenses**	209	95	74	15	25
Depreciation, depletion and amortization	1,159	127	490	401	141
Total costs and expenses	3,170	796	1,234	817	323
Results of operations before income taxes	3,354	436	1,818	820	280
Provision for income taxes	1,870	161	1,009	609	91
Results of operations	$1,484	$ 275	$ 809	$ 211	$189

Required

a. Prepare a vertical common-size analysis for results of operations for oil and gas producing activities for 2006. Use total revenues as the base.
b. Prepare a horizontal common-size analysis for 2006. Use total as the base.
c. Comment on the common-size analysis in (a) and (b).

*Hess Corporation "is a global integrated energy company that operates in two segments, Exploration and Production (E&P) and Marketing and Refining (M&R)." 10-K

**Includes accrued severance and costs for vacated office space of approximately $30 million and $15 million in 2006 and 2004, respectively.

Case	
12-3	ALLOWANCE FOR LOAN LOSSES

Indymac Bancorp, Inc.,* included the following in its 2006 annual report:

Note 6—ALLOWANCE FOR LOAN LOSSES

Our determination of the level of the allowance for loan losses and, correspondingly, the provision for loan losses, is based upon management's judgments and assumptions regarding various matters, including general economic conditions, loan portfolio composition, loan demand, delinquency trends, and prior loan loss experience. The allowance for loan losses of $62.4 million is considered adequate to cover probable losses inherent in the loan portfolio at December 31, 2006. However, no assurance can be given that we will not, in any particular period, sustain loan losses that exceed the allowance, or that subsequent evaluation of the loan portfolio, in light of then-prevailing factors, including economic conditions, credit quality of the assets comprising the portfolio and the ongoing examination process, will not require significant changes in the allowance for loan losses.

The table below summarizes the changes to the allowance for loan losses for the years ended:

	December 31,		
	2006	**2005**	**2004**
	(Dollars in thousands)		
Balance, beginning of period	$ 55,168	$ 52,891	$52,645
Provision for loan losses	19,993	9,978	8,170
Charge-offs, net of recoveries:			
SFR mortgage loans	(7,324)	(1,428)	(3,060)
Land and other mortgage loans	—	(168)	—
Builder construction	—	—	—
Consumer construction	(3,318)	(2,127)	(1,463)
Discontinued product lines(1)	(2,133)	(3,978)	(3,401)
Charge-offs, net of recoveries	(12,775)	(7,701)	(7,924)
Balance, end of period	$ 62,386	$ 55,168	$52,891

(1)Includes manufactured home loans and home improvement loans.

Required   Give your opinion of trends in the allowance for loan losses.

*"Indymac Bancorp, Inc. "originates mortgages in all 50 states of the U.S. and the largest savings and loan headquartered in Los Angeles County, California." 10-K

Case	
12-4	YOU CAN BANK ON IT

Sovereign Bancorp
Consolidated Balance Sheet

	At December 31,	
(In thousands, except share data)	**2004**	**2003**
Assets		
Cash and amounts due from depository institutions	$ 1,160,922	$ 950,302
Investment securities available for sale	7,642,558	10,102,619
Investment securities held to maturity (fair value of $3,889,002 in 2004 and $2,507,710 in 2003)	3,904,319	2,516,352
Loans (including loans held for sale of $137,478 in 2004 and $137,154 in 2003)	36,631,079	26,148,659
Allowance for loan losses	(408,716)	(327,894)
Net loans	36,222,363	25,820,765
Premises and equipment	353,337	273,278

"Sovereign's primary business consists of attracting deposits from its network of community banking offices, and originating small business and middle market commercial loans, residential mortgage loans, home equity lines of credit, and auto and other consumer loans in the communities served by those offices." 10-K

(continued)

YOU CAN BANK ON IT (Continued)

	At December 31,	
	2004	**2003**
Accrued interest receivable	226,012	190,714
Goodwill	2,125,081	1,027,292
Core deposit intangibles, net of accumulated amortization of $445,559 in 2004 and $372,924 in 2003	256,694	268,759
Bank owned life insurance	885,807	801,535
Other assets	1,694,220	1,553,713
Total Assets	**$54,471,313**	**$43,505,329**
Liabilities		
Deposits and other customer accounts	$32,555,518	$27,344,008
Borrowings and other debt obligations	16,140,128	12,197,603
Advance payments by borrowers for taxes and insurance	30,542	17,966
Other liabilities	552,847	483,210
Total Liabilities	49,279,035	40,042,787
Minority interest-preferred securities of subsidiaries	203,906	202,136
Stockholders Equity		
Preferred stock; no par value; $50 liquidation preference; 7,500,000 shares authorized; 0 shares issued and outstanding	—	—
Common stock; no par value; 800,000,000 shares authorized; 350,261,512 issued in 2004 and 298,111,799 in 2003	2,949,870	1,892,126
Warrants and employee stock options issued	317,842	13,944
Unallocated common stock held by the Employee Stock Ownership Plan (3,285,872 shares in 2004 and 3,550,268 shares in 2003, at cost)	(23,707)	(26,078)
Treasury stock (1,200,470 shares in 2004 and 1,450,668 shares in 2003, at cost)	(19,136)	(21,927)
Accumulated other comprehensive loss	(108,092)	(52,924)
Retained earnings	1,871,595	1,455,265
Total Stockholders Equity	4,988,372	3,260,406
Total Liabilities and Stockholders Equity	$54,471,313	$43,505,329

Sovereign Bancorp
Consolidated Statements of Operations

	For the Year Ended December 31,		
(In thousands, except share data)	**2004**	**2003**	**2002**
Interest Income:			
Interest-earning deposits	$ 4,734	$ 2,141	$ 4,620
Investment securities:			
Available for sale	501,471	584,697	614,761
Held to maturity	152,680	27,123	46,967
Interest on loans	1,565,259	1,315,790	1,393,192
Total interest income	2,224,144	1,929,751	2,059,540
Interest Expense:			
Deposits and other customer accounts	303,045	320,689	458,287
Borrowings and other debt obligations	516,282	403,434	441,637
Total interest expense	819,327	724,123	899,924
Net interest income	1,404,817	1,205,628	1,159,616
Provision for loan losses	127,000	161,957	146,500
Net interest income after provision for loan losses	1,277,817	1,043,671	1,013,116
Non-interest Income:			
Consumer banking fees	242,587	208,819	179,402
Commercial banking fees	123,837	107,973	95,083
Mortgage banking revenue	22,509	50,018	28,571
Capital markets revenue	19,943	27,014	14,995
Bank-owned life insurance	39,272	43,338	43,456
Miscellaneous income	19,921	18,357	17,247
Total fees and other income	468,069	455,519	378,754
Net gain on investment securities	14,229	66,057	51,431
Total non-interest income	482,298	521,576	430,185

(continued)

	For the Year Ended December 31,		
	2004	2003	2002
General and Administrative Expenses:			
Compensation and benefits	448,142	388,750	362,813
Occupancy and equipment	220,673	210,761	210,044
Technology expense	77,359	73,032	69,424
Outside services	53,315	53,436	49,235
Marketing expense	46,523	38,824	35,852
Other administrative	96,649	87,561	86,416
Total general and administrative expenses	942,661	852,364	813,784
Other Expenses:			
Amortization of intangibles	72,635	73,835	80,274
Trust Preferred Securities and other minority			
interest expense (see Note 1)	22,006	42,813	62,835
Loss on debt extinguishment	63,761	29,838	—
Merger related and restructuring charges	46,359	—	15,871
Equity method investments	31,471	11,498	3,982
Total other expenses	236,232	157,984	162,962
Income before income taxes	581,222	554,899	466,555
Income tax provision	127,670	153,048	124,570
Net Income	$ 453,552	$ 401,851	$ 341,985
Earnings per share:			
Basic	$1.41	$1.45	$1.32
Diluted	$1.36	$1.38	$1.23
Dividends Declared Per Common Share	$0.115	$0.10	$0.10

Notes to Consolidated Financial Statements (in Part)
Note 7. Loans (in Part)
The activity in the allowance for loan losses is as follows (in thousands):

	Year Ended December 31,		
	2004	2003	2002
Balance, beginning of period	$327,894	$298,750	$264,667
Allowance acquired from acquisitions	64,105		14,877
Provision for loan losses	127,000	161,957	146,500
Charge-offs:			
Residential[1]	1,890	4,313	8,186
Commercial	77,499	101,597	85,931
Consumer	73,859	59,478	68,528
Total charge-offs	153,248	165,388	162,645
Recoveries:			
Residential	847	1,465	525
Commercial	12,825	7,531	6,082
Consumer	29,293	23,579	28,744
Total recoveries	42,965	32,575	35,351
Charge-offs, net of recoveries	110,283	132,813	127,294
Balance, end of period	$408,716	$327,894	$298,750

[1]The 2002 residential charge-offs include $4.6 million of charge-offs incurred as part of accelerated dispositions of non-performing residential loans sold during the first and fourth quarters of 2002.

Required   a. Prepare a horizontal common-size analysis for 2004, 2003, and 2002 for the following items from the consolidated statements of operations (use 2002 as the base):

   1. Total interest income
   2. Total interest expense

(continued)

YOU CAN BANK ON IT (Continued)

3. Provision for loan losses
4. Total fees and other income
5. Total general and administrative
6. Total other expenses
7. Net income

b. Comment on the trends indicated in (a).

c. Compute the following for 2004 and 2003 (use ending balance sheet accounts):

1. Earning assets to total assets
2. Interest margin to average earning assets
3. Loan loss coverage ratio
4. Equity capital to total assets (use year-end numbers)
5. Deposits times capital (use year-end numbers)
6. Loans to deposits (use year-end net loans and year-end deposits)

d. Comment on the trends indicated by the ratios computed in (c).

YOU'RE COVERED

Exhibit 12-20 on pages 523–524 includes the consolidated statement of income for The Chubb Corporation.

Required

a. Prepare a horizontal common-size analysis of this statement. Use 2004 as the base.

b. Comment on trends found in (a).

Thomson One *Business School Edition*

Please complete the Web case that covers material discussed in this chapter at academic.cengage .com/accounting/Gibson. You'll be using Thomson One Business School Edition, a powerful tool, that combines a full range of fundamental financial information, earnings estimates, market data, and source documents for 500 publicly traded companies.

Endnotes

1. Arthur Andersen & Co., *Insurance* (Essex, England: Saffren Press Ltd., 1983), p. 87.
2. *Statement of Financial Accounting Standards No. 60*, "Accounting and Reporting by Insurance Enterprises" (Stamford, Conn.: Financial Accounting Standards Board, 1982), par. 13.
3. *Statement of Financial Accounting Standards No. 60*, par. 15.
4. *Statement of Financial Accounting Standards No. 97*, "Accounting and Reporting by Insurance Enterprises for Certain Long-Duration Contracts and for Realized Gains and Losses from the Sale of Investments" (Stamford, Conn.: Financial Accounting Standards Board, 1987), par. 15.
5. "SEC Broadens Role to Investigate Insurance Industry," *The Blade* (April 8, 2005), Sec. B, p. 14.
6. Ibid.

Chapter 13

Personal Financial Statements and Accounting for Governments and Not-for-Profit Organizations

This chapter briefly covers three types of financial reporting that have not been discussed in previous chapters: (1) personal financial statements, (2) governments, and (3) not-for-profit organizations other than governments.

Personal Financial Statements

Personal financial statements of individuals, husband and wife, or a larger family group are prepared for obtaining credit, income tax planning, retirement planning, and estate planning. *Statement of Position 82-1 (SOP 82-1)* covers guidelines for the preparation of personal financial statements.[1] SOP 82-1 concludes that:

> *The primary users of personal financial statements normally consider estimated current value information to be more relevant for their decisions than historical cost information. Lenders require estimated current value information to assess collateral, and most personal loan applications require estimated current value information. Estimated current values are required for estate, gift, and income tax planning, and estimated current value information about assets is often required in federal and state filings of candidates for public office.*[2]

SOP 82-1 concludes that personal financial statements should present assets at their estimated current values and liabilities at their estimated current amounts at the date of the financial statements. This contrasts with commercial financial statements, which predominantly use historical cost information. SOP 82-1 provides guidelines for determining the estimated current value of an asset and the estimated current amount of a liability.[3]

FORM OF THE STATEMENTS

The basic and most important statement prepared for personal financial statements, a statement of financial condition, resembles a balance sheet. It states assets at estimated current values and liabilities at estimated current amounts. A tax liability is estimated on the difference between the stated amounts of the assets and liabilities and the tax basis of these assets and liabilities. For example, land may cost $10,000, which would be the tax basis, but may have an estimated current value of $25,000. The estimated tax liability on the difference between the $10,000 and the $25,000 would be estimated.

The difference between the total assets and total liabilities, designated net worth, is equivalent to the equity section in a commercial balance sheet. The statement of financial condition is prepared on the accrual basis. Assets and liabilities are presented in order of liquidity and maturity, without classification as current and noncurrent.

The optional statement of changes in net worth presents the major changes (sources of increases and decreases) in net worth. This statement combines income and other changes because of the mix of business and personal items. Examples of changes in net worth would be income, increases in the estimated current value of assets, and decreases in estimated income taxes. The statement of changes in net worth presents changes in terms of realized increases (decreases) and unrealized increases (decreases). Examples of realized increases (decreases) are salary, dividends, income taxes, and personal expenditures. Examples of unrealized increases (decreases) are an increase in the value of securities, an increase in the value of a residence, a decrease in the value of a boat, and estimated income taxes on the differences between the estimated current values of assets and the estimated current amounts of liabilities and their tax bases. Comparative financial statements may be more informative than statements of only one period.

For personal financial statements, the statement of changes in net worth replaces the income statement. SOP 82-1 includes guidelines on disclosure. These guidelines are not all-inclusive. Examples of disclosure include the methods used in determining current values of major assets, descriptions of intangible assets, and assumptions used to compute the estimated income taxes.

Most individuals do not maintain a complete set of records, so the necessary data must be gathered from various sources. These sources include brokers' statements, income tax returns, safe deposit boxes, insurance policies, real estate tax returns, checkbooks, and bank statements.

SUGGESTIONS FOR REVIEWING THE STATEMENT OF FINANCIAL CONDITION

1. Usually the most important figure, the net worth amount, indicates the level of wealth.
2. Determine the amount of the assets that you consider to be very liquid (cash, savings accounts, marketable securities, and so on). These assets are readily available.
3. Observe the due date of the liabilities. In general, we would prefer the liabilities to be relatively long-term. Long-term liabilities do not represent an immediate pressing problem.
4. When possible, compare specific assets with their related liabilities. This will indicate the net investment in the asset. For example, a residence with a current value of $90,000 and a $40,000 mortgage represents a net investment of $50,000.

SUGGESTIONS FOR REVIEWING THE STATEMENT OF CHANGES IN NET WORTH

1. Review realized increases in net worth. Determine the principal sources of realized net worth.
2. Review realized decreases in net worth. Determine the principal items in realized decreases in net worth.
3. Observe whether the net realized amount increased or decreased and by how much.
4. Review unrealized increases in net worth. Determine the principal sources of the increases.
5. Review unrealized decreases in net worth. Determine the principal sources of the decreases.
6. Observe whether the net unrealized amount increased or decreased and the amount.
7. Observe whether the net change increased or decreased and the amount.
8. Observe the net worth at the end of the year. (This indicates the level of wealth.)

ILLUSTRATION OF PREPARATION OF THE STATEMENT OF FINANCIAL CONDITION

For Bill and Mary, assume that assets and liabilities, effective income tax rates, and the amount of estimated income taxes are as follows at December 31, 2008:

Account	Tax Bases	Estimated Current Value	Excess of Estimated Current Values over Tax Bases	Effective Income Tax Rates	Amount of Estimated Income Taxes
Cash	$ 8,000	$ 8,000	—	—	—
Savings accounts	20,000	20,000	—	—	—
Marketable securities	50,000	60,000	$10,000	28%	$ 2,800
Options	0	20,000	20,000	28%	5,600
Royalties	0	10,000	10,000	28%	2,800
Auto	15,000	10,000	(5,000)	—	—
Boat	12,000	8,000	(4,000)	—	—
Residence	110,000	130,000	20,000	28%	5,600*
Furnishings	30,000	25,000	(5,000)	—	—
Mortgage payable	(60,000)	(60,000)	—	—	—
Auto loan	(5,000)	(5,000)	—	—	—
Credit cards	(5,000)	(4,000)	—	—	—
Total estimated income tax					$16,800

*The residence may not be taxed.

Bill and Mary
Statement of Financial Condition
December 31, 2008

Assets:	
Cash	$ 8,000
Savings accounts	20,000
Marketable securities	60,000
Options	20,000
Royalties	10,000
Auto	10,000
Boat	8,000
Residence	130,000
Furnishings	25,000
Total assets	$291,000
Liabilities:	
Credit cards	$ 4,000
Auto loan	5,000
Mortgage payable	60,000
Total liabilities	69,000
Estimated income taxes on the difference between the estimated current values of assets and the estimated current amounts of liabilities and their tax bases	16,800
Net worth	205,200
Total liabilities and net worth	$291,000

Comments

1. Many would consider the net worth, $205,200, a relatively high amount.

2. Liquid assets total $88,000 (cash, $8,000; savings accounts, $20,000; and marketable securities, $60,000).

3. Most of the liabilities appear to be long-term (mortgage payable, $60,000).

4. Compare specific assets with related liabilities:

Auto:		Residence:	
Current value	$10,000	Current value	$130,000
Auto loan	5,000	Mortgage payable	60,000
Net investment	$ 5,000	Net investment	$ 70,000

ILLUSTRATION OF PREPARATION OF THE STATEMENT OF CHANGES IN NET WORTH

For Bill and Mary, the data relating to changes in net worth for the year ended December 31, 2008, follow:

Realized increases in net worth:	
Salary	$ 70,000
Dividend income	5,000
Interest income	6,000
Gain on sale of marketable securities	2,000
Realized decreases in net worth:	
Income taxes	20,000
Real estate taxes	2,000
Personal expenditures	28,000
Unrealized increases in net worth:	
Marketable securities	11,000
Residence	3,000
Unrealized decreases in net worth:	
Boat	2,000
Furnishings	4,000
Estimated income taxes on the differences between the estimated current values of assets and current amounts of liabilities and their tax bases	12,000
Net worth at the beginning of year	176,200

Bill and Mary
Statement of Changes in Net Worth
For the Year Ended December 31, 2008

Realized increases in net worth:	
Salary	$ 70,000
Dividend income	5,000
Interest income	6,000
Gain on sale of marketable securities	2,000
	83,000
Realized decreases in net worth:	
Income taxes	20,000
Real estate taxes	2,000
Personal expenditures	28,000
	50,000
Net realized increase in net worth	33,000
Unrealized increases in net worth:	
Marketable securities	11,000
Residence	3,000
	14,000
Unrealized decreases in net worth:	
Boat	2,000
Furnishings	4,000
Estimated income taxes on the differences between the estimated current values of assets and the estimated current amounts of liabilities and their tax base	12,000
	18,000
Net unrealized decreases in net worth	4,000
Net increase in net worth	29,000
Net worth at the beginning of year	176,200
Net worth at the end of the year	$205,200

Comments

1. Most of the realized increase in net worth is salary ($70,000).

2. The major decreases in realized net worth are income taxes ($20,000) and personal expenditures ($28,000).

3. The net realized increase in net worth totaled $33,000.
4. The principal unrealized increase in net worth is marketable securities ($11,000).
5. The principal unrealized decreases in net worth are estimated income taxes on the differences between the estimated current value of assets and the estimated current amounts of liabilities and their tax bases ($12,000).
6. The net unrealized decreases in net worth totaled $4,000.
7. The net increase in net worth totaled $29,000.
8. The net worth at the end of the year totaled $205,200.

Accounting for Governments

The accounting terminology utilized by governments differs greatly from that used by profit-oriented enterprises. Governments use such terms as *appropriations* and *general fund*. Definitions of some of the terms that will be encountered follow:

- **Appropriations.** Provision for necessary resources and the authority for their disbursement.
- **Debt service.** Cash receipts and disbursements related to the payment of interest and principal on long-term debt.
- **Capital projects.** Cash receipts and disbursements related to the acquisition of long-lived assets.
- **Special assessments.** Cash receipts and disbursements related to improvements or services for which special property assessments have been levied.
- **Enterprises.** Operations that are similar to private businesses in which service users are charged fees.
- **Internal services.** Service centers that supply goods or services to other governmental units on a cost reimbursement basis.
- **General fund.** All cash receipts and disbursements not required to be accounted for in another fund.
- **Proprietary funds.** Funds whose purpose is to maintain the assets through cost reimbursement by users or partial cost recovery from users and periodic infusion of additional assets.
- **Fiduciary funds (nonexpendable funds).** Funds whose principal must remain intact (revenues earned may be distributed).
- **Encumbrances.** Future commitments for expenditures.

Thousands of state and local governments in the United States account for a large segment of the gross national product. State and local governments have a major impact on the citizens. No organization had a clear responsibility for providing accounting principles for state and local governments. The American Institute of Certified Public Accountants (AICPA), the National Council on Governmental Accounting, and the Municipal Finance Officers Association have provided significant leadership in establishing accounting principles for state and local governments.

During the early 1980s, many thought that governmental accounting could benefit from the establishment of a board similar to the Financial Accounting Standards Board (FASB). A group of government accountants and CPAs organized a committee known as the Governmental Accounting Standards Board Organizing Committee. The Committee recommended the establishment of a separate standard-setting body for governmental accounting.

In April 1984, the Financial Accounting Foundation amended its articles of incorporation to accommodate a Governmental Accounting Standards Board (GASB). Thus, the GASB became a branch of the Financial Accounting Foundation. The GASB has a seven-member board. A simple majority of four votes is needed to issue a pronouncement.

Governmental Accounting Standards Board Statement No. 1, Appendix B, addresses the jurisdictional hierarchy of the GASB and the FASB. It establishes the following priorities for governmental units:

1. Pronouncements of the Governmental Accounting Standards Board.
2. Pronouncements of the Financial Accounting Standards Board.
3. Pronouncements of bodies composed of expert accountants that follow a due process procedure, including broad distribution of proposed accounting principles for public comment, for the intended purpose of establishing accounting principles or describing existing practices that are generally accepted.

4. Practices or pronouncements that are widely recognized as being generally accepted because they represent prevalent practice in a particular industry or the knowledgeable application to specific circumstances of pronouncements that are generally accepted.

5. Other accounting literature.[4]

Governmental Accounting Standards Board Statement No. 1 also adopts the National Council on Governmental Accounting pronouncements and the American Institute of Certified Public Accountants audit guide entitled *Audits of State and Local Governmental Units* as the basis for currently existing GAAP for state and local governmental units.

In 1984, the GASB codified all existing governmental accounting and financial reporting standards, interpretations, and technical bulletins in a joint effort with the Government Finance Officers Association (GFOA). This book, *Codification of Governmental Accounting and Financial Reporting Standards*, is periodically updated for subsequent changes.

State and local governments serve as stewards over public funds. This stewardship responsibility dominates state and local government accounting.

State and local government accounting revolves around fund accounting. A **fund** is defined as an:

> *Independent fiscal and accounting entity with a self-balancing set of accounts recording cash and/or other resources together with all related liabilities, obligations, reserves, and equities which are segregated for the purpose of carrying on specific activities or attaining certain objectives in accordance with special regulations, restrictions, or limitations.*[5]

Government transactions are recorded in one or more funds designed to emphasize control and budgetary limitations. Examples of funds, established for a specific purpose, are highway maintenance, parks, debt repayment, endowment, and welfare. The number of funds utilized depends on the responsibilities of the particular state or local government and the grouping of these responsibilities. For example, highway maintenance and bridge maintenance may be grouped together.

Some governments do their accounting using a method that resembles a cash basis, others use a modified accrual basis, and some use an accrual basis. A single government unit may use more than one basis, depending on the fund. The trend is away from the cash basis and toward the modified accrual basis or accrual basis.

Under the GASB, the most substantial pronouncement has been GASB Statement No. 34, which was issued in 1999. GASB No. 34 redefines what constitutes basic financial statements for state and local governments. This includes states, cities, towns, and special-purpose governments such as school districts.

GASB Statement No. 34 provides minimum requirements for general-purpose external financial statements. Exhibit 13-1 shows a diagram illustrating the minimum requirements.

The basic financial statements are to be preceded by the management's discussion and analysis (MD&A). The "MD&A should provide an objective and easily readable analysis of the government's financial activities based on currently known facts, decisions, or conditions."[6] The "MD&A provides financial managers with the opportunity to present both a short-term and a long-term analysis of the government's activities."[7]

The MD&A must include:

-   An objective discussion of the basic financial statements and condensed financial information comparing current and prior years.
-   An analysis of the overall financial position and results of operations.
-   Analysis of balances and transactions of individual funds.
-   Analysis of significant variations between the original and final budget and the final budget and actual results for the general fund.
-   A description of significant capital—asset and long-term debt activity during the year.
-   Known facts, decisions, or conditions expected to have a significant impact on financial position or results of operations.[8]

GASB Statement No. 34 makes it clear that neither government-wide statements nor fund statements are considered superior or subordinate to the other. For the government-wide

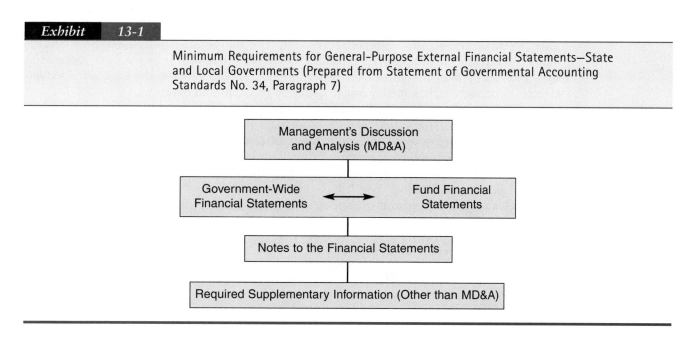

Exhibit   13-1

Minimum Requirements for General-Purpose External Financial Statements—State and Local Governments (Prepared from Statement of Governmental Accounting Standards No. 34, Paragraph 7)

Management's Discussion and Analysis (MD&A)

Government-Wide Financial Statements ⟷ Fund Financial Statements

Notes to the Financial Statements

Required Supplementary Information (Other than MD&A)

statements, governmental activities are to be presented separately from the financial statements of business-type activities. Examples of governmental activities are police and fire departments. Examples of business-type activities are airports and utilities.

The government-wide financial statements are to be prepared on an accrual basis for all of the government's activities. These government-wide financial statements help users:[9]

- Assess the finances of the government in its entirety, including the year's operating results.
- Determine whether the government's overall financial position improved or deteriorated.
- Evaluate whether the government's current-year revenues were sufficient to pay for current-year services.
- See the cost of providing services to its citizenry.
- See how the government finances its programs—through user fees and other program revenues versus general tax revenues.
- Understand the extent to which the government has invested in capital assets, including roads, bridges, and other infrastructure assets.
- Make better comparisons between governments.

As indicated previously, the government entity will continue to present fund statements. The government entity uses funds to maintain its financial records during the year. The funds enable the government entity to segregate transactions related to certain functions or activities in separate funds in order to aid financial management and to demonstrate legal compliance.

A fund is defined as a fiscal and accounting entity with a self-balancing set of accounts. The three categories of funds are governmental, proprietary, and fiduciary.

Governmental funds are those through which most governmental functions are financed. These funds are used to account for the general operations of government.

Proprietary funds focus on maintaining capital or producing income, or both. Fiduciary funds focus on assets held in a trustee or agency capacity on behalf of others external to the government entity.

Government funds use the modified accrual basis of accounting. Proprietary and fiduciary funds use the accrual basis of accounting. The differences in the accrual and modified accrual bases of accounting come from the recognition of revenue, from the recording of deferred revenue, and in the presentation of expenses versus expenditures.

A required reconciliation is to be presented reconciling the "government-wide financial statements at the bottom of the fund financial statements or in an accompanying schedule."[10]

Notes to the financial statements are similar to notes of corporate statements in that they provide information to aid the user's understanding of the basic financial statements. In addition, the notes must contain budgetary information that includes the original budget and revised budgets. The budget, being a detailed plan of operations for each period, includes an item-by-item estimate of expenditures when the representatives of the citizens (city council, town meeting, and so on) approve the budget. The individual expenditures then become limits. An increase in an approved expenditure will require approval by the same representatives who set up a legal control over expenditures. This differs from the budget for a commercial business, which is merely a plan of future revenues and expenses.

In addition to the notes to the financial statements, the typical governmental entity provides a statistical section. This statistical section includes important information that aids in the understanding of the governmental entity. It also often presents historical, financial, analytical, economic, and demographic information that may be useful for analysis. Exhibit 13-2 includes parts of Schedule 2 of the statistical section from the 2006 comprehensive annual financial report of the City of Toledo, Ohio. It includes expenses for governmental activities. A review of this schedule provides insight of expenses for areas such as public safety and health.

| *Exhibit* | **13-2** | SCHEDULE 2, CITY OF TOLEDO, OHIO |

Changes in Net Assets, Last Five Fiscal Years (in Part)
Accrual Basis of Accounting
Amounts in Thousands

	Fiscal Year				
	2002	**2003**	**2004**	**2005**	**2006**
Expenses					
Governmental activities:					
General Government	$ 27,694	$ 26,790	$ 26,721	$ 25,960	$ 27,250
Public Service	42,036	45,757	48,204	52,706	52,891
Public Safety	142,256	148,446	151,217	153,085	158,499
Public Utilities	1,143	1,085	808	—	46
Community Environment	23,240	19,465	17,918	14,895	20,589
Health	16,490	17,347	17,030	17,638	18,207
Parks and Recreation	7,834	7,488	7,765	7,345	7,563
Interest and Fiscal Charges	15,679	16,437	9,408	8,973	7,833
Total Governmental Activities	$276,372	$282,815	$279,071	$280,602	$292,878

Source: City of Toledo, Finance Department, Comprehensive Annual Report, For the Year Ended December 31, 2006, p. s–4.

Exhibit 13-3 shows Schedule 12 of the statistical section from the 2006 comprehensive annual financial report of the City of Toledo, Ohio. It includes the ratio of net bonded debt to assessed value and net bonded debt per capita.

The comprehensive annual financial report will include a "Report of Independent Auditors." Review this report in detail. It could include important information relating to the financial statements and the internal controls of the government entity.

In addition to the primary financial statements, the government entity will report on any "component units," which are legally separate organizations that hold the elected officials of the primary government financially accountable. The financial data of the component units are also included because of the significance of their operational or financial relationships with the government entity.

To determine if the government entity has one or more component units, review the management's discussion and analysis, government-wide financial statements, fund financial statements, and notes for disclosure of component units. Also, review the Report of Independent Auditors. "Financial statements of component units should be on an accrual basis of accounting."[11] The 2006 comprehensive annual financial report of the City of Toledo, Ohio, did not disclose component units, but the comprehensive annual financial report of Lucas County, Ohio, did reveal component units.

The Lucas County report provides a separate statement combining statements of net assets of discretely presented component units and a separate statement of activities of discretely presented component units. The government-wide financial statements include a separate component unit column to emphasize that they are legally separate from the county.

| Exhibit | 13-3 | SCHEDULE 12, CITY OF TOLEDO, OHIO |

Ratio of net bonded debt to assessed value and net bonded debt per capita, last ten fiscal years.

Fiscal Year	Population[1]	Assessed Value[2]	Gross General Bonded Debt[2]	Less Balance in Debt Service Fund[1][3]	Net General Bonded Debt[2]	Ratio of Net Bonded Debt to Assessed Value	Net Bonded Debt per Capita
1997	332,943	3,450,882	106,213	864	105,349	3.0%	312.51
1998	332,943	3,451,238	131,859	899	130,960	3.8%	393.34
1999	332,943	3,472,027	127,636	1,023	126,613	3.7%	380.28
2000	313,619	4,084,141	126,046	1,156	124,890	3.1%	398.22
2001	313,619	4,025,806	123,810	579	123,231	3.1%	392.93
2002	313,619	4,009,940	127,805	215	127,590	3.2%	406.83
2003	313,619	4,411,593	125,978	29	125,949	2.9%	401.60
2004	313,619	4,423,240	127,241	38	127,203	2.9%	405.63
2005	313,619	4,369,616	128,474	38	128,436	2.9%	409.53
2006	313,619	4,813,232	126,683	45	126,638	2.6%	403.80

[1]From the U.S. Bureau of the Census.

[2]Amounts shown in thousands of dollars. From the Lucas County Auditor.

[3]The city has paid its general bonded debt service for the tax years shown from current income tax revenues. The amount required is transferred to the debt service funds from the capital improvement fund.

Footnote "A" describes the component units in detail. One of the component units is the Toledo Mud Hens Baseball Club, Inc. Partial disclosure of the Toledo Mud Hens Baseball Club is as follows:

"Toledo Mud Hens Baseball Club, Inc. is organized to own, manage, and operate a professional baseball club. Upon dissolution, any remaining net assets become property of the Board of County Commissioners, and new appointments to the Board of Directors requires concurrence of the Commissioners. The county receives rent from the Mud Hens to retire non-tax revenue bonds issued to finance the construction of the baseball stadium."

The management's discussion and analysis discloses that "the bonds for the baseball stadium have been rated "A2" by Moody's, "A" by Standard and Poor's, and "AA" by Fitch."

The Report of Independent Auditors includes this comment: "We did not audit the financial statements of the Toledo Mud Hens Baseball Club, Inc., Lott Industries, Inc., and Preferred Properties, Inc., which represent 100 percent of the assets, net assets, and revenues of the aggregate discretely presented component units. Those financial statements were audited by other auditors whose reports have been furnished to us, and our opinion, insofar as it relates to the amounts included for the discretely presented component units, is based on the reports of the other auditors."

Review a governmental accounting book for a detailed discussion of state and local government accounting procedures. A typical governmental comprehensive annual financial report will be 200 pages or longer. A detailed review of the contents of these financial reports is beyond the scope of this book.

A great variance exists in the quality of disclosure in the financial reporting of state and local governments. Some poorly reported items have been pension liabilities, marketable securities, inventories, fixed assets, and lease obligations.

The Government Finance Officers Association of the United States and Canada presents a Certificate of Achievement for Excellence in Financial Reporting to governmental units and public employee retirement systems whose comprehensive annual financial reports are judged to conform substantially to program standards. These standards are considered to be very rigorous.

The municipal bond rating of the governmental unit should also be determined. Standard & Poor's, Fitch, and Moody's evaluate and grade the quality of a bond relative to the probability of default. One rating is assigned to all general obligation bonds (backed by the full faith and credit of the governmental unit). Bonds not backed by the full faith and credit of the governmental unit, such as industrial revenue bonds, are rated individually. These ratings do not represent the probability of default by the governmental unit.

When reviewing a governmental financial statement, the following suggestions are helpful:

1. Determine if a Certificate of Achievement has been received.
2. a. Determine the bond rating of the governmental unit for its general obligation bonds. Since the rating from Standard & Poor's, Fitch, and Moody's may differ, determine the rating from each.
   b. Determine the bond rating of bonds not backed by the full faith and credit of the governmental unit. Again, determine the rating from Standard & Poor's, Fitch, and Moody's.
3. Review the Report of Independent Auditors.
4. Review the management's discussion and analysis.
5. Review the notes to the financial statements.
6. Review the government-wide financial statements.
7. Review the fund financial statements.
8. Review the supplementary information.
9. Look for component units. If component units are present, then determine the obligation of the government unit to the component unit.
10. Review the statistical section.

Accounting for Not-for-Profit Organizations Other Than Governments

Not-for-profit organizations account for a substantial portion of economic activity in the United States. There are over 20,000 not-for-profit organizations in the United States.[12] Examples of not-for-profit organizations include hospitals, religious institutions, professional organizations, universities, and museums.

Not-for-profit accounting principles were derived from numerous not-for-profit industry accounting manuals and audit guides. Examples were AICPA audit guides for Colleges and Universities, Audits of Voluntary Health and Welfare Organizations, and audits of providers of Health Care Services.

The FASB was concerned about the lack of uniformity in the accounting for not-for-profit organizations and the lack of overall quality of not-for-profit organizations' financial reporting. To address this concern, four accounting standards relating to not-for-profits were issued by the FASB. These standards are: (1) SFAS No. 93, "Recognition of Depreciation by Not-for-Profit Organizations," (2) SFAS No. 116, "Accounting for Contributions Received and Contributions Made," (3) SFAS No. 117, "Financial Statements of Not-for-Profit Organizations," and (4) SFAS No. 124, "Accounting for Certain Investments Held by Not-for-Profit Organizations." A brief description of these accounting standards and how they impact financial reports follows:

1. SFAS No. 93, "Recognition of Depreciation by Not-for-Profit Organizations"[13]

Prior to SFAS No. 93, most not-for-profit organizations did not recognize depreciation. SFAS No. 93 requires not-for-profit organizations to recognize depreciation on long-lived tangible assets. SFAS No. 93 includes these requirements relating to depreciation.

1. Disclose the amount of depreciation expense for each period.
2. Disclose depreciable assets by major classes as of the balance sheet date.
3. Disclose accumulated depreciation for each asset class or in total as of the balance sheet date.
4. Disclose the methods used to calculate depreciation.

SFAS No. 93 exempts individual works of art or historical treasures from the depreciation requirements. For this exemption, two requirements must be met.

1. The asset must have "cultural, aesthetic, or historical value that is worth preserving perpetually."
2. The organization that owns the artwork or historical treasure must be able to preserve the asset so that its potentially unlimited service potential will remain intact.

2. SFAS No. 116, "Accounting for Contributions Received and Contributions Made"[14]

SFAS No. 116 applies to all *not-for-profit organizations as well as to any entity that receives or makes contributions*. Some key aspects of SFAS No. 116 will be summarized.

Contributions Received

Contributions received are to be recognized as revenues or gains in the period received. In addition, these contributions are to be recognized as assets, decreases in liabilities, or as expenses in the same period. Contributions received are to be measured at their fair values and reported as restricted support or unrestricted support.

Contributed services received are to be recognized if one of the following conditions holds:

1. The service creates or enhances nonfinancial assets; or
2. These services involve specialized skills that would most likely be paid for if they were not donated (i.e., electrical services, plumbing services, accounting services, etc.).

Contributed services recognized should be disclosed by nature and amount for the period. Service contributions are to be valued at the fair value of the services or the resulting increase in assets.

Under SFAS No. 116, donated works of art, historical treasures, or similar assets can be excluded if the following conditions are met:

1. Contributed items are held for public service purposes rather than for financial gain.
2. Contributed items must be protected, kept unencumbered, cared for, and preserved.
3. The organization must have a policy of using funds from the sales of collected items to purchase additional collection pieces.

Contributions received are to be segregated into permanent restrictions, temporary restrictions, and unrestricted support imposed by donors. Restricted contributions shall be reported as an increase in either permanently restricted net assets or temporarily restricted net assets. Unrestricted contributions received are to be reported as unrestricted support and increases in unrestricted net assets. Contributions received are to be measured at fair value.

Conditional promises are to be recognized in the financial statements when the condition(s) has been substantially met. If the nature of the conditional promise is ambiguous, it should be interpreted as conditional.

Contributions Made

Contributions made are to be recognized as expenses in the period in which they are made. These contributions are to be reported as decreases in assets or increases in liabilities. Contributions made are to be measured at the fair value of the asset contributed or the liability discharged. Conditional promises to give are recognized when the conditions are substantially met.

3. SFAS No. 117, "Financial Statements of Not-for-Profit Organizations"[15]

Prior to SFAS No. 117, there were significant differences in the financial reports of not-for-profit organizations. The intent of SFAS No. 117 is to provide consistency in the financial statements of not-for-profit organizations. SFAS No. 117 addresses financial statements, the content of financial statements, and the classification of financial statement information.

Not-for-profit organizations are to present three aggregated financial statements. These include a statement of financial position, a statement of activities, and a statement of cash flows. SFAS No. 117 specifies the content of each of these required financial statements.

Concerning the statement of financial position, SFAS No. 117 directs that it is to include aggregated information about the assets, liabilities, and net assets. SFAS No. 117 requires the statement of activity to provide information concerning the effects of transactions on the amount and nature of net assets, the interrelationships between those transactions and other events, and how resources are used by the organization to provide services. The statement of activity is also to disclose the changes in the amounts of permanently restricted net assets, temporarily restricted net assets, and unrestricted net assets.

In regards to the content of the statement of cash flows, SFAS No. 117 requires that not-for-profit organizations comply with SFAS No. 95, "Statement of Cash Flows." In addition, SFAS No. 117 amends SFAS No. 95 concerning its description of financing activities. Financing activities now include receipts of donations restricted for acquiring, constructing, or improving long-lived assets or establishing or increasing permanent or term endowments.

For the statement of financial position, SFAS No. 117 requires that assets and liabilities should be reported in relatively homogeneous groups. They should also be classified to provide information about their interrelationships, liquidity, and financial flexibility. New assets are to be classified as either permanently restricted, temporarily restricted, or unrestricted. Revenues, expenses, gains, and losses are to be separated into reasonably homogeneous groups for the statement of activities. They also are to be classified as affecting permanently restricted, temporarily restricted, or unrestricted net assets.

4. SFAS No. 124, "Accounting for Certain Investments Held by Not-for-Profit Organizations"[16]

This statement applies to investments in equity securities that have a readily determinable fair value and to all investments in debt securities. These investments are to be shown at their fair values in the statement of financial position. This statement does not apply to investments in equity securities that are accounted for under the equity method or to investments in consolidated subsidiaries. Disclosure requirements in the statement of financial position include the aggregate carrying value of investments by major categories and the basis for determining the carrying values of equity securities without readily determinable fair market values. Any shortfall in the fair value of donor-restricted endowment funds below the amount required by donor stipulations or by law must also be disclosed.

For the statement of activities, any realized or unrealized gains and losses are to be shown. Some of the disclosure requirements for the statement of activities include the composition of the investment return, which consists of investment income, realized gains and losses on investments not reported at fair value, and net gains and losses on investments that are reported at fair value.

APPLICABILITY OF GAAP TO NOT-FOR-PROFIT ORGANIZATIONS

Some individuals were of the opinion that the applicability of GAAP to not-for-profit organizations was unclear. SOP 94-2 was issued to address the applicability of GAAP to not-for-profit organizations.[17]

SOP 94-2 concludes that not-for-profit organizations should follow the guidance in effective provisions of ARBs, APB Opinions, and FASB Statements and Interpretations unless the specific pronouncement explicitly exempts not-for-profit organizations or their subject matter precludes such applicability (SOP 94-2, paragraph .09).

Exhibit 13-4 contains the consolidated statement of financial position and the consolidated statement of activities for The Ohio Society of Certified Public Accountants. These statements are for the year ended April 30, 2007. Not included in Exhibit 13-4 are the report of independent auditors, consolidated statements of cash flows, and notes to consolidated financial statements.

| Exhibit | 13-4 | THE OHIO SOCIETY OF CERTIFIED PUBLIC ACCOUNTANTS |

CONSOLIDATED STATEMENT OF FINANCIAL POSITION
April 30, 2007

ASSETS

Cash and cash equivalents	$ 62,000
Accounts receivable, net of allowance for doubtful accounts of $28,000	84,000
Prepaid expenses and deposits	75,000
Investments	3,945,000
Property, net of accumulated depreciation and amortization of $1,768,000	1,435,000
Total Assets	$5,601,000

LIABILITIES AND NET ASSETS

LIABILITIES	
Accounts payable and earned liabilities	$ 797,000
Deferred revenue	665,000
Short-term borrowings	905,000
Accrued pension	222,000
Mortgage payable	1,190,000
Total liabilities	3,779,000
NET ASSETS	
Unrestricted	913,000
Temporarily restricted	74,000
Permanently restricted	835,000
	1,822,000
TOTAL LIABILITIES AND NET ASSETS	$5,601,000

CONSOLIDATED STATEMENT OF ACTIVITIES
Year Ended April 30, 2007

	Unrestricted	Temporarily Restricted	Permanently Restricted	Total
REVENUE				
Dues	$4,464,000	$ —	$ —	$4,464,000
Education and training course fees	2,388,000	—	—	2,388,000
Peer review fees	510,000	—	—	510,000
Member Connections	481,000	—	—	481,000
Public relations and publications	375,000	—	—	375,000
Investment income, net	288,000	40,000	43,000	371,000
Other	165,000	—	—	165,000
Membership affinity programs	124,000	—	—	124,000
Educational Foundation contributions	78,000	—	—	78,000
Scholarships released from restrictions	26,000	(26,000)	—	—
Net assets reclassified	(66,000)	(47,000)	113,000	—
Total revenue	8,833,000	(33,000)	156,000	8,956,000
EXPENSES				
Education and training course program	2,647,000	—	—	2,647,000
Public relations and publications	1,880,000	—	—	1,880,000
Member Connections and sections	1,288,000	—	—	1,288,000
General and administrative	1,227,000	—	—	1,227,000
Governmental affairs	747,000	—	—	747,000
Membership services	638,000	—	—	638,000
Peer review	555,000	—	—	555,000
Interest	67,000	—	—	67,000
Educational Foundation scholarships	50,000	—	—	50,000
Total expenses	9,099,000	—	—	9,099,000

(continued)

Exhibit	13-4	THE OHIO SOCIETY OF CERTIFIED PUBLIC ACCOUNTANTS (Continued)

	Unrestricted	Temporarily Restricted	Permanently Restricted	Total
CHANGE IN NET ASSETS	(266,000)	(33,000)	156,000	(143,000)
NET ASSETS—Beginning of year, as restated (Note 11)	1,179,000	107,000	679,000	1,965,000
NET ASSETS—End of year	$ 913,000	$ 74,000	$835,000	$1,822,000

Source: The Ohio Society of Certified Public Accountants Consolidated Statements of Financial Position, April 30, 2007.

BUDGETING BY OBJECTIVES AND/OR MEASURES OF PRODUCTIVITY

Accounting for nonprofit institutions differs greatly from accounting for a profit-oriented enterprise. The accounting for a profit-oriented business centers on the entity concept and the efficiency of the entity. The accounting for governments and accounting for not-for-profit organizations do not include an entity concept or efficiency. The accounting for a profit-oriented business has a bottom-line net income. The accounting for governments and accounting for not-for-profit organizations do not have a bottom line.

Some governments and not-for-profit organizations have added budgeting by objectives and/or measures of productivity to their financial reporting to incorporate measures of efficiency. The article, "Budgeting by Objectives: Charlotte's Experience," reported several objectives incorporated in the budget of Charlotte, North Carolina. Four primary objectives guided the budget: (1) the property tax rate should not increase, (2) continued emphasis should be placed on making the best use of city employees and the present computer capability, (3) any budget increase should be held to a minimum, and (4) a balanced program of services should be presented.[18]

This article also reports measures of productivity that Charlotte has used. These measures of productivity include: (1) customers served per $1,000 of sanitation expense, (2) number of tons of refuse per $1,000 expense, and (3) street miles flushed per $1,000 expense.[19]

Budgeting by objectives and/or measures of productivity could be added to the financial reporting of any not-for-profit institution. The objectives and measures of productivity should be applicable to the particular not-for-profit institution.

Summary

This chapter reviewed financial reporting for personal financial statements and accounting for governments and other not-for-profit organizations. Accounting for these areas differs greatly from accounting for profit-oriented businesses. This difference has been narrowed substantially for not-for-profit organizations other than governments.

Statement of Position 82-1 presents guidelines for the preparation of personal financial statements. SOP 82-1 concludes that personal financial statements should present assets at their estimated current values and liabilities at their estimated current amounts at the date of the financial statements. This differs from commercial financial statements that predominantly use historical information.

GASB Statement No. 34 redefines what constitutes basic financial statements for state and local governments. Minimum requirements for general-purpose external financial statements—state and local governments include management discussion and analysis (MD&A), government-wide financial statements, fund financial statements, and required supplementary information (other than MD&A).

Not-for-profit accounting for organizations, other than governments, has changed substantially. It now resembles accounting for profit organizations. A major difference is that not-for-profit organizations issue a statement of activities instead of an income statement.

Some not-for-profit institutions have added budgeting by objectives and/or measures of productivity to their financial reporting to incorporate measures of efficiency.

1. Go to the GASB Web site (http://www.gasb.org). Click on "GASB FACTS." Click on "GASB Fact Sheets." Print the page "GASB at a Glance Fact Sheet." Be prepared to discuss the following:
   a. What is the GASB?
   b. Why is the work of the GASB important?
   c. How does the GASB carry out its mission?
   d. Who are the primary users of the information that results from GASB standards?
   e. How is the GASB structured?
   f. Who provides financial support for the GASB?
   g. Why is independent standards setting important?
   h. What the GASB is NOT.

2. Go to the GASB Web site (http://www.gasb.org). Click on "STRATEGIC PLAN." Click on "Summary of the Plan." Print the "Summary of the Plan." Be prepared to discuss the following:
   a. Vision
   b. Mission
   c. Goals
      Goal I.   Standards Setting
      Goal II. Constituent Relations and Communications
      Goal III. Education
      Goal IV. Organizational Effectiveness
   d. Core Values

3. Go to the GASB Web site (http://www.gasb.org). Click on "PERFORMANCE REPORTING." Click on "Measurement initiatives." Click on "Local government." For each of the following, describe a measurement initiative:
   a. City government
   b. County government

Questions

Q 13-1.   May personal financial statements be prepared only for an individual? Comment.

Q 13-2.   What is the basic personal financial statement?

Q 13-3.   Is a statement of changes in net worth required when presenting personal financial statements?

Q 13-4.   Are comparative financial statements required when presenting personal financial statements?

Q 13-5.   When preparing a personal statement of financial condition, should assets and liabilities be presented on the basis of historical cost or estimated current value?

Q 13-6.   In a personal statement of financial condition, what is the equity section called?

Q 13-7.   What personal financial statement should be prepared when an explanation of changes in net worth is desired?

Q 13-8.   Is the presentation of a personal income statement appropriate?

Q 13-9.   GAAP as they apply to personal financial statements use the cash basis. Comment.

Q 13-10. Is the concept of working capital used with personal financial statements? Comment.

Q 13-11. List some sources of information that may be available when preparing personal financial statements.

Q 13-12. Give examples of disclosure in notes with personal financial statements.

Q 13-13. If quoted market prices are not available, a personal financial statement cannot be prepared. Comment.

Q 13-14.   List some objectives that could be incorporated into the financial reporting of a professional accounting organization.

Q 13-15.   Do not-for-profit organizations, other than governments, use fund accounting? Comment.

Q 13-16.   The accounting for governments is centered on the entity concept and the efficiency of the entity. Comment.

Q 13-17.   For governmental accounting, define the following types of funds:
1. General fund
2. Proprietary fund
3. Fiduciary fund

Q 13-18.   How many funds will be used by a state or local government?

Q 13-19.   The budget for a state or local government is not as binding as a budget for a commercial business. Comment.

Q 13-20.   Which organization provides a service whereby it issues a certificate of conformance to governmental units with financial reports that meet its standards?

Q 13-21.   The rating on an industrial revenue bond is representative of the probability of default of bonds issued with the full faith and credit of a governmental unit. Comment.

Q 13-22.   The accounting for not-for-profit institutions does not typically include the concept of efficiency. Indicate how the concept of efficiency can be incorporated in the financial reporting of a not-for-profit institution.

Q 13-23.   Could a profit-oriented enterprise use fund accounting practices? Comment.

Q 13-24.   How many members serve on the GASB? How many votes are needed to issue a pronouncement?

Q 13-25.   What is the purpose of the book, *Codification of Governmental Accounting and Financial Reporting Standards*?

Q 13-26.   Under GASB, which statement has been the most substantial pronouncement?

Q 13-27.   For the government-wide statements, governmental activities are to be presented separately from the financial statements of business-type activities. Give one example of a governmental activity and one example of a business-type activity.

Q 13-28.   Why are the financial data of a component unit included with the government entities reporting entity?

Problems

P 13-1.   For each of these situations, indicate the amount to be placed on a statement of financial condition at December 31, 2008.

    a. Bill and Pat Konner purchased their home at 2829 Willow Road in Stow, Ohio, in August 1994 for $80,000. The unpaid mortgage is $20,000. Immediately after purchasing the home, Bill and Pat added several improvements totaling $10,000. Real estate prices in Stow have increased 40% since the time of purchase.

       From the facts given, determine the estimated current value of the home.

    b. Joe Best drives a Toyota, for which he paid $20,000 when it was new. Joe believes that since he maintains the car in good condition, he could sell it for $12,000. The average selling price for this model of Toyota is $9,000.

       From the facts given, determine the estimated current value of Joe's car.

c. Sue Bell is 40 years old and has an IRA with a balance of $20,000. The IRS penalty for early withdrawal is 10%. The marginal tax rate for Sue Bell is 30% (tax on gross amount).

What is the estimated current value of the IRA and the estimated income taxes on the difference between the estimated current values of assets and the estimated current amounts of liabilities and their tax bases?

d. Bill Kell guaranteed a loan of $8,000 for his girlfriend to buy a car. She is behind in payments on the car.

What liability should be shown on Bill Kell's statement of financial condition?

e. Dick Better bought a home in 1996 for $70,000. Currently, the mortgage on the home is $45,000. Because of the current high interest rates, the bank has offered to retire the mortgage for $40,000.

What is the estimated current value of this liability?

P 13-2. For each of these situations, indicate the amount to be placed on a statement of financial condition at December 31, 2008.

a. Raj Reel owns the following securities:

1,000 shares of Ree's

2,000 shares of Bell's

Ree's is traded on the New York Stock Exchange. The prices from the most recent trade day follow:

Open   19

High $20\frac{1}{2}$

Low   19

Close   20

Bell's is a local company whose stock is sold by brokers on a workout basis. (The broker tries to find a buyer.) The most recent selling price was $8.

What is the estimated current value of these securities? (Assume that the commission on Ree's would be $14 and the commission on Bell's would be $17.)

b. Charlie has a certificate of deposit with a $10,000 balance. Accrued interest is $500. The penalty for early withdrawal would be $300.

What is the estimated current value of the certificate of deposit?

c. Jones has an option to buy 500 shares of ABC Construction at a price of $20 per share. The option expires in one year. ABC Construction shares are presently selling for $25.

What is the estimated current value of these options?

d. Carl Jones has a whole-life insurance policy with the face amount of $100,000, cash value of $50,000, and a loan outstanding against the policy of $20,000. Susan Jones is the beneficiary.

What is the estimated current value of the insurance policy?

e. Larry Solomon paid $60,000 for a home 10 years ago. The unpaid mortgage on the home is $30,000. Larry estimates the current value of the home to be $90,000. This estimate is partially based on the selling price of homes recently sold in the neighborhood. Larry's home is assessed for tax purposes at $50,000. Assessments in the area average one-half of market value. The house has not been inspected for assessment during the past two years. Larry would sell through a broker, who would charge 5% of the selling price.

What is the estimated current value of the home?

P 13-3. For Barb and Carl, the assets and liabilities and the effective income tax rates at December 31, 2008, follow:

Accounts	Tax Bases	Estimated Current Value	Excess of Estimated Current Values over Tax Bases	Effective Income Tax Rates	Amount of Estimated Income Taxes
Cash	$ 20,000	$ 20,000	$ —	—	_____
Marketable securities	45,000	50,000	5,000	28%	_____
Life insurance	50,000	50,000	—	—	_____
Residence	100,000	125,000	25,000	28%	_____
Furnishings	40,000	25,000	(15,000)	—	_____
Jewelry	20,000	20,000	—	—	_____
Autos	20,000	12,000	(8,000)	—	_____
Mortgage payable	(90,000)	(90,000)	—	—	_____
Note payable	(30,000)	(30,000)	—	—	_____
Credit cards	(10,000)	(10,000)	—	—	_____

Required   a. Compute the estimated tax liability on the differences between the estimated current value of the assets and liabilities and their tax bases.

b. Present a statement of financial condition for Barb and Carl at December 31, 2008.

c. Comment on the statement of financial condition.

P 13-4.   For Mary Lou and Ernie, the assets and liabilities and the effective income tax rates at December 31, 2008, follow:

Accounts	Tax Bases	Estimated Current Value	Excess of Estimated Current Values over Tax Bases	Effective Income Tax Rates	Amount of Estimated Income Taxes
Cash	$ 20,000	$ 20,000	$ —	—	_____
Marketable securities	80,000	100,000	20,000	28%	_____
Options	0	30,000	30,000	28%	_____
Residence	100,000	150,000	50,000	28%	_____
Royalties	0	20,000	20,000	28%	_____
Furnishings	40,000	20,000	(20,000)	—	_____
Auto	20,000	15,000	(5,000)	—	_____
Mortgage	(70,000)	(70,000)	—	—	_____
Auto loan	(10,000)	(10,000)	—	—	_____

Required   a. Compute the estimated tax liability on the differences between the estimated current value of the assets and liabilities and their tax bases.

b. Present a statement of financial condition for Mary Lou and Ernie at December 31, 2008.

c. Comment on the statement of financial condition.

P 13-5.   For Bob and Sue, the changes in net worth for the year ended December 31, 2008, follow:

Realized increases in net worth:	
Salary	$ 60,000
Dividend income	2,500
Interest income	2,000
Gain on sale of marketable securities	500
Realized decreases in net worth:	
Income taxes	20,000
Interest expense	6,000
Personal expenditures	29,000
Unrealized increases in net worth:	
Stock options	3,000
Land	7,000
Residence	5,000
Unrealized decreases in net worth:	
Boat	3,000
Jewelry	1,000
Furnishings	4,000
Estimated income taxes on the differences between the estimated current values of assets and the estimated current amounts of liabilities and their tax bases	15,000
Net worth at the beginning of year	150,000

Required   a. Prepare a statement of changes in net worth for the year ended December 31, 2008.

b. Comment on the statement of changes in net worth.

P 13-6.   For Jim and Carrie, the changes in net worth for the year ended December 31, 2008, are shown below.

Realized increases in net worth:	
Salary	$ 50,000
Interest income	6,000
Realized decreases in net worth:	
Income taxes	15,000
Interest expense	3,000

Personal property taxes	$ 1,000
Real estate taxes	1,500
Personal expenditures	25,000
Unrealized increases in net worth:	
Marketable securities	2,000
Land	5,000
Residence	3,000
Stock options	4,000
Unrealized decreases in net worth:	
Furnishings	3,000
Estimated income taxes on the differences	
between the estimated current values of	
assets and the estimated current amounts	
of liabilities and their tax bases	12,000
Net worth at the beginning of year	130,000

Required
a. Prepare a statement of changes in net worth for the year ended December 31, 2008.
b. Comment on the statement of changes in net worth.

P 13-7.   Use Exhibit 13-2, City of Toledo, Ohio, Expenses, Governmental activities.

Required
a. Prepare a horizontal common-size statement for 2002–2006. Use 2002 as the base.
b. Comment on significant items in the horizontal common-size analysis.

P 13-8.   Use Exhibit 13-2, City of Toledo, Ohio, Expenses, Governmental activities.

Required
a. Prepare a vertical common-size statement. Use total governmental activities as the base.
b. Comment on significant items in the vertical common-size analysis.

P 13-9.   Use Exhibit 13-3, City of Toledo, Ohio, Ratio of Net Bonded Debt to Assessed Value and Net Bonded Debt per Capita, Last 10 Fiscal Years.

Required
a. Prepare a vertical common-size statement. Use 1997 as the base. Include assessed value, net general bonded debt, and net bonded debt per capita.
b. Comment on significant items in the vertical common-size analysis.

P 13-10.   Use Exhibit 13-4, The Ohio Society of Certified Public Accountants's financial report.

Required
a. Prepare a vertical common-size analysis for the consolidated statement of financial position. For April 30, 2007, use total assets as the base. Comment on significant items in total assets, liabilities, and net assets.
b. Prepare a vertical common-size analysis for the consolidated statement of activities. Work up the vertical common-size analysis for unrestricted and total. Use total expenses as the base. Comment on significant items.

P 13-11.   The Ohio Society of Certified Public Accountants's financial report for the year ended April 30, 2007, included this note.

Note 1. Organization

The Ohio Society of Certified Public Accountants was organized in 1908 as a not-for-profit corporation. The mission of the society is to act on behalf of its members and provide necessary support to assure that members serve the public by performing quality professional services.

Required   Using Exhibit 13-4, The Ohio Society of Certified Public Accountants's consolidated statement of activities, comment on items which indicate that the society is achieving its mission.

P 13-12.

Required   Answer the following multiple-choice questions related to personal financial statements:
a. For the personal financial statement, statement of changes in net worth, which of the following would be a realized increase in net worth?
   1. Dividend income
   2. Change in value of land

   3. Decrease in value of house
   4. Personal expenditures
   5. None of the above

b. For the personal financial statement, statement of changes in net worth, which of the following would be an unrealized increase in net worth?
   1. Increase in value of land
   2. Decrease in value of furnishings
   3. Personal expenditures
   4. Salary
   5. None of the above

c. Which of the following is *not* a suggestion for reviewing the statement of financial condition?
   1. Review realized decreases in net worth.
   2. Review the net worth amount.
   3. Determine the amount of the assets that you consider to be very liquid.
   4. Observe the due period of the liabilities.
   5. Compare specific assets with any related liabilities.

d. Which of the following would be a source of information for personal financial statements?
   1. Bank statements
   2. Checkbooks
   3. Real estate tax returns
   4. Insurance policies
   5. All of the above

e. Which of the following would *not* be an acceptable presentation on the statement of financial condition?
   1. A car may be presented at cost.
   2. Payables and other liabilities are presented at the discounted amounts of cash to be paid.
   3. Investments in real estate should be presented at their estimated current values.
   4. The liability for income taxes payable should include unpaid income taxes for completed tax years and an estimated amount for income taxes accrued for the elapsed portion of the current tax year to the date of the financial statements.
   5. All of the above

P 13-13.

Required   Answer the following multiple-choice questions related to state and local governments:

a. Proprietary funds are a type of funds used by governments. A reasonable definition of proprietary funds would be
   1. Funds whose purpose is to maintain the assets through cost reimbursement by users or partial cost recovery from users and periodic infusion of additional assets.
   2. Funds whose principal must remain intact.
   3. Funds that handle all cash receipts and disbursements not required to be accounted for in another fund.
   4. Funds that cash receipts and disbursements related to the payment of interest and principal on long-term debt.
   5. None of the above.

b. Government transactions are recorded in one or more funds designed to emphasize control and budgetary limitations. A fund may be established for which of the following specific purposes?
   1. Highway maintenance
   2. Parks
   3. Debt repayment
   4. Endowment fund
   5. All of the above

c. Which of the following is *not* a minimum requirement for general-purpose external financial statements—state and local governments?
   1. Statement of cash flow
   2. Management discussion and analysis
   3. Government-wide financial statements

   4. Fund financial statements

   5. Notes to the financial statements

d. For state and local governments, the MD&A must include all but which of the following?

   1. An objective discussion of the basic financial statements and condensed financial information comparing current and prior years

   2. An analysis of the overall financial position and results of operations

   3. Analysis of balances and transactions of individual funds

   4. Analysis of significant variations between the original and final budget and the final budget and actual results for the general fund

   5. Known facts, decisions, or conditions expected to have an impact on financial position or results of operations

e. Which of the following statements is *not* true?

   1. The government-wide financial statements are to be prepared on an accrual basis for all of the government's activities.

   2. Under GASB Statement No. 34, the government entity will continue to present fund statements.

   3. Under GASB Statement No. 34, government-wide statements are superior to fund statements.

   4. Government-wide financial statements are prepared on an accrual basis.

   5. Government transactions are recorded in one or more funds designed to emphasize central and budgetary limitations.

P 13-14.

Required   Answer the following multiple-choice questions:

a. Which of the following is *not* true?

   1. SFAS No. 93 requires not-for-profit organizations to recognize depreciation on long-lived tangible assets.

   2. Under SFAS No. 116, "Accounting for Contributions Received and Contributions Made," contributions are to be segregated into permanent restrictions, temporary restrictions, and unrestricted support imposed by donors.

   3. Prior to SFAS No. 117, "Financial Statements of Not-for-Profit Organizations," there were significant differences in the financial reports of not-for-profit organizations.

   4. Not-for-profit organizations are to present two aggregated financial statements.

   5. According to SFAS No. 124, "Accounting for Certain Investments Held by Not-for-Profit Organizations," equity securities should be shown at their fair values in the statement of financial position.

b. Which of the following is an example of a profit institution?

   1. Bank

   2. State government

   3. Church

   4. University

   5. None of the above

c. Which of the following is *not* true?

   1. SOP 94-2 concludes that not-for-profit organizations should follow the guidance in effective provisions of GAAP, unless the specific pronouncement explicitly exempts not-for-profit organizations or their subject matter precludes such applicability.

   2. Not-for-profit organizations account for a substantial portion of economic activity in the United States.

   3. Prior to SOP 94-2, not-for-profit accounting principles were derived solely from AICPA audit guides.

   4. Under SFAS No. 116, "Accounting for Contributions Received and Contributions Made," contributions received are to be recognized as revenues or gains in the period received.

   5. For a not-for-profit organization, the statement of activities should show realized or unrealized gains and losses.

d. Which of the following is *not* true?

   1. The accounting for a not-for-profit institution does not include an entity concept or efficiency.

   2. The accounting for a not-for-profit institution has a bottom-line net income.

   3. Some not-for-profit institutions have added budgeting by objectives and/or productivity to their financial reporting to incorporate measures of efficiency.

   4. Budgeting by objectives and/or measures of productivity could be added to the financial reporting of any not-for-profit institution.

   5. Accounting for not-for-profit institutions differs greatly from accounting for a profit-oriented enterprise.

Case	DEFICIT BUDGET?
13-1	

In July 2003, the Medical College of Ohio (MCO) (now part of The University of Toledo) approved its first deficit budget of $3.4 million, but no programs or faculty members were cut.

MCO announced a "mission-based" study of all programs and an examination of how financially viable they are, as well as how essential they are.

MCO was projected to lose money because of recognizing depreciation expense. Without depreciation expense, MCO would have a $5 million profit for fiscal year 2004.

In recognizing depreciation expense, MCO was adopting a new accounting standard passed in 2000 that requires colleges (universities) to account for depreciation. Many colleges adopted the new standard by disclosing in a note in their audited financial statements, not their operating budgets.

Required   a. In your opinion, should colleges and universities recognize depreciation expense? Comment.

b. Is recognizing depreciation expense in a note equivalent to recognizing depreciation expense in the statements? Comment.

c. Should the standard be explicit on how a college or university recognizes depreciation expense? Comment.

Note: Information relating to this case comes from "MCO Board Votes Its 1st Deficit Budget," *The Blade*, Toledo, Ohio, July 29, 2003, Section B, pp. 1–2.

Case	MY MUD HENS
13-2	

Toledo Mud Hens Baseball Club, Inc., is a not-for-profit organization that is a separate legal entity and can be sued in its own right.

The Toledo Mud Hens are probably the most famous team in all of minor league baseball. They have been named the Toledo Mud Hens since 1896 when the team played at Bay View Park. The surrounding marshland was frequented by these strange birds.

Famous people such as Casey Stengel, Jamie Farr, and Bob Costas, have helped bring the team nationwide fame. Players who have contributed to the team's fame include Moses Fleetwood Walker, Addie Joss, Tony Clark, Kirby Puckett, Travis Fryman, and Kirk Gibson.

An Ohio Historical Marker at the corner of N. Huron and Washington in Toledo, Ohio, reads as follows:

Moses Fleetwood Walker Square
In honor of baseball's first
African-American
Major League Player
Toledo Blue Stockings—1889
Ohio Historical Marker
Moses Fleetwood Walker

Moses Fleetwood Walker was born on October 7, 1856, in Ohio to Moses M. Walker, a physician, and Caroline, a midwife. He attended and played baseball at Oberlin College and the University of Michigan. In 1883, Walker joined the newly formed Toledo Blue Stockings and became the first African-American major league baseball player when Toledo joined the major league-sanctioned American Association the following year. As a barehanded catcher, his biggest assets were his catching ability, powerful throwing arm, and aggressive base running. He endured racial prejudice from teammates, opponents, and baseball fans and eventually left to become a writer, inventor, civil rights advocate, and entrepreneur. Walker was

(continued)

Case	MY MUD HENS (Continued)
13-2	

elected to the Ohio Baseball Hall of Fame in 1991. He died in 1924 and is buried in Steubenville, Ohio, in the family plot at Union Cemetery.

There is now a Moses Fleetwood Walker Society in Toledo, Ohio. It has an annual dinner after the World Series. The dinner and dues help raise money to buy baseball items for underprivileged kids.

By 1889 blacks were barred from the high minor leagues and the major leagues. It remained that way until 1947 when Jackie Robinson joined the Brooklyn Dodgers.

Casey Stengel skippered six Toledo teams, including the 1927 squad that won the Junior World Series.

In 2002, the team moved into a new facility. The County issued $20 million in economic development revenue bonds and $6 million in economic development revenue anticipation notes in March 2001. The County retired the notes in March 2002 after receiving revenue for the naming rights (Fifth Third Field) and the lease of the luxury suites.

Lucas County receives rent from the Mud Hens that in the County's opinion is substantially below market rate. The board of the Mud Hens is approved by the Board of County Commissioners.

The Mud Hens' ball park was named by *Newsweek Magazine* as the best minor league park. The largest video board in minor league baseball was added to the park in 2005. This video board complements the 2002 video board.

The Lucas County, Ohio, comprehensive annual financial report included the Toledo Mud Hens Baseball Club, Inc., financial information for the fiscal year ended December 31, 2006.

Lucas County, Ohio
Statement of Net Assets*
Discretely Presented Component Unit
December 31, 2006
(Amounts in 000's)

	Toledo Mud Hens Baseball Club, Inc.
Assets:	
Current assets	
Pooled cash and cash equivalents	$6,107
Pooled investments	60
Receivables, net of allowances for uncollectibles accounts	172
Prepaid expense	70
Inventory: Materials and supplies	156
Total current assets	6,565
Noncurrent assets	
Furniture, fixtures and equipment	1,735
Total noncurrent assets	1,735
Total assets	$8,300
Liabilities	
Current liabilities	
Accounts payable	$ 742
Accrued wages and benefits	1,008
Deferred revenue	612
Total current liabilities	2,362
Net assets	
Unrestricted	5,938
Total liabilities and net assets	$8,300

*Adapted from Lucas County, Ohio, Combining Statement of Net Assets, Discretely Presented Component Units, December 31, 2006.

(continued)

Case 13-2

MY MUD HENS (Continued)

Lucas County, Ohio
Statement of Activities*
Discretely Presented Component Unit
Year Ended December 31, 2006
(Amounts in 000's)

Toledo Mud Hens Baseball Club, Inc.	Expenses	Program Revenues Charges for Services	Toledo Mud Hens Baseball Club, Inc.
Recreation	$10,649	$4,652	$(5,997)
General revenues:			
Miscellaneous			7,840
Total general revenues			7,840
Changes in net assets			1,843
Net assets—beginning			4,095
Net assets—ending			$5,938

Required

  a. What form would the Mud Hens statement take?

  b. Why does Lucas County, Ohio, include financial and descriptive information relating to the Mud Hens in its financial report?

  c. Based on the statement of activities, did the Mud Hens have a good year in 2006? Comment.

  d. Based on the statement of net assets, does it appear that the Mud Hens were in a good financial condition at December 31, 2006? Comment.

*Adapted from Lucas County, Ohio, Statement of Activities, Discretely Presented Component Units, Year Ended December 31, 2006.

Sources: "Square Is Named for Walker," *The Blade* (October 2, 2002), Sec. B, p. 1; Lucas County, Ohio, Comprehensive Annual Financial Report, For Fiscal Year Ended December 31, 2006; and "The Toledo Mud Hens—History in the Making," provided by Toledo Mud Hens Baseball Club, Inc. The source also includes Lucas County, Ohio, Comprehensive Annual Financial Report, For Fiscal Year Ended December 31, 2006.

Case 13-3

JEEP

DaimlerChrysler completed its first year of production of the Jeep Liberty in 2001. This production was in a new plant that cost $1.2 billion.

DaimlerChrysler was assisted in financing this new plant by the federal government, state government, the City of Toledo, and Lucas County. The county pledged $2 million by 2002 to help the City of Toledo acquire and improve the site for the new plant.

Required   How would the county account for its $2 million expenditure?

Case 13-4

GOVERNOR LUCAS—THIS IS YOUR COUNTY

Lucas County, Ohio, presented this table in its comprehensive annual financial report for the fiscal year ended December 31, 2006.

(continued)

Case 13-4	GOVERNOR LUCAS—THIS IS YOUR COUNTY (Continued)

Table 5
Lucas County, Ohio
Tax Revenues by Source
Last Ten Fiscal Years
(Amounts in 000's)

Fiscal Year	General Property Tax	Tangible Personal Tax[1]	Property Transfer Tax	County Sales Tax	Total	Fiscal Year
1997	$63,821	$12,289	$3,006	$61,935	$141,051	1997
1998	66,516	12,799	3,629	65,045	147,989	1998
1999	69,124	14,021	3,638	70,441	157,224	1999
2000	69,697	15,960	3,598	71,574	160,829	2000
2001	76,203	13,953	3,760	70,480	164,396	2001
2002	86,817	16,948	3,879	68,211	175,855	2002
2003	88,799	16,226	4,398	67,007	176,430	2003
2004	90,769	15,170	4,718	69,958	180,615	2004
2005	91,873	15,169	5,183	70,601	182,826	2005
2006	87,093	16,051	4,557	70,824	178,525	2006

[1]Tangible personal tax includes personal property tax, mobile home tax, and grain tax.
Source: Lucas County Auditor, p. 186.

Required
a. Complete a horizontal common-size analysis. Use the Total column as the base.
b. Comment on the results of the horizontal common-size analysis.
c. Complete a vertical common-size analysis. Use 1997 as the base.
d. Comment on the results of the vertical common-size analysis.

Case 13-5	COUNTY-WIDE

Lucas County, Ohio, presented the following within its management's discussion and analysis with its comprehensive annual financial report for the fiscal year ended December 31, 2006. It was presented as part of the county-wide financial analysis.

Table 1
Net Assets
(Amounts in 000's)

	Governmental Activities		Business-Type Activities		Total	
	2006	2005	2006	2005	2006	2005
Assets						
Current and other assets	$ 395,505	$ 371,057	$ 23,225	$ 22,561	$ 418,730	$ 393,618
Capital assets, net	248,405	252,056	111,761	112,523	360,166	364,579
Total assets	643,910	623,113	134,986	135,084	778,896	758,197
Liabilities						
Current and other liabilities	(46,517)	(43,617)	(1,116)	(1,027)	(47,633)	(44,644)
Long-term liabilities due within one year	(13,411)	(13,515)	(963)	(893)	(14,374)	(14,408)
Long-term liabilities due in more than one year	(81,433)	(85,382)	(30,529)	(31,242)	(111,962)	(116,624)
Total liabilities	(141,361)	(142,514)	(32,608)	(33,162)	(173,969)	(175,676)

(continued)

Case
13-5

COUNTY-WIDE (Continued)

	2006	2005	2006	2005	2006	2005
Net assets						
Invested in capital assets, net of debt	154,881	163,910	80,269	80,389	235,150	244,299
Restricted:						
Capital projects	9,806	10,345	—	—	9,806	10,345
Debt service	5,140	7,682	—	—	5,140	7,682
Unrestricted	332,722	298,662	22,109	21,533	354,831	320,195
Total net assets	$ 502,549	$ 480,599	$102,378	$101,922	$ 604,927	$ 582,521

Source: Lucas County Auditor, comprehensive annual report for the fiscal year ended December 31, 2006, p. 18.

Required   Prepare a descriptive county-wide financial analysis.

Endnotes

1. *Statement of Position 82-1,* "Accounting and Financial Reporting for Personal Financial Statements" (New York: American Institute of Certified Public Accountants, October 1982).
2. *Statement of Position 82-1,* p. 6.
3. A good article on this subject is Michael D. Kinsman and Bruce Samuelson, "Personal Financial Statements: Valuation Challenges and Solutions," *Journal of Accountancy* (September 1987), p. 138.
4. *Governmental Accounting Standards Board Statement No. 1* (July 1984), Appendix B, par. 4.
5. *Governmental Accounting, Auditing, and Financial Reporting* (Chicago: Municipal Finance Officers Association of the United States and Canada, 1968), p. 6.
6. *Statement of Governmental Accounting Standards No. 34,* "Basic Financial Statements— Management's Discussion and Analysis—For State and Local Governments" (Governmental Accounting Standard Board, 1999), par. 8.
7. Ibid., par. 8.
8. Edward M. Klasny and James M. Williams, "Government Reporting Fares an Overhaul," *Journal of Accountancy* (January 2000), pp. 49–51.
9. Ibid., preface.
10. Ibid., preface.
11. Ibid., par. 107.
12. Walter Robbins and Paul Polinski, "Financial Reporting by Nonprofits," *National Public Accountant* (October 1995), p. 29.
13. *Statement of Financial Accounting Standards No. 93,* "Recognition of Depreciation by Not-for-Profit Organizations" (Stamford, Conn.: Financial Accounting Standards Board, 1987).
14. *Statement of Financial Accounting Standards No. 116,* "Accounting for Contributions Received and Contributions Made" (Norwalk, Conn.: Financial Accounting Standards Board, 1993).
15. *Statement of Financial Accounting Standards No. 117,* "Financial Statements of Not-for-Profit Organizations" (Norwalk, Conn.: Financial Accounting Standards Board, 1993).
16. *Statement of Financial Accounting Standards No. 124,* "Accounting for Certain Investments Held by Not-for-Profit Organizations" (Norwalk, Conn.: Financial Accounting Standards Board, 1995).
17. *Statement of Position 94-2,* "The Application of the Requirements of Accounting Research Bulletins, Opinions of the Accounting Principles Board and Statements of Interpretations of the Financial Accounting Standards Board to Not-for-Profit Organizations" (New York: American Institute of Certified Public Accountants, September 1994).
18. Charles H. Gibson, "Budgeting by Objectives: Charlotte's Experience," *Management Accounting* (January 1978), p. 39.
19. Ibid., pp. 39, 48.

Many of the terms in this glossary are explained in the text. Terms not explained in the text are included because they represent terms frequently found in annual reports and the financial literature.

A

Accelerated Cost Recovery System (ACRS): Depreciation method introduced for tax purposes in 1981 and subsequently modified. See Modified Accelerated Cost Recovery System (MACRS).

Accelerated depreciation: Any depreciation method in which the charges in earlier periods exceed those in later periods.

Account: A record used to classify and summarize transactions.

Accountant: One who performs accounting services.

Account form of balance sheet: A balance sheet that presents assets on the left-hand side and liabilities and owners' equity on the right-hand side.

Accounting: The systematic process of measuring the economic activity of an entity to provide useful information to those who make business and economic decisions.

Accounting changes: A term used to describe the use of a different accounting principle, estimate, or reporting entity than used in a prior year.

Accounting controls: Procedures concerned with safeguarding the assets or the reliability of the financial statements.

Accounting cycle: A series of steps used for analyzing, recording, classifying, and summarizing transactions.

Accounting equation: Assets = Liabilities + Owners' Equity.

Accounting errors: Mistakes resulting from mathematical errors, improper application of accounting principles, or omissions of material facts.

Accounting period: The time to which accounting reports are related. The time is usually annual, quarterly, or monthly.

Accounting policies: The accounting principles and practices adopted by a company to report its financial results.

Accounting Principles Board (APB): A board established by the AICPA that issued opinions establishing accounting standards during the period 1959–1973.

Accounting process: The procedures used for analyzing, recording, classifying, and summarizing the information to be presented in accounting reports.

Accounting Research Bulletins (ARBs): Publications of the Committee on Accounting Procedure of the AICPA that established accounting standards during the years 1939–1959.

Accounting system: The procedures and methods used to collect and report accounting data.

Accounts payable: Amounts owed for inventory, goods, or services acquired in the normal course of business.

Accounts receivable (trade receivables): Monies due on accounts from customers arising from sales or services rendered.

Accounts receivable factoring: The sale of receivables without recourse for cash to a third party.

Accrual basis: The accrual basis of accounting dictates: revenue is recognized when realized (realization concept) and expenses are recognized when incurred (matching concept).

Accrued expenses: Expenses incurred but not recognized in the accounts.

Accrued liability: A liability resulting from the recognition of an expense before the payment of cash.

Accrued pension cost: The difference between the amount of pension recorded as an expense and the amount of the funding payment.

Accrued revenues: Revenues for services performed or for goods delivered that have not been recorded.

Accumulated Benefit Obligation (ABO): The present value of pension benefits earned to date based on employee service and compensations to that date.

Accumulated depreciation: Depreciation allocates the cost of buildings and machinery over the periods of benefits. The depreciation expense taken each period accumulates in the account, Accumulated Depreciation.

Accumulated Postretirement Benefit Obligation (APBO): The present value of postretirement benefits earned to date based on employee service to that date.

Acquisition: A business combination in which one corporation acquires control over the operations of another entity.

Acquisition cost: The amount that includes all of the cost normally necessary to acquire an asset and prepare it for its intended use.

Acquisitions: Companies that have been acquired.

Actuarial assumptions: Assumptions about future events based on historic data such as employee turnover, service lives, and longevity that are used to estimate future costs such as pension benefits.

Actuarial present value: The present value of pension obligations determined by using stated actuarial assumptions and estimates.

Additional paid-in capital: The investment by stockholders in excess of the stocks par or stated value as well as invested capital from other sources, such as donations of property or sale of treasury stock.

Additions: Enlargements and extensions of existing facilities.

Adjusting entries: Entries made at the end of each accounting period to update the accounts.

Administrative controls: Procedures concerned with efficient operation of the business and adherence to managerial policies.

Administrative expense: Result from the general administration of the company's operation.

Adverse opinion: An audit opinion issued whenever financial statements contain departures from GAAP that are too material to warrant only a qualification. This opinion states that the financial statements do not present fairly the financial position, results of operations, or cash flows of the entity in conformity with GAAP.

Aging of accounts receivables: A method of reviewing for uncollectible trade receivables by which an estimate of the bad debts expense is determined. The receivable balances are classified into age categories and then an estimate of noncollection is applied.

Aging schedule: A form used to categorize the various individual accounts receivable according to the length of time each has been outstanding.

Allowance for Funds Used During Construction (AFUDC): The recording of AFUDC is a utility accounting practice prescribed by the state utility commission. It represents the estimated debt and equity costs of financing construction work in progress. AFUDC does not represent a current source of cash, but under regulatory rate practices, a return on and recovery of AFUDC is permitted in determining rates charged for utility services. Some utilities report the estimated debt and equity costs of financing construction work in progress in separate accounts.

Allowance for uncollectible accounts: A contra accounts receivable account showing an estimate of the accounts receivable that will not be collected.

Allowance method: A method of estimating bad debts on the basis of either the net credit sales of the period or the accounts receivable at the end of the period.

American Accounting Association (AAA): An accounting organization of accounting professors and practicing accountants. (http://aaahq.org)

American Institute of Certified Public Accountants (AICPA): The AICPA is the national professional organization for certified public accountants (http://www.aicpa.org).

Amortization: The periodic allocation of the cost of an intangible asset over its useful life.

Analyze: To evaluate the condition of an accounting-related item and possible reasons for discrepancies.

Annualize: To extend an item to an annual basis.

Annual report: A formal presentation containing financial statements and other important information prepared by the management of a corporation once a year.

Annuity: A series of equal payments (receipts) over a specified number of equal time periods.

Antidilution of earnings: Assumed conversion of convertible securities or exercise of stock options that results in an increase in earnings per share or a decrease in loss per share.

Antidilutive securities: Securities whose assumed conversion or exercise results in an increase in earnings per share or a decrease in loss per share.

Appreciation: An increase in the value of an asset.

Appropriated retained earnings: A restriction of retained earnings that indicates that a portion of a company's assets are to be used for purposes other than paying dividends.

Appropriations (government accounting): Budget authorizations of expenditures.

Arm's-length transaction: Transactions that are conducted by independent parties, each acting in their own self-interest.

Asset impairment: Condition where a resource's expected future cash flow is less than its reported book value. The income statement reports losses on impaired assets.

Assets: Probable future economic benefits obtained or controlled by a particular entity as a result of past transactions or events.

Assignment of receivables: The borrowing of money with receivables pledged as security.

Attestation: Any service performed by a CPA resulting in a written communication that expresses a conclusion about the reliability of a written assertion that is the responsibility of investigating another party.

Audit committee: A committee of the board of directors comprised mainly of outside directors having no management ties to the organization.

Audit report: The mechanism for communicating the results of an audit.

Auditing: A systematic process of objectively obtaining and evaluating evidence regarding assertions and communicating the results to interested users.

Auditor: A person who conducts an audit.

Authorized stock: The maximum number of shares a corporation may issue without changing its charter with the state.

Available-for-sale securities: Stocks and bonds that are not classified as either held-to-maturity or trading securities.

Average cost method (inventory): Averaging methods lump the costs of inventory to determine an average.

B

Bad debt: An account or note receivable that proves to be entirely or partially uncollectible.

Bad debt expense: An account on the income statement representing estimated uncollectible credit sales for the current accounting period.

Bad debt recovery: Represents an account receivable previously written off as uncollectible and is now collected.

Balance sheet (classified): A form that segregates the assets and liabilities between current and noncurrent.

Balance sheet (financial position form): A form that deducts current liabilities from current assets to show working capital. The form adds remaining assets and deducts the remaining liabilities to derive the residual stockholders' equity.

Balance sheet (statement of financial position): The financial statement which shows the financial position of an accounting entity as of a specific date. The balance sheet lists assets, the resources of the firm; liabilities, the debts of the firm; and stockholders' equity, the owners' interest in the firm.

Balance sheet (unclassified): A form that does not segregate the assets and liabilities between current and non-current.

Balancing equation: Assets = Liabilities + Stockholders' Equity.

Bankruptcy protection: Legal arrangement in which creditor claims are suspended while a court appointed trustee reorganizes the bankrupt firm.

Bargain purchase option: Provision granting the lessee the right, but not the obligation, to purchase leased property at a price that, at the inception date, is sufficiently below the expected fair value of the property at exercise date to provide reasonable assurance of exercise.

Bargain renewal option: Provision granting the lessee the right, but not the obligation, to renew the lease at a rental that, at inception, is sufficiently below the expected fair rental at exercise date to provide reasonable assurance of renewal.

Basic earnings per share: The amount of earnings for the period available to each share of common stock outstanding during the reporting period.

Basis: A figure or value that is the starting point in computing gain or loss.

Bearer (coupon) bonds: Bonds whose ownership is determined by possession and for which interest is paid to the holder (bearer) of an interest coupon.

Benchmark: In the content of outcomes and performance discussion, the term refers to desired program results. It may include a target or standard for the program to achieve. It is also used to denote best practices.

BestCalls.com: This site has live broadcasts and recordings of earnings announcements and management interviews (http://www.bestcalls.com).

Big bath: The concept that a company expecting to have a series of hits to earnings in future years is better off to try to recognize all of the bad news in one year, leaving future years unencumbered by continuing losses.

Board of directors: A body of individuals who are elected by the stockholders to be their representatives in managing the company.

Bond: A security, usually long-term, representing money borrowed by a corporation. Normally issued with $1,000 face value.

Bond discount: The difference between the face value and the sales price when bonds are sold below their face value.

Bond indenture: The contract between the issuing entity and the bondholders specifying the terms, rights, and obligations of the contracting parties.

Bond issue price: The present value of the annuity interest payments plus the present value of the principal.

Bond premium: The difference between the face value and the sales price when bonds are sold above their face value.

Bond refinancing: Issuing new bonds to replace outstanding bonds either at maturity or prior to maturity.

Bond sinking fund: A fund established by the segregation of assets over the life of the bond issue to pay the bondholders at maturity.

Bonds (serial): A bond issue which matures in installments.

Book value: The original cost of an asset less any accumulated depreciation (depletion or amortization) taken to date.

Book value per share: The dollar amount of the net assets of a company per share of common stock.

Bottom line: The financial vernacular for net income.

Budget: A quantitative plan of activities and programs expressed in terms of assets, liabilities, revenues, and expenses.

Buildings: A structure used in a business operation.

Business combination: One or more businesses that are merged together as one accounting entity.

Business entity: The viewpoint that the business (or entity) for which the financial statements are prepared is separate and distinct from the owners of the entity.

Business (source) document: Business record used as the basis for analyzing and recording transactions; examples include invoices, check stubs, receipts, and similar business papers.

C

Calendar year: The accounting year ends on December 31.

Callable bonds: Bonds that a corporation has the option of buying back and retiring at a given price before maturity.

Callable obligation: A debt instrument payable on demand of the company that issued the obligation.

Callable preferred stock: Preferred stock that may be redeemed and retired by the corporation at its option.

Capital: Owners' equity in an unincorporated firm.

Capital expenditures: Costs that increase the future economic benefits of an asset above those originally expected.

Capital lease: Long-term lease in which the risk of ownership lies with the lessee and whose terms resemble a purchase or sale; recorded as an asset with a corresponding liability at the present value of the lease payments.

Capital stock: The portion of the contribution by stockholders assignable to the shares of stock as par or stated value.

Capital structure: Amount, types, and proportion of an entity's liabilities and shareholders' equity.

Capitalization: The process of assigning value to a balance sheet account (asset or liability).

Capitalized interest: Interest added to the cost of a fixed asset instead of being expensed.

Carrying value: The face of a bond plus the amount of unamortized premium or minus the amount of unamortized discount.

Cash: The most liquid asset that includes negotiable checks, unrestricted balances in checking accounts, and cash on hand.

Cash basis accounting: A system of accounting that records revenues when received and expenses when paid.

Cash dividend: The payment (receipt) of a dividend in cash.

Cash equivalents: A company's highly liquid short-term investments considered to be cash equivalents and usually classified with cash on the balance sheet.

Cash flows from financing activities: Cash flows relating to liability and owners' equity accounts.

Cash flows from investing activities: Cash flows relating to lending money and to acquiring and selling investments and productive long-term assets.

Cash flows from operating activities: Generally, the cash effects of transactions and other events that determine net income.

Cash (sales) discount: A reduction in sales price allowed if payment is received within a specified period, usually offered to customers to encourage prompt payment.

Cash surrender value: The investment portion of a life insurance policy, payable to the policyholder if the policyholder cancels the policy.

Certified Management Accountant (CMA): An accountant that has met the admission criteria and demonstrated the competency of technical knowledge in management accounting required by the Institute of Management Accountants.

Certified Public Accountant (CPA): An accountant who has received a certificate stating that he/she has met the requirements of state law.

Change in an accounting estimate: A change in the estimation of the effects of future events.

Change in an accounting principle: Adoption of a generally accepted accounting principle different from the one used previously for reporting purposes.

Change in reporting entity: An accounting change that reflects financial statements for a different unit of accountability.

Chart of accounts: A listing of all accounts used by a company.

Chief accountant of the SEC: An appointed official of the Securities and Exchange Commission.

Chief Financial Officer (CFO): Executive responsible for overseeing the financial operations of an organization.

Classified balance sheet: A balance sheet that segregates the assets and liabilities as current and noncurrent.

Closing entries: Temporary account balances are transferred to the permanent stockholders' equity account, Retained Earnings.

Collateral: Security for loans or other forms of indebtedness.

Commercial paper: Short-term obligations or promissory notes, unsecured, interest bearing with flexible maturities.

Commitment fee: A fee for committing to holding a credit facility available over a period of time to a borrower.

Common-size analysis (horizontal): Common-size analysis expresses comparisons in percentages. Horizontal analysis indicates proportionate change over a period of time.

Common-size analysis (vertical): Common-size analysis expresses comparisons in percentages. Vertical analysis indicates the proportionate expression of each item in a given period to a base figure selected from that same period.

Common stock (capital stock): The stock representing the most basic rights to ownership of a corporation.

Common stock equivalent shares: A security that is not in the form of a common stock, but that contains provisions that enable its holder to acquire common stock.

Comparability: For accounting information, the quality that allows a user to analyze two or more companies and look for similarities and differences.

Comparative statements: Financial statements for two or more periods.

Compensated absences: Payments to employees for vacation, holiday, illness, or other personal activities.

Compensating balance requirements: Provisions in loan agreements requiring the borrower to maintain minimum cash balances with the lending institution.

Compensatory option plans: Stock option plans offered to a select group of employees.

Compilation: A professional service in which the CPA presents information that is the representation of management without undertaking to express any assurance on the statements.

Complex capital structure: Capital structure that has potentially dilutive securities such as convertible debt, preferred stock, and options.

Completed-contract method: A method that recognizes revenues on long-term construction contracts only when the contract is completed.

Composite depreciation: A depreciation method which aggregates dissimilar assets and computes depreciation for the aggregation based on a weighted average life expectancy.

Compound interest: The process of earning interest on interest from previous periods.

Comprehensive income: Net income plus the period's change in accumulated other comprehensive income (accumulated other comprehensive income is a category within stockholders' equity).

Conglomerates: Complex companies that operate in multiple industries.

Conservatism: The concept that directs that the measurement with the least favorable effect on net income and financial position in the current period be selected.

Conservative analysis: This perspective represents a relatively strict interpretation of the value of assets and what constitutes debt.

Consigned goods: Inventory physically located at a dealer but another company retains title until the consignee sells the inventory.

Consignment: A transfer of property without a transfer of title and risk of ownership. The recipient of the property (consignee) acts as a selling agent on behalf of the owner (consignor).

Consistency: The concept requiring the entity to give the same treatment to comparable transactions from period to period.

Consolidated financial statements: The combined financial statements of a parent company and its subsidiary.

Constant dollar accounting (price-level accounting): The method of reporting financial statement elements in dollars having similar purchasing power. Constant dollar accounting measures general changes in prices of goods and services.

Construction-in-process: Fixed asset account where construction costs are recorded until construction is completed.

Contingencies: Conditions which may result in gains and losses, and that will be resolved by the occurrence of future events.

Contingent asset: An asset that may arise in the future if certain events occur.

Contingent liabilities: Liabilities whose payment is dependent on a particular occurrence such as settlement of litigation or a ruling of a tax court.

Contra account: An account used to offset a primary account in order to show a net valuation, e.g., Accounts Receivable (primary account) less Allowance for Doubtful Accounts (contra account).

Contributed capital: The sum of the capital stock accounts and the capital in excess of par (or stated) value accounts.

Contributory pension plan: A pension plan in which employees make contributions to the plan and thus bear part of the cost.

Control account: The general ledger account that is supported by a subsidiary ledger.

Controller: The chief accounting officer for a company. This individual usually reports to the chief financial officer (CFO).

Convertible bonds: Bonds that may be exchanged for other securities of the corporation, usually common stock.

Convertible preferred stock: Preferred stock that can be converted into common stock.

Convertible securities: Securities whose terms permit the holder to convert the investment into common stock of the issuing companies.

Copyright: An exclusive right granted by the federal government to publish and sell literary, musical, and other artistic materials.

Corporate officers: Senior executive managers of the company identified by title and name.

Corporation: A separate legal entity having its own rights, privileges, and liabilities distinct from those of its owners.

Cost accounting: Determines product costs and other relevant information used.

Cost/benefit: The process of determining that the benefit of an act or series of acts exceeds the cost of performing the act(s).

Cost of goods manufactured: The total cost of goods completed in the manufacturing process during an accounting period.

Cost of goods sold: Cost of goods available for sale minus ending inventory.

Cost of goods sold or cost of sales: The cost of goods sold during an accounting period.

Cost principle: The accounting principle that records historical cost as the appropriate basis of initial accounting recognition of all acquisitions, liabilities, and owners' equity.

Cost recovery: A revenue recognition method which requires recovery of the total cost prior to the recognition of revenue.

Coupon rate: The stated interest rate in a bond contract. Also referred to as the nominal, stated, or face rate.

Covenants: Conditions placed in a loan or credit agreement by the lender to protect its position as a creditor of the borrowing.

Credit: An entry on the right side of an account.

Credit agreement: A contractual arrangement between a lender and a borrower which sets the terms and conditions for borrowing.

Credit ratings: Formal credit risk evaluations by credit rating agencies of a company's ability to repay principal and interest on its debt obligations.

Credit risk: Uncertainty that the party on the other side of an agreement will abide by the terms of the agreement.

Creditor: A party who lends money to a company.

Cumulative effect of change in accounting principle: The effect that a new accounting principle would have had on net income of prior periods if it had been used instead of the old principle.

Cumulative preferred stock: Preferred stock on which unpaid dividends accumulate over time and must be satisfied in any given year before a dividend may be paid to common stockholders.

Currency swap: An exchange of two currencies as part of an agreement to reverse the exchange on a specific future date.

Current assets: Current assets are assets (1) in the form of cash, (2) that will normally be realized in cash, or (3) that conserve the use of cash during the operating cycle of a firm or for one year, whichever is longer.

Current cost: The current replacement cost of the same asset owned, adjusted for the value of any operating advantages or disadvantages.

Current liabilities: Obligations whose liquidation is reasonably expected to require the use of existing resources properly classifiable as current assets or the creation of other current liabilities.

Current market value: The amount of cash, or its equivalent, that could be obtained by selling an asset in an orderly liquidation.

Current maturity of long-term debt: The portion of a long-term debt payable within the next operating cycle or one year, whichever is longer.

Current replacement cost: The estimated cost of acquiring the best asset available to undertake the function of the asset owned.

Current value: The amount of cash, or its equivalent, that could be received by selling an asset currently.

D

Debenture bonds: Bonds issued on the general credit of a company.

Debit: An entry on the left side of an account.

Debt: Considered to be funds a company has borrowed from a creditor.

Debt securities: Investments in debt instruments such as commercial paper or bonds.

Debt service: A term used by bankers, which refers to a borrower's requirement to make payment of the current maturities on outstanding debt.

Decentralization: The freedom for managers at lower levels of the organization to make decisions.

Decision usefulness: The overriding quality or characteristic of accounting information.

Declining-balance method: The declining-balance method applies double the straight-line depreciation rate times the declining book value (cost minus accumulated depreciation) to achieve a declining depreciation charge over the estimated life of the asset.

Default: A failure of a debtor to meet principal or interest payment on a debt at the due date.

Default risk: The probability that a company will be unable to meet its obligations.

Defeasance: A method of early retirement of debt in which risk-free securities are purchased and then placed in a trust account to be used to retire the outstanding debt at its maturity.

Deferral: The postponement of the recognition of an expense already paid or of a revenue already received.

Deferred charge: A long-term expense prepayment amortized to expense.

Deferred expense: An asset resulting from the payment of cash before the incurrence of expense.

Deferred financing costs, net: An asset account usually classified under other assets; costs associated with the issuance of long-term bonds that have not been amortized.

Deferred revenue: A liability resulting from the receipt of cash before the recognition of revenue.

Deferred taxes: A balance sheet account; classified as an asset or liability depending on the nature of the timing differences. The differences are the result of any situation that recognizes revenue or expense in a different time period for tax purposes than for the financial statements.

Deficiency: An additional tax liability that the IRS deems to be curved by a taxpayer.

Deficit: A negative (debit) balance in retained earnings.

Defined benefit pension plan: A pension plan that defines the benefits that employees will receive at retirement.

Defined contribution pension plan: A pension plan that specifies the employer's contributions and bases benefits solely on the amount contributed.

Deflation: A general decrease in prices.

Depletion: Recognition of the wearing away or using up of a natural resource.

Depreciable cost: The cost of a fixed asset less salvage value.

Depreciation expense: The process of allocating the cost of buildings, machinery, and equipment over the periods benefitted.

Derivative instruments: Financial instruments or other contracts where rights or obligations meet the definitions of assets or liabilities.

Devaluation: A downward adjustment of the exchange rate between two currencies.

Diluted earnings per share: The amount of earnings for the period available to each share of common stock outstanding during the reporting period and to each share that would have been outstanding assuming the issuance of common shares for all dilutive potential common shares outstanding during the reporting period.

Dilution: Refers to the effect on earnings calculations when the number of shares issued increases disproportionately to the growth in the earnings.

Direct financing type lease: A capital lease in which the lessor receives income only from financing the "purchase" of the leased asset.

Direct method: For preparing the operating activities section of the statement of cash flows, the approach in which cash receipts and cash payments are reported.

Direct write-off method: A method of recognizing specific accounts receivable determined to be uncollectible.

Disbursement: A payment by cash or check.

Disclaimer of opinion: Inability to render an audit opinion because of lack of sufficient evidence or lack of independence.

Discontinued operations: The disposal of a major segment of a business.

Discount on bonds: A bond is issued below its face amount, indicating that the coupon rate is lower than the market rate for similar bonds.

Discount on notes payable: A contra liability that represents interest deducted from a loan in advance.

Discount rate: The interest rate used to compute the present value.

Discounted Cash Flow (DCF): Measures all expected future cash inflows and outflows as if they occurred at a single point in time.

Discounted note: A non-interest-bearing note where the interest charge has been deducted from the principal in advance.

Discounting: The process of selling a promissory note.

Discussion Memorandum (DM): A document issued by the FASB that identifies the principal issues involved with financial accounting and reporting topics. It includes a discussion of the various points of view as to the resolution of issues but does not reach a specific conclusion.

Divestitures: Companies that have been disposed of.

Dividends (cash): Cash payment from current or past income to the owners of a corporation.

Dividends in arrears: The accumulated unpaid dividends from prior years on cumulative preferred stock.

Dividends payable: A current liability on the balance sheet resulting from the declaration of dividends by the board of directors.

Dividends (stock): A percentage of outstanding stock issued as new shares to existing shareholders.

Dollar-value LIFO: An adaptation of LIFO that measures inventory by total dollar amount rather than by individual units. LIFO increment layers are determined based on total dollar changes.

Domestic Corporation: A company established under U.S. or state law.

Donated assets: Receipt of assets without being required to give goods or services in return.

Donated capital: Assets donated to the company by stockholders, creditors, or other parties.

Double-declining-balance depreciation: A method of calculating depreciation by which a percentage equal to twice the straight-line percentage is multiplied by the declining book value to determine the depreciation expense for the period (salvage value is ignored when calculating).

Double-entry accounting: A system of recording transactions in a way that maintains the equality of the equation: Assets = Liabilities + Stockholders' Equity.

Dry holes: Wells drilled which do not find commercial quantities of oil or gas.

E

Early extinguishment of debt: The retirement of debt prior to the maturity date.

Earnings: A term used interchangeably with income and profit.

Earnings per share: A company's bottom line stated on a per-share basis.

Economic substance: The "real" nature of a transaction, as opposed to its legal form.

EDGAR system: The SEC's electronic data gathering analysis and retrieval system.

Effective rate of interest: The yield or true rate of interest.

Efficient market hypothesis: A theory to explain the functioning of capital markets in which share prices reflect all publicly available information.

Emerging Issues Task Force (EITF): A task force of representatives from the accounting profession created by the FASB to deal with emerging issues of financial reporting.

Employee Retirement Income Security Act (ERISA): A legislative act passed by Congress in 1974 that made significant changes in requirements for employer pension plans. This act has been amended several times since 1974.

Employee stock ownership plans (ESOPS): A qualified stock-bonus, or combination stock-bonus and money purchase, pension plan designed to invest in primarily the employer's securities.

Enterprise funds (governmental accounting): Funds used to report any activity for which a fee is charged to external users for goods or services.

Entity assumption: Accounting records are kept for the business entity as distinct from the entity's owners.

Equipment: Assets used in the production of goods or in providing services.

Equity: Equity is the residual interest in the assets of an entity that remains after deducting its liabilities. Synonymous with the expression *shareholders' equity*.

Equity in earnings of nonconsolidated subsidiaries: When a firm has investments in stocks, uses the equity method of accounting, and the investment is not consolidated, then the investor firm reports equity earnings (the proportionate share of the earnings of the investee).

Equity method: A method to value intercorporate equity investments by adjusting the investor's cost basis for the percentage ownership in the investee's earnings (or losses) and for any dividends paid by the investee.

Equity-oriented deferred compensation: The amount of compensation cost deferred and amortized to future periods as the services are provided.

Equity securities: Securities issued by corporations as a form of ownership in the business.

ERISA: The acronym for the Employee Retirement Income Security Act of 1974.

Estimated economic life of leased property: The useful life of leased property estimated at inception under conditions of normal maintenance and repairs.

Estimated liability: An obligation of the entity whose exact amount cannot be determined until a later date.

Estimated residual value of leased property: The expected fair or market value of leased property at the end of the lease term.

Estimated useful life: The period of time that a company establishes in order to depreciate a fixed asset.

Ethics: A set of principles referring to ideals of character and conduct.

Event: A happening of consequence to an entity.

Exchange rate: The rate at which one unit of currency may be purchased by another unit of currency.

Executory costs: Insurance, maintenance, and local and property taxes on leased property.

Expectations gap: The disparity between users' and CPAs' perceptions of professional services, especially audit services.

Expenses: Outflows or uses of assets or incurrences of liabilities (or a combination of both) during the process of an entity's revenue-generating operations.

Exposure Draft (ED): A proposed Statement of Financial Accounting Standards.

External expansion: Occurs as firms take over, or merge with, other existing firms.

Extraordinary items: Material events and transactions distinguished by their unusual nature and infrequent occurrence.

F

Face amount, maturity value: The amount that will be paid on a bond (note) at the maturity date.

Face rate of interest: The rate of interest on the bond certificate.

Factor: Selling accounts receivable for cash.

Fair value: The amount at which an asset (liability) could be bought (incurred) or sold (settled) in a current transaction between willing parties.

Feedback value: An ingredient of relevant accounting information.

Fiduciary duty: Management's obligation to protect the interests of equity investors.

Fiduciary funds (governmental accounting): Funds used to report assets held in a trustee or agency capacity for others.

FIFO method: An inventory costing method that assigns the most recent costs to ending inventory.

Financial accounting: Recording and communication of financial information under GAAP.

Financial Accounting Standards Board (FASB): A body that has responsibility for developing and issuing rules on accounting practice in the United States (http://www.fasb.org).

Financial analysis: Describes the process of studying a company's financial report.

Financial leverage: The amount of debt financing in relation to equity financing.

Financial news: For a wealth of information about the economy and specific companies and industries (The Wall Street Journal, http://www.wsj.com; The New York Times, http://www.nyt.com; Financial Times, http://www.ft.com; Investor's Business Daily, http://www.investors.com).

Financial portals: These sites have financial news, information about companies, and other financial information. There are many such sites. Some popular sites are Microsoft's Money Central (http://www.moneycentral.msn.com), Yahoo! Finance (http://finance.yahoo.com), and The Street.com (http://www.thestreet.com).

Financial Reporting Release (FRR): SEC statement dealing with reporting and disclosure requirements in documents filed with the SEC.

Financial statement (report) analysis: The process of reviewing, analyzing, and interpreting the basic financial reports.

Financial statements: Generally considered to be the balance sheet, income statement, and statement of cash flows.

Financial summary: A section of the annual report which provides a 5-, 10-, or 11-year summary of selected financial data.

Financing activities: Activities concerned with the raising and repayment of funds in the form of debt and equity.

Finished goods: A manufacturer's inventory that is complete and ready for sale.

First-in, first-out (FIFO) (inventory): The flow pattern assumes that the first unit purchased is the first sold.

Fiscal year: Any 12-month accounting period used by an economic entity, which closes at the end of a month other than December.

Fixed assets: Tangible, long-lived assets, primarily property, plant, and equipment. They are expected to provide service benefit for more than one year.

Fixed cost: Cost that remains unchanged in total for a given time period, despite wide changes in the related level of total activity or volume.

Forecasted transaction: A transaction that is expected to occur for which there is no firm commitment.

Foreign Corrupt Practices Act: Legislation intended to increase the accountability of management for accurate records and reliable financial statements.

Foreign currency: A currency other than the entity's functional currency.

Foreign currency transactions: Transactions that are settled with a nondomestic currency.

Foreign exchange rate: Specifies the number of U.S. dollars (from a U.S. perspective) that are needed to obtain one unit of a specific foreign currency.

Foreign operations: Operational activities that take place in a foreign country.

Forgery: The act of fabricating or producing something falsely.

Form 8-K: A special SEC filing required when a material event or transaction occurs between Form 10-Q filing dates.

Form 10-K: It is like an annual report but with more detail. It is provided to the SEC.

Form 10-Q: An SEC form required to be filed at the end of a company's first, second, and third fiscal year quarters. It contains interim information on a company's operations and financial position.

Form 20-F: The annual financial report filing with the SEC required of all foreign companies whose debt or equity capital is available for purchase/sale on a U.S. exchange.

Form S-1: Form filed with the Securities and Exchange Commission listing securities to be traded on a national stock market.

Form S-4: Form filed with the Securities and Exchange Commission that registers securities used to effect a business combination.

Form versus substance: Form refers to the legal nature of a transaction or event; substance refers to the economic aspects of the transaction or event.

Forward contract: Agreement to purchase or sell commodities, securities, or currencies on a specified future date at a specified price.

Forward exchange rate: A rate quoted currently for the exchange of currency at some future specified date.

Fractional share: A unit of stock that is less than one full share.

Franchise: A contractual privilege granted by one person to another permitting the sale of a product, use of trade name, or provision of a service within a specified territory and/or in a specified manner.

Fraud: Intent to deceive.

Fraudulent transfer: A transfer of an interest or an obligation incurred by the debtor within one year prior to the date of filing a bankruptcy petition with the intent to defraud creditors.

Fringe benefit: The compensation or other benefit provided by the employer to the employee at no charge that is above and beyond salary or wages.

Full-costing method: The method of accounting that capitalizes all costs of exploring for and developing oil and gas reserves within a defined area subject only to the limitation that costs attributable to developed reserves should not exceed their estimated present value.

Full disclosure: Accounting reports must disclose all facts that may influence the judgment of an informed reader.

Functional currency: The currency a company uses to conduct its business.

Fund accounting: Accounting procedures in which a self-balancing group of accounts is provided for each accounting entity established by legal, contractual, or voluntary action.

Funded debt: The long-term debt of a business.

Fund financial statements (governmental accounting): Consist of a series of statements that focus on information about the government's major governmental and enterprise funds, including its blended component units.

Funding payment: A payment made by the employer to the pension fund on its trustee.

Furniture and fixtures: A noncurrent depreciable asset consisting of office or store equipment.

Future contract: Exchange-traded contract for future acceptance or delivery of a standardized quantity of a commodity or financial instrument on a specified future date at a specified price.

Future value of an annuity: Amount accumulated in the future when a series of payments is invested and accrues interest.

G

Gain or loss on redemption: The difference between the carrying value and the redemption price at the time bonds are redeemed.

Gains: Profits realized from activities that are incidental to a firm's primary operating activities.

General fund (governmental accounting): This fund is used to account for all financial resources not accounted for in another fund.

General journal: A journal used to record transactions not maintained in special journals.

General ledger: A record of all accounts used by a company.

General partnership: An association in which each partner has unlimited liability.

Generally Accepted Accounting Principles (GAAP): Accounting principles that have substantial authoritative support.

Generally Accepted Auditing Standards (GAAS): GAAS are the standards governing the conduct of independent audits of nonpublic companies by CPAs.

Going concern or continuity: Assumes that the entity being accounted for will remain in business for an indefinite period of time.

Golden Parachute Agreement: A highly lucrative contract giving a senior corporate executive monetary or other benefits if his or her job is lost in a merger or acquisition.

Goodwill: An intangible asset representing the unrecorded assets of a firm. It appears in the accounting records only if the firm is acquired for a price in excess of the fair market value of its net assets.

Government-wide financial statements: These financial statements consist of a statement of net assets and a statement of activities. These statements should report all of the assets, liabilities, revenues, expenses, and gains and losses of the government.

Governmental Accounting Standards Board (GASB): The standards-setting body for governmental accounting and financial reporting.

Governmental funds: General, special revenue, project, debt service, and special assessment funds; each designed for a specific purpose and used by a state or local government to account for its normal operations.

Grant date: The date at which an employer and an employee reach a mutual understanding of the key terms and conditions of a share-based payment award.

Gross profit margin: Gross profit margin equals the difference between net sales revenue and the cost of goods sold.

Group depreciation: A depreciation method which groups like assets together and computes depreciation for the group rather than for individual assets.

Guarantee of Employee Stock Ownership Plan (ESOPs): An employee stock bonus plan used as a financing vehicle for an employer which borrows money to purchase its own stock. The stock is security for the loan, and the ESOP repays the loan from employer contributions.

Guaranteed residual value: A guarantee by lessee of a minimum value for the residual value of a leased asset. If the residual value is less than the guarantee, the lessee must pay the difference to the lessor.

H

Harmonization of accounting principles: The attempt by various organizations (e.g., the FASB, IASB) to establish a common set of international accounting and reporting standards.

Hedge: A process of buying or selling commodities, forward contracts, or options for the explicit purpose of reducing or eliminating foreign exchange risk.

Hedging contract: A contract to buy or sell foreign currencies in the forward market to protect against the risks of foreign exchange rate fluctuations.

Held-to-maturity securities: Investments in bonds of other companies in which the investor has the positive intent and the ability to hold the securities to maturity.

Historical cost: The cash equivalent price of goods or services at the date of acquisition.

Horizontal analysis: A comparison of financial statement items over a period of time.

Human resource accounting: Attempts to account for the services of employees.

Hybrid securities: A security that is neither clearly debt nor clearly equity.

I

Impairment: A temporary or permanent reduction in asset value.

Implicit interest rate: The interest rate that would discount the minimum lease payments to the fair market value of the leased asset at the lease signing date.

Imputed interest rate: A rate of interest applied to a note when the effective rate was either not evident or determinable by other factors involved in the exchange.

Income smoothing: An accounting practice that attempts to present a stable measure of income (usually an increasing amount).

Income Summary: A temporary account in which revenues and expenses are closed at the end of the year.

In-substance defeasance of debt: The debtor irrevocably places cash or other assets in a trust to be used solely for satisfying the payments of both interest and principal on a specific debt obligation.

Income statement (statement of earnings): A statement that summarizes revenues and expenses.

Income taxes: Taxes levied by federal, state, and local governments on reported accounting profit. Income tax expense includes both tax paid and deferred.

Inconsistency: A change in accounting principle from one period to the next, requiring an explanatory paragraph following the opinion paragraph of the auditor's report.

Incorporated: A legal state of existence signifying that a corporate entity has been recognized.

Incorporation by reference: Direction of the reader's attention to information included in source other than the Form 10-K, rather than reporting such information in Form 10-K.

Incremental borrowing rate: The interest rate at which the lessee could borrow the amount of money necessary to purchase the leased asset, taking into consideration the lessee's financial situation and the current conditions in the marketplace.

Indentures: Provisions and restrictions attached to a bond that make the bond more attractive for investors.

Indexed bond: An obligation with interest payments tied to an inflation index.

Indirect cost: An expense that is difficult to trace directly to a specific costing object.

Indirect method: For preparing the operating activities section of the statement of cash flows, the approach in which net income is reconciled to net cash flow from operations.

Industry practices: Practices leading to accounting reports that do not conform to the general theory that underlies accounting.

Industry ratios: Financial ratios for a particular industry.

Industry segment: A component of an organization providing a product or related products (or services) to outside parties.

Inflation: An increase in the general price level of goods and services.

Information overload: Amount of data that unnecessarily complicates analysis.

Initial direct costs: Costs such as commissions, legal fees, and preparation of documents that are incurred by the lessor or negotiating and completing a lease transaction.

Initial Public Offering (IPO): The first or initial sale of voting stock to the general market by a previously privately held concern.

Insolvent: A condition in which a company is unable to pay its debts.

Installment method: The method in which revenue is recognized at the time cash is collected.

Installment sales: A type of sale which requires periodic payments over an extended length of time.

Institute of Management Accountants (IMA): An organization of management accountants concerned with the internal use of accounting data.

Intangibles: Nonphysical assets, such as legal rights, recorded at historical cost, then reduced by systematic amortization.

Intercompany profit: The profit resulting when one related company sells to another related company.

Intercompany receivables and payables: Receivables and payables among a parent company and its subsidiary(ies).

Interest: The cost for the use of money. It is a cost to the borrower and revenue to the lender.

Interest-bearing note: A debt instrument (note) that pays interest at a stated rate for a stated period.

Interest rate: A rate, usually expressed as a percentage per annum charged on money borrowed or lent.

Internal reporting: Represents financial data or other information accumulated by one individual to be communicated to another within the business entity.

Interest rate risk: Uncertainty about future interest rates and their impact on future cash flows as well as on the fair value of existing assets and liabilities.

Interest rate swaps: An agreement to exchange variable rate interest payments based on a specific index for a fixed rate or a variable rate stream of payments based on another index.

Interim reports: Financial reports that cover fiscal periods of less than one year.

Internal auditing: The department responsible in a company for the review and appraisal of its accounting and administrative controls.

Internal control: The process effected by an entity to provide reasonable assurance regarding the achievement of objectives. It consists of three parts—operations controls, financial reporting controls, and compliance controls.

Internal event: An event occurring entirely within an entity.

Internal financing: Financing provided from cash generated from business operations.

Internal Revenue Service (IRS): U.S. government agency responsible for administering U.S. income tax rules.

International Accounting Standards (IAS): The accounting standards adopted by the IASC and later by the IASB.

International Accounting Standards Board (IASB): Established in January 2001 to replace the IASC. The new structure has characteristics similar to that of the FASB. The IASB sets global financial accounting and reporting standards (http://www.iasb.org).

International Accounting Standards Committee (IASC): An organization established in 1973 by the leading professional groups of the major industrial countries.

International Federation of Accountants (IFAC): An association of professional accounting organizations founded in 1977.

Interperiod: Of or related to more than one reporting period.

Interperiod tax allocation: The process of allocating the taxes paid by a company over the periods in which the taxes are recognized for accounting purposes.

Intraperiod: Of or related to one reporting period.

Intrinsic value method: Method of accounting for stock-based compensation in which the difference between the exercise price and the market price per share at the grant date is used to measure compensation expense.

Introductory paragraph: The first paragraph of the standard audit report, which identifies the financial statements covered by the audit report and clearly differentiates management's responsibility for preparing the financial statements from the auditor's responsibility for expressing an opinion on them.

Inventories: The balance of goods on hand.

Inventory-lower-of-cost-or-market (LCM) rule: An inventory pricing method which prices the inventory at an amount below cost if the replacement (market) value is less than cost.

Investing activities: Describes a firm's uses of cash to acquire other assets. A category shown on the cash flow statement.

Investments: Usually stocks and bonds of other companies held for the purpose of maintaining a business relationship or exercising control. To be classified as long term, it must be the intent of management to hold these assets as such. Long-term investments are differentiated from marketable securities, where the intent is to hold the assets for short-term profits and to achieve liquidity.

Investors: Owners and potential owners of a company.

Invoice: Form sent by the seller to the buyer as evidence of a sale.

Issued stock: The shares of stock sold or otherwise transferred to stockholders.

J

Joint venture: An association of two or more businesses established for a special purpose; some in the form of partnerships and unincorporated joint ventures; others in the form of corporations jointly owned by two or more other firms.

Journalizing: The act of recording journal entries.

Journals: Initial recordings of a company's transactions.

Junk bonds: High-risk, high-yield bonds issued by companies in a weak financial condition.

K

Kiting: A type of misrepresentation fraud used to conceal bank overdrafts or cash misappropriations.

L

Labor intensive: Activities, companies, and industries that are dominated by human effort.

Land: Realty used for business purposes. It is shown at acquisition cost and not depreciated. Land containing resources that will be used up, however, such as mineral deposits and timberlands, is subject to depletion.

Land improvements: Expenditures incurred in the process of putting land into a usable condition, e.g., clearing, grading, paving, etc.

Lapping: A form of concealment that involves crediting current customer remittances to the accounts of customers who have remitted previously.

Last-in, first-out (LIFO) (inventory): The flow pattern assumes that those units purchased last are sold first.

Lease: An agreement conveying the right to use property, plant, or equipment (land and/or depreciable assets) for a stated period of time.

Lease improvement: An improvement to leased property that becomes the property of the lessor at the end of the lease.

Lease term: The noncancelable period of a lease designated in the lease contract plus the period of any bargain renewal periods over which the lease is likely to be renewed.

Leasehold: A payment made to secure the right to a lease.

Ledger: Summarizes the effects of transactions upon individual accounts.

Lessee: The party to a lease who acquires the right to use the property, plant, and equipment.

Lessor: The party to a lease giving up the right to use the property, plant, and equipment.

Letter to the shareholders: A section of the annual report that presents a message from the company's chairman of the board or president.

Leverage: The use of borrowed funds and amounts contributed by preferred stockholders to earn an overall return higher than the cost of these funds.

Leveraged buyout (LBO): A purchase of a company where a substantial amount of the purchase price is debt financed.

Liabilities: Future sacrifices of economic benefits arising from present obligations to other entities.

License: Rights to engage in a particular activity.

Life cycle: Progression of a product, company, or industry from inception, through growth, to maturity, and into decline.

LIFO conformity rule: A federal tax regulation that requires the use of LIFO for financial reporting purposes if LIFO is used for income tax purposes.

LIFO inventory pool: A group of inventory items having common characteristics and assumed to be the same when applying LIFO.

LIFO layer: An incremental group of LIFO inventory items created in any year in which the number of units purchased or produced exceeds the number sold.

LIFO liquidation: The reduction or elimination of old LIFO layers because total purchases or production in the current period is less than sales.

LIFO method: An inventory method that assigns the most recent costs to the cost of goods sold.

LIFO reserves (LIFO valuation adjustment): The amount that would need to be added back to the LIFO inventory in order for the inventory account to approximate current cost.

Limited liability: The concept that stockholders in a corporation are not held personally liable.

Line of credit: A prearranged loan allowing borrowing up to a certain maximum amount.

Liquid assets: Current assets that either are in cash or can be readily converted to cash.

Liquidating dividend: A dividend that exceeds the balance in retained earnings.

Liquidation: The process of selling off the assets of a business, paying any outstanding debts, and distributing any remaining cash to the owners.

Liquidity: The nearness to cash of the assets and liabilities.

Listed company: A company whose shares or bonds have been accepted for trading on a securities exchange.

Loan covenant: Provision of a loan contract restricting the actions of the borrower or allowing for some monitoring of the borrower's actions.

Loan defaults: Violations of loan agreements that could result in loan principal and interest becoming immediately due.

Loan (mortgage) amortization: The process by which payments on a loan are allocated between principal and interest components.

Loan restructuring: Revision of loan terms in a manner mutually acceptable to the lender and borrower.

Long-term liabilities: Long-term liabilities are those due in a period exceeding one year or one operating cycle, whichever is longer.

Loss on sale of asset: The amount by which selling price is less than book value.

Losses: Losses realized from activities that are incidental to a firm's primary activities.

Lower of cost or market: A method to value inventories and marketable securities.

M

Machinery: An asset listed at historical cost, including delivery and installation, plus any material improvements that extend its life or increase the quantity or quality of service; depreciated over its estimated useful life.

Maintenance: Expenditures made to maintain plant assets in good operating condition.

Management accounting: The branch of accounting concerned with providing management with information to facilitate planning and control.

Management report: Management statements to shareholders that acknowledge management's responsibility for the preparation and integrity of financial statements.

Management's discussion and analysis (MD&A): Part of the annual report package required by the Securities and Exchange Commission. Management comments on the results of operations, liquidity, and capital resources for the years under review in the financial statements.

Market capitalization: Total value of an entity's outstanding shares at a point in time which reflects the value investors place on a company. It is computed by multiplying the number of common shares outstanding by the share price.

Market value (stock): The price investors are willing to pay for a share of stock.

Marketable securities: Ownership and debt instruments of the government and other companies that can be readily converted into cash.

Matching: The concept that determines the revenue and then matches the appropriate cost incurred in generating this revenue.

Materiality: The concept that exempts immaterial items from the concepts and principles that bind the accountant, and allows these items to be handled in the most economical and expedient manner possible.

Maturity date: Date on which the principal of a note becomes due.

Maturity value: The amount of cash the maker is to pay the payee on the maturity of the note.

Merchandise inventory: The account wholesalers and retailers use to report inventory held for sale.

Merger: A combination of one or more companies into a single corporate entity.

Minimum lease payments: The lease payments required over the lease term plus any amount to be paid for the residual value either through a bargain purchase option or a guarantee of residual value.

Minority interest (balance sheet account): The ownership of minority shareholders in the equity of consolidated subsidiaries that are less than wholly owned.

Minority share of earnings: The portion of income that belongs to the minority owners of a firm that has been consolidated.

Misappropriation: The fraudulent transfer of assets from the firm to one or more employees.

Modified Accelerated Cost Recovery System (MACRS): The accelerated cost recovery system as revised by The Tax Reform Act of 1986.

Monetary assets: Cash and other assets that represent the right to receive a specific amount of cash.

Monetary liabilities: Accounts payable and other liabilities that represent the obligation to pay a specific amount of cash.

Monetary unit: The unit used to measure financial transactions.

Mortgage: A loan backed by an asset with the asset title pledged to the lender.

Mortgage payable: A liability secured by real property.

Moving average: The name given to an average cost method when it is used with a perpetual inventory system.

Multinational enterprise: Entity engages in transnational business activities.

Multiple-step income statement: Form of the income statement that arrives at net income in steps.

Municipal debt: Debt securities issued by state, county, and local governments and their agencies.

N

NASDAQ (OTC): The National Association of Securities Dealers Automated Quotations. Represents a computerized communication network that handles the securities transactions of the over-the-counter market (http://www.nasdaq.com).

Natural business year: A 12-month period ending on a date that coincides with the end of an operating cycle.

Natural resources: Assets produced by nature such as petroleum, minerals, and timber.

Negative goodwill: Term used to describe the amount paid for another company that is less than the fair value of the company's net identifiable assets.

Negligence: An accountant's failure to conduct an audit with "due care."

Negotiable notes: Notes that are legally transferable by endorsement and delivery.

Net assets: Total assets less total liabilities (equivalent to shareowners' equity).

Net income: Amount by which total revenues exceed total expenses. The bottom line on the income statement.

Net of tax: Indicates that expected tax effects have already been considered as part of a particular calculation or figure. Indicates that taxes have been deducted from a particular financial component.

Net operating loss carryback: When tax-deductible expenses exceed taxable revenues, a company may carry the net operating loss back three years and receive refunds for income taxes paid in those years.

Net operating loss carryforward: When tax-deductible expenses exceed taxable revenues, a company may carry an operating loss forward and offset future taxable income.

Net periodic pension expense: The amount recognized in an employer's financial statements as an expense of a pension plan for a period.

Net realizable value: The nondiscounted amount of cash, or its equivalent, into which an asset is expected to be converted less direct costs necessary to make that conversion.

Net sales: Gross sales revenue less any allowances or discounts.

Net worth: Synonymous with shareholders' equity.

Neutrality: A qualitative characteristic of accounting information that involves the faithful reporting of business activity without bias to one or another view.

New York Stock Exchange (NYSE): The New York Stock Exchange is the world's largest securities exchange (http://www.nyse.com).

Nominal accounts: The name given to revenue, expense, and dividend accounts because they are temporary and are closed at the end of the period.

Noncancelable: A lease contract that can be cancelled only under very unlikely circumstances or with extremely expensive penalties to the lessee.

Noncash investing and financing activities: A category of investing and financing activities that does not involve cash flows.

Noncontributory pension plans: Plans in which the employer bears the total cost of the plan.

Noncumulative preferred stock: Preferred stock that has no claim on any prior year dividends that may have been "passed."

Noncurrent or long-term assets: Assets that do not qualify as current assets. In general, they take longer than a year to be converted to cash or to conserve cash in the long run.

Nondetachable warrants: Stock warrants that cannot be traded separately from the security with which they were originally issued.

Non-profit accounting: Accounting policies, procedures, and techniques employed by non-profit organizations.

Nonpublic company: A company whose equity or debt securities are not publicly traded on a stock exchange or in the over-the-counter market.

Nonrecurring: Earnings that do not represent the normal, recurring earnings from operations.

Nontrade notes payable: Notes issued to nontrade creditors for purposes other than to purchase goods or services.

Nontrade receivables: Any receivables arising from transactions that are not directly associated with the normal operating activities of a business.

Not sufficient funds (NSF) check: A check that is not honored by a bank because of insufficient cash in the maker's account.

Note: A written promise to pay signed by the debtor.

Note payable: Payables in the form of a written promissory note.

Note receivable: An asset resulting from the acceptance of a promissory note from another company.

Notes: Present additional information on items included in the financial statements and additional financial information.

Notes to the financial statements: Information that clarifies and extends the material presented in the financial statements with narrative and detail.

O

Objective acceleration clause: A clause in a debt agreement that identifies specific conditions that will cause the debt to be callable immediately.

Objectivity: Represents freedom from subjective valuation and bias in making an accounting decision.

Obsolescence: This represents a major factor in depreciation, resulting from technological or market changes.

Off-balance-sheet financing: Refers to a company taking advantage of debt-like resources without these obligations appearing as debt on the face of the balance sheet.

On account: Purchases or sales on credit.

Operating activities: One of three major categories included in a statement of cash flows; includes transactions and events that normally enter into the determination of net income, including interest and taxes.

Operating cycle: The period of time elapsing between the acquisition of goods and the final cash realization resulting from sales and subsequent collections.

Operating expenses: Consist of two types: selling and administrative. Selling expenses result from the company's effort to create sales. Administrative expenses relate to the general administration of the company's operation.

Operating lease (lessee): Periodic payment for the right to use an asset, recorded in a manner similar to the recording of rent expense payments.

Opportunity cost: This represents revenue forfeited by rejecting an alternative use of time or facilities.

Option: A financial instrument that conveys to its owner the right, but not the obligation, to buy or sell a security, commodity, or currency at a specific price over a specified time period or at a specific date.

Organization costs: The costs of forming a corporation.

Organizational costs: The legal costs incurred when organizing a business; carried as an asset and usually written off over a period of five years or longer.

Original entry: Represents recording a business transaction in a journal.

Other assets: Represents a balance sheet category for minor assets not classified under the typical headings.

Other income and expenses: Income and expenses from secondary activities of the firm not directly related to the operations.

Outstanding shares: The number of authorized shares of capital stock sold to stockholders that are currently in the possession of stockholders (issues shares less treasury shares).

Owners' equity (stockholders' equity, shareholders' equity): The residual ownership interest in the assets of an entity that remains after deducting its liabilities.

P

Paid-in capital in excess of par value (or stated value): The proceeds from the sale of capital stock in excess of the par value (or stated value) of the capital stock.

Par value: An amount set by the firm's board of directors and approved by the state. (The par value does not relate to the market value.)

Parent: Tax term applied to the buyer company in a business combination.

Parent company: A company that owns a controlling interest in another company.

Participating preferred stock: Preferred stock that provides for additional dividends to be paid to preferred stockholders after dividends of a specified amount are paid to common stockholders.

Partnership: An unincorporated business owned by two or more individuals.

Patent: Exclusive legal rights granted to an inventor for a period of 17 years.

Payables (trade): Short-term obligations created by the acquisition of goods and services, such as accounts payable, wages payable, and taxes payable.

Payee: The party that will receive the money from a promissory note at some future date.

Pension Benefit Guaranty Corporation: A U.S. government agency that insures the pension benefits of workers.

Pension fund: A fund established through contributions from an employer and sometimes from employees that pays pension benefits to employees after retirement.

Pension plan: An arrangement whereby an employer provides benefits (payments) to employees after they retire for services they provided while they were working.

Pension plan—contributory: A pension plan where the employees bear part of the cost of the stated benefits or voluntarily make payments to increase their benefits.

Pension plan—funded: A pension plan where the employer sets funds aside for future pension benefits by making payments to a funding agency that is responsible for accumulating the assets of the pension fund and for making payments to the recipients as the benefits become due.

Pension plan—noncontributory: A pension plan in which the employer bears the entire cost.

Pension plan—qualified: A pension plan in accord with federal income tax requirements that permit deductibility of the employer's contributions to the pension fund and tax-free status of earnings from pension fund assets.

Percentage-of-completion method: A revenue recognition method which recognizes profit each period during the life of the contract in proportion to the amount of the contract completed during the period.

Period cost: Cost that is recognized as an expense during the period in which it is incurred.

Periodic inventory method: A method of accounting for inventory that determines inventory at the end of the period.

Permanent accounts: All balance sheet accounts.

Permanent differences: Nondeductible expenses or nontaxable revenues that are recognized for financial reporting purposes but that are never part of taxable income.

Perpetual inventory method: A method of accounting for inventory that records continuously the sales and purchases of individual items of inventory.

Personal financial statements: Financial statements of individuals, husband and wife, or a larger family group.

Petty cash (fund): Small quantity of funds kept on hand for incidental expenditures requiring quick cash.

Pledging: Using assets as collateral for a bank loan.

Pooling of interest: A method of accounting for a business combination that combines all asset, liability, and stockholders' equity accounts.

Post-balance sheet event: Event occurring between the balance sheet date and the date financial statements are issued and made available to external users (also called subsequent event).

Posting: Transcribing the amounts from journal entries into the general ledger.

Postretirement benefits other than pensions: Benefits other than pensions that accrue to employees upon retirement, such as medical insurance and life insurance contracts.

Predictive value: Helps a decision maker predict future consequences based on information about past transactions and events.

Preferred stock: Stock that has some preference over common stock.

Premium: An amount paid in excess of the face value of a security (stock or bond).

Prepaid: An expenditure made in advance of the use of the service or goods.

Present value consideration: The characteristic that money to be received or paid out in the future is not worth as much as money available today. Accountants consider the time value of money when preparing the financial statements for such areas as long-term leases, pensions, and other long-term situations where the future payments or receipts are not indicative of the present value of the asset or the obligation.

Present value factor: Using multiplication, converts a future value to its present value.

Present value of an annuity: The amount at a present time that is equivalent to a series of payments and interest in the future.

Primary earnings per share: Net income applicable to common stock divided by the sum of the weighted-average common stock and common stock equivalents.

Principal: The original or base amount of a loan or investment.

Prior-period adjustments: Reported as restatements of retained earnings. They include corrections of errors of prior periods, a change in accounting entity, certain changes in accounting principles, and adjustments that result from the realization of income tax benefits of preacquisition operating loss carryforwards of purchased subsidiaries.

Prior service cost: When a defined pension plan is adopted or amended, credit is often given to employees for years of service provided before the date of adoption or amendment. The cost of taking on this added commitment is called the prior service cost.

Privatization: The sale of all or part of a previously government-controlled entity to the general public.

Pro forma amount: Hypothetical or projected amount. Synonymous with "what if" analyses. Pro forma statements indicate what would have happened under specified circumstances.

Productive-output depreciation: A depreciation method in which the depreciable cost is divided by the total estimated output to determine the depreciation rate per unit of output.

Profitability: The relative success of a company's operations.

Projected benefit obligation (PBO): The present value of pension benefits earned to date based on past service and an estimate of future compensation levels for pay-related plans.

Promissory note: A formal written promise to pay a certain amount of money at a specified future date.

Property dividend: A dividend in a form of an asset other than cash.

Property, plant, and equipment: Tangible assets of a long-term nature used in the continuing operation of the business.

Proportionate consolidation: A method of consolidating the financial results of a parent company and its subsidiary in which only the proportion of net assets owned by the parent are consolidated.

Proprietary funds (governmental accounting): Funds used to report assets held in a trustee or agency capacity for others.

Proprietorship: A business owned by one person. The owner and business are not separate legal entities but are separate accounting entities.

Prospectus: A document describing the nature of a business and its recent financial history.

Proxy: A legal document granting another party the right to vote for a shareholder on matters involving a shareholder vote.

Proxy statement: Information provided in a formal written form to shareholders prior to a company's regular annual meeting.

Public company: A company whose voting shares are listed for trading on a recognized securities exchange or are otherwise available for purchase by public investors.

Public Company Accounting Oversight Board (PCAOB): The PCAOB is a regulatory body created by the Sarbanes-Oxley Act of 2002. It regulates audits of SEC registrants. The PCAOB operates under the U.S. Securities and Exchange Commission. It has the authority for registration, inspection, and discipline of firms auditing SEC registrants and sets standards for public company audits (http://www.pcaobus.org).

Purchase accounting: The assets and liabilities of an acquired company accounted for on the books of the acquiring company at their relative fair market values to the acquiring company at the date of acquisition.

Put option: Contract giving the owner the right, but not the obligation, to sell an asset at a specified price.

Q

Qualified opinion: An audit opinion rendered under circumstances of one or more material scope restrictions or departures from GAAP.

Qualitative characteristics: Standards for judging the information accountants provide to decision makers; the primary criteria are relevance and reliability.

Quarterly statements: Interim financial statements on a quarterly basis.

Quasi-reorganization: An accounting procedure equivalent to an accounting fresh start. A company with a deficit balance in retained earnings "starts over" with a zero balance rather than a deficit. A quasi-reorganization may also include a restatement of the carrying values of assets and liabilities to reflect current values.

R

Ratio analysis: A comparison of relationships among account balances.

Raw materials: Goods purchased for direct use in manufacturing that become part of the product.

Real accounts: The name given to balance sheet accounts because they are permanent and are not closed at the end of the period.

Realization (revenue recognition): A concept that generally recognizes revenue when (1) the earning process is virtually complete and (2) the exchange value can be objectively determined.

Receivables: Claims arising from the selling of merchandise or services on account to customers are referred to as trade receivables. Other claims may be from sources such as loans to employees or a federal tax refund.

Recognition: Recording a transaction on the accounting records.

Recourse: The right of one company to collect money from another company in the event that a third party fails to pay its obligation to the first company.

Redeemable preferred stock: Preferred stock subject to mandatory redemption requirements, or with a redemption feature that is outside the control of the issuer.

Registrar: An independent agent that maintains a record of the number of a company's shares of capital stock that have been issued and to whom.

Relevance: Qualitative characteristic requiring that accounting information bear directly on the economic decision for which it is to be used; one of the primary qualitative characteristics of accounting information.

Reliability: Qualitative characteristic requiring that accounting information be faithful to the original data and that it be neutral and verifiable; one of the primary qualitative characteristics of accounting information.

Repairs: Expenditures made to restore assets to good operating condition upon their breakdown or to restore and replace broken parts.

Replacement cost: The cost to reproduce or replace an asset.

Report form of balance sheet: A balance sheet presentation which presents assets, liabilities, and stockholders' equity in a vertical format.

Reporting currency: The currency used to measure and report.

Representational faithfulness: The agreement of information with what it is supposed to represent.

Research and Development (R&D): Funds spent to improve existing products and develop new ones.

Reserves: Accounts classified under liabilities resulting from an expense to the income statement and an equal increase in the reserve account on the balance sheet. These reserve accounts do not represent definite commitments to pay out funds in the future, but they do represent an estimate of funds that will be paid out in the future.

Residual value (salvage value): The estimated net scrap or trade-in value of a tangible asset at the date of disposal.

Restrictive covenants: Limitations imposed by a creditor on a debtor's actions. Covenants are often based on accounting measurements of assets, liabilities, and/or income.

Restructure: The term used to describe corporate downsizing and refocus of operations.

Retail inventory method: An inventory method that converts the retail value of inventory to an estimated cost.

Retained earnings: The undistributed earnings of a corporation consisting of the net income for all past periods minus the dividends that have been declared.

Retained earnings restricted: The amount of retained earnings that has been restricted for specific purposes.

Retroactively: The method of accounting for accounting principle changes whereby past years' financial statements are restated to reflect the use of the new method.

Revenue recognition: A basic accounting concept that is applied to determine when revenue should be recognized (recorded). Generally, under this principle, revenues are recognized when two criteria are met; the earnings process is substantially complete, and the revenues are realized, or realizable.

Revenues: Inflows or other enhancements of assets of an entity or settlements of its liabilities (or a combination of both) from delivering or producing goods, rendering services, or other activities that constitute the entity's ongoing major or central operations.

Risk: The uncertainty surrounding estimates of future cash flows.

Royalties: Payment for a right over some natural resource or payment to an author or composer.

S

Sale and leaseback: Sale of an asset with the purchaser concurrently leasing the asset to the seller.

Sales discounts: Contra-revenue account used to record discounts given customers for early payment of their accounts.

Sales or revenues: Income from the sale of goods or services and lease or royalty payments.

Sales returns and allowances: Contra-revenue account used to record both refunds to customers and reduction of their accounts.

Sales-type lease: A capital lease that generates two income streams. One from the sale of the asset and a second from the financing of the asset.

Salvage value (residual value): The estimated net scrap or trade-in value of a tangible asset at the date of disposal.

Scope paragraph: That paragraph of the audit report that tells what the auditor did. Specifically, it states whether or not the audit was conducted in accordance with GAAS.

SEC EDGAR database: Contains electronic copies of SEC filings by publicly traded companies (http://www.edgar-online.com and http://www.tenkwizard.com).

Secured bonds: Bonds for which assets are pledged to guarantee repayment.

Secured loan: A loan backed by certain assets as collateral.

Securities Act of 1933: A federal statute governing the registration of new securities issues traded in interstate commerce.

Securities Act of 1934: A federal statute establishing recurring reporting requirements for public companies once their securities have been registered with the SEC.

Securities and Exchange Commission (SEC): An agency of the federal government that has the legal power to set and enforce accounting practices (http://www.sec.gov).

Segment reporting (product segment information): When operations are diversified, the firm may report results on a segmented basis.

Self insurance: A coverage borne by the person or company itself against the risk of loss that may occur if property is destroyed or damaged from some cause.

Selling expenses: Result from the company's effort to create sales.

Senior debt: Debt obligations that would have a prior claim over junior debt and equity holders on the assets of a company in liquidation.

Serial bonds: Bonds that do not all have the same due date; a portion of the bonds comes due each time period.

Service cost: A component of net periodic pension expense representing the actuarial present value of benefits accruing to employees for services rendered during that period.

Service lives: Working years of employees prior to retirement, as used in accounting for postretirement benefit obligations.

Short-term debt: Represents money payable by the debtor to the creditor within one year.

Shrinkage: The amount of inventory that is lost, stolen, or spoiled.

Simple capital structure: A corporate structure that includes only common and noncovertible preferred stock and has no convertible securities, stock options, warrants, or other rights outstanding.

Simple interest: Interest computed on the principal amount only.

Single-employer pension plans: Pension plans established for a single employer.

Single-step income statement: Form of the income statement that arrives at net income in a single step.

Sinking fund: An accumulation of cash or securities in a special fund dedicated to paying, or redeeming, an issue of bonds or preferred stock.

Social accounting: Attempts to account for the benefits to the social environment within which the firm operates.

Sole proprietorship: A business with a single owner.

Solvency: The ability of a company to remain in business over the long term.

Special journal: An accounting record used to list a particular type of frequently recurring transaction.

Specific identification (inventory): Identifies the items in inventory as coming from specific purchases.

Staff Accounting Bulletin (SAB): Accounting interpretations made by the staff of the SEC. SABs do not necessarily represent official positions of the SEC.

Stakeholders: All parties interested in the performance of a company.

Standard audit report: The form of audit report recommended by the Auditing Standards Board of the AICPA. This report is rendered at the conclusion of an audit in which the auditor encountered no material scope limitations, and the financial statements conform to GAAP in all material respects.

Stated (contract) rate: The rate of interest printed on the bond.

Stated value: A value assigned by the board of directors to no-par stock.

Statement of cash flows: Provides detailed information on cash flows resulting from operating, investing, and financing activities.

Statement of owners' equity (statement of shareholders' equity): An accounting statement describing transactions affecting the owners' equity.

Statement of retained earnings: A summary of the changes to retained earnings for an accounting period.

Statements of Financial Accounting Concepts (SFACs): Issued by the Financial Accounting Standards Board and provide the Board with a common foundation and basic reasons for considering the merits of various alternative accounting principles.

Statements of Financial Accounting Standards (SFASs): These statements establish generally accepted accounting principles (GAAP) for specific accounting issues.

Statements of Position (SOPs): Issued by the Accounting Standards Division of the AICPA to influence the development of accounting standards.

Stock appreciation rights: Give the holder the right to receive compensation at some future date based on the market price of the stock at the date of exercise over a pre-established price.

Stock certificate: A document issued to a stockholder indicating the number of shares of stock owned.

Stock dividend: A dividend in the form of additional shares of a company's stock.

Stock options: Allow the holder to purchase a company's stock at favorable terms.

Stock rights: Rights issued to existing shareholders to buy shares of stock in order to maintain their proportionate ownership interests.

Stock split: Increase in the number of shares of a class of capital stock, with no change in the total dollar amount of the class, but with a converse reduction in the par or stated value of the shares.

Stockholder (shareholder): The owner of one or more shares of stock in an incorporated business.

Stockholders' (shareholders') equity: Total owners' equity of a corporation.

Straight-line amortization of bonds: Writes off an equal amount of bond premium or discount each period.

Straight-line method: A method of depreciation that allocates the cost of a tangible asset in a constant over the life of the asset.

Subordinated debt: A form of long-term debt which is "junior," or in a secondary position vis-à-vis the claim on a company's assets for the payment of its other debt obligations.

Subscription: A contract between the purchaser of stock and the issuer in which the purchaser promises to buy shares of the issuing company's stock.

Subsequent events: Events that occur after the balance sheet date, but before the statements are issued.

Subsidiary: An entity economically controlled by another company, despite its independent legal status.

Subsidiary account: One of the accounts in a particular subsidiary ledger.

Subsidiary ledger: Provides detailed information regarding a particular general ledger account.

Successful-efforts method: The method of accounting which capitalizes only the costs that result in the discovery of oil and gas reserves.

Sum-of-the-years'-digits method: This method of depreciation takes a fraction each year times the cost less salvage value. The numerator of the fraction is the remaining number of years of life. The denominator remains constant and is the sum of the digits of the years of life.

Summary annual report: A simplified annual report in which data required by the SEC is supplied in the proxy statement and the Form 10-K.

Summary of significant accounting policies: A description of all significant accounting policies of the company. An integral part of the financial statements, this information is typically presented as the first footnote.

Supplies: Items used indirectly in the production of goods or services.

T

T-account: A form of ledger page used to record (or illustrate) the entry of debits and credits into ledger accounts.

Take-or-pay contract: An executory contract by which one party agrees to pay for the product regardless of whether the product is physically received or not.

Tangible assets: The physical facilities used in the operation of the business.

Tax benefit: A reduction in taxes, or a tax credit or refund, due to a particular action or expense incurred by a taxable entity.

Taxable income: Income determined in accordance with income tax regulation.

Taxes payable: Represents unpaid taxes that are owed to a governmental unit.

Technical analysis: A method of predicting stock prices based on historical price and trading patterns.

Temporal method of translation: A method of translating foreign financial statements in which cash, receivables, and payables are translated at the exchange rate in effect at the balance sheet date. Other assets and liabilities are translated at historical rates while revenues and expenses are translated at the weighted average rate for the period.

Temporary accounts: Accounts closed at the end of an accounting period: includes all income statement accounts and the dividends account.

Temporary differences: Revenue and expense recognized in one period for financial reporting but recognized in an earlier or later period for income tax purposes.

10-K Report: Mandatory report filed by a company on an annual basis with the Securities and Exchange Commission.

10-Q Report: Mandatory report filed by a company on a quarterly basis with the Securities and Exchange Commission.

Term bonds: Bonds that mature in one lump sum at a specified future date.

Time period: Assumes that the entity can be accounted for with reasonable accuracy for a particular period of time.

Time value of money: The concept that money earns interest over time. This implies that a dollar to be received a year from now is worth less than a dollar received today.

Timeliness: The qualitative characteristic indicating that accounting information should reach the user in time to help in making a decision.

Trademarks: Rights to use distinctive names or symbols granted to the holder for 28 years with option for renewal.

Trading on equity: Financial leverage, or the use of borrowed funds, particularly long-term debt, in the capital structure of a firm.

Trading securities: Securities held by firms for brief periods of time that are intended to generate profits from short-term differences in price.

Transaction approach: The recording of events that affect the financial position of the entity and that can be reasonably determined in monetary terms.

Translation adjustments (foreign currency translation adjustment): An account classified under stockholders' equity that represents foreign currency translation gains and losses that have not been charged to the income statement.

Translation gains and losses: Gains and losses due to fluctuations in exchange rates.

Treadway Commission: Popular name for the National Commission on Fraudulent Reporting that has issued a number of recommendations for the prevention of fraud in financial reports, ethics, and effective internal controls.

Treasurer: The officer responsible in a firm for the safeguarding and efficient use of a company's liquid assets.

Treasury stock: Capital stock of a company, either common or preferred, that has been issued and reacquired by the issuing company but has not been reissued or retired. It reduces stockholders' equity.

Trend analysis: Analysis over more than one accounting period to identify the trend of a company's results.

Trial balance: A listing of all general ledger accounts and their balances for the purpose of verifying that total debits equal total credits.

Troubled debt restructuring: A concession by creditors to allow debtors to eliminate or modify debt obligations.

U

Unappropriated retained earnings: The unrestricted retained earnings.

Unaudited: A term applied to information in the annual or quarterly reports, which is outside the audit conducted by the auditors.

Unconsolidated subsidiaries: Subsidiaries whose financial statements are not combined with the parent company.

Understandability: A user-specific quality directing that accounting information be understandable to users who have a reasonable knowledge of business and economic activities and who are willing to study the information with reasonable diligence.

Unearned income: A liability, either current or long-term, for income received prior to the delivery of goods or the rendering of services (also described as deferred income).

Unexpended industrial revenue bond proceeds: An asset account, classified under other assets, representing funds that have not yet been used for the purpose indicated when the bonds were issued.

Unit-of-production method: Relates depreciation to the output capacity of the asset, estimated for the life of the asset.

Unlimited liability: Each partner is liable for all partnership debts. Limited partners in a limited partnership, which is allowed in some states, do not have unlimited liability.

Unlisted securities: Securities which are not listed on an organized stock exchange.

Unqualified opinion: An audit opinion not qualified for any material scope restrictions or departures from GAAP.

Unrealized decline in market value of noncurrent equity investments: A stockholders' equity account that results from adjusting long-term equity securities to the lower of cost or market value.

Unrealized (gain) loss: A (gain) loss recognized in the financial statements but not associated with an asset sale.

Unsecured (debenture) bonds: Bonds for which no specific collateral has been pledged.

Unusual or infrequent item: Certain income statement items that are unusual or occur infrequently, but not both.

Useful life: Length of time over which a long-term asset is forecasted to provide economic benefits.

V

Valuation: A process of estimating the value of a firm or some component of a firm.

Venture capital: Funding by investment firms that specialize in financing unproven but potentially profitable businesses.

Verifiability: The qualitative characteristic indicating that accounting information can be confirmed or duplicated by independent parties using the same measurement technique.

Vertical analysis: A comparison of various financial statement items within a single period with the use of common-size statements.

Vertical integration: The combination of firms with operations in different but successive stages of production and/or distribution.

Vested benefit obligation (VBO): The portion of the pension benefit obligation that does not depend on future employee service.

Vesting: The accrual to an employee of pension rights, arising from employer contributions, not contingent upon the employee's continuing service with the employer.

W

Warrant: A security that gives the holder the right to purchase shares of common stock in accordance with the terms of the instrument, usually upon payment of a specified amount.

Warranties: Obligations of a company to provide free service on units failing to perform satisfactorily or to replace defective goods.

Warranty obligations: Estimated obligations arising out of product warranties.

Weighted average cost method: An inventory costing method that assigns the same unit cost to all units available for sale during the period.

Weighted average of outstanding common stock: Gives the proportional shares outstanding in their fraction of the fiscal year.

Work in process: Goods started, but not ready for sale.

Working capital: The excess of current assets over current liabilities.

Write-off: A write-off recognizes that the asset no longer has any value to the firm.

Z

Zero coupon bond: A bond that does not pay periodic interest, but promises to pay a fixed amount at the maturity date.

Z-score: Statistically derived combination of weighted ratios to predict the likelihood of bankruptcy.

Bibliography

1. Introduction to Financial Reporting

Aier, Jagadison K., Joseph Comprix, Matthew T. Gunlock, and Deanna Lee. "The Financial Expertise of CFOs and Accounting Restatements," *Accounting Horizons* (September 2005), 123–135.

Ashbaugh, H., R. LaFond, and B. W. Mayhew. "Do Nonaudit Services Compromise Auditor Independence? Further Evidence," *The Accounting Review* (78: 2003), 611–639.

Ashbaugh, Holles, Karia M. Johnstone, and Terry D. Warfield. "Corporate Reporting on the Internet," *Accounting Horizons* (September 1999), 241–257.

Bannister, James W. and Harry A. Newman. "Analysis of Corporate Disclosures on Relative Performance Evaluation," *Accounting Horizons* (September 2003), 235–246.

Beresford, D. R. "The Balancing Act in Setting Accounting Standards," *Accounting Horizons* (March 1988), 1–7.

Beresford, Dennis. "How to Succeed as a Standard Setter by Trying Really Hard," *Accounting Horizons* (September 1997), 79–90.

Bierman, Harold. "Extending the Usefulness of Accrual Accounting," *Accounting Horizons* (September 1988), 10–14.

Brody, Richard G., D. Jordan Lowe, and Kurt Pany. "Could $51 Million Be Immaterial When Enron Reports Income of $10.5 Million?" *Accounting Horizons* (June 2003), 153–160.

Carpenter, Tina D., M. G. Fennema, Phillip Z. Fretwell, and William Hillson. "A Changing Corporate Culture," *Journal of Accountancy* (March 2004), 57–61.

Chen, Shimin, Zzheng Sun, and Yuetang Wang. "Evidence from China on Whether Harmonized Accounting Standards Harmonize Accounting Practices," *Accounting Horizons* (September 2002), 183–197.

Cheney, Glen. "Differential Problems & Possibilities," *Financial Executive* (March/April 2004), 20–22.

Cotter, J. and I. Zimmer. "Disclosure Versus Recognition: The Case of Asset Revaluations," *Asia Pacific Journal of Accounting and Economics* (June 2003), 81–99.

Ge, Weili and Sarah McVay. "The Disclosure of Material Weaknesses in Internal Control After the Sarbanes-Oxley Act," *Accounting Horizons* (September 2005), 137–158.

Geiger, M. A., Raghunandan, and D. V. Rama. "Costs Associated with Going-Concern Modified Audit Opinions. An Analysis of Auditor Changes, Subsequent Opinions, and Client Failures," *Advances in Accounting* (16: 1998), 117–139.

Geiger, Marshall A. and K. Raghunandan. "Going-Concern Opinions in the New Legal Environment," *Accounting Horizons* (March 2002), 17–26.

Geiger, Marshall A. and Dasaratha V. Rama. "Audit Firm Size and Going-Concern Reporting Accuracy," *Accounting Horizons* (March 2006), 1–17.

Geiger, Marshall A. and Porcher L. Taylor III. "CEO and CFO Certifications of Financial Information," *Accounting Horizons* (December 2003), 357–368.

Gerboth, Dale L. "The Conceptual Framework: Not Definitions, But Professional Values," *Accounting Horizons* (September 1987), 1–8.

Goldwasser, D. L. "Independence in a Changing Accounting Profession: Is it Possible to Achieve?" *The CPA Journal* (October 1999), 46–51.

Grady, Robert E. "The Sarbox Monster," *The Wall Street Journal* (April 26, 2007), A29.

Hirshleifer, D., S. Lim, and S. Teoh. "Limited Attention, Information Disclosure, and Financial Reporting," *Journal of Accounting and Economics* (36: 2003), 332–386.

Holder-Webb, Lora M. and Michael S. Wilkins. "The Incremental Information Content of SAS No. 559 Going-Concern Opinions," *Journal of Accounting Research* (Spring 2000), 209–219.

James, Kevin L. "The Effects of Internal Audit Structure on Perceived Financial Statement Fraud Prevention," (December 2003), 315–327.

Kahn, Jeremy. "Accounting's White Knight," *Fortune* (September 30, 2002), 117, 118, 120, 122.

Klein, April. "Likely Effects of Stock Exchange Governance Proposals and Sarbanes-Oxley on Corporate Boards and Financial Reporting," *Accounting Horizons* (December 2003), 343–355.

Koeppen, David R. "Using the FASB's Conceptual Framework: Fitting the Pieces Together," *Accounting Horizons* (June 1988), 18–26.

Levitt, A. "The Importance of High Quality Accounting Standards," *Accounting Horizons* (March 1998), 79–82.

Lobo, Gerald J. and Jian Zhou. "Did Conservatism in Financial Reporting Increase After the Sarbanes-Oxley Act? Initial Evidence," *Accounting Review* (March 2006), 57–73.

Martin, Alyssa. "How Section 404 Can Help Deter Fraud," *Financial Executive* (May 2005), 45–47.

McEwen, Ruth Ann, Thomas J. Joey, and John A. Brozousky. "The FASB's Codification Project: A Critical Step Toward Simplification," *Accounting Horizons* (December 2006), 391–398.

Mercer, Molly. "How Do Investors Assess the Credibility of Management Disclosures?" *Accounting Horizons* (September 2004), 185–196.

Nelson, M. "Behavioral Evidence on the Effects of Principles and Rules Bases Standards," *Accounting Horizons* (March 2003), 91–104.

Nobes, Christopher W. "Rules-Based Standards and the Lack of Principles in Accounting," *Accounting Horizons* (March 2005), 25–34.

Nogler, G. "The Resolution of Auditor Going-Concern Opinions," *Auditing: A Journal of Practice & Theory* (Fall 1995), 54–73.

Parfet, W. V. "Accounting Subjectivity and Earnings Management: A Prepared Perspective," *Accounting Horizons* (December 2000), 481–488.

Ramos, Michael. "Section 404 Compliance in the Annual Report," *Journal of Accountancy* (October 2004), 43–48.

Reed, Ronald O., William M. Sinnett, Thomas Buchman, and Richard Wobbekind. "Should Private Companies Implement Sarbanes-Oxley?" *Financial Executive* (April 2005), 54–57.

Reilly, David. "What's Better in Accounting, Rules or 'Feel'?" *The Wall Street Journal* (April 30, 2007), C1–2.

Reither, Cheri L. "How the FASB Approaches a Standard-Setting Issue," *Accounting Horizons* (December 1997), 91–104.

Rogero, L. H. "Characteristics of High Quality Accounting Standards," *Accounting Horizons* (June 1998), 177–183.

Shafer, W. E., R. E. Morris, and A. A. Ketchand. "The Effects of Formal Sanctions on Auditor Independence," *Auditing: A Journal of Practice & Theory* (Supplement 1999), 85–101.

Sinnett, William M. and Ellen M. Heffes. "Section 404 Implementation: Is the Gain Worth the Pain?" *Financial Executive* (May 2005), 30–32.

Special Report. "The Case for Private Company GAAP," *Journal of Accountancy* (May 2005), 27–29.

Stamp, Edward. "Why Can Accounting Not Become a Science Like Physics?" *Abacus* (Spring 1981), 13–27.

Sutton, Michael H. "Financial Reporting in U.S. Capital Markets: International Dimensions," *Accounting Horizons* (June 1997), 96–102.

Vorhies, James Brady. "The New Importance of Materiality," *Journal of Accountancy* (May 2005), 53–59.

Watts, Ross L. "Conservatism in Accounting Part I: Expla-nations and Implications," *Accounting Horizons* (September 2003), 207–221.

Watts, Ross L. "Conservationism in Accounting Part II: Evidence and Research Opportunities," *Accounting Horizons* (December 2003), 287–301.

Wyatt, Arthur. "Accounting Standards: Conceptual or Political?" *Accounting Horizons* (September 1990), 83–88.

Wyatt, Arthur R. "Accounting Professionalism—They Just Don't Get It!" *Accounting Horizons* (March 2004), 45–53.

Zeff, Stephen A. "How the U.S. Accounting Profession Got Where it is Today: Part I," *Accounting Horizons* (September 2003), 189–205.

Zeff, Stephen A. "How the U.S. Accounting Profession Got Where it is Today: Part II," *Accounting Horizons* (December 2003), 267–286.

2.   Introduction to Financial Statements and Other Financial Reporting Topics

Adhikari, Ajay and Shawn Z. Wang. "Accounting for China," *Management Accounting* (April 1995), 27–32.

Ali, Ashiq and Lee-Seok Hwang. "Country-Specific Factors Related to Financial Reporting and the Value Relevance of Accounting Data," *Journal of Accounting Research* (Spring 2000), 1–22.

Atkins, Paul S. "Is Excessive Regulation and Litigation Eroding U.S. Financial Competitiveness?" Remarks by SEC Commissioner, Conference Co-Sponsored by the American Enterprise Institute and the Brookings Institution, Washington, D.C. (April 20, 2007), http://www.sec.gov/ news/speech.

Badal, Jaclyne and Phred Dvorak. "Sarbanes-Oxley Gains Adherents," *The Wall Street Journal* (August 14, 2006), B3.

Bauer, Christopher. "A Preventative Maintenance Approach to Ethics," *Financial Executive* (May 2005), 18–20.

Benston, Gi and A. Hartgraves. "Enron: What Happened and What We Can Learn From It," *Journal of Accounting and Public Policy* (August 2002), 105–127.

Bruns, William J. and Kenneth A. Merchant. "The Dangerous Morality of Managing Earnings," *Management Accounting* (August 1990), 22–25.

Campos, Roel C. "SEC Regulation Outside the United States," Remarks by SEC Commissioner Before the Governance for Owners Conference in London, England (March 8, 2007), http://www.sec.gov/news/speech/2007.

Carbridge, Curtis, Walter W. Austin, and David J. Lemak. "Germany's Accrual Accounting Practices," *Management Accounting* (August 1993), 45–47.

Cheney, Glenn A. "If IFRS Offer the Answer, They Sure Raise a Lot of Questions," *Financial Executive* (November 2007), 21–23.

Cheney, Glenn A. "Soviet-American Financial Coexistence," *Journal of Accountancy* (January 1990), 68–72.

Choi, Frederick D. "A Cluster Approach to Accounting Harmonization," *Management Accounting* (August 1981), 27–31.

Collett, Peter H., Jayne M. Godfrey, and Sue L. Hrasky. "International Harmonization: Cautions from the Australian Experience," *Accounting Horizons* (June 2001), 171–182.

Cook, J. Michael and Michael H. Sutton. "Summary Annual Reporting: A Cure For Information Overload," *Financial Executive* (January/February 1995), 12–15.

Copeland, Jr., James E. "Ethics as an Imperative," *Accounting Horizons* (March 2005), 35–43.

Cox, Christopher. "Chairman's Address to the SEC Roundtable on International Financial Reporting Standards," (March 6, 2007), http://www.sec.gov/news.

Cox, Christopher. "Securing America's Competitiveness," Remarks by the SEC Chairman to the U.S. Chamber of Commerce (March 14, 2007), http://www.sec.gov/news.

Davidson, Ronald A., Alexander M. G. Gelardi, and Fangyve Li. "Analysis of the Conceptual Framework of China's New Account-ing System," *Journal of Accountancy* (March 1996), 58–74.

DeFond, M., K. Raghunandan, and K. Jubramanyam. "Do Non-Audit Service Fees Impair Auditor Independence? Evidence from Going Concern Audit Opinions," *Journal of Accounting Research* (September 2002), 1247–1274.

deMesa Graziano, Cheryl and William M. Sinnett. "How Low Can Sarbanes-Oxley Section 404 Costs Go?" *Financial Executive* (July/August 2007), 61–63.

Duska, Ronald F. and Brenda Shay Duska. "Accounting Ethics," (Cambridge, MA: Blackwell, 2003).

Dye, Ronald A. and Shyam Sunder. "Why Not Allow FASB and IASB Standards to Compete in the U.S.?" *Accounting Horizons* (September 2001), 257–271.

Epstein, Marc J. and Moses L. Pava. "Profile of an Annual Report," *Financial Executive* (January/February 1994), 41–43.

Erickson, Merle, Brian W. Mayhew, and William L. Felix, Jr. "Why Do Audits Fail? Evidence from Lincoln Savings and Loan," *Journal of Accounting Research* (Spring 2000), 165–194.

Firth, Michael. "Auditor-Provided Consultancy Services and Their Associations with Audit Fees and Audit Opinions," *Journal of Business Finance & Accounting* (June/July 2002), 661–694.

Frankel, R., M. Johnson, and K. Nelson. "The Relation Between Auditor's Fees for Non-Audit Services and Earnings Quality," *The Accounting Review* (77 Supplement 2002), 71–105.

Gannon, D. J. and Alex Ashwal. "Financial Reporting Goes Global," *Journal of Accountancy* (September 2004), 43–47.

Gibson, A. M. and A. H. Frakes. "Truth or Consequences: A Study of Critical Issues and Decision Making in Accounting," *Journal of Business Ethics* (16 (2) 1997), 161–171.

Gill, M. Lawrence. "IFRS: Coming to America," *Journal of Accountancy* (June 2007), 70–71.

Graham, Roger C., Raymond D. King, and Cameron K. J. Merrill. "Decision Usefulness of Alternative Joint Venture Reporting Methods," *Accounting Horizons* (June 2003), 123–137.

Grant, C. Terry, Chaunsey M. Deproe, Jr., and Gerry H. Grant. "Earnings Management and the Abuse of Materiality," *Journal of Accountancy* (September 2000), 41–44.

Hartgraves, Al L. and George J. Benston. "The Evolving Accounting Standards for Special Purpose Entities and Consolidations," *Accounting Horizons* (September 2002), 245–258.

Heffes, Ellen M. and Cheryl deMesa Graziano. "Accounting Without Borders: Has Its Time Come," *Financial Executive* (September 2007), 22–26.

Heiman, V. "Auditors' Assessments of the Likelihood of Analytical Review Explanations," *The Accounting Review* (65: 1990), 875–890.

Heiman-Hoffman, V. B., K. P. Morgan, and J. M. Patton. "The Warning Signs of Fraudulent Financial Reporting," *Journal of Accountancy* (October 1996), 75–77.

Herrmann, Don and Ian P. N. Hague. "Convergence: In Search of the Best," *Journal of Accountancy* (January 2006), 69–73.

Hitlebeitel, K. M. and S. K. Jones. "Initial Evidence on the Impact of Integrating Ethics into Accounting Education," *Issues in Accounting Education* (6: 1991), 262–275.

Huss, H. Fenwick and Denise M. Palterson. "Ethics in Accounting: Values Education Without Indoctrination," *Journal of Business Ethics* (March 1993), 235–243.

Ingberman, M. and G. H. Sorter. "The Role of Financial Statements in an Efficient Market," *Journal of Accounting, Auditing, and Finance* (Fall 1978), 58–62.

Kinney, W. R. and R. D. Martin. "Does Auditing Reduce Bias in Financial Reporting? A Review of Audit-Related Adjustments Studies," *Auditing: A Journal of Practice & Theory* (13 (1) 1994), 149–156.

Krall, Karen M. "More Talk, More Action," *Journal of Accountancy* (May 2005), 67–70; 72–74.

Lee, Charles and Dale Morse. "Summary Annual Reports," *Accounting Horizons* (March 1990), 39–50.

Lowe, Herman J. "Ethics In Our 100-Year History," *Journal of Accountancy* (May 1987), 78–87.

McEnroe, John E. and Stanley C. Martens. "Auditors' and Investors' Perceptions of the Expectation Gap," *Accounting Horizons* (December 2001), 345–358.

McKinnon, John D. "U.S., EU to Streamline Accounting," *The Wall Street Journal* (May 1, 2007), A8.

Meiers, Donald H. "The MD&A Challenge," *Journal of Accountancy* (January 2006), 59–60, 62, 64, 66.

Millman, Gregory J. "New Scandals, Old Lessons: Financial Ethics After Enron," *Financial Executive* (July/August 2002), 16–19.

Nagy, Albert L. "Mandatory Audit Firm Turnover, Financial Reporting Quality, and Client Bargaining Power: The Case of Arthur Anderson," *Accounting Horizons* (June 2005), 51–68.

Nair, R. D. and Larry E. Rittenberg. "Summary Annual Reports: Background and Implications for Financial Reporting and Auditing," *Accounting Horizons* (March 1990), 25–38.

Orenstein, Edith. "Ask FERF About . . . International Standard-Setting Organizations," *Financial Executive* (March 2005), 64.

Pacter, Paul. "Should U.S. Private Companies Use IFRS for SMEs?" *Financial Executive* (October 2007), 16–17.

Perera, M. H. "Towards a Framework to Analyzing the Impact of Culture on Accounting," *International Journal of Accounting* (1989), 42–56.

Ponemon, L. and A. Glazer. "Accounting Education and Ethical Development; The Influence of Liberal Learning on Students and Alumni in Accounting Practice," *Issues in Accounting Education* (5: 1990), 195–208.

Price, Jennifer Tisone. "A Brave New World: The Future of Audit Standards," *Catalyst* (September/October 2003), 8–10.

Raghununandan, K., William J. Read, and J. Scott Whisenant. "Initial Evidence on the Association Between Nonaudit Fees and Restated Financial Statements," *Accounting Horizons* (September 2003), 223–224.

Rama, Dasaratha V. and William J. Read. "Resignations by the Big 4 and the Market for Audit Services," *Accounting Horizons* (June 2006), 97–109.

Reilly, David. "What's Better in Accounting, Rules or 'Feel'," *The Wall Street Journal* (April 30, 2007), C1–2.

Rich, Anne J. "Understanding Global Standards," *Management Accounting* (April 1995), 51–54.

Sainty, Barbara J., Gary K. Taylor, and David D. Williams. "Investor Dissatisfaction Toward Auditors," *Journal of Accounting, Auditing, & Finance* (Spring 2002), 111–136.

Schroeder, Nicholas W. and Charles H. Gibson. "Are Summary Annual Reports Successful?" *Accounting Horizons* (June 1992), 28–37.

Schroeder, Nicholas W. and Charles H. Gibson. "Improving Annual Reports by Improving the Readability of Footnotes," *The Woman CPA* (April 1988), 13–16.

SEC Special Studies Archive, "Report and Recommendations Pursuant to Section 401(c) of the Sarbanes-Oxley Act of 2002 on Arrangements with Off-Balance Sheet Implications, Special Purpose Entities, and Transparency of Filings by Issuers," (June 15, 2005), http://www.sec.gov/news/studiesarchive.

Shafer, William E., D. Jordan Lowe, and Timothy J. Fogarty. "The Effects of Corporate Ownership on Public Accountants' Professionalism and Ethics," *Accounting Horizons* (June 2002), 109–124.

"Simplify Global Accounting," *Journal of Accountancy* (July 2007), 36–38.

Smith, Dr. L. Murphy. "A Fresh Look at Accounting Ethics (or Dr. Smith Goes to Washington)," *Accounting Horizons* (March 2003), 47–49.

Snyder, Lisa A. "Streamlining Ethics Enforcement," *Journal of Accountancy* (August 2003), 51–56.

U.S. Securities and Exchange Commission. "SEC Announces Next Steps Relating to International Financial Reporting Standards," (April 24, 2007), 2007-72, http://www.sec.gov/news/press.

Wallace, Wanda A. and John Walsh. "Apples-to-Apples Profits Abroad," *Financial Executives* (May/June 1995), 28–31.

Wells, Joseph T. "So That's Why It's Called A Pyramid Scheme," *Journal of Accountancy* (October 2000), 91–95.

Wells, Joseph T. "Timing Is of the Essence," *Journal of Accountancy* (May 2001), 78; 81–82; 85–87.

Wilks, T. Jeffery and Mark F. Zimbelman. "Using Game Theory and Strategic Reasoning Concepts to Prevent and Detect Fraud," *Accounting Horizons* (September 2004), 173–184.

Wyatt, Arthur R. and Joseph F. Yospe. "Wake-Up Call to U.S. Business: International Accounting Standards Are On The Way," *Journal of Accountancy* (July 1993), 80–85.

Zeff, S. "Political Lobbying on Proposed Standards: A Challenge to the IASB," *Accounting Horizons* (January 2002), 43–54.

Zeff, S. "Political Lobbying on Proposed Standards: A Challenge to the IASB," *Accounting Horizons* (March 2002), 45–54.

Zimbelman, M. F. "The Effects of SAS No. 82 on Auditor's Attention to Fraud Risk Factors and Audit Planning Decision," *Journal of Accounting Research* (Supplement 1997), 75–97.

3. Balance Sheet

Bahnam, Russ. "Valuing IP Post-Sarbanes-Oxley," *Journal of Accounting* (November 2005), 72–78.

Barron, Orie E., Donal Byard, Charles Kite, and Edward J. Riedl. "High-Technology Intangibles and Analysts Forecasts," *Journal of Accounting Research* (May 2002), 289–320.

Botosan, Christine A., Lisa Koonce, Stephen G. Ryan, Mary S. Stone, and James M. Wahlen. "Accounting for Liabilities: Conceptual Issues, Standard Setting, and Evidence from Academic Research," *Accounting Horizons* (September 2005), 159–186.

Donohue, James and Cynthia Waller Vallario. "A New Scorecard for Intellectual Property," *Journal of Accountancy* (April 2002), 75–79.

Flamholtz, Eric G., D. Gerald Searfoss, and Russell Coff. "Developing Human Resource Accounting As a Human Resource Decision Support System," *Accounting Horizons* (September 1988), 1–9.

Frischmann, Peter J., Paul D. Kimmel, and Terry D. Warfield. "Innovation in Preferred Stock: Current Developments and Implications for Financial Reporting," *Accounting Horizons* (September 1999), 201–218.

Gibson, Charles H. "Quasi-Reorganizations in Practice," *Accounting Horizons* (September 1988), 83–89.

Healy, Paul M., Stewart C. Myers, and Christopher D. Howe. "The R & D Accounting and the Tradeoff Between Relevance and Objectivity," *Journal of Accounting Research* (June 2002), 677–710.

Kim, M. and G. Moore. "Economics vs. Accounting Depreciation," *Journal of Accounting and Economics* (April 1988), 111–125.

Leu, Baruch. "Intangibles At a Crossroads: What's Next?" *Financial Executive* (March/April 2002), 34–36; 38–39.

Moehrle, Stephen R., Jennifer A. Reynolds-Moehrle, and James S. Wallace. "How Informative Are Earnings Numbers That Exclude Goodwill Amortization," *Accounting Horizons* (September 2001), 243–255.

Mueller, Jennifer M. "Amortization of Certain Intangible Assets," *Journal of Accountancy* (December 2004), 74–78.

Sanders, George, Paul Munter, and Tommy Moures. "Software-The Unrecorded Asset," *Management Accounting* (August 1994), 57–61.

4. Income Statement

Asquith, Paul, Paul Healy, and Krishna Palepu. "Earnings and Stock Splits," *The Accounting Review* (July 1989), 387–403.

Bauman, Mark P. "The Impact and Valuation of Off-Balance–Sheet Activities Concealed by Equity Method Accounting," *Accounting Horizons* (December 2003), 303–314.

Burgstahler, David, James Jiambolvo, and Terry Shevlin. "Do Stock Prices Fully Reflect the Implications of Special Items for Future Earnings?" *Journal of Accounting Research* (June 2002), 585–612.

Cheng, Q. "What Determines Residual Income?" *The Accounting Review* (January 2005), 85–112.

Davis, M. L. and J. A. Largay III. "Financial Reporting of 'Significant-Influence Equity Investments: Analysis and Managerial Issues," *Journal of Managerial Issues* (11: 1999), 280–298.

Elliott, J. A. and D. R. Philbrick. "Accounting Changes and Earnings Predictability," *The Accounting Review* (January 1990), 157–174.

Lilien, Steven, Martin Mellman, and Victor Pastena. "Accounting Changes: Successful Versus Unsuccessful Firms," *The Accounting Review* (October 1988), 642–656.

McGough, Eugene. "Anatomy of a Stock Split," *Management Accounting* (September 1993), 58–61.

Pincus, Morton and Charles Wasley. "The Incidence of Accounting Changes and Characteristics of Firms Making Accounting Changes," *Journal of Accountancy* (June 1994), 1–24.

5. Basics of Analysis

Chang, L. S., K. S. Most, and C. W. Brain. "The Utility of Annual Reports: An International Study," *Journal of International Business Studies* (Spring/Summer 1983), 63–84.

Gibson, C. H. and P. A. Boyer. "Need for Disclosure of Uniform Financial Ratios," *Journal of Accountancy* (May 1980), 78.

Wells, Joseph T. "Irrational Ratios," *Journal of Accountancy* (August 2001), 80–83.

Wittington, G. "Some Basic Properties of Accounting Ratios," *Journal of Business Finance and Accounting* (Summer 1980), 219–232.

6. Liquidity of Short-Term Assets; Related Debt-Paying Ability

Boer, Germain. "Managing the Cash GAP," *Journal of Accountancy*, (October 1999), 27–32.

Davis, H. Z., N. Kahn, and E. Rosen. "LIFO Inventory Liquidations: An Empirical Study," *Journal of Accounting Research* (Autumn 1984), 480–496.

Dopuch, N. and M. Pincus. "Evidence on the Choice of Inventory Accounting Methods: LIFO Versus FIFO," *Journal of Accounting Research* (Spring 1988), 28–59.

Heath, L. C. "Is Working Capital Really Working?" *Journal of Accountancy* (August 1980), 55–62.

Hunt, H. G. III. "Potential Determinants of Corporate Inventory Accounting Decisions," *Journal of Accounting Research* (Autumn 1985), 448–467.

Payne, Stephen. "Working Capital Optimization Can Yield Real Gains," *Financial Executive* (September 2002), 40–42.

7. Long-Term Debt-Paying Ability

Deakin, Edward B. "Accounting for Contingencies: The Pennzoil-Texaco Case," *Accounting Horizons* (March 1989), 21–28.

Dietrich, J. and R. S. Kaplan. "Empirical Analysis of the Commercial Loan Classification Decision," *Accounting Review* (January 1982), 18–38.

Heian, James B. and James B. Thies. "Consolidation of Finance Subsidiaries: $230 Billion in Off-Balance-Sheet Financing Comes Home To Roost," *Accounting Horizons* (March 1989), 1–9.

Leib, Barclay. "Questioning the Basic Assumptions," *Financial Executive* (September 2002), 35–38.

Schipper, Katherine and Teri Lombardi Yohn. "Standard-Setting Issues and Academic Research Related to the Accounting for Financial Asset Transfers," *Accounting Horizons* (March 2007), 59–80.

Thomas, J. K. "Why Do Firms Terminate Their Overfunded Pension Plans?" *Journal of Accounting and Economics* (November 1989), 361–398.

Williams, Georgina and Thomas J. Phillips. "Cleaning Up Our Act: Accounting For Environmental Liabilities," *Management Accounting* (February 1994), 30–33.

8. Profitability

Albrecht, David W. and Niranjan Chipalkalti. "New Segment Reporting," *The CPA Journal* (May 1998), 46–52.

Bhattacharya, N., E. L. Black, T. E. Christensen, and C. R. Larson. "Assessing the Relative Informativeness and Performance of Pro Forma Earnings and GAAP Operating Earnings," *Journal of Accounting and Economics* (36: 2003), 285–319.

Bhattacharya, Nilabhra, Ervin L. Black, Theodore E. Christensen, and Richard D. Mergenthaler. "Empirical Evidence on Recent Trends in Pro Forma Reporting," *Accounting Horizons* (March 2004), 27–43.

Bradshaw, Mark T. and Richard G. Sloan. "GAAP versus the Street: An Empirical Assessment of Two Alternative Definitions of Earnings," *Journal of Accounting Research* (March 2002), 41–66.

Entwistle, G. M., G. D. Feltham, and C. Mbagwu. "Financial Reporting Regulation and the Reporting of Pro Forma Earnings," *Accounting Horizons* (March 2006), 39–55.

Glover, Jonathan C., Yuja Ijiri, Carolyn B. Levine, and Pierre Jinghong Liang. "Separating Facts from Forecasts in Financial Statements," *Accounting Horizons* (December 2005), 267–282.

Guidry, F., A. J. Leone, and S. Rock. "Earnings-Based Bonus Plans and Earnings Management by Business-Unit Managers," *Journal of Accounting and Economics* (26: 1999), 113–142.

Healy, P. M. and J. M. Wahlen. "A Review of the Earnings Management Literature and Its Implications for Standard Setting," *Accounting Horizons* (October 13, 1999), 365–383.

Hodge, Frank D. "Investors' Perceptions of Earnings Quality, Auditor Independence, and the Usefulness of Audited Financial Information," *Accounting Horizons* (2003 Supplement), 37–48.

Leibowitz, M. "Market-to-Book Ratios and Positive and Negative Returns on Equity," *Journal of Financial Statement Analysis* (Winter 1999), 21–30.

Lipe, R. C. "The Information Contained in the Components of Earnings," *Journal of Accounting Research* (Supplement 1986), 37–64.

Liv, Jing and Jacob Thomas. "Stock Returns and Accounting Earnings," *Journal of Accounting Research* (Spring 2000), 71–102.

Lougee, B. A. and C. A. Marquardt. "Earnings Informativeness and Strategic Disclosure: An Empirical Examination of 'Pro Forma' Earnings," *The Accounting Review* (2004), 769–795.

MacDonald, Elizabeth. "Accounting in the Danger Zone," *Forbes* (September 2, 2002), 138.

McNichols, M. and G. P. Wilson. "Evidence of Earnings Management from the Provision for Bad Debts," *Journal of Accounting Research* (Supplement 26, 1988), 1–31.

Moses, D. "Income Smoothing and Incentives: Empirical Tests Using Accounting Changes," *The Accounting Review* (April 1987), 358–377.

Nelson, M. W., J. A. Elliot, and R. L. Tarpley. "Evidence from Auditors About Managers' and Auditors Earnings Management Decisions," *The Accounting Review* (Supplement 2002), 175–202.

Nelson, Mark W., John A. Elliot, and Robin L. Tarpley. "How Are Earnings Managed? Examples from Auditors," *Accounting Horizons* (2003 Supplement), 17–35.

Phillips, T., M. Luehlfing, and C. Vallario. "Hazy Reporting," *Journal of Accountancy* (August 2002), 47–50.

Securities and Exchange Commission (SEC). Final Rule: Conditions for Use of Non-GAAP Financial Measures, Release No. 33-8176; 34-47226; FR-65. Washington D.C.: Government Printing Office, 2003.

Worthy, F. S. "Manipulating Profits: How It's Done," *Fortune* (June 15, 1984), 50–54.

9. For the Investor

Aharony, J. and A. Dotan. "A Comparative Analysis of Auditor, Manager, and Financial Analyst Interpretations of SFAS No. 5 Disclosure Guidelines," *Journal of Business Finance & Accounting* (April/May 2004), 475–504.

Ball, Ray. "The Earnings-Price Anomaly," *Journal of Accounting and Economics* (June/September 1992), 319–346.

Balsam, Steven, Sebastian O'Keefe, and Mark M. Wiedemer. "Frontline Reaction to FASB 123(R)," *Journal of Accountancy* (April 2007), 55–56.

Beaver, W. and D. Morse. "What Determines Price-Earnings Ratios?" *Financial Analysts Journal* (July/August 1978), 65–76.

Bens, Daniel A., Venky Nagar, and M. H. Franco Wong. "Real Investment Implications of Employee Stock Options Exercises," *Journal of Accounting Research* (May 2002), 359–406.

Block, Frank E. "A Study of the Price to Book Relationship," *Financial Analysts Journal* (January/February 1995), 63–73.

Botosan, Christine, A. and Marlene A. Plumlee. "Stock Options Expense: The Sword of Damocles Revealed," *Accounting Horizons* (December 2001), 311–327.

Butler, Kirt C. and Larry H. P. Lang. "The Forecast Accuracy of Individual Analysts: Evidence of Systematic Optimism and Pessimism," *Journal of Accounting Research* (Spring 1991), 150–156.

Chambers, A. E. and S. H. Penman. "Timeliness of Reporting and the Stock Price Reaction to Earnings Announcements," *Journal of Accounting Research* (Spring 1984), 21–47.

Clarkson, P., Y. La, and G. Richardson. "The Market Valuation of Environmental Capital Expenditures by Pulp and Paper Companies," *The Accounting Review* (April 2004), 329–345.

Clemente, Holly A. "What Wall Street Sees When It Looks At Your P/E Ratio," *Financial Executive* (May/June 1990), 40–44.

Coggin, T. D. and J. E. Hunter. "Analysts EPS Forecasts Nearer Actual Than Statistical Models," *The Journal of Business Forecasting* (Winter 1982–1983), 20–23.

Cole, Kevin, Jean Helwege, and David Laster. "Stock Market Valuation Indicators: Is This Time Different?" *Financial Analysts Journal* (May/June 1996), 56–64.

Core, John and Wayne Guay. "Estimating the Value of Employee Stock Option Portfolios Volatility," *Journal of Accounting Research* (June 2002), 613–630.

Dykewrcz, Paul. "Options Alert," *Kiplinger's* (June 2005), 65.

Eaton, Tim V. and Brian A. Pruryk. "No Longer an 'Option'," *Journal of Accountancy* (April 2005), 63–68.

Farber, David B., Marilyn F. Johnson, and Kathy R. Petroni. "Congressional Intervention in the Standard-Setting Process: An Analysis of the Stock Option Accounting Reforms Act of 2004," *Accounting Horizons* (March 2007), 1–22.

Griffin, P. A. "Got Information? Investor Response to Form 10-K and Form 10-Q EDGAR Filing," *Review of Accounting Studies* (8: 2003), 433–460.

Holthausen, Robert W. and D. F. Larcker. "The Prediction of Stock Returns Using Financial Statement Information," *Journal of Accounting and Economics* (June/September 1992), 373–411.

Kohlbeck, Mark and Terry D. Warfield. "Unrecorded Intangible Assets: Abnormal Earnings and Valuation," *Accounting Horizons* (March 2007), 23–41.

Levitt, A. "The Numbers Game. Remarks Delivered at the NYU Center for Law and Business," New York, NY (September 28, 1998), http://www.sec.gov (press release, 1998).

Liv, Jing, Doron Nissim, and Jacob Thomas. "Equity Valuation Using Multiples," *Journal of Accounting Research* (March 2002), 135–173.

MacDonald, Elizabeth. "An Expensive Option," *Forbes* (August 16, 2004), 116–117.

Molodovsky, Nicholas. "A Theory of Price-Earnings Ratios," *Financial Analysts Journal* (January/February 1995), 29–43.

Nichols, D. Craig and James M Wahlen. "How Do Earnings Numbers Relate to Stock Returns? A review of Classic Accounting Research with Updated Evidence," *Accounting Horizons* (December 2004), 263–286.

Ou, Jane A. and Stephen H. Penman. "Financial Statement Analysis and the Prediction of Stock Returns," *Journal of Accounting and Economics* (November 1989), 295–329.

Ou, Jane A. and James F. Jepen. "Analysts Earnings Forecasts and the Roles of Earnings and Book Value in Equity Valuation," *Journal of Business Finance & Accounting* (April/May 2002), 287–316.

Roberts, David and Thomas Roberts. "Option Expensing Spawn New Options," *Financial Executive* (May 2005), 26–28.

Schilit, H. "Financial Shenanigans: How to Detect Accounting Gimmicks and Fraud in Financial Reports," 1993. New York, NY: McGraw-Hill.

Skinner, D. and R. Sloan. "Earning Surprises, Growth Expectations, and Stock Returns or Don't Let an Earnings Torpedo Sink Your Portfolio," *Review of Accounting Studies* (7: 2002), 289–312.

Wallace, W. "Pro Forma Before and After the SEC's Warning: A Quantification of Reporting Variances from GAAP," 2002. Morristown, NJ: FEI. Research Foundation.

Weil, J. "Companies Pollute Earnings Reports Leaving P/E Ratios Hard to Calculate" *Wall Street Journal* (August 21, 2001), 1a.

Zarowin, P. "What Determines Earnings-Price Ratios Revisited," *Journal of Accounting Auditing and Finance* (Summer 1990), 439–454.

Zhang, X. "Conservative Accounting and Equity Valuation," *Journal of Accounting & Economics* (29: 2000), 125–149.

10. Statement of Cash Flows

Adhikari, Ajay and Augustine Duru. "Voluntary Disclosure of Free Cash Flow Information," *Accounting Horizons* (December 2006), 311–332.

Casey, C. J. and N. J. Bartczak. "Cash Flow—It's Not the Bottom Line," *Harvard Business Review* (July/August 1984), 61–66.

Comiskey, Eugene E. "The Classification by Real Estate Investment Trusts of Distributions from Unconsolidated Entities," *Accounting Horizons* (June 2006), 111–132.

DeFond, M. and M. Hung. "An Empirical Analysis of Analysts' Cash Flow Forecasts," *Journal of Accounting & Economics* (35: 2003), 73–100.

Gullapalli, D. "Free Cash Flow Gets Scrutiny," *The Wall Street Journal* (November 18, 2004), C3.

Largay, J. A. III and C. P. Stickney. "Cash Flows, Ratio Analysis and the W. T. Grant Company Bankruptcy," *Financial Analysts Journal* (July/August 1980), 51–54.

Livnat, Joshua and Paul Zarowin. "The Incremental Informational Content of Cash-Flow Components," *Journal of Accounting and Economics* (May 1990), 25–46.

Kronquist, Stacey L. and Nancy Newman-Limata. "Reporting Corporate Cash Flows," *Management Accounting* (July 1990), 31–36.

Nurnberg, Hugo. "Inconsistencies and Ambiguities in Cash Flow Statements Under FASB Statement No. 95," *Accounting Horizons* (June 1993), 60–75.

Perez, Evan. "Delta to Record $1.65 Billion in Noncash Charges for Quarter," *The Wall Street Journal* (July 14, 2004), A3.

Rapoport, Michael. "'Cash Flow' Isn't What It Used To Be," *The Wall Street Journal* (March 24, 2005), C3.

Rappaport, Alfred. "Show Me the Cash Flow," *Fortune* (September 16, 2002), 192, 194.

Rayburn, J. "The Association of Operating Cash Flow and Accruals with Security Returns," *Journal of Accounting Research* (Supplement 1986), 121–133.

Reichalstein, Stefan. "Providing Managerial Incentives: Cash Flows Versus Accrual Accounting," *Journal of Accounting Research* (Autumn 2000), 243–270.

Wasley, C. E. and J. S. Wu. "Why Do Managers Voluntarily Issue Cash Flow Forecasts?" *Journal of Accounting Research* (May 2006), 389–429.

Summary Analysis-Nike, Inc.

Beneish, Messod D. "The Dedication of Earnings Manipulation," *Financial Analysts Journal*(September/ October 1999).

Kang, Stephanie. "Just Do It: Nike Gets Revelatory," *The Wall Street Journal* (April 13, 2005), B11.

Roth, Daniel. "Can Nike Still Do It Without Phil Knight?" *Fortune* (April 4, 2005), 59–64, 66, 68.

Tkacik, Maureen. "Protection Go?" *The Wall Street Journal* (January 10, 2003), B1.

Valokh, Eugene. "Nike and the Free-Speech Knot," *The Wall Street Journal* (June 30, 2003), A16.

11. Expanded Analysis

Altman, E. I. "Financial Ratios, Discriminant Analysis and the Prediction of Corporate Bankruptcy," *Journal of Finance* (September 1968), 589–609.

Altman, E. I. and M. Brenner. "Information Effects and Stock Market Response to Signs of Firm Deterioration," *Journal of Financial and Quantitative Analysis* (March 1981), 35–51.

Altman, E. I. *Corporate Financial Distress* (New York: John Wiley & Sons, 1993).

Arya, Anil, Jonathan C. Glover, and Shyam Sunder. "Are Unmanaged Earnings Always Better for Shareholders?" *Accounting Horizons* (Supplement 2003), 111–116.

Asquith, Paul, Michael B. Mikhail, and Andrea S. Au. "Information Content of Equity Analyst Reports," *Journal of Financial Economics* (75: 2005), 245–282.

Ballou, Brian, Norman H. Godwin, and Rebecca Toppe Shortridge. "Firm Value and Employee Attitudes on Workplace Quality," *Accounting Horizons* (December 2003), 329–341.

Barber, B., R. Lehavy, M. McNichols, and B. Trueman. "Can Investors Profit from the Prophets? Security Analyst Recommendations and Stock Returns," *The Journal of Finance* (56: 2001), 531–563.

Barker, Richard G. "Survey and Market-Based Evidence of Industry-Dependence in Analysts' Preferences Between the Dividend Yield and Price-Earnings Ratio Valuation Models," *Journal of Business Finance and Accounting* (April/May 1999), 393–418.

Barker, Richard G. "The Role of Dividends in Valuation Models Used by Analysts and Fund Managers," *The European Accounting Review* (8:2 1999), 195–218.

Barrett, A. "Slammed! Investors Are Telling Companies that Creative Accounting Will No Longer Fly," *Business Week* (March 4, 2002), 34.

Barwiv, Ran, Anurag Aggarwal, and Robert Leach. "Predicting Bankruptcy Resolution," *Journal of Business Finance & Accounting* (April/May 2002), 497–520.

Beasley, M. S. "An Empirical Analysis of the Relation Between the Board of Director Composition and Finance Statement Fraud," *The Accounting Review* (October 1996), 443–465.

Bell, T. B. and J. V. Carcello. "A Decision Aid for Assessing the Likelihood of Fraudulent Financial Reporting," *Auditing: A Journal of Practice & Theory* (Spring 1999), 169–184.

Beneish, Messod P. "The Detection of Earnings Manipulation," *Financial Analysts Journal* (September/October 1999), 24–36.

Bernard, V. L. "The Feltham-Ohlson Framework: Implications for Empiricists," *Contemporary Accounting Research* (11: 1995), 733–748.

Burgstahler, D. C. and I. D. Dichev. "Earnings Adaptation and Equity Value," *Accounting Review* (2: 1997), 187–216.

Bradshaw, M. T. "How Do Analysts Use Their Earnings Forecasts in Generating Stock Recommendations?" *The Accounting Review* (January 2004), 25–50.

Burgess, Deanna Qender. "Graphical Sleight of Hand," *Journal of Accountancy* (February 2002), 45–48, 51.

Burkert, Rod P. "A Good Deal Depends on Preparation," *Journal of Accountancy* (November 2003), 47–52.

Casey, C. J. and N. J. Bartczak. "Using Operating Cash Flow Data to Predict Financial Distress: Some Extensions," *Journal of Accounting Research* (Spring 1985), 384–401.

Chandra, Uday, Bradley D. Childs, and Bturvg T. Ro. "The Association Between LIFO Reserve and Equity Risk: An Empirical Assessment," *Journal of Accounting Auditing & Finance* (Summer 2002), 185–208.

Copeland, Tom, Tim Kaller, and Jack Murrin. "Valuation, Measuring, and Managing the Value of Companies, Third Edition," (New York: John Wiley & Sons, Inc. 2000), 1–494.

Dambolena, I. G. and S. J. Khorvry. "Ratio Stability and Corporate Failure," *Journal of Finance* (September 1980), 1017–1026.

Dechow, P. A., R. G. Sloan, and A. P. Sweeney. "Causes and Consequences of Earnings Manipulation: An Analysis of Firms Subject to Enforcement Actions by the SEC," *Contemporary Accounting Research* (Spring 1996), 1–36.

Demirakos, Efthimios G., Norman C. Strong, and Martin Walker. "What Valuation Models Do Analysts Use?" *Accounting Horizons* (December 2004), 221–240.

Dutta, Sunil and Frank Gigler. "The Effect of Earnings Forecasts on Earnings Management," *Journal of Accounting Research* (June 2002), 631–656.

Frankel, R., M. Johnson, and K. Nelson. "Auditor Independence and Earnings Quality," *The Accounting Review* (Supplement 2002), 71–105.

Gombola, M. J. and J. E. Ketz. "Financial Ratio Patterns in Retail and Manufacturing Organizations," *Financial Management* (Summer 1983), 45–56.

Gramlich, Jeffrey D. and James E. Wheeler. "How Chevron, Texaco, and the Indonesian Government Structured Transactions to Avoid Billions in U.S. Income Taxes," *Accounting Horizons* (June 2003), 107–122.

Grent, C. Terry, Chaunrey M. Depree, Jr., and Gerry H. Grant. "Earnings Management and the Abuse of Materiality," *Journal of Accountancy* (September 2000), 41–44.

Hodge, Frank D. "Investors' Perceptions of Earnings Quality, Auditor Independence, and the Usefulness of Audited Financial Information," *Accounting Horizons* (Supplement 2003), 37–48.

Howell, Robert A. "Fixing Financial Reporting: Financial Statement Overhaul," *Financial Executive* (March/April 2002), 40–42.

Jaggi, B. "Which Is Better, D & B or Zeta in Forecasting Credit Risk?" *Journal of Business Forecasting* (Summer 1984), 13–16, 22.

Kasznik, Ron and Maureen F. McNichols. "Does Meeting Earnings Expectations Matter? Evidence from Analyst Forecast Revisions and Share Prices," *Journal of Accounting Research* (June 2002), 727–760.

Kirschenheiter, Michael and Nahum D. Melumad. "Can 'Big Bath' and Earnings Smoothing Co-Exist as Equilibrium Financial Reporting Strategies?" *Journal of Accounting Research* (June 2002), 761–796.

Largay, James A. "Lessons from Enron," *Accounting Horizons* (June 2002), 153–156.

Lennox, C. S. "The Accuracy and Incremental Information Content of Audit Reports in Predicting Bankruptcy," *Journal of Business Finance & Accounting* (June/July 1999), 757–778.

Liv, Jing, Nissim Doren, and Thomas Jacob. "Equity Valuation Using Multiples," *Journal of Accounting Research* (March 2002), 135–172.

Lo, K. and T. Lys. "The Ohlson Model: Contribution to Valuation Theory, Limitations, and Empirical Applications," *Journal of Accounting, Auditing, and Finance* (13, 3: Summer 2000), 337–367.

Makeever, D. A. "Predicting Business Failures," *The Journal of Commercial Bank Lending* (January 1984), 14–18.

Marquardt, C. and C. Wiedman. "Earnings Management Through Transaction Structuring Contingent Convertible Debt and Diluted EPS," *Journal of Accounting Research* (May 2005), 205–244.

Mendenhall, Richard R. "How Naive Is the Market's Use of Firm-Specific Earnings Information?" *Journal of Accounting Research* (June 2002), 841–864.

Miller, Paul B. "Quality Financial Reporting," *Journal of Accountancy* (April 2002), 70–74.

Mills, J., L. Bible, and R. Mason. "Defining Free Cash Flow," *The CPA Journal* (January 2002), 37–41.

Moriarty, G. and P. Livingston. "Quantitative Measures of the Quality of Financial Reporting," *Financial Executive* (July 2001), 17.

Nelson, Mark W., John A. Elliott, and Robin L. Tarpley. "How Are Earnings Managed? Examples From Auditors," *Accounting Horizons* (Supplement 2003), 17–35.

Nichols, D. Craig and James M. Wahlon. "How Do Earnings Numbers Relate to Stock Returns? A Review of Classic Accounting Research with Updated Evidence," *Accounting Horizons* (December 2004), 263–286.

Ohlson, J. A. "Earnings, Book Values, and Dividends in Equity Valuation," *Contemporary Accounting Research* (11 (2): 1995), 661–687.

Patell, J. M. and M. A. Wolfson. "The Intraday Speed of Adjustment of Stock Prices to Earnings and Dividend Announcements," *Journal of Financial Economics* (June 1984), 223–252.

Patrone, F. L. and D. duBois, "Financial Ratio Analysis in the Small Business," *Journal of Small Business Management* (January 1981), 35–40.

Parsons, O. "Using Financial Statement Data to Identify Factors Associated with Fraudulent Financial Reporting," *Journal of Applied Business Research* (Summer 1995), 38–46.

Peterson, M. "Putting Extra Fizz Into Profits; Critics Say Coca-Cola Dumps Debt on Spin Off," *New York Times* (August 4, 1998), D1.

Rama, D. V., K. Raghunandan, and M. A. Gerger. "The Association Between Audit Reports and Bankruptcies: Further Evidence," *Advances in Accounting* (1997 15), 1–15.

Rege, V. P. "Accounting Ratios to Locate Take-Over Targets," *Journal of Business Finance and Accounting* (Autumn 1984), 301–311.

Richardson, F. M., G. D. Kane, and P. Lobingier. "The Impact of Recession on the Prediction of Corporate Failure," *Journal of Business Finance & Accounting* (January/March 1998), 167, 186.

Schipper, Katherine and Linda Vincent. "Earnings Quality," *Accounting Horizons* (Supplement 2003), 97–110.

Shelton, Sandra Waller, O. Ray Whittington, and David Landsittel. "Auditing Firms' Fraud Risk Assessment Practices," *Accounting Horizons* (March 2001), 19–33.

Steinbart, Paul John. "The Auditor's Responsibility for the Accuracy of Graphs in Annual Reports: Some Evidence of the Need for Additional Guidance," *Accounting Horizons* (September 1989), 60–70.

Stober, T. L. "The Incremental Information Content of Financial Statement Disclosures: The Case of LIFO Liquidations," *Journal of Accounting Research* (Supplement 1986), 138–160.

Summers, S. L. and J. T. Sweeney. "Fraudulently Misstated Financial Statements and Insider Trading: An Empirical Analysis," *The Accounting Review* (January 1998), 131–146.

Trombetta, Marco. "Discussion of Implied Cost of Equity Capital in Earnings-Based Valuation: International Evidence," *Accounting and Business Research* (Volume 34, Number 4, 2004), 345–348.

Tse, S. "LIFO Liquidations," *Journal of Accounting Research* (Spring 1990), 229–238.

U.S. Government Accounting Office, "Financial Restatements: Update of Public Company Trends, Market Impacts, and Regulatory Enforcement Activities," (July 2006), GAO-06-678, http://www.gao.gov/research.

Williams, Patricia A. "The Search for a Better Market Model Expectation of Earnings," *Journal of Accounting Literature* (14: 1995), 140–168.

Williamson, R. W. "Evidence on the Selective Reporting of Financial Ratios," *The Accounting Review* (April 1984), 296–299.

Wright, P., B. Dunford, and S. A. Snell. "Human Resources and the Resource-Based View of the Firm," *Journal of Management* (27: 2001), 701–721.

Xie, B., W. Davidson, and P. DaDalt. "Earnings Management and Corporate Governance: The Role of the Board and Audit Committee," *Journal of Corporate Finance* (9: 2003), 295–316.

York, Timothy. "Start a BV Engagement the Right Way," *Journal of Accountancy* (August 2003), 35–40.

12.   Special Industries: Banks, Utilities, Oil and Gas, Transportation, Insurance, Real Estate Companies

Agnich, J. F. "How Utilities Account to the Regulators," *Management Accounting* (February 1981), 17–22.

Barniv, Ran. "Accounting Procedures, Market Data, Cash-Flow Figures, and Insolvency Classification: The Case of the Insurance Industry," *The Accounting Review* (July 1990), 578–604.

Begley, J., S. Chamberlain, and Y. La. "Modeling Goodwill for Banks: A Residual Income Approach with Empirical Tests," *Contemporary Accounting Research* (23: 2006), 31–68.

Christensen, Theodore E. "The Effects of Uncertainty on the Informativeness of Earnings: Evidence from the Insurance Industry in the Wake of Catastrophic Events," *Journal of Business Finance & Accounting* (January/March 2002), 223–256.

Gaver, J. J. and J. S. Paterson. "Managing Insurance Company Financial Statements to Meet Regulatory and Tax Reporting Goals," *Contemporary Accounting Research* (16: summer 1999), 207–241.

Gore, R. and D. Stott. "Toward a More Informative Measure of Operating Performance in the REIT Industry: Net Income vs. Funds from Operations," *Accounting Horizons* (12: 1998), 323–339.

Hirst, E., P. Hopkins, and J. Wahlen. "Fair Values, Income Measurement, and Bank Analysts' Risk and Valuation Judgments," *The Accounting Review* (79: 2004), 453–472.

Ho, T. and A. Saunders. "A Catastrophe Model of Bank Failure," *The Journal of Finance* (December 1980), 1189–1207.

Kohlbec, M. "Investor Valuation and Measuring Bank Intangible Assets," *Journal of Accounting, Auditing, and Finance* (Winter 2004), 29–60.

Owhoso, Vincent E., William F. Messer, Jr., and John G. Lynch, Jr. "Error Detection by Industry-Specialized Teams During Sequential Audit Review," *Journal of Accounting Research* (June 2002), 883–900.

Palmon, Dan and Lee J. Zeidler. "Current Value Reporting of Real Estate Companies and a Possible Example of Market Inefficiency," *The Accounting Review* (July 1978), 776–790.

Rose, P. L. and W. L. Scott. "Return-on-Equity Analysis of Eleven Largest U.S. Bank Failures," *Review of Business and Economic Research* (Winter 1980–81), 1–11.

Serwer, Andy. "Oh, the Games Insurance Companies Love to Play," *Fortune* (May 30, 2005), 53.

Shick, R. A. and L. F. Sherman. "Bank Stock Prices as an Early Warning System for Changes in Condition," *Journal of Bank Research* (Autumn 1980), 136–146.

Solomon, Deborah. "SEC Brings New Federal Oversight to Insurance Industry with Probes," *The Wall Street Journal* (April 1, 2005), 1, A4.

Wahlen, J. "The Nature of Information in Commercial Bank Loan Loss Disclosures," *The Accounting Review* (69 (3) 1994), 455–478.

Zuckerman, Gregory and Ellen Byron. "Big Investors: Too Sold on Retail?" *The Wall Street Journal* (April 14, 2005), C1, C4, Column 2.

13. Personal Financial Statements and Accounting for Governments and Not-for-Profit Organizations

Baber, William R., Andrea Alston Roberts, and Gnanakumar Visuana Dran. "Charitable Organizations' Strategies and Program-Spending Ratios," *Accounting Horizons* (December 2001), 329–343.

Barrett, W. "Look Before You Give," *Forbes* (December 27, 1999), 206–214.

Bernstein, David J. "Local Government Measurement Use in Focus on Performance and Results," *Evaluation and Program Planning, Vol. 24, No. 1* (January 2001), 95–101.

Brevl, Jonathan D. "The Government Performance and Results Act—10 Years Later," *Journal of Financial Management* (Spring 2003), 58–64.

Brown, Trevor L. and Matthew Potoski. "Managing Contract Performance: A Transaction Costs Approach," *Policy Analysis and Management* (Spring 2003), 275–298.

Brown, Victor H. and Susan E. Weiss. "Toward Better Not-For-Profit Accounting and Reporting," *Management Accounting* (July 1993), 48–52.

Chandra, Uday, Michael L. Ettrdge, and Mary S. Stone. "Enron-Era Disclosure of Off-Balance-Sheet Entities," *Accounting Horizons* (September 2006), 231–252.

Charnes, A. and W. Cooper. "Auditing and Accounting for Program Efficiency and Management Effectiveness in Not-for-Profit Entities," *Accounting Organizations and Society 5* (1980), 87–108.

Chase, Bruce. "New Reporting Standards For Not-For-Profits," *Management Accounting* (October 1995), 34–37.

Chase, Bruce W. and Laura B. Triggs. "How to Implement GASB Statement No. 34," *Journal of Accountancy* (November 2001), 71–79.

Coggbum, Jerrell D. and Saundra Schrieder. "The Relationship Between State Government Performance and State Quality of Life," *International Journal of Public Administration, Vol. 26, No. 12* (October 2003), 1337–1354.

Downs, G. W. and D. M. Rocke. "Municipal Budget Forecasting with Multivariate ARMA Models," *Journal of Forecasting* (October/December 1983), 377–387.

Eisenberg, Daniel. "Evaluating the Effectiveness of Policies Related to Drunk Driving," *Policy Analysis and Management* (Spring 2003), 249–274.

Freeman, Robert J. and Craig D. Shoulders. "GASB Statement 34: A Bold Step Forward," *The Government Accountants Journal* (Spring 2000), 8–17.

Gordon, Teresa P., Janet S. Greenlee, and Denise Nitterhouse. "Tax-Exempt Organization Financial Data: Availability and Limitations," *Accounting Horizons* (June 1999), 113–128.

Hu, Shih-Jen Kathy and Linda Achey Kidwell, "A Survey of Management Techniques Implemented by Municipal Administrators," *The Government Accountants Journal* (Spring 2000), 46–52.

Holder, William W., Kenneth R. Schermann, and Ray Whittington. "Materiality Considerations," *Journal of Accountancy* (November 2003), 61–66.

Ives, Martin, "The Governmental Accounting Standards Board: Factors Influencing Its Operation and Initial Technical Agenda," *The Government Accountants Journal* (Spring 2000), 22–28.

Johnson, Laurence E. and David R. Bean. "GASB Statement No. 34: The Dawn of a New Governmental Financial Reporting Model," *The CPA Journal* (December 1999), 14–24.

Kelly, Janet M. and David Swindell. "A Multiple Indicator Approach to Municipal Service Evaluation: Correlating Performance Measurement and Citizen Satisfaction Across Jurisdictions," *Public Administrative Review* (September/October 2002), 610–619.

Kinsman, Michael D. and Bruce Samuelson. "Personal Financial Statements: Valuation Challenges and Solutions," *Journal of Accountancy* (September 1987), 138–148.

Klasny, Edward M. and James M. Williams. "Government Reporting Faces an Overhaul," *Journal of Accountancy* (January 2000), 49–51.

Meeting, David T., Randall W. Luecke, and Edward J. Giniat. "Understanding and Implementing FASB 124," *Journal of Accountancy* (March 1996), 62–66.

Revell, Janice. "The Great State Health-Care Giveaway," *Fortune* (May 2, 2005), 43–44; 46.

Revenbark, William C. and Carla M. Pizzarella. "Auditing Performance Data in Local Government," *Public Performance and Management Review, Vol. 25* (June 2002), 412–420.

Sacco, John. "GASB Statement 34, Part of Changing Political and Global Market Pressures," The *Government Accountants Journal* (Spring 2000), 20–21.

Statement of Position of the Accounting Standards Division 82-1, "Accounting and Financial Reporting for Personal Financial Statements," New York: American Institute of Certified Public Accountants, 1982.

Index

DON'T THROW THIS CARD AWAY!
THIS MAY BE REQUIRED FOR YOUR COURSE!

THOMSON ONE Business School Edition

Congratulations!

Your purchase of this NEW textbook includes complimentary access to THOMSON ONE – Business School Edition for Accounting. THOMSON ONE – Business School Edition is a Web-based portal product that provides integrated access to Thomson Financial content for the purpose of financial analysis. This is an educational version of the same financial resources used by Wall Street analysts on a daily basis!

For hundreds of companies, this online resource provides seamless access to:

- **Current and Past Company Data:** Worldscope which includes company profiles, financials and accounting results, market per-share data, annual information, and monthly prices going back to 1980.

- **Financial Analyst Data and Forecasts:** I/B/E/S Consensus Estimates which provides consensus estimates, analyst-by-analyst earnings coverage, and analysts' forecasts.

- **SEC Disclosure Statements:** Disclosure SEC Database which includes company profiles, annual and quarterly company financials, pricing information, and earnings.

- **And More!**

THOMSON

SOUTH-WESTERN

THOMSON ONE
Business School Edition

ACCESS CODE

PNWZ32JPPGVXT7

HOW TO REGISTER YOUR ACCESS CODE

1. Launch a web browser and go to **http://tabseacct.swlearning.com**.

2. Click the "Register" button to enter your access code.

3. Enter your access code **exactly** as it appears here and create a unique User ID, or enter an existing User ID if you have previously registered for a different South-Western product via an access code.

4. When prompted, create a password (or enter an existing password, if you have previously registered for a different product via an access code.) Submit the necessary information when prompted. **Record your User ID and password in a secure location.**

5. Once registered, return to the URL above and select the "Enter" button; have your User ID and password handy.

NOTE: The duration of your access to the product begins when registration is complete.

For technical support, contact 1-800-423-0563 or email **tl.support@thomson.com**

INVESTOR ANALYSIS

$$\text{Degree of Financial Leverage} = \frac{\text{Earnings Before Interest and Tax}}{\text{Earnings Before Tax}}$$

$$\text{All-Inclusive Degree of Financial Leverage} = \frac{\substack{\text{Earnings Before Interest, Tax,} \\ \text{Minority Share of Earnings,} \\ \text{Equity Income, and Nonrecurring Items}}}{\substack{\text{Earnings Before Tax, Minority Share of Earnings,} \\ \text{Equity Income, and Nonrecurring Items}}}$$

$$\text{Earnings per Common Share} = \frac{\text{Net Income} - \text{Preferred Dividends}}{\substack{\text{Diluted Weighted Average Number of} \\ \text{Common Shares Outstanding}}}$$

$$\text{Operating Cash Flow per Share} = \frac{\text{Operating Cash Flow} - \text{Preferred Dividends}}{\text{Diluted Weighted Average Common Shares Outstanding}}$$

$$\text{Price/Earnings Ratio} = \frac{\text{Market Price per Share}}{\text{Diluted Earnings per Share, before Nonrecurring Items}}$$

$$\text{Percentage of Earnings Retained} = \frac{\text{Net Income before Nonrecurring Items} - \text{All Dividends}}{\text{Net Income before Nonrecurring Items}}$$

$$\text{Dividend Payout} = \frac{\text{Dividends per Common Share}}{\text{Diluted Earnings per Share before Nonrecurring Items}}$$

$$\text{Dividend Yield} = \frac{\text{Dividends per Common Share}}{\text{Market Price per Common Share}}$$

$$\text{Book Value per Share} = \frac{\text{Total Stockholders' Equity} - \text{Preferred Stock Equity}}{\text{Number of Common Shares Outstanding}}$$

$$\text{Operating Cash Flow/Cash Dividends} = \frac{\text{Operating Cash Flow}}{\text{Cash Dividends}}$$

$$\text{Materiality of Options} = \frac{\substack{\text{Net Income before} \\ \text{Nonrecurring Items Not} \\ \text{Including Option Expense}} - \substack{\text{Net Income before} \\ \text{Nonrecurring Items} \\ \text{Including Option Expense}}}{\substack{\text{Net Income before Nonrecurring Items} \\ \text{Not Including Option Expense}}}$$